The Heritage Foundation

W9-BEM-369

2017
INDEX OF
ECONOMIC FREEDOM

INSTITUTE FOR ECONOMIC FREEDOM

Terry Miller
Anthony B. Kim

2017
INDEX OF
ECONOMIC
FREEDOM

INSTITUTE FOR ECONOMIC FREEDOM

CONTENTS

Preface..vii

Foreword..ix

Executive Highlights...1

Chapter 1: The Growth and Impact of Economic Freedom.................................9
  Ambassador Terry Miller and Anthony B. Kim

Chapter 2: Defining Economic Freedom...19
  Ambassador Terry Miller and Anthony B. Kim

Chapter 3: Economic Freedom by Region and Country......................................27

  The Americas..29

  Asia-Pacific...101

  Europe...197

  Middle East/North Africa...297

  Sub-Saharan Africa...341

Appendix..447

Methodology..455

Major Works Cited...471

Our International Partners..473

PREFACE

2016 was yet another year of startling changes around the globe. Three of the most notable political developments during the year—the United Kingdom's "Brexit," America's election of Donald Trump as President, and the passing of Cuban dictator Fidel Castro—have powerfully reminded us that freedom matters, and we must act to guard and nurture it.

The British exit from the European Union, a supranational entity, has been a long time coming. To a growing number of Brits, the EU has become an overregulated and undemocratic institution. In a historic referendum, by a margin of a million votes, the British people chose to leave the EU. Brexit embodies the very principles and ideals of conservatism: self-determination, limited government, democratic accountability, and economic liberty.

In my own country, the people have spoken too and have rejected failed liberal policies. For too long, the policy agenda in Washington has been defined by well-connected special interests that have severely undercut economic freedom for ordinary hardworking Americans. Beyond the walls of the backrooms where deep-pocketed elites secure favors from their friends in government, almost no one in Washington had seemed to be listening to the American people. The election of Donald Trump has clearly disrupted that deplorable status quo.

In Cuba, the death of brutal tyrant Fidel Castro marked the long-awaited end of a dark era for countless Cubans. Or perhaps it is just the beginning of the end, as the same repressive government that he created, with its hostility toward freedom, remains strong. The tragedy that Castro's Communist dictatorship has inflicted on the Cuban people for nearly six decades is beyond description. The death of Fidel opens an opportunity for change if the Cuban people can seize it.

As echoed in these three notable events of 2016, we know from history that the human spirit thrives on fairness, opportunity, and liberty. Yet there are those who persist in attacking freedom in the name of collectivism, solidarity, and social justice. These false idols of a socialist nirvana may have emotional appeal for some, but the real-life results when they become the touchstones of government policy are all too predictable: economic stagnation, poverty, deprivation, and oppression. If we are going to continue to safeguard societies from errors that have brought nothing but misery throughout history, we must win the battle of ideas. The fight for freedom is a never-ending struggle, but people will not fight for freedom unless they understand it, value it, and believe it is at risk.

We free-market conservatives cannot afford complacency; we must tend the flames of liberty, side by side with our allies, new and old, around the globe.

The 2017 *Index of Economic Freedom*, our 23rd edition, provides ample evidence of the dynamic gains that flow from greater economic freedom, both for individuals and for societies. It is gratifying to see overall global progress in advancing economic freedom reflected in rising scores in dozens of countries. The lesson is clear: The human spirit is the real wellspring of economic prosperity. That spirit is at its most inspired when it is unleashed from the chains in which it has been bound.

The imperative to advance economic freedom and thereby revitalize vibrant entrepreneurial growth is stronger than ever. It should be noted that free-market capitalism built on the principles of economic freedom does not just conserve. In many cases, it overturns and transforms. It pushes out the old to make way for the new so that real and true progress can take place. It leads to innovation in all realms: better jobs, better goods and services, and better societies.

A recurring theme in human history has been resilience and revival. The country profiles presented in the 2017 *Index* provide many such examples of countries that have accelerated their economic and social progress. Their successes can be emulated by others. Indeed, they are a sure guide for ensuing greater prosperity—but only a guide. What truly will matter are the creative solutions to pressing world problems that are certain to flow from individuals who are, in the words of the late Milton and Rose Friedman, "free to choose."

Jim DeMint, President
The Heritage Foundation
December 2016

FOREWORD

Economic freedom is a critical element of human well-being and a vital linchpin in sustaining a free civil society. As Friedrich A. Hayek foresaw decades ago, "The guiding principle in any attempt to create a world of free men must be this: a policy of freedom for the individual is the only truly progressive policy." Indeed, the best path to prosperity is the path of freedom: letting individuals decide for themselves how best to achieve their dreams and aspirations and those of their families. It is that path whose course is charted in the *Index of Economic Freedom.*

FOSTERING INCLUSIVE AND SUSTAINABLE GROWTH

In practice, each country's path to growth and development must be tailored to its own culture, history, and unique conditions, but there are certain fundamental characteristics of that path that are common to all countries. Nations with higher degrees of economic freedom prosper because they tend to capitalize more fully on the knowledge and ability of all individuals in society. Given a chance, the free-market system provides a framework for organizing, without coercion, the skills, talents, and effort of individuals toward the production of the goods and services most in demand by their fellow citizens. For society as a whole, this generates dynamic economic growth and promotes innovation through the efficient allocation of resources.

In addition, policies that promote freedom, whether through improvements in the rule of law, the promotion of efficiency through competition and openness, or suitable restraints on the size and economic reach of government, create an environment that is conducive to practical solutions to a wide range of economic and social challenges that face the world's societies.

As the country profiles in the 2017 *Index of Economic Freedom* document, the link between economic freedom and prosperity has never been clearer. Since the dawn of the modern age, a central question for policymakers has been: "What can government do to spur growth?" The data provide an obvious answer: "Adopt policies that advance economic freedom."

Chart 1, which compares income per capita and levels of economic freedom, illustrates the significant differences in income between countries with low levels of economic freedom and those that provide the greatest scope for individual initiative and choice. It also plots the impact that changes in economic freedom have on economic growth rates. Countries can get an immediate boost to economic growth by taking steps to increase economic freedom through policies that reduce taxes, rationalize the regulatory environment, open the economy to greater competition, and fight corruption.

WITH ECONOMIC FREEDOM COMES PROSPERITY AND MORE RAPID GROWTH

Equally important, of course, are the things that government should *not* do. Policies that subsidize specific industries, impose one-size-fits-all central planning, attempt to buy growth through government "stimulus"

WITH ECONOMIC FREEDOM COMES PROSPERITY AND MORE RAPID GROWTH

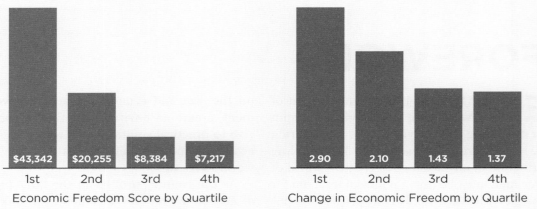

GDP per Capita, Purchasing Power Parity, Current U.S. Dollars

$43,342	$20,255	$8,384	$7,217
1st	2nd	3rd	4th

Economic Freedom Score by Quartile

GDP per Capita, Purchasing Power Parity, 5–Year Growth Rate

2.90	2.10	1.43	1.37
1st	2nd	3rd	4th

Change in Economic Freedom by Quartile

SOURCES: Terry Miller and Anthony B. Kim, *2017 Index of Economic Freedom* (Washington: The Heritage Foundation, 2017), http://www.heritage.org/index; International Monetary Fund, World Economic Outlook Database, April 2016, https://www.imf.org/external/pubs/ft/weo/2016/01/weodata/index.aspx (accessed December 13, 2016); and The World Bank, World Development Indicators Online, http://databank.worldbank.org/data/reports.aspx?source=world-development-indicators (accessed December 13, 2016).

Chart 1 ☎ heritage.org

spending, or rack up excessive debt by accumulating budget deficits are highly counterproductive. The evidence is overwhelming that any gains from such strategies will be ephemeral at best. The economic distortions they create reduce efficiency, productivity, and ultimately growth. That is too high a price to pay for any short-term benefits that such strategies might yield.

ECONOMIC FREEDOM: MORE THAN A GOOD BUSINESS ENVIRONMENT

To be sure, economic freedom is about much more than a business environment in which entrepreneurship and prosperity can flourish. With its far-reaching impacts on various aspects of human development, economic freedom empowers people, unleashes powerful forces of choice and opportunity, gives nourishment to other liberties, and improves the overall quality of life.

While the *Index of Economic Freedom* is concerned exclusively with the measurement of freedom in the economic sphere of life, it is clear that economic freedom is also connected to civil and political freedom. A free economy is a fertile environment for the promotion of democracy. By giving people greater control of their daily lives, economic freedom nurtures self-reliance and the acquisition of varied skills and resources—key attributes of a middle class.

The pursuit of greater economic freedom can thus be an important stepping-stone to democratic governance. Freedom in the economic sphere encourages individual initiative and promotes decentralized decision-making throughout society. It nurtures precisely those personal attributes that allow individuals to challenge entrenched interests and compete for political power.

The dispersion of power in a well-functioning market system easily accommodates

DEMOCRATIC GOVERNANCE AND ECONOMIC FREEDOM

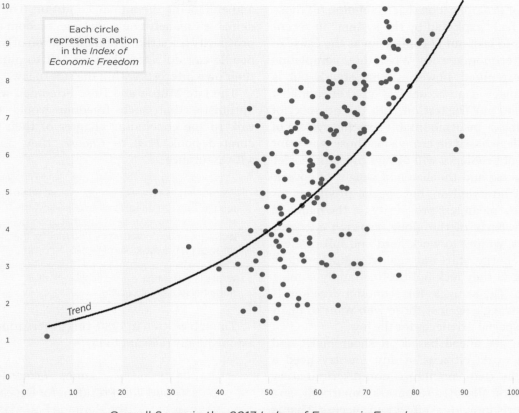

Democratic Governance

Each circle represents a nation in the *Index of Economic Freedom*

Trend

Overall Score in the *2017 Index of Economic Freedom*

SOURCES: Terry Miller and Anthony B. Kim, *2017 Index of Economic Freedom* (Washington: The Heritage Foundation, 2017), http://www.heritage.org/index, and The Economist Intelligence Unit, "Democracy Index 2015," http://www.eiu.com/Handlers/WhitepaperHandler.ashx?fi=EIU-Democracy-Index-2015.pdf&mode=wp&campaignid=DemocracyIndex2015 (accessed December 13, 2016).

Chart 2 ☎ heritage.org

diversity of thought and action. In fact, perhaps the greatest benefit of the free-market system is that it can provide a powerful yet peaceful organizing principle for today's pluralistic societies. And on a wider scale, the mutually beneficial interactions of freely trading societies may be the best hope for a peaceful world.

Undoubtedly, achieving greater political freedom and creating a well-functioning democracy can be a messy and often excruciating process. However, as shown in Chart 2, the positive relationship between economic freedom and effective democratic governance is unmistakable.

THE STRUGGLE CONTINUES

Now, as we progress further into the 21st century, more countries, whether politically free or not, have realized the critical necessity of establishing institutional frameworks that can enhance economic freedom for their citizens as the best path to development. Yet the struggle for economic freedom continues to face determined opposition.

For example, it has been common for those who feel "exploited by the system" in recent years to lash out at capitalism as the cause of their economic woes. When their complaints are examined, however, what stands out is not anger at an actual free-market capitalist system, but frustration with the prospect of an almost insurmountable existing system of privilege based on cronyism. Those who want special privileges will always pressure societies to expand the size and weight of government intervention, but special privileges for the few mean less prosperity for the many. In many parts of the globe, aspiring entrepreneurs, willing to work hard and full of ideas and energy, start out against a stacked deck because they lack political or family connections. The struggle for economic freedom is the struggle against those who want to maintain special privileges for the few.

To get ahead based on sheer merit and hard work, citizens of any country need a system that maintains non-discriminatory markets, allocates resources impartially, and rewards individual effort and success. That is the recipe for economic freedom—and for the opportunity to escape poverty and build lasting prosperity.

No alternative systems—and many have been tried—come close to the record of free-market capitalism in promoting growth and enhancing the human condition. The undeniable link between economic freedom and prosperity is a striking demonstration of what people can do when they are left to pursue their own interests within the rule of law.

The late Milton and Rose Friedman were optimistic that such freedom would prevail. In the concluding chapter of their celebrated book *Free to Choose*, they noted with assurance:

> Fortunately, we are waking up. We are again recognizing the dangers of an over-governed society, coming to understand that good objectives can be perverted by bad means, that reliance on the freedom of people to control their own lives in accordance with their own values is the surest way to achieve the full potential of a great society.

Though written in 1980, this observation is astonishingly relevant today.

James Wallner, PhD
Group Vice President for Research
The Heritage Foundation
December 2016

EXECUTIVE HIGHLIGHTS

The *Index of Economic Freedom* provides compelling evidence of the wide-ranging tangible benefits of living in freer societies. Now in its 23rd edition, the *Index* analyzes economic policy developments in 186 countries. Countries are graded and ranked on 12 measures of economic freedom that evaluate the rule of law, government size, regulatory efficiency, and the openness of markets.

KEY FINDINGS OF THE 2017 *INDEX*

- Per capita incomes are much higher in countries that are more economically free. Economies rated "free" or "mostly free" in the 2017 *Index* generate incomes that are more than double the average levels in other countries and more than five times higher than the incomes of people living in countries with "repressed" economies.

- Not only are higher levels of economic freedom associated with higher per capita incomes, but greater economic freedom is also strongly correlated to overall well-being, taking into account such factors as health, education, environment, innovation, societal progress, and democratic governance.

- No matter what their existing level of development may be, countries can get an immediate boost in their economic growth by implementing steps to increase economic freedom through policies that reduce taxes, rationalize the regulatory environment, open the economy to greater competition, and fight corruption.

THE GROWTH OF ECONOMIC FREEDOM

- Economic freedom has advanced in a majority of the world's countries over the past year. Global average economic freedom increased by 0.2 point to a record level of 60.9 on the 0–100 scale used in the *Index of Economic Freedom*. Since the inception of the *Index* in 1995, average scores have increased by over 5 percent.

- In the 2017 *Index*, 103 countries, most of which are less developed or emerging economies, showed advances in economic freedom. Remarkably, 49 countries achieved their highest economic freedom scores ever. Two large economies (China and Russia) are included in this group.

- While two countries (Mauritius and the United Kingdom) recorded no change in score, 73 experienced declines in economic freedom. Sixteen of these 73 countries, including notably the Bahamas, Bahrain, El Salvador, Pakistan, Venezuela, and the United States, recorded their lowest economic freedom scores ever.

- The Asia–Pacific region is home to nine of the 20 most improved countries: Fiji, Kiribati, Kazakhstan, China, Turkmenistan, Uzbekistan, Vanuatu, Tajikistan, and the Solomon Islands all recorded score gains of four points or more. On the other hand, Sub-Saharan Africa has the most countries (Cabo Verde, Djibouti, Ghana, Guinea, Kenya, The Gambia, and Madagascar) recording notable score declines, followed by the Americas (Barbados, the Bahamas, Venezuela, Suriname, Saint Lucia, and Brazil).

- Of the 180 economies whose economic freedom has been graded and ranked in the 2017 *Index*, only five (Hong Kong, Singapore, New Zealand, Switzerland, and Australia) have sustained very high freedom scores of 80 or more, putting them in the ranks of the economically "free."

- A further 29 countries, including Chile, the United Arab Emirates, the United Kingdom, Georgia, the United States, and Mauritius, have been rated as "mostly free" economies with scores between 70 and 80.

- A total of 92 economies, just over half of those graded in the 2017 *Index*, have earned a designation of "moderately free" or better. These economies provide institutional environments in which individuals and private enterprises benefit from at least a moderate degree of economic freedom in the pursuit of greater competitiveness, growth, and prosperity.

- On the opposite side of the spectrum, nearly half of the countries graded in the *Index*—88 economies—have registered economic freedom scores below 60. Of those economies, 65 are considered "mostly unfree" (scores of 50–60), and 23 are considered "repressed" (scores below 50).

THE INTANGIBLE BENEFITS OF ECONOMIC FREEDOM

Economic freedom is about much more than a business environment in which entrepreneurship and prosperity can flourish.

- With its far-reaching impacts on various aspects of human development, economic freedom empowers people, unleashes powerful forces of choice and opportunity, gives nourishment to other liberties, and improves the overall quality of life.

- It is true that in practice, each country's path to growth and development must be tailored to its own conditions and even what is politically possible. However, there are some fundamentals to bear in mind. Nations with higher degrees of economic freedom prosper because they tend to capitalize more fully on the ability of the free-market system not only to generate economic growth, but also to reinforce dynamic growth through efficient resource allocation, value creation, and innovation.

WHAT'S NEW IN THE 2017 *INDEX*?

The *Index of Economic Freedom*, The Heritage Foundation's flagship product, has become an essential reference tool and policy guidebook for many leaders and scholars around the world over the past 23 years. During that time, a number of improvements have been made in data collection, evaluation, and display in an effort to enhance the substance and overall quality of the publication. Following that tradition, the 2017 edition of the *Index* incorporates a number of enhancements that are intended to ensure that it remains a practical resource that is both credible and relevant to a changing world while remaining true to its roots as an objective source of data-driven analysis and policy recommendations.

Specific enhancements this year include:

- **New Country Page Design.** Individual country pages of the *Index* are intended to provide both a quick visual snapshot of a country's overall economic freedom and as much detailed information as space allows about developments and conditions in various aspects of that freedom. To improve the user-friendliness of the country pages, the 2017 *Index* incorporates a new page layout and full color charts that illustrate a country's overall economic freedom score in a more intuitive and visually attractive way.

- **Presentation of Country Pages by Region.** The country pages in the 2017 *Index* are now grouped by region and presented in alphabetical order following a brief summary of regional developments. All countries of the Western Hemisphere are now grouped in a single Americas region.

- **Enhanced Methodology.** The number of components of economic freedom that are separately evaluated and graded has increased from 10 to 12. The increased reliability and availability of worldwide data from a variety of sources has permitted the incorporation of new components specifically addressing "Judicial Effectiveness" and "Fiscal Health." The former Freedom from Corruption component has been refined, incorporating additional sub-factors and underlying data sources that are significantly more comprehensive than those formerly used, and renamed "Government Integrity." Finally, the Fiscal Freedom component of the *Index* has been renamed "Tax Burden" to better reflect exactly what is being measured. Details of these methodological changes are provided in the Methodology Appendix.

- **Equal Weighting.** The four pillars of economic freedom—Rule of Law, Government Size, Regulatory Efficiency, and Open Markets—now carry equal weight in the computation of the overall economic freedom score. Each now includes three equally weighted components, presenting opportunities for new types of analytical comparisons reflecting the impact of reforms in broader policy areas.

World Rank	Regional Rank	Country	Overall Score	Change from 2016	Property Rights	Judicial Effectiveness	Government Integrity	Tax Burden	Government Spending	Fiscal Health	Business Freedom	Labor Freedom	Monetary Freedom	Trade Freedom	Investment Freedom	Financial Freedom
1	1	Hong Kong	89.8	1.2	93.7	84.0	80.3	93.0	90.0	100	94.6	89.1	83.2	90.0	90	90
2	2	Singapore	88.6	0.8	97.1	91.5	87.9	90.5	90.1	80.7	95.1	90.8	84.3	90.0	85	80
3	3	New Zealand	83.7	2.1	96.1	88.5	89.9	70.8	46.5	97.8	91.8	86.2	90.1	87.4	80	80
4	1	Switzerland	81.5	0.5	86.9	77.6	80.3	70.9	67.5	95.8	76.8	72.2	84.4	90.0	85	90
5	4	Australia	81.0	0.7	81.7	92.9	74.8	63.2	59.0	84.6	89.3	84.1	86.4	86.2	80	90
6	2	Estonia	79.1	1.9	82.6	82.8	69.9	81.2	55.8	99.8	77.0	56.9	85.7	87.0	90	80
7	1	Canada	78.5	0.5	88.3	80.8	81.6	77.4	52.3	80.3	81.9	73.1	77.8	88.4	80	80
8	1	United Arab Emirates	76.9	4.3	76.7	85.0	74.2	96.4	67.4	99.2	81.1	80.9	78.4	83.5	40	60
9	3	Ireland	76.7	-0.6	85.8	78.3	78.3	72.7	57.1	60.3	80.3	73.6	87.6	87.0	90	70
10	2	Chile	76.5	-1.2	68.2	63.7	70.5	77.6	82.2	96.1	72.3	64.3	82.2	86.4	85	70
11	5	Taiwan	76.5	1.8	86.5	67.7	70.5	75.3	89.5	83.7	93.4	55.0	85.2	86.2	65	60
12	4	United Kingdom	76.4	0.0	93.8	93.0	78.3	65.1	41.9	40.4	89.9	72.8	85.0	87.0	90	80
13	5	Georgia	76.0	3.4	55.1	66.5	65.0	87.3	74.4	93.5	87.2	75.9	78.2	88.6	80	60
14	6	Luxembourg	75.9	2.0	85.8	77.0	78.3	64.5	46.0	99.0	68.6	43.8	86.2	87.0	95	80
15	7	Netherlands	75.8	1.2	87.4	69.9	85.7	53.2	37.0	83.0	80.2	70.5	85.8	87.0	90	80
16	8	Lithuania	75.8	0.6	73.0	62.4	69.7	86.9	64.1	93.6	79.1	63.6	90.0	87.0	70	70
17	3	United States	75.1	-0.3	81.3	75.1	78.1	65.3	55.9	53.3	84.4	91.0	80.1	87.1	80	70
18	9	Denmark	75.1	-0.2	86.7	68.5	84.9	37.2	5.7	95.4	93.9	85.8	85.5	87.0	90	80
19	10	Sweden	74.9	2.9	88.6	82.2	87.4	44.4	21.7	93.4	90.8	53.2	85.3	87.0	85	80
20	11	Latvia	74.8	4.4	72.6	59.7	67.3	84.7	57.4	95.0	79.8	72.0	86.5	87.0	75	60
21	1	Mauritius	74.7	0.0	64.4	72.6	44.3	92.0	81.5	74.9	78.2	68.8	81.1	88.7	80	70
22	12	Iceland	74.4	1.1	85.0	71.5	71.5	70.9	41.1	90.6	90.2	62.6	81.2	88.0	80	60
23	6	South Korea	74.3	2.6	77.8	59.9	67.3	73.7	68.9	97.4	90.6	57.0	84.0	79.5	65	70
24	13	Finland	74.0	1.4	90.6	82.7	90.0	66.6	0.0	77.3	90.2	53.4	85.1	87.0	85	80
25	14	Norway	74.0	3.2	86.7	83.3	88.3	55.6	38.5	98.4	89.5	48.8	75.8	87.7	75	60
26	15	Germany	73.8	-0.6	82.9	79.5	77.7	61.9	41.4	89.9	86.6	42.8	85.9	87.0	80	70
27	7	Malaysia	73.8	2.3	85.3	67.3	51.8	85.3	78.7	76.5	90.8	73.1	85.3	81.2	60	50
28	16	Czech Republic	73.3	0.1	70.3	55.9	55.9	82.9	45.3	92.0	67.2	77.7	85.8	87.0	80	80
29	2	Qatar	73.1	2.4	74.8	63.0	59.0	99.6	71.2	97.4	68.1	65.4	80.6	83.1	55	60
30	17	Austria	72.3	0.6	86.0	81.8	75.2	50.3	19.3	79.7	76.9	67.6	83.4	87.0	90	70
31	18	Macedonia	70.7	3.2	67.0	61.4	52.0	91.9	68.9	72.6	81.5	66.7	80.8	86.1	60	60
32	8	Macau	70.7	0.6	60.0	60.0	37.1	72.3	92.8	100	60.0	50.0	70.8	90.0	85	70
33	19	Armenia	70.3	3.3	55.5	42.5	43.4	83.7	81.7	82.9	78.5	72.4	72.8	80.2	80	70
34	2	Botswana	70.1	-1.0	58.1	54.0	57.6	77.1	61.2	99.4	68.8	68.6	77.9	83.8	65	70
35	9	Brunei Darussalam	69.8	2.5	62.5	39.9	40.9	85.6	61.2	100	76.6	90.4	76.1	89.1	65	50
36	3	Israel	69.7	-1.0	71.9	82.0	47.6	61.0	50.5	71.8	69.9	64.3	84.9	88.0	75	70
37	4	Colombia	69.7	-1.1	63.8	25.2	39.6	80.1	74.2	89.8	77.1	77.9	77.0	81.6	80	70
38	5	Uruguay	69.7	0.9	70.2	66.8	70.3	77.5	69.4	77.2	74.8	62.9	71.3	80.6	85	30

2017 INDEX OF ECONOMIC FREEDOM WORLD RANKINGS

World Rank	Regional Rank	Country	Overall Score	Change from 2016	Property Rights	Judicial Effectiveness	Government Integrity	Tax Burden	Government Spending	Fiscal Health	Business Freedom	Labor Freedom	Monetary Freedom	Trade Freedom	Investment Freedom	Financial Freedom
39	20	Romania	69.7	4.1	63.9	58.5	45.9	87.4	65.3	90.9	65.9	62.5	83.6	87.0	75	50
40	10	Japan	69.6	-3.5	89.4	73.8	86.1	68.5	52.3	9.5	82.3	77.5	83.0	82.6	70	60
41	6	Jamaica	69.5	2.0	58.0	61.5	38.2	81.0	77.5	79.9	78.9	73.7	79.5	75.3	80	50
42	11	Kazakhstan	69.0	5.4	56.1	56.5	38.0	93.3	85.7	98.9	74.5	82.5	73.9	78.5	40	50
43	7	Peru	68.9	1.5	58.3	28.2	38.8	80.3	85.1	98.4	69.4	62.8	83.3	87.1	75	60
44	4	Bahrain	68.5	-5.8	64.2	53.7	55.5	99.9	69.8	12.0	69.4	78.7	80.7	82.8	75	80
45	21	Poland	68.3	-1.0	60.8	58.0	55.5	76.0	46.9	76.1	67.8	61.5	84.7	87.0	75	70
46	22	Kosovo	67.9	6.5	70.3	58.0	45.9	93.5	77.8	88.9	68.8	65.3	80.0	70.8	65	30
47	23	Bulgaria	67.9	2.0	62.5	38.9	41.8	91.0	58.4	86.4	66.7	68.3	83.3	87.0	70	60
48	24	Cyprus	67.9	-0.8	75.4	60.7	53.6	73.0	48.8	72.9	75.8	58.6	83.3	87.0	75	50
49	25	Belgium	67.8	-0.6	83.3	69.3	71.5	44.1	9.6	66.3	82.0	61.1	84.9	87.0	85	70
50	26	Malta	67.7	1.0	67.7	62.9	53.6	62.8	44.9	85.1	62.5	57.2	83.5	87.0	85	60
51	3	Rwanda	67.6	4.5	64.4	68.8	45.9	79.8	77.3	83.3	59.0	81.8	80.0	70.3	60	40
52	12	Vanuatu	67.4	6.6	65.5	33.0	70.5	97.0	80.4	99.1	51.4	58.1	74.8	73.9	65	40
53	5	Jordan	66.7	-1.6	60.1	49.5	49.8	91.3	73.3	55.5	63.9	58.1	86.7	82.0	70	60
54	8	Panama	66.3	1.5	61.1	21.5	40.9	85.2	83.1	84.9	74.4	43.0	78.4	77.8	75	70
55	13	Thailand	66.2	2.3	51.3	41.7	40.7	81.0	85.3	96.3	69.9	62.8	72.9	82.8	50	60
56	27	Hungary	65.8	-0.2	60.1	51.8	41.5	79.3	25.3	79.3	64.0	64.4	91.7	87.0	75	70
57	28	Slovak Republic	65.7	-0.9	69.0	38.0	39.6	79.7	47.2	82.9	64.9	54.4	81.1	87.0	75	70
58	14	Philippines	65.6	2.5	49.2	37.1	38.7	78.9	89.4	97.2	62.6	57.2	80.6	76.4	60	60
59	9	St. Vincent and the Grenadines	65.2	-3.6	37.3	68.8	47.6	72.8	71.7	66.7	80.3	74.5	82.9	65.2	75	40
60	29	Turkey	65.2	3.1	61.3	52.5	40.7	75.5	57.7	95.7	64.3	48.5	72.2	79.4	75	60
61	6	Kuwait	65.1	2.4	55.5	56.4	41.3	97.7	40.8	99.8	61.2	61.5	73.6	78.7	55	60
62	11	St. Lucia	65.0	-5.0	65.5	68.8	39.6	76.4	71.6	53.8	77.2	68.7	82.3	71.6	65	40
63	10	Costa Rica	65.0	-2.4	51.6	55.6	55.4	79.4	88.5	42.4	68.1	53.9	80.8	84.7	70	50
64	7	Saudi Arabia	64.4	2.3	62.0	65.0	45.9	99.7	54.5	65.7	73.8	68.5	70.1	78.2	40	50
65	30	Albania	64.4	-1.5	54.0	28.5	39.7	86.9	72.5	51.5	79.3	50.7	81.4	87.7	70	70
66	12	El Salvador	64.1	-1.0	45.3	35.4	31.7	79.0	85.9	74.7	57.3	54.5	79.2	86.5	80	60
67	13	Dominica	63.7	-3.3	43.8	67.7	40.9	73.2	67.5	72.6	72.1	59.0	89.5	72.6	75	30
68	15	Azerbaijan	63.6	3.4	50.5	33.0	37.6	87.7	57.5	97.4	71.5	75.0	73.6	74.4	55	50
69	31	Spain	63.6	-4.9	71.2	53.9	57.2	62.5	41.4	26.9	66.9	55.3	85.5	87.0	85	70
70	14	Mexico	63.6	-1.6	58.1	38.7	30.0	74.9	76.7	66.8	70.7	57.9	78.8	80.0	70	60
71	16	Fiji	63.4	4.6	67.7	41.9	32.7	80.7	72.5	84.1	61.3	70.5	75.5	68.8	55	50
72	32	France	63.3	1.0	85.0	72.7	69.7	47.6	2.0	57.0	78.0	44.1	81.6	82.0	70	70
73	17	Tonga	63.0	3.4	65.5	19.8	47.6	86.9	74.4	79.6	76.1	86.0	80.6	79.7	40	20
74	15	Guatemala	63.0	1.2	45.0	27.8	27.5	79.2	94.8	93.5	58.7	48.2	79.4	87.0	65	50
75	4	Côte d'Ivoire	63.0	3.0	42.6	45.8	34.3	78.4	84.6	87.0	62.1	50.6	73.2	72.3	75	50

2017 INDEX OF ECONOMIC FREEDOM WORLD RANKINGS

World Rank	Regional Rank	Country	Overall Score	Change from 2016	Property Rights	Judicial Effectiveness	Government Integrity	Tax Burden	Government Spending	Fiscal Health	Business Freedom	Labor Freedom	Monetary Freedom	Trade Freedom	Investment Freedom	Financial Freedom
76	16	Dominican Republic	62.9	1.9	56.1	25.3	30.9	84.6	90.2	90.1	52.8	56.2	76.7	77.0	75	40
77	33	Portugal	62.6	-2.5	73.3	68.9	59.0	59.8	25.1	32.1	86.4	43.4	85.9	87.0	70	60
78	5	Namibia	62.5	0.6	53.8	50.6	41.3	65.2	55.6	66.4	67.6	84.4	77.2	83.5	65	40
79	34	Italy	62.5	1.3	74.6	55.4	44.7	54.9	22.3	66.9	69.8	52.9	86.9	87.0	85	50
80	17	Paraguay	62.4	0.9	38.2	23.3	32.6	96.2	83.0	95.1	62.4	28.5	78.3	76.6	75	60
81	6	South Africa	62.3	0.4	67.6	59.7	47.6	70.2	68.4	70.0	62.0	58.9	75.8	77.3	40	50
82	8	Oman	62.1	-5.0	60.8	52.3	47.6	98.5	20.5	36.3	68.4	70.3	80.6	85.2	65	60
83	35	Montenegro	62.0	-2.9	58.0	50.4	43.4	83.1	33.1	44.3	72.0	67.4	82.5	84.7	75	50
84	18	Indonesia	61.9	2.5	48.3	39.3	44.7	83.6	89.9	90.1	49.1	48.9	74.0	80.5	35	60
85	7	Seychelles	61.8	-0.4	55.2	42.6	44.3	78.8	63.9	90.7	63.4	55.9	78.3	83.4	55	30
86	9	Morocco	61.5	0.2	55.0	41.9	37.1	71.7	69.4	55.0	67.7	33.8	82.7	84.0	70	70
87	18	Trinidad and Tobago	61.2	-1.7	54.7	48.7	36.8	81.4	57.7	51.8	67.7	71.4	75.9	78.6	60	50
88	8	Swaziland	61.1	1.4	53.5	33.3	30.9	74.8	71.6	93.2	57.5	64.4	75.6	88.9	50	40
89	19	Kyrgyz Republic	61.1	1.5	50.9	17.2	30.3	93.7	55.2	78.9	73.7	79.8	68.5	75.3	60	50
90	19	Bahamas	61.1	-9.8	45.3	48.7	38.2	97.1	83.8	42.3	68.5	71.5	77.0	50.6	50	60
91	9	Uganda	60.9	1.6	39.3	34.6	28.7	73.7	91.0	78.1	42.4	84.6	80.3	78.3	60	40
92	36	Bosnia and Herzegovina	60.2	1.6	41.2	40.0	32.7	83.5	33.7	89.3	47.4	59.3	84.0	86.6	65	60
93	10	Burkina Faso	59.6	0.5	38.2	28.4	31.7	82.6	82.5	88.4	46.4	53.3	84.6	69.2	70	40
94	20	Cambodia	59.5	1.6	42.4	22.1	12.8	90.2	88.1	95.7	29.6	62.0	81.0	80.3	60	50
95	37	Croatia	59.4	0.3	65.5	56.8	43.4	66.8	31.3	44.7	58.2	43.3	80.3	87.4	75	60
96	11	Benin	59.2	-0.1	36.0	29.4	31.3	68.6	85.9	71.3	51.9	52.4	85.4	68.7	80	50
97	38	Slovenia	59.2	-1.4	75.0	55.1	53.6	58.7	28.6	6.1	80.6	60.2	85.3	87.0	70	50
98	20	Nicaragua	59.2	0.6	31.1	15.9	27.4	77.2	80.8	96.1	59.0	55.6	71.2	81.0	65	50
99	39	Serbia	58.9	-3.2	50.3	40.2	38.2	83.3	40.3	46.9	62.9	65.9	80.8	77.8	70	50
100	21	Honduras	58.8	1.1	45.0	38.2	32.2	83.3	74.7	64.1	56.9	31.2	77.3	78.4	65	60
101	22	Belize	58.6	1.2	43.5	48.7	35.0	81.3	68.6	60.5	62.7	53.6	79.6	70.1	50	50
102	12	Mali	58.6	2.1	36.7	33.8	34.3	69.4	88.0	87.8	44.2	51.1	83.0	70.1	65	40
103	13	Gabon	58.6	-0.4	35.9	26.7	37.6	77.0	81.0	96.1	50.6	58.4	83.0	61.8	55	40
104	40	Belarus	58.6	9.8	50.9	56.3	37.6	89.8	48.7	92.8	71.3	74.6	60.4	80.6	30	10
105	14	Tanzania	58.6	0.1	33.8	28.8	29.2	80.3	89.5	76.6	50.1	64.3	69.6	76.0	55	50
106	23	Guyana	58.5	3.1	37.7	34.1	33.9	68.0	72.8	80.9	63.2	70.9	79.8	70.7	60	30
107	21	Bhutan	58.4	-1.1	60.1	50.7	44.7	83.1	73.6	61.7	72.6	77.6	67.1	60.0	20	30
108	22	Samoa	58.4	-5.1	51.3	22.6	37.1	80.4	51.9	66.6	77.0	73.3	84.5	70.7	55	30
109	23	Tajikistan	58.2	6.9	45.5	45.6	32.7	90.9	74.1	95.8	65.6	49.2	69.8	73.9	25	30
110	41	Moldova	58.0	0.6	49.6	23.9	28.6	86.1	54.8	90.6	65.9	38.9	72.0	80.0	55	50
111	24	China	57.4	5.4	48.3	60.7	41.6	70.0	73.0	92.5	53.9	63.4	71.8	73.6	20	20
112	25	Sri Lanka	57.4	-2.5	48.0	48.3	30.0	85.3	90.2	31.2	72.8	57.5	76.0	74.5	35	40
113	15	Madagascar	57.4	-3.7	34.8	21.4	25.0	91.0	93.2	79.8	43.3	43.8	73.3	78.0	55	50

World Rank	Regional Rank	Country	Overall Score	Change from 2016	Property Rights	Judicial Effectiveness	Government Integrity	Tax Burden	Government Spending	Fiscal Health	Business Freedom	Labor Freedom	Monetary Freedom	Trade Freedom	Investment Freedom	Financial Freedom
114	42	Russia	57.1	6.5	47.6	44.5	38.2	81.8	61.5	93.4	74.8	50.8	57.3	75.2	30	30
115	16	Nigeria	57.1	-0.4	35.3	33.2	12.2	85.2	95.2	87.2	48.9	73.9	71.3	62.3	40	40
116	17	Cabo Verde	56.9	-9.6	42.6	50.2	41.8	78.3	70.7	1.2	65.5	43.2	86.7	68.2	75	60
117	18	Congo, Dem. Rep. of	56.4	10.0	40.6	48.7	28.6	73.4	94.7	99.3	59.9	38.4	78.6	64.6	30	20
118	19	Ghana	56.2	-7.3	51.6	40.9	35.5	84.5	76.3	9.2	59.6	57.4	64.5	65.1	70	60
119	20	Guinea-Bissau	56.1	4.3	33.8	48.7	28.7	89.0	87.5	75.3	46.7	60.9	77.7	65.2	30	30
120	21	Senegal	55.9	-2.2	44.0	39.3	42.1	70.9	74.3	51.8	50.8	38.9	86.0	73.1	60	40
121	22	Comoros	55.8	3.4	37.3	22.6	30.0	64.6	81.2	98.6	58.5	50.6	81.5	70.2	45	30
122	23	Zambia	55.8	-3.0	49.6	39.8	35.0	73.1	81.6	21.6	66.6	48.2	70.7	78.3	55	50
123	10	Tunisia	55.7	-1.9	49.6	39.9	37.3	73.7	73.4	53.4	80.6	56.1	75.9	63.8	35	30
124	24	São Tomé and Príncipe	55.4	-1.3	37.7	15.9	39.7	87.8	67.9	67.1	65.0	47.2	69.6	71.8	65	30
125	26	Nepal	55.1	4.2	37.3	32.0	26.7	84.9	89.5	98.4	64.6	47.6	72.2	68.1	10	30
126	27	Solomon Islands	55.0	8.0	39.3	41.9	33.9	62.8	34.4	99.8	68.5	70.5	81.0	83.0	15	30
127	43	Greece	55.0	1.8	52.5	56.1	41.3	61.1	5.4	58.1	74.3	51.0	78.2	82.0	60	40
128	28	Bangladesh	55.0	1.7	34.9	26.0	19.1	72.8	94.0	78.7	53.4	68.7	68.6	63.6	50	30
129	29	Mongolia	54.8	-4.6	51.3	28.4	36.8	87.1	57.6	0.0	67.2	76.6	72.3	74.9	45	60
130	24	Barbados	54.5	-13.8	55.5	33.0	34.3	74.0	39.0	0.0	69.6	67.7	83.7	62.2	75	60
131	25	Mauritania	54.4	-0.4	22.5	13.8	29.2	81.2	73.2	77.1	64.4	57.4	81.9	62.3	50	40
132	30	Micronesia	54.1	2.3	30.0	30.0	40.7	90.7	0.0	98.6	57.8	67.7	83.6	85.6	35	30
133	31	Lao P.D.R.	54.0	4.2	35.3	35.9	32.6	86.1	76.6	61.2	66.3	54.4	70.2	74.6	35	20
134	26	Lesotho	53.9	3.3	51.6	50.9	39.6	55.7	0.0	92.2	52.2	57.7	76.4	80.2	50	40
135	27	Kenya	53.5	-4.0	45.1	42.7	24.7	78.5	77.9	14.4	50.0	62.4	73.8	67.2	55	50
136	28	Gambia	53.4	-3.7	39.1	38.8	38.2	74.9	74.3	3.2	52.8	65.6	63.8	65.0	75	50
137	11	Lebanon	53.3	-6.2	43.8	25.3	23.3	91.8	76.1	0.0	51.5	49.5	78.4	84.4	65	50
138	29	Togo	53.2	-0.4	33.8	39.9	36.8	68.2	79.8	45.1	50.3	46.2	77.5	71.3	60	30
139	30	Burundi	53.2	-0.7	25.7	19.8	24.6	73.8	69.5	69.6	53.5	67.4	75.2	74.2	55	30
140	25	Brazil	52.9	-3.6	55.0	49.7	33.4	70.1	53.1	22.8	61.3	52.3	67.0	69.4	50	50
141	32	Pakistan	52.8	-3.1	36.4	34.1	30.5	78.9	87.3	30.8	61.2	37.8	74.8	67.2	55	40
142	31	Ethiopia	52.7	1.2	32.6	29.6	37.6	77.1	90.3	86.5	50.0	57.2	65.7	65.1	20	20
143	33	India	52.6	-3.6	55.4	44.4	44.3	77.2	77.4	11.0	52.8	41.6	75.0	72.6	40	40
144	12	Egypt	52.6	-3.4	35.4	56.3	32.7	86.1	63.0	4.6	66.8	51.3	69.6	70.2	55	40
145	32	Sierra Leone	52.6	0.3	37.4	27.0	18.9	81.3	90.2	76.2	49.6	29.7	71.1	69.4	60	20
146	34	Burma	52.5	3.8	23.0	12.9	29.6	86.2	81.5	89.9	50.1	77.1	65.4	74.2	20	20
147	35	Vietnam	52.4	-1.6	49.7	32.0	24.6	79.6	74.6	21.1	61.2	62.2	76.0	83.1	25	40
148	36	Uzbekistan	52.3	6.3	48.0	41.9	27.5	90.7	66.2	99.8	64.8	50.4	61.1	66.8	0	10
149	33	Malawi	52.2	0.4	36.0	44.2	31.3	79.1	69.8	33.5	45.3	56.9	54.7	70.5	55	50
150	34	Cameroon	51.8	-2.4	43.5	29.6	17.4	75.4	84.4	60.9	44.3	47.8	80.1	53.4	35	50
151	35	Central African Republic	51.8	6.6	12.6	33.0	28.7	65.8	94.1	84.1	27.2	42.7	68.2	55.2	80	30

World Rank	Regional Rank	Country	Overall Score	Change from 2016	Property Rights	Judicial Effectiveness	Government Integrity	Tax Burden	Government Spending	Fiscal Health	Business Freedom	Labor Freedom	Monetary Freedom	Trade Freedom	Investment Freedom	Financial Freedom
152	37	Papua New Guinea	50.9	-2.3	37.7	54.0	32.7	67.8	64.5	16.7	59.8	67.4	69.8	85.4	25	30
153	38	Kiribati	50.9	4.7	48.0	33.0	37.6	73.6	0.0	99.5	51.5	71.9	82.0	58.2	25	30
154	36	Niger	50.8	-3.5	33.8	22.6	35.0	76.3	73.4	38.5	39.1	46.1	83.3	66.4	55	40
155	13	Iran	50.5	7.0	32.4	36.0	29.6	81.1	92.7	94.9	64.8	54.5	55.5	54.5	0	10
156	26	Argentina	50.4	6.6	32.4	39.6	38.2	62.6	54.6	56.4	57.3	46.1	50.9	66.7	50	50
157	39	Maldives	50.3	-3.6	45.1	33.0	31.4	93.0	51.5	9.4	80.6	70.4	76.3	47.8	35	30
158	37	Mozambique	49.9	-3.3	40.6	32.4	30.9	73.2	58.2	22.7	58.8	41.0	79.9	76.7	35	50
159	27	Haiti	49.6	-1.7	12.6	25.1	19.1	80.3	81.0	51.8	49.4	62.1	73.8	70.6	40	30
160	28	Ecuador	49.3	0.7	38.7	22.3	33.9	79.1	46.1	56.4	55.4	47.3	67.7	69.7	35	40
161	38	Liberia	49.1	-3.1	33.6	41.0	31.4	83.6	60.1	36.2	53.1	48.5	71.8	60.1	50	20
162	39	Chad	49.0	2.7	30.6	24.1	24.6	46.0	87.2	74.6	27.5	44.9	74.3	54.7	60	40
163	40	Afghanistan	48.9	N/A	12.6	28.4	27.5	91.6	79.9	97.3	54.2	59.9	69.3	66.0	0	0
164	40	Sudan	48.8	N/A	31.1	19.8	18.9	86.5	95.1	85.5	53.9	49.7	59.3	50.5	15	20
165	41	Angola	48.5	-0.4	36.4	19.8	12.8	87.7	58.6	70.7	58.5	40.4	70.6	56.7	30	40
166	44	Ukraine	48.1	1.3	41.4	22.6	29.2	78.6	38.2	67.9	62.1	48.8	47.4	85.9	25	30
167	29	Suriname	48.0	-5.8	45.1	15.4	31.7	70.1	69.6	16.2	48.6	76.1	75.1	68.4	30	30
168	30	Bolivia	47.7	0.3	25.7	15.4	32.6	86.1	49.1	81.4	58.9	35.8	66.4	76.0	5	40
169	42	Guinea	47.6	-5.7	15.6	13.1	27.5	69.1	78.4	34.2	55.8	54.8	71.1	61.2	50	40
170	41	Turkmenistan	47.4	5.5	32.4	5.0	29.6	95.3	92.3	98.9	30.0	20.0	74.8	80.0	0	10
171	43	Djibouti	46.7	-9.3	12.3	10.3	32.6	80.9	39.5	13.8	51.6	59.0	75.3	54.9	80	50
172	14	Algeria	46.5	-3.6	38.2	29.6	31.7	81.1	51.0	19.8	62.1	49.5	67.0	63.3	35	30
173	42	Timor-Leste	46.3	0.5	6.8	10.3	29.2	64.7	65.6	20.0	72.2	63.9	77.5	80.0	45	20
174	44	Equatorial Guinea	45.0	1.3	35.4	13.1	24.6	75.4	53.6	46.4	50.9	38.5	78.3	53.8	40	30
175	45	Zimbabwe	44.0	5.8	27.3	26.1	14.7	61.1	75.2	90.6	36.2	33.1	76.5	52.8	25	10
176	46	Eritrea	42.2	-0.5	36.4	10.3	27.5	81.3	74.7	0.0	56.7	69.7	61.0	69.2	0	20
177	47	Congo, Rep. of	40.0	-2.8	34.8	22.6	30.5	66.8	36.2	11.6	32.1	37.5	76.1	52.2	50	30
178	31	Cuba	33.9	4.1	32.4	10.0	41.8	51.3	0.0	81.2	20.0	20.0	66.0	64.5	10	10
179	32	Venezuela	27.0	-6.7	6.8	10.3	11.6	72.5	51.5	15.2	39.7	28.5	16.8	60.7	0	10
180	43	North Korea	4.9	2.6	32.4	5.0	11.6	0.0	0.0	0.0	5.0	5.0	0.0	0.0	0	0
N/A	N/A	Iraq	N/A	N/A	37.3	15.9	19.1	N/A	36.1	11.3	61.2	68.0	76.9	N/A	N/A	N/A
N/A	N/A	Libya	N/A	N/A	6.8	22.6	26.7	95	0	11.4	65.0	52.5	69.2	80.0	N/A	N/A
N/A	N/A	Liechtenstein	N/A	N/A	N/A	N/A	N/A	N/A	N/A	N/A	92.3	85.7	N/A	90.0	85	80
N/A	N/A	Somalia	N/A	N/A	6.8	N/A	11.6	100	N/A	0.0	92.3	91.8	N/A	N/A	N/A	N/A
N/A	N/A	Syria	N/A	N/A	37.3	22.6	30.0	N/A	N/A	0.0	66.4	55.7	N/A	56.6	N/A	N/A
N/A	N/A	Yemen	N/A	N/A	37.3	22.6	17.4	N/A	77.2	10.6	51.4	54.2	59.7	N/A	N/A	N/A

CHAPTER 1

THE GROWTH AND IMPACT OF ECONOMIC FREEDOM

Ambassador Terry Miller and Anthony B. Kim

Economic freedom has advanced in over 100 countries over the past year. Global average economic freedom increased by 0.2 point to a record level of 60.9 on the 0–100 scale used in the *Index of Economic Freedom*. In the years since the inception of the *Index* in 1995, average scores have increased by over 5 percent.

Behind this record of advancing economic freedom are stories of human progress and the achievements of countries and their citizens—literally billions of people around the world whose lives have been measurably improved. There also are stories of policy failure, backsliding, and continuing repression.

GAINS AND LOSSES

In the 2017 *Index*, 103 countries, the majority of which are less developed or emerging economies, showed advances in economic freedom over the past year. Remarkably, 49 countries achieved their highest economic freedom scores ever. Two large economies (China and Russia) are included in this group.

While two countries (Mauritius and the United Kingdom) recorded no change in score, 73 experienced declines in economic freedom, and 16 countries, including notably the Bahamas, Bahrain, El Salvador, Pakistan, Venezuela, and the United States, recorded their lowest economic freedom scores ever.

The Asia–Pacific region is home to nine of the 20 most improved countries: Fiji, Kiribati, Kazakhstan, China, Turkmenistan, Uzbekistan, Vanuatu, Tajikistan, and the Solomon Islands all recorded score gains of four points or more. On the other hand, Sub-Saharan Africa has the

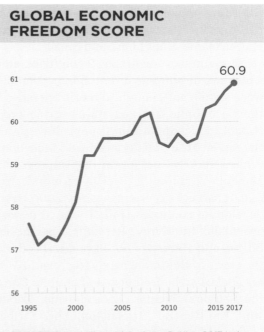

GLOBAL ECONOMIC FREEDOM SCORE

60.9

SOURCE: Terry Miller and Anthony B. Kim, *2017 Index of Economic Freedom* (Washington: The Heritage Foundation, 2017), http://www.heritage.org/index.

Chart 1 ☎ heritage.org

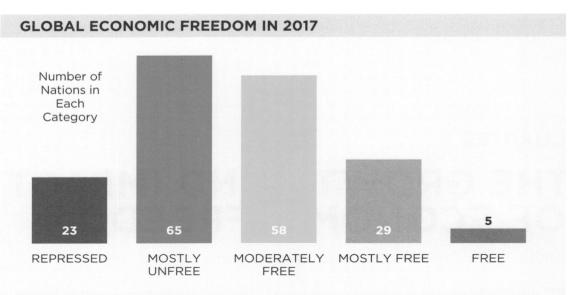

GLOBAL ECONOMIC FREEDOM IN 2017

Number of Nations in Each Category

REPRESSED	MOSTLY UNFREE	MODERATELY FREE	MOSTLY FREE	FREE
23	65	58	29	5

SOURCE: Terry Miller and Anthony B. Kim, *2017 Index of Economic Freedom* (Washington: The Heritage Foundation, 2017), http://www.heritage.org/index.

Chart 2 ☎ heritage.org

most countries (Cabo Verde, Djibouti, Ghana, Guinea, Kenya, The Gambia, and Madagascar) recording notable score declines, followed by the Americas (Barbados, the Bahamas, Venezuela, Suriname, Saint Lucia, and Brazil).

Score improvements in 19 countries, all of which are developing or emerging economies, were significant enough to merit upgrades in their economic freedom status in the *Index*. Notably, Macedonia and Armenia have joined the ranks of the "mostly free," with Macedonia ranked "mostly free" for the first time ever and Armenia regaining a level of economic freedom it had not experienced since 2006. Seven developing countries (Fiji, Tonga, Indonesia, Swaziland, the Kyrgyz Republic, Uganda, and Bosnia and Herzegovina) have advanced into the ranks of the "moderately free," and 10 others (Belarus, the Democratic Republic Congo, the Solomon Islands, Laos, Burma, Uzbekistan, the Central African Republic, Kiribati, Iran, and Argentina) have escaped the status of economically "repressed."

Of the 180 economies whose economic freedom has been graded and ranked in the 2017 *Index*, only five have sustained very high freedom scores of 80 or more, putting them in the ranks of the economically "free." The five are Hong Kong, Singapore, New Zealand, Switzerland, and Australia. A further 29 countries, including Chile, the United Arab Emirates, the United Kingdom, Georgia, the United States, and Mauritius, have been rated as "mostly free" economies with scores between 70 and 80.

A total of 92 economies, or about 51 percent of all nations and territories graded in the 2017 *Index*, have earned a designation of "moderately free" or better. These economies provide institutional environments in which individuals and private enterprises benefit from at least a moderate degree of economic freedom in the pursuit of greater competitiveness, growth, and prosperity. On the opposite side of the spectrum, nearly half of the countries graded in the *Index*—88 economies—have registered economic freedom scores below 60. Of those, 65 economies are considered "mostly unfree" (scores of 50–60), and 23 are considered "repressed" (scores below 50).

Despite the global progress recorded over the 23-year history of the *Index*, the number

ECONOMIC FREEDOM AND PER CAPITA INCOME

GDP per Capita (Purchasing Power Parity)

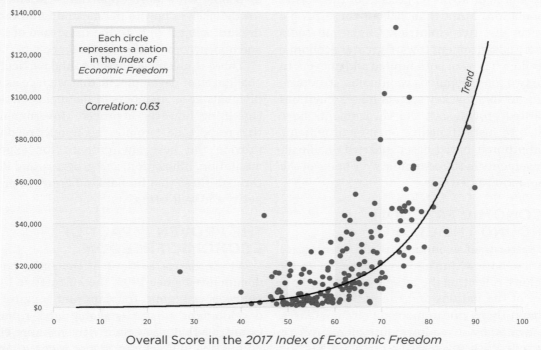

Each circle represents a nation in the *Index of Economic Freedom*

Correlation: 0.63

Trend

Overall Score in the *2017 Index of Economic Freedom*

GDP per Capita (Purchasing Power Parity)

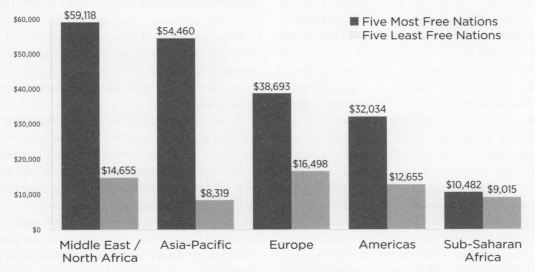

■ Five Most Free Nations
  Five Least Free Nations

	Five Most Free	Five Least Free
Middle East / North Africa	$59,118	$14,655
Asia-Pacific	$54,460	$8,319
Europe	$38,693	$16,498
Americas	$32,034	$12,655
Sub-Saharan Africa	$10,482	$9,015

SOURCES: Terry Miller and Anthony B. Kim, *2017 Index of Economic Freedom* (Washington: The Heritage Foundation, 2017), http://www.heritage.org/index, and International Monetary Fund, World Economic Outlook Database, April 2016, https://www.imf.org/external/pubs/ft/weo/2016/01/weodata/index.aspx (accessed December 13, 2016).

Chart 3 ☎ heritage.org

of people suffering from a lack of economic freedom remains disturbingly high: around 4.5 billion, or about 65 percent of the world's population. More than half of these people live in just two countries, China and India, where advancement toward greater economic freedom has been both limited and uneven. In the two most populous economies, structural reforms in a few key sectors have sometimes boosted growth, but the governments have failed to institutionalize open environments that promote broad-based and sustainable improvements in the economic well-being of the population as a whole.

ECONOMIC FREEDOM AROUND THE GLOBE

Patterns of economic freedom are quite diverse both within and among the five *Index* regions, reflecting the unique culture and history of the nations and the individuals that inhabit them, not to mention circumstances of geography or endowments of natural resources. With an average score of 68, Europe has recorded the highest level of average economic freedom among the regions. Despite the ongoing economic and political turmoil in a number of countries in the Middle East and North Africa, the region as a whole has still achieved an average economic freedom score slightly above 60 due to high ratings of economic freedom in the United Arab Emirates, Qatar, Israel, and Bahrain. Despite some progress in recent years, the average economic freedom score in Sub-Saharan Africa continues to be below 60.

As demonstrated in previous editions of the *Index*, it is notable that despite varying degrees of economic freedom across the regions, the fundamentally positive relationship between economic freedom and prosperity is readily apparent worldwide. Chart 3 shows that, no matter the region, the higher a country's level of economic freedom is, the higher its income per capita also is.

The diversity of the world's peoples and cultures implies that there will be many paths to economic development and prosperity. The whole idea of economic freedom is to empower people with more opportunity to choose for themselves how to pursue and fulfill their dreams, subject only to the basic rule of law and honest competition from others.

There is no single answer to the particular challenges of development that we face as individuals or as members of distinct societies. One thing, however, is proven: Governments that respect and promote economic freedom provide the best environment for experimentation, innovation, and progress, and it is through these that humankind grows in prosperity and well-being.

THE PROVEN IMPACT OF ECONOMIC FREEDOM

As successive editions of the *Index* have documented since 1995, the affirmative link between economic freedom and long-term development is unmistakable and robust. Countries that allow their citizens more economic freedom achieve higher incomes and better standards of living. People in economically free societies have longer lives. They have better health and access to more effective education. They are able to be better stewards of the environment, and they push forward the frontiers of human achievement in science and technology through greater innovation.

It has become quite apparent that despite ups and downs, the principles and lessons of economic freedom have been widely understood, accepted, and implemented in practice by a significant number of countries around the globe. Their progress is seen in the score changes. The poorer-performing countries, by contrast, have tried only some of the ideas, adulterated others, or even in a few cases rejected them outright.

The economic performance of countries with various rankings in the *Index* provides numerous examples of the consequences of the rise and fall of economic freedom around the globe. For example:

AS ECONOMIC FREEDOM RISES, THE GLOBAL ECONOMY EXPANDS AND POVERTY FALLS

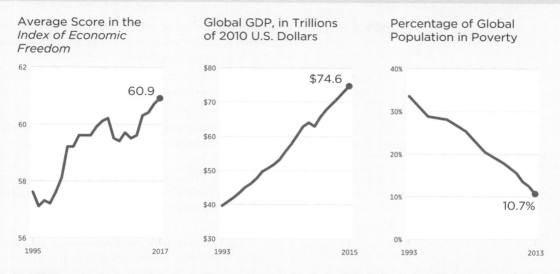

Average Score in the *Index of Economic Freedom*

60.9

Global GDP, in Trillions of 2010 U.S. Dollars

$74.6

Percentage of Global Population in Poverty

10.7%

SOURCES: Terry Miller and Anthony B. Kim, *2017 Index of Economic Freedom* (Washington: The Heritage Foundation, 2017), http://www.heritage.org/index.org/index; The World Bank, World Development Indicators, http://databank.worldbank.org/data/reports.aspx?source=world-development-indicators (accessed December 16, 2016); and The World Bank, PovcalNet, http://iresearch.worldbank.org/PovcalNet/povDuplicateWB.aspx (accessed December 16, 2016). Some figures have been interpolated.

Chart 4 ☎ heritage.org

- Countries that allow private ownership of property protected by an effective judicial system encourage more entrepreneurial initiative than do countries that require collective or government ownership or control of economic resources.

- Governments that dominate their countries' economies with heavy taxation and deficit spending end up impoverishing their citizens through prolonged economic stagnation exacerbated by high debt burdens.

- Open competition, facilitated by regulatory efficiency, promotes greater productivity and ensures better-organized allocation of resources than do systems of central planning.

- Countries that practice some version of free-market capitalism, with economies open to global trade, investment, and financial markets, do better than those that are protectionist or that shun economic linkages with others.

Policies that promote economic freedom, whether through improvements in the rule of law, the promotion of efficiency and openness, or suitable restraints on the size and reach of government, therefore provide the environment that can best inspire people to develop practical solutions to the economic and social challenges that confront our world.

GREATER ECONOMIC FREEDOM MEANS GREATER HUMAN DEVELOPMENT

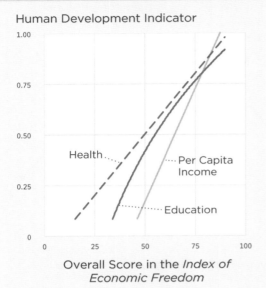

Human Development Indicator

Overall Score in the *Index of Economic Freedom*

SOURCES: Terry Miller and Anthony B. Kim, *2017 Index of Economic Freedom* (Washington: The Heritage Foundation, 2017), http://www.heritage.org/index, and U.N. Human Development Programme, *Human Development Report 2015*, http://hdr.undp.org/en/2015-report (accessed December 16, 2016). Human Development values have been converted to a 0–1 scale.

Chart 5 ☎ heritage.org

ECONOMIC FREEDOM ALLEVIATES POVERTY AND PROMOTES OVERALL HUMAN DEVELOPMENT

The free-market system that is rooted in the principles of economic freedom has fueled unprecedented economic growth around the world. As the global economy has moved toward greater economic freedom over the past two decades, real world GDP has increased by about 80 percent, and the global poverty rate has been cut in half, lifting hundreds of millions of people out of poverty.

Achieving greater overall prosperity that goes beyond the materialistic and monetary dimensions of well-being is equally important.

The societal benefits of economic freedom extend far beyond reductions in poverty. Countries with higher levels of economic freedom enjoy higher levels of human development in terms of life expectancy, literacy, education, and overall quality of life.

As Chart 5 shows, governments that choose policies that increase economic freedom are placing their societies on the path to more education opportunities, better health care, and higher standards of living for their citizens.

ECONOMIC FREEDOM FACILITATES INNOVATION AND BETTER ENVIRONMENTAL PROTECTION

The positive link between economic freedom and higher levels of innovation ensures greater economic dynamism in coping with various developmental challenges by spurring a virtuous cycle of investment, innovation (including in greener technologies), and dynamic entrepreneurial growth.

In recent years, government policies and actions concerning the environment have become more intrusive and economically distortionary. Many governments have promoted programs to tax carbon emissions and increase taxes on gasoline, have organized non-transparent and sometimes corrupt exchanges for the buying and selling of carbon emissions, and have provided subsidies for "clean" energy to politically favored firms. Such policies impose a huge direct cost on society and retard economic growth—and all for uncertain environmental benefits.

In addition, the fact that the most remarkable improvements in clean energy use and energy efficiency over the past decades have occurred not as a result of government regulation, but rather as a result of advances in technology and trade should not be overlooked. Around the world, economic freedom has been a key factor in enhancing countries' capacity for innovation and, by so doing, in improving their overall environmental performance.

ECONOMIC FREEDOM, INNOVATION, AND THE ENVIRONMENT

Innovation Index Score

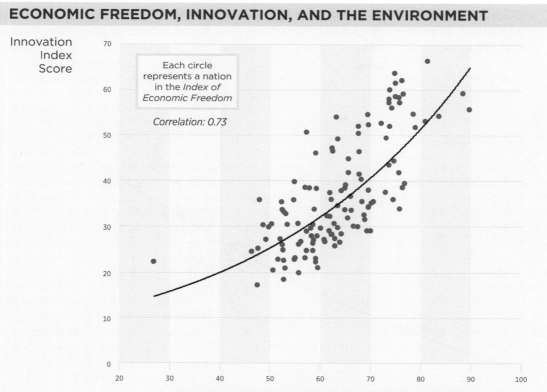

Each circle represents a nation in the *Index of Economic Freedom*

Correlation: 0.73

Overall Score in the *2017 Index of Economic Freedom*

Environmental Performance Index

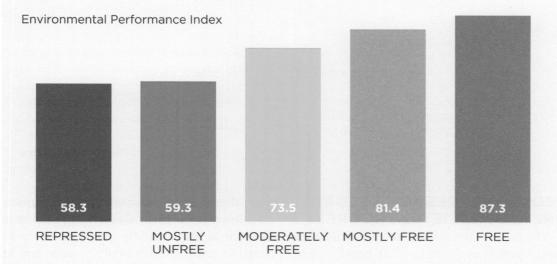

| 58.3 | 59.3 | 73.5 | 81.4 | 87.3 |
| REPRESSED | MOSTLY UNFREE | MODERATELY FREE | MOSTLY FREE | FREE |

SOURCES: Terry Miller and Anthony B. Kim, *2017 Index of Economic Freedom* (Washington: The Heritage Foundation, 2017), http://www.heritage.org/index; Cornell University, INSEAD, and World Intellectual Property Organization, *The Global Innovation Index 2016* (Geneva: World Intellectual Property Organization, 2016), https://www.globalinnovationindex.org/gii-2016-report (accessed December 16, 2016); and Yale University, "2016 Environmental Performance Index," http://epi.yale.edu/reports/2016-report (accessed December 16, 2016).

Chart 6 ☎ heritage.org

ECONOMIC FREEDOM AND SOCIAL PROGRESS

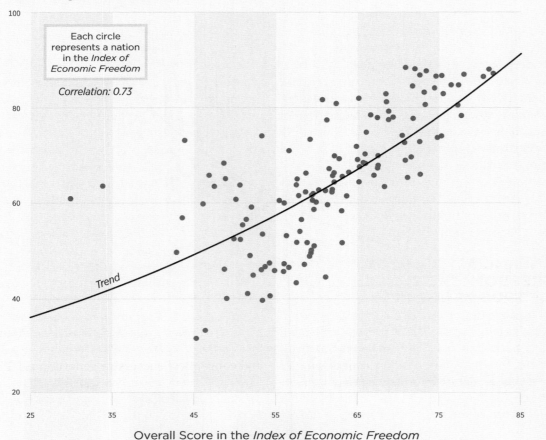

Social Progress Index Score

Each circle represents a nation in the *Index of Economic Freedom*

Correlation: 0.73

Trend

Overall Score in the *Index of Economic Freedom*

SOURCES: Terry Miller and Anthony B. Kim, *2017 Index of Economic Freedom* (Washington: The Heritage Foundation, 2017), http://www.heritage.org/index, and Social Progress Imperative, "Social Progress Index 2015," http://www.socialprogressimperative.org/data/spi (accessed December 8, 2016).

Chart 7 ☎ heritage.org

ECONOMIC FREEDOM ENSURES GREATER SOCIETAL PROGRESS

The massive improvements in global indicators of income and quality of life largely reflect a paradigm shift in the debate about how societies should be structured to achieve the most optimal outcome. Over the past two decades, this debate has largely been won by capitalism. However, fears that the immediate benefits of capitalism are fading have led to concerns about economic mobility and economic freedom.

At the heart of ensuring upward economic mobility is the task of advancing economic freedom so that ordinary people in a free society can enjoy the fruits of dynamic and inclusive growth. Economic freedom is critical to generating the broader-based economic growth that brings more opportunities for a greater number of people to work, produce, and save. In other words, ensuring greater economic freedom is directly related to preserving and enhancing dynamic upward mobility.

Not surprisingly, societies based on economic freedom are the ones that have demonstrated the strongest social progress. As shown in Chart 7, countries that more fully embrace economic freedom have provided the institutional environments that are most conducive to societal progress. Countries that have improved their competitiveness and have opened their societies to new ideas have largely achieved the high levels of societal progress that their citizens demand. It is not massive redistributions of wealth or government dictates on income levels that produce the most positive societal outcomes. Instead, mobility and progress require lower barriers to market entry, freedom to engage with the world, and less government intrusion.

ADVANCING ECONOMIC FREEDOM: THE SOURCE OF TRUE PROGRESS

Regrettably, it has been an avoidable human tragedy that not all of the world's people have participated in our era's spread of economic freedom. Free-market capitalism, given a chance, does benefit the greatest number of people. No other systems that have been tried have come close in terms of providing broad-based prosperity. Countries that have not joined the march of freedom have left their citizens lagging behind and even, in the worst cases, stuck in poverty or destitution.

Such failures are inexcusable. Most important, they are preventable.

Advancing the free market is the most democratic and effective way to challenge big government, concentrated government power, and the status quo. Perhaps one of the critical lessons of the past years is that the fundamental superiority and value of economic liberty must be retaught to a new generation of political leaders, either by their peers who have lived in less free systems and less free times or by their own citizens, who understand instinctively that when individuals are allowed to decide for themselves how best to pursue their dreams and aspirations, their collective achievements can add up to a better society for all.

As Friedrich A. Hayek once observed, "If old truths are to retain their hold on men's minds, they must be restated in the language and concepts of successive generations." The *Index of Economic Freedom* provides the basis for such a dialogue and a foundation for economic revival in the years ahead.

CHAPTER 2

DEFINING ECONOMIC FREEDOM

Ambassador Terry Miller and Anthony B. Kim

Economic freedom is at its heart about individual autonomy, concerned chiefly with the freedom of choice enjoyed by individuals in acquiring and using economic goods and resources. The underlying assumption of those who favor economic freedom is that individuals know their needs and desires best and that a self-directed life, guided by one's own philosophies and priorities rather than those of a government or technocratic elite, is the foundation of a fulfilling existence. Independence and self-respect flow from the ability and responsibility to take care of oneself and one's family and are invaluable contributors to human dignity and equality.

Living in societies as we do, individual autonomy can never be considered absolute. Many individuals regard the well-being of their families and communities as equal in importance to their own, and the personal rights enjoyed by one person may well end at his neighbor's doorstep. Decisions and activities that have an impact or potential impact on others are rightly constrained by societal norms and, in the most critical areas, by government laws or regulations.

In a market-oriented economy, societal norms, not government laws and regulations, are the primary regulator of behavior. Such norms grow organically out of society itself, reflecting its history, its culture, and the experience of generations learning how to live with one another. They guide our understanding of ethics, the etiquette of personal and professional relationships, and consumer tastes. Democratic political systems, at their best, reflect societal norms in their laws and regulations, but even democratic governments, if unconstrained by constitutional or other traditional limits, may pose substantial threats to economic freedom. A constraint imposed on economic freedom by majority rule is no less a constraint than one imposed by an absolute ruler or oligarch. It is thus not so much the type of government that determines the degree of economic freedom as it is the extent to which government has limits beyond which it may not, or at least does not, go.

Inevitably, any discussion of economic freedom will focus on the critical relationship between individuals and the government. In general, state action or government control that interferes with individual autonomy limits economic freedom.

However, the goal of economic freedom is not simply the absence of government coercion or constraint, but rather the creation and maintenance of a mutual sense of liberty for all. Some government action is necessary for the citizens of a nation to defend themselves and to promote the peaceful evolution of civil society, but when government action rises beyond the minimal necessary level, it is likely infringing on someone's economic or personal freedom.

Throughout history, governments have imposed a wide array of constraints on economic activity. Such constraints, though sometimes imposed in the name of equality or some other ostensibly noble societal purpose, are in fact imposed most often for the benefit of societal elites or special interests. As Milton and Rose Friedman once observed:

> A society that puts equality—in the sense of equality of outcome—ahead of freedom will end up with neither equality nor freedom. The use of force to achieve equality will destroy freedom, and the force, introduced for good purposes, will end up in the hands of people who use it to promote their own interests.[1]

Government's excessive intrusion into wide spheres of economic activity comes with a high cost to society as a whole. By substituting political judgments for those of the marketplace, government diverts entrepreneurial resources and energy from productive activities to rent-seeking, the quest for economically unearned benefits. The result is lower productivity, economic stagnation, and declining prosperity.

MEASURING ECONOMIC FREEDOM

The *Index of Economic Freedom* takes a comprehensive view of economic freedom. Some of the aspects of economic freedom that are evaluated are concerned with a country's interactions with the rest of the world (for example, the extent of an economy's openness to global investment or trade). Most, however, focus on policies within a country, assessing the liberty of individuals to use their labor or finances without undue restraint and government interference.

Each of the measured aspects of economic freedom plays a vital role in promoting and sustaining personal and national prosperity. All are complementary in their impact, however, and progress in one area is often likely

to reinforce or even inspire progress in another. Similarly, repressed economic freedom in one area (for example, a lack of respect for property rights) may make it much more difficult to achieve high levels of freedom in other categories.

The 12 aspects of economic freedom measured in the *Index* may be grouped into four broad categories:

- **Rule of law** (property rights, judicial effectiveness, and government integrity);

- **Government size** (tax burden, government spending, and fiscal health);

- **Regulatory efficiency** (business freedom, labor freedom, and monetary freedom); and

- **Market openness** (trade freedom, investment freedom, and financial freedom).

RULE OF LAW

Property Rights. In a market economy, the ability to accumulate private property and wealth is a central motivating force for workers and investors. The recognition of private property rights and an effective rule of law to protect them are vital features of a fully functioning market economy. Secure property rights give citizens the confidence to undertake entrepreneurial activity, save their income, and make long-term plans because they know that their income, savings, and property (both real and intellectual) are safe from unfair expropriation or theft.

Property rights are a primary factor in the accumulation of capital for production and investment. Secure titling is key to unlocking the wealth embodied in real estate, making natural resources available for economic use, and providing collateral for investment financing. It is also through the extension and protection of property rights that societies avoid the "tragedy of the commons," the phenomenon that leads to the degradation and exploitation of property that is held communally and for which no one is accountable. A key aspect of property rights protection is the enforcement of contracts. The voluntary undertaking of contractual obligations is the foundation of the market system and the basis for economic specialization, gains from commercial exchange, and trade among nations. Even-handed government enforcement of private contracts is essential to ensuring equity and integrity in the marketplace.

Judicial Effectiveness. Well-functioning legal frameworks protect the rights of all citizens against infringement of the law by others, including by governments and powerful parties. As an essential component of the rule of law, judicial effectiveness requires efficient and fair judicial systems to ensure that laws are fully respected, with appropriate legal actions taken against violations.

Judicial effectiveness, especially for developing countries, may be the area of economic freedom that is most important in laying the foundations for economic growth, and in advanced economies, deviations from judicial effectiveness may be the first signs of serious problems that will lead to economic decline.

There is plenty of evidence from around the world that judicial effectiveness is a critical factor in empowering individuals, ending discrimination, and enhancing competition. In the never-ending struggle to improve the human condition and achieve greater prosperity, an institutional commitment to the preservation and advancement of judicial effectiveness is critical.

Government Integrity. In a world characterized by social and cultural diversity, practices regarded as corrupt in one place may simply reflect traditional interactions in another. For example, small informal payments to service providers or even government officials may be regarded variously as a normal means of compensation, a "tip" for unusually good service, or a corrupt form of extortion.

While such practices may indeed constrain an individual's economic freedom, their impact on the economic system as a whole is likely to be modest. Of far greater concern is the systemic corruption of government institutions by practices such as bribery, nepotism, cronyism, patronage, embezzlement, and graft. Though not all are crimes in every society or circumstance, these practices erode the integrity of government wherever they are practiced. By allowing some individuals or special interests to gain government benefits at the expense of others, they are grossly incompatible with the principles of fair and equal treatment that are essential ingredients of an economically free society.

There is a direct relationship between the extent of government intervention in economic activity and the prevalence of corruption. In particular, excessive and redundant government regulations provide opportunities for bribery and graft. In addition, government regulations or restrictions in one area may create informal markets in another. For example, by imposing numerous burdensome barriers to conducting business, including regulatory red tape and high transaction costs, a government can incentivize bribery and encourage illegitimate and secret interactions that compromise the transparency that is essential for the efficient functioning of a free market.

GOVERNMENT SIZE

Tax Burden. All governments impose fiscal burdens on economic activity through taxation and borrowing. Governments that permit individuals and businesses to keep and manage a larger share of their income and wealth for their own benefit and use, however, maximize economic freedom.

The higher the government's share of income or wealth, the lower the individual's reward for economic activity and the lower the incentive to undertake work at all. Higher tax rates reduce the ability of individuals and firms to pursue their goals in the marketplace and thereby lower the level of overall private-sector activity.

Individual and corporate income tax rates are an important and direct constraint on an individual's economic freedom and are reflected as such in the *Index*, but they are not a comprehensive measure of the tax burden. Governments impose many other indirect taxes, including payroll, sales, and excise taxes, as well as tariffs and value-added taxes (VATs). In the *Index of Economic Freedom*, the burden of these taxes is captured by measuring the overall tax burden from all forms of taxation as a percentage of total gross domestic product (GDP).

Government Spending. The cost, size, and intrusiveness of government taken together are a central economic freedom issue that is measured in the *Index* in a variety of ways (see, for example, Tax Burden and Regulatory Efficiency). Government spending comes in many forms, not all of which are equally harmful to economic freedom. Some government spending (for example, to provide infrastructure, fund research, or improve human capital) may be considered investment. Government also spends on public goods, the benefits of which accrue broadly to society in ways that markets cannot price appropriately.

All government spending, however, must eventually be financed by higher taxation and entails an opportunity cost. This cost is the value of the consumption or investment that would have occurred had the resources involved been left in the private sector.

Excessive government spending runs a great risk of crowding out private economic activity. Even if an economy achieves faster growth through more government spending, such economic expansion tends to be only temporary, distorting the market allocation of resources and private investment incentives. Even worse, a government's insulation from market discipline often leads to bureaucracy, lower productivity, inefficiency, and mounting public debt that imposes an even greater burden on future generations.

Fiscal Health. A government's budget is one of the clearest indicators of the extent to which it respects the principle of limited government. By delineating priorities and allocating resources, a budget signals clearly the areas in which government will intervene in economic activity and the extent of that intervention. Beyond that, however, a budget reflects a government's commitment (or lack thereof) to sound financial management of resources, which is both essential for dynamic long-term economic expansion and critical to the advancement of economic freedom.

Widening deficits and a growing debt burden, both of which are direct consequences of poor government budget management, lead to the erosion of a country's overall fiscal health. Deviations from sound fiscal positions often disturb macroeconomic stability, induce economic uncertainty, and thus limit economic freedom.

Debt is an accumulation of budget deficits over time. In theory, debt financing of public spending could make a positive contribution to productive investment and ultimately to economic growth. Debt could also be a mechanism for positive macroeconomic countercyclical interventions or even long-term growth policies. On the other hand, high levels of public debt may have numerous negative impacts such as raising interest rates, crowding out private investment, and limiting government's flexibility in responding to economic crises. Mounting public debt driven by persistent budget deficits, particularly spending that merely boosts government consumption or transfer payments, often undermines overall productivity growth and leads ultimately to economic stagnation rather than growth.

REGULATORY EFFICIENCY

Business Freedom. An individual's ability to establish and run an enterprise without undue interference from the state is one of the most fundamental indicators of economic freedom. Burdensome and redundant regulations are the most common barriers to the free conduct of entrepreneurial activity. By increasing the costs of production, regulations can make it difficult for entrepreneurs to succeed in the marketplace.

Although many regulations hinder business productivity and profitability, the ones that most inhibit entrepreneurship are often those that are associated with licensing new businesses. In some countries, as well as many states in the United States, the procedure for obtaining a business license can be as simple as mailing in a registration form with a minimal fee. In Hong Kong, for example, obtaining a business license requires filling out a single form, and the process can be completed in a few hours. In other economies, such as India and parts of South America, the process of obtaining a business license can take much longer and involve endless trips to government offices and repeated encounters with officious and sometimes corrupt bureaucrats.

Once a business is open, government regulation may interfere with the normal decision-making or price-setting process. Interestingly, two countries with the same set of regulations can impose different regulatory burdens. If one country applies its regulations evenly and transparently, it can lower the regulatory burden by facilitating long-term business planning. If the other applies regulations inconsistently, it raises the regulatory burden by creating an unpredictable business environment.

Labor Freedom. The ability of individuals to find employment opportunities and work is a key component of economic freedom. By the same token, the ability of businesses to contract freely for labor and dismiss redundant workers when they are no longer needed is essential to enhancing productivity and sustaining overall economic growth.

The core principle of any economically free market is voluntary exchange. That is just as true in the labor market as it is in the market for goods.

State intervention generates the same problems in the labor market that it produces in any other market. Government labor regulations take a variety of forms, including minimum wages or other wage controls, limits on hours worked or other workplace conditions, restrictions on hiring and firing, and other constraints. In many countries, unions play an important role in regulating labor freedom and, depending on the nature of their activity, may be either a force for greater freedom or an impediment to the efficient functioning of labor markets.

Onerous labor laws penalize businesses and workers alike. Rigid labor regulations prevent employers and employees from freely negotiating changes in terms and conditions of work, and the result is often a chronic mismatch of labor supply and demand.

Monetary Freedom. Monetary freedom requires a stable currency and market-determined prices. Whether acting as entrepreneurs or as consumers, economically free people need a steady and reliable currency as a medium of exchange, unit of account, and store of value. Without monetary freedom, it is difficult to create long-term value or amass capital.

The value of a country's currency can be influenced significantly by the monetary policy of its government. With a monetary policy that endeavors to fight inflation, maintain price stability, and preserve the nation's wealth, people can rely on market prices for the foreseeable future. Investments, savings, and other longer-term plans can be made more confidently. An inflationary policy, by contrast, confiscates wealth like an invisible tax and distorts prices, misallocates resources, and raises the cost of doing business.

There is no single accepted theory of the right monetary policy for a free society. At one time, the gold standard enjoyed widespread support. What characterizes almost all monetary theories today, however, is support for low inflation and an independent central bank. There is also widespread recognition that price controls corrupt market efficiency and lead to shortages or surpluses.

MARKET OPENNESS

Trade Freedom. Many governments place restrictions on their citizens' ability to interact freely as buyers or sellers in the international marketplace. Trade restrictions can manifest themselves in the form of tariffs, export taxes, trade quotas, or outright trade bans. However, trade restrictions also appear in more subtle ways, particularly in the form of regulatory barriers related to health or safety.

The degree to which government hinders the free flow of foreign commerce has a direct bearing on the ability of individuals to pursue their economic goals and maximize their productivity and well-being. Tariffs, for example, directly increase the prices that local consumers pay for foreign imports, but they also distort production incentives for local producers, causing them to produce either a good in which they lack a comparative advantage or more of a protected good than is economically ideal. This impedes overall economic efficiency and growth.

In many cases, trade limitations also put advanced-technology products and services beyond the reach of local entrepreneurs, limiting their own productive development.

Investment Freedom. A free and open investment environment provides maximum entrepreneurial opportunities and incentives for expanded economic activity, greater productivity, and job creation. The benefits of such an environment flow not only to the individual companies that take the entrepreneurial risk in expectation of greater return, but also to society as a whole. An effective investment framework is characterized by transparency and equity, supporting all types of firms rather than just large or strategically important companies, and encourages rather than discourages innovation and competition.

Restrictions on the movement of capital, both domestic and international, undermine the efficient allocation of resources and reduce productivity, distorting economic decision-making. Restrictions on cross-border investment can limit both inflows and outflows of capital, thereby shrinking markets and reducing opportunities for growth.

In an environment in which individuals and companies are free to choose where and how to invest, capital can flow to its best uses: to the sectors and activities where it is most needed and the returns are greatest. State action to redirect the flow of capital and limit choice is an imposition on the freedom of both the investor and the person seeking capital. The more restrictions a country imposes on investment, the lower its level of entrepreneurial activity.

Financial Freedom. An accessible and efficiently functioning formal financial system ensures the availability of diversified savings, credit, payment, and investment services to individuals. By expanding financing opportunities and promoting entrepreneurship, an open banking environment encourages competition in order to provide the most efficient financial intermediation between households and firms as well as between investors and entrepreneurs.

Through a process driven by supply and demand, markets provide real-time information on prices and immediate discipline for those who have made bad decisions. This process depends on transparency in the market and the integrity of the information being made available. A prudent and effective regulatory system, through disclosure requirements and independent auditing, ensures both.

Increasingly, the central role played by banks is being complemented by other financial services that offer alternative means for raising capital or diversifying risk. As with the banking system, the useful role for government in regulating these institutions lies in ensuring transparency and integrity and promoting disclosure of assets, liabilities, and risks.

Banking and financial regulation by the state that goes beyond the assurance of transparency and honesty in financial markets can impede efficiency, increase the costs of financing entrepreneurial activity, and limit competition. If the government intervenes in the stock market, for instance, it contravenes the choices of millions of individuals by interfering with the pricing of capital—the most critical function of a market economy.

ECONOMIC FREEDOM: A FORMULA FOR SUCCESS

As a vital component of human dignity, autonomy, and personal empowerment, economic freedom is valuable as an end itself. Just as important, however, is the fact that economic freedom provides a formula for economic success.

We know from the data we collect to build the *Index* that each measured aspect of economic freedom has a significant effect on economic growth and prosperity. Policies that allow greater freedom in any of the areas measured tend to spur growth. Growth, in turn, is an essential element in building lasting prosperity.

Economic freedom is not a single system, however. In many respects, it is the absence of a single dominating system. As previous editions of the *Index* have elaborated, economic freedom is not a dogmatic ideology. It represents instead a philosophy that rejects dogma and embraces diverse and even competing strategies for economic advancement. The *Index* also reveals that it is not the policies we fail to implement that hold back economic growth. Rather, it is the dreadful policies that, all too often, we put in place.

In other words, those who believe in economic freedom believe in the right of individuals to decide for themselves how to direct their lives. The added benefit from society's point of view is the proven power of self-directed individuals, whether working alone or working together in associations or corporations, to create the goods and services that best respond to the needs and desires of their fellow citizens.

No country provides perfect freedom to its citizens, and those that do permit high levels of freedom differ with respect to which aspects they believe are most important. That is consistent with the nature of liberty, which allows individuals and societies to craft their own unique paths to prosperity.

Throughout the *Index of Economic Freedom*, we explore many aspects of the relationships between individuals and governments. In measuring economic freedom, we have focused on a comprehensive yet far from exhaustive range of policy areas in which governments typically act, for good or ill. However, the concept of freedom, by its very nature, resists a narrow definition, and each year seems to bring new challenges from those who seek to impose their own views or control the economic actions of others. As new threats to economic freedom arise around the world, our definitions and methodologies will continue to evolve so that we can provide as true a picture as possible of the state of economic freedom around the world.

ENDNOTE:

1.   Milton Friedman and Rose D. Friedman, *Free to Choose: A Personal Statement* (New York: Harcourt Brace Jovanovich, 1979).

CHAPTER 3

ECONOMIC FREEDOM BY REGION AND COUNTRY

The *Index of Economic Freedom* chronicles and benchmarks the many factors underpinning economic freedom in countries throughout the world.

The country profiles in the *Index*, organized regionally in five groupings (the Americas, Asia and the Pacific, Europe, the Middle East and North Africa, and Sub-Saharan Africa), provide many real-world examples of the impact, both positive and negative, of government economic policies. Those that enhance economic freedom tend to be associated with greater economic and social progress and can be emulated by other countries that are willing to reform. Successful countries are those that chart not just one path to development, but as many as the ingenuity of humans can produce when they are free to experiment and innovate.

Of the 186 countries included in this edition, 180 are fully scored and ranked. Because of insufficient data, six countries (Iraq, Libya, Somalia, Syria, Yemen, and Liechtenstein) are evaluated but not graded. In the 2017 *Index*, Afghanistan has been graded and ranked for the first time, and Sudan has returned to the rankings for the first time since 2000.

For analytical understanding and presentational clarity, the 12 economic freedoms are grouped into four pillars of economic freedom:

- **Rule of law** (property rights, judicial effectiveness, and government integrity);

- **Government size** (tax burden, government spending, and fiscal health);

- **Regulatory efficiency** (business freedom, labor freedom, and monetary freedom); and

- **Market openness** (trade freedom, investment freedom, and financial freedom).

Ranked countries are given a score ranging from 0 to 100 on each of the 12 components of economic freedom, and these scores are then averaged (using equal weights) to compute a country's final economic freedom score.

In addition to the scores, the country pages include a brief overview describing economic strengths and weaknesses and providing the political and economic background that may have influenced the country's performance. A statistical profile includes the country's main economic and demographic indicators.

ECONOMIC FREEDOM: REGIONAL VARIATIONS
(REGIONAL AVERAGE)

Regional Ranking	The Americas (60.0)	Asia-Pacific (60.3)	Europe (68.0)	Middle East + North Africa (61.9)	Sub-Saharan Africa (55.0)
1	Canada	Hong Kong	Switzerland	United Arab Emirates	Mauritius
2	Chile	Singapore	Estonia	Qatar	Botswana
3	United States	New Zealand	Ireland	Israel	Rwanda
4	Colombia	Australia	United Kingdom	Bahrain	Côte d'Ivoire
5	Uruguay	Taiwan	Georgia	Jordan	Namibia
6	Jamaica	South Korea	Luxembourg	Kuwait	South Africa
7	Peru	Malaysia	Netherlands	Saudi Arabia	Seychelles
8	Panama	Macau	Lithuania	Oman	Swaziland
9	Saint Vincent and the Grenadines	Brunei Darussalam	Denmark	Morocco	Uganda
10	Costa Rica	Japan	Sweden	Tunisia	Burkina Faso
11	Saint Lucia	Kazakhstan	Latvia	Lebanon	Benin
12	El Salvador	Vanuatu	Iceland	Egypt	Mali
13	Dominica	Thailand	Finland	Iran	Gabon
14	Mexico	Philippines	Norway	Algeria	Tanzania
15	Guatemala	Azerbaijan	Germany	Iraq	Madagascar
16	Dominican Republic	Fiji	Czech Republic	Libya	Nigeria
17	Paraguay	Tonga	Austria	Syria	Cabo Verde
18	Trinidad and Tobago	Indonesia	Macedonia	Yemen	Congo, Dem. Rep. of
19	Bahamas	Kyrgyz Republic	Armenia		Ghana
20	Nicaragua	Cambodia	Romania		Guinea-Bissau
21	Honduras	Bhutan	Poland		Senegal
22	Belize	Samoa	Kosovo		Comoros
23	Guyana	Tajikistan	Bulgaria		Zambia
24	Barbados	China	Cyprus		São Tomé and Príncipe
25	Brazil	Sri Lanka	Belgium		Mauritania
26	Argentina	Nepal	Malta		Lesotho
27	Haiti	Solomon Islands	Hungary		Kenya
28	Ecuador	Bangladesh	Slovak Republic		Gambia
29	Suriname	Mongolia	Turkey		Togo
30	Bolivia	Micronesia	Albania		Burundi
31	Cuba	Laos	Spain		Ethiopia
32	Venezuela	Pakistan	France		Sierra Leone
33		India	Portugal		Malawi
34		Burma	Italy		Cameroon
35		Vietnam	Montenegro		Central African Republic
36		Uzbekistan	Bosnia and Herzegovina		Niger
37		Papua New Guinea	Croatia		Mozambique
38		Kiribati	Slovenia		Liberia
39		Maldives	Serbia		Chad
40		Afghanistan	Belarus		Sudan
41		Turkmenistan	Moldova		Angola
42		Timor-Leste	Russia		Guinea
43		North Korea	Greece		Djibouti
44			Ukraine		Equatorial Guinea
45			Liechtenstein		Zimbabwe
46					Eritrea
47					Congo, Rep. of
48					Somalia

Economic Freedom Scores
- 80–100   Free
- 70–79.9   Mostly Free
- 60–69.9   Moderately Free
- 50–59.9   Mostly Unfree
- 0–49.9   Repressed
- Not Graded

THE AMERICAS

THE AMERICAS

The countries of the Americas range from the continent-spanning advanced economies of Canada and the United States to the island microstates of the Caribbean. The region is one of the world's most economically diverse. Poor nations of Central America, for example, share culture and history but little else with potential South American economic powerhouses like Brazil or Argentina. Ideological differences are strong as well: The tragic legacy of Cuba's Fidel Castro includes a few states in the region still experimenting with discredited Communist/socialist economic theories that for the most part have lost sway in other regions.

The overall population of the Americas is 965 million, second only to Asia. Among the five regions, the Americas has the second highest population-weighted average per capita income. Across the region, economies have expanded at an average rate of 2.4 percent over the past five years. Regional average rates of unemployment and inflation have been over 8 percent.

The lack—and in some cases erosion—of economic freedom in the Americas reflects reversals of free-market policies in some countries and a failure in others to commit fully to the pursuit of economic reform. Despite some progress in moving away from the authoritarian cronyism that has held back development in Latin America, the stark common reality across the region is that the foundations of a well-functioning free market remain fragile, with widespread corruption and the weak protection of property rights aggravating systemic shortcomings such as regulatory inefficiency and monetary instability caused by various government-driven market distortions.

Chart 1 shows the distribution of countries in the Americas in terms of economic freedom. The region does not have any economically "free" countries. Three of the 32 countries in the Americas region (Canada, Chile, and the United States) are rated "mostly free." Most countries in the region fall in the category of "moderately free" and "mostly unfree." Six countries (Haiti, Ecuador, Suriname, Bolivia, Cuba, and Venezuela) are rated "repressed."

An examination of the various components of economic freedom evaluated in the *Index* reveals that the countries of the Americas as a whole perform better than the world average in only four of the 12 categories. Scores for tax burden and government spending indicate broad regional acceptance of the principle of limited government, and levels of market openness are consistent with world standards. On the other hand, as shown in Table 1, the rule of law and regulatory efficiency are major problem areas, reflecting long-standing weakness in the protection of property rights, ineffectiveness in the judiciary, and lack of government integrity.

Chart 2, which highlights the vivid positive correlation between high levels of economic freedom and high GDP per capita, reveals a large freedom gap within the Americas. The failed populist policies implemented by such

THE AMERICAS: QUICK FACTS

TOTAL POPULATION: 965.4 million

POPULATION WEIGHTED AVERAGES

GDP PER CAPITA (PPP): $28,484

GROWTH: 1.0%

5 YEAR GROWTH: 2.4%

INFLATION: 8.3%

UNEMPLOYMENT: 5.9%

PUBLIC DEBT: 71.0%

SOURCE: Terry Miller and Anthony B. Kim,
2017 Index of Economic Freedom
(Washington: The Heritage Foundation, 2017),
http://www.heritage.org/index.

☎ heritage.org

AMERICAS

Canada

United States

Mexico

Cuba

Jamaica

Belize

Guatemala

El Salvador

Costa Rica

Panama

Bahamas

Haiti

Dominican Republic

Honduras

Nicaragua

Dominica

St. Lucia

St. Vincent & Grenadines

Barbados

Trinidad and Tobago

Venezuela

Guyana

Suriname

Colombia

Ecuador

Peru

Brazil

Bolivia

Chile

Paraguay

Argentina

Uruguay

Economic Freedom Scores

- 80–100   Free
- 70–79.9   Mostly Free
- 60–69.9   Moderately Free
- 50–59.9   Mostly Unfree
- 0–49.9   Repressed
- Not Graded

SOURCE: Terry Miller and Anthony B. Kim, *2017 Index of Economic Freedom* (Washington: The Heritage Foundation, 2017), http://www.heritage.org/index.

☎ heritage.org

THE AMERICAS: ECONOMIC FREEDOM SUMMARY

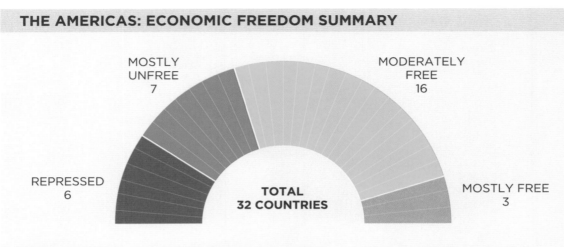

MOSTLY
UNFREE
7

MODERATELY
FREE
16

REPRESSED
6

**TOTAL
32 COUNTRIES**

MOSTLY FREE
3

SOURCE: Terry Miller and Anthony B. Kim, *2017 Index of Economic Freedom* (Washington: The Heritage Foundation, 2017), http://www.heritage.org/index.

Chart 1 ☎ heritage.org

leaders of repressive economies as Venezuela's Nicolás Maduro and Bolivia's Evo Morales continue to threaten regional development and stability, trapping millions in poverty while their neighbors in freer countries leap ahead.

As shown in Chart 3, it is also notable that countries with greater degrees of economic freedom tend to achieve the higher levels of social progress that their citizens demand.

For the Americas as a whole, there has been little change in economic freedom over the past year. Sixteen countries in the region posted gains in economic freedom, and 16 recorded declines. Such a starkly divided trend is indicative of a region that is still searching for its true economic identity. It is noteworthy that after a prolonged period of populist domination, the pendulum has swung back to the center-right in a number of the region's

THE AMERICAS: GDP PER CAPITA, BY ECONOMIC FREEDOM CATEGORY

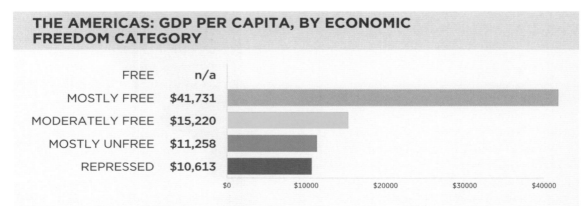

FREE	n/a
MOSTLY FREE	$41,731
MODERATELY FREE	$15,220
MOSTLY UNFREE	$11,258
REPRESSED	$10,613

$0 $10000 $20000 $30000 $40000

SOURCES: Terry Miller and Anthony B. Kim, *2017 Index of Economic Freedom* (Washington: The Heritage Foundation, 2017), http://www.heritage.org/index, and International Monetary Fund, World Economic Outlook Database, April 2016, https://www.imf.org/external/pubs/ft/weo/2016/01/weodata/index.aspx (accessed December 13, 2016).

Chart 2 ☎ heritage.org

THE AMERICAS: COMPONENTS OF ECONOMIC FREEDOM

		AVERAGES	
		Region	World
OVERALL		**60.0**	60.9
RULE OF LAW	Property Rights	**48.5**	53.0
	Judicial Effectiveness	**40.3**	45.0
	Government Integrity	**39.8**	43.0
GOVERNMENT SIZE	Tax Burden	**77.3**	77.1
	Government Spending	**68.5**	63.4
	Fiscal Health	**65.4**	68.0
REGULATORY EFFICIENCY	Business Freedom	**64.1**	64.6
	Labor Freedom	**57.5**	59.2
	Monetary Freedom	**74.5**	76.4
MARKET OPENNESS	Trade Freedom	**75.1**	75.9
	Investment Freedom	**60.5**	57.2
	Financial Freedom	**48.4**	48.2

SOURCE: Terry Miller and Anthony B. Kim, *2017 Index of Economic Freedom* (Washington: The Heritage Foundation, 2017), http://www.heritage.org/index.

Table 1 ☎ heritage.org

countries, including Argentina, Brazil, Chile, and Peru, but the region remains ideologically in flux overall.

NOTABLE COUNTRIES

- Argentina has implemented a number of significant changes in its economic policies since December 2015. President Mauricio Macri's administration has swiftly adopted critical reforms such as modernization of the import regime, measures against inflation, and reform of the national statistics system. The 2016 settlement with creditors has allowed Argentina to access international capital markets for the first time in 15 years.

- The Brazilian economy has been in deep recession. Coupled with a political crisis, the sharp contraction of economic growth, exacerbated by falling commodity prices, has helped to undermine the confidence of consumers and investors. Brazil's fiscal condition has been severely damaged by a combination of high inflation, political paralysis, and widening budget deficits that have increased the burden of public debt.

- Cuba's bloated government sector continues to account for much of that country's economic activity, although the government has eased the rules on private employment in an effort to improve efficiency. In the absence of significant future oil subsidies from nearly bankrupt Venezuela,

THE AMERICAS: ECONOMIC FREEDOM AND SOCIAL PROGRESS

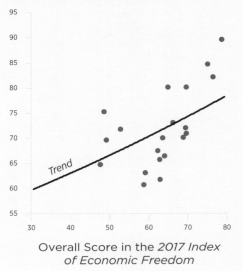

Each circle represents a nation in the *Index of Economic Freedom*

Social Progress Index Score

Overall Score in the *2017 Index of Economic Freedom*

SOURCES: Terry Miller and Anthony B. Kim, *2017 Index of Economic Freedom* (Washington: The Heritage Foundation, 2017), http://www.heritage.org/index, and Social Progress Imperative, "2016 Social Progress Index," http://www.socialprogressimperative.org/global-index/ (accessed December 13, 2016).

Chart 3 ☎ heritage.org

Cuba's dysfunctional economy is even more dependent on external assistance such as remittances from Cuban émigrés.

- Peru was one of the year's most positive stories, thanks to a move toward market-based democracy through the election of President Pedro Pablo Kuczynski, a conservative 77-year-old former World Bank economist and investment banker who defeated right-wing populist Keiko Fujimori, daughter of autocratic former President Alberto Fujimori.

- The United States continued its string of discouraging trends in the 2017 *Index*, registering its lowest economic freedom score ever and now not even one of the world's 15 freest economies. The substantial expansion in the size and scope of the U.S. government, increased regulatory and tax burdens in many sectors, and the loss of trust and confidence that has accompanied a growing perception of cronyism have severely undermined America's global competitiveness.

ECONOMIC FREEDOM IN THE AMERICAS

World Rank	Regional Rank	Country	Overall Score	Change from 2016	Property Rights	Judicial Effectiveness	Government Integrity	Tax Burden	Government Spending	Fiscal Health	Business Freedom	Labor Freedom	Monetary Freedom	Trade Freedom	Investment Freedom	Financial Freedom
7	1	Canada	78.5	0.5	88.3	80.8	81.6	77.4	52.3	80.3	81.9	73.1	77.8	88.4	80	80
10	2	Chile	76.5	-1.2	68.2	63.7	70.5	77.6	82.2	96.1	72.3	64.3	82.2	86.4	85	70
17	3	United States	75.1	-0.3	81.3	75.1	78.1	65.3	55.9	53.3	84.4	91.0	80.1	87.1	80	70
37	4	Colombia	69.7	-1.1	63.8	25.2	39.6	80.1	74.2	89.8	77.1	77.9	77.0	81.6	80	70
38	5	Uruguay	69.7	0.9	70.2	66.8	70.3	77.5	69.4	77.2	74.8	62.9	71.3	80.6	85	30
41	6	Jamaica	69.5	2.0	58.0	61.5	38.2	81.0	77.5	79.9	78.9	73.7	79.5	75.3	80	50
43	7	Peru	68.9	1.5	58.3	28.2	38.8	80.3	85.1	98.4	69.4	62.8	83.3	87.1	75	60
54	8	Panama	66.3	1.5	61.1	21.5	40.9	85.2	83.1	84.9	74.4	43.0	78.4	77.8	75	70
59	9	Saint Vincent and the Grenadines	65.2	-3.6	37.3	68.8	47.6	72.8	71.7	66.7	80.3	74.5	82.9	65.2	75	40
63	10	Costa Rica	65.0	-2.4	51.6	55.6	55.4	79.4	88.5	42.4	68.1	53.9	80.8	84.7	70	50
62	11	Saint Lucia	65.0	-5.0	65.5	68.8	39.6	76.4	71.6	53.8	77.2	68.7	82.3	71.6	65	40
66	12	El Salvador	64.1	-1.0	45.3	35.4	31.7	79.0	85.9	74.7	57.3	54.5	79.2	86.5	80	60
67	13	Dominica	63.7	-3.3	43.8	67.7	40.9	73.2	67.5	72.6	72.1	59.0	89.5	72.6	75	30
70	14	Mexico	63.6	-1.6	58.1	38.7	30.0	74.9	76.7	66.8	70.7	57.9	78.8	80.0	70	60
74	15	Guatemala	63.0	1.2	45.0	27.8	27.5	79.2	94.8	93.5	58.7	48.2	79.4	87.0	65	50
76	16	Dominican Republic	62.9	1.9	56.1	25.3	30.9	84.6	90.2	90.1	52.8	56.2	76.7	77.0	75	40
80	17	Paraguay	62.4	0.9	38.2	23.3	32.6	96.2	83.0	95.1	62.4	28.5	78.3	76.6	75	60
87	18	Trinidad and Tobago	61.2	-1.7	54.7	48.7	36.8	81.4	57.7	51.8	67.7	71.4	75.9	78.6	60	50
90	19	Bahamas	61.1	-9.8	45.3	48.7	38.2	97.1	83.8	42.3	68.5	71.5	77.0	50.6	50	60
98	20	Nicaragua	59.2	0.6	31.1	15.9	27.4	77.2	80.8	96.1	59.0	55.6	71.2	81.0	65	50
100	21	Honduras	58.8	1.1	45.0	38.2	32.2	83.3	74.7	64.1	56.9	31.2	77.3	78.4	65	60
101	22	Belize	58.6	1.2	43.5	48.7	35.0	81.3	68.6	60.5	62.7	53.6	79.6	70.1	50	50
106	23	Guyana	58.5	3.1	37.7	34.1	33.9	68.0	72.8	80.9	63.2	70.9	79.8	70.7	60	30
130	24	Barbados	54.5	-13.8	55.5	33.0	34.3	74.0	39.0	0.0	69.6	67.7	83.7	62.2	75	60
140	25	Brazil	52.9	-3.6	55.0	49.7	33.4	70.1	53.1	22.8	61.3	52.3	67.0	69.4	50	50
156	26	Argentina	50.4	6.6	32.4	39.6	38.2	62.6	54.6	56.4	57.3	46.1	50.9	66.7	50	50
159	27	Haiti	49.6	-1.7	12.6	25.1	19.1	80.3	81.0	51.8	49.4	62.1	73.8	70.6	40	30
160	28	Ecuador	49.3	0.7	38.7	22.3	33.9	79.1	46.1	56.4	55.4	47.3	67.7	69.7	35	40
167	29	Suriname	48.0	-5.8	45.1	15.4	31.7	70.1	69.6	16.2	48.6	76.1	75.1	68.4	30	30
168	30	Bolivia	47.7	0.3	25.7	15.4	32.6	86.1	49.1	81.4	58.9	35.8	66.4	76.0	5	40
178	31	Cuba	33.9	4.1	32.4	10.0	41.8	51.3	0.0	81.2	20.0	20.0	66.0	64.5	10	10
179	32	Venezuela	27.0	-6.7	6.8	10.3	11.6	72.5	51.5	15.2	39.7	28.5	16.8	60.7	0	10

ARGENTINA

The government of Argentina has implemented several significant economic policy changes since December 2015, including such critical reforms as modernization of the import regime, reduction of inflation, and reform of the national statistics system. The 2016 settlement with creditors has allowed Argentina to access international capital markets for the first time in 15 years.

Substantial policy adjustments have sent a strong signal that the new government is committed to reform, ending the former government's period of heavy government interventionism. The economy has been placed on a sounder footing, but much remains to be done in terms of further institutional and structural reform to restore Argentina to its former levels of economic freedom.

WORLD RANK: **156** REGIONAL RANK: **26**

ECONOMIC FREEDOM STATUS:
MOSTLY UNFREE

ECONOMIC FREEDOM SCORE

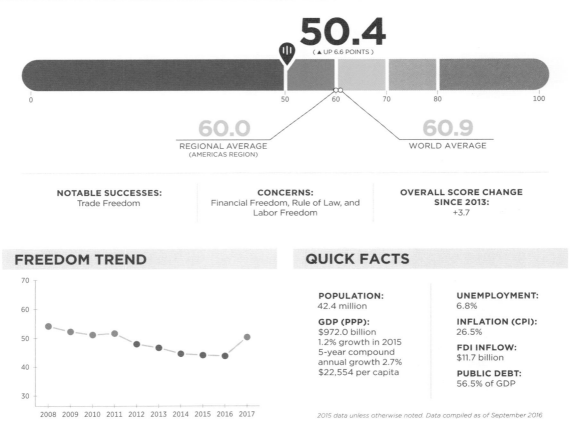

50.4
(▲ UP 6.6 POINTS)

0   50   60   70   80   100

60.0
REGIONAL AVERAGE
(AMERICAS REGION)

60.9
WORLD AVERAGE

NOTABLE SUCCESSES:
Trade Freedom

CONCERNS:
Financial Freedom, Rule of Law, and Labor Freedom

OVERALL SCORE CHANGE SINCE 2013:
+3.7

FREEDOM TREND

70
60
50
40
30

2008 2009 2010 2011 2012 2013 2014 2015 2016 2017

QUICK FACTS

POPULATION:
42.4 million

GDP (PPP):
$972.0 billion
1.2% growth in 2015
5-year compound
annual growth 2.7%
$22,554 per capita

UNEMPLOYMENT:
6.8%

INFLATION (CPI):
26.5%

FDI INFLOW:
$11.7 billion

PUBLIC DEBT:
56.5% of GDP

2015 data unless otherwise noted. Data compiled as of September 2016

BACKGROUND: Argentina, once one of the world's wealthiest nations, is South America's second-largest country. It has vast agricultural and mineral resources and a highly educated population, but its long history of political and economic instability is the biggest challenge confronting center-right President Mauricio Macri. Upon taking office in December 2015, Macri immediately floated the peso exchange rate, reentered global capital markets, reduced costly electricity and other energy subsidies, and scaled back belligerent claims to the Falkland Islands. Macri's more moderate policy agenda has repositioned an Argentina that had drifted far outside the mainstream of the international community into a country that is increasingly attractive to foreign investors.

12 ECONOMIC FREEDOMS | ARGENTINA

RULE OF LAW

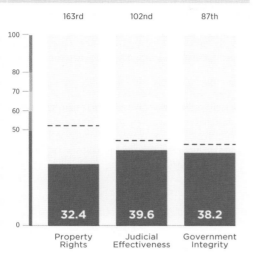

Rank: 163rd | 102nd | 87th

Property Rights: 32.4
Judicial Effectiveness: 39.6
Government Integrity: 38.2

Secured interests in property are recognized and enforced. The government adheres to most treaties and international agreements on intellectual property, although deficiencies persist within the patent and regulatory data protection regimes. Given the president's minority position in Congress, the pace of reforms to reduce bureaucracy and corruption and enhance the effectiveness and independence of the judiciary will be slow.

GOVERNMENT SIZE

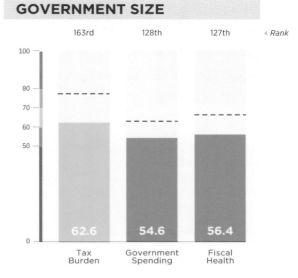

163rd | 128th | 127th ◄ Rank

Tax Burden: 62.6
Government Spending: 54.6
Fiscal Health: 56.4

The top individual and corporate tax rates remain at 35 percent. Other taxes include a value-added tax, a wealth tax, and a tax on financial transactions. The overall tax burden equals 35.9 percent of total domestic income. Government spending has amounted to 38.9 percent of total output (GDP) over the past three years, and budget deficits have averaged 4.8 percent of GDP. Public debt is equivalent to 56.5 percent of GDP.

REGULATORY EFFICIENCY

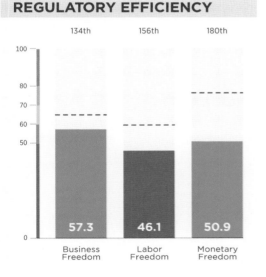

134th | 156th | 180th

Business Freedom: 57.3
Labor Freedom: 46.1
Monetary Freedom: 50.9

The Macri administration has pursued a range of measures to improve the efficiency of business regulation. In May 2016, the president vetoed a labor law that would have kept firms from dismissing workers, arguing that it would depress the employment outlook by deterring investment. The new government has reduced subsidies on electricity and raised prices on gas, water, and public transportation in an effort to cut the budget deficit.

OPEN MARKETS

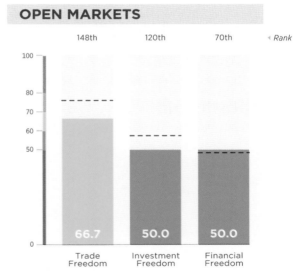

148th | 120th | 70th ◄ Rank

Trade Freedom: 66.7
Investment Freedom: 50.0
Financial Freedom: 50.0

Trade is moderately important to Argentina's economy; the value of exports and imports taken together equals 29 percent of GDP. The average applied tariff rate is 6.6 percent. Nontariff barriers interfere with trade, but barriers to foreign exchange have been relaxed. The small financial sector accounts for less than 3 percent of GDP. The presence of foreign banks has increased, and total assets have risen to approximately 30 percent.

THE BAHAMAS

WORLD RANK: **90**   REGIONAL RANK: **19**

ECONOMIC FREEDOM STATUS:
MODERATELY FREE

There is little momentum for economic reform in the Bahamas, which appears gradually to be losing competitiveness vis-à-vis other nations that are moving more rapidly to expand economic opportunity. The emergence of a more dynamic and sustainable private sector is held back by the weak rule of law, lingering protectionism, and bureaucracy that undermines the investment environment.

Nevertheless, the overall regulatory system is conducive to entrepreneurial activity, and there are no individual or corporate income taxes. Relatively sound management of fiscal policy contributes to macroeconomic stability, and investment management and financial services play a vital role in sustaining overall economic strength.

ECONOMIC FREEDOM SCORE

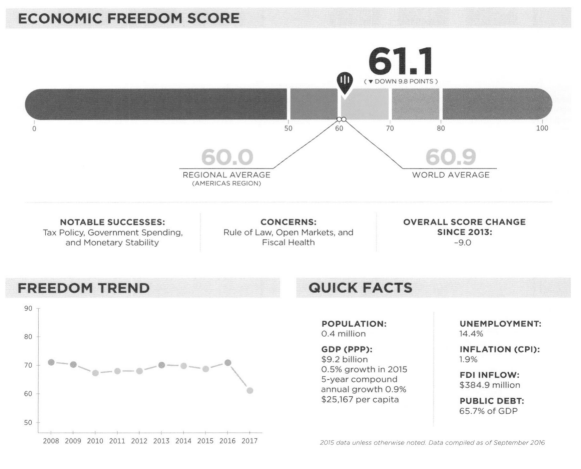

61.1
(▼ DOWN 9.8 POINTS)

0   50   60   70   80   100

60.0
REGIONAL AVERAGE
(AMERICAS REGION)

60.9
WORLD AVERAGE

NOTABLE SUCCESSES:
Tax Policy, Government Spending, and Monetary Stability

CONCERNS:
Rule of Law, Open Markets, and Fiscal Health

OVERALL SCORE CHANGE SINCE 2013:
–9.0

FREEDOM TREND

90
80
70
60
50

2008 2009 2010 2011 2012 2013 2014 2015 2016 2017

QUICK FACTS

POPULATION:
0.4 million

GDP (PPP):
$9.2 billion
0.5% growth in 2015
5-year compound
annual growth 0.9%
$25,167 per capita

UNEMPLOYMENT:
14.4%

INFLATION (CPI):
1.9%

FDI INFLOW:
$384.9 million

PUBLIC DEBT:
65.7% of GDP

2015 data unless otherwise noted. Data compiled as of September 2016

BACKGROUND: Prime Minister Perry Christie of the long-dominant center-left Progressive Liberal Party, in office since 2012, says he will seek another five-year term in the May 2017 elections. Although tourism accounts for more than 60 percent of GDP, a record-high murder rate in 2015 heightened concerns that violent crime will have a negative impact. The Bahamas will soon set a record for the longest-running accession to the World Trade Organization, having initiated the still-incomplete process in 2001. Politicians and the private sector remain at loggerheads about how to replace the tariff revenues that would be lost. The Bahamas is a major transshipment point both for smuggling illegal drugs into the United States and Europe and for smuggling illegal migrants into the U.S.

12 ECONOMIC FREEDOMS | THE BAHAMAS

RULE OF LAW

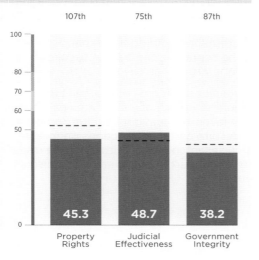

107th	75th	87th	◄ Rank
Property Rights **45.3**	Judicial Effectiveness **48.7**	Government Integrity **38.2**	

Property registration is difficult and time-consuming, but the introduction of new rules of civil procedure has made enforcement of contracts easier. Although the independent legal system is based on British common law, the inefficiency of the judicial process causes trials to be delayed. Retaliatory crimes against both witnesses and alleged perpetrators have increased. Money laundering and corruption are problems at all levels of government.

GOVERNMENT SIZE

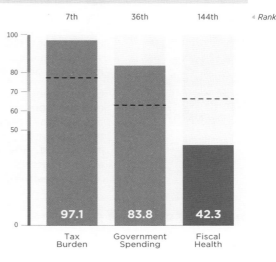

7th	36th	144th	◄ Rank
Tax Burden **97.1**	Government Spending **83.8**	Fiscal Health **42.3**	

The government imposes national insurance, property, and stamp taxes but no income, corporate income, capital gains, value-added, or wealth taxes. The overall tax burden equals 16.9 percent of total domestic income. Government spending has amounted to 23.3 percent of total output (GDP) over the past three years, and budget deficits have averaged 5.5 percent of GDP. Public debt is equivalent to 65.7 percent of GDP.

REGULATORY EFFICIENCY

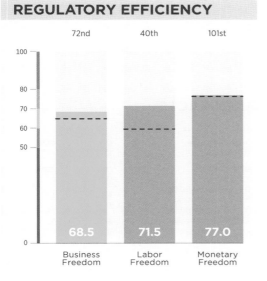

72nd	40th	101st
Business Freedom **68.5**	Labor Freedom **71.5**	Monetary Freedom **77.0**

There is no minimum capital requirement for starting a company, but it takes almost a month on average to launch a business. No major reforms have been implemented in recent years. The labor market is relatively flexible, but the existing labor codes are not enforced effectively. Subsidies to the state-owned Bahamas Electricity Corporation and the Water and Sewerage Corporation continue to be a drag on government finances.

OPEN MARKETS

180th	120th	39th	◄ Rank
Trade Freedom **50.6**	Investment Freedom **50.0**	Financial Freedom **60.0**	

Trade is important to the Bahamas' economy; the value of exports and imports taken together equals 93 percent of GDP. Government finances are heavily reliant on tariffs, and the average applied tariff rate is 19.7 percent. Financial services are competitive, and domestic and offshore activities contribute around 15 percent of GDP. The diversified banking sector remains stable, although the number of nonperforming loans has increased.

BARBADOS

WORLD RANK: **130** | **REGIONAL RANK:** **24**

ECONOMIC FREEDOM STATUS:
MOSTLY UNFREE

Barbados has transformed itself from a low-income agricultural economy producing mainly sugar and rum into a middle-income economy built on tourism and offshore banking that generates one of the Caribbean's highest per capita incomes. However, increased government spending has expanded the state's influence within the economy, and a large fiscal deficit has made government debt larger than the size of the economy.

Government economic policies are focused on attracting international companies. Regulatory efficiency facilitates private-sector growth. Transparency levels the playing field for domestic and foreign businesses despite certain restrictions on foreign investment. However, policies intended to buttress open trade and productivity growth are undercut by bureaucracy, discouraging investment expansion.

ECONOMIC FREEDOM SCORE

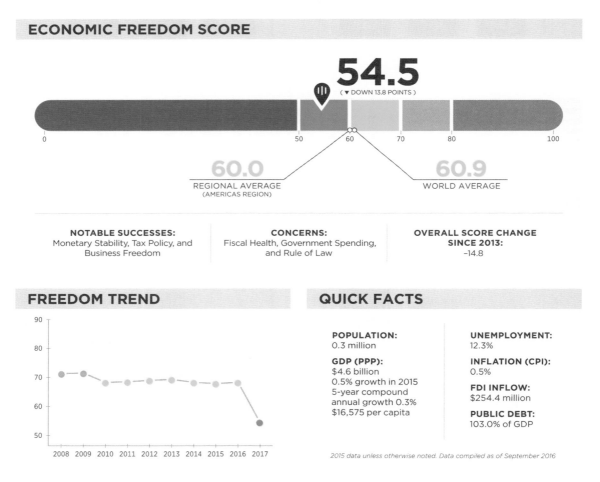

54.5
(▼ DOWN 13.8 POINTS)

0   50   60   70   80   100

60.0
REGIONAL AVERAGE
(AMERICAS REGION)

60.9
WORLD AVERAGE

NOTABLE SUCCESSES:
Monetary Stability, Tax Policy, and Business Freedom

CONCERNS:
Fiscal Health, Government Spending, and Rule of Law

OVERALL SCORE CHANGE SINCE 2013:
–14.8

FREEDOM TREND

90
80
70
60
50
2008 2009 2010 2011 2012 2013 2014 2015 2016 2017

QUICK FACTS

POPULATION:
0.3 million

GDP (PPP):
$4.6 billion
0.5% growth in 2015
5-year compound annual growth 0.3%
$16,575 per capita

UNEMPLOYMENT:
12.3%

INFLATION (CPI):
0.5%

FDI INFLOW:
$254.4 million

PUBLIC DEBT:
103.0% of GDP

2015 data unless otherwise noted. Data compiled as of September 2016

BACKGROUND: Barbados was uninhabited when first settled by the British in 1627. African slaves worked the sugar plantations until 1834 when slavery was abolished. Independent from the United Kingdom since 1966, Barbados is a stable parliamentary constitutional monarchy. Prime Minister Freundel Stuart of the center-left Democratic Labour Party won a five-year term in 2013. Stuart wanted Barbados to become a republic in 2016, the 50th anniversary of its independence from the U.K., but the public views that politically complicated process as a low priority as the country continues its struggle to recover from years of economic stagnation. Tourism receipts have improved, but serious challenges to medium-term economic growth remain.

12 ECONOMIC FREEDOMS | BARBADOS

RULE OF LAW

◄ Rank

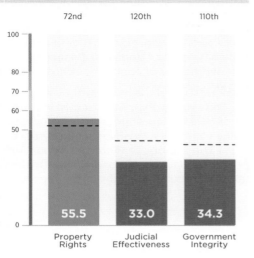

Property Rights	Judicial Effectiveness	Government Integrity
72nd	120th	110th
55.5	33.0	34.3

Property registration in Barbados is very time-consuming. The court system is based on British common law and is generally unbiased and efficient. The protection of property rights is strong, and the rule of law is respected. Corruption is not a major problem in Barbados, but violence related to transshipment drug trafficking from Venezuela is a serious problem.

GOVERNMENT SIZE

◄ Rank

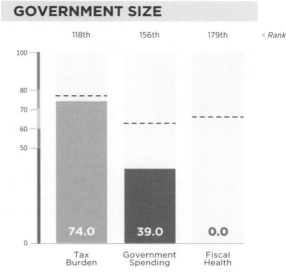

Tax Burden	Government Spending	Fiscal Health
118th	156th	179th
74.0	39.0	0.0

The top income tax rate is 35 percent, and the top corporate tax rate is 25 percent. Other taxes include a value-added tax and a property tax. The overall tax burden equals 27.4 percent of total domestic income. Government spending has amounted to 45.1 percent of total output (GDP) over the past three years, and budget deficits have averaged 9.1 percent of GDP. Public debt is equivalent to 103.0 percent of GDP.

REGULATORY EFFICIENCY

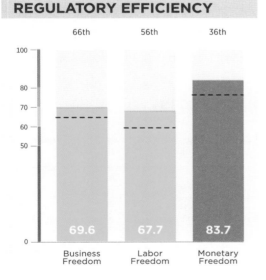

Business Freedom	Labor Freedom	Monetary Freedom
66th	56th	36th
69.6	67.7	83.7

Transparent policies and straightforward laws generally facilitate regulatory efficiency. The overall process for obtaining licenses and starting a business is not burdensome. The labor market remains relatively flexible, and employers are not legally obligated to recognize unions. To meet a 2017 deadline set by the World Trade Organization, the government took steps in 2016 to phase out subsidies to manufacturing firms.

OPEN MARKETS

◄ Rank

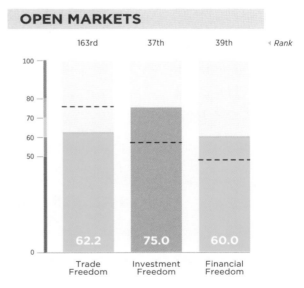

Trade Freedom	Investment Freedom	Financial Freedom
163rd	37th	39th
62.2	75.0	60.0

Trade is important to Barbados's economy; the value of exports and imports taken together equals 81 percent of GDP. Government finances are heavily reliant on tariffs, and the average applied tariff rate is 13.9 percent. The investment climate has improved, but much investment activity is subject to government approval. The banking sector provides a wide range of services for investors, although securities markets are relatively illiquid.

BELIZE

Belize has an uneven record in economic reform, and more dynamic growth is constrained by lingering policy weaknesses in many parts of the economy. Entrepreneurial activity remains limited, and recovery from the recent economic slowdown has been narrowly based. Burdensome tariff and nontariff barriers, together with the high cost of domestic financing, hinder private-sector development and economic diversification.

Overall economic freedom in Belize remains limited by other institutional weaknesses. The regulatory infrastructure is inefficient and raises the cost of conducting entrepreneurial activity. The judicial system remains vulnerable to political interference, and corruption is common. The Caribbean Financial Action Task Force has tightened anti–money laundering and antiterrorism financing controls in Belize, particularly in light of the recent Panama Papers leaks.

ECONOMIC FREEDOM SCORE

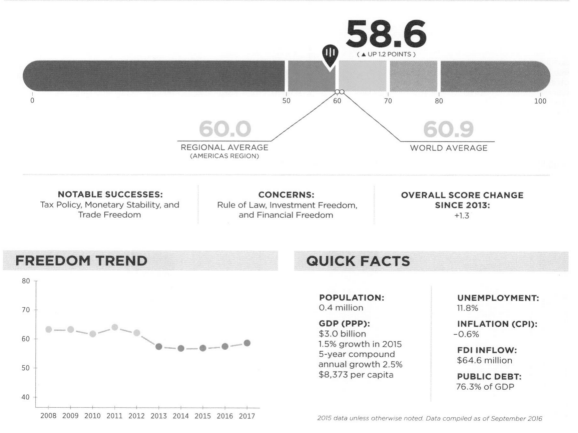

58.6
(▲ UP 1.2 POINTS)

0   50   60   70   80   100

60.0
REGIONAL AVERAGE
(AMERICAS REGION)

60.9
WORLD AVERAGE

NOTABLE SUCCESSES:
Tax Policy, Monetary Stability, and Trade Freedom

CONCERNS:
Rule of Law, Investment Freedom, and Financial Freedom

OVERALL SCORE CHANGE SINCE 2013:
+1.3

FREEDOM TREND

80

70

60

50

40

2008 2009 2010 2011 2012 2013 2014 2015 2016 2017

QUICK FACTS

POPULATION:
0.4 million

GDP (PPP):
$3.0 billion
1.5% growth in 2015
5-year compound
annual growth 2.5%
$8,373 per capita

UNEMPLOYMENT:
11.8%

INFLATION (CPI):
-0.6%

FDI INFLOW:
$64.6 million

PUBLIC DEBT:
76.3% of GDP

2015 data unless otherwise noted. Data compiled as of September 2016

BACKGROUND: Belize is a parliamentary democracy. Prime Minister Dean Barrow of the center-right United Democratic Party was elected in 2015 to his third and constitutionally final consecutive five-year term. The economy relies primarily on tourism, followed by exports of marine products, citrus, sugar, and bananas. Although tourism receipts are up, economic growth slowed considerably after agriculture and fisheries contracted sharply in 2015, with shrimp farms affected by bacterial infection and banana production affected by severe drought. Multimillion-dollar compensation to the former owners of Belize Telemedia, nationalized by the government in 2009, will add to budgetary pressures.

12 ECONOMIC FREEDOMS | BELIZE

RULE OF LAW

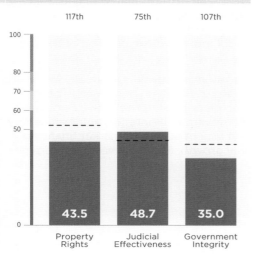

117th	75th	107th
Property Rights **43.5**	Judicial Effectiveness **48.7**	Government Integrity **35.0**

Unreliable land title certificates have led to numerous property disputes involving foreign investors and landowners. The judiciary, although independent, is often influenced by the executive. Belize is the only Central American country that is not a party to the U.N. Convention Against Corruption. Since 2009, Transparency International has not had access to enough data to include Belize in its annual *Corruption Perceptions Index*.

GOVERNMENT SIZE

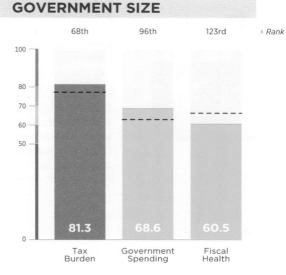

68th	96th	123rd	◄ Rank
Tax Burden **81.3**	Government Spending **68.6**	Fiscal Health **60.5**	

The top income and corporate tax rates are 25 percent; petroleum profits are taxed at 40 percent. Other taxes include a goods and services tax and a stamp duty. The overall tax burden equals 24.8 percent of total domestic income. Government spending has amounted to 32.3 percent of total output (GDP) over the past three years, and budget deficits have averaged 4.2 percent of GDP. Public debt is equivalent to 76.3 percent of GDP.

REGULATORY EFFICIENCY

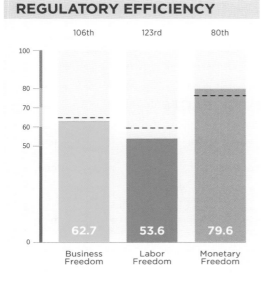

106th	123rd	80th
Business Freedom **62.7**	Labor Freedom **53.6**	Monetary Freedom **79.6**

Entrepreneurial activity often faces such challenges as poor enforcement of the commercial code and lack of transparency. The nonsalary cost of employing a worker is relatively low, and terminating labor contracts is not cumbersome. However, a formal labor market has not been fully developed. The government maintains price controls on various products such as rice, sugar, and flour and subsidizes the cost of electricity.

OPEN MARKETS

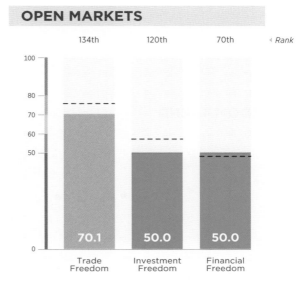

134th	120th	70th	◄ Rank
Trade Freedom **70.1**	Investment Freedom **50.0**	Financial Freedom **50.0**	

Trade is extremely important to Belize's economy; the value of exports and imports taken together equals 126 percent of GDP. The average applied tariff rate is 10.0 percent. Bureaucratic barriers may discourage foreign investment. The financial system is small but growing, and obtaining credit is relatively straightforward. The government influences the allocation of credit through the quasi-government banks.

BOLIVIA

WORLD RANK: **168**   REGIONAL RANK: **30**

ECONOMIC FREEDOM STATUS:
REPRESSED

Bolivia's overall economic development remains severely hampered by structural and institutional problems. Heavily dependent on the hydrocarbon sector, the economy suffers from a lack of dynamism. Poor economic infrastructure and a weak regulatory framework impede diversification of the productive base.

The state's presence in economic activity is gradually increasing through nationalization, and judicial independence is becoming more vulnerable to political interference. The rule of law is weak in many areas, with government integrity undermined by pervasive corruption. The lack of access to market financing precludes entrepreneurial growth, and the investment regime lacks transparency.

ECONOMIC FREEDOM SCORE

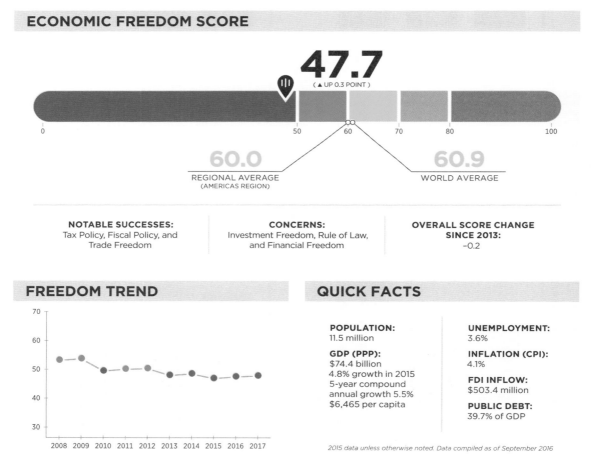

47.7
(▲ UP 0.3 POINT)

0   50   60   70   80   100

60.0
REGIONAL AVERAGE
(AMERICAS REGION)

60.9
WORLD AVERAGE

NOTABLE SUCCESSES:
Tax Policy, Fiscal Policy, and Trade Freedom

CONCERNS:
Investment Freedom, Rule of Law, and Financial Freedom

OVERALL SCORE CHANGE SINCE 2013:
−0.2

FREEDOM TREND

70
60
50
40
30

2008 2009 2010 2011 2012 2013 2014 2015 2016 2017

QUICK FACTS

POPULATION:
11.5 million

GDP (PPP):
$74.4 billion
4.8% growth in 2015
5-year compound
annual growth 5.5%
$6,465 per capita

UNEMPLOYMENT:
3.6%

INFLATION (CPI):
4.1%

FDI INFLOW:
$503.4 million

PUBLIC DEBT:
39.7% of GDP

2015 data unless otherwise noted. Data compiled as of September 2016

BACKGROUND: Landlocked, resource-rich Bolivia is one of the world's largest producers of coca leaf and a major transit zone for Peruvian cocaine. President Evo Morales began his third consecutive term in 2015. In 2016, voters rejected his plan to run for a fourth term in 2019, but his ruling Movement Toward Socialism (MAS) party is trying to promote another referendum on that question. In a bid to drum up support, Morales has increased nationalistic rhetoric (particularly over Bolivia's border dispute with Chile) and has sought to silence critical voices in the media and nongovernment organizations. His government also has threatened some opposition politicians. Bolivia maintains strong alliances with Cuba, Venezuela, and Iran. Nearly four out of 10 Bolivians live below the poverty line.

12 ECONOMIC FREEDOMS | BOLIVIA

RULE OF LAW

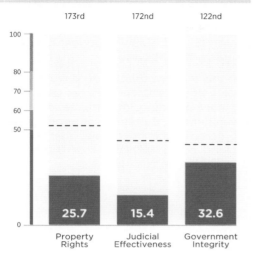

	173rd	172nd	122nd
	Property Rights	Judicial Effectiveness	Government Integrity
	25.7	15.4	32.6

An unreliable dispute resolution process and the lack of adequate land title verification create risk and uncertainty in real property acquisition. Although Bolivia's highest courts have occasionally asserted some independence from the executive, the ruling MAS party tightly controls all institutions. Moreover, the judicial system remains highly discredited as a result of ongoing scandals, corruption, and influence-peddling.

GOVERNMENT SIZE

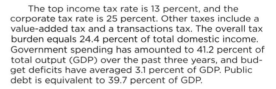

	43rd	139th	78th	◄ Rank
	Tax Burden	Government Spending	Fiscal Health	
	86.1	49.1	81.4	

The top income tax rate is 13 percent, and the corporate tax rate is 25 percent. Other taxes include a value-added tax and a transactions tax. The overall tax burden equals 24.4 percent of total domestic income. Government spending has amounted to 41.2 percent of total output (GDP) over the past three years, and budget deficits have averaged 3.1 percent of GDP. Public debt is equivalent to 39.7 percent of GDP.

REGULATORY EFFICIENCY

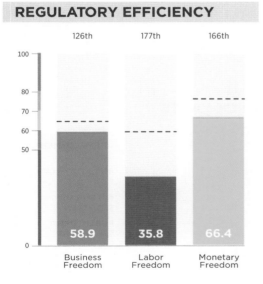

	126th	177th	166th
	Business Freedom	Labor Freedom	Monetary Freedom
	58.9	35.8	66.4

The entrepreneurial environment is burdened by red tape, corruption, and inconsistent enforcement of commercial regulations. Employment regulations are rigid and not conducive to productivity growth. There are government-established minimum wages for the public and private sectors. The cost of state gasoline, diesel, kerosene, natural gas, liquefied petroleum gas, jet fuel, and fuel oil subsidies is nearly 8 percent of GDP.

OPEN MARKETS

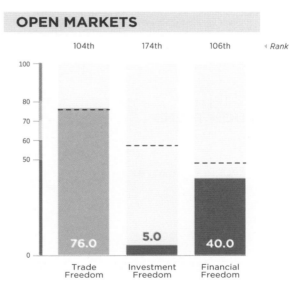

	104th	174th	106th	◄ Rank
	Trade Freedom	Investment Freedom	Financial Freedom	
	76.0	5.0	40.0	

Trade is important to Bolivia's economy; the value of exports and imports taken together equals 85 percent of GDP. The average applied tariff rate is 4.5 percent. The government prioritizes domestic investment over foreign investment. The financial sector is vulnerable to state interference and poorly developed. Credit to the private sector has expanded very slowly. Political unrest hinders the development of a modern capital market.

BRAZIL

A political crisis that, along with declines in commodity prices, contributed to a sharp contraction of the economy has undermined consumer and investor confidence. Brazil's fiscal condition has been severely compromised by a combination of high inflation, political paralysis, and widening budget deficits that have elevated the burden of public debt.

The state's interference in the economy has been heavy. The efficiency and overall quality of government services remain poor despite high government spending. Implementation of any reform program has proven difficult. Barriers to entrepreneurial activity include burdensome taxes, inefficient regulation, poor access to long-term financing, and a rigid labor market. The judicial system remains vulnerable to corruption.

WORLD RANK: **140** REGIONAL RANK: **25**

ECONOMIC FREEDOM STATUS:
MOSTLY UNFREE

ECONOMIC FREEDOM SCORE

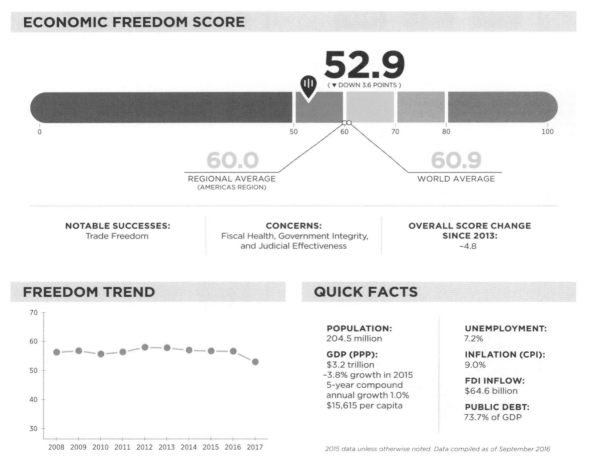

52.9
(▼ DOWN 3.6 POINTS)

0   50   60   70   80   100

60.0
REGIONAL AVERAGE
(AMERICAS REGION)

60.9
WORLD AVERAGE

NOTABLE SUCCESSES:
Trade Freedom

CONCERNS:
Fiscal Health, Government Integrity, and Judicial Effectiveness

OVERALL SCORE CHANGE SINCE 2013:
–4.8

FREEDOM TREND

70 — 60 — 50 — 40 — 30

2008 2009 2010 2011 2012 2013 2014 2015 2016 2017

QUICK FACTS

POPULATION:
204.5 million

GDP (PPP):
$3.2 trillion
–3.8% growth in 2015
5-year compound
annual growth 1.0%
$15,615 per capita

UNEMPLOYMENT:
7.2%

INFLATION (CPI):
9.0%

FDI INFLOW:
$64.6 billion

PUBLIC DEBT:
73.7% of GDP

2015 data unless otherwise noted. Data compiled as of September 2016

BACKGROUND: Brazil, the world's fifth-largest country, is dominated by the Amazon River basin and the world's largest rain forest. The population of more than 200 million is heavily concentrated on the coast, where a dozen major metropolitan areas with populations of a million or more offer direct access to the Atlantic Ocean. The current democratic constitution dates from 1988. Workers' Party President Dilma Rousseff, who sought to further the leftist and populist policy agenda begun by her predecessor, Luiz Inacio "Lula" da Silva, was impeached and removed from office in 2016. New President Michel Temer faces continuing corruption scandals and ongoing political turmoil.

12 ECONOMIC FREEDOMS | BRAZIL

RULE OF LAW

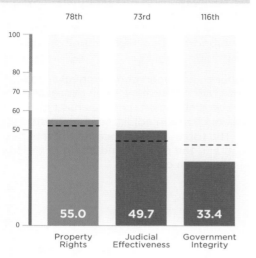

78th	73rd	116th
Property Rights **55.0**	Judicial Effectiveness **49.7**	Government Integrity **33.4**

The judiciary, though largely independent, is over-burdened, inefficient, and often subject to intimidation and other external influences, especially in rural areas. Corruption scandals have undermined trust in both public and private institutions and contributed to Brazil's decline in the World Economic Forum's 2016 *Global Competitiveness Index*. Many members of the ruling PMDB party, for example, are deeply involved in the Petrobras scandal.

GOVERNMENT SIZE

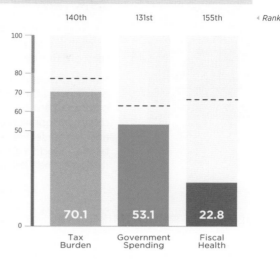

140th	131st	155th	◄ *Rank*
Tax Burden **70.1**	Government Spending **53.1**	Fiscal Health **22.8**	

The personal income tax rate is 27.5 percent. The standard corporate rate is 15 percent, but other taxes, including a financial transactions tax, bring the effective rate to 34 percent. The overall tax burden equals 32.8 percent of domestic income. Government spending has amounted to 39.5 percent of total output (GDP) over the past three years, and budget deficits have averaged 6.4 percent of GDP. Public debt is equivalent to 73.7 percent of GDP.

REGULATORY EFFICIENCY

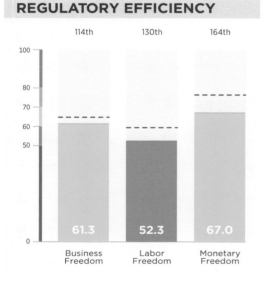

114th	130th	164th
Business Freedom **61.3**	Labor Freedom **52.3**	Monetary Freedom **67.0**

Organizing new businesses remains cumbersome and bureaucratic. It is costly and time-consuming to launch or expand a business. Rigid and outmoded labor regulations undermine employment growth, and the nonsalary cost of employing a worker is burden-some. The new government has pursued more ortho-dox policies than its predecessor and plans to cap increases in budget spending and eliminate automatic indexation of entitlements.

OPEN MARKETS

136th	120th	70th	◄ *Rank*
Trade Freedom **69.4**	Investment Freedom **50.0**	Financial Freedom **50.0**	

Trade is moderately important to Brazil's economy; the value of exports and imports taken together equals 27 percent of GDP. The average applied tariff rate is 7.8 percent. Trade and investment face bureaucratic and regulatory hurdles. The financial sector is diversified and competitive, but the government's involvement remains considerable, and public banks now account for over 50 percent of total loans to the private sector.

CANADA

Canada's economic competitiveness has been sustained by the solid institutional foundations of an open-market system. The independent judiciary provides strong protection of property rights and upholds the rule of law. The economy is open to global commerce and supported by a high degree of regulatory efficiency.

Management of public finance has been comparatively prudent, but the size and scope of government have been expanding over the past year. The government's policy focus has tilted toward income redistribution through adjustments in taxation and increased spending. The top individual income tax rate has been raised to 33 percent, and the planned reduction of the tax rate for small businesses has been canceled.

WORLD RANK: 7

REGIONAL RANK: 1

ECONOMIC FREEDOM STATUS:
MOSTLY FREE

ECONOMIC FREEDOM SCORE

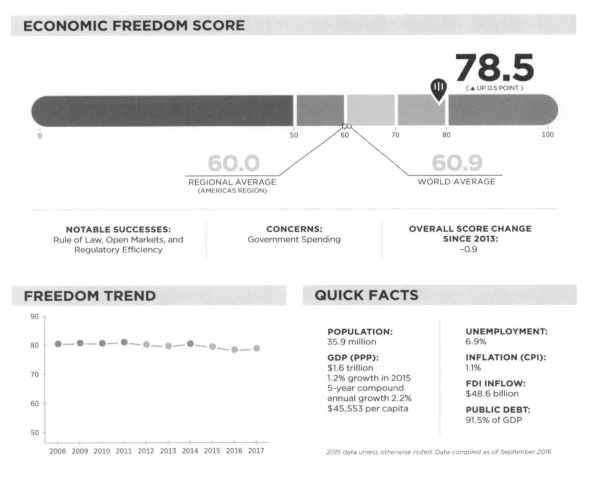

78.5
(▲ UP 0.5 POINT)

0   50   60   70   80   100

60.0
REGIONAL AVERAGE
(AMERICAS REGION)

60.9
WORLD AVERAGE

NOTABLE SUCCESSES:
Rule of Law, Open Markets, and Regulatory Efficiency

CONCERNS:
Government Spending

OVERALL SCORE CHANGE SINCE 2013:
–0.9

FREEDOM TREND

90
80
70
60
50

2008 2009 2010 2011 2012 2013 2014 2015 2016 2017

QUICK FACTS

POPULATION:
35.9 million

GDP (PPP):
$1.6 trillion
1.2% growth in 2015
5-year compound
annual growth 2.2%
$45,553 per capita

UNEMPLOYMENT:
6.9%

INFLATION (CPI):
1.1%

FDI INFLOW:
$48.6 billion

PUBLIC DEBT:
91.5% of GDP

2015 data unless otherwise noted. Data compiled as of September 2016

BACKGROUND: Liberal Party candidate Justin Trudeau was elected prime minister in October 2015 after promising to revive Canada's economy. After a decade of Conservative rule, Trudeau has reshaped Canadian politics. In March 2016, the prime minister announced a $46 billion stimulus plan targeted at improving public transportation, water systems, and housing. The government has also accepted 25,000 Syrian refugees into the country and has taken the lead in increasing aid to Syria. Canada's 13 provinces and territories have significant autonomy from the federal government. Canada produces commodities like automobiles, forest products, manufactured goods, minerals, and oil. Its leading export market is the United States.

12 ECONOMIC FREEDOMS | CANADA

RULE OF LAW

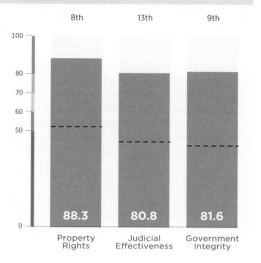

| | 8th | 13th | 9th | ◄ Rank |

- Property Rights: 88.3
- Judicial Effectiveness: 80.8
- Government Integrity: 81.6

Although 89 percent of Canada's land area is owned by the state, the property rights to the 11 percent that is privately owned are well protected. Intellectual property rights meet world standards. Enforcement of contracts is secure, and expropriation is highly unusual. Canada has a reputation for clean government. Its judicial system has an impeccable record of independence and transparency, and cases of corruption are prosecuted vigorously.

GOVERNMENT SIZE

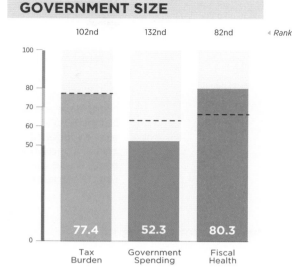

| | 102nd | 132nd | 82nd | ◄ Rank |

- Tax Burden: 77.4
- Government Spending: 52.3
- Fiscal Health: 80.3

The top federal personal income tax rate has been raised to 33 percent. The top corporate tax rate is 15 percent. Other taxes include a value-added tax and a property tax. The overall tax burden equals 30.8 percent of total domestic income. Government spending has amounted to 39.9 percent of total output (GDP) over the past three years, and budget deficits have averaged 1.4 percent of GDP. Public debt is equivalent to 91.5 percent of GDP.

REGULATORY EFFICIENCY

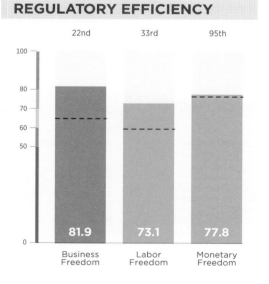

| | 22nd | 33rd | 95th |

- Business Freedom: 81.9
- Labor Freedom: 73.1
- Monetary Freedom: 77.8

The transparent regulatory framework facilitates commercial activity, allowing the processes of business formation and operation to be efficient and dynamic. Relatively flexible labor regulations enhance employment growth. In 2016, Canadian aerospace company Bombardier and the provincial Quebec government agreed to a $1 billion rescue package, but the federal government has not yet approved an additional $1 billion bailout.

OPEN MARKETS

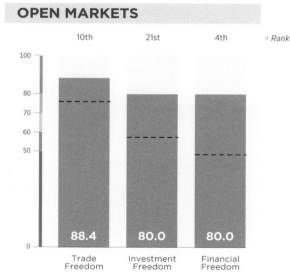

| | 10th | 21st | 4th | ◄ Rank |

- Trade Freedom: 88.4
- Investment Freedom: 80.0
- Financial Freedom: 80.0

Trade is important to Canada's economy; the value of exports and imports taken together equals 65 percent of GDP. The average applied tariff rate is 0.8 percent. Foreign investment in sectors including aviation and telecommunications is capped by the government. The banking sector remains sound and stable. A wide range of nonbank financial companies operates in a prudent business environment, and securities markets are well developed.

CHILE

Chile's openness to global trade and investment provides a solid basis for economic dynamism. A transparent regulatory environment buttressed by well-secured property rights provides commercial security for the resilient private sector. The independent judicial system continues to sustain the rule of law.

However, several recent policy shifts have put Chile's economic freedom on a downward trend. The size and scope of government have expanded, substantially undercutting adherence to the principle of limited government. Along with the introduction of redistributive tax measures, the corporate tax rate has been raised and is slated to rise further. Labor reforms have focused on increasing the minimum wage and strengthening union bargaining.

ECONOMIC FREEDOM SCORE

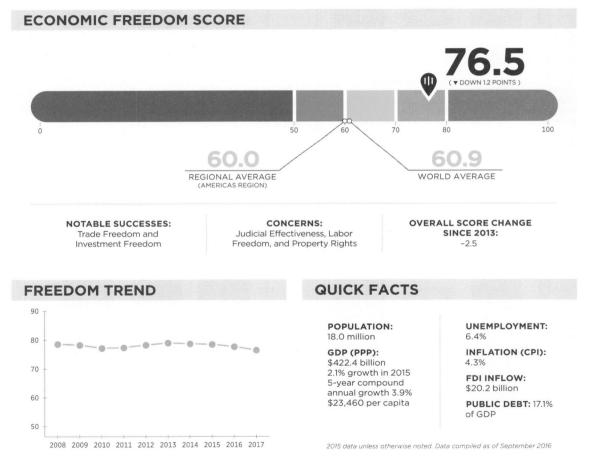

76.5
(▼ DOWN 1.2 POINTS)

0   50   60   70   80   100

60.0
REGIONAL AVERAGE
(AMERICAS REGION)

60.9
WORLD AVERAGE

NOTABLE SUCCESSES:
Trade Freedom and
Investment Freedom

CONCERNS:
Judicial Effectiveness, Labor
Freedom, and Property Rights

**OVERALL SCORE CHANGE
SINCE 2013:**
–2.5

FREEDOM TREND

90
80
70
60
50

2008 2009 2010 2011 2012 2013 2014 2015 2016 2017

QUICK FACTS

POPULATION:
18.0 million

GDP (PPP):
$422.4 billion
2.1% growth in 2015
5-year compound
annual growth 3.9%
$23,460 per capita

UNEMPLOYMENT:
6.4%

INFLATION (CPI):
4.3%

FDI INFLOW:
$20.2 billion

PUBLIC DEBT: 17.1%
of GDP

2015 data unless otherwise noted. Data compiled as of September 2016

BACKGROUND: Socialist President Michelle Bachelet, who began her second nonconsecutive four-year term in 2014, has strayed from the policies of her first term, which largely supported Chile's successful free-market institutions. She has pushed through major and sometimes flawed tax, labor, education, and other constitutional reforms, and the public perception that she turned a blind eye to her son's alleged wrongdoing in an ongoing corruption case has undermined her reputation for trustworthiness and moral probity. Nonetheless, Chile retains the region's best investment profile and benefits from its membership in the Pacific Alliance and a vast network of free-trade agreements. Chile is the world's leading producer of copper.

12 ECONOMIC FREEDOMS | CHILE

RULE OF LAW

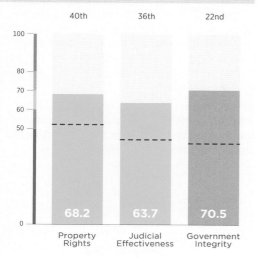

	40th	36th	22nd

- Property Rights: 68.2
- Judicial Effectiveness: 63.7
- Government Integrity: 70.5

Property rights and contracts are strongly respected, and expropriation is rare. The judiciary is independent, and the courts are generally competent and free from political interference. Although Chile remains one of South America's least corrupt countries, several scandals (including one involving the president's son) continue to shake public confidence. Corruption was the top political concern of more than one-third of Chileans in 2016.

GOVERNMENT SIZE

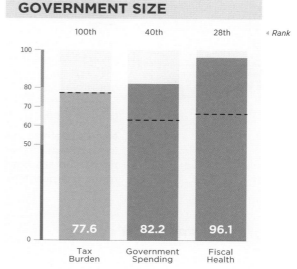

	100th	40th	28th	◄ Rank

- Tax Burden: 77.6
- Government Spending: 82.2
- Fiscal Health: 96.1

The top individual income tax rate has been cut to 35 percent, but the top corporate tax rate has increased to 25 percent. Other taxes include a value-added tax. The overall tax burden equals 19.8 percent of total domestic income. Government spending has amounted to 24.3 percent of total output (GDP) over the past three years, and budget deficits have averaged 1.4 percent of GDP. Public debt is equivalent to 17.1 percent of GDP.

REGULATORY EFFICIENCY

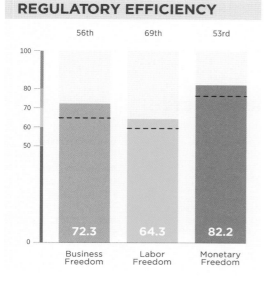

	56th	69th	53rd

- Business Freedom: 72.3
- Labor Freedom: 64.3
- Monetary Freedom: 82.2

The overall regulatory framework facilitates entrepreneurial activity and productivity growth. However, barriers to market entry remain, and bankruptcy procedures are cumbersome and costly. Increases in the minimum wage have exceeded overall productivity growth in recent years. Rapid expansion of the privately owned power generation sector without government subsidies has included the development of renewable energy sources.

OPEN MARKETS

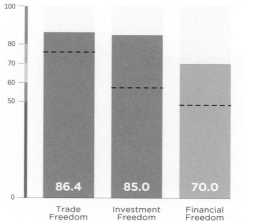

	47th	9th	17th	◄ Rank

- Trade Freedom: 86.4
- Investment Freedom: 85.0
- Financial Freedom: 70.0

Trade is important to Chile's economy; the value of exports and imports taken together equals 60 percent of GDP. The average applied tariff rate is 1.8 percent. The investment climate is generally open, but numerous state-owned enterprises distort the economy. The financial system remains one of the region's most stable and developed, and foreign and domestic banks compete on an equal footing.

COLOMBIA

Colombia has maintained strong economic fundamentals, including macroeconomic stability and openness to global trade and finance. The relatively sound economic policy framework has contributed to economic expansion averaging over 4.5 percent annually over the past five years. Recent reforms have focused on regulatory improvements and fostering a stronger private sector. A founding member of the Pacific Alliance, Colombia has free trade agreements with the U.S. and many other nations.

More sustained growth in economic freedom will require deeper institutional reforms that include better protection of property rights and strengthening of the judicial system. Corruption remains a problem in many sectors of the economy.

ECONOMIC FREEDOM SCORE

69.7
(▼ DOWN 1.1 POINTS)

0   50   60   70   80   100

60.0
REGIONAL AVERAGE
(AMERICAS REGION)

60.9
WORLD AVERAGE

NOTABLE SUCCESSES:
Trade Freedom, Fiscal Policy, and Investment Freedom

CONCERNS:
Judicial Effectiveness and Government Integrity

OVERALL SCORE CHANGE SINCE 2013:
+0.1

FREEDOM TREND

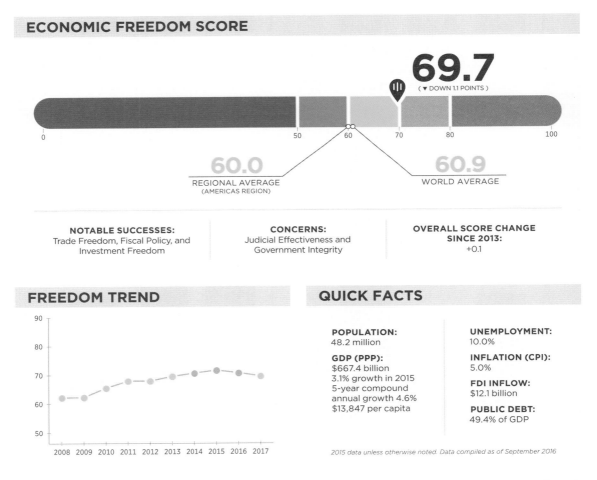

QUICK FACTS

POPULATION:
48.2 million

GDP (PPP):
$667.4 billion
3.1% growth in 2015
5-year compound annual growth 4.6%
$13,847 per capita

UNEMPLOYMENT:
10.0%

INFLATION (CPI):
5.0%

FDI INFLOW:
$12.1 billion

PUBLIC DEBT:
49.4% of GDP

2015 data unless otherwise noted. Data compiled as of September 2016

BACKGROUND: A large, geographically and ethnically diverse country in the northwestern corner of South America, Colombia is Latin America's oldest democracy. A costly five-decade guerilla insurgency, principally led by the leftist, narco-funded Revolutionary Armed Forces of Colombia (FARC), caused hundreds of thousands of casualties. President Juan Manuel Santos, reelected in 2014, made peace with the FARC his top priority and signed a cease-fire in June 2016. In an October 2016 referendum, however, skeptical voters narrowly rejected the controversial final peace treaty that would have mainstreamed demobilized FARC members, given them impunity for past crimes, and allowed them to run for political office.

12 ECONOMIC FREEDOMS | COLOMBIA

RULE OF LAW

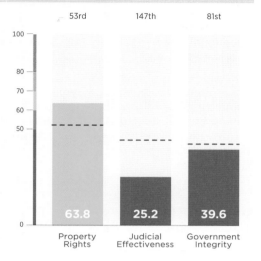

	53rd	147th	81st
Property Rights	63.8		
Judicial Effectiveness		25.2	
Government Integrity			39.6

Property rights are recognized and generally enforced. The justice system is compromised by corruption and extortion, although the Constitutional Court and the Supreme Court have shown independence from the executive in recent years. Drug trafficking and the violence and corruption that it engenders continue to erode institutions. Colombia was ranked 126th for corruption and 134th for security in the World Economic Forum's 2016 *Global Competitiveness Index*.

GOVERNMENT SIZE

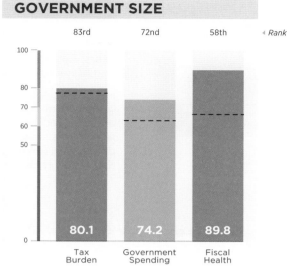

83rd	72nd	58th	◄ Rank
Tax Burden 80.1	Government Spending 74.2	Fiscal Health 89.8	

The top individual income tax rate is 33 percent, and the top corporate tax rate is 25 percent. Other taxes include a value-added tax and a financial transactions tax. The overall tax burden equals 16.7 percent of total domestic income. Government spending has amounted to 29.3 percent of total output (GDP) over the past three years, and budget deficits have averaged 1.8 percent of GDP. Public debt is equivalent to 49.4 percent of GDP.

REGULATORY EFFICIENCY

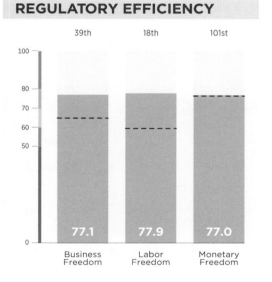

39th	18th	101st
Business Freedom 77.1	Labor Freedom 77.9	Monetary Freedom 77.0

Simplified procedures for establishing and running a business have improved the efficiency of the overall business environment. The regulatory framework is generally conducive to private business activity and job growth, but reforms are needed to lower nonwage costs. A May 2016 IMF report reflects that Colombia has made progress in bringing its subsidies in line with "OECD best practices" except for increased spending on housing subsidies.

OPEN MARKETS

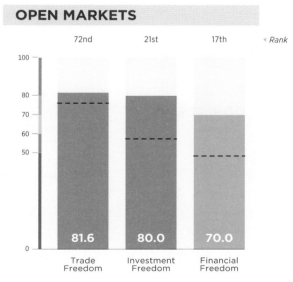

72nd	21st	17th	◄ Rank
Trade Freedom 81.6	Investment Freedom 80.0	Financial Freedom 70.0	

Trade is moderately important to Colombia's economy; the value of exports and imports taken together equals 39 percent of GDP. The average applied tariff rate is 4.2 percent. Foreign and domestic investors are generally treated equally, but investment in some sectors of the economy is restricted. Domestic banks continue to dominate the banking sector, although the presence of foreign banks has increased.

COSTA RICA

WORLD RANK: **63** | REGIONAL RANK: **10**

ECONOMIC FREEDOM STATUS:
MODERATELY FREE

Costa Rica's economic fundamentals, including macroeconomic stability and openness to global trade and finance, remain relatively strong. The economy has expanded by an average of approximately 3.5 percent annually over the past five years. Recent reforms have focused on regulatory improvements and fostering a stronger private sector.

However, deeper institutional reforms are needed. Excessive government bureaucracy continues to discourage dynamic entrepreneurial activity, and the pace of privatization and fiscal reform has slowed. Widening budget deficits have put public debt on an upward trend. The judicial system, while transparent and not corrupt, remains inefficient.

ECONOMIC FREEDOM SCORE

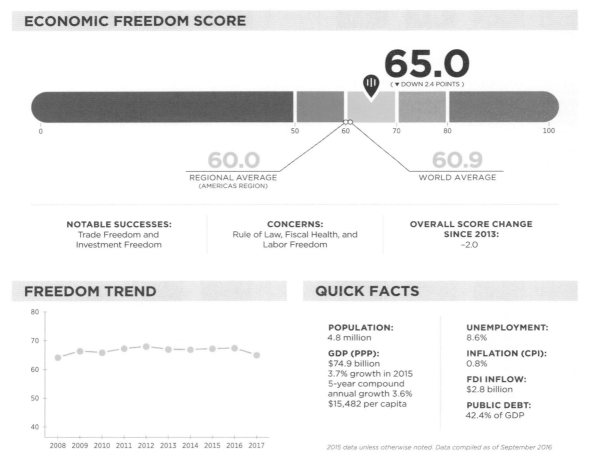

65.0
(▼ DOWN 2.4 POINTS)

0   50   60   70   80   100

60.0
REGIONAL AVERAGE
(AMERICAS REGION)

60.9
WORLD AVERAGE

NOTABLE SUCCESSES:
Trade Freedom and
Investment Freedom

CONCERNS:
Rule of Law, Fiscal Health, and
Labor Freedom

**OVERALL SCORE CHANGE
SINCE 2013:**
–2.0

FREEDOM TREND

80
70
60
50
40

2008 2009 2010 2011 2012 2013 2014 2015 2016 2017

QUICK FACTS

POPULATION:
4.8 million

GDP (PPP):
$74.9 billion
3.7% growth in 2015
5-year compound
annual growth 3.6%
$15,482 per capita

UNEMPLOYMENT:
8.6%

INFLATION (CPI):
0.8%

FDI INFLOW:
$2.8 billion

PUBLIC DEBT:
42.4% of GDP

2015 data unless otherwise noted. Data compiled as of September 2016

BACKGROUND: The most prosperous of the five countries in the Central American Common Market, Costa Rica has a long history of democratic stability and enjoys one of Latin America's highest levels of foreign direct investment per capita. Luis Guillermo Solís of the center-left Partido Acción Ciudadana began his four-year term as president in 2014. A fractious legislature complicates policymaking because the PAC holds the fewest seats of any ruling party in Costa Rican history. Costa Rica has a long-standing border dispute with Nicaragua that is related to the San Juan River. Traditional agricultural exports of bananas, coffee, and sugar are still the backbone of the country's commodity-driven export economy, and high-value-added goods and services have further bolstered exports.

12 ECONOMIC FREEDOMS | COSTA RICA

RULE OF LAW

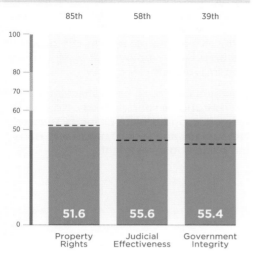

| | 85th | 58th | 39th | ◄ Rank |

Property Rights	Judicial Effectiveness	Government Integrity
51.6	55.6	55.4

Property rights are secure, and contracts are generally upheld, although they are sometimes difficult to enforce. The judicial branch is independent, but its processes are often slow. Despite ongoing efforts to combat drug trafficking, the country's fiscal challenges threaten to undermine the security and justice sectors. A complex bureaucracy slows the pace of capacity-building, and corruption remains a nagging issue.

GOVERNMENT SIZE

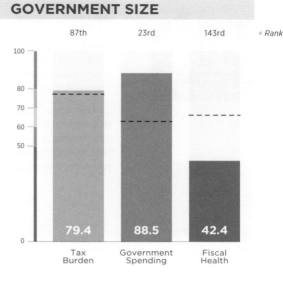

| 87th | 23rd | 143rd | ◄ Rank |

Tax Burden	Government Spending	Fiscal Health
79.4	88.5	42.4

The top personal income tax rate is 25 percent, and the top corporate tax rate is 30 percent. Other taxes include a general sales tax and a real property tax. The overall tax burden equals 23.1 percent of total domestic income. Government spending has amounted to 19.6 percent of total output (GDP) over the past three years, and budget deficits have averaged 5.8 percent of GDP. Public debt is equivalent to 42.4 percent of GDP.

REGULATORY EFFICIENCY

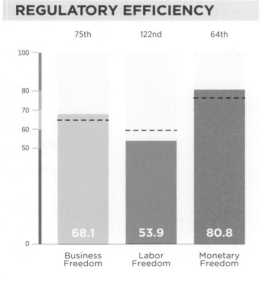

| 75th | 122nd | 64th |

Business Freedom	Labor Freedom	Monetary Freedom
68.1	53.9	80.8

The overall business framework does not adequately support entrepreneurial activity. Licensing requirements have been reduced, but procedures for launching a business remain cumbersome. The nonsalary cost of employing a worker remains high. To fulfill its commitment to forswear the use of fossil fuels, the government subsidizes the cost to consumers of hydroelectric power generated by the state-owned electric utility.

OPEN MARKETS

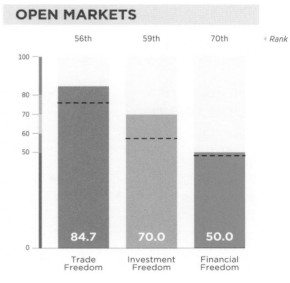

| 56th | 59th | 70th | ◄ Rank |

Trade Freedom	Investment Freedom	Financial Freedom
84.7	70.0	50.0

Trade is important to Costa Rica's economy; the value of exports and imports taken together equals 72 percent of GDP. The average applied tariff rate is 2.7 percent. The government restricts investment in some sectors of the economy. The growing financial sector functions relatively well. Banking remains dominated by state-owned institutions, but they have given up a considerable portion of the market to private-sector banks.

CUBA

WORLD RANK:
178

REGIONAL RANK:
31

ECONOMIC FREEDOM STATUS:
REPRESSED

State control of Cuba's economy is both pervasive and inefficient, hampering any meaningful development of a job-creating private sector. As the largest source of employment, the bloated government sector soaks up much of the labor force. After decades without effective economic reform, the government has eased the rules on private employment in an effort to reshape the economy and improve efficiency.

Cuba's potential entrepreneurs have long been shackled by tight government control and institutional shortcomings. No courts are free of political interference, and private property is strictly regulated. Excessive bureaucracy and lack of regulatory transparency continue to limit trade and investment.

ECONOMIC FREEDOM SCORE

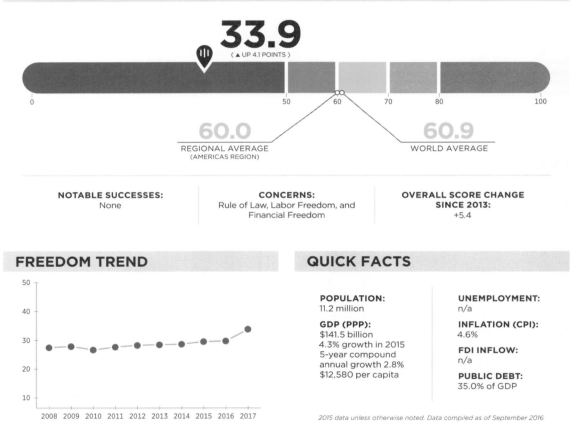

33.9
(▲ UP 4.1 POINTS)

0   50   60   70   80   100

60.0
REGIONAL AVERAGE
(AMERICAS REGION)

60.9
WORLD AVERAGE

NOTABLE SUCCESSES:	CONCERNS:	OVERALL SCORE CHANGE SINCE 2013:
None	Rule of Law, Labor Freedom, and Financial Freedom	+5.4

FREEDOM TREND

50

40

30

20

10

2008 2009 2010 2011 2012 2013 2014 2015 2016 2017

QUICK FACTS

POPULATION:
11.2 million

GDP (PPP):
$141.5 billion
4.3% growth in 2015
5-year compound
annual growth 2.8%
$12,580 per capita

UNEMPLOYMENT:
n/a

INFLATION (CPI):
4.6%

FDI INFLOW:
n/a

PUBLIC DEBT:
35.0% of GDP

2015 data unless otherwise noted. Data compiled as of September 2016

BACKGROUND: Although Fidel Castro died in November 2016, his 85-year-old younger brother Raúl continues to lead both the government and the Cuban Communist Party. Raúl's only son, Colonel Alejandro Castro Espín, and former son-in-law, General Luis Alberto Rodríguez López-Callejas, are being groomed to perpetuate the family's political and economic control of the island. Ironically, violent repression of civil society and religious persecution actually increased in the run-up to President Barack Obama's March 2016 visit that showcased weakened U.S. economic sanctions and looser travel restrictions on Americans visiting Cuba. In the absence of significant future oil subsidies from nearly bankrupt Venezuela, Cuba's dysfunctional economy is even more dependent on external assistance such as remittances from Cuban émigrés.

12 ECONOMIC FREEDOMS | CUBA

RULE OF LAW

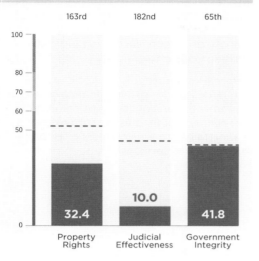

163rd	182nd	65th
Property Rights	Judicial Effectiveness	Government Integrity
32.4	10.0	41.8

Most means of production are owned by the state. Seizures of property by police without legal justification are common. The nominally independent but heavily politicized judiciary is directly subordinate to the National Assembly and the Communist Party, which may remove or appoint judges at any time. Corruption is a serious problem, with widespread illegality permeating both the limited private enterprises and the vast state-controlled economy.

GOVERNMENT SIZE

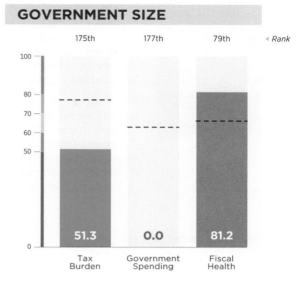

175th	177th	79th	◂ Rank
Tax Burden	Government Spending	Fiscal Health	
51.3	0.0	81.2	

The top individual income tax rate is 50 percent, and the top corporate tax rate is 30 percent. Other taxes include a tax on property transfers and a sales tax. The overall tax burden equals 38.3 percent of total domestic income. Government spending has amounted to 63.3 percent of total output (GDP) over the past three years, and budget deficits have averaged 3.2 percent of GDP. Public debt is equivalent to 35.0 percent of GDP.

REGULATORY EFFICIENCY

185th	184th	167th
Business Freedom	Labor Freedom	Monetary Freedom
20.0	20.0	66.0

Only limited private economic activity is permitted. Inconsistent and nontransparent application of regulations impedes entrepreneurship. State control of the formal labor market has led to the creation of a large informal economy. Prices are tightly controlled to contain inflation, but in 2016, the government backpedaled from plans to eliminate its dual currency system, which has long been a source of economic distortions.

OPEN MARKETS

157th	172nd	173rd	◂ Rank
Trade Freedom	Investment Freedom	Financial Freedom	
64.5	10.0	10.0	

Trade is only moderately important to Cuba's economy; the value of exports and imports taken together equals 26.4 percent of GDP. The average applied tariff rate is 7.7 percent. State-owned enterprises significantly distort the economy. Access to credit for private-sector activity is severely impeded by the shallow financial market. Despite a decade of incremental changes, the state remains firmly in control.

DOMINICA

WORLD RANK:
67

REGIONAL RANK:
13

ECONOMIC FREEDOM STATUS:
MODERATELY FREE

A process of gradual reform, including simplification of the business start-up process, has helped to improve Dominica's overall investment framework. The independent legal system generally adjudicates business disputes effectively and encourages a relatively low level of corruption, sustaining judicial effectiveness and government integrity.

However, policies to open markets further have not been advanced, and the lack of access to long-term financing prevents more dynamic economic expansion. Despite some cuts, public spending remains relatively high, a fiscal burden that is exacerbated by budget shortfalls and a rising level of public debt. The efficiency of government services has been poor, undermining overall productivity.

ECONOMIC FREEDOM SCORE

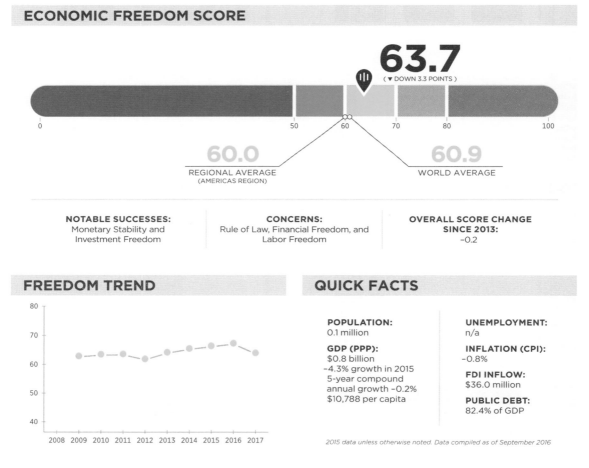

63.7
(▼ DOWN 3.3 POINTS)

0   50   60   70   80   100

60.0
REGIONAL AVERAGE
(AMERICAS REGION)

60.9
WORLD AVERAGE

NOTABLE SUCCESSES:	CONCERNS:	OVERALL SCORE CHANGE
Monetary Stability and Investment Freedom	Rule of Law, Financial Freedom, and Labor Freedom	SINCE 2013: −0.2

FREEDOM TREND

80
70
60
50
40

2008 2009 2010 2011 2012 2013 2014 2015 2016 2017

QUICK FACTS

POPULATION:
0.1 million

GDP (PPP):
$0.8 billion
−4.3% growth in 2015
5-year compound
annual growth −0.2%
$10,788 per capita

UNEMPLOYMENT:
n/a

INFLATION (CPI):
−0.8%

FDI INFLOW:
$36.0 million

PUBLIC DEBT:
82.4% of GDP

2015 data unless otherwise noted. Data compiled as of September 2016

BACKGROUND: Dominica has a unicameral parliamentary government with a president and prime minister. Prime Minister Roosevelt Skerrit of the Dominica Labour Party took office in 2004 and was reelected in 2009 and again in 2014. In 2008, Dominica made an ill-advised decision to join the Bolivarian Alliance for the Peoples of Our America (ALBA), a restrictive trade and political organization led by authoritarian socialist Venezuela that aims to undermine free-market democratic institutions and regional trade integration. Deteriorating economic conditions in Venezuela, however, have greatly reduced ALBA's material benefit and influence. In an effort to diversify the economy, the government of Dominica encourages investments in nontraditional agricultural exports such as coffee, exotic fruits, and cut flowers.

12 ECONOMIC FREEDOMS | DOMINICA

RULE OF LAW

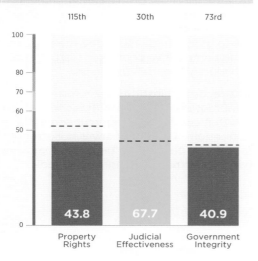

115th	30th	73rd
Property Rights	Judicial Effectiveness	Government Integrity
43.8	67.7	40.9

Private property rights are generally respected, although pirated copyrighted material is sold openly. Dominica has an independent but short-staffed judiciary. Public trials are considered fair. Despite the fact that anticorruption statutes are not always implemented effectively, corruption is not a major problem. Nonbank financial institutions are monitored to combat money laundering and the financing of terrorism.

GOVERNMENT SIZE

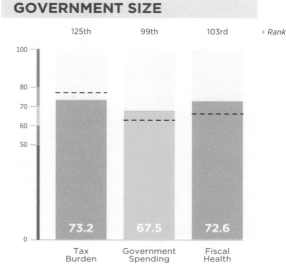

Rank

125th	99th	103rd
Tax Burden	Government Spending	Fiscal Health
73.2	67.5	72.6

The top individual income tax rate is 35 percent, and the top corporate tax rate is 30 percent. Other taxes include a value-added tax and an environmental tax. The overall tax burden equals 23.6 percent of total domestic income. Government spending has amounted to 32.9 percent of total output (GDP) over the past three years, and budget deficits have averaged 2.9 percent of GDP. Public debt is equivalent to 82.4 percent of GDP.

REGULATORY EFFICIENCY

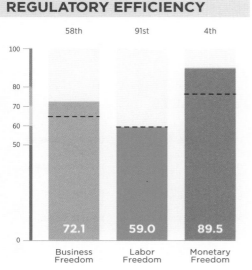

58th	91st	4th
Business Freedom	Labor Freedom	Monetary Freedom
72.1	59.0	89.5

Dominica has made progress in eliminating regulatory bottlenecks and reducing the overall cost of conducting business. The nonsalary cost of employing a worker is moderate, but the labor market lacks flexibility in other areas. An ongoing and comprehensive government restructuring of the economy to meet IMF requirements, including elimination of price controls, has been underway for more than a decade.

OPEN MARKETS

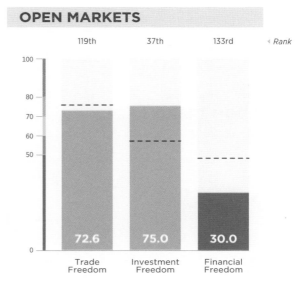

Rank

119th	37th	133rd
Trade Freedom	Investment Freedom	Financial Freedom
72.6	75.0	30.0

Trade is important to Dominica's economy; the value of exports and imports taken together equals 81 percent of GDP. The average applied tariff rate is 8.7 percent. Foreign investment may be screened by the government. The financial sector remains underdeveloped. Shallow markets and a lack of available financial instruments restrict overall access to credit and undercut prospects for faster economic development.

DOMINICAN REPUBLIC

WORLD RANK: **76** | REGIONAL RANK: **16**

ECONOMIC FREEDOM STATUS:
MODERATELY FREE

Wide-ranging reforms have led to some progress in regulatory efficiency, enhancing the Dominican Republic's entrepreneurial environment. Gradual economic diversification has strengthened resilience to external shocks. A relatively high degree of openness to global trade has aided the ongoing transition to a modern and competitive economic system, and modest tax rates have encouraged competitiveness.

The Dominican Republic's record on institutional reform has been uneven, and more vibrant economic growth is constrained by structural weaknesses that continue to undercut some of the four pillars of economic freedom. The rule of law is not strongly sustained by the judicial system, particularly because of growing corruption that undermines government integrity and judicial effectiveness.

ECONOMIC FREEDOM SCORE

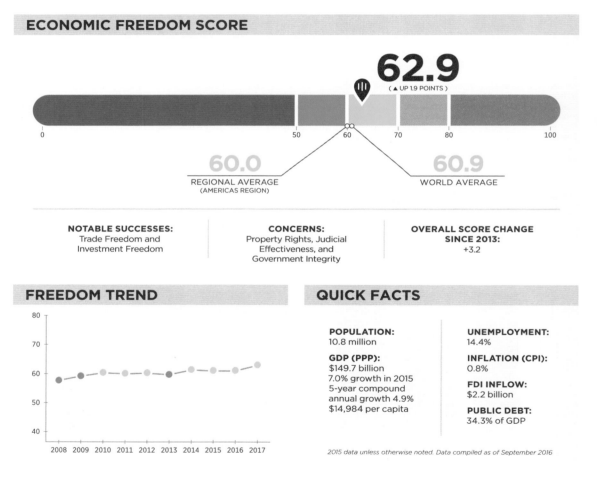

62.9
(▲ UP 1.9 POINTS)

0   50   60   70   80   100

60.0
REGIONAL AVERAGE
(AMERICAS REGION)

60.9
WORLD AVERAGE

NOTABLE SUCCESSES:
Trade Freedom and
Investment Freedom

CONCERNS:
Property Rights, Judicial
Effectiveness, and
Government Integrity

**OVERALL SCORE CHANGE
SINCE 2013:**
+3.2

FREEDOM TREND

80
70
60
50
40

2008 2009 2010 2011 2012 2013 2014 2015 2016 2017

QUICK FACTS

POPULATION:
10.8 million

GDP (PPP):
$149.7 billion
7.0% growth in 2015
5-year compound
annual growth 4.9%
$14,984 per capita

UNEMPLOYMENT:
14.4%

INFLATION (CPI):
0.8%

FDI INFLOW:
$2.2 billion

PUBLIC DEBT:
34.3% of GDP

2015 data unless otherwise noted. Data compiled as of September 2016

BACKGROUND: The Dominican Republic has long been viewed primarily as an exporter of sugar, coffee, and tobacco. After its two principal parties entered into an agreement to cooperate and support common candidates, President Danilo Medina of the center-right Dominican Liberation Party took office for a second four-year term in August 2016, and his party retained majority control of Congress. Journalists face intimidation and violence when investigating such issues as drug trafficking and corruption. In recent years, growth driven by mining activity and such service-based sectors as tourism and finance has made the economy one of the most vibrant in the Caribbean.

12 ECONOMIC FREEDOMS | DOMINICAN REPUBLIC

RULE OF LAW

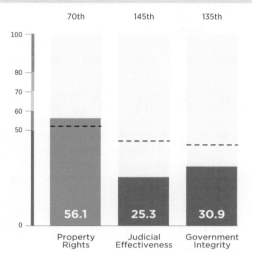

	70th	145th	135th
	Property Rights	Judicial Effectiveness	Government Integrity
	56.1	25.3	30.9

Private property rights are respected, although enforcement of intellectual property rights is poor. Despite the increasing independence of the judiciary, instances of political influence in decision-making are still evident. Corruption is a serious systemic problem at all levels of the government, the judiciary, the security forces, and the private sector. Institutionalized graft is linked to significant levels of narco-trafficking.

GOVERNMENT SIZE

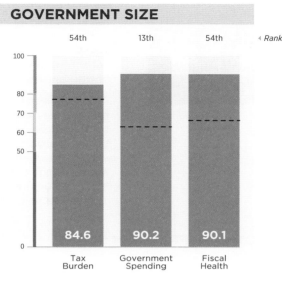

◀ Rank

	54th	13th	54th
	Tax Burden	Government Spending	Fiscal Health
	84.6	90.2	90.1

The top individual income tax rate is 25 percent, and the top corporate tax rate is 27 percent. Other taxes include a value-added tax, an estate tax, and a net wealth tax. The overall tax burden equals 13.8 percent of total domestic income. Government spending has amounted to 18.1 percent of total output (GDP) over the past three years, and budget deficits have averaged 2.2 percent of GDP. Public debt is equivalent to 34.3 percent of GDP.

REGULATORY EFFICIENCY

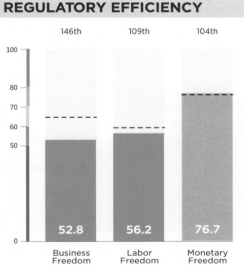

	146th	109th	104th
	Business Freedom	Labor Freedom	Monetary Freedom
	52.8	56.2	76.7

The cost of completing licensing requirements has been reduced, and the process for launching a business has been streamlined. The nonsalary cost of employing a worker is moderate, but restrictions on work hours are rigid. The Medina government still funds electricity subsidies that are estimated at approximately 2 percent of GDP and has yet to push forward with energy-sector reforms.

OPEN MARKETS

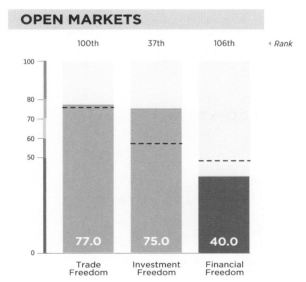

◀ Rank

	100th	37th	106th
	Trade Freedom	Investment Freedom	Financial Freedom
	77.0	75.0	40.0

Trade is important to the Dominican Republic's economy; the value of exports and imports taken together equals 54 percent of GDP. The average applied tariff rate is 6.5 percent. In general, the government does not discriminate against or screen foreign investment. The small financial sector has been consolidated, but confidence in banking has been unsteady. Capital markets are underdeveloped, and long-term financing is hard to obtain.

ECUADOR

WORLD RANK: **160** | REGIONAL RANK: **28**

ECONOMIC FREEDOM STATUS:
REPRESSED

Ecuador's government continues to expand its reach into economic sectors beyond the petroleum industry. Pervasive corruption undermines the rule of law and weakens property rights. The private sector is struggling to operate and compete with the growing public sector in what has become a restrictive entrepreneurial environment.

Private investment has shrunk as costly regulations and uncertainty have made planning for expansion more difficult. The trade regime has become more restrictive, reducing competition and eroding productivity. Ecuador's underdeveloped and state-controlled financial sector limits access to credit and adds costs for entrepreneurs. The overall investment climate has become uncertain as the government's economic policies continue to evolve rapidly in a repressive political environment.

ECONOMIC FREEDOM SCORE

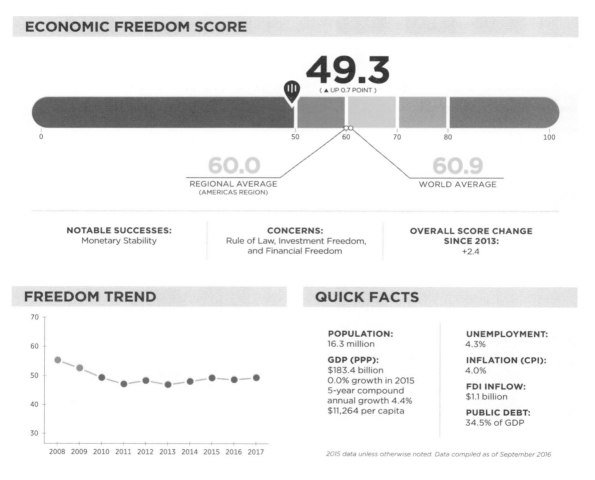

49.3
(▲ UP 0.7 POINT)

0   50   60   70   80   100

60.0
REGIONAL AVERAGE
(AMERICAS REGION)

60.9
WORLD AVERAGE

NOTABLE SUCCESSES:
Monetary Stability

CONCERNS:
Rule of Law, Investment Freedom, and Financial Freedom

OVERALL SCORE CHANGE SINCE 2013:
+2.4

FREEDOM TREND

Chart showing years 2008–2017 with values declining from about 55 to roughly 49.

QUICK FACTS

POPULATION:
16.3 million

GDP (PPP):
$183.4 billion
0.0% growth in 2015
5-year compound annual growth 4.4%
$11,264 per capita

UNEMPLOYMENT:
4.3%

INFLATION (CPI):
4.0%

FDI INFLOW:
$1.1 billion

PUBLIC DEBT:
34.5% of GDP

2015 data unless otherwise noted. Data compiled as of September 2016

BACKGROUND: President Rafael Correa, reelected to an unprecedented third term in 2013, is laying the groundwork to run again in 2017 and appears to hope to remain president indefinitely. The world's largest banana exporter, Ecuador belongs to the socialist, Venezuela-led Alliance for the Peoples of Our America (ALBA). The judiciary is not independent, and the Inter-American Human Rights Commission has criticized Correa's government for restricting freedom of the press. Ecuador continues to be a major narco-trafficking transit country. Its dollarized economy depends substantially on its petroleum resources, which have accounted for more than half of export earnings and approximately one-quarter of public-sector revenues in recent years.

12 ECONOMIC FREEDOMS | ECUADOR

RULE OF LAW

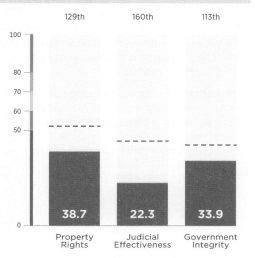

129th	160th	113th
Property Rights	Judicial Effectiveness	Government Integrity
38.7	22.3	33.9

Protection of property rights is weak, and violation of intellectual property rights has been decriminalized altogether. A weak judiciary and lack of investigative capacity contribute to an environment of impunity. Some judges accept bribes for favorable decisions and faster resolution of legal cases. Persistent corruption is fueled in part by cronyism and government persecution of media investigative reporters.

GOVERNMENT SIZE

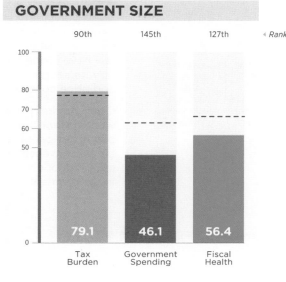

◄ Rank

90th	145th	127th
Tax Burden	Government Spending	Fiscal Health
79.1	46.1	56.4

The top personal income tax rate is 35 percent, and the corporate tax rate is 22 percent. Other taxes include a value-added tax and an inheritance tax. The overall tax burden equals 19.6 percent of total domestic income. Government spending has amounted to 42.4 percent of total output (GDP) over the past three years, and budget deficits have averaged 5.1 percent of GDP. Public debt is equivalent to 34.5 percent of GDP.

REGULATORY EFFICIENCY

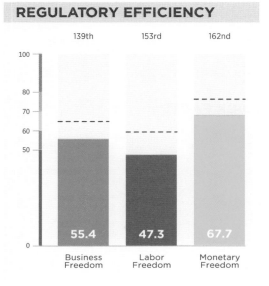

139th	153rd	162nd
Business Freedom	Labor Freedom	Monetary Freedom
55.4	47.3	67.7

The regulatory complexity resulting from inconsistent application of existing commercial laws increases the cost of conducting business. Cumbersome labor regulations inhibit dynamic expansion of employment opportunities and foster the informal labor market. Although dollarization generates a modicum of monetary stability, the government continues to impose price controls and fund subsidies.

OPEN MARKETS

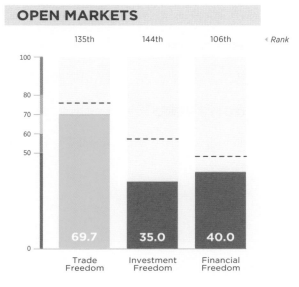

◄ Rank

135th	144th	106th
Trade Freedom	Investment Freedom	Financial Freedom
69.7	35.0	40.0

Trade is moderately important to Ecuador's economy; the value of exports and imports taken together equals 45 percent of GDP. The average applied tariff rate is 5.2 percent. Nontariff barriers interfere with trade, and state-owned enterprises distort the economy. The financial sector remains poorly developed. The number of nonperforming loans has been rising, and state interference in banking has expanded.

EL SALVADOR

WORLD RANK:
66

REGIONAL RANK:
12

ECONOMIC FREEDOM STATUS:
MODERATELY FREE

El Salvador's economy, once considered to be among the region's most promising, has been suffering from a gradual decline in economic freedom. Institutional weaknesses continue to slow development, and judicial independence and the rule of law have eroded in recent years. Government interference in the private sector has increased, with populist spending measures and price controls further distorting markets.

Open-market policies that support El Salvador's engagement with the world through trade and investment are still largely in place, but overall competitiveness is increasingly constrained by chronic fiscal deficits and regulatory inefficiency. A growing perception of corruption has undermined popular trust in government.

ECONOMIC FREEDOM SCORE

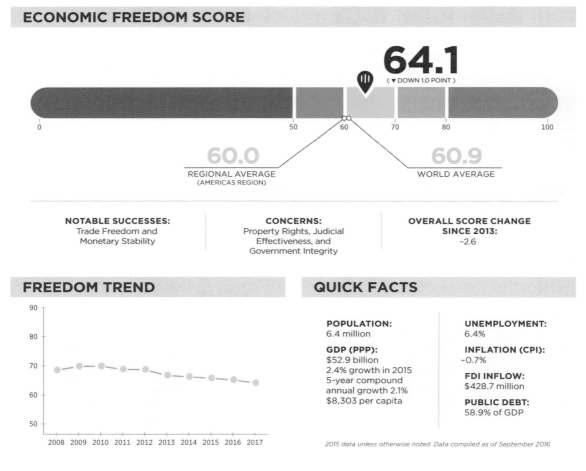

64.1
(▼ DOWN 1.0 POINT)

0   50   60   70   80   100

60.0
REGIONAL AVERAGE
(AMERICAS REGION)

60.9
WORLD AVERAGE

NOTABLE SUCCESSES:
Trade Freedom and
Monetary Stability

CONCERNS:
Property Rights, Judicial
Effectiveness, and
Government Integrity

**OVERALL SCORE CHANGE
SINCE 2013:**
−2.6

FREEDOM TREND

90

80

70

60

50

2008 2009 2010 2011 2012 2013 2014 2015 2016 2017

QUICK FACTS

POPULATION:
6.4 million

GDP (PPP):
$52.9 billion
2.4% growth in 2015
5-year compound
annual growth 2.1%
$8,303 per capita

UNEMPLOYMENT:
6.4%

INFLATION (CPI):
−0.7%

FDI INFLOW:
$428.7 million

PUBLIC DEBT:
58.9% of GDP

2015 data unless otherwise noted. Data compiled as of September 2016

BACKGROUND: Since 2009, governments of the leftist Farabundo Martí National Liberation Front have increased the state's role in the economy and strengthened their alliance with the socialist, Venezuela-led Alliance for the Peoples of Our America (ALBA). The term of the current president, Salvador Sánchez Cerén, will end in 2019. He has pursued relatively moderate policies but has lost popularity as a result of anemic economic growth, weak government effectiveness, a surge in violence and drug trafficking, and rising gang-related homicides. The economy relies on exports of coffee, sugar, textiles and apparel, gold, ethanol, chemicals, and the assembly of intermediate goods. Remittances account for nearly one-fifth of GDP.

12 ECONOMIC FREEDOMS | EL SALVADOR

RULE OF LAW

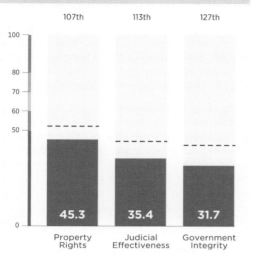

107th	113th	127th
45.3	35.4	31.7
Property Rights	Judicial Effectiveness	Government Integrity

Property rights are not strongly respected, and enforcement efforts to protect them are uneven. No single natural or legal person can own more than 245 hectares (605 acres) of land. Substantial corruption in the judicial system contributes to a high level of impunity, undermining the rule of law and the public's respect for the judiciary. Narcotics-related corruption within El Salvador's political system remains a serious problem.

GOVERNMENT SIZE

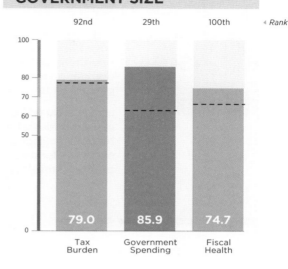

92nd	29th	100th	◀ Rank
79.0	85.9	74.7	
Tax Burden	Government Spending	Fiscal Health	

The top personal income and corporate tax rates are 30 percent. Other taxes include a value-added tax and excise taxes. The overall tax burden equals 17.3 percent of total domestic income. Government spending has amounted to 21.7 percent of total output (GDP) over the past three years, and budget deficits have averaged 3.4 percent of GDP. Public debt is equivalent to 58.9 percent of GDP.

REGULATORY EFFICIENCY

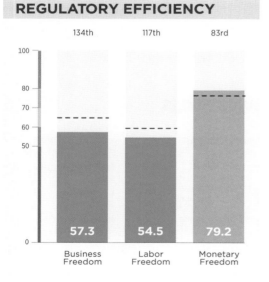

134th	117th	83rd
57.3	54.5	79.2
Business Freedom	Labor Freedom	Monetary Freedom

Despite some progress, regulations are enforced inconsistently. The inefficient labor market lacks flexibility, and imbalances persist in the demand for and supply of skilled workers. The government imposes price controls on a range of goods and services. In its report on El Salvador's fiscal deficit in 2016, the IMF noted the government's failure to reform poorly targeted subsidies, especially for electricity, liquefied petroleum gas, and transportation.

OPEN MARKETS

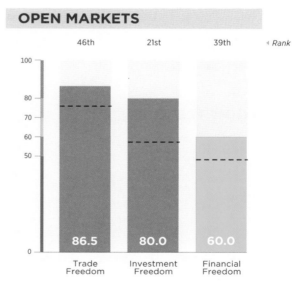

46th	21st	39th	◀ Rank
86.5	80.0	60.0	
Trade Freedom	Investment Freedom	Financial Freedom	

Trade is important to El Salvador's economy; the value of exports and imports taken together equals 68 percent of GDP. The average applied tariff rate is 1.8 percent. In general, foreign and domestic investors are treated equally, and there is no screening of foreign investment. Banking is highly concentrated, with four private banks accounting for over 70 percent of total assets.

GUATEMALA

WORLD RANK: **74** | REGIONAL RANK: **15**

ECONOMIC FREEDOM STATUS:
MODERATELY FREE

Policy failures and structural inadequacies continue to hinder broad-based economic growth in Guatemala. The government's fiscal deficits remain contained, but efforts to improve management of public finance and government effectiveness have had little impact, and the inefficient public sector continues to undermine private-sector development. More than half of the population lives below the national poverty line, and almost 40 percent of the indigenous population lives in extreme poverty.

Long-standing constraints on Guatemala's economic freedom include widespread government corruption and fragile protection of property rights under the weak rule of law. Lack of access to long-term financing is a significant impediment to business development and job growth.

ECONOMIC FREEDOM SCORE

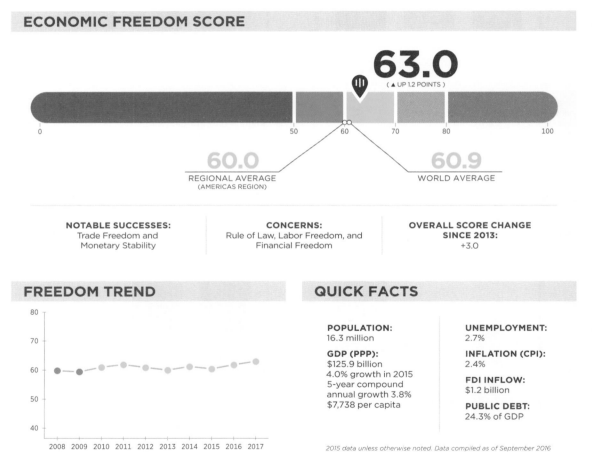

63.0
(▲ UP 1.2 POINTS)

0   50   60   70   80   100

60.0
REGIONAL AVERAGE
(AMERICAS REGION)

60.9
WORLD AVERAGE

NOTABLE SUCCESSES:
Trade Freedom and
Monetary Stability

CONCERNS:
Rule of Law, Labor Freedom, and
Financial Freedom

**OVERALL SCORE CHANGE
SINCE 2013:**
+3.0

FREEDOM TREND

80

70

60

50

40

2008 2009 2010 2011 2012 2013 2014 2015 2016 2017

QUICK FACTS

POPULATION:
16.3 million

GDP (PPP):
$125.9 billion
4.0% growth in 2015
5-year compound
annual growth 3.8%
$7,738 per capita

UNEMPLOYMENT:
2.7%

INFLATION (CPI):
2.4%

FDI INFLOW:
$1.2 billion

PUBLIC DEBT:
24.3% of GDP

2015 data unless otherwise noted. Data compiled as of September 2016

BACKGROUND: Guatemala won its independence from Spain in 1821. A long guerrilla war that left more than 200,000 dead and led to the out-migration of about a million Guatemalans ended with a peace agreement in 1996. Since then, Guatemala has pursued important reforms and macroeconomic stabilization and has attracted foreign investment. Instability spiked anew when the rightist Patriotic Party government collapsed in November 2015. The new president, political neophyte Jimmy Morales, began his five-year term in early 2016 but has made little progress on promised improvements in health care, education, and security. Guatemala remains a major drug trafficking transit country. Gang violence continues to impede economic development.

12 ECONOMIC FREEDOMS | GUATEMALA

RULE OF LAW

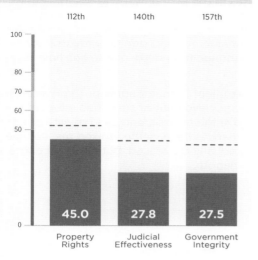

112th	140th	157th
45.0	27.8	27.5
Property Rights	Judicial Effectiveness	Government Integrity

Although the government has stepped up efforts to enforce property rights, it can be difficult to obtain and enforce eviction notices when rightful ownership is in dispute. The judiciary is hobbled by corruption, inefficiency, insufficient capacity, and the intimidation of judges and prosecutors. Widespread corruption and mismanagement remain problems, especially in the customs and tax agencies.

GOVERNMENT SIZE

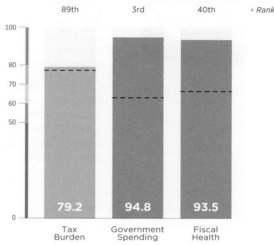

89th	3rd	40th	◂ Rank
79.2	94.8	93.5	
Tax Burden	Government Spending	Fiscal Health	

The top individual income and corporate tax rates are 31 percent. Other taxes include a value-added tax and a tax on real estate. The overall tax burden equals 12.5 percent of total domestic income. Government spending has amounted to 13.1 percent of total output (GDP) over the past three years, and budget deficits have averaged 1.8 percent of GDP. Public debt is equivalent to 24.3 percent of GDP.

REGULATORY EFFICIENCY

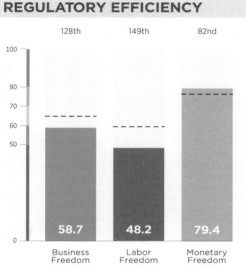

128th	149th	82nd
58.7	48.2	79.4
Business Freedom	Labor Freedom	Monetary Freedom

Bureaucratic hurdles, including lengthy processes for launching a business and obtaining necessary permits, remain common. Outmoded labor regulations are rigid. A large portion of the workforce is employed in the informal sector. The state maintains few price controls but subsidizes public transport in Guatemala City, diesel fuel for trucks and buses, and electricity for low-income families.

OPEN MARKETS

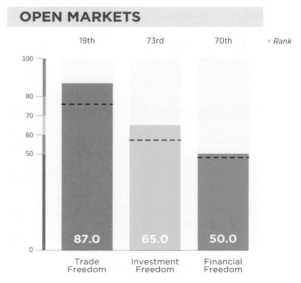

19th	73rd	70th	◂ Rank
87.0	65.0	50.0	
Trade Freedom	Investment Freedom	Financial Freedom	

Trade is important to Guatemala's economy; the value of exports and imports taken together equals 51 percent of GDP. The average applied tariff rate is 1.5 percent. Foreign and domestic investors are generally treated equally under the law, but the judicial and regulatory systems may discourage investment. The small financial system is dominated by bank-centered financial conglomerates. The foreign bank presence is small.

GUYANA

Broad-based economic growth in Guyana is held back by structural weaknesses in the economy. Long-standing constraints on economic freedom include widespread corruption in government, fragile protection of property rights, and weak rule of law. Inefficient bureaucracy and significant restrictions on foreign investment continue to undermine the entrepreneurial environment.

Guyana's oversized government is an impediment to private-sector development and the achievement of sustained economic growth. Actions to improve the transparency and quality of its management of public finances have yielded mixed results. The average tariff rate has gradually decreased, but nontariff barriers continue to limit trade freedom.

ECONOMIC FREEDOM SCORE

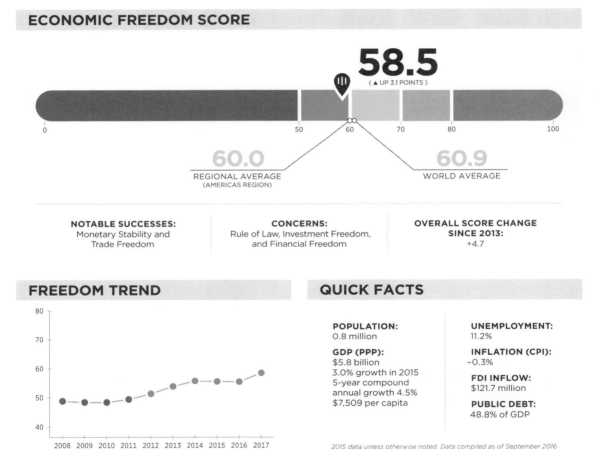

58.5
(▲ UP 3.1 POINTS)

0   50   60   70   80   100

60.0
REGIONAL AVERAGE
(AMERICAS REGION)

60.9
WORLD AVERAGE

NOTABLE SUCCESSES:	CONCERNS:	OVERALL SCORE CHANGE
Monetary Stability and Trade Freedom	Rule of Law, Investment Freedom, and Financial Freedom	**SINCE 2013:** +4.7

FREEDOM TREND

80

70

60

50

40

2008 2009 2010 2011 2012 2013 2014 2015 2016 2017

QUICK FACTS

POPULATION:
0.8 million

GDP (PPP):
$5.8 billion
3.0% growth in 2015
5-year compound
annual growth 4.5%
$7,509 per capita

UNEMPLOYMENT:
11.2%

INFLATION (CPI):
-0.3%

FDI INFLOW:
$121.7 million

PUBLIC DEBT:
48.8% of GDP

2015 data unless otherwise noted. Data compiled as of September 2016

BACKGROUND: Originally a Dutch colony, Guyana had become a British possession by 1815. The abolition of slavery led to settlement of urban areas by former slaves and the importation of indentured servants from India to work the sugar plantations. The resulting ethno-cultural divide has persisted and has led to political turbulence. Since gaining independence in 1966, Guyana has been ruled mostly by socialist-oriented governments. A multiracial coalition government led by President David Granger was elected in 2015. Political tensions between the coalition government and the formerly ruling Indo-Guyanese PPC/Civic parties eased slightly following successful local elections in March 2016. Exports of sugar, gold, bauxite, shrimp, timber, and rice represent nearly 60 percent of formal GDP.

12 ECONOMIC FREEDOMS | GUYANA

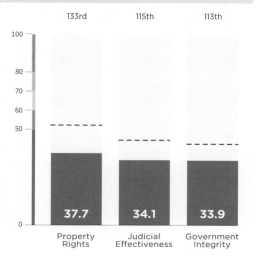

RULE OF LAW

| 133rd | 115th | 113th | ◄ Rank |

Property Rights — 37.7
Judicial Effectiveness — 34.1
Government Integrity — 33.9

Guyana's property rights system is overly bureau-cratic and complex, with regulations that are overlap-ping and competing, overloaded, and nontransparent. The judicial system is generally perceived as slow and ineffective in enforcing contracts or resolving disputes. There is a widespread public perception of corruption involving officials at all levels, including the police and the judiciary.

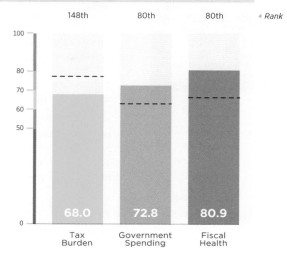

GOVERNMENT SIZE

| 148th | 80th | 80th | ◄ Rank |

Tax Burden — 68.0
Government Spending — 72.8
Fiscal Health — 80.9

The top personal income tax rate is 33.3 percent, and the top corporate tax rate is 40 percent. Other taxes include a property tax and a value-added tax. The overall tax burden equals 22.1 percent of total domestic income. Government spending has amounted to 30.1 percent of total output (GDP) over the past three years, and budget deficits have averaged 3.0 percent of GDP. Public debt is equivalent to 48.8 percent of GDP.

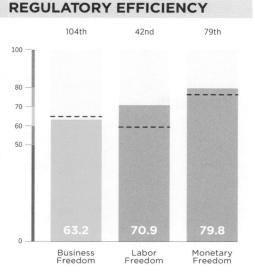

REGULATORY EFFICIENCY

| 104th | 42nd | 79th |

Business Freedom — 63.2
Labor Freedom — 70.9
Monetary Freedom — 79.8

Enforcement of existing regulations is not always consistent, and a lack of regulatory certainty often increases the cost of doing business. Labor regulations are relatively flexible, but the size of the public sector has prevented the emergence of an efficient labor market. Government-subsidized rice used to be sold to Venezuela for rates that were higher than market rates, but by 2016, Venezuela could no longer afford to buy it.

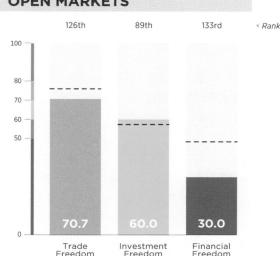

OPEN MARKETS

| 126th | 89th | 133rd | ◄ Rank |

Trade Freedom — 70.7
Investment Freedom — 60.0
Financial Freedom — 30.0

Trade is extremely important to Guyana's economy; the value of exports and imports taken together equals 121 percent of GDP. The average applied tariff rate is 7.1 percent. In general, foreign and domestic investors are treated equally under the law. The underdeveloped financial sector continues to suffer from a poor institu-tional framework. Scarce access to financing remains a barrier to more dynamic entrepreneurial activity.

HAITI

H aiti, the Western Hemisphere's poorest and most deforested country, is plagued by corruption, gang violence, drug trafficking, organized crime, and a general lack of economic opportunity. Poor economic management and crippling natural disasters have taken a terrible human and economic toll. A devastating earthquake destroyed much of the basic economic infrastructure in 2010, and more recent hurricane damage has compounded the problem. The international community has assisted in recovery and rebuilding efforts.

Haiti's institutional capacity for economic policymaking has been complicated by the absence of a stable government since February 2016. The effectiveness of public finance has been severely undermined by political volatility that further weakens an already weak rule of law.

WORLD RANK: 159 | **REGIONAL RANK:** 27

ECONOMIC FREEDOM STATUS:
REPRESSED

ECONOMIC FREEDOM SCORE

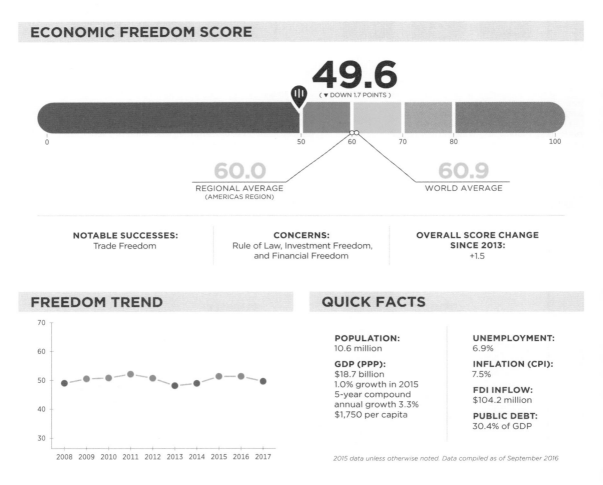

49.6
(▼ DOWN 1.7 POINTS)

0   50   60   70   80   100

60.0
REGIONAL AVERAGE
(AMERICAS REGION)

60.9
WORLD AVERAGE

NOTABLE SUCCESSES:	CONCERNS:	OVERALL SCORE CHANGE SINCE 2013:
Trade Freedom	Rule of Law, Investment Freedom, and Financial Freedom	+1.5

FREEDOM TREND

70

60

50

40

30

2008 2009 2010 2011 2012 2013 2014 2015 2016 2017

QUICK FACTS

POPULATION:
10.6 million

GDP (PPP):
$18.7 billion
1.0% growth in 2015
5-year compound
annual growth 3.3%
$1,750 per capita

UNEMPLOYMENT:
6.9%

INFLATION (CPI):
7.5%

FDI INFLOW:
$104.2 million

PUBLIC DEBT:
30.4% of GDP

2015 data unless otherwise noted. Data compiled as of September 2016

BACKGROUND: Haiti was politically paralyzed after Michel Martelly's five-year term as president expired in February 2016 with no elected successor in place. Martelly's tenure was marked by political stalemate and fragmentation, delayed elections, and accelerating deterioration of already dysfunctional democratic institutions. After a series of interim presidents, Jovenel Moïse, a businessman, political newcomer, and Martelly protégé, was finally elected president in November 2016. Commercial and diplomatic relations with the neighboring Dominican Republic have been gridlocked since Santo Domingo began to deport tens of thousands of undocumented Dominican-born people of Haitian descent.

12 ECONOMIC FREEDOMS | HAITI

RULE OF LAW

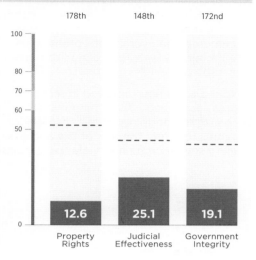

178th	148th	172nd
Property Rights	Judicial Effectiveness	Government Integrity
12.6	25.1	19.1

Real property interests are negatively affected by the absence of a comprehensive civil registry, and the authenticity of titles is difficult to confirm. The judicial system performs poorly because of antiquated penal and criminal procedure codes, opaque court proceedings, lack of judicial oversight, and widespread judicial corruption. There has never been a successful conviction on drug trafficking or corruption-related charges in Haitian courts.

GOVERNMENT SIZE

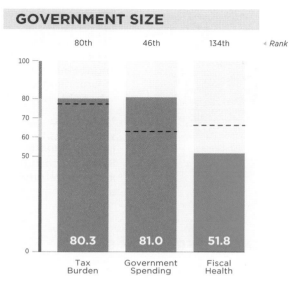

80th	46th	134th	◂ Rank
Tax Burden	Government Spending	Fiscal Health	
80.3	81.0	51.8	

The top personal income and corporate tax rates are 30 percent. Other taxes include a value-added tax and a capital gains tax. The overall tax burden equals 13.2 percent of total domestic income. Government spending has amounted to 25.2 percent of total output (GDP) over the past three years, and budget deficits have averaged 5.4 percent of GDP. Public debt is equivalent to 30.4 percent of GDP.

REGULATORY EFFICIENCY

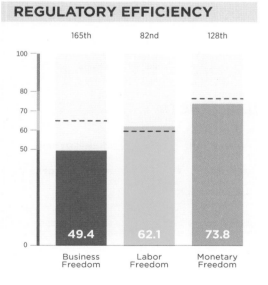

165th	82nd	128th
Business Freedom	Labor Freedom	Monetary Freedom
49.4	62.1	73.8

Political instability has hurt the business environment. A large portion of the workforce has been dependent on the informal sector. In May 2016, despite criticism that the donation could damage Haitian agriculture, the U.S. government planned to ship a million pounds of peanuts to Haiti that were produced in excess of market demand because of U.S. farm subsidies. Overall, foreign and domestic subsidies have harmed Haiti's economy.

OPEN MARKETS

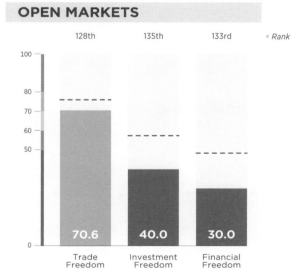

128th	135th	133rd	◂ Rank
Trade Freedom	Investment Freedom	Financial Freedom	
70.6	40.0	30.0	

Trade is important to Haiti's economy; the value of exports and imports taken together equals 70 percent of GDP. The average applied tariff rate is 7.2 percent. Bureaucratic barriers may discourage foreign investment. Haiti's already strained financial infrastructure has become even more fragile. Many economic transactions are conducted outside of the formal banking sector, and scarce access to financing severely hinders entrepreneurial activity.

HONDURAS

Broader implementation of deeper institutional reforms remains critical to spurring dynamic economic growth throughout the Honduran economy. Despite the implementation of policies that aim to sustain market openness and facilitate engagement in global commerce, the overall entrepreneurial environment continues to be hurt by weak protection of property rights and political instability.

Management of public expenditures has improved in recent years. In April 2016, Congress approved a fiscal responsibility law intended to institutionalize the ongoing fiscal consolidation. Systemic corruption continues to erode the rule of law and trust in the government. Reducing severe crime and violence remains a priority.

WORLD RANK: **100**
REGIONAL RANK: **21**

ECONOMIC FREEDOM STATUS:
MOSTLY UNFREE

ECONOMIC FREEDOM SCORE

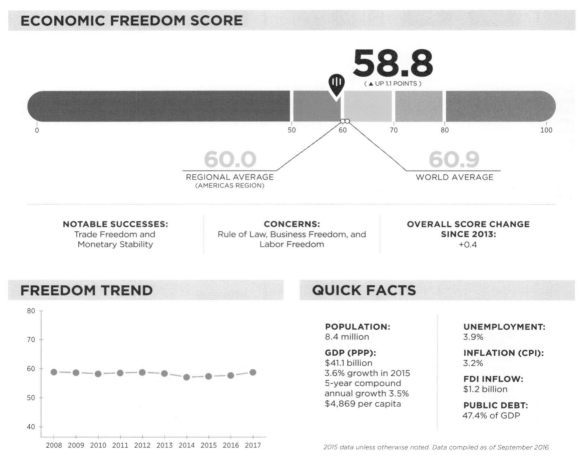

58.8
(▲ UP 1.1 POINTS)

0   50   60   70   80   100

60.0
REGIONAL AVERAGE
(AMERICAS REGION)

60.9
WORLD AVERAGE

NOTABLE SUCCESSES:	CONCERNS:	OVERALL SCORE CHANGE
Trade Freedom and Monetary Stability	Rule of Law, Business Freedom, and Labor Freedom	SINCE 2013: +0.4

FREEDOM TREND

80
70
60
50
40

2008 2009 2010 2011 2012 2013 2014 2015 2016 2017

QUICK FACTS

POPULATION:
8.4 million

GDP (PPP):
$41.1 billion
3.6% growth in 2015
5-year compound
annual growth 3.5%
$4,869 per capita

UNEMPLOYMENT:
3.9%

INFLATION (CPI):
3.2%

FDI INFLOW:
$1.2 billion

PUBLIC DEBT:
47.4% of GDP

2015 data unless otherwise noted. Data compiled as of September 2016

BACKGROUND: Honduras, the second-poorest country in Central America, has one of the highest homicide rates in the world as street gangs and transnational organized criminal networks prey on communities, often in collusion with authorities. In 2015, the country's Supreme Court struck down a controversial term limit and cleared the way for President Juan Orlando Hernández to seek a second term in 2017. Hernández has promoted foreign investment and has encouraged leaders of El Salvador and Guatemala to join him in making Central America more competitive. Continuing high levels of violence, extensive narco-related money laundering, and reports of government corruption reaching the highest levels have undermined the country's international image.

12 ECONOMIC FREEDOMS | HONDURAS

RULE OF LAW

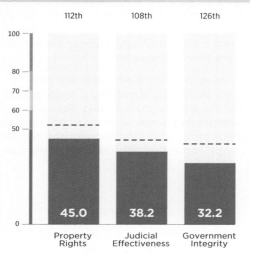

| | 112th | 108th | 126th |

Property Rights: **45.0**
Judicial Effectiveness: **38.2**
Government Integrity: **32.2**

Approximately 80 percent of the privately held land in Honduras is either untitled or improperly titled. Resolution of title disputes in court often takes years, partly because of the judicial system's weakness. Rampant corruption and weak state institutions make it virtually impossible to combat threats posed by violent transnational gangs and organized criminal groups. Honduras has one of the world's highest murder rates.

GOVERNMENT SIZE

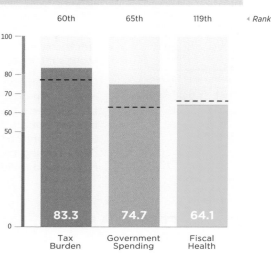

60th   65th   119th   ◂ Rank

Tax Burden: **83.3**
Government Spending: **74.7**
Fiscal Health: **64.1**

The top individual income and corporate tax rates are 25 percent (27.5 percent for corporations with an added social contribution tax). The overall tax burden equals 20.6 percent of total domestic income. Government spending has amounted to 29.1 percent of total output (GDP) over the past three years, and budget deficits have averaged 4.4 percent of GDP. Public debt is equivalent to 47.4 percent of GDP.

REGULATORY EFFICIENCY

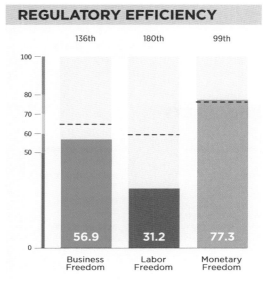

136th   180th   99th

Business Freedom: **56.9**
Labor Freedom: **31.2**
Monetary Freedom: **77.3**

The inefficient regulatory environment does not encourage dynamic entrepreneurship, and the cost of forming a business is burdensome. Labor regulations are outmoded, and a large proportion of the labor force is dependent on the informal sector. The government is continuing to overhaul the struggling state-owned ENEE electricity utility but maintains price controls for basic food items along with water, telecommunications, and port services.

OPEN MARKETS

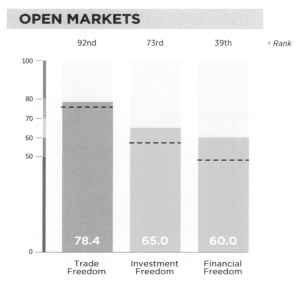

92nd   73rd   39th   ◂ Rank

Trade Freedom: **78.4**
Investment Freedom: **65.0**
Financial Freedom: **60.0**

Trade is extremely important to Honduras's economy; the value of exports and imports taken together equals 109 percent of GDP. The average applied tariff rate is 5.8 percent. In general, the government does not screen or discriminate against foreign investment. The financial sector has regained stability following the liquidation of Banco Continental in late 2015. Capital markets are not fully developed.

JAMAICA

Jamaica's economy depends heavily on tourism and other service sectors. The government has struggled with balancing the budget but has reduced its crippling debt to around 120 percent of GDP. Some structural reforms and cuts in fuel and electricity subsidies in the most recent budget show the government's intent to improve its financial health.

Despite some reforms to make paying taxes easier for businesses, the government has increased stamp duty, property tax, property transfer tax, and education tax rates. Bureaucracy hinders the ability of investors and entrepreneurs to do business. Government corruption and crime also remain serious problems, undercutting the confidence and competitiveness of both businesses and individuals.

ECONOMIC FREEDOM SCORE

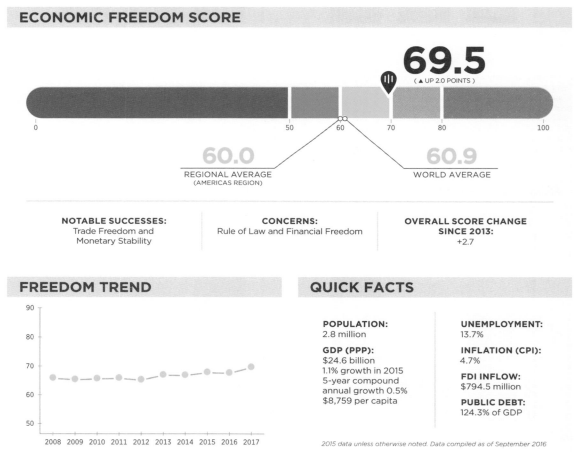

69.5
(▲ UP 2.0 POINTS)

| 0 | 50 | 60 | 70 | 80 | 100 |

60.0
REGIONAL AVERAGE
(AMERICAS REGION)

60.9
WORLD AVERAGE

NOTABLE SUCCESSES:
Trade Freedom and Monetary Stability

CONCERNS:
Rule of Law and Financial Freedom

OVERALL SCORE CHANGE SINCE 2013:
+2.7

FREEDOM TREND

QUICK FACTS

POPULATION:
2.8 million

GDP (PPP):
$24.6 billion
1.1% growth in 2015
5-year compound annual growth 0.5%
$8,759 per capita

UNEMPLOYMENT:
13.7%

INFLATION (CPI):
4.7%

FDI INFLOW:
$794.5 million

PUBLIC DEBT:
124.3% of GDP

2015 data unless otherwise noted. Data compiled as of September 2016

BACKGROUND: Jamaica gained full independence from the United Kingdom in 1962. Deteriorating economic conditions during the 1970s led to recurrent violence as rival gangs affiliated with the major political parties evolved into powerful and still active organized crime networks that are involved in international drug smuggling and money laundering. Prime Minister Andrew Holness's center-left Jamaica Labour Party narrowly won election in February 2016. Once a major sugar producer, Jamaica is now a net sugar importer, and services account for more than 70 percent of GDP. Most foreign exchange comes from remittances, tourism, and bauxite. Agricultural production rebounded in 2016, primarily due to more favorable weather conditions.

12 ECONOMIC FREEDOMS | JAMAICA

RULE OF LAW

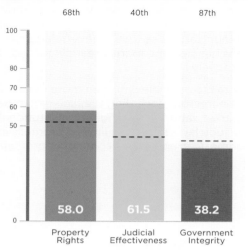

68th   40th   87th

Property Rights	Judicial Effectiveness	Government Integrity
58.0	61.5	38.2

The government has increased the percentage of land with clear title, but much remains to be done; squatters make up nearly 20 percent of the population. The inefficient legal system weakens the security of property rights and the rule of law. Long-standing ties between elected representatives and organized criminals allow some gangs to operate with impunity, contributing to high levels of corruption and crime.

GOVERNMENT SIZE

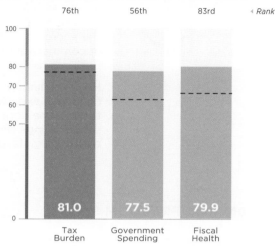

76th   56th   83rd   ‹ Rank

Tax Burden	Government Spending	Fiscal Health
81.0	77.5	79.9

Jamaica's top individual and corporate income tax rates are 25 percent. Other taxes include a property transfer tax and a general consumption tax. The overall tax burden equals 25.5 percent of total domestic income. Government spending has amounted to 27.4 percent of total output (GDP) over the past three years, and budget deficits have averaged 0.3 percent of GDP. Public debt is equivalent to 124.3 percent of GDP.

REGULATORY EFFICIENCY

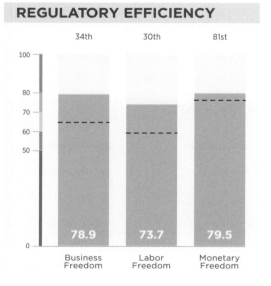

34th   30th   81st

Business Freedom	Labor Freedom	Monetary Freedom
78.9	73.7	79.5

The overall process for obtaining licenses and starting a business has been streamlined, and enforcement of the commercial code is relatively strong. The nonsalary cost of employing a worker is moderate, but dismissing an employee is costly. Regulations on work hours are flexible. In May 2016, the new government presented its first budget, which included significant cuts in subsidies for fuels and electricity.

OPEN MARKETS

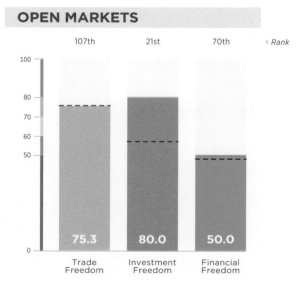

107th   21st   70th   ‹ Rank

Trade Freedom	Investment Freedom	Financial Freedom
75.3	80.0	50.0

Trade is important to Jamaica's economy; the value of exports and imports taken together equals 77 percent of GDP. The average applied tariff rate is 7.3 percent. Jamaica is relatively open to foreign investment, but state-owned enterprises distort the economy. Restoring stability in the financial sector has enabled Jamaica to regain access to the international financial market, but high financing costs continue to hamper private-sector growth.

MEXICO

Prudent fiscal and monetary policies have enhanced Mexico's macroeconomic performance. The pace of change has accelerated in recent years as previously unthinkable structural reforms have been adopted in parts of the economy that include the energy and telecommunications sectors. The regulation of commercial operations has become more streamlined, and business formation is relatively easy.

However, lingering constraints on achieving even more dynamic economic expansion are numerous, including the lack of competition in the domestic market, labor market rigidity, institutional shortcomings within the judicial system, and limited progress in curbing high levels of crime. Corruption is a continuing problem.

ECONOMIC FREEDOM SCORE

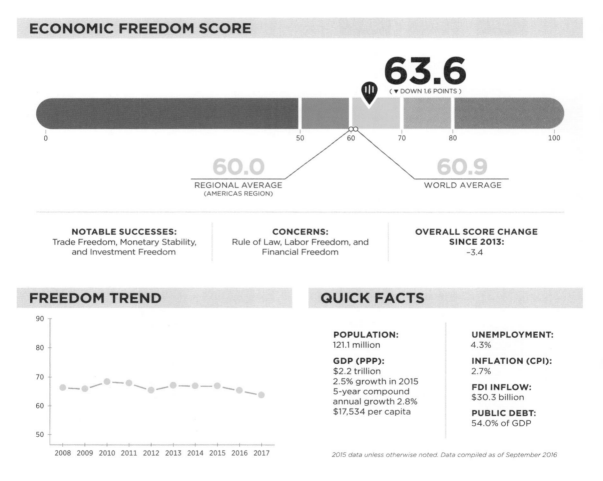

63.6
(▼ DOWN 1.6 POINTS)

0   50   60   70   80   100

60.0
REGIONAL AVERAGE
(AMERICAS REGION)

60.9
WORLD AVERAGE

NOTABLE SUCCESSES:
Trade Freedom, Monetary Stability, and Investment Freedom

CONCERNS:
Rule of Law, Labor Freedom, and Financial Freedom

OVERALL SCORE CHANGE SINCE 2013:
-3.4

FREEDOM TREND

90
80
70
60
50

2008 2009 2010 2011 2012 2013 2014 2015 2016 2017

QUICK FACTS

POPULATION:
121.1 million

GDP (PPP):
$2.2 trillion
2.5% growth in 2015
5-year compound
annual growth 2.8%
$17,534 per capita

UNEMPLOYMENT:
4.3%

INFLATION (CPI):
2.7%

FDI INFLOW:
$30.3 billion

PUBLIC DEBT:
54.0% of GDP

2015 data unless otherwise noted. Data compiled as of September 2016

BACKGROUND: Mexico has the largest Spanish-speaking population of any country in the world. Following the 1910 Mexican Revolution, the center-left Institutional Revolutionary Party (PRI) governed the country unchallenged for decades until its defeat by the center-right National Action Party in 2000. The PRI regained the presidency in 2012 with the election of current President Enrique Peña Nieto, whose single six-year term of office runs through 2018. After pushing through most of his ambitious structural reform agenda in 2013–2014, Peña Nieto has focused on implementation and on boosting sluggish growth. Rising drug-related crime has resulted in homicides, and widespread corruption has increased public dissatisfaction about the effectiveness of anticorruption efforts by weak government institutions.

12 ECONOMIC FREEDOMS | MEXICO

RULE OF LAW

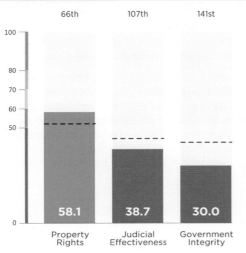

| | | | ◄ Rank |
| 66th | 107th | 141st | |

- Property Rights: **58.1**
- Judicial Effectiveness: **38.7**
- Government Integrity: **30.0**

In 2016, Freedom House reported that property rights in Mexico are protected by a modern legal framework but that the weakness of the judicial system, frequent solicitation of bribes by bureaucrats and officials, widespread impunity, and the high incidence of extortion harm security of property for many individuals and businesses. Corruption, deeply embedded culturally, is pervasive and fed by billions of narco-dollars. Drug-related crime has risen.

GOVERNMENT SIZE

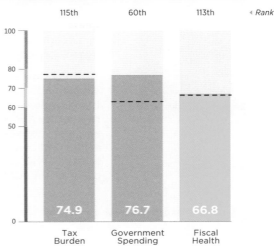

| 115th | 60th | 113th | ◄ Rank |

- Tax Burden: **74.9**
- Government Spending: **76.7**
- Fiscal Health: **66.8**

The top individual income tax rate is 35 percent, and the corporate tax rate is 30 percent. Other taxes include a value-added tax. The overall tax burden equals 19.7 percent of total domestic income. Government spending has amounted to 27.9 percent of total output (GDP) over the past three years, and budget deficits have averaged 4.1 percent of GDP. Public debt is equivalent to 54.0 percent of GDP.

REGULATORY EFFICIENCY

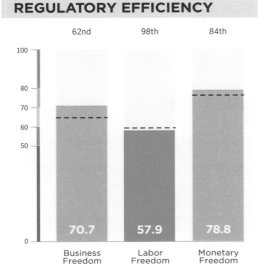

| 62nd | 98th | 84th | |

- Business Freedom: **70.7**
- Labor Freedom: **57.9**
- Monetary Freedom: **78.8**

There is no minimum capital requirement for launching a business, but completion of necessary licensing requirements remains costly. Rigid labor laws continue to give incentives for small companies to operate outside the formal sector, making the hiring and dismissing of employees costly. Mexico maintained no formal price controls as of mid-2016, although the government does set price recommendations for pharmaceuticals.

OPEN MARKETS

| 81st | 59th | 39th | ◄ Rank |

- Trade Freedom: **80.0**
- Investment Freedom: **70.0**
- Financial Freedom: **60.0**

Trade is important to Mexico's economy; the value of exports and imports taken together equals 73 percent of GDP. The average applied tariff rate is 5.0 percent. Mexico participates in numerous free-trade agreements. The state-owned oil company has begun to accept foreign investment. The financial sector is competitive and open. The banking system remains relatively well capitalized, and foreign participation has grown.

NICARAGUA

WORLD RANK: **98** | REGIONAL RANK: **20**

ECONOMIC FREEDOM STATUS:
MOSTLY UNFREE

Nicaragua's efforts to improve macroeconomic stability and enhance economic growth have been modest. Relatively well-controlled government spending has strengthened the management of public finance, but inefficiency and uncertainty in such other key policy areas as the regulatory and investment frameworks have impeded dynamic growth.

Overall, Nicaragua's structural reform effort has been sluggish, and privatization has stalled. Significant state interference in the economy through state-owned enterprises or inconsistent regulatory administration introduces uncertainty into the market. Institutional weaknesses persist in protection of property rights and combating corruption. The inefficient judicial system enforces contracts inconsistently and is subject to political interference.

ECONOMIC FREEDOM SCORE

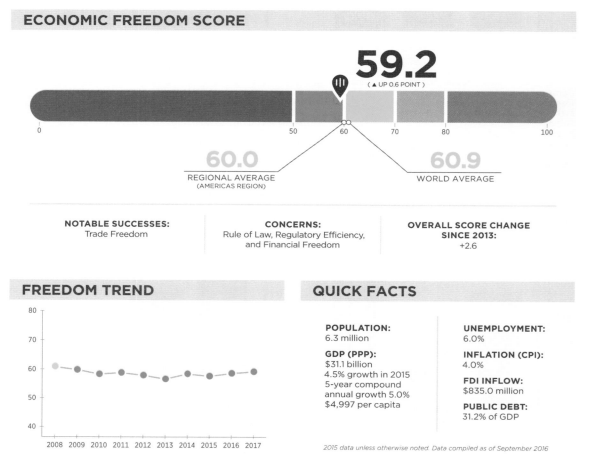

59.2
(▲ UP 0.6 POINT)

0   50   60   70   80   100

60.0
REGIONAL AVERAGE
(AMERICAS REGION)

60.9
WORLD AVERAGE

NOTABLE SUCCESSES:
Trade Freedom

CONCERNS:
Rule of Law, Regulatory Efficiency,
and Financial Freedom

**OVERALL SCORE CHANGE
SINCE 2013:**
+2.6

FREEDOM TREND

80
70
60
50
40

2008 2009 2010 2011 2012 2013 2014 2015 2016 2017

QUICK FACTS

POPULATION:
6.3 million

GDP (PPP):
$31.1 billion
4.5% growth in 2015
5-year compound
annual growth 5.0%
$4,997 per capita

UNEMPLOYMENT:
6.0%

INFLATION (CPI):
4.0%

FDI INFLOW:
$835.0 million

PUBLIC DEBT:
31.2% of GDP

2015 data unless otherwise noted. Data compiled as of September 2016

BACKGROUND: In the late 1970s, the Sandinista National Liberation Front, led by Daniel Ortega, overthrew the authoritarian Somoza political dynasty. Ortega became de facto ruler of a provisional FSLN-led government before free and fair elections in 1990, 1996, and 2001. Ortega lost all of these elections but was finally elected to a five-year presidential term with 38 percent of the vote in 2006. Since then, he has been reelected twice and has engineered constitutional changes that may permit him to retain power indefinitely. Despite his revolutionary rhetoric, Ortega has governed fairly pragmatically, accepting billions in subsidized oil shipments from Venezuela while embracing the U.S.–Central America–Dominican Republic Free Trade Agreement.

12 ECONOMIC FREEDOMS | NICARAGUA

RULE OF LAW

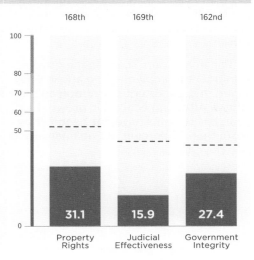

168th	169th	162nd
31.1	**15.9**	**27.4**
Property Rights	Judicial Effectiveness	Government Integrity

Private property rights are not protected effectively, especially for foreign investors, and contracts are not always secure. The judicial system suffers from corruption and long delays, and the politicized Supreme Court is controlled by Sandinista judges. Bribery of public officials remains a major challenge. The authoritarian and open-ended rule by President Daniel Ortega and his family is the greatest threat to the rule of law.

GOVERNMENT SIZE

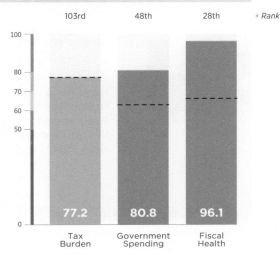

103rd	48th	28th	◂ Rank
77.2	**80.8**	**96.1**	
Tax Burden	Government Spending	Fiscal Health	

The top individual income and corporate tax rates are 30 percent. Other taxes include a value-added tax and a capital gains tax. The overall tax burden equals 21.9 percent of total domestic income. Government spending has amounted to 25.3 percent of total output (GDP) over the past three years, and budget deficits have averaged 1.1 percent of GDP. Public debt is equivalent to 31.2 percent of GDP.

REGULATORY EFFICIENCY

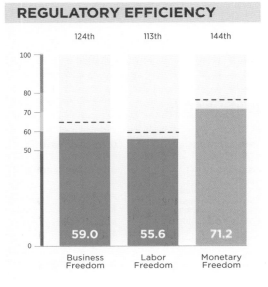

124th	113th	144th
59.0	**55.6**	**71.2**
Business Freedom	Labor Freedom	Monetary Freedom

The regulatory system lacks both transparency and clarity. The lack of employment opportunities has caused chronic underemployment. The state regulates and heavily subsidizes the energy and water sectors. The Ortega government was able to consolidate power partly because of the inflows of hundreds of millions of dollars of Venezuelan PetroCaribe oil subsidies.

OPEN MARKETS

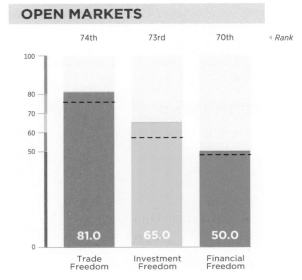

74th	73rd	70th	◂ Rank
81.0	**65.0**	**50.0**	
Trade Freedom	Investment Freedom	Financial Freedom	

Trade is important to Nicaragua's economy; the value of exports and imports taken together equals 93 percent of GDP. The average applied tariff rate is 2.0 percent. The judicial and regulatory systems impede foreign investment, and state-owned enterprises distort the economy. Inadequate levels of financing reflect the low level of financial intermediation in the economy and continue to undermine private-sector growth.

PANAMA

Panama has been working to expand trade by exploring entry into the Pacific Alliance and negotiating a trade agreement with South Korea. Reforms such as simplification of business start-ups and reduction of the corporate tax rate have contributed to economic growth.

Following the April 2016 Panama Papers scandal, the government reaffirmed its commitment to implementing anti–money laundering reforms. Despite this, persistent corruption continues to undermine the rule of law. Although economic growth has been strong in recent years, its benefits have not been felt by the entire population. More than 25 percent of Panamanians in rural areas live in extreme poverty.

ECONOMIC FREEDOM SCORE

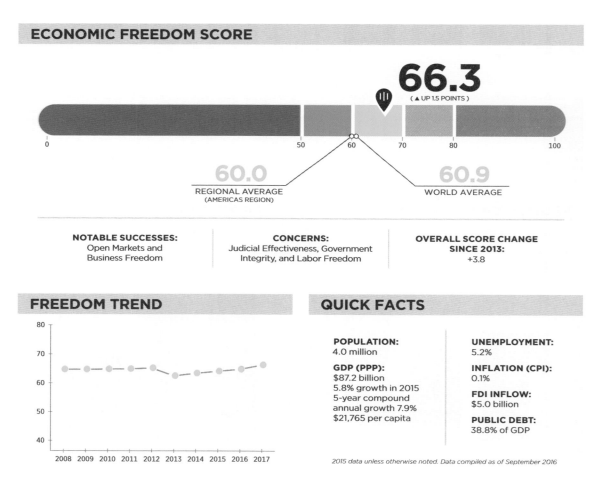

66.3
(▲ UP 1.5 POINTS)

0   50   60   70   80   100

60.0
REGIONAL AVERAGE
(AMERICAS REGION)

60.9
WORLD AVERAGE

NOTABLE SUCCESSES:
Open Markets and
Business Freedom

CONCERNS:
Judicial Effectiveness, Government
Integrity, and Labor Freedom

**OVERALL SCORE CHANGE
SINCE 2013:**
+3.8

FREEDOM TREND

80
70
60
50
40

2008 2009 2010 2011 2012 2013 2014 2015 2016 2017

QUICK FACTS

POPULATION:
4.0 million

GDP (PPP):
$87.2 billion
5.8% growth in 2015
5-year compound
annual growth 7.9%
$21,765 per capita

UNEMPLOYMENT:
5.2%

INFLATION (CPI):
0.1%

FDI INFLOW:
$5.0 billion

PUBLIC DEBT:
38.8% of GDP

2015 data unless otherwise noted. Data compiled as of September 2016

BACKGROUND: Panama's isthmian canal in Central America connecting the Caribbean and the Pacific Ocean has been a vital conduit for global commerce since it opened in 1914. In 2016, an ambitious expansion project was completed that more than doubles the canal's capacity. President Juan Carlos Varela began his single five-year term in 2014. His popularity has waned, however, in the wake of negative fallout from publication of the Panama Papers, sanctions by the U.S. government in May 2016 related to an extensive drug money-laundering network based in Panama, and a deadly outbreak of swine flu in June 2016. Panama's U.S. dollar-based economy rests primarily on a well-developed services sector.

12 ECONOMIC FREEDOMS | PANAMA

RULE OF LAW

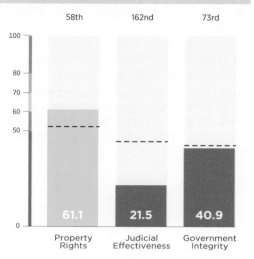

	58th	162nd	73rd
	Property Rights	Judicial Effectiveness	Government Integrity
	61.1	21.5	40.9

Panama's weak capacity to resolve contractual and property disputes is illustrated by its low rating for judicial independence (119th out of 140 countries) in the World Economic Forum's 2015–2016 *Global Competitiveness Report*. Corruption is widespread, especially in the security services, customs, and justice system. The Panama Papers scandal tarnished the current president politically, and his predecessor is being investigated for corruption.

GOVERNMENT SIZE

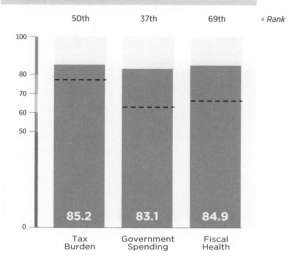

	50th	37th	69th	◄ *Rank*
	Tax Burden	Government Spending	Fiscal Health	
	85.2	83.1	84.9	

The top personal income and corporate tax rates are 25 percent. Other taxes include a value-added tax and a capital gains tax. The overall tax burden equals 15.2 percent of total domestic income. Government spending has amounted to 23.8 percent of total output (GDP) over the past three years, and budget deficits have averaged 2.7 percent of GDP. Public debt is equivalent to 38.8 percent of GDP.

REGULATORY EFFICIENCY

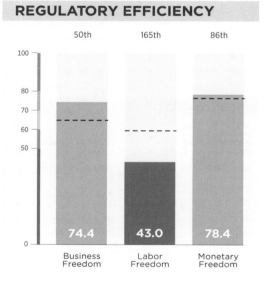

	50th	165th	86th
	Business Freedom	Labor Freedom	Monetary Freedom
	74.4	43.0	78.4

The overall freedom to form and operate a business is relatively well protected within an efficient regulatory environment. The labor market lacks flexibility, and the nonsalary cost of hiring a worker is relatively high. About 75 percent of subsidies to the energy sector are untargeted, and electricity subsidies have been increasing. The IMF urged Panama to end price controls on food and fuel; instead, the government extended them twice.

OPEN MARKETS

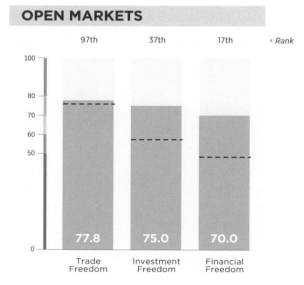

	97th	37th	17th	◄ *Rank*
	Trade Freedom	Investment Freedom	Financial Freedom	
	77.8	75.0	70.0	

Trade is extremely important to Panama's economy; the value of exports and imports taken together equals 115 percent of GDP. The average applied tariff rate is 6.1 percent. In general, the government does not screen or discriminate against foreign investment. The financial sector, vibrant and generally well regulated, provides a wide range of services. Banking continues to expand, albeit slowly.

PARAGUAY

WORLD RANK: **80** | REGIONAL RANK: **17**

ECONOMIC FREEDOM STATUS:
MODERATELY FREE

The agriculture, retail, and construction sectors continue to be driving forces for economic growth in Paraguay. One of the region's lowest tax burdens enhances competitiveness. However, the informal economy remains large, and private-sector growth is hindered by institutional weaknesses that undermine the rule of law. Foreign investment is not subject to screening, and foreign entities are permitted to own property.

Despite some improvement, a persistent lack of transparency at all levels of government hurts investor confidence and slows the emergence of a broader-based private sector. State-owned enterprises are present in several sectors of the economy, and most operate as monopolies.

ECONOMIC FREEDOM SCORE

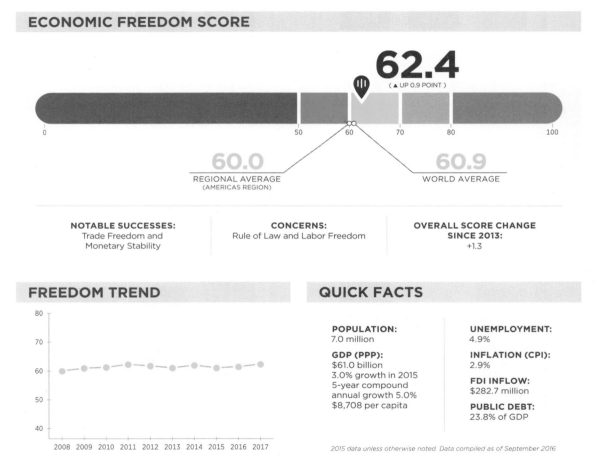

62.4
(▲ UP 0.9 POINT)

0   50   60   70   80   100

60.0
REGIONAL AVERAGE
(AMERICAS REGION)

60.9
WORLD AVERAGE

NOTABLE SUCCESSES:
Trade Freedom and
Monetary Stability

CONCERNS:
Rule of Law and Labor Freedom

**OVERALL SCORE CHANGE
SINCE 2013:**
+1.3

FREEDOM TREND

80

70

60

50

40

2008 2009 2010 2011 2012 2013 2014 2015 2016 2017

QUICK FACTS

POPULATION:
7.0 million

GDP (PPP):
$61.0 billion
3.0% growth in 2015
5-year compound
annual growth 5.0%
$8,708 per capita

UNEMPLOYMENT:
4.9%

INFLATION (CPI):
2.9%

FDI INFLOW:
$282.7 million

PUBLIC DEBT:
23.8% of GDP

2015 data unless otherwise noted. Data compiled as of September 2016

BACKGROUND: Paraguay is a major producer of hydroelectricity, and the Itaipú dam on the Paraná River is the world's largest generator of renewable energy. President Horacio Cartes of the historically dominant Colorado Party was elected to a five-year term in 2013. He has made progress in public-sector reform and has increased investment in infrastructure, but conservative factions within his party are expected to oppose his plans for further structural reforms and are likely to challenge any attempt to reelect him in 2018. Economic growth depends heavily on exports of electricity and soybeans. Attempts to reduce smuggling and counter suspected terrorist groups in the triborder area with Brazil and Argentina have not been successful.

12 ECONOMIC FREEDOMS | PARAGUAY

RULE OF LAW

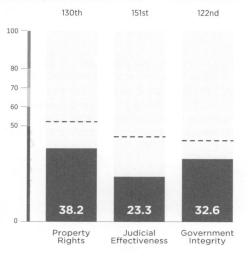

	130th	151st	122nd
	Property Rights	Judicial Effectiveness	Government Integrity
	38.2	23.3	32.6

A lack of consistent property surveys and registries often makes it difficult to acquire title documents for land. Cases languish for years in the court system without resolution, and offenses often go unpunished due to political influence in the judiciary. Corruption is widespread. Officials at all levels of government, the judiciary, and the police frequently engage in corrupt practices with impunity, particularly in the Ciudad del Este area.

GOVERNMENT SIZE

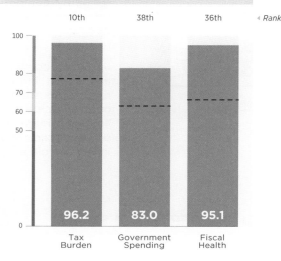

	10th	38th	36th	◄ Rank
	Tax Burden	Government Spending	Fiscal Health	
	96.2	83.0	95.1	

The top personal income and corporate tax rates are 10 percent. Other taxes include a value-added tax and a property tax. The overall tax burden equals 13.5 percent of total domestic income. Government spending has amounted to 23.8 percent of total output (GDP) over the past three years, and budget deficits have averaged 1.5 percent of GDP. Public debt is equivalent to 23.8 percent of GDP.

REGULATORY EFFICIENCY

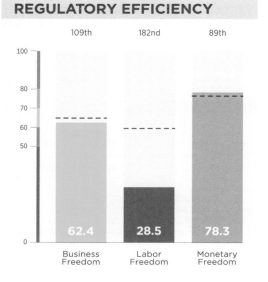

	109th	182nd	89th
	Business Freedom	Labor Freedom	Monetary Freedom
	62.4	28.5	78.3

The overall regulatory framework remains less than fully conducive to more dynamic entrepreneurial investment and production. Labor regulations are outmoded and restrictive. The government subsidizes major state-owned entities performing a wide range of activities, from public utilities to commercial activities, that include fuel importation and distribution, telecommunications, and the production of alcoholic beverages and cement.

OPEN MARKETS

	102nd	37th	39th	◄ Rank
	Trade Freedom	Investment Freedom	Financial Freedom	
	76.6	75.0	60.0	

Trade is important to Paraguay's economy; the value of exports and imports taken together equals 82 percent of GDP. The average applied tariff rate is 4.2 percent. In general, foreign and domestic investors are treated equally under the law. State-owned enterprises distort the economy. Financial intermediation has gradually been improving as credit to the private sector has grown and the number of nonperforming loans has declined.

PERU

WORLD RANK:
43

REGIONAL RANK:
7

ECONOMIC FREEDOM STATUS:
MODERATELY FREE

S tructural reforms in recent years have sustained Peru's economic competitiveness. During the 2015–2016 fiscal year, the government reduced the corporate tax rate from 30 percent to 28 percent as part of a planned gradual decrease over the next few years.

Peru's economy is relatively open and welcomes most foreign investment, but regulatory delays and a lack of predictability in regulations are problematic for foreign investors. Government corruption is a serious problem, and drug trafficking has grown, limiting foreign investor confidence in the economy. State-owned enterprises remain very active in the economy, especially in the petroleum sector.

ECONOMIC FREEDOM SCORE

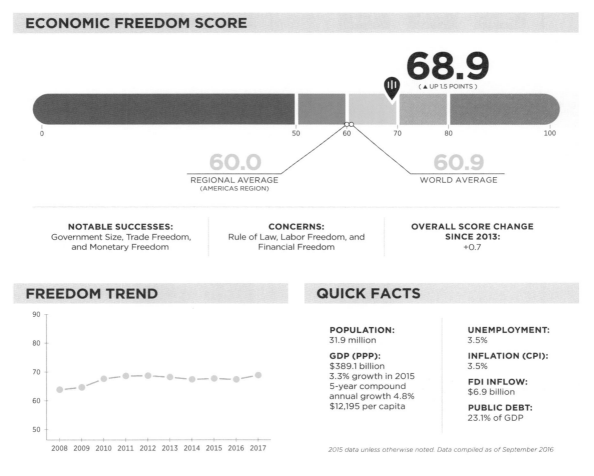

68.9
(▲ UP 1.5 POINTS)

0   50   60   70   80   100

60.0
REGIONAL AVERAGE
(AMERICAS REGION)

60.9
WORLD AVERAGE

NOTABLE SUCCESSES:
Government Size, Trade Freedom, and Monetary Freedom

CONCERNS:
Rule of Law, Labor Freedom, and Financial Freedom

OVERALL SCORE CHANGE SINCE 2013:
+0.7

FREEDOM TREND

90

80

70

60

50

2008 2009 2010 2011 2012 2013 2014 2015 2016 2017

QUICK FACTS

POPULATION:
31.9 million

GDP (PPP):
$389.1 billion
3.3% growth in 2015
5-year compound
annual growth 4.8%
$12,195 per capita

UNEMPLOYMENT:
3.5%

INFLATION (CPI):
3.5%

FDI INFLOW:
$6.9 billion

PUBLIC DEBT:
23.1% of GDP

2015 data unless otherwise noted. Data compiled as of September 2016

BACKGROUND: Pedro Pablo Kuczynski, a center-right 78-year-old former World Bank economist and investment banker better known by his initials, "PPK," narrowly defeated a populist campaign by former President Alberto Fujimori's daughter in the presidential election of June 2016. Outgoing President Ollanta Humala of the leftist Peruvian Nationalist Party governed moderately during his five-year term, but he did not deepen liberalization and was undermined by allegations of corruption. Nevertheless, poverty rates have been reduced, and Peru has benefited from significant foreign investment in mining and manufacturing. Peru has entered into numerous trade agreements with the U.S. and other countries and is a founding member of the Pacific Alliance.

12 ECONOMIC FREEDOMS | PERU

RULE OF LAW

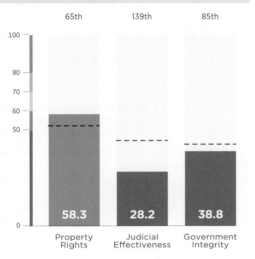

65th	139th	85th
Property Rights	Judicial Effectiveness	Government Integrity
58.3	28.2	38.8

Although Peruvian law recognizes secured interests in both movable and immovable property, the judicial system (with the exception of the commercial courts) has a large backlog and is extremely slow to hear cases and issue decisions. Corruption is a serious problem in the government, the security forces, the judiciary, customs agencies, and the ports, as well as in local governments, where the influence of drug traffickers has grown.

GOVERNMENT SIZE

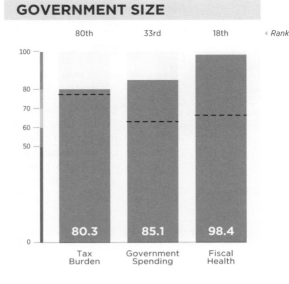

80th	33rd	18th	◄ Rank
Tax Burden	Government Spending	Fiscal Health	
80.3	85.1	98.4	

The top personal income tax rate is 30 percent, and the top corporate tax rate is 28 percent. Other taxes include a value-added tax and a financial transactions tax. The overall tax burden equals 16.8 percent of total domestic income. Government spending has amounted to 22.3 percent of total output (GDP) over the past three years, and budget deficits have averaged 0.6 percent of GDP. Public debt is equivalent to 23.1 percent of GDP.

REGULATORY EFFICIENCY

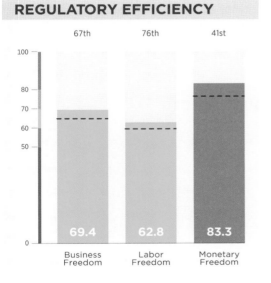

67th	76th	41st
Business Freedom	Labor Freedom	Monetary Freedom
69.4	62.8	83.3

Recent reforms have dismantled some barriers to launching private enterprises, but the formation and operation of private businesses can still be costly. Labor regulations continue to evolve, with more flexibility gradually being introduced. Most price controls had been eliminated as of mid-2016 except for the regulation of rates set by private companies in telecommunications, energy and mining, public transport, and sanitation services.

OPEN MARKETS

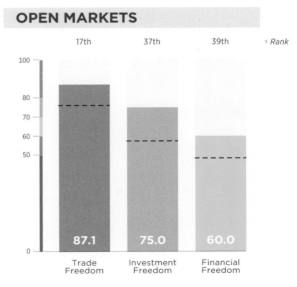

17th	37th	39th	◄ Rank
Trade Freedom	Investment Freedom	Financial Freedom	
87.1	75.0	60.0	

Trade is moderately important to Peru's economy; the value of exports and imports taken together equals 45 percent of GDP. The average applied tariff rate is 1.4 percent. Investment in most sectors of the economy is not screened, but state-owned enterprises distort the economy. The banking sector has been transformed through consolidation. Foreign ownership is substantial, and credit to the private sector has increased steadily.

SAINT LUCIA

WORLD RANK: **62** **REGIONAL RANK:** **11**

ECONOMIC FREEDOM STATUS:
MODERATELY FREE

S aint Lucia's economy has benefited from a well-developed legal and commercial infrastructure and a tradition of entrepreneurial dynamism in the private sector. The business environment is generally efficient and transparent, and the regulatory framework has become more streamlined. An educated workforce and improved roads, communications, and port facilities have attracted foreign investment in tourism and transshipment.

Open-market policies, however, are not firmly institutionalized. Trade freedom is limited by tariff and nontariff barriers, and the investment regime lacks efficiency. Greater access to financing opportunities remains critical to private-sector development. In recent years, expansionary government spending has driven up public debt to around 65 percent of GDP.

ECONOMIC FREEDOM SCORE

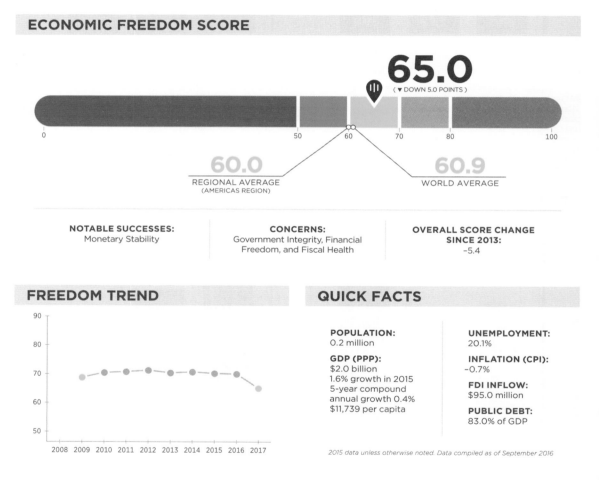

65.0
(▼ DOWN 5.0 POINTS)

| 0 | 50 | 60 | 70 | 80 | 100 |

60.0
REGIONAL AVERAGE
(AMERICAS REGION)

60.9
WORLD AVERAGE

NOTABLE SUCCESSES:
Monetary Stability

CONCERNS:
Government Integrity, Financial Freedom, and Fiscal Health

OVERALL SCORE CHANGE SINCE 2013:
−5.4

FREEDOM TREND

QUICK FACTS

POPULATION:
0.2 million

GDP (PPP):
$2.0 billion
1.6% growth in 2015
5-year compound
annual growth 0.4%
$11,739 per capita

UNEMPLOYMENT:
20.1%

INFLATION (CPI):
−0.7%

FDI INFLOW:
$95.0 million

PUBLIC DEBT:
83.0% of GDP

2015 data unless otherwise noted. Data compiled as of September 2016

BACKGROUND: Saint Lucia, an island nation in the Lesser Antilles well known for its two distinctive "Piton" mountains, is a two-party democracy with a bicameral parliament. Prime Minister Allen Chastanet of the United Workers Party, a former tourism minister, took office in June 2016. Saint Lucia is a member of the Caribbean Community and Common Market and hosts the headquarters of the Organization of Eastern Caribbean States. The economy depends primarily on tourism and banana production, along with some light manufacturing. Faced with the uncertain future of the banana industry, the government has encouraged farmers to diversify into such crops as cocoa, mangos, and avocados.

12 ECONOMIC FREEDOMS | SAINT LUCIA

RULE OF LAW

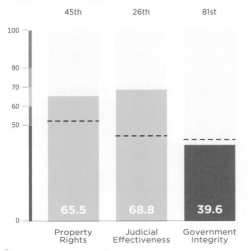

45th	26th	81st
Property Rights **65.5**	Judicial Effectiveness **68.8**	Government Integrity **39.6**

Saint Lucia has a wide legislative framework to protect property rights, although enforcement of intellectual property rights is generally weak. The independent judicial system's highest court is the Eastern Caribbean Supreme Court; lower courts are understaffed and slow. Saint Lucia has one of the lowest levels of corruption in the West Indies, but enforcement of anticorruption statutes is not always effective.

GOVERNMENT SIZE

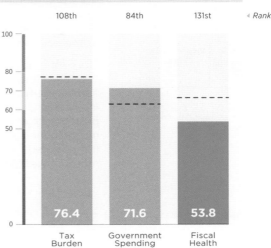

108th	84th	131st	◄ Rank
Tax Burden **76.4**	Government Spending **71.6**	Fiscal Health **53.8**	

The top personal income and corporate tax rates are 30 percent. Other taxes include a consumption tax and a property transfer tax. The overall tax burden equals 23.7 percent of total domestic income. Government spending has amounted to 30.7 percent of total output (GDP) over the past three years, and budget deficits have averaged 4.5 percent of GDP. Public debt is equivalent to 83.0 percent of GDP.

REGULATORY EFFICIENCY

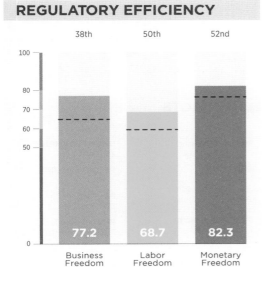

38th	50th	52nd
Business Freedom **77.2**	Labor Freedom **68.7**	Monetary Freedom **82.3**

The regulatory environment for businesses facilitates entrepreneurial activity that fosters development of the private sector. Labor regulations are flexible, but an efficient labor market has not been fully developed. Application of existing labor codes is uneven, although the nonsalary cost of employing a worker is low. In 2016, the IMF recommended that the government eliminate nontargeted liquefied petroleum gas and food subsidies.

OPEN MARKETS

123rd	73rd	106th	◄ Rank
Trade Freedom **71.6**	Investment Freedom **65.0**	Financial Freedom **40.0**	

Trade is important to Saint Lucia's economy; the value of exports and imports taken together equals 95 percent of GDP. The average applied tariff rate is 9.2 percent. Some agricultural imports face additional barriers. Foreign investment is screened by the government. There is a small offshore financial sector, and the banking sector is dominated by commercial banking. Saint Lucia is a member of the Eastern Caribbean Currency Union.

SAINT VINCENT AND THE GRENADINES

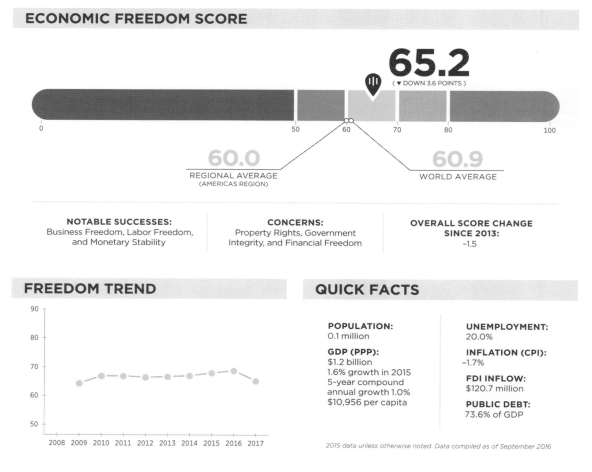

Saint Vincent and the Grenadines performs relatively well in some fundamental aspects of economic freedom: flexible regulations, an efficient legal system that secures private property, and macroeconomic stability. Tourism is the primary driver of the economy and the main draw for foreign investment.

More vibrant entrepreneurial activity remains stifled by limited access to financing in an underdeveloped financial environment and by inefficient open-market policies that impede trade and international investment. Fiscal policy is constrained by rising public debt and an uncompetitive tax regime. The challenging global economic environment makes external borrowing for long-term projects like the construction of a new airport more challenging.

WORLD RANK:
59

REGIONAL RANK:
9

ECONOMIC FREEDOM STATUS:
MODERATELY FREE

ECONOMIC FREEDOM SCORE

65.2
(▼ DOWN 3.6 POINTS)

0   50   60   70   80   100

60.0
REGIONAL AVERAGE
(AMERICAS REGION)

60.9
WORLD AVERAGE

NOTABLE SUCCESSES:
Business Freedom, Labor Freedom, and Monetary Stability

CONCERNS:
Property Rights, Government Integrity, and Financial Freedom

OVERALL SCORE CHANGE SINCE 2013:
–1.5

FREEDOM TREND

90

80

70

60

50

2008 2009 2010 2011 2012 2013 2014 2015 2016 2017

QUICK FACTS

POPULATION:
0.1 million

GDP (PPP):
$1.2 billion
1.6% growth in 2015
5-year compound
annual growth 1.0%
$10,956 per capita

UNEMPLOYMENT:
20.0%

INFLATION (CPI):
–1.7%

FDI INFLOW:
$120.7 million

PUBLIC DEBT:
73.6% of GDP

2015 data unless otherwise noted. Data compiled as of September 2016

BACKGROUND: Saint Vincent and the Grenadines became an independent parliamentary democracy in 1979. Prime Minister Ralph Gonsalves, in office since 2001, was reelected to a fourth term when his center-left Unity Labour Party won the most recent election in December 2015. The country is a member of the Caribbean Community, the Venezuela-led Bolivarian Alliance for the Peoples of Our America, and the Organization of Eastern Caribbean States. Exports benefit from the Caribbean Basin Initiative, which provides duty-free access to the U.S. market. Agriculture and tourism employ a significant portion of the workforce, but formal-sector unemployment is high. The economy is vulnerable to global price fluctuations and natural disasters.

12 ECONOMIC FREEDOMS | SAINT VINCENT AND THE GRENADINES

KEY: − − WORLD AVERAGE

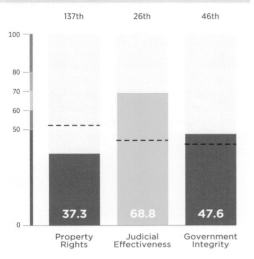

RULE OF LAW

Property Rights	Judicial Effectiveness	Government Integrity
137th	26th	46th
37.3	68.8	47.6

Saint Vincent and the Grenadines' relatively independent and efficient judicial system, based on English common law, protects property rights and enforces contracts. Enforcement of intellectual property rights statutes, however, has been viewed as generally weak. In comparison with some of its neighbors, the rule of law remains strong and corruption is not pervasive, although drug-related money laundering has been a problem.

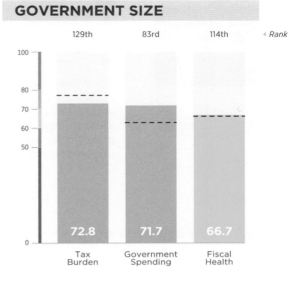

GOVERNMENT SIZE

Tax Burden	Government Spending	Fiscal Health	◂ Rank
129th	83rd	114th	
72.8	71.7	66.7	

The top personal income and corporate tax rates are 32.5 percent. Other taxes include a property tax and a value-added tax. The overall tax burden equals 23.9 percent of total domestic income. Government spending has amounted to 30.7 percent of total output (GDP) over the past three years, and budget deficits have averaged 3.7 percent of GDP. Public debt is equivalent to 73.6 percent of GDP.

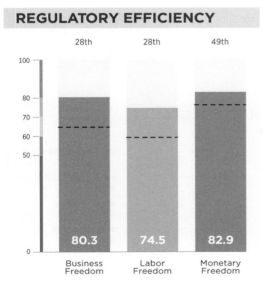

REGULATORY EFFICIENCY

Business Freedom	Labor Freedom	Monetary Freedom
28th	28th	49th
80.3	74.5	82.9

Operation of a private enterprise is not burdened by excessive government interference, and enforcement of commercial regulations is relatively effective. Much of the labor force is employed in the agricultural and tourism sectors. The nonsalary cost of employing a worker is moderate. In 2015, the IMF estimated that limiting subsidies and transfers to state-owned enterprises during the 2015–2019 period would save more than 3 percent of GDP.

OPEN MARKETS

Trade Freedom	Investment Freedom	Financial Freedom	◂ Rank
151st	37th	106th	
65.2	75.0	40.0	

Trade is important to Saint Vincent and the Grenadines' economy; the value of exports and imports taken together equals 78 percent of GDP. The average applied tariff rate is 12.4 percent. In general, foreign and domestic investors are treated equally under the law, but foreign investment is screened by the government. Businesses lack adequate access to a wide variety of financing instruments, and the capital market is underdeveloped.

SURINAME

The entrepreneurial environment in Suriname remains constrained by a burdensome and inefficient regulatory framework. Despite recent progress in achieving some macroeconomic stability and market reforms, there has been little overall development of a more dynamic private sector.

Privatization has been slow and uneven. Direct state involvement in the economy through ownership or control remains considerable. Poor policy choices and the uncertainty generated by weak management of fiscal and monetary policy have increased the risks for entrepreneurs. Pervasive corruption continues to undermine the judicial system and the rule of law.

ECONOMIC FREEDOM SCORE

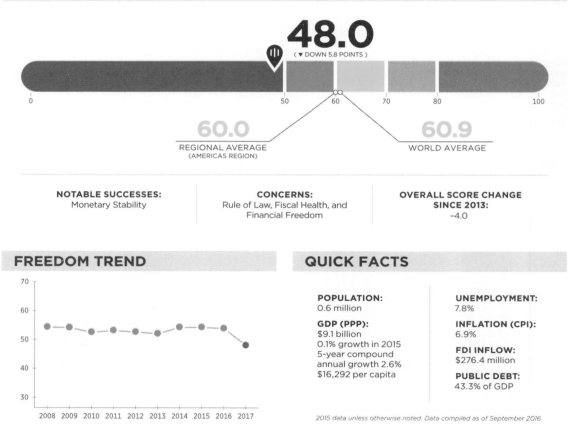

48.0
(▼ DOWN 5.8 POINTS)

0   50   60   70   80   100

60.0
REGIONAL AVERAGE
(AMERICAS REGION)

60.9
WORLD AVERAGE

NOTABLE SUCCESSES:
Monetary Stability

CONCERNS:
Rule of Law, Fiscal Health, and Financial Freedom

OVERALL SCORE CHANGE SINCE 2013:
–4.0

FREEDOM TREND

70
60
50
40
30

2008 2009 2010 2011 2012 2013 2014 2015 2016 2017

QUICK FACTS

POPULATION:
0.6 million

GDP (PPP):
$9.1 billion
0.1% growth in 2015
5-year compound
annual growth 2.6%
$16,292 per capita

UNEMPLOYMENT:
7.8%

INFLATION (CPI):
6.9%

FDI INFLOW:
$276.4 million

PUBLIC DEBT:
43.3% of GDP

2015 data unless otherwise noted. Data compiled as of September 2016

BACKGROUND: Former dictator and convicted narco-trafficker Desire "Dési" Bouterse of the National Democratic Party began a second consecutive five-year term as president in 2015. Bouterse first took power in 1980 when he led the "Sergeants Coup" that overthrew the civilian government and installed a military regime that ruled until 1987. Also in 2015, Bouterse's son, Dino, began serving a 16-year prison sentence after pleading guilty in New York to charges of drug trafficking and providing material support to a terrorist organization. Legislative amnesty for the president's role in the1982 murders of 15 politically prominent young men who had criticized the military dictatorship was invalidated in 2016, increasing the possibility of political turmoil. The economy is dominated by the exploitation of natural resources.

12 ECONOMIC FREEDOMS | SURINAME

RULE OF LAW

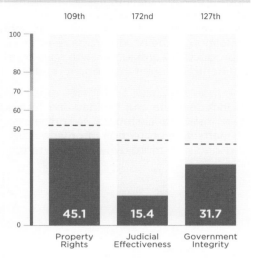

109th   172nd   127th

Property Rights	Judicial Effectiveness	Government Integrity
45.1	15.4	31.7

Property rights are not well protected. Organized criminal gangs have fueled increases in crime, narco-trafficking, and human trafficking, hampering governance and undermining the judicial system. Corruption is most pervasive in government procurement, issuance of licenses, land policy, and taxation. The trial of Suriname's president for the 1982 deaths of political opponents was cleared to resume in 2016 after a military court invalidated an amnesty law.

GOVERNMENT SIZE

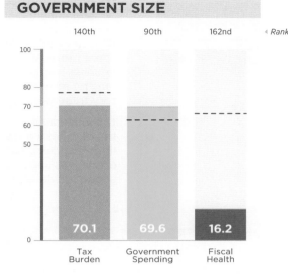

140th   90th   162nd   ◀ Rank

Tax Burden	Government Spending	Fiscal Health
70.1	69.6	16.2

The top personal income tax rate is 38 percent, and the top corporate tax rate is 36 percent. Other taxes include a property tax and an excise tax. The overall tax burden equals 15.7 percent of total domestic income. Government spending has amounted to 31.8 percent of total output (GDP) over the past three years, and budget deficits have averaged 8.1 percent of GDP. Public debt is equivalent to 43.3 percent of GDP.

REGULATORY EFFICIENCY

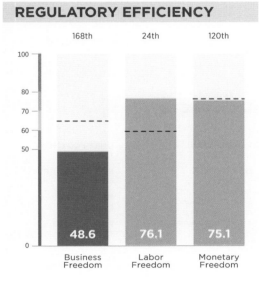

168th   24th   120th

Business Freedom	Labor Freedom	Monetary Freedom
48.6	76.1	75.1

Licensing requirements are quite burdensome, and procedures for launching a business are time-consuming. Enforcement of the labor code is not effective in practice, and the formal labor market is not fully developed. Under an IMF program, the government has undertaken measures to reduce electricity tariff subsidies. The program calls for the complete elimination of these subsidies along with an increase in fuel taxes.

OPEN MARKETS

142nd   154th   133rd   ◀ Rank

Trade Freedom	Investment Freedom	Financial Freedom
68.4	30.0	30.0

Trade is important to Suriname's economy; the value of exports and imports taken together equals 91 percent of GDP. The average applied tariff rate is 10.8 percent. Foreign investment is screened by the government, and land and natural resources are owned by the state. The financial system remains underdeveloped and vulnerable to government influence. Financial regulations are antiquated, and supervision is poor.

TRINIDAD AND TOBAGO

Trinidad and Tobago's record in advancing economic freedom and enhancing its entrepreneurial climate has been mixed in recent years. Overdependence on oil and gas continues to hold back private-sector development, although there has been some progress in diversification of the economic base, as in the financial sector. Non-oil productivity and job growth have been hurt by an inefficient and nontransparent investment regulatory framework.

The judiciary is relatively independent, and Trinidad and Tobago benefits from a tradition of institutional stability. Nevertheless, lingering corruption and ineffective protection of private property rights undermine prospects for more dynamic long-term economic development.

ECONOMIC FREEDOM SCORE

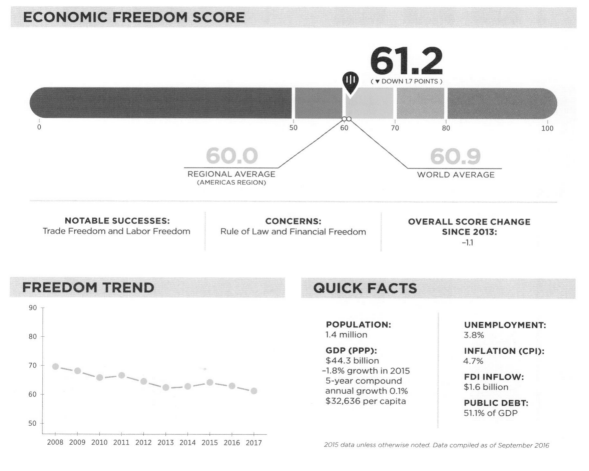

61.2
(▼ DOWN 1.7 POINTS)

0   50   60   70   80   100

60.0
REGIONAL AVERAGE
(AMERICAS REGION)

60.9
WORLD AVERAGE

NOTABLE SUCCESSES:
Trade Freedom and Labor Freedom

CONCERNS:
Rule of Law and Financial Freedom

OVERALL SCORE CHANGE SINCE 2013:
–1.1

FREEDOM TREND

90

80

70

60

50

2008 2009 2010 2011 2012 2013 2014 2015 2016 2017

QUICK FACTS

POPULATION:
1.4 million

GDP (PPP):
$44.3 billion
–1.8% growth in 2015
5-year compound
annual growth 0.1%
$32,636 per capita

UNEMPLOYMENT:
3.8%

INFLATION (CPI):
4.7%

FDI INFLOW:
$1.6 billion

PUBLIC DEBT:
51.1% of GDP

2015 data unless otherwise noted. Data compiled as of September 2016

BACKGROUND: Trinidad and Tobago is one of the Caribbean's wealthiest nations. Hydrocarbons account for more than 40 percent of GDP and 80 percent of exports. Prime Minister Dr. Keith Rowley of the center-left People's National Movement, a geologist by training, took office in September 2015 and was immediately confronted by economic policy challenges stemming from low energy prices and declining natural gas reserves that caused the economy to begin contracting in 2015. Oil production has declined over the past decade as the country has focused on natural gas. In 2016, Trinidad and Tobago's government bond rating was downgraded because of concern that the government lacks an effective fiscal consolidation strategy.

12 ECONOMIC FREEDOMS | TRINIDAD AND TOBAGO

RULE OF LAW

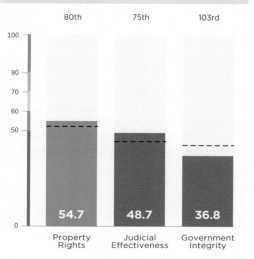

80th	75th	103rd

Property Rights	Judicial Effectiveness	Government Integrity
54.7	48.7	36.8

Property rights are well protected. The judiciary is independent but somewhat subject to political pressures. Rising crime rates and very high levels of violent crime, much of it drug-related, have led to delays in the judicial system. The quality of the bureaucracy remains relatively poor, and narcotics-related graft is endemic in the police force. A long history of corruption and mismanagement under successive governments stretches back to colonial times.

GOVERNMENT SIZE

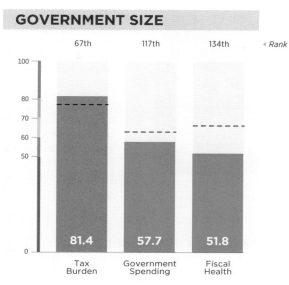

67th	117th	134th	◄ Rank

Tax Burden	Government Spending	Fiscal Health
81.4	57.7	51.8

Both the top personal income tax rate and the standard corporate tax rate are 25 percent. Other taxes include a value-added tax and a property tax. The overall tax burden equals 24.7 percent of total domestic income. Government spending has amounted to 37.6 percent of total output (GDP) over the past three years, and budget deficits have averaged 5.2 percent of GDP. Public debt is equivalent to 51.1 percent of GDP.

REGULATORY EFFICIENCY

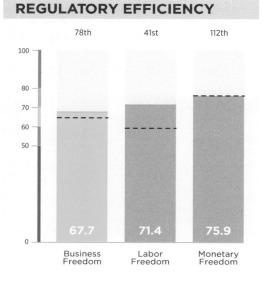

78th	41st	112th

Business Freedom	Labor Freedom	Monetary Freedom
67.7	71.4	75.9

The regulatory system lacks transparency and clarity, and regulations are enforced inconsistently, injecting uncertainty into entrepreneurial decision-making and holding back lasting economic development. The relatively flexible labor market facilitates the matching of jobs with available workers. Fuel subsidies have dropped as a result of lower global oil prices, and the government has announced its intention to phase them out completely.

OPEN MARKETS

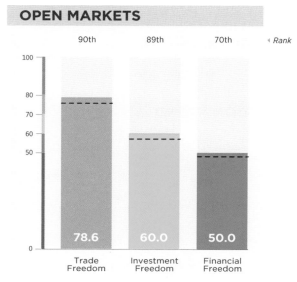

90th	89th	70th	◄ Rank

Trade Freedom	Investment Freedom	Financial Freedom
78.6	60.0	50.0

Trade is important to Trinidad and Tobago's economy; the value of exports and imports taken together equals 60 percent of GDP. The average applied tariff rate is 5.7 percent. The regulatory and judicial systems sometimes impede trade, and numerous state-owned enterprises distort the economy. The financial sector is relatively well developed, with capital markets centered on the stock exchange, and state interference in the sector is not substantial.

UNITED STATES

Large budget deficits and a high level of public debt, both now reflected in the *Index* methodology, have contributed to the continuing decline in America's economic freedom. Having registered its lowest economic freedom score ever, the United States is no longer among the world's 15 freest economies.

The anemic economic recovery since the great recession has been characterized by a lack of labor market dynamism and depressed levels of investment. The substantial expansion of government's size and scope, increased regulatory and tax burdens, and the loss of confidence that has accompanied a growing perception of cronyism, elite privilege, and corruption have severely undermined America's global competitiveness.

WORLD RANK: **17**   **REGIONAL RANK:** **3**

ECONOMIC FREEDOM STATUS:
MOSTLY FREE

ECONOMIC FREEDOM SCORE

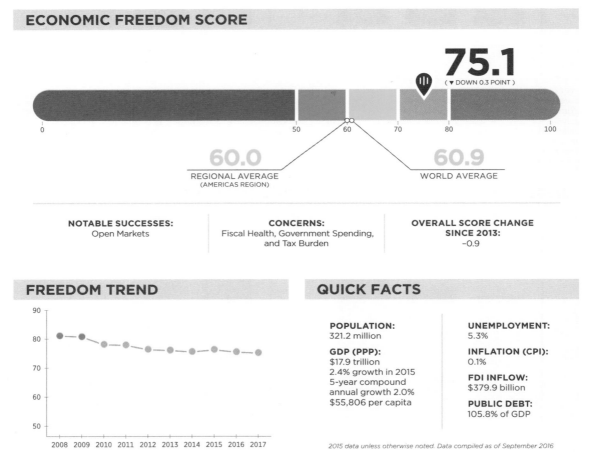

75.1
(▼ DOWN 0.3 POINT)

0   50   60   70   80   100

60.0
REGIONAL AVERAGE
(AMERICAS REGION)

60.9
WORLD AVERAGE

NOTABLE SUCCESSES:	CONCERNS:	OVERALL SCORE CHANGE
Open Markets	Fiscal Health, Government Spending, and Tax Burden	SINCE 2013: −0.9

FREEDOM TREND

90

80

70

60

50

2008 2009 2010 2011 2012 2013 2014 2015 2016 2017

QUICK FACTS

POPULATION:
321.2 million

GDP (PPP):
$17.9 trillion
2.4% growth in 2015
5-year compound
annual growth 2.0%
$55,806 per capita

UNEMPLOYMENT:
5.3%

INFLATION (CPI):
0.1%

FDI INFLOW:
$379.9 billion

PUBLIC DEBT:
105.8% of GDP

2015 data unless otherwise noted. Data compiled as of September 2016

BACKGROUND: The United States, with the world's largest and most diversified economy, is still suffering through a protracted period of slow growth that has held down job creation and labor market participation. The population remains sharply divided over appropriate remedies. Donald Trump, elected President in November 2016, has promised a sharp break with the regulatory, tax, and trade policies of his predecessor, including dismantling such major legislation as the Affordable Care Act and the Dodd–Frank financial regulatory bill. Because of its size and inherent strength, the U.S. economy has shown considerable resilience. Services account for about 80 percent of GDP, but manufacturing output and productivity are at historic highs.

12 ECONOMIC FREEDOMS | UNITED STATES

RULE OF LAW

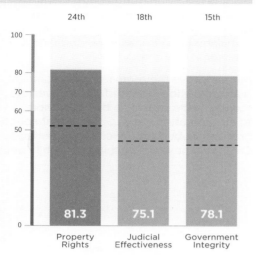

	24th	18th	15th

- Property Rights: 81.3
- Judicial Effectiveness: 75.1
- Government Integrity: 78.1

Although property rights are guaranteed and the judiciary functions independently and predictably, protection of property rights has been uneven. For example, rising civil asset forfeitures by law enforcement agencies and a vast expansion of occupational licensing have directly encroached on U.S. citizens' property rights. The Pew Research Center reported in late 2015 that just 19 percent of Americans trust the government always or most of the time.

GOVERNMENT SIZE

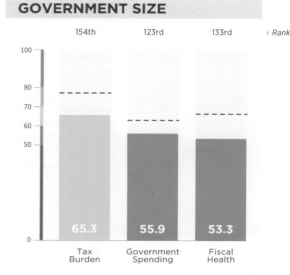

	154th	123rd	133rd	◂ Rank

- Tax Burden: 65.3
- Government Spending: 55.9
- Fiscal Health: 53.3

The top individual income tax rate is 39.6 percent, and the top corporate tax rate remains among the world's highest at 35 percent. The overall tax burden equals 26.0 percent of total domestic income. Government spending at all levels has amounted to 38.3 percent of total output (GDP) over the past three years, and federal budget deficits have averaged 4.1 percent of GDP. Public debt is equivalent to 105.8 percent of GDP.

REGULATORY EFFICIENCY

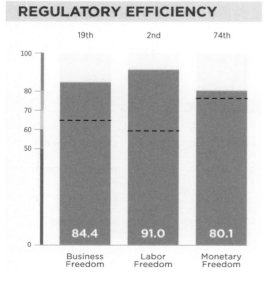

	19th	2nd	74th

- Business Freedom: 84.4
- Labor Freedom: 91.0
- Monetary Freedom: 80.1

The number of federal regulations has increased substantially, raising total annual compliance costs to more than $100 billion in just seven years. Labor regulations are not rigid, but other government policies restrict dynamic job growth. Federal welfare programs, combined with federal subsidies for agriculture, health care, green energy, corporate welfare, and other special interests, contribute to large deficits.

OPEN MARKETS

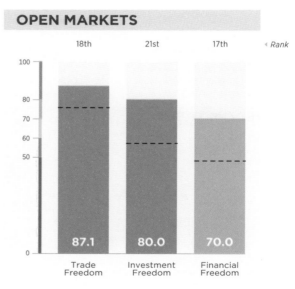

	18th	21st	17th	◂ Rank

- Trade Freedom: 87.1
- Investment Freedom: 80.0
- Financial Freedom: 70.0

Trade is moderately important to the United States economy; the value of exports and imports taken together equals 28 percent of GDP. The average applied tariff rate is 1.4 percent. Over one-third of all land is owned by government. The overall financial sector remains competitive, but the banking sector remains vulnerable to uncertainty and bureaucratic interference related to the 2,300-page Dodd–Frank legislation.

URUGUAY

U ruguay's economy stands out in the region because of its relative openness, supported by a strong commitment to maintaining the rule of law. Uruguay is considered the least corrupt country in Latin America. The majority of Uruguayans enjoy economic prosperity, and poverty has been dramatically reduced over the past decade.

Reforms in recent years to improve the regulatory environment have made Uruguay an attractive location for foreign investors, but the government recently made starting a business more expensive by increasing incorporation costs. Government spending continues to be a problem as budget deficits have remained around 3 percent of GDP in recent years, pushing up public debt.

WORLD RANK:	REGIONAL RANK:
38	**5**

ECONOMIC FREEDOM STATUS:
MODERATELY FREE

ECONOMIC FREEDOM SCORE

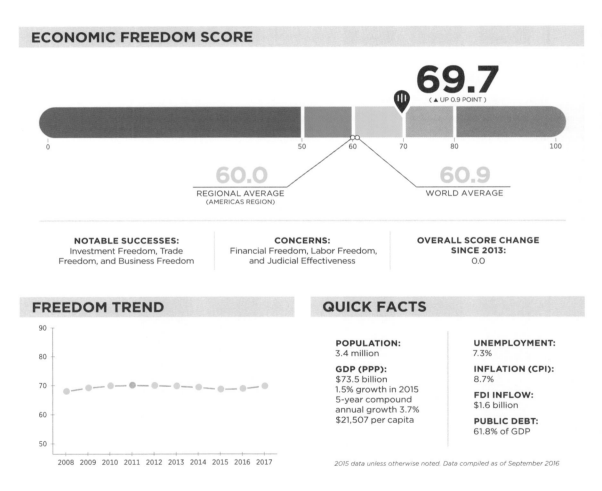

69.7
(▲ UP 0.9 POINT)

0   50   60   70   80   100

60.0
REGIONAL AVERAGE
(AMERICAS REGION)

60.9
WORLD AVERAGE

NOTABLE SUCCESSES:
Investment Freedom, Trade Freedom, and Business Freedom

CONCERNS:
Financial Freedom, Labor Freedom, and Judicial Effectiveness

OVERALL SCORE CHANGE SINCE 2013:
0.0

FREEDOM TREND

90
80
70
60
50

2008 2009 2010 2011 2012 2013 2014 2015 2016 2017

QUICK FACTS

POPULATION:
3.4 million

GDP (PPP):
$73.5 billion
1.5% growth in 2015
5-year compound annual growth 3.7%
$21,507 per capita

UNEMPLOYMENT:
7.3%

INFLATION (CPI):
8.7%

FDI INFLOW:
$1.6 billion

PUBLIC DEBT:
61.8% of GDP

2015 data unless otherwise noted. Data compiled as of September 2016

BACKGROUND: Uruguay's political and labor conditions are among the freest in Latin America. Public outrage at the Tupamaros, a violent 1960s Marxist guerrilla movement, facilitated a military takeover of the government in 1973. Civilian rule was not restored until 1985. The 2004 election victory of the center-left Frente Amplio Coalition (FAC) party ended 170 years of political control by the center-right Colorado and Blanco parties. President Tabaré Vázquez of the FAC began his second (nonconsecutive) five-year term in 2015 but has faced a significantly tougher political landscape because of a regional economic slowdown that has forced spending cuts in programs that are popular with his political base.

12 ECONOMIC FREEDOMS | URUGUAY

RULE OF LAW

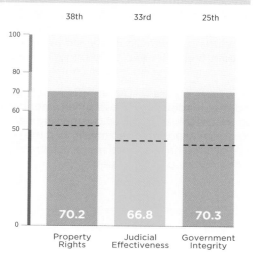

	38th	33rd	25th
Property Rights	70.2		
Judicial Effectiveness		66.8	
Government Integrity			70.3

Private property is generally secure, expropriation is unlikely, and contracts are enforced. The judiciary is transparent and relatively independent, but the courts function slowly. Uruguay surpassed Chile as the least corrupt country in Latin America in Transparency International's 2015 *Corruption Perceptions Index*. A three-member Advisory Economic and Financial Board works to promote government transparency and implement anticorruption measures.

GOVERNMENT SIZE

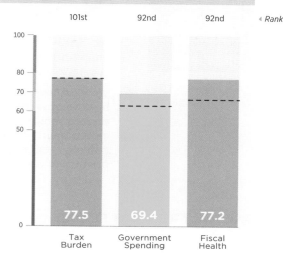

Rank: 101st, 92nd, 92nd

Tax Burden 77.5 | Government Spending 69.4 | Fiscal Health 77.2

The top individual income tax rate is 30 percent, and the top corporate tax rate is 25 percent. Other taxes include a value-added tax and a capital gains tax. The overall tax burden equals 26.9 percent of total domestic income. Government spending has amounted to 31.9 percent of total output (GDP) over the past three years, and budget deficits have averaged 3.1 percent of GDP. Public debt is equivalent to 61.8 percent of GDP.

REGULATORY EFFICIENCY

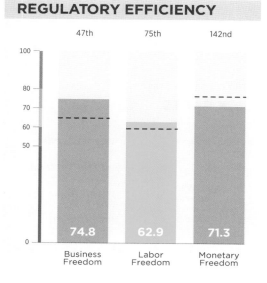

47th, 75th, 142nd

Business Freedom 74.8 | Labor Freedom 62.9 | Monetary Freedom 71.3

Recent reforms have considerably enhanced regulatory efficiency and reduced the cost of completing licensing requirements. The nonsalary cost of employing a worker is relatively low. The government has eliminated most price controls, but it continues to fix prices for electricity, fuels, interdepartmental transport, medicines, natural gas, pasteurized milk, taxi fares, tolls, and water.

OPEN MARKETS

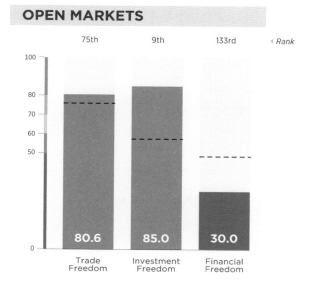

Rank: 75th, 9th, 133rd

Trade Freedom 80.6 | Investment Freedom 85.0 | Financial Freedom 30.0

Trade is moderately important to Uruguay's economy; the value of exports and imports taken together equals 45 percent of GDP. The average applied tariff rate is 4.7 percent. The economy is relatively open to foreign investment, but state-owned enterprises distort the economy. Although the financial sector continues to evolve, capital markets are underdeveloped and concentrated in government debt. The state continues to influence the allocation of credit.

VENEZUELA

Worsening shortages of food, medicines, and other consumer goods, combined with triple-digit inflation that has eroded monetary stability, have drastically undermined Venezuela's already fragile economy. Years of interventionist and market-distorting policies, including nationalizations and restrictions on imports, have resulted in dire economic conditions. There is a substantial risk that civil unrest may spiral out of control.

Venezuela's economy has been stifled by blatant disregard for both the rule of law and the principle of limited government. The private sector has been severely marginalized by institutional impediments related to government encroachment into the marketplace. The judicial system has become more vulnerable to political interference, and corruption is prevalent.

ECONOMIC FREEDOM SCORE

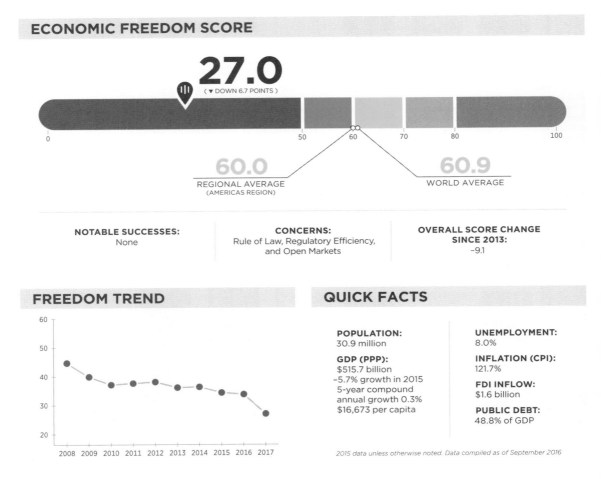

27.0
(▼ DOWN 6.7 POINTS)

0   50   60   70   80   100

60.0
REGIONAL AVERAGE
(AMERICAS REGION)

60.9
WORLD AVERAGE

NOTABLE SUCCESSES:	CONCERNS:	OVERALL SCORE CHANGE
None	Rule of Law, Regulatory Efficiency, and Open Markets	**SINCE 2013:** −9.1

FREEDOM TREND

60
50
40
30
20

2008 2009 2010 2011 2012 2013 2014 2015 2016 2017

QUICK FACTS

POPULATION:
30.9 million

GDP (PPP):
$515.7 billion
−5.7% growth in 2015
5-year compound
annual growth 0.3%
$16,673 per capita

UNEMPLOYMENT:
8.0%

INFLATION (CPI):
121.7%

FDI INFLOW:
$1.6 billion

PUBLIC DEBT:
48.8% of GDP

2015 data unless otherwise noted. Data compiled as of September 2016

BACKGROUND: After decades under generally benevolent military rule, Venezuela's modern democratic era began in 1959. Under the late Hugo Chávez, president from 1999 to 2013, and his handpicked successor, current President Nicolás Maduro, the executive branch has exercised increasingly authoritarian control, and democratic institutions have deteriorated. Venezuelans enjoy few civil liberties and little economic freedom. Violent crime is rampant. A founding member of the Organization of Petroleum Exporting Countries (OPEC), Venezuela has the world's largest proven oil reserves and is highly dependent on oil revenues, which account for almost all exports and half of state revenues. Production has fallen due to government mismanagement of state-owned oil company PDVSA.

12 ECONOMIC FREEDOMS | VENEZUELA

RULE OF LAW

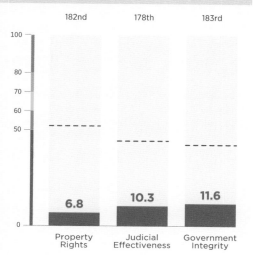

182nd	178th	183rd
6.8	10.3	11.6
Property Rights	Judicial Effectiveness	Government Integrity

Expropriations, weak public-sector institutions, and lack of judicial independence undermine real property rights. The government's economic policies, particularly currency and price controls, have greatly increased opportunities for corruption, black-market activity, and collusion between public officials and organized crime networks. Spiraling rates of violent crime have encouraged the outmigration of skilled workers.

GOVERNMENT SIZE

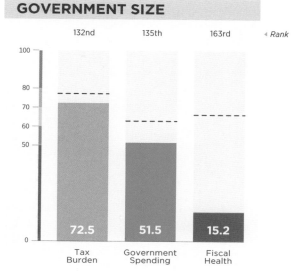

132nd	135th	163rd	◂ Rank
72.5	51.5	15.2	
Tax Burden	Government Spending	Fiscal Health	

Both the top personal income tax rate and the top corporate tax rate are 34 percent. Other taxes include a value-added tax. The overall tax burden equals 20.9 percent of total domestic income. Government spending has amounted to 40.2 percent of total output (GDP) over the past three years, and budget deficits have averaged 16.1 percent of GDP. Public debt is equivalent to 48.8 percent of GDP.

REGULATORY EFFICIENCY

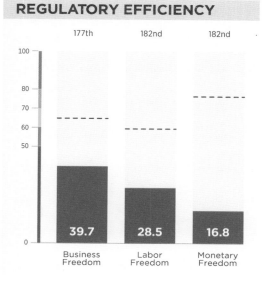

177th	182nd	182nd
39.7	28.5	16.8
Business Freedom	Labor Freedom	Monetary Freedom

Bureaucratic interference has severely undercut regulatory efficiency and productivity growth. The labor market remains rigidly controlled and severely impedes dynamic employment creation. Although the central bank did not release any official inflation statistics in 2016, a Caracas think tank (CENDA) has estimated that annual inflation is more than 600 percent, driven by the severe scarcity of imported goods.

OPEN MARKETS

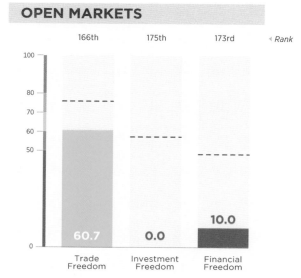

166th	175th	173rd	◂ Rank
60.7	0.0	10.0	
Trade Freedom	Investment Freedom	Financial Freedom	

Trade is moderately important to Venezuela's economy; the value of exports and imports taken together equals 37 percent of GDP. The average applied tariff rate is 9.7 percent. Numerous government policies discourage foreign investment, and state-owned enterprises significantly distort the economy. The financial system remains hobbled by state interference and uncertainty about the direction of economic policies.

ASIA-PACIFIC

ASIA-PACIFIC

The Asia–Pacific region spans the world's largest surface area, stretching from Japan and New Zealand in the East to Azerbaijan in the West. With 4.1 billion inhabitants, this region contains over half of the world's population, with much of this population concentrated in just two countries: China and India.

Despite the challenging global economic environment, the region has achieved an average annual economic growth rate of close to 6.5 percent over the past five years, driven largely by China, India, and other trade-oriented economies. The region also has one of the lowest average unemployment rates (4.3 percent) and the lowest average inflation rate (3.3 percent).

More notably, what makes the Asia–Pacific region unique from other regions is the extraordinary disparity in its countries' levels of economic freedom. The contrast between North Korea and South Korea, for example, provides a vivid demonstration of the benefits of economic freedom.

Chart 1 shows the distribution within the *Index* of Asia–Pacific countries in terms of economic freedom. Four of the world's five truly "free" economies (Hong Kong, Singapore, Australia, and New Zealand) are in this region. Another four of the region's 43 countries(Taiwan, South Korea, Malaysia, and Macau) are rated "mostly free." The majority of the other countries remain "mostly unfree." Four countries, including Turkmenistan, Timor-Leste and Afghanistan, have economies that are rated "repressed." North Korea, which continues to reject any form of free-market activity, remains the least free economy in both the region and the world.

Although its overall economic freedom score is below the world average of 60.9 in the 2017 *Index*, the Asia–Pacific region continues to score higher than world averages in five of the 12 economic freedom categories related to government size and regulatory efficiency: tax burden, government spending, fiscal health, business freedom, and labor freedom. (See Table 1.) Typically lower government expenditures result in a regional government spending score that is over five points better than the world average. The region's labor freedom score also beats the world average by about five points, although many small Pacific island economies still lack fully developed formal labor markets. In other critical areas of economic freedom such as protection of property rights, judicial effectiveness, government integrity, investment freedom, and financial freedom, the Asia–Pacific region as a whole lags behind world averages.

As shown in Chart 2, the eight freest Asia–Pacific countries far outpace other countries in the region in per capita income. It is the less free countries in the region, however—notably China and India, both "mostly unfree" and ranked only 111th and 143rd, respectively, in the world—that have the highest growth rates. One of the most interesting findings of the *Index* is that economic growth is more highly correlated with improvements in economic freedom than with its absolute level. It

ASIA-PACIFIC: QUICK FACTS

TOTAL POPULATION: 4.1 billion

POPULATION WEIGHTED AVERAGES

GDP PER CAPITA (PPP):	$11,494
GROWTH:	6.1%
5 YEAR GROWTH:	6.4%
INFLATION:	3.3%
UNEMPLOYMENT:	4.3%
PUBLIC DEBT:	56.2%

SOURCE: Terry Miller and Anthony B. Kim, *2017 Index of Economic Freedom* (Washington: The Heritage Foundation, 2017), http://www.heritage.org/index.

☎ heritage.org

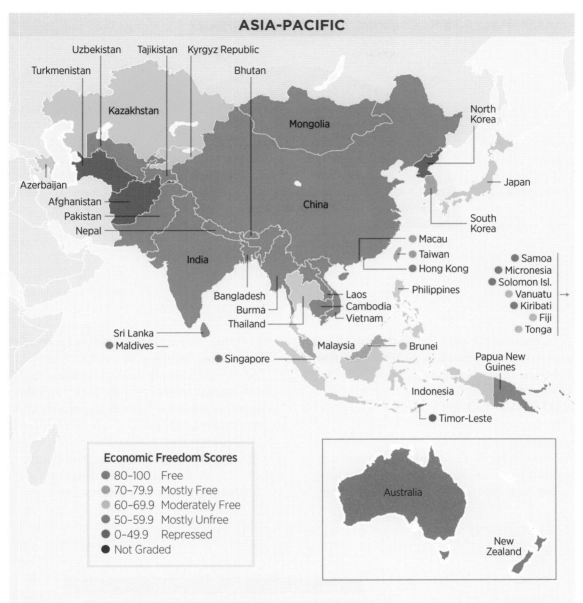

ASIA-PACIFIC

Turkmenistan
Uzbekistan
Tajikistan
Kyrgyz Republic
Bhutan
Kazakhstan
Mongolia
North Korea
Japan
Azerbaijan
Afghanistan
Pakistan
Nepal
China
South Korea
India
Macau
Taiwan
Hong Kong
Samoa
Micronesia
Solomon Isl.
Philippines
Vanuatu
Bangladesh
Laos
Cambodia
Vietnam
Kiribati
Burma
Fiji
Thailand
Tonga
Sri Lanka
Maldives
Malaysia
Brunei
Singapore
Papua New Guines
Indonesia
Timor-Leste

Economic Freedom Scores
- 80–100   Free
- 70–79.9 Mostly Free
- 60–69.9 Moderately Free
- 50–59.9 Mostly Unfree
- 0–49.9   Repressed
- Not Graded

Australia

New Zealand

SOURCE: Terry Miller and Anthony B. Kim, *2017 Index of Economic Freedom* (Washington: The Heritage Foundation, 2017), http://www.heritage.org/index.

☎ heritage.org

is interesting to note in this context that economic freedom scores in both China and India have improved by over five points over the life of the *Index*. Nevertheless, the foundations of economic freedom continue to be fragile in both countries, with reforms often stymied by those who have a political interest in maintaining the status quo. There is therefore room for considerable further progress.

As depicted in Chart 3, it is clear that greater economic freedom is also strongly correlated with overall well-being, which takes into account such factors as health, education, security, and personal freedom.

ASIA-PACIFIC: ECONOMIC FREEDOM SUMMARY

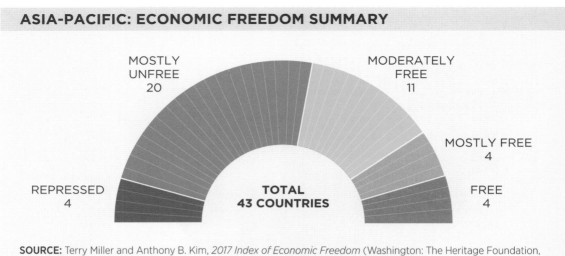

MOSTLY UNFREE
20

MODERATELY FREE
11

MOSTLY FREE
4

REPRESSED
4

TOTAL
43 COUNTRIES

FREE
4

SOURCE: Terry Miller and Anthony B. Kim, *2017 Index of Economic Freedom* (Washington: The Heritage Foundation, 2017), http://www.heritage.org/index.

Chart 1 ☎ heritage.org

In the 2017 *Index*, the scores of 32 countries in the Asia–Pacific region have improved, and those of 11 have declined.

NOTABLE COUNTRIES

- Burma's economy has undergone significant changes. Economic sanctions have been eased or lifted, and the government has launched reforms to modernize the economic system. A new banking and finance law that lays the foundations for more efficient licensing of financial institutions has been ratified. In 2016, the lower house of parliament also approved a new investment law.

- China, with its low deficits and moderate level of public debt, benefited significantly this year in the rankings from

ASIA-PACIFIC: GDP PER CAPITA, BY ECONOMIC FREEDOM CATEGORY

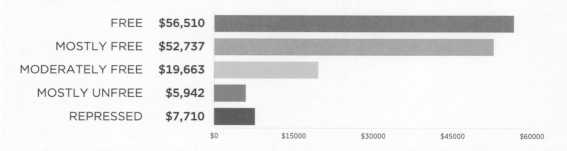

FREE	$56,510
MOSTLY FREE	$52,737
MODERATELY FREE	$19,663
MOSTLY UNFREE	$5,942
REPRESSED	$7,710

$0 $15000 $30000 $45000 $60000

SOURCES: Terry Miller and Anthony B. Kim, *2017 Index of Economic Freedom* (Washington: The Heritage Foundation, 2017), http://www.heritage.org/index, and International Monetary Fund, World Economic Outlook Database, April 2016, https://www.imf.org/external/pubs/ft/weo/2016/01/weodata/index.aspx (accessed December 13, 2016).

Chart 2 ☎ heritage.org

ASIA-PACIFIC: COMPONENTS OF ECONOMIC FREEDOM

LOWER THAN WORLD AVERAGE ●——| |——● HIGHER THAN WORLD AVERAGE

		AVERAGES		
		Region	World	
OVERALL		**60.3**	60.9	●
RULE OF LAW	Property Rights	**52.8**	53.0	●
	Judicial Effectiveness	**41.8**	45.0	●—|
	Government Integrity	**42.1**	43.0	◖
GOVERNMENT SIZE	Tax Burden	**80.3**	77.1	|—●
	Government Spending	**68.9**	63.4	|——●
	Fiscal Health	**72.6**	68.0	|—●
REGULATORY EFFICIENCY	Business Freedom	**66.2**	64.6	|●
	Labor Freedom	**64.0**	59.2	|——●
	Monetary Freedom	**74.4**	76.4	●—|
MARKET OPENNESS	Trade Freedom	**74.7**	75.9	●|
	Investment Freedom	**44.2**	57.2	●————|
	Financial Freedom	**41.8**	48.2	●——|

SOURCE: Terry Miller and Anthony B. Kim, *2017 Index of Economic Freedom* (Washington: The Heritage Foundation, 2017), http://www.heritage.org/index.

Table 1 ☎ heritage.org

the incorporation of those two factors in the *Index* methodology. Regrettably, there seems to be little momentum for significant economic reform, and the government, confronting a period of economic slowdown, has increased expansionary fiscal and monetary interventions. Deep-seated structural problems, including a state-controlled financial sector and regulatory inefficiency, remain unaddressed.

- Economic freedom continues to decline in Japan, and the economy remains stagnant. Scores in the economic freedom categories related to the size of government are far below average, but much of the government's political capital has been expended in efforts related to the country's defense and security posture rather than economic reform, which would challenge well-established special interests and traditions.

- Despite the difficult global economic environment, the Philippines has achieved notable economic expansion, driven by the economy's strong export performance and inflows of remittances that have bolstered private consumption. The government has pursued a series of legislative reforms to enhance the overall entrepreneurial environment and develop a stronger private sector, but the country still lags in business freedom, labor freedom, and the rule of law.

ASIA-PACIFIC: ECONOMIC FREEDOM AND OVERALL WELL-BEING

- Capitalizing on its gradual integration into the global trade and investment system, Vietnam is transforming into a more market-oriented economy. Reforms have included partial privatization of state-owned enterprises, liberalization of the trade regime, and increasing recognition of private property rights. The economy has registered annual growth rates averaging about 6 percent over the past five years.

Each circle represents a nation in the *Index of Economic Freedom*

Prosperity Index Score

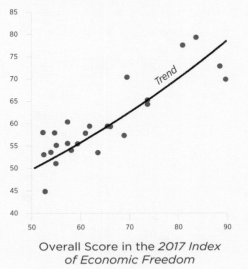

Overall Score in the *2017 Index of Economic Freedom*

SOURCES: Terry Miller and Anthony B. Kim, *2017 Index of Economic Freedom* (Washington: The Heritage Foundation, 2017), http://www.heritage.org/index, and Legatum Institute Foundation, "The Legatum Prosperity Index 2016," 2016, http://www.prosperity.com/rankings (accessed December 13, 2016).

Chart 3 ☎ heritage.org

ECONOMIC FREEDOM IN ASIA-PACIFIC

World Rank	Regional Rank	Country	Overall Score	Change from 2016	Property Rights	Judicial Effectiveness	Government Integrity	Tax Burden	Government Spending	Fiscal Health	Business Freedom	Labor Freedom	Monetary Freedom	Trade Freedom	Investment Freedom	Financial Freedom
1	1	Hong Kong	89.8	1.2	93.7	84.0	80.3	93.0	90.0	100	94.6	89.1	83.2	90.0	90	90
2	2	Singapore	88.6	0.8	97.1	91.5	87.9	90.5	90.1	80.7	95.1	90.8	84.3	90.0	85	80
3	3	New Zealand	83.7	2.1	96.1	88.5	89.9	70.8	46.5	97.8	91.8	86.2	90.1	87.4	80	80
5	4	Australia	81.0	0.7	81.7	92.9	74.8	63.2	59.0	84.6	89.3	84.1	86.4	86.2	80	90
11	5	Taiwan	76.5	1.8	86.5	67.7	70.5	75.3	89.5	83.7	93.4	55.0	85.2	86.2	65	60
23	6	South Korea	74.3	2.6	77.8	59.9	67.3	73.7	68.9	97.4	90.6	57.0	84.0	79.5	65	70
27	7	Malaysia	73.8	2.3	85.3	67.3	51.8	85.3	78.7	76.5	90.8	73.1	85.3	81.2	60	50
32	8	Macau	70.7	0.6	60.0	60.0	37.1	72.3	92.8	100	60.0	50.0	70.8	90.0	85	70
35	9	Brunei Darussalam	69.8	2.5	62.5	39.9	40.9	85.6	61.2	100	76.6	90.4	76.1	89.1	65	50
40	10	Japan	69.6	-3.5	89.4	73.8	86.1	68.5	52.3	9.5	82.3	77.5	83.0	82.6	70	60
42	11	Kazakhstan	69.0	5.4	56.1	56.5	38.0	93.3	85.7	98.9	74.5	82.5	73.9	78.5	40	50
52	12	Vanuatu	67.4	6.6	65.5	33.0	70.5	97.0	80.4	99.1	51.4	58.1	74.8	73.9	65	40
55	13	Thailand	66.2	2.3	51.3	41.7	40.7	81.0	85.3	96.3	69.9	62.8	72.9	82.8	50	60
58	14	Philippines	65.6	2.5	49.2	37.1	38.7	78.9	89.4	97.2	62.6	57.2	80.6	76.4	60	60
68	15	Azerbaijan	63.6	3.4	50.5	33.0	37.6	87.7	57.5	97.4	71.5	75.0	73.6	74.4	55	50
71	16	Fiji	63.4	4.6	67.7	41.9	32.7	80.7	72.5	84.1	61.3	70.5	75.5	68.8	55	50
73	17	Tonga	63.0	3.4	65.5	19.8	47.6	86.9	74.4	79.6	76.1	86.0	80.6	79.7	40	20
84	18	Indonesia	61.9	2.5	48.3	39.3	44.7	83.6	89.9	90.1	49.1	48.9	74.0	80.5	35	60
89	19	Kyrgyz Republic	61.1	1.5	50.9	17.2	30.3	93.7	55.2	78.9	73.7	79.8	68.5	75.3	60	50
94	20	Cambodia	59.5	1.6	42.4	22.1	12.8	90.2	88.1	95.7	29.6	62.0	81.0	80.3	60	50
107	21	Bhutan	58.4	-1.1	60.1	50.7	44.7	83.1	73.6	61.7	72.6	77.6	67.1	60.0	20	30
108	22	Samoa	58.4	-5.1	51.3	22.6	37.1	80.4	51.9	66.6	77.0	73.3	84.5	70.7	55	30
109	23	Tajikistan	58.2	6.9	45.5	45.6	32.7	90.9	74.1	95.8	65.6	49.2	69.8	73.9	25	30
111	24	China	57.4	5.4	48.3	60.7	41.6	70.0	73.0	92.5	53.9	63.4	71.8	73.6	20	20
112	25	Sri Lanka	57.4	-2.5	48.0	48.3	30.0	85.3	90.2	31.2	72.8	57.5	76.0	74.5	35	40
125	26	Nepal	55.1	4.2	37.3	32.0	26.7	84.9	89.5	98.4	64.6	47.6	72.2	68.1	10	30
126	27	Solomon Islands	55.0	8.0	39.3	41.9	33.9	62.8	34.4	99.8	68.5	70.5	81.0	83.0	15	30
128	28	Bangladesh	55.0	1.7	34.9	26.0	19.1	72.8	94.0	78.7	53.4	68.7	68.6	63.6	50	30
129	29	Mongolia	54.8	-4.6	51.3	28.4	36.8	87.1	57.6	0.0	67.2	76.6	72.3	74.9	45	60
132	30	Micronesia	54.1	2.3	30.0	30.0	40.7	90.7	0.0	98.6	57.8	67.7	83.6	85.6	35	30
133	31	Laos	54.0	4.2	35.3	35.9	32.6	86.1	76.6	61.2	66.3	54.4	70.2	74.6	35	20
141	32	Pakistan	52.8	-3.1	36.4	34.1	30.5	78.9	87.3	30.8	61.2	37.8	74.8	67.2	55	40
143	33	India	52.6	-3.6	55.4	44.4	44.3	77.2	77.4	11.0	52.8	41.6	75.0	72.6	40	40
146	34	Burma	52.5	3.8	23.0	12.9	29.6	86.2	81.5	89.9	50.1	77.1	65.4	74.2	20	20
147	35	Vietnam	52.4	-1.6	49.7	32.0	24.6	79.6	74.6	21.1	61.2	62.2	76.0	83.1	25	40
148	36	Uzbekistan	52.3	6.3	48.0	41.9	27.5	90.7	66.2	99.8	64.8	50.4	61.1	66.8	0	10
152	37	Papua New Guinea	50.9	-2.3	37.7	54.0	32.7	67.8	64.5	16.7	59.8	67.4	69.8	85.4	25	30

(CONTINUED ON NEXT PAGE)

ECONOMIC FREEDOM IN ASIA-PACIFIC

World Rank	Regional Rank	Country	Overall Score	Change from 2016	Property Rights	Judicial Effectiveness	Government Integrity	Tax Burden	Government Spending	Fiscal Health	Business Freedom	Labor Freedom	Monetary Freedom	Trade Freedom	Investment Freedom	Financial Freedom
153	38	Kiribati	50.9	4.7	48.0	33.0	37.6	73.6	0.0	99.5	51.5	71.9	82.0	58.2	25	30
157	39	Maldives	50.3	-3.6	45.1	33.0	31.4	93.0	51.5	9.4	80.6	70.4	76.3	47.8	35	30
163	40	Afghanistan	48.9	N/A	12.6	28.4	27.5	91.6	79.9	97.3	54.2	59.9	69.3	66.0	0	0
170	41	Turkmenistan	47.4	5.5	32.4	5.0	29.6	95.3	92.3	98.9	30.0	20.0	74.8	80.0	0	10
173	42	Timor-Leste	46.3	0.5	6.8	10.3	29.2	64.7	65.6	20.0	72.2	63.9	77.5	80.0	45	20
180	43	North Korea	4.9	2.6	32.4	5.0	11.6	0.0	0.0	0.0	5.0	5.0	0.0	0.0	0	0

AFGHANISTAN

Afghanistan's economic freedom is graded for the first time in the 2017 *Index*, reflecting the improved availability of key economic data. Over the past decade, the country has achieved rapid yet volatile economic growth. Construction and agriculture have been the key contributors to economic expansion. Afghanistan became a member of the World Trade Organization in 2016.

Political uncertainty and security challenges remain formidable. The rule of law continues to be fragile and uneven across the country; the inability to deliver even basic services reliably has eroded public confidence in the government; and systemic corruption has undermined the effectiveness of the courts, the banking sector, and other parts of the economy.

ECONOMIC FREEDOM SCORE

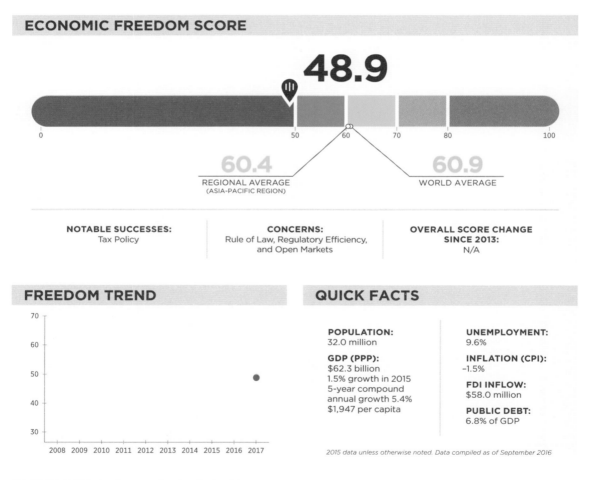

48.9

0   50   60   70   80   100

60.4
REGIONAL AVERAGE
(ASIA-PACIFIC REGION)

60.9
WORLD AVERAGE

NOTABLE SUCCESSES:	CONCERNS:	OVERALL SCORE CHANGE SINCE 2013:
Tax Policy	Rule of Law, Regulatory Efficiency, and Open Markets	N/A

FREEDOM TREND

70
60
50
40
30

2008 2009 2010 2011 2012 2013 2014 2015 2016 2017

QUICK FACTS

POPULATION:
32.0 million

GDP (PPP):
$62.3 billion
1.5% growth in 2015
5-year compound
annual growth 5.4%
$1,947 per capita

UNEMPLOYMENT:
9.6%

INFLATION (CPI):
–1.5%

FDI INFLOW:
$58.0 million

PUBLIC DEBT:
6.8% of GDP

2015 data unless otherwise noted. Data compiled as of September 2016

BACKGROUND: Mohammad Ashraf Ghani became president following an election marred by allegations of vote-rigging in 2014. After three months of political wrangling, Ghani and former Foreign Minister Abdullah Abdullah agreed to form a unity government with Abdullah as chief executive officer. Taliban insurgents stepped up their attacks during the past year and now hold more territory than they have held at any other time since 2001 when they were ousted from power. In response to this offensive, President Obama decided to slow the withdrawal of U.S. troops from Afghanistan and keep about 8,400 U.S. forces in the country through the end of his term.

12 ECONOMIC FREEDOMS | AFGHANISTAN

RULE OF LAW

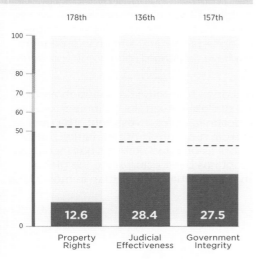

Protection of property rights is weak due to the lack of a comprehensive land titling system, disputed land titles, and the incapacity of commercial courts. The judicial system operates haphazardly; in many places, justice is administered by inadequately trained judges according to a mixture of legal codes. Corruption is endemic throughout society, and demands for bribery at border crossings hamper development of a market economy.

GOVERNMENT SIZE

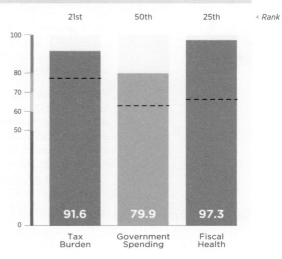

The top income and corporate tax rates are 20 percent. The overall tax burden equals 6.5 percent of total domestic income. Government spending has amounted to 26.4 percent of total output (GDP) over the past three years, and budget deficits have averaged 1.3 percent of GDP. Public debt is equivalent to 6.8 percent of GDP. Years of political and security uncertainty have caused increased budgetary uncertainty and fiscal vulnerability.

REGULATORY EFFICIENCY

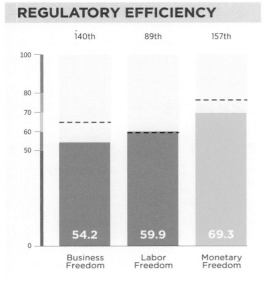

Processes for establishing businesses and obtaining necessary licenses are relatively streamlined, but other structural barriers persist. The presence of a large informal economy continues to dampen development of a functioning labor market. Due to the severe underdevelopment of Afghanistan's financial system, the government has very limited influence on monetary policy.

OPEN MARKETS

Trade is important to Afghanistan's economy; the value of exports and imports taken together equals 53 percent of GDP. The average applied tariff rate is 7.0 percent, and regulatory barriers deter trade and investment. Security concerns and the financial system's weak capacity have slowed investment growth. The financial sector remains underdeveloped, and trust in the banking system has been undermined.

AFGHANISTAN

WORLD RANK: **5** REGIONAL RANK: **4**

ECONOMIC FREEDOM STATUS:
FREE

AUSTRALIA

A ustralia, a vibrant free-market democracy, has recorded impressive economic progress unmarred by recession for more than 25 years. In addition to abundant natural resources, the economy has benefited from an effective system of government, a well-functioning legal system, and an independent bureaucracy, all of which have facilitated robust entrepreneurial development.

With almost all industries open to foreign competition and a skilled workforce readily available, Australia continues to be an attractive and dynamic destination for investment. The government has withdrawn from most areas of the market, and competition in such sectors as financial services has increased. Although government debt has been rising since the global financial crisis, it remains substantially lower than in most other advanced economies.

ECONOMIC FREEDOM SCORE

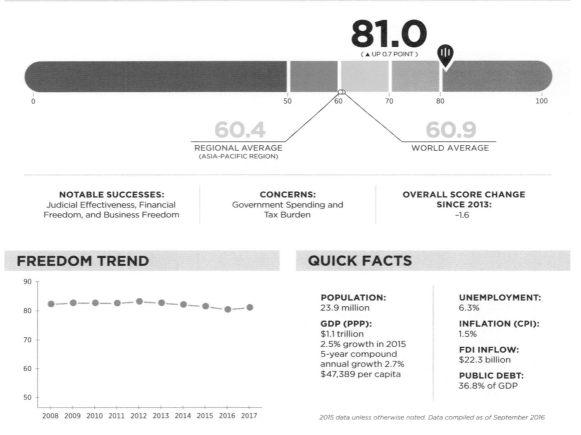

81.0
(▲ UP 0.7 POINT)

0   50   60   70   80   100

60.4
REGIONAL AVERAGE
(ASIA-PACIFIC REGION)

60.9
WORLD AVERAGE

NOTABLE SUCCESSES:
Judicial Effectiveness, Financial Freedom, and Business Freedom

CONCERNS:
Government Spending and Tax Burden

OVERALL SCORE CHANGE SINCE 2013:
–1.6

FREEDOM TREND

90
80
70
60
50

2008 2009 2010 2011 2012 2013 2014 2015 2016 2017

QUICK FACTS

POPULATION:
23.9 million

GDP (PPP):
$1.1 trillion
2.5% growth in 2015
5-year compound annual growth 2.7%
$47,389 per capita

UNEMPLOYMENT:
6.3%

INFLATION (CPI):
1.5%

FDI INFLOW:
$22.3 billion

PUBLIC DEBT:
36.8% of GDP

2015 data unless otherwise noted. Data compiled as of September 2016

BACKGROUND: Australia is one of the wealthiest Asia–Pacific nations and has enjoyed more than two decades of economic expansion. It emerged from the 2009 global recession relatively unscathed, but stimulus spending by the previous Labor government generated a fiscal deficit that has continued under subsequent Liberal governments. Australia is internationally competitive in services, technologies, and high-value-added manufactured goods. Mining and agriculture are important sources of exports. Malcolm Turnbull, a former businessman and communications minister, replaced Tony Abbott as head of the ruling Liberal–National coalition and as prime minister in September 2015.

12 ECONOMIC FREEDOMS | AUSTRALIA

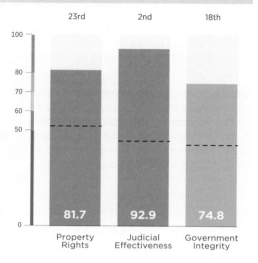

RULE OF LAW

23rd	2nd	18th
Property Rights	Judicial Effectiveness	Government Integrity
81.7	92.9	74.8

Strong rule of law protects property rights and helps to minimize corruption. Expropriation is highly unusual, and enforcement of contracts is reliable. Australia's stable political environment supports transparent and well-established political processes, a strong legal system, competent governance, and an independent bureaucracy. The judicial system operates independently and impartially. Anti-corruption measures are generally effective.

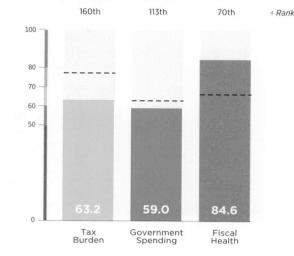

GOVERNMENT SIZE

◄ Rank

160th	113th	70th
Tax Burden	Government Spending	Fiscal Health
63.2	59.0	84.6

The top income tax rate is 45 percent, and the flat corporate tax rate is 30 percent. Other taxes include a value-added tax and a capital gains tax. The overall tax burden equals 27.5 percent of total domestic income. Government spending has amounted to 37 percent of total output (GDP) over the past three years, and budget deficits have averaged 2.8 percent of GDP. Public debt is equivalent to 36.8 percent of GDP.

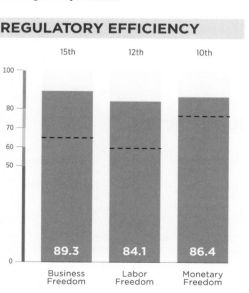

REGULATORY EFFICIENCY

15th	12th	10th
Business Freedom	Labor Freedom	Monetary Freedom
89.3	84.1	86.4

Australia's regulatory environment is one of the world's most transparent and efficient and is highly conducive to entrepreneurship. It takes only three procedures to launch a business. The labor market is well supported by the modern and flexible employment code. The Reserve Bank of Australia has reacted prudently to the slowdown in growth among the country's trading partners, and inflation remains below target levels.

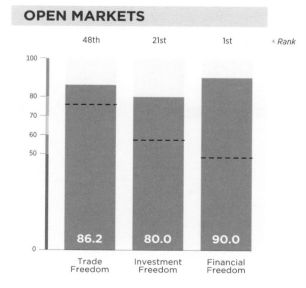

OPEN MARKETS

◄ Rank

48th	21st	1st
Trade Freedom	Investment Freedom	Financial Freedom
86.2	80.0	90.0

Trade is moderately important to Australia's economy; the value of exports and imports taken together equals 41 percent of GDP. The average applied tariff rate is 1.9 percent. Some regulations impede agricultural trade. Most state-owned enterprises have been privatized. Foreign firms compete on equal terms with domestic banks and other financial institutions in Australia's highly developed and competitive financial system.

AUSTRALIA

AZERBAIJAN

Openness to global trade and investment, supported by some improvements in regulatory efficiency, has aided Azerbaijan's transition to a more market-based economic system. Continued transformation and restructuring are needed to capitalize on the well-educated labor force and broaden the production base. Economic growth has been driven mainly by development of the energy sector.

Challenges to diversification and sustainable growth remain substantial. Deeper systemic reforms are critically needed to advance and institutionalize economic freedom more firmly. Despite some progress, property rights are weak, and corruption remains widespread. State involvement in banking is still excessive, and lingering financial instability adds to uncertainty.

ECONOMIC FREEDOM SCORE

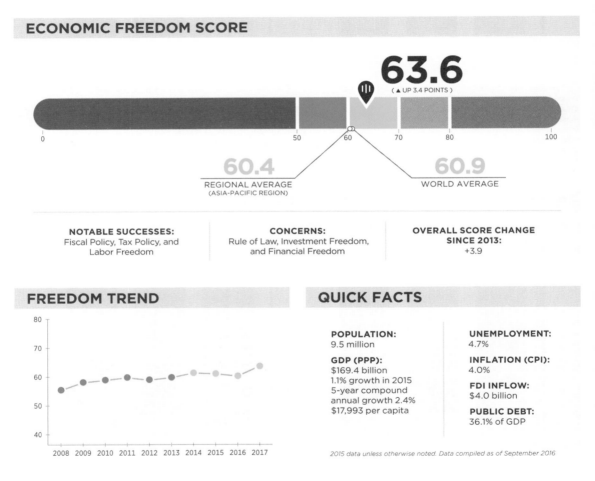

63.6
(▲ UP 3.4 POINTS)

0   50   60   70   80   100

60.4
REGIONAL AVERAGE
(ASIA-PACIFIC REGION)

60.9
WORLD AVERAGE

NOTABLE SUCCESSES:
Fiscal Policy, Tax Policy, and Labor Freedom

CONCERNS:
Rule of Law, Investment Freedom, and Financial Freedom

OVERALL SCORE CHANGE SINCE 2013:
+3.9

FREEDOM TREND

80

70

60

50

40

2008 2009 2010 2011 2012 2013 2014 2015 2016 2017

QUICK FACTS

POPULATION:
9.5 million

GDP (PPP):
$169.4 billion
1.1% growth in 2015
5-year compound annual growth 2.4%
$17,993 per capita

UNEMPLOYMENT:
4.7%

INFLATION (CPI):
4.0%

FDI INFLOW:
$4.0 billion

PUBLIC DEBT:
36.1% of GDP

2015 data unless otherwise noted. Data compiled as of September 2016

BACKGROUND: President Ilham Aliyev was elected to a third term in 2013 amid allegations of electoral fraud. His father, Heydar, ruled Azerbaijan as a Soviet republic and later as an independent country until his death in 2003, when his son succeeded him. Armenia currently occupies the Nagorno–Karabakh region and seven neighboring districts that amount to almost 20 percent of Azerbaijan's internationally recognized territory. An upsurge in violence between Armenian and Azerbaijani forces in April 2016 threatened to exacerbate regional instability. Falling oil production is expected to be partially offset by increased natural gas exports. In 2015, construction began on the Trans-Anatolian Natural Gas Pipeline to export Azerbaijani gas through Turkey and ease Europe's energy dependence on Russia.

12 ECONOMIC FREEDOMS | AZERBAIJAN

RULE OF LAW

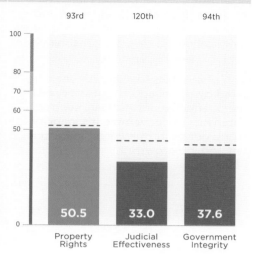

93rd   120th   94th

Property Rights	Judicial Effectiveness	Government Integrity
50.5	33.0	37.6

The state has seized property for development projects that involved forced evictions and unlawful and inadequately compensated expropriations. The corrupt and inefficient judiciary is largely subservient to the president and ruling party. Outcomes frequently appear to be predetermined. Corruption is widespread. Opposition politicians are subject to arbitrary arrest, physical violence, and other forms of intimidation.

GOVERNMENT SIZE

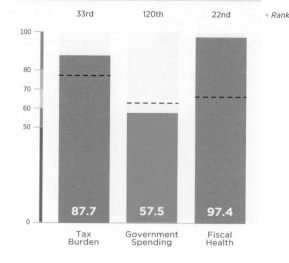

33rd   120th   22nd   ◄ *Rank*

Tax Burden	Government Spending	Fiscal Health
87.7	57.5	97.4

The top individual income tax rate is 25 percent, and the top corporate tax rate is 20 percent. Other taxes include a value-added tax and a property tax. The overall tax burden equals 14.2 percent of total domestic income. Government spending has amounted to 37.6 percent of total output (GDP) over the past three years, and budget surpluses have averaged 0.3 percent of GDP. Public debt is equivalent to 36.1 percent of GDP.

REGULATORY EFFICIENCY

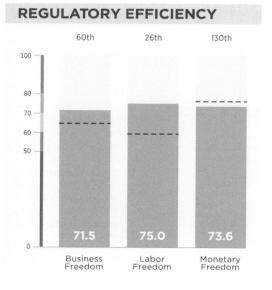

60th   26th   130th

Business Freedom	Labor Freedom	Monetary Freedom
71.5	75.0	73.6

Despite progress in streamlining the process for launching a business, other time-consuming requirements reduce regulatory efficiency. Labor regulations have become somewhat more flexible, but enforcement of the labor code remains uneven. After two steep devaluations, the central bank moved to a managed float exchange rate regime and raised interest rates in 2016 to address rising inflation.

OPEN MARKETS

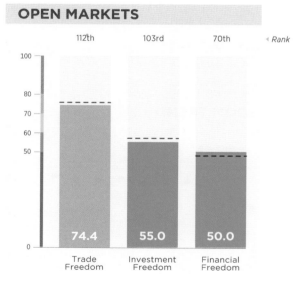

112th   103rd   70th   ◄ *Rank*

Trade Freedom	Investment Freedom	Financial Freedom
74.4	55.0	50.0

Trade is important to Azerbaijan's economy; the value of exports and imports taken together equals 73 percent of GDP. The average applied tariff rate is 5.3 percent, and bureaucratic and regulatory barriers impede international trade and investment. The financial sector faces a range of challenges that include a currency devaluation. The banking sector is dominated by a large state bank, and small private banks remain fragmented.

AZERBAIJAN

BANGLADESH

WORLD RANK: **128** | REGIONAL RANK: **28**

ECONOMIC FREEDOM STATUS:
MOSTLY UNFREE

The fragile rule of law continues to undermine economic development in Bangladesh. Corruption and marginal enforcement of property rights drive people and enterprises into the informal economy, and poor economic management, worsened by repeated political crises, severely constrains economic dynamism.

Despite some streamlining of business regulations, entrepreneurial activity is hampered by an uncertain regulatory environment and the absence of effective institutional support for private-sector development. The government's inability to provide even minimal public goods further limits opportunities for business development and job growth.

ECONOMIC FREEDOM SCORE

55.0
(▲ UP 1.7 POINTS)

| 0 | 50 | 60 | 70 | 80 | 100 |

60.4
REGIONAL AVERAGE
(ASIA–PACIFIC REGION)

60.9
WORLD AVERAGE

| **NOTABLE SUCCESSES:** | **CONCERNS:** | **OVERALL SCORE CHANGE** |
| Government Spending, Fiscal Policy, and Tax Policy | Rule of Law, Business Freedom, and Open Markets | **SINCE 2013:** +2.4 |

FREEDOM TREND

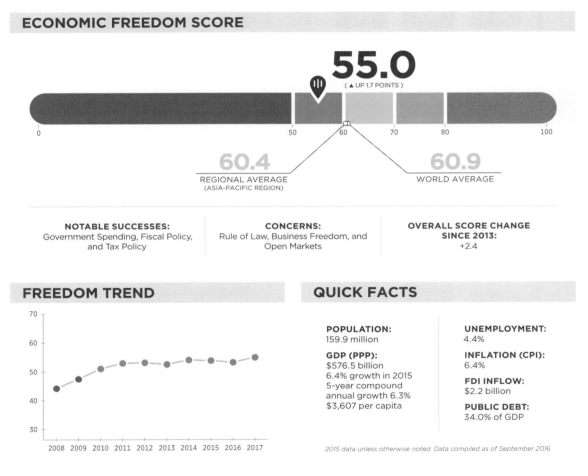

QUICK FACTS

POPULATION:
159.9 million

GDP (PPP):
$576.5 billion
6.4% growth in 2015
5-year compound
annual growth 6.3%
$3,607 per capita

UNEMPLOYMENT:
4.4%

INFLATION (CPI):
6.4%

FDI INFLOW:
$2.2 billion

PUBLIC DEBT:
34.0% of GDP

2015 data unless otherwise noted. Data compiled as of September 2016

BACKGROUND: Prime Minister Sheikh Hasina was reelected in January 2014 in an election marred by an opposition boycott. A year later, when antigovernment demonstrations and a transport blockade fueled violence that killed over 120 people, the government jailed over 7,000 opposition members. Extremist attacks against liberal bloggers, religious minorities, and foreigners have risen alarmingly since 2013. A major terrorist attack on a café in Dhaka in July 2016 that killed 22 people has led to concern that international terrorist groups like the Islamic State and al-Qaeda are linking up with local militant groups. Despite the political turmoil, a decade of fairly rapid economic growth has contributed to progress against persistent poverty.

12 ECONOMIC FREEDOMS | BANGLADESH

RULE OF LAW

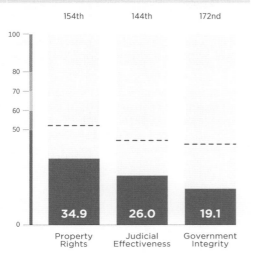

154th   144th   172nd

Property Rights	Judicial Effectiveness	Government Integrity
34.9	26.0	19.1

Property laws are antiquated, and property rights are enforced unevenly. The judiciary is not independent. Procedures for contract enforcement and dispute settlement are inefficient. Endemic corruption and criminality, weak rule of law, limited bureaucratic transparency, and political polarization have undermined government accountability. Anticorruption efforts are weakened by politicized enforcement and subversion of the judicial process.

GOVERNMENT SIZE

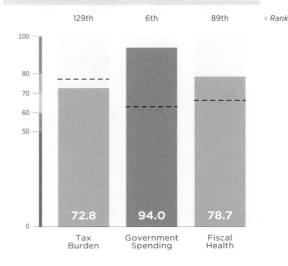

129th   6th   89th   ◄ Rank

Tax Burden	Government Spending	Fiscal Health
72.8	94.0	78.7

The top income tax rate is 25 percent, and the top corporate tax rate is 45 percent. Other taxes include a value-added tax that is being reformed. The overall tax burden equals 8.6 percent of total domestic income. Government spending has amounted to 14.1 percent of total output (GDP) over the past three years, and budget deficits have averaged 3.4 percent of GDP. Public debt is equivalent to 34.0 percent of GDP.

REGULATORY EFFICIENCY

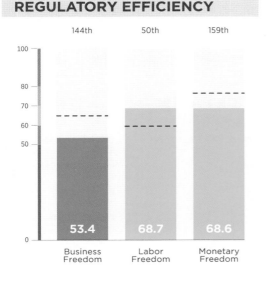

144th   50th   159th

Business Freedom	Labor Freedom	Monetary Freedom
53.4	68.7	68.6

The costs of getting necessary permits and establishing a company have been reduced considerably. A well-functioning labor market has not been fully developed, but labor productivity growth has been slightly higher than wage hikes. Although somewhat less costly in 2016 due to low oil prices, the government's extensive subsidizing of basic food staples, fuels, fertilizers, and electricity continues to hamper economic growth.

OPEN MARKETS

159th   120th   133rd   ◄ Rank

Trade Freedom	Investment Freedom	Financial Freedom
63.6	50.0	30.0

Trade is moderately important to Bangladesh's economy; the value of exports and imports taken together equals 42 percent of GDP. The average applied tariff rate is 10.7 percent, and the government has taken steps to reduce bureaucratic barriers to trade and investment. Government ownership and interference in the financial sector remain considerable, undermining efficiency and growth.

WORLD RANK:
107

REGIONAL RANK:
21

ECONOMIC FREEDOM STATUS:
MOSTLY UNFREE

BHUTAN

Bhutan has made progress in modernizing its economic structure and reducing poverty. The public sector has long been the main source of economic growth, but the government now recognizes that private-sector growth is crucial. Higher priority is being given to economic diversification, particularly in light of demographic shifts that will bring more young people into the labor market.

The government has taken steps to ensure greater security for property rights. However, lingering constraints on private-sector development include an inefficient regulatory framework, pervasive nontariff barriers to trade, and a rudimentary investment code. The financial sector remains small and without adequate regulation or supervision.

ECONOMIC FREEDOM SCORE

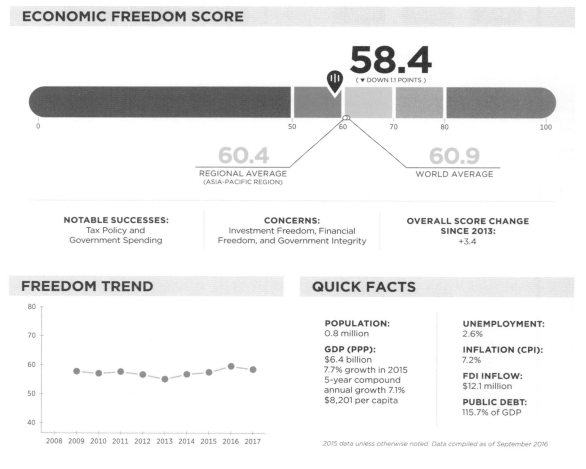

58.4
(▼ DOWN 1.1 POINTS)

0   50   60   70   80   100

60.4
REGIONAL AVERAGE
(ASIA-PACIFIC REGION)

60.9
WORLD AVERAGE

NOTABLE SUCCESSES:
Tax Policy and
Government Spending

CONCERNS:
Investment Freedom, Financial
Freedom, and Government Integrity

**OVERALL SCORE CHANGE
SINCE 2013:**
+3.4

FREEDOM TREND

80

70

60

50

40

2008 2009 2010 2011 2012 2013 2014 2015 2016 2017

QUICK FACTS

POPULATION:
0.8 million

GDP (PPP):
$6.4 billion
7.7% growth in 2015
5-year compound
annual growth 7.1%
$8,201 per capita

UNEMPLOYMENT:
2.6%

INFLATION (CPI):
7.2%

FDI INFLOW:
$12.1 million

PUBLIC DEBT:
115.7% of GDP

2015 data unless otherwise noted. Data compiled as of September 2016

BACKGROUND: Bhutan is a small Himalayan constitutional monarchy that made the transition from absolute monarchy to parliamentary democracy in March 2008. In July 2013, it completed its second democratic handover of power after Prime Minister Tshering Tobgay's People's Democratic Party won the majority of seats in the National Assembly. Bhutan has one of the world's smallest and least-developed economies. Until a few decades ago, it was agrarian with few roads, little electricity, and no modern hospitals. Recent interregional economic cooperation, particularly involving trade with Bangladesh and India, is helping to encourage economic growth. Connections to global markets are limited and dominated significantly by India.

12 ECONOMIC FREEDOMS | BHUTAN

BHUTAN

RULE OF LAW

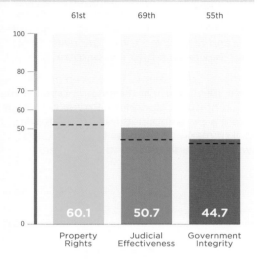

61st	69th	55th
60.1	**50.7**	**44.7**
Property Rights	Judicial Effectiveness	Government Integrity

Introduction of a computerized land information system has made it easier to transfer property. Since 2007, Bhutan has moved decisively toward the judicially based rule of law, and its judiciary is now considered generally independent. The law provides criminal penalties for corruption by officials, and the government generally implements those laws effectively, although there are isolated reports of government corruption.

GOVERNMENT SIZE

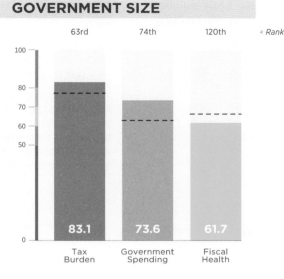

63rd	74th	120th	◄ Rank
83.1	**73.6**	**61.7**	
Tax Burden	Government Spending	Fiscal Health	

The top income tax rate is 25 percent, and the corporate tax rate is 30 percent. Other taxes include a property tax and an excise tax. The overall tax burden equals 13.0 percent of total domestic income. Government spending has amounted to 29.6 percent of total output (GDP) over the past three years, and budget deficits have averaged 3.4 percent of GDP. Public debt is equivalent to 115.7 percent of GDP.

REGULATORY EFFICIENCY

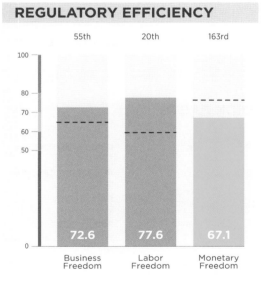

55th	20th	163rd
72.6	**77.6**	**67.1**
Business Freedom	Labor Freedom	Monetary Freedom

A modern regulatory framework has not been fully developed. Despite recent efforts, the business climate remains hampered by inconsistent enforcement of regulations and a lack of transparency. The labor supply-and-demand imbalance persists. India provides subsidized liquefied petroleum gas and kerosene to Bhutan and is cofinancing numerous hydropower projects. The state maintains significant financial and commercial controls.

OPEN MARKETS

168th	166th	133rd	◄ Rank
60.0	**20.0**	**30.0**	
Trade Freedom	Investment Freedom	Financial Freedom	

Trade is extremely important to Bhutan's economy; the value of exports and imports taken together equals 116 percent of GDP. The average applied tariff rate is 10.0 percent. Investment in some sectors is restricted. Bhutan needs a more efficient banking sector to mobilize savings and channel long-term capital to facilitate private-sector development. An underdeveloped regulatory framework limits access to capital.

WORLD RANK: **35** | REGIONAL RANK: **9**

ECONOMIC FREEDOM STATUS:
MODERATELY FREE

BRUNEI

Oil and gas revenue have helped to make Brunei one of the world's richest economies, but long-standing efforts to modernize the economic structure have met with only limited success. Recently, a higher priority has been placed on measures to diversify the economy and attract more foreign investment, and the corporate tax rate has been cut to 18.5 percent.

With oil revenues down, fiscal adjustments have been at the forefront of reform efforts, particularly in terms of improving the efficiency and composition of public spending. Brunei continues to benefit from moderately well-maintained monetary stability and a relatively high level of market openness that facilitates engagement with the world through trade and investment.

ECONOMIC FREEDOM SCORE

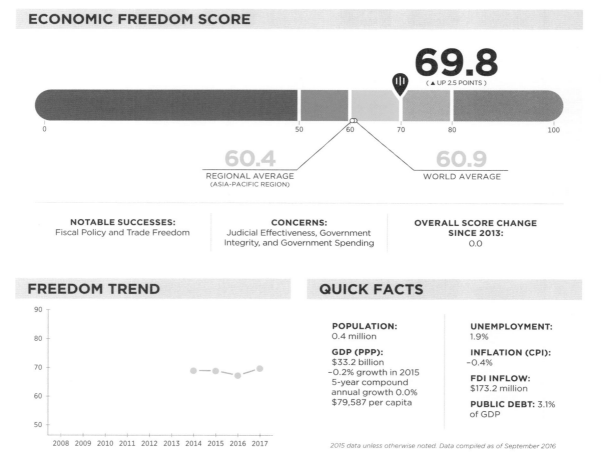

69.8
(▲ UP 2.5 POINTS)

0   50   60   70   80   100

60.4
REGIONAL AVERAGE
(ASIA-PACIFIC REGION)

60.9
WORLD AVERAGE

NOTABLE SUCCESSES:
Fiscal Policy and Trade Freedom

CONCERNS:
Judicial Effectiveness, Government Integrity, and Government Spending

OVERALL SCORE CHANGE SINCE 2013:
0.0

FREEDOM TREND

90
80
70
60
50

2008 2009 2010 2011 2012 2013 2014 2015 2016 2017

QUICK FACTS

POPULATION:
0.4 million

GDP (PPP):
$33.2 billion
–0.2% growth in 2015
5-year compound
annual growth 0.0%
$79,587 per capita

UNEMPLOYMENT:
1.9%

INFLATION (CPI):
–0.4%

FDI INFLOW:
$173.2 million

PUBLIC DEBT: 3.1%
of GDP

2015 data unless otherwise noted. Data compiled as of September 2016

BACKGROUND: Brunei, two small disconnected enclaves surrounded by the Malaysian state of Sarawak, lies on the northern coast of Borneo. The sultan serves as his own prime minister, minister of defense, foreign minister, and minister of finance. He is advised by several councils, including a Legislative Council and Privy Council, which he appoints. The oil and gas industry accounts for over half of GDP and 90 percent of government revenues. However, it generates only a small fraction of employment, and most of the population works directly for the government. Brunei has extremely low manufacturing capacity and imports most of its manufactured goods and food.

12 ECONOMIC FREEDOMS | BRUNEI

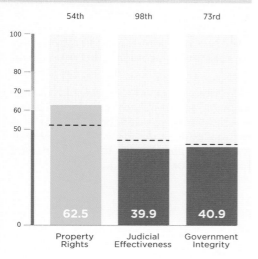

RULE OF LAW

54th	98th	73rd
Property Rights	Judicial Effectiveness	Government Integrity
62.5	39.9	40.9

Protection of private property is weak. Only citizens may purchase land; foreign firms must have a local partner. The constitution does not provide for an independent judiciary. Brunei is one of the world's last remaining autocracies, and Sultan Hassanal Bolkiah wields nearly absolute powers. In 2016, the government slowed the planned full implementation of sharia (Islamic) law because it might jeopardize Brunei's inclusion in the Trans-Pacific Partnership trade pact.

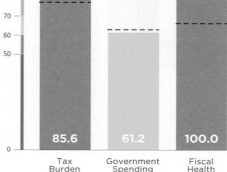

GOVERNMENT SIZE

47th	110th	1st	◄ Rank
Tax Burden	Government Spending	Fiscal Health	
85.6	61.2	100.0	

Brunei has no personal income tax. The top corporate tax rate is 18.5 percent for most companies; the rate for oil and gas companies is 55 percent. The overall tax burden equals 33.1 percent of total domestic income. Government spending has amounted to 36 percent of total output (GDP) over the past three years, and budget surpluses have averaged 1.9 percent of GDP. Public debt is equivalent to 3.1 percent of GDP.

BRUNEI

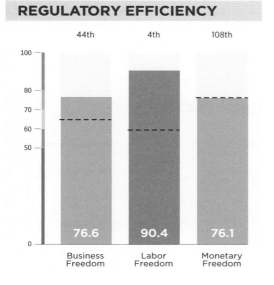

REGULATORY EFFICIENCY

44th	4th	108th
Business Freedom	Labor Freedom	Monetary Freedom
76.6	90.4	76.1

Registration requirements for starting a business have been simplified, and a one-stop shop now facilitates the overall operation of small and medium-size enterprises. The labor market is relatively flexible. The government provides large price-distorting subsidies for nearly everything the average citizen needs (for example, fuel, power, food, health care, and education).

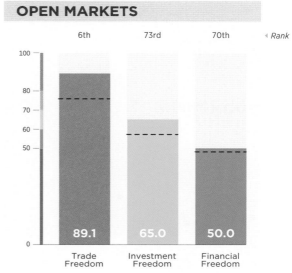

OPEN MARKETS

6th	73rd	70th	◄ Rank
Trade Freedom	Investment Freedom	Financial Freedom	
89.1	65.0	50.0	

Trade is extremely important to Brunei's economy; the value of exports and imports taken together equals 107 percent of GDP. The average applied tariff rate is only 0.5 percent. State-owned enterprises distort the economy, and foreign ownership of land is restricted. The small financial sector remains dominated by banks, which are well capitalized. Islamic financial services have grown considerably in recent years.

BURMA

WORLD RANK: **146**   **REGIONAL RANK:** **34**

ECONOMIC FREEDOM STATUS:
MOSTLY UNFREE

Burma's economy has undergone notable changes. Economic sanctions have been eased or lifted, and the government has launched reforms to modernize the economic system. A new banking and finance law that lays the foundations for more efficient licensing of financial institutions has been ratified. In 2016, the lower house of parliament also approved a new investment law.

Long-standing structural problems include poor public finance management and underdeveloped legal and regulatory frameworks. Fragile monetary stability largely reflects excessive money creation to fund fiscal deficits. Arbitrary taxation policies and marginal enforcement of property rights have driven many enterprises into the informal sector.

ECONOMIC FREEDOM SCORE

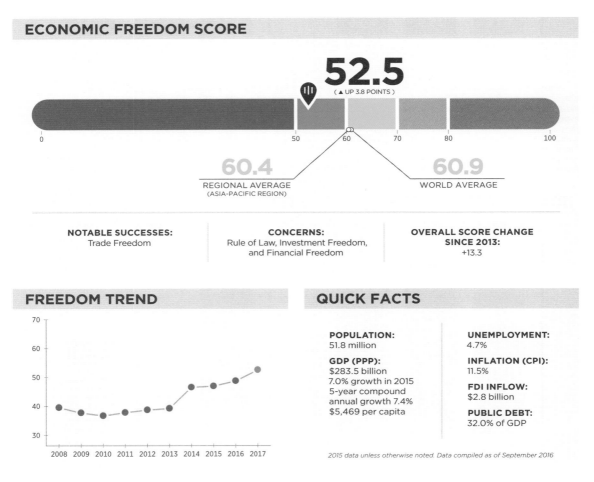

52.5
(▲ UP 3.8 POINTS)

0   50   60   70   80   100

60.4
REGIONAL AVERAGE
(ASIA-PACIFIC REGION)

60.9
WORLD AVERAGE

NOTABLE SUCCESSES:	CONCERNS:	OVERALL SCORE CHANGE SINCE 2013:
Trade Freedom	Rule of Law, Investment Freedom, and Financial Freedom	+13.3

FREEDOM TREND

70

60

50

40

30

2008 2009 2010 2011 2012 2013 2014 2015 2016 2017

QUICK FACTS

POPULATION:
51.8 million

GDP (PPP):
$283.5 billion
7.0% growth in 2015
5-year compound
annual growth 7.4%
$5,469 per capita

UNEMPLOYMENT:
4.7%

INFLATION (CPI):
11.5%

FDI INFLOW:
$2.8 billion

PUBLIC DEBT:
32.0% of GDP

2015 data unless otherwise noted. Data compiled as of September 2016

BACKGROUND: Burma's slow transition from military dictatorship continues. Beginning in 2010, it experimented with some political and economic reform. National League for Democracy leader Aung San Suu Kyi, released from jail in November 2010, now acts as state counsellor and leader of the NLD. Following a general election in 2015 that gave the NLD an absolute majority, parliament elected Suu Kyi confidant Htin Kyaw as president. The army remains a major political force and controls several cabinet portfolios, including defense, foreign, border, and home affairs. The United States and the European Union have continued to ease sanctions in response to political changes, but sectarian violence and persecution of Muslims and Christians continue.

12 ECONOMIC FREEDOMS | BURMA

RULE OF LAW

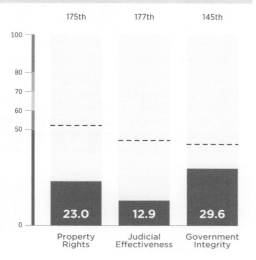

175th	177th	145th
23.0	12.9	29.6
Property Rights	Judicial Effectiveness	Government Integrity

Protection of property rights is weak. There continue to be numerous cases of sometimes violent land-grabs and forced evictions without sufficient compensation by state security officials. The judiciary is not independent, and judicial decisions are heavily influenced by the executive. The budget process has become more open, but the government has not taken significant steps to curb rampant national and local corruption.

GOVERNMENT SIZE

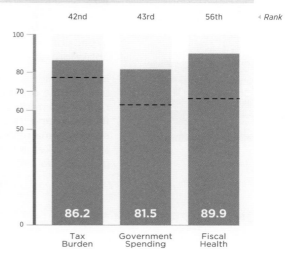

42nd	43rd	56th	◄ Rank
86.2	81.5	89.9	
Tax Burden	Government Spending	Fiscal Health	

The top individual income tax rate is 20 percent, and the top corporate tax rate is 30 percent. Other taxes include commercial and capital gains taxes. The overall tax burden equals 9.2 percent of total domestic income. Government spending has amounted to 24.8 percent of total output (GDP) over the past three years, and budget deficits have averaged 2.2 percent of GDP. Public debt is equivalent to 32.0 percent of GDP.

REGULATORY EFFICIENCY

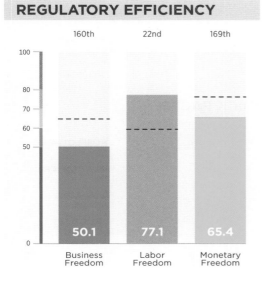

160th	22nd	169th
50.1	77.1	65.4
Business Freedom	Labor Freedom	Monetary Freedom

The regulatory system lacks transparency and clarity, and inconsistent enforcement of regulations injects uncertainty into business decision-making. The labor market lacks flexibility, and informal-sector employment is substantial. The government intends to make public spending more efficient, improve budget transparency, and privatize some loss-making state-owned enterprises.

OPEN MARKETS

113th	166th	162nd	◄ Rank
74.2	20.0	20.0	
Trade Freedom	Investment Freedom	Financial Freedom	

Trade is moderately important to Burma's economy; the value of exports and imports taken together equals 34 percent of GDP. The average applied tariff rate is 2.9 percent. Several sectors, including land ownership, are closed to foreign investment, and state-owned enterprises significantly distort the economy. Four foreign banks were permitted to operate in 2016, adding to the nine that were licensed in 2014. State-owned banks still account for more than half of total banking-sector assets.

CAMBODIA

WORLD RANK:
94

REGIONAL RANK:
20

ECONOMIC FREEDOM STATUS:
MOSTLY UNFREE

Cambodia's continuing efforts to integrate more fully into the global trading framework have contributed to high growth rates. Public finance is sound, with modest deficits and a moderate level of debt. Promotion of foreign investment and expansion of small and medium-size enterprises are important priorities.

However, lingering institutional weaknesses hold back the emergence of a more dynamic private sector. Weak property rights and pervasive corruption continue to constrain economic freedom, and institutionalization of a more independent judicial system remains a key area for reform. The rigidity of the formal labor market is partly responsible for the existence of an underground dual labor market.

ECONOMIC FREEDOM SCORE

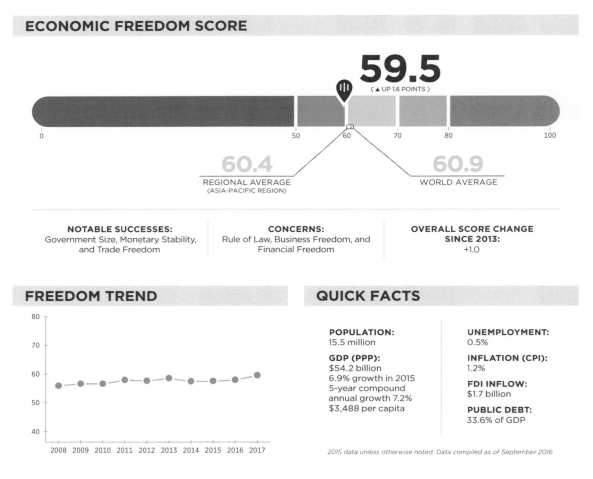

59.5
(▲ UP 1.6 POINTS)

0   50   60   70   80   100

60.4
REGIONAL AVERAGE
(ASIA-PACIFIC REGION)

60.9
WORLD AVERAGE

NOTABLE SUCCESSES:
Government Size, Monetary Stability, and Trade Freedom

CONCERNS:
Rule of Law, Business Freedom, and Financial Freedom

OVERALL SCORE CHANGE SINCE 2013:
+1.0

FREEDOM TREND

80
70
60
50
40

2008 2009 2010 2011 2012 2013 2014 2015 2016 2017

QUICK FACTS

POPULATION:
15.5 million

GDP (PPP):
$54.2 billion
6.9% growth in 2015
5-year compound
annual growth 7.2%
$3,488 per capita

UNEMPLOYMENT:
0.5%

INFLATION (CPI):
1.2%

FDI INFLOW:
$1.7 billion

PUBLIC DEBT:
33.6% of GDP

2015 data unless otherwise noted. Data compiled as of September 2016

BACKGROUND: Nominally a democracy, Cambodia has been ruled by former Khmer Rouge member Prime Minister Hun Sen since 1985. The general election victory of Hun Sen's Cambodian People's Party in 2013 was hotly contested by the opposition Cambodia National Rescue Party. In July 2014, after Hun Sen promised to initiate electoral reform, both parties agreed to suspend protests and reconvene government. Those reforms were only partially implemented. In 2016, democracy was in retreat. Opposition leaders have been silenced, government security forces allegedly beat up opposition parliamentarians, and at least 27 people are being held as political prisoners. Cambodia's economy remains heavily dependent on tourism and apparel assembly.

12 ECONOMIC FREEDOMS | CAMBODIA

RULE OF LAW

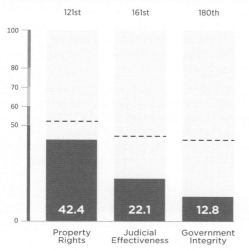

121st — Property Rights: **42.4**
161st — Judicial Effectiveness: **22.1**
180th — Government Integrity: **12.8**

Property rights are regularly abused in the name of development. Powerful politicians, bureaucrats, and military officers have used state-sanctioned seizures to grab an estimated 12 percent or more of Cambodia's land. The judiciary is politicized and marred by inefficiency, poorly trained judges, and a lack of independence. Corruption remains a serious obstacle to economic development and social stability.

GOVERNMENT SIZE

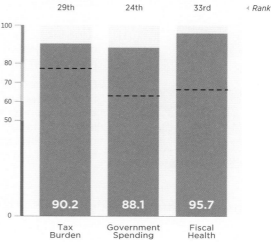

29th — Tax Burden: **90.2**
24th — Government Spending: **88.1**
33rd — Fiscal Health: **95.7**

◂ Rank

The top individual income and corporate tax rates are 20 percent. Other taxes include an excise tax and a value-added tax. The overall tax burden equals 13.4 percent of total domestic income. Government spending has amounted to 19.9 percent of total output (GDP) over the past three years, and budget deficits have averaged 1.1 percent of GDP. Public debt is equivalent to 33.6 percent of GDP.

REGULATORY EFFICIENCY

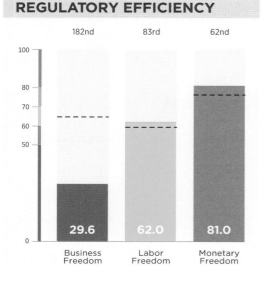

182nd — Business Freedom: **29.6**
83rd — Labor Freedom: **62.0**
62nd — Monetary Freedom: **81.0**

Measures to modernize commercial codes and facilitate private-sector development have been implemented in recent years. All sectors of the economy are open to foreign competition and investment. Labor force participation is high, but many jobs are informal. In 2016, drought conditions led the government to introduce de facto subsidies by exempting agricultural products from the value-added tax.

OPEN MARKETS

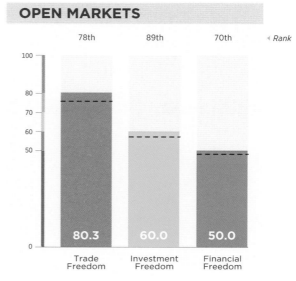

78th — Trade Freedom: **80.3**
89th — Investment Freedom: **60.0**
70th — Financial Freedom: **50.0**

◂ Rank

Trade is extremely important to Cambodia's economy; the value of exports and imports taken together equals 142 percent of GDP. The average applied tariff rate is 4.9 percent. New foreign investment may be screened by the government. Privatization and consolidation have gradually improved the efficiency of the banking sector. Banking has become more market-oriented, and credit to the private sector has increased.

CHINA

China's economy remains "mostly unfree," and there is little momentum for reform. Despite a nominal openness to trade and investment, bureaucratic hurdles and resistance from vested interests in the state sector are substantial barriers to more dynamic economic development. Confronting a period of economic slowdown, the government has increased expansionary fiscal and monetary interventions.

Deep-seated structural problems, including a state-controlled financial sector and regulatory inefficiency, have become more acute. Accumulating debt at various levels of the economy increases long-term risks. The legal system's vulnerability to political influence and Communist Party directives undercuts the rule of law and adds uncertainty to economic activity.

WORLD RANK:
111

REGIONAL RANK:
24

ECONOMIC FREEDOM STATUS:
MOSTLY UNFREE

ECONOMIC FREEDOM SCORE

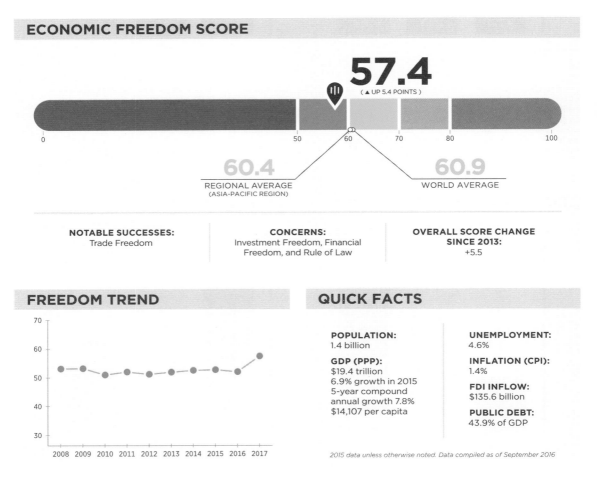

57.4
(▲ UP 5.4 POINTS)

| 0 | 50 | 60 | 70 | 80 | 100 |

60.4
REGIONAL AVERAGE
(ASIA-PACIFIC REGION)

60.9
WORLD AVERAGE

NOTABLE SUCCESSES:
Trade Freedom

CONCERNS:
Investment Freedom, Financial Freedom, and Rule of Law

OVERALL SCORE CHANGE SINCE 2013:
+5.5

FREEDOM TREND

QUICK FACTS

POPULATION:
1.4 billion

GDP (PPP):
$19.4 trillion
6.9% growth in 2015
5-year compound annual growth 7.8%
$14,107 per capita

UNEMPLOYMENT:
4.6%

INFLATION (CPI):
1.4%

FDI INFLOW:
$135.6 billion

PUBLIC DEBT:
43.9% of GDP

2015 data unless otherwise noted. Data compiled as of September 2016

BACKGROUND: After more than three years in power, Communist Party General Secretary Xi Jinping's regime has failed to produce any significant progress in economic reform. State-owned enterprises still dominate the financial sector and many basic industries. Total national debt (household, corporate, and government) has approached 300 percent of GDP, a level comparable to crisis-ridden southern Europe. The anticorruption campaign is popular with the public but has reduced provincial spending and economic growth. The slowdown in economic growth, which may be more severe than reflected in official statistics, poses serious challenges for a government whose legitimacy, more now than in the past, depends on its ability to increase living standards throughout the large population.

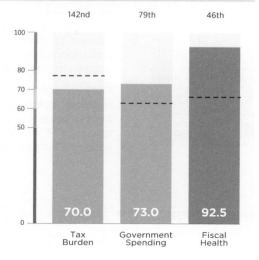

KEY: — — WORLD AVERAGE

12 ECONOMIC FREEDOMS | CHINA

RULE OF LAW

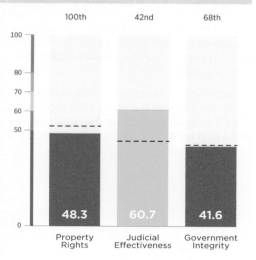

100th	42nd	68th
48.3	60.7	41.6
Property Rights	Judicial Effectiveness	Government Integrity

The state owns all land, and protection of foreign intellectual property continues to erode. Xi Jinping's anticorruption campaign accelerated in 2016, but corruption remains endemic, and the leadership has rejected more fundamental reforms such as requiring public disclosure of assets by officials, creating genuinely independent oversight bodies, or lifting political constraints on journalists and law enforcement agencies.

GOVERNMENT SIZE

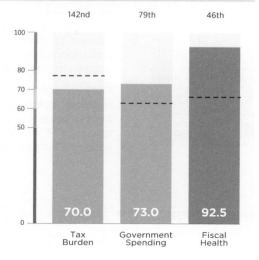

142nd	79th	46th	◄ Rank
70.0	73.0	92.5	
Tax Burden	Government Spending	Fiscal Health	

The top personal income tax rate is 45 percent, and the top corporate tax rate is 25 percent. Other taxes include a value-added tax and a real estate tax. The overall tax burden equals 18.7 percent of total domestic income. Government spending has amounted to 30 percent of total output (GDP) over the past three years, and budget deficits have averaged 1.5 percent of GDP. Public debt is equivalent to 43.9 of GDP.

REGULATORY EFFICIENCY

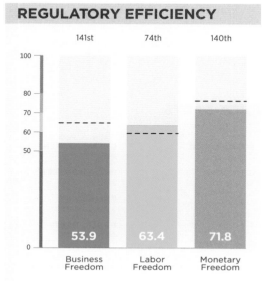

141st	74th	140th
53.9	63.4	71.8
Business Freedom	Labor Freedom	Monetary Freedom

Elimination of the minimum capital requirement has made it easier to launch a new business, but the overall regulatory framework remains complex, arbitrary, and uneven. The labor regime continues to be repressive. The government props up numerous inefficient state-owned enterprises and funds a vast array of subsidies for manufactured exports, energy, agriculture, and consumer goods.

OPEN MARKETS

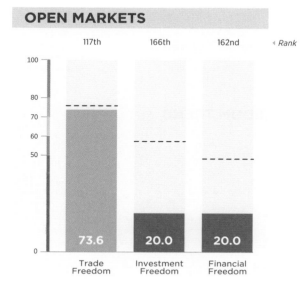

117th	166th	162nd	◄ Rank
73.6	20.0	20.0	
Trade Freedom	Investment Freedom	Financial Freedom	

Overall, trade is only moderately important to China's economy; the value of exports and imports taken together equals 41 percent of GDP. The average applied tariff rate is 3.2 percent. Numerous state-owned enterprises distort the economy, and the state maintains its tight grip on the financial system. The government controls almost all of China's banks, which are facing a rise in the number of nonperforming loans.

CHINA

FIJI

Fiji's record in reforming underperforming institutions has been uneven, and economic growth is limited by lingering structural and policy weaknesses that constrain economic freedom. The rule of law is not strongly supported by the judicial system, particularly because of growing corruption. Inefficient and high public spending has resulted in a considerable fiscal burden imposed on the population.

The government has implemented a series of pro-business reforms, including simplification of the business start-up process, in an effort to enhance regulatory efficiency. However, the pace of reform has slowed in recent years, and policies to open markets further have not been advanced.

WORLD RANK: **71** **REGIONAL RANK:** **16**

ECONOMIC FREEDOM STATUS:
MODERATELY FREE

ECONOMIC FREEDOM SCORE

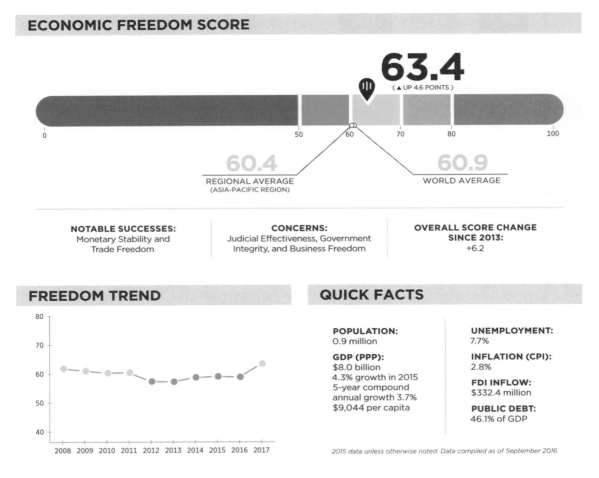

63.4
(▲ UP 4.6 POINTS)

0   50   60   70   80   100

60.4
REGIONAL AVERAGE
(ASIA-PACIFIC REGION)

60.9
WORLD AVERAGE

NOTABLE SUCCESSES:
Monetary Stability and Trade Freedom

CONCERNS:
Judicial Effectiveness, Government Integrity, and Business Freedom

OVERALL SCORE CHANGE SINCE 2013:
+6.2

FREEDOM TREND

QUICK FACTS

POPULATION:
0.9 million

GDP (PPP):
$8.0 billion
4.3% growth in 2015
5-year compound annual growth 3.7%
$9,044 per capita

UNEMPLOYMENT:
7.7%

INFLATION (CPI):
2.8%

FDI INFLOW:
$332.4 million

PUBLIC DEBT:
46.1% of GDP

2015 data unless otherwise noted. Data compiled as of September 2016

BACKGROUND: Military strongman Commodore Frank Bainimarama has ruled the Pacific island nation of Fiji for a decade. There is a long history of ethnic tension between the indigenous, mostly Christian population and a large minority of Hindu and Muslim Indo–Fijians. Sanctions imposed in 2006 by Fiji's main trading partners, including the European Union and Australia, in reaction to the coup that installed Bainimarama hurt vital agriculture, apparel, and fishing industries. In September 2014, in Fiji's first election since 2006, Bainimarama was elected prime minister. Soon after the election, Australia and the United States lifted their sanctions. Fiji's economy relies heavily on tourism, remittances, and the sugar industry.

12 ECONOMIC FREEDOMS | FIJI

RULE OF LAW

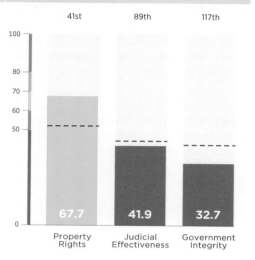

	41st	89th	117th
Property Rights	67.7		
Judicial Effectiveness		41.9	
Government Integrity			32.7

Protection of property rights is highly uncertain. Obtaining land titles is difficult. Only 8 percent of land is freehold; the rest is indigenous and government land and can only be leased. The judiciary is constitutionally independent but subject to executive influence. The parliamentary opposition is pushing for more transparent administration, but the government's heavy-handed tactics seriously undermine democratic accountability.

GOVERNMENT SIZE

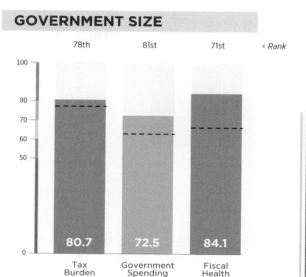

	78th	81st	71st	◄ Rank
Tax Burden	80.7			
Government Spending		72.5		
Fiscal Health			84.1	

The top individual income tax rate is 29 percent, and the top corporate tax rate is 20 percent. Other taxes include a value-added tax and a land sales tax. The overall tax burden equals 26.3 percent of total domestic income. Government spending has amounted to 30.3 percent of total output (GDP) over the past three years, and budget deficits have averaged 2.7 percent of GDP. Public debt is equivalent to 46.1 percent of GDP.

REGULATORY EFFICIENCY

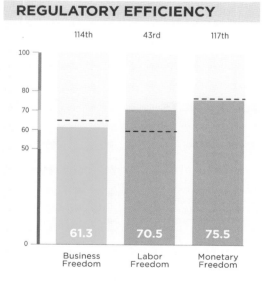

	114th	43rd	117th
Business Freedom	61.3		
Labor Freedom		70.5	
Monetary Freedom			75.5

Despite some progress, procedures for establishing and running a private enterprise are still time-consuming and costly. Labor regulations remain rigid, and an efficient labor market has not been developed. The government's budget for fiscal year 2016–2017 contained subsidies on imported building materials for post-cyclone rebuilding of roads, bridges, water supplies, sanitation, and rural electrification.

OPEN MARKETS

	140th	103rd	70th	◄ Rank
Trade Freedom	68.8			
Investment Freedom		55.0		
Financial Freedom			50.0	

Trade is extremely important to Fiji's economy; the value of exports and imports taken together equals 137 percent of GDP. The average applied tariff rate is 10.6 percent. Foreign investment is screened, and investment in land is restricted. State-owned enterprises distort the economy. The government has withdrawn from commercial banking, and foreign participation is significant. Controls on foreign exchange have been eased.

HONG KONG

WORLD RANK: 1 | **REGIONAL RANK:** 1

ECONOMIC FREEDOM STATUS:
FREE

Hong Kong has demonstrated a high degree of economic resilience and remains one of the world's most competitive financial and business hubs. The high-quality legal framework, which provides effective protection of property rights and strong support for the rule of law, continues to be a cornerstone of strength for this dynamic city. There is little tolerance for corruption, and government integrity is buttressed by a high degree of transparency.

Regulatory efficiency and openness to global commerce strongly support entrepreneurial activity. Interaction with China has become more intense through strengthened financial and other noneconomic linkages, and Hong Kong is by far the most significant transit point for exports and imports to and from China.

ECONOMIC FREEDOM SCORE

89.8
(▲ UP 1.2 POINTS)

0   50   60   70   80   100

60.4
REGIONAL AVERAGE
(ASIA-PACIFIC REGION)

60.9
WORLD AVERAGE

NOTABLE SUCCESSES:
Government Size, Open Markets, and Regulatory Efficiency

CONCERNS:
Government Integrity and Judicial Effectiveness

OVERALL SCORE CHANGE SINCE 2013:
+0.5

FREEDOM TREND

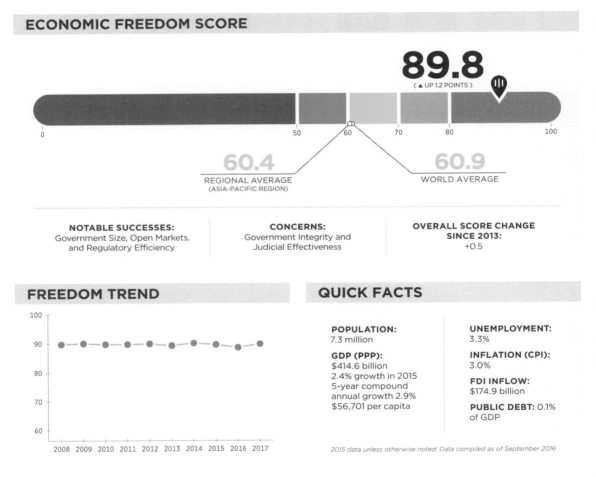

QUICK FACTS

POPULATION:
7.3 million

GDP (PPP):
$414.6 billion
2.4% growth in 2015
5-year compound
annual growth 2.9%
$56,701 per capita

UNEMPLOYMENT:
3.3%

INFLATION (CPI):
3.0%

FDI INFLOW:
$174.9 billion

PUBLIC DEBT: 0.1%
of GDP

2015 data unless otherwise noted. Data compiled as of September 2016

BACKGROUND: Hong Kong became part of the People's Republic of China (PRC) in 1997. Under the "one country, two systems" agreement, China promised not to impose its socialist policies on Hong Kong and to allow Hong Kong a high degree of autonomy in all matters except foreign and defense policy for 50 years. This autonomy policy has been stressed by political interference from the PRC in recent years. Major industries include financial services and shipping; manufacturing has largely migrated to Mainland China and other Southeast Asian economies.

12 ECONOMIC FREEDOMS | HONG KONG

RULE OF LAW

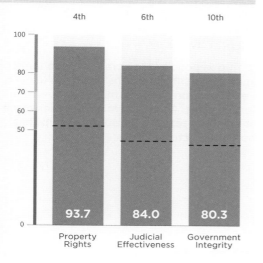

	Property Rights	Judicial Effectiveness	Government Integrity
Rank	4th	6th	10th
Score	93.7	84.0	80.3

Private ownership of property is enshrined in the Basic Law, which is Hong Kong's constitution. Commercial and company laws provide for effective enforcement of contracts and protection of corporate rights. The judiciary is independent, but Beijing reserves the right to make final interpretations of the Basic Law, effectively limiting the power of Hong Kong's Court of Final Appeal. Hong Kong has an excellent track record in combating corruption.

GOVERNMENT SIZE

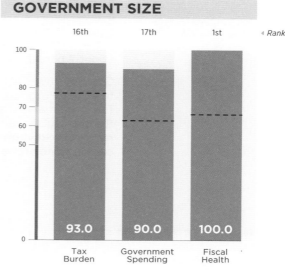

	Tax Burden	Government Spending	Fiscal Health	◄ Rank
Rank	16th	17th	1st	
Score	93.0	90.0	100.0	

The standard individual income tax rate is 15 percent, and the top corporate tax rate is 16.5 percent. The tax system is simple and efficient. The overall tax burden equals 14.4 percent of total domestic income. Government spending has amounted to 18.3 percent of total output (GDP) over the past three years, and budget surpluses have averaged 2.0 percent of GDP. Public debt is equivalent to 0.1 percent of GDP.

REGULATORY EFFICIENCY

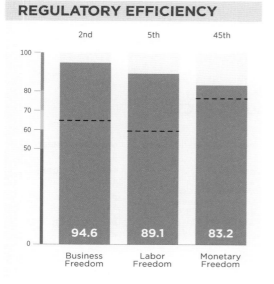

	Business Freedom	Labor Freedom	Monetary Freedom
Rank	2nd	5th	45th
Score	94.6	89.1	83.2

Business freedom is well protected within an efficient regulatory framework. Transparency encourages entrepreneurship, and the overall environment is conducive to the formation and operation of start-up businesses. The labor code is strictly enforced but not burdensome. Hong Kong has very few price controls, but it does fund some subsidies and regulates residential rents and prices for telecommunications, public transport, and electricity.

OPEN MARKETS

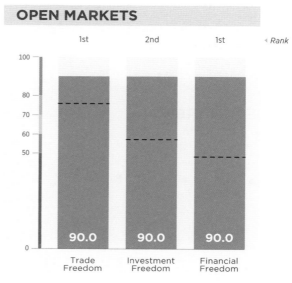

	Trade Freedom	Investment Freedom	Financial Freedom	◄ Rank
Rank	1st	2nd	1st	
Score	90.0	90.0	90.0	

Trade is extremely important to Hong Kong's economy; the value of exports and imports taken together equals 400 percent of GDP. The average applied tariff rate is zero percent. Hong Kong is very open to global trade and investment. The financial regulatory and legal environment focuses on ensuring transparency and enforcing prudent minimum standards. There are no restrictions on foreign banks, which are treated the same as domestic institutions.

WORLD RANK:
143

REGIONAL RANK:
33

ECONOMIC FREEDOM STATUS:
MOSTLY UNFREE

INDIA

India is a significant force in world trade. Corruption, under-developed infrastructure, and poor management of public finance continue to undermine overall development, although the economy has sustained an average annual growth rate of about 7 percent over the past five years.

Growth is not deeply rooted in policies that preserve economic freedom. Progress on market-oriented reforms has been uneven. The state maintains an extensive presence in many areas through public-sector enterprises. A restrictive and burdensome regulatory environment discourages the entrepreneurship that could provide broader private-sector growth.

ECONOMIC FREEDOM SCORE

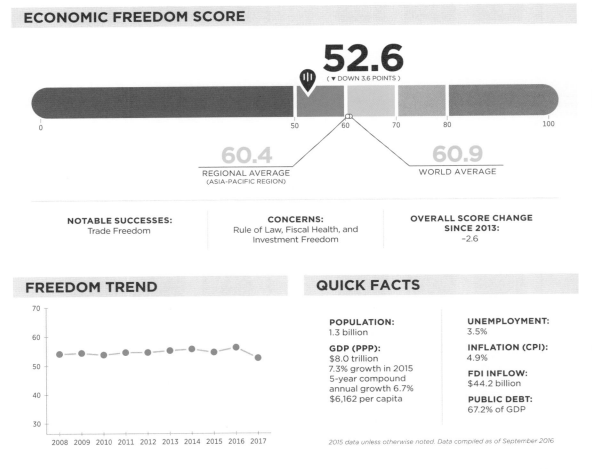

52.6
(▼ DOWN 3.6 POINTS)

0   50   60   70   80   100

60.4
REGIONAL AVERAGE
(ASIA-PACIFIC REGION)

60.9
WORLD AVERAGE

NOTABLE SUCCESSES:
Trade Freedom

CONCERNS:
Rule of Law, Fiscal Health, and Investment Freedom

OVERALL SCORE CHANGE SINCE 2013:
−2.6

FREEDOM TREND

70

60

50

40

30

2008 2009 2010 2011 2012 2013 2014 2015 2016 2017

QUICK FACTS

POPULATION:
1.3 billion

GDP (PPP):
$8.0 trillion
7.3% growth in 2015
5-year compound
annual growth 6.7%
$6,162 per capita

UNEMPLOYMENT:
3.5%

INFLATION (CPI):
4.9%

FDI INFLOW:
$44.2 billion

PUBLIC DEBT:
67.2% of GDP

2015 data unless otherwise noted. Data compiled as of September 2016

BACKGROUND: India is a stable democracy. It is 80 percent Hindu but also home to one of the world's largest Muslim populations. Prime Minister Narendra Modi, leader of the Bharatiya Janata Party, took office in 2014 and is credited with reinvigorating India's foreign policy. Modi, who in June 2016 made his fourth visit to the United States in two years, has bolstered ties with the U.S., particularly in defense cooperation. India has technology and manufacturing sectors as advanced as any in the world as well as traditional sectors characteristic of a lesser developed economy. Extreme wealth and poverty coexist as the nation both modernizes rapidly and struggles to find paths to inclusive development for its large and diverse population.

132   2017 Index of Economic Freedom

12 ECONOMIC FREEDOMS | INDIA

RULE OF LAW

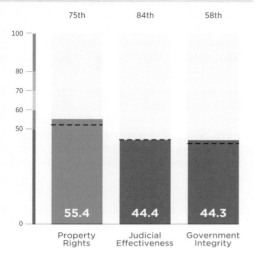

75th   84th   58th

55.4 Property Rights
44.4 Judicial Effectiveness
44.3 Government Integrity

Real property rights are generally well enforced in metropolitan areas, although titling remains unclear in many other urban and rural areas. The judiciary is independent, but courts are understaffed and lack the technology necessary to clear an enormous backlog. Domestic and international pressure led to passage of legislation aimed at addressing corruption, but there is little evidence that it is being implemented effectively.

GOVERNMENT SIZE

103rd   57th   170th   ◄ *Rank*

77.2 Tax Burden
77.4 Government Spending
11.0 Fiscal Health

The top individual income tax rate is 30.9 percent (including an education tax). The top corporate tax rate is 34.6 percent. The overall tax burden equals 16.6 percent of total domestic income. Government spending has amounted to 27.4 percent of total output (GDP) over the past three years, and budget deficits have averaged 7.3 percent of GDP. Public debt is equivalent to 67.2 percent of GDP.

REGULATORY EFFICIENCY

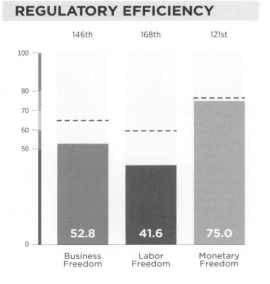

146th   168th   121st

52.8 Business Freedom
41.6 Labor Freedom
75.0 Monetary Freedom

The regulatory framework is burdensome, and the legal framework is weak. Labor regulations continue to evolve, and the informal economy is an important source of employment. Although the IMF reported in 2016 that India's "major subsidies" (e.g., on fuels and fertilizer) dropped below 2 percent of GDP, the government is introducing a new basic foods subsidy for around two-thirds of the population.

OPEN MARKETS

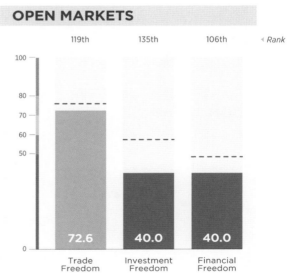

119th   135th   106th   ◄ *Rank*

72.6 Trade Freedom
40.0 Investment Freedom
40.0 Financial Freedom

Trade is moderately important to India's economy; the value of exports and imports taken together equals 49 percent of GDP. The average applied tariff rate is 6.2 percent. Foreign investment is screened, but ownership restrictions in some economic sectors have been reduced. State-owned enterprises distort the economy. Despite some liberalization and modernization, state-owned institutions dominate the banking sector and capital markets.

INDIA

84

REGIONAL RANK:
18

ECONOMIC FREEDOM STATUS:
MODERATELY FREE

INDONESIA

Indonesia's reform-minded government has undertaken some necessary structural adjustments with a focus on stamping out corruption, better managing public finance, and improving the business environment. Fuel subsidies have been cut dramatically in an effort to narrow fiscal deficits. The administration has also moved to dismantle some of the barriers that had been imposed on foreign investment.

Despite this progress, however, lingering institutional short-comings continue to undercut momentum for more dynamic economic development. In the absence of a well-functioning legal and regulatory framework, corruption remains a serious impediment to the emergence of a more dynamic private sector. The state's presence in the economy remains extensive through state-owned enterprises.

ECONOMIC FREEDOM SCORE

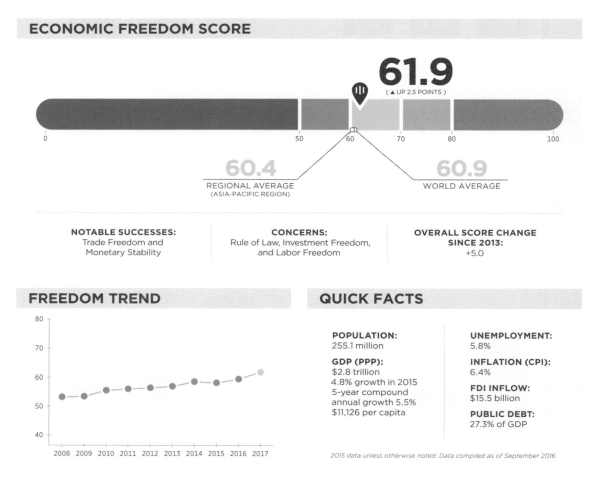

61.9
(▲ UP 2.5 POINTS)

0   50   60   70   80   100

60.4
REGIONAL AVERAGE
(ASIA-PACIFIC REGION)

60.9
WORLD AVERAGE

NOTABLE SUCCESSES:
Trade Freedom and
Monetary Stability

CONCERNS:
Rule of Law, Investment Freedom,
and Labor Freedom

**OVERALL SCORE CHANGE
SINCE 2013:**
+5.0

FREEDOM TREND

80
70
60
50
40

2008 2009 2010 2011 2012 2013 2014 2015 2016 2017

QUICK FACTS

POPULATION:
255.1 million

GDP (PPP):
$2.8 trillion
4.8% growth in 2015
5-year compound
annual growth 5.5%
$11,126 per capita

UNEMPLOYMENT:
5.8%

INFLATION (CPI):
6.4%

FDI INFLOW:
$15.5 billion

PUBLIC DEBT:
27.3% of GDP

2015 data unless otherwise noted. Data compiled as of September 2016

BACKGROUND: Indonesia is the world's most populous Muslim-majority democracy. Since 1998, when long-serving authoritarian ruler General Suharto stepped down, Indonesia's 250 million people have enjoyed a widening range of political freedoms, and participation in the political process is high. Joko Widodo, former businessman and governor of Jakarta, won a tight race for the presidency in 2014, pledging to end corruption and promote economic reform. As a member of the G20 and a driving force within the Association of Southeast Asian Nations, Indonesia plays a growing role at the multilateral level.

12 ECONOMIC FREEDOMS | INDONESIA

RULE OF LAW

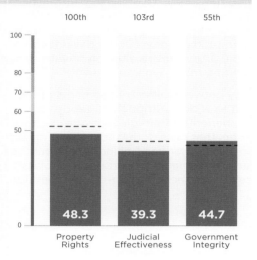

	100th	103rd	55th
	Property Rights **48.3**	Judicial Effectiveness **39.3**	Government Integrity **44.7**

Property rights are generally respected, but enforcement is inefficient and uneven, and registering property can be difficult. The judiciary has demonstrated independence in some cases, but the court system remains plagued by corruption and other weaknesses. The World Economic Forum's *Global Competitiveness Index* reports that anticorruption efforts are nevertheless paying off, with Indonesia improving on almost all measures related to bribery and ethics.

GOVERNMENT SIZE

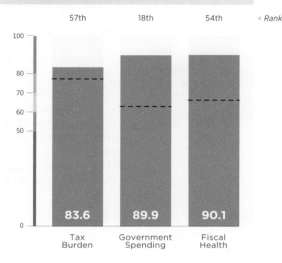

◀ Rank

	57th	18th	54th
	Tax Burden **83.6**	Government Spending **89.9**	Fiscal Health **90.1**

The top individual income tax rate is 30 percent, and the top corporate tax rate is 25 percent. Other taxes include a value-added tax and a property tax. The overall tax burden equals 10.9 percent of total domestic income. Government spending has amounted to 18.4 percent of total output (GDP) over the past three years, and budget deficits have averaged 2.3 percent of GDP. Public debt is equivalent to 27.3 percent of GDP.

REGULATORY EFFICIENCY

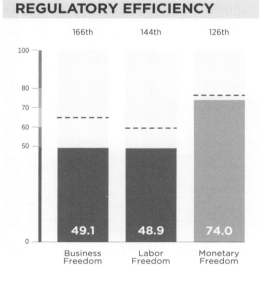

	166th	144th	126th
	Business Freedom **49.1**	Labor Freedom **48.9**	Monetary Freedom **74.0**

Indonesia's overall regulatory environment has improved over the years, but more commitment to reform is necessary to boost private investment and increase employment opportunities. The IMF commended Indonesia in 2016 for a "very successful" fuel subsidy reform that "serves as a model for other countries." Government energy subsidies are provided now only to the poorest consumers.

OPEN MARKETS

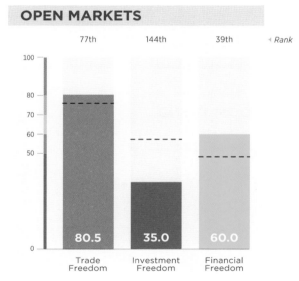

◀ Rank

	77th	144th	39th
	Trade Freedom **80.5**	Investment Freedom **35.0**	Financial Freedom **60.0**

Trade is moderately important to Indonesia's economy; the value of exports and imports taken together equals 42 percent of GDP. The average applied tariff rate is 2.3 percent. Foreign investment in several sectors of the economy is restricted, and state-owned enterprises distort the economy. Overall, banking supervision has been strengthened, and the efficiency of the system has increased. The state still owns a number of banks.

INDONESIA

JAPAN

WORLD RANK: **40** | REGIONAL RANK: **10**

ECONOMIC FREEDOM STATUS:
MODERATELY FREE

Economic freedom in Japan is buttressed by political stability and a well-maintained rule of law. Overcoming entrenched economic stagnation, however, will require serious efforts at reform that challenge long-established economic and cultural interests. A large public debt, the highest in the developed world as a percentage of GDP, has taken a toll on private-sector economic activity, preventing more dynamic growth.

Disparities in productivity between different segments of the economy have continued to widen. Although its export-oriented economy has long benefited from global trade, Japan still maintains nontariff barriers that raise domestic prices and hurt overall efficiency. Japan also has lagged behind other countries in pursuing bilateral trade agreements, in part because of its unwillingness to expose certain sectors to foreign competition.

ECONOMIC FREEDOM SCORE

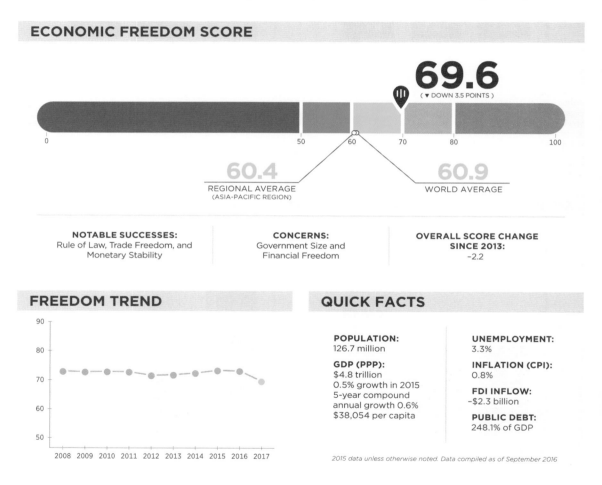

69.6
(▼ DOWN 3.5 POINTS)

0   50   60   70   80   100

60.4
REGIONAL AVERAGE
(ASIA-PACIFIC REGION)

60.9
WORLD AVERAGE

NOTABLE SUCCESSES:
Rule of Law, Trade Freedom, and Monetary Stability

CONCERNS:
Government Size and Financial Freedom

OVERALL SCORE CHANGE SINCE 2013:
−2.2

FREEDOM TREND

90
80
70
60
50

2008 2009 2010 2011 2012 2013 2014 2015 2016 2017

QUICK FACTS

POPULATION:
126.7 million

GDP (PPP):
$4.8 trillion
0.5% growth in 2015
5-year compound
annual growth 0.6%
$38,054 per capita

UNEMPLOYMENT:
3.3%

INFLATION (CPI):
0.8%

FDI INFLOW:
−$2.3 billion

PUBLIC DEBT:
248.1% of GDP

2015 data unless otherwise noted. Data compiled as of September 2016

BACKGROUND: Prime Minister Shinzo Abe has energized Japan's international security role by reducing constraints on the allowable roles and missions of its Self-Defense Forces. Japan and the United States have made sweeping changes in the bilateral alliance guidelines, enabling greater integrated security operations worldwide. Japan will now play a larger role in addressing international security challenges, including collective self-defense. Previously, for example, Japan was precluded from protecting U.S. forces deployed to defend Japan or even from transporting American munitions on Japanese ships.

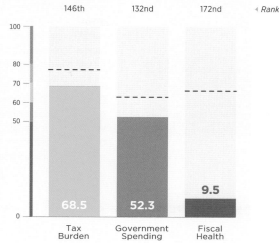

12 ECONOMIC FREEDOMS | JAPAN

RULE OF LAW

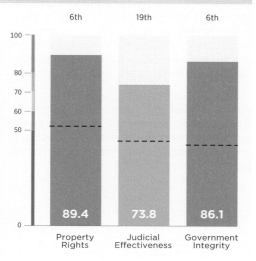

	6th	19th	6th
	Property Rights	Judicial Effectiveness	Government Integrity
	89.4	73.8	86.1

Japan's judiciary is independent and fair. It provides secure protection of real and intellectual property. The direct exchange of cash for favors from government officials is extremely rare. However, a web of close relationships among companies, politicians, government agencies, and other groups fosters a business climate that is conducive to corruption, most often seen in the rigging of bids on government public works projects.

GOVERNMENT SIZE

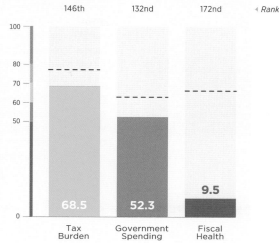

	146th	132nd	172nd	◀ Rank
	Tax Burden	Government Spending	Fiscal Health	
	68.5	52.3	9.5	

The top personal income tax rate is 40.8 percent. The top corporate tax rate is 23.9 percent, which local taxes and an enterprise tax can increase significantly. The overall tax burden equals 30.3 percent of total domestic income. Government spending has amounted to 39.9 percent of total output (GDP) over the past three years, and budget deficits have averaged 6.6 percent of GDP. Public debt is equivalent to 248.1 percent of GDP.

REGULATORY EFFICIENCY

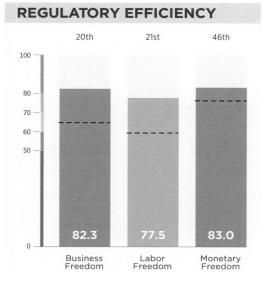

	20th	21st	46th
	Business Freedom	Labor Freedom	Monetary Freedom
	82.3	77.5	83.0

The process for establishing a business is relatively streamlined, but bureaucracy is sometimes stifling, and structural problems discourage entrepreneurial growth. A propensity for lifetime employment guarantees and seniority-based wages impedes the development of a dynamic and flexible labor market. The government has continued its efforts to scale back institutionalized farm subsidies and liberalize electricity markets.

OPEN MARKETS

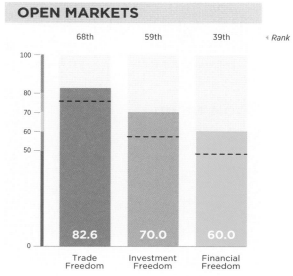

	68th	59th	39th	◀ Rank
	Trade Freedom	Investment Freedom	Financial Freedom	
	82.6	70.0	60.0	

Trade is moderately important to Japan's economy; the value of exports and imports taken together equals 37 percent of GDP. The average applied tariff rate is 1.2 percent. Many agricultural imports are restricted, and foreign investment in some sectors of the economy is screened by the government. The financial sector is competitive, but state involvement persists. Banks are well capitalized, and the share of nonperforming loans is low.

JAPAN

KAZAKHSTAN

WORLD RANK: **42** | **REGIONAL RANK:** **11**

ECONOMIC FREEDOM STATUS:
MODERATELY FREE

Kazakhstan's economy has benefited substantially from increased openness and flexibility over the past decade. Although the state continues to maintain its ownership in key enterprises, particularly in the energy sector, the economy is mostly in private hands, and more privatization is being sought. Beneficial structural reforms have included bank privatization, implementation of competitive flat tax rates, and modernization of the trade regime.

Deeper institutional reforms to reduce barriers to investment and increase the efficiency of the judiciary are critical to further success. Despite measures to expand the non-energy sector, the overall regulatory framework needs to be more streamlined to enhance competitiveness.

ECONOMIC FREEDOM SCORE

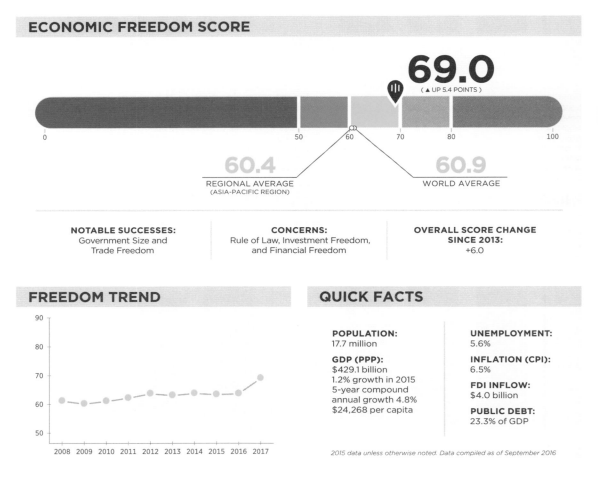

69.0
(▲ UP 5.4 POINTS)

0   50   60   70   80   100

60.4
REGIONAL AVERAGE
(ASIA-PACIFIC REGION)

60.9
WORLD AVERAGE

NOTABLE SUCCESSES:
Government Size and Trade Freedom

CONCERNS:
Rule of Law, Investment Freedom, and Financial Freedom

OVERALL SCORE CHANGE SINCE 2013:
+6.0

FREEDOM TREND

(chart: 2008 2009 2010 2011 2012 2013 2014 2015 2016 2017, values ranging approximately 60 to 69)

QUICK FACTS

POPULATION:
17.7 million

GDP (PPP):
$429.1 billion
1.2% growth in 2015
5-year compound annual growth 4.8%
$24,268 per capita

UNEMPLOYMENT:
5.6%

INFLATION (CPI):
6.5%

FDI INFLOW:
$4.0 billion

PUBLIC DEBT:
23.3% of GDP

2015 data unless otherwise noted. Data compiled as of September 2016

BACKGROUND: President Nursultan Nazarbayev, whose rule began in 1989 when Kazakhstan was still a Soviet republic, won a sixth five-year term in 2015. The opposition is marginalized, and the lack of a succession plan creates longer-term political uncertainty. Kazakhstan joined the Eurasian Economic Union, which includes Russia and Belarus, on January 1, 2015. The past year has been tumultuous for Kazakhstan. In April 2016, there were widespread protests against government land-reform plans. In June, a terrorist attack in the northwestern city of Aqtobe left 28 people dead. Modernization of the Atyrau, Shymkent, and Pavlodar refineries is due to be completed in 2018. Kazakhstan is also the world's largest producer of uranium.

12 ECONOMIC FREEDOMS | KAZAKHSTAN

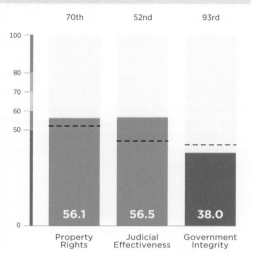

RULE OF LAW

70th	52nd	93rd
Property Rights	Judicial Effectiveness	Government Integrity
56.1	56.5	38.0

Property rights are not protected effectively, although the government has made enforcement of contracts easier by introducing a simplified fast-track procedure for small claims. Judges are subject to political influence, and bias is evident throughout the judicial system. Corruption is widespread, and those in positions of authority and individuals with ties to government or law enforcement officials may act with impunity.

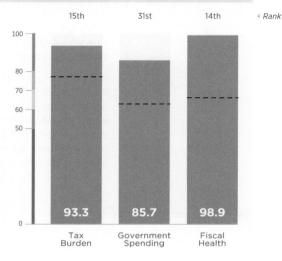

GOVERNMENT SIZE

15th	31st	14th	◂ Rank
Tax Burden	Government Spending	Fiscal Health	
93.3	85.7	98.9	

The flat personal income tax rate is 10 percent, and the standard corporate tax rate is 20 percent. Other taxes include a value-added tax and excise taxes. The overall tax burden equals 13.2 percent of total domestic income. Government spending has amounted to 21.8 percent of total output (GDP) over the past three years, and budget surpluses have averaged 0.5 percent of GDP. Public debt is equivalent to 23.3 percent of GDP.

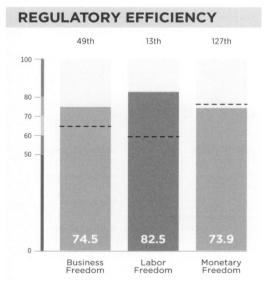

REGULATORY EFFICIENCY

49th	13th	127th
Business Freedom	Labor Freedom	Monetary Freedom
74.5	82.5	73.9

The regulatory framework has undergone a series of reforms. The private sector now faces fewer constraints, although there is still much room for institutional reform. Labor regulations are relatively flexible, facilitating the development of a more dynamic labor market. Kazakhstan is subsidizing renewable energy with the goal of having 10 percent of its needs met by renewables by 2030.

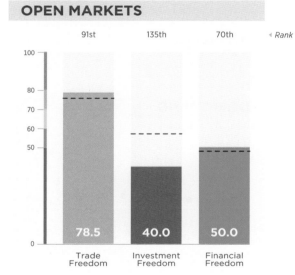

OPEN MARKETS

91st	135th	70th	◂ Rank
Trade Freedom	Investment Freedom	Financial Freedom	
78.5	40.0	50.0	

Trade is important to Kazakhstan's economy; the value of exports and imports taken together equals 53 percent of GDP. The average applied tariff rate is 3.3 percent. Foreign investment in some sectors of the economy is restricted, and state-owned enterprises distort the economy. The state has been providing additional support to the banking sector since 2014. The number of nonperforming loans continues to be high.

KAZAKHSTAN

KIRIBATI

Kiribati's economy is dominated by a public sector that accounts for two-thirds of formal employment and about half of GDP. Only a small proportion of the total labor force is employed on salaries, however; the rest work in subsistence farming or fishing. The economy relies heavily on foreign assistance and remittances.

Economic growth continues to be undermined by inefficient state-owned enterprises and regulations that hinder private-sector development. The government has tried to decentralize economic activity from the main islands, but progress has been very limited. The financial sector remains underdeveloped, leaving much of the population without formal access to banking services.

ECONOMIC FREEDOM SCORE

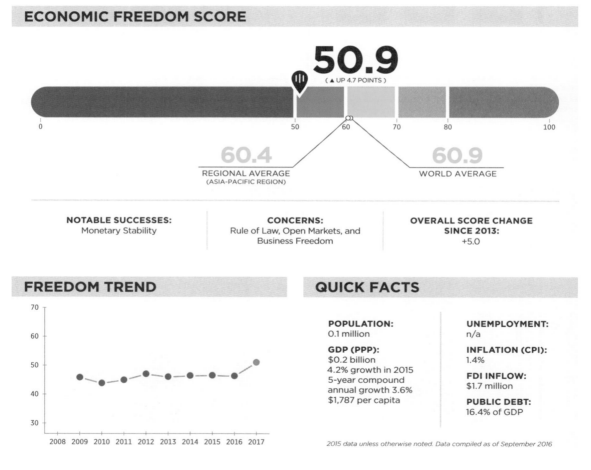

50.9
(▲ UP 4.7 POINTS)

0   50   60   70   80   100

60.4
REGIONAL AVERAGE
(ASIA-PACIFIC REGION)

60.9
WORLD AVERAGE

NOTABLE SUCCESSES:
Monetary Stability

CONCERNS:
Rule of Law, Open Markets, and Business Freedom

OVERALL SCORE CHANGE SINCE 2013:
+5.0

FREEDOM TREND

70

60

50

40

30

2008 2009 2010 2011 2012 2013 2014 2015 2016 2017

QUICK FACTS

POPULATION:
0.1 million

GDP (PPP):
$0.2 billion
4.2% growth in 2015
5-year compound annual growth 3.6%
$1,787 per capita

UNEMPLOYMENT:
n/a

INFLATION (CPI):
1.4%

FDI INFLOW:
$1.7 million

PUBLIC DEBT:
16.4% of GDP

2015 data unless otherwise noted. Data compiled as of September 2016

BACKGROUND: The Pacific archipelago of Kiribati gained its independence from Britain in 1979, and its government functions democratically. Elections in February 2016 ushered in new leadership, with Taneti Maamau of the Tobwaan Kiribati Party becoming president after 12 years of rule by Anote Tong of the Boutokaan te Koaua. Economic activity in Kiribati once centered on the mining of phosphates, but deposits were exhausted in 1979. However, a $500 million Revenue Equalization Reserve Fund created with mining revenues continues to provide significant revenue. Reliance on foreign assistance, remittances from overseas, fishing licenses, exports of fish and coconuts, and tourism is also heavy. Crippling algae in the corals surrounding Kiribati seriously threaten the fishing industry.

12 ECONOMIC FREEDOMS | KIRIBATI

RULE OF LAW

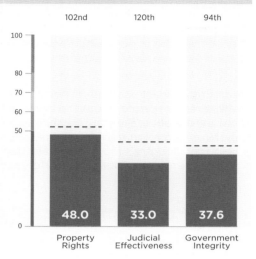

| 102nd | 120th | 94th | ◄ Rank |

| 48.0 | 33.0 | 37.6 |
| Property Rights | Judicial Effectiveness | Government Integrity |

Property rights are weak. The judicial system is modeled on English common law and provides adequate due process rights, but the rule of law remains uneven across the country. Enforcement of contracts is weak, and courts are relatively inexperienced in commercial litigation. Official corruption and abuse are serious problems, and international donors continue to demand improved governance and transparency.

GOVERNMENT SIZE

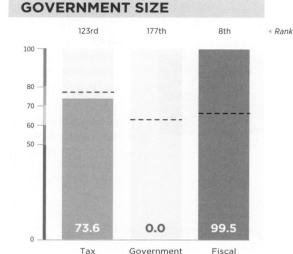

| 123rd | 177th | 8th | ◄ Rank |

| 73.6 | 0.0 | 99.5 |
| Tax Burden | Government Spending | Fiscal Health |

The top individual income and corporate tax rates are 35 percent. Taxation remains erratic and poorly administered. The overall tax burden equals 13.8 percent of total domestic income. Government spending has amounted to 94.9 percent of total output (GDP) over the past three years, and budget surpluses have averaged 9.4 percent of GDP. Public debt is equivalent to 16.4 percent of GDP.

REGULATORY EFFICIENCY

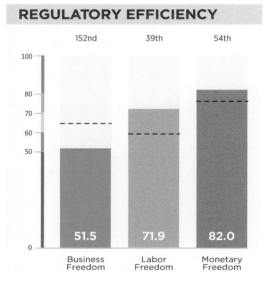

| 152nd | 39th | 54th |

| 51.5 | 71.9 | 82.0 |
| Business Freedom | Labor Freedom | Monetary Freedom |

Kiribati's regulatory environment is quite rudimentary. Existing commercial regulations are not enforced consistently. The government is the major source of formal employment, providing jobs in public service and state-owned enterprises. It also funds price-distorting subsidies for some agricultural products such as coconut oil. Inflows of development aid and assistance account for as much as 25 percent of GDP.

OPEN MARKETS

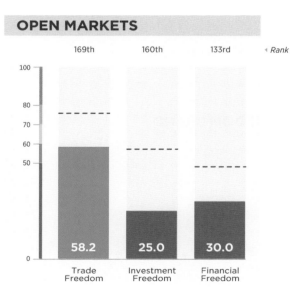

| 169th | 160th | 133rd | ◄ Rank |

| 58.2 | 25.0 | 30.0 |
| Trade Freedom | Investment Freedom | Financial Freedom |

Trade is extremely important to Kiribati's economy; the value of exports and imports taken together equals 104 percent of GDP. The average applied tariff rate is 15.9 percent. Foreign investors may not own land, and investment in other sectors of the economy is screened by the government. High credit costs impede development of the private sector. A large proportion of the population remains outside the formal banking system.

KIRIBATI

NORTH KOREA

North Korea remains an unreformed and closed state as Kim Jong-un maintains a despotic regime that resists economic reform. The government has experimented with a few market reforms but mainly administers a system of centralized planning and state control of the economy. The impoverished population is heavily dependent on food rations and government housing subsidies.

North Korea may be attempting modest economic opening by encouraging limited foreign direct investment, but the dominant influence of the military establishment makes any meaningful near-term change unlikely. Normal foreign trade is minimal, with China and South Korea being the country's most important trading partners. No courts are independent of political interference.

WORLD RANK:
180

REGIONAL RANK:
43

ECONOMIC FREEDOM STATUS:
REPRESSED

ECONOMIC FREEDOM SCORE

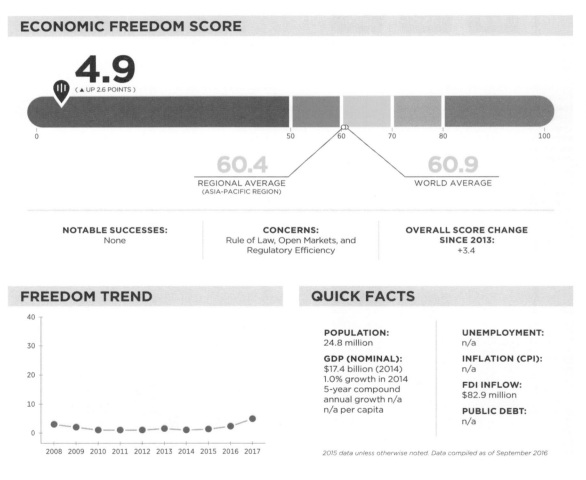

4.9
(▲ UP 2.6 POINTS)

0   50   60   70   80   100

60.4
REGIONAL AVERAGE
(ASIA–PACIFIC REGION)

60.9
WORLD AVERAGE

NOTABLE SUCCESSES:
None

CONCERNS:
Rule of Law, Open Markets, and Regulatory Efficiency

OVERALL SCORE CHANGE SINCE 2013:
+3.4

FREEDOM TREND

40

30

20

10

0

2008 2009 2010 2011 2012 2013 2014 2015 2016 2017

QUICK FACTS

POPULATION:
24.8 million

GDP (NOMINAL):
$17.4 billion (2014)
1.0% growth in 2014
5-year compound annual growth n/a
n/a per capita

UNEMPLOYMENT:
n/a

INFLATION (CPI):
n/a

FDI INFLOW:
$82.9 million

PUBLIC DEBT:
n/a

2015 data unless otherwise noted. Data compiled as of September 2016

BACKGROUND: In May 2016, North Korea convened the first Korea Workers' Party Congress in 36 years and only the seventh in North Korean history, generating speculation about possible sweeping policy changes, but the congress merely affirmed North Korea's dogged pursuit of nuclear weapons and continuance of socialist policies. Kim Jong-un has warned that opening the country would expose it to the contagion of foreign influences. In 2016, North Korea conducted more nuclear and long-range missile tests in defiance of U.N. resolutions, earning widespread condemnation. The regime continues to threaten nuclear attacks on the United States and its allies and is augmenting its nuclear and missile-delivery capabilities.

12 ECONOMIC FREEDOMS | NORTH KOREA

RULE OF LAW

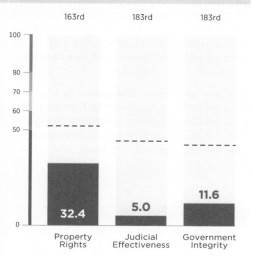

163rd   183rd   183rd

Property Rights: 32.4
Judicial Effectiveness: 5.0
Government Integrity: 11.6

Almost all property belongs to the state. Government control extends even to chattel property (domestically produced goods and all imports and exports). A functioning, modern, and independent judiciary does not exist. Bribery is pervasive, and corruption is endemic at every level of the state and economy. The ruling Workers' Party, the Korean People's Army, and members of the cabinet run companies that compete to earn foreign exchange.

GOVERNMENT SIZE

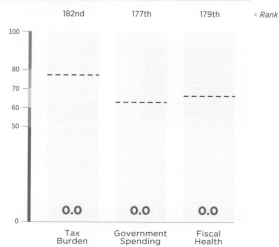

182nd   177th   179th   ◂ Rank

Tax Burden: 0.0
Government Spending: 0.0
Fiscal Health: 0.0

No effective tax system is in place. The government commands almost every part of the economy. The government sets production levels for most products, and state-owned industries account for nearly all GDP. The state directs all significant economic activity. Disproportionately high military spending further drains scarce resources. Despite an attempted state crackdown, black markets have grown.

REGULATORY EFFICIENCY

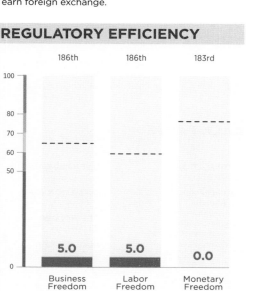

186th   186th   183rd

Business Freedom: 5.0
Labor Freedom: 5.0
Monetary Freedom: 0.0

The state continues to regulate the economy heavily through central planning and control. Entrepreneurial activity remains virtually impossible. As the main source of employment, the state determines wages. Factory managers have had limited autonomy to offer incentives to workers. North Korea receives extensive food and energy subsidies from China. Its monetary regime is completely controlled, leading to a total distortion of prices.

OPEN MARKETS

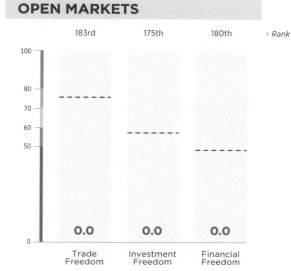

183rd   175th   180th   ◂ Rank

Trade Freedom: 0.0
Investment Freedom: 0.0
Financial Freedom: 0.0

Trade and investment flows are impeded by the North Korean government and by actions that have resulted in multilateral economic sanctions. There is virtually no functioning financial sector. Access to financing is very limited and constrained by the repressive economic system. The government provides most funding for industries and takes a percentage from enterprises.

NORTH KOREA

SOUTH KOREA

South Korea's economy is at a crossroads. Despite its relatively well-maintained macroeconomic stability and openness to global commerce, the economy has been flagging, with momentum for growth increasingly subdued in the absence of decisive policy reforms to improve overall efficiency and flexibility. Ongoing political instability and uncertainty have made structural economic reform almost impossible.

The rule of law has been fairly well institutionalized in South Korea, supporting such other pillars of economic freedom as regulatory efficiency and market openness. However, repeated high-profile corruption scandals have raised concerns about government integrity and eroded the public's trust and confidence in government.

ECONOMIC FREEDOM SCORE

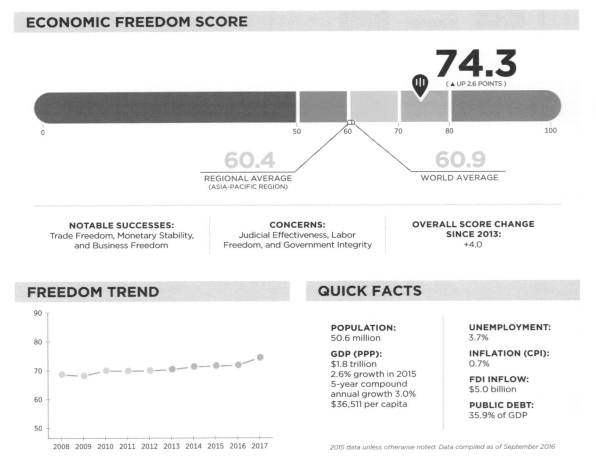

74.3
(▲ UP 2.6 POINTS)

0   50   60   70   80   100

60.4
REGIONAL AVERAGE
(ASIA–PACIFIC REGION)

60.9
WORLD AVERAGE

NOTABLE SUCCESSES:
Trade Freedom, Monetary Stability, and Business Freedom

CONCERNS:
Judicial Effectiveness, Labor Freedom, and Government Integrity

OVERALL SCORE CHANGE SINCE 2013:
+4.0

FREEDOM TREND

90

80

70

60

50

2008 2009 2010 2011 2012 2013 2014 2015 2016 2017

QUICK FACTS

POPULATION:
50.6 million

GDP (PPP):
$1.8 trillion
2.6% growth in 2015
5-year compound
annual growth 3.0%
$36,511 per capita

UNEMPLOYMENT:
3.7%

INFLATION (CPI):
0.7%

FDI INFLOW:
$5.0 billion

PUBLIC DEBT:
35.9% of GDP

2015 data unless otherwise noted. Data compiled as of September 2016

BACKGROUND: The South Korean political landscape is in flux following the impeachment of President Park Geun-hye. Though Park remains in office, she was required to transfer her presidential powers to Prime Minister Hwang Kyo-ahn pending final resolution by the Constitutional Court. Park's corruption scandal led to a fracturing of the ruling conservative party and increased the likelihood that a progressive candidate might win the presidential election. Progressive candidates advocate greater focus on resolving domestic economic disparity and reforming the economy away from reliance on the chaebol (large family-owned conglomerates). Progressives would also push for reduced reliance on the alliance with the U.S., reopening economic ventures with North Korea, and more timid implementation of sanctions for Pyongyang's repeated violations of U.N. resolutions.

12 ECONOMIC FREEDOMS | SOUTH KOREA

RULE OF LAW

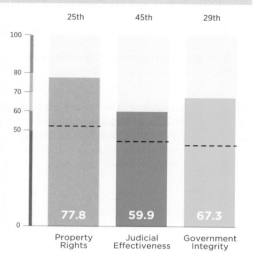

	25th	45th	29th
	Property Rights	Judicial Effectiveness	Government Integrity
	77.8	59.9	67.3

Private property rights are protected, and the judicial system is independent and efficient. Nevertheless, encounters with graft, influence peddling, and extortion continue to occur despite the government's anticorruption efforts. Piracy of copyrighted material is significant, and protection of intellectual property rights needs to be improved. The importance that the government places on IPR protection, however, has increased considerably.

GOVERNMENT SIZE

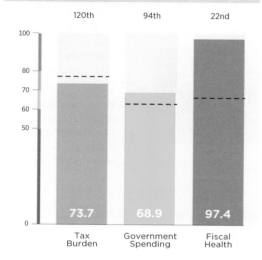

120th   94th   22nd   ◄ Rank

	Tax Burden	Government Spending	Fiscal Health
	73.7	68.9	97.4

The top personal income tax rate is 35 percent, and the top corporate tax rate is 22 percent. A 10 percent surtax is imposed on individual and corporate rates. The overall tax burden equals 24.6 percent of total domestic income. Government spending has amounted to 32.2 percent of total output (GDP) over the past three years, and budget surpluses have averaged 0.3 percent of GDP. Public debt is equivalent to 35.9 percent of GDP.

REGULATORY EFFICIENCY

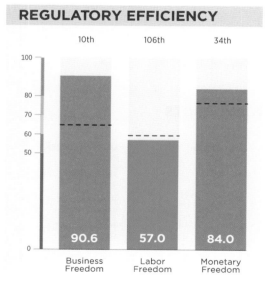

10th   106th   34th

	Business Freedom	Labor Freedom	Monetary Freedom
	90.6	57.0	84.0

The competitive regulatory framework facilitates entrepreneurial activity and innovation. Business formation and operating rules are relatively efficient. The labor market is dynamic, but there are lingering regulatory rigidities, and powerful trade unions add to the cost of doing business. Monetary stability has been well maintained. The government subsidizes rice farmers and sets price controls on items that include fuel, rice, and electricity.

OPEN MARKETS

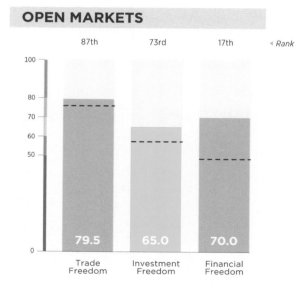

87th   73rd   17th   ◄ Rank

	Trade Freedom	Investment Freedom	Financial Freedom
	79.5	65.0	70.0

Trade is important to South Korea's economy; the value of exports and imports taken together equals 85 percent of GDP. The average applied tariff rate is 5.2 percent. Foreign investment in some sectors is restricted, and state-owned enterprises distort the economy. The financial sector has become more competitive, although business start-ups still struggle to obtain financing. The banking sector remains largely stable.

SOUTH KOREA

KYRGYZ REPUBLIC

The Kyrgyz Republic is one of Central Asia's poorest countries and is sharply divided along ethnic lines. Despite implementation of some reforms, overall improvement in the entrepreneurial environment has been slow and uneven. Political turmoil has contributed to policy volatility and uncertainty, hampering economic development. Political rivalries and powerful vested interests have held back implementation of deeper structural reforms.

With remnants of the former Communist system evident in many areas, the economy lacks the institutional foundations necessary for the advancement of economic freedom. Weak rule of law fosters pervasive corruption and ownership insecurity, undermining private-sector investment and business growth.

WORLD RANK:
89

REGIONAL RANK:
19

ECONOMIC FREEDOM STATUS:
MODERATELY FREE

ECONOMIC FREEDOM SCORE

61.1
(▲ UP 1.5 POINTS)

0   50   60   70   80   100

60.4
REGIONAL AVERAGE
(ASIA-PACIFIC REGION)

60.9
WORLD AVERAGE

NOTABLE SUCCESSES:	CONCERNS:	OVERALL SCORE CHANGE
Trade Freedom	Rule of Law and Financial Freedom	SINCE 2013: +1.5

FREEDOM TREND

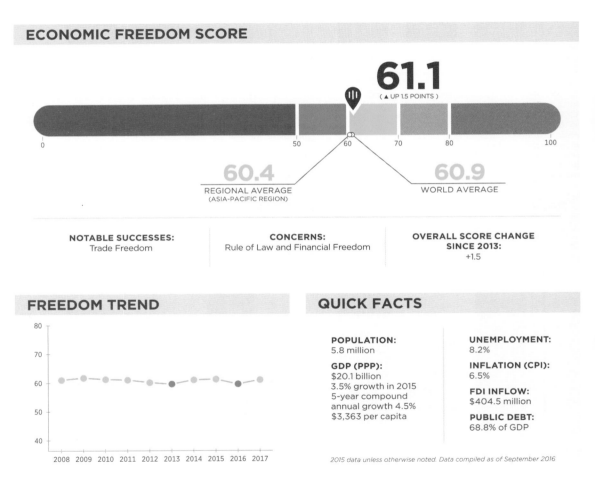

80
70
60
50
40

2008 2009 2010 2011 2012 2013 2014 2015 2016 2017

QUICK FACTS

POPULATION:
5.8 million

GDP (PPP):
$20.1 billion
3.5% growth in 2015
5-year compound
annual growth 4.5%
$3,363 per capita

UNEMPLOYMENT:
8.2%

INFLATION (CPI):
6.5%

FDI INFLOW:
$404.5 million

PUBLIC DEBT:
68.8% of GDP

2015 data unless otherwise noted. Data compiled as of September 2016.

BACKGROUND: Weak governance under President Almazbek Atambayev, elected in 2011 with Moscow's support, has encouraged extremist threats, organized crime, and corruption. The Kyrgyz Republic is a member of the Eurasian Economic Union. The economy depends heavily on gold exports and remittances from Kyrgyzstani migrant workers, primarily in Russia, who have been negatively affected by declines in the Russian economy. Cotton, tobacco, wool, and meat are the main agricultural products, but only tobacco and cotton are exported in any quantity. Foreign investment from Russia has been strong in the past, but its continuation is far from certain. This has led many in the political elite to question Russia's reliability as a long-term partner.

12 ECONOMIC FREEDOMS | KYRGYZ REPUBLIC

RULE OF LAW

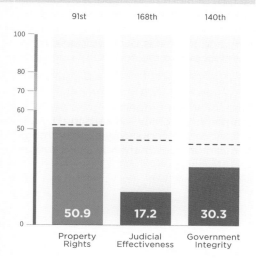

91st	168th	140th
50.9	17.2	30.3
Property Rights	Judicial Effectiveness	Government Integrity

Protection of property rights is weak. The judiciary is not independent and is dominated by the executive branch. There are numerous credible reports that judges pay bribes to attain their positions. Corruption is pervasive in Kyrgyzstani society. Despite some anticorruption efforts, the country is trapped in a cycle in which predatory political elites use government resources to reward clients, including organized crime figures, and punish opponents.

GOVERNMENT SIZE

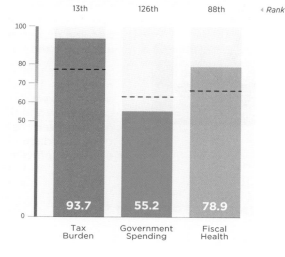

13th	126th	88th	◀ Rank
93.7	55.2	78.9	
Tax Burden	Government Spending	Fiscal Health	

The personal income and corporate tax rates are a flat 10 percent. Taxation remains erratic and poorly administered. The overall tax burden equals 20.8 percent of total domestic income. Government spending has amounted to 38.7 percent of total output (GDP) over the past three years, and budget deficits have averaged 2.7 percent of GDP. Public debt is equivalent to 68.8 percent of GDP.

REGULATORY EFFICIENCY

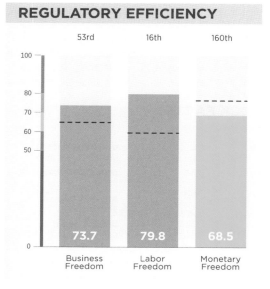

53rd	16th	160th
73.7	79.8	68.5
Business Freedom	Labor Freedom	Monetary Freedom

The overall regulatory environment is still hampered by bureaucratic impediments to private-sector production and investment. Reforms have not yet resulted in the structural changes that are needed to foster efficiency. The formal labor market has not been fully developed. Agricultural sector growth has been financed by subsidized lending. In 2016, the government told the IMF that it intends to reduce subsidies and transfers to 3 percent of GDP.

OPEN MARKETS

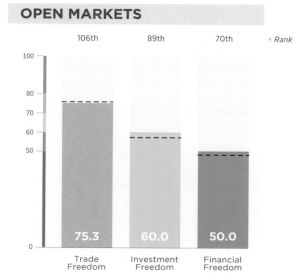

106th	89th	70th	◀ Rank
75.3	60.0	50.0	
Trade Freedom	Investment Freedom	Financial Freedom	

Trade is extremely important to the Kyrgyz Republic's economy; the value of exports and imports taken together equals 125 percent of GDP. The average applied tariff rate is 2.3 percent. In 2016, the government banned the use of foreign currency. State-owned enterprises distort the economy. Financial intermediation has continued to increase, but credit costs remain high. The banking sector remains vulnerable to political interference.

LAOS

The Laotian economy has shown notable resilience, growing at an average annual rate of more than 7 percent over the past five years. Laos continues to integrate more fully into the system of global trade and investment. The trade regime has become more transparent, and there has been progress in improving the management of public finances.

Substantial challenges remain, particularly in implementing deeper institutional and systemic reforms that are critical to advancing economic freedom. Weak property rights, pervasive corruption, and burdensome bureaucracy, exacerbated by lingering government interference and regulatory controls, continue to reduce the dynamism of investment flows and overall economic efficiency.

WORLD RANK:
133

REGIONAL RANK:
31

ECONOMIC FREEDOM STATUS:
MOSTLY UNFREE

ECONOMIC FREEDOM SCORE

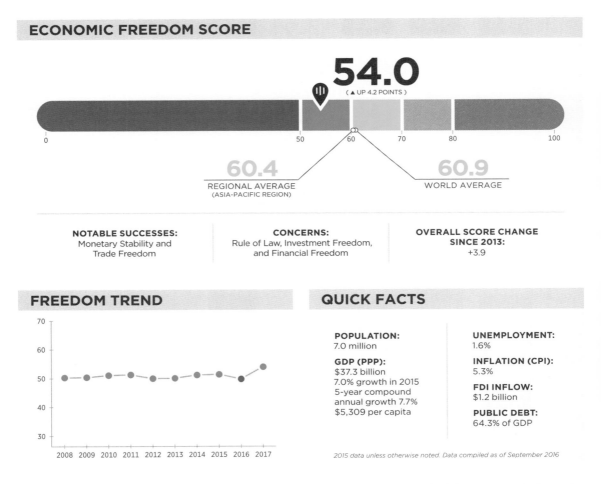

54.0
(▲ UP 4.2 POINTS)

0   50   60   70   80   100

60.4
REGIONAL AVERAGE
(ASIA–PACIFIC REGION)

60.9
WORLD AVERAGE

NOTABLE SUCCESSES:
Monetary Stability and Trade Freedom

CONCERNS:
Rule of Law, Investment Freedom, and Financial Freedom

OVERALL SCORE CHANGE SINCE 2013:
+3.9

FREEDOM TREND

70

60

50

40

30

2008 2009 2010 2011 2012 2013 2014 2015 2016 2017

QUICK FACTS

POPULATION:
7.0 million

GDP (PPP):
$37.3 billion
7.0% growth in 2015
5-year compound
annual growth 7.7%
$5,309 per capita

UNEMPLOYMENT:
1.6%

INFLATION (CPI):
5.3%

FDI INFLOW:
$1.2 billion

PUBLIC DEBT:
64.3% of GDP

2015 data unless otherwise noted. Data compiled as of September 2016

BACKGROUND: The Communist government of Laos, in power since 1975, wrecked the economy in the early years of its rule. Minimal liberalization, begun in 1986, has yielded some progress. To advance its "state-managed market-orientated economy," the government has taken on increasing levels of external public and publicly guaranteed debt since 2012 to subsidize construction of hydropower and mining megaprojects. Basic civil liberties are heavily restricted. Seventy-three percent of the workforce is employed in subsistence farming. In 2013, after 15 years of negotiations, Laos became a member of the World Trade Organization. It also served as the 2016 chair for the Association of Southeast Asian Nations. Since 2016, 79-year-old Bounnhang Vorachith has served as president of Laos and general secretary of the Lao People's Revolutionary Party.

12 ECONOMIC FREEDOMS | LAOS

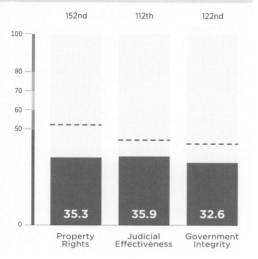

RULE OF LAW

152nd   112th   122nd

35.3	35.9	32.6
Property Rights	Judicial Effectiveness	Government Integrity

Protection of property rights is weak. The judicial system is inefficient, corrupt, and controlled by the ruling party. Corruption and graft by government officials are serious problems in Laos, fueling public discontent and causing gaps in revenue collection and degraded public services. Several anticorruption laws have been passed, but enforcement remains weak, and no high-profile cases have been brought to trial.

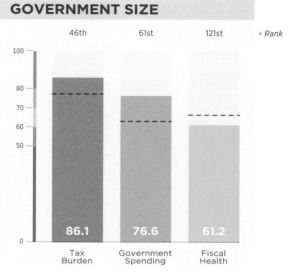

GOVERNMENT SIZE

46th   61st   121st   ◂ Rank

86.1	76.6	61.2
Tax Burden	Government Spending	Fiscal Health

The top personal income and corporate tax rates are 24 percent. Other taxes include a vehicle tax and excise taxes. The overall tax burden equals 15.5 percent of total domestic income. Government spending has amounted to 27.9 percent of total output (GDP) over the past three years, and budget deficits have averaged 4.4 percent of GDP. Public debt is equivalent to 64.3 percent of GDP.

LAOS

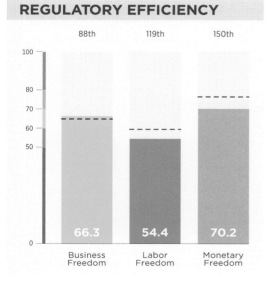

REGULATORY EFFICIENCY

88th   119th   150th

66.3	54.4	70.2
Business Freedom	Labor Freedom	Monetary Freedom

The poor regulatory infrastructure continues to impede private-sector development. The labor market does not promote flexibility or economic diversification and has not provided dynamic employment opportunities for the growing labor supply. To advance its socialist "state-managed market-orientated economy," the government influences many prices through subsidies and state-owned enterprises, especially in the hydropower and mining sectors.

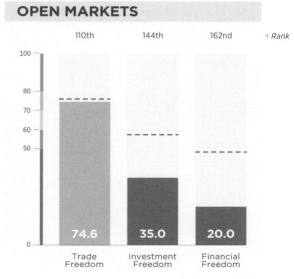

OPEN MARKETS

110th   144th   162nd   ◂ Rank

74.6	35.0	20.0
Trade Freedom	Investment Freedom	Financial Freedom

Trade is important to the Laotian economy; the value of exports and imports taken together equals 79 percent of GDP. The average applied tariff rate is 5.2 percent. State-owned enterprises distort the economy, and foreign investors may not own land. The financial system is underdeveloped and subject to government involvement. High credit costs and scarce access to financing severely impede private-sector development.

MACAU

WORLD RANK:
32

REGIONAL RANK:
8

ECONOMIC FREEDOM STATUS:
MOSTLY FREE

As a free port, Macau has long benefited from global trade and investment. The entrepreneurial environment is generally efficient and streamlined, and property rights are generally well respected. Taxation is low and relatively efficient. Since opening up the gaming industry in 2002, Macau has attracted more foreign investment. Other growth areas include finance, insurance, and real estate. New measures to accelerate the registration processes for trademarks and patents have been implemented.

The services sector accounts for almost 90 percent of GDP and over 70 percent of total employment. Investment in resort and entertainment projects and related infrastructure has transformed Macau into one of the world's leading tourism destinations.

ECONOMIC FREEDOM SCORE

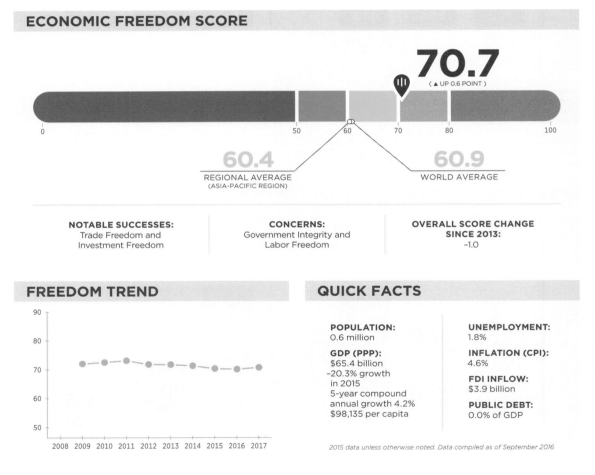

70.7
(▲ UP 0.6 POINT)

0   50   60   70   80   100

60.4
REGIONAL AVERAGE
(ASIA-PACIFIC REGION)

60.9
WORLD AVERAGE

NOTABLE SUCCESSES:
Trade Freedom and
Investment Freedom

CONCERNS:
Government Integrity and
Labor Freedom

**OVERALL SCORE CHANGE
SINCE 2013:**
–1.0

FREEDOM TREND

QUICK FACTS

POPULATION:
0.6 million

GDP (PPP):
$65.4 billion
–20.3% growth
in 2015
5-year compound
annual growth 4.2%
$98,135 per capita

UNEMPLOYMENT:
1.8%

INFLATION (CPI):
4.6%

FDI INFLOW:
$3.9 billion

PUBLIC DEBT:
0.0% of GDP

2015 data unless otherwise noted. Data compiled as of September 2016

BACKGROUND: Macau, colonized by the Portuguese in the 16th century, became a Special Administrative Region of China in 1999, and its chief executive is appointed by Beijing. Macau is one of the world's largest gaming centers and the only place in China where casinos are legal. Gaming-related taxes account for approximately 80 percent of government revenue. Over the past three years, China's anticorruption campaign has caused tourism and gambling traffic from the mainland to decrease. As a result, the city's small economy shrank by 20 percent last year. Two ongoing structural problems are a lack of attractions for nongambling tourists and high travel expenses.

12 ECONOMIC FREEDOMS | MACAU

RULE OF LAW

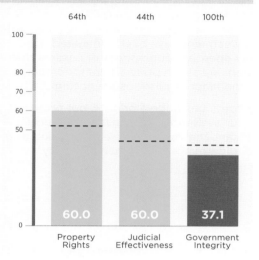

| 64th | 44th | 100th |

- Property Rights: **60.0**
- Judicial Effectiveness: **60.0**
- Government Integrity: **37.1**

Private ownership of property and contractual rights are well established. There are no restrictions on foreign ownership of property. Macau has its own judicial system with a high court, and its legal framework is based largely on Portuguese law. Although the population was politically quiescent in the past, the frequency of public protests against a range of issues such as corruption, favoritism, and nepotism has increased in recent years.

GOVERNMENT SIZE

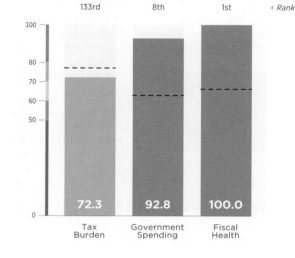

| 133rd | 8th | 1st | ◄ Rank |

- Tax Burden: **72.3**
- Government Spending: **92.8**
- Fiscal Health: **100.0**

The top personal income tax rate is 12 percent, and the top corporate tax rate is 39 percent. Gambling tax revenues are quite high. The overall tax burden equals 33.2 percent of total domestic income. Government spending has amounted to 15.5 percent of total output (GDP) over the past three years, and budget surpluses have averaged 21.4 percent of GDP. Macau has no public debt.

REGULATORY EFFICIENCY

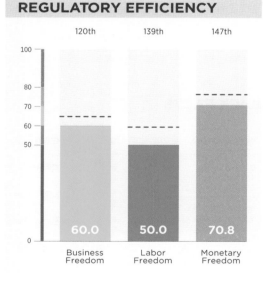

| 120th | 139th | 147th |

- Business Freedom: **60.0**
- Labor Freedom: **50.0**
- Monetary Freedom: **70.8**

The overall regulatory environment is relatively transparent and efficient, with license requirements varying by type of economic activity. The economy lacks a dynamic and broad-based labor market. The government sets minimum standards for the terms and conditions of employment. Monetary stability has been relatively well maintained, but the government funds generous subsidies to households, the elderly, and students.

OPEN MARKETS

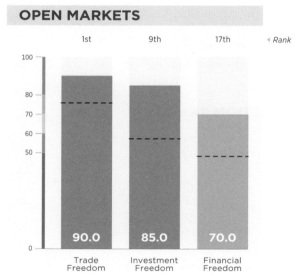

| 1st | 9th | 17th | ◄ Rank |

- Trade Freedom: **90.0**
- Investment Freedom: **85.0**
- Financial Freedom: **70.0**

Trade is extremely important to Macau's economy; the value of exports and imports taken together equals 115 percent of GDP. The average applied tariff rate is 0.0 percent. There are few nontariff barriers to trade, and Macau is relatively open to foreign investment. The small financial system functions without undue government influence. Credit is allocated on market terms, and relatively sound regulation assures free flows of financial resources.

MACAU

MALAYSIA

Ongoing economic reforms have enhanced Malaysia's competitiveness. The financial sector has undergone regulatory adjustments that include easing the limits on foreign ownership in financial subsectors. Numerous domestic equity requirements that restricted foreign investment have been eliminated. The trade regime is relatively open, although nontariff barriers that limit overall trade freedom are still in place. There is no mandated minimum wage, and labor regulations are not rigid.

Improving fiscal health continues to be a priority, but progress has been slow. The judicial system's vulnerability to political influence poses a significant challenge to the effective and even-handed rule of law and undermines government integrity.

WORLD RANK: 27
REGIONAL RANK: 7
ECONOMIC FREEDOM STATUS:
MOSTLY FREE

ECONOMIC FREEDOM SCORE

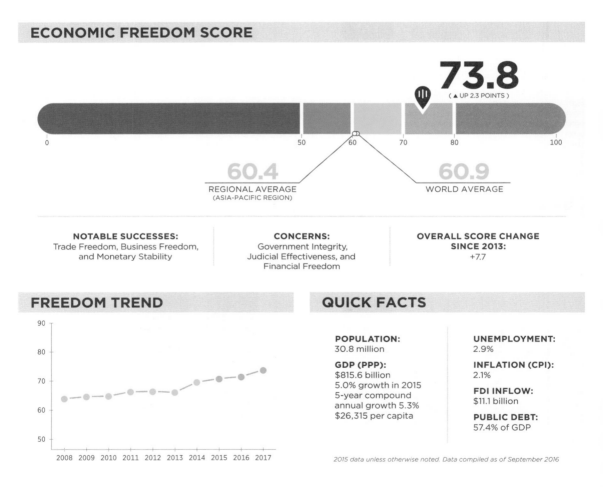

73.8
(▲ UP 2.3 POINTS)

0   50   60   70   80   100

60.4
REGIONAL AVERAGE
(ASIA-PACIFIC REGION)

60.9
WORLD AVERAGE

NOTABLE SUCCESSES:
Trade Freedom, Business Freedom, and Monetary Stability

CONCERNS:
Government Integrity, Judicial Effectiveness, and Financial Freedom

OVERALL SCORE CHANGE SINCE 2013:
+7.7

FREEDOM TREND

90
80
70
60
50

2008 2009 2010 2011 2012 2013 2014 2015 2016 2017

QUICK FACTS

POPULATION:
30.8 million

GDP (PPP):
$815.6 billion
5.0% growth in 2015
5-year compound
annual growth 5.3%
$26,315 per capita

UNEMPLOYMENT:
2.9%

INFLATION (CPI):
2.1%

FDI INFLOW:
$11.1 billion

PUBLIC DEBT:
57.4% of GDP

2015 data unless otherwise noted. Data compiled as of September 2016

BACKGROUND: The United Malays National Organization (UMNO) has ruled the ethnically and religiously diverse constitutional monarchy of Malaysia since independence in 1957. In 2013 elections, the UMNO-led coalition retained power but for the first time failed to win more than 50 percent of the popular vote. Since 2015, Prime Minister Najib Razak has been embroiled in a scandal involving the misappropriation of $3.5 billion in state funds. Despite this, Najib's UNMO won two special parliamentary elections in June 2016. The government maintains investments in such key sectors as banking, media, automobiles, and airlines. Malaysia is a leading exporter of electronics and information-technology products.

12 ECONOMIC FREEDOMS | MALAYSIA

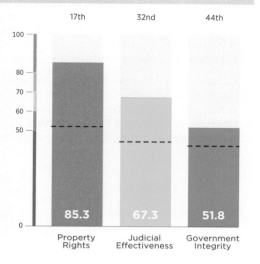

RULE OF LAW

17th	32nd	44th
Property Rights **85.3**	Judicial Effectiveness **67.3**	Government Integrity **51.8**

Malaysian courts protect real property ownership rights, but protection of intellectual property rights is weaker. Judicial independence is marred by heavy executive influence, and arbitrary or politically motivated verdicts are common. Favoritism and blurred distinctions between public and private enterprises create conditions conducive to corruption. A multibillion-dollar corruption scandal involving the prime minister has dominated the headlines during the past year.

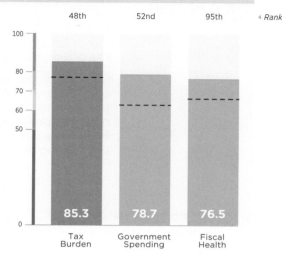

GOVERNMENT SIZE

48th	52nd	95th	◂ Rank
Tax Burden **85.3**	Government Spending **78.7**	Fiscal Health **76.5**	

The top individual income tax rate has been raised to 28 percent. The top corporate tax rate has been cut to 24 percent. Other taxes include a capital gains tax. The overall tax burden equals 14.8 percent of total domestic income. Government spending has amounted to 25.8 percent of total output (GDP) over the past three years, and budget deficits have averaged 3.2 percent of GDP. Public debt is equivalent to 57.4 percent of GDP.

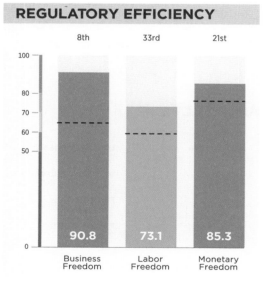

REGULATORY EFFICIENCY

8th	33rd	21st
Business Freedom **90.8**	Labor Freedom **73.1**	Monetary Freedom **85.3**

A new Companies Act, which was enacted in 2016 to facilitate the establishment and operations of domestic firms, is expected to take effect in 2017. There is no national minimum wage, and restrictions on work hours are relatively flexible. The International Monetary Fund has praised the government's bold multi-year drive to reduce costly and untargeted subsidies (for example, on electricity and fuel).

OPEN MARKETS

73rd	89th	70th	◂ Rank
Trade Freedom **81.2**	Investment Freedom **60.0**	Financial Freedom **50.0**	

Trade is extremely important to Malaysia's economy; the value of exports and imports taken together equals 134 percent of GDP. The average applied tariff rate is 4.4 percent. Investment in some sectors is restricted, and state-owned enterprises distort the economy. The financial sector continues to grow, and its competitiveness is increasing. Supervision of banking has been strengthened, and measures to liberalize capital markets have progressed.

MALAYSIA

MALDIVES

Tourism and related industries drive the Maldives' economy, which needs diversification to protect it from global slowdowns. Reforms to improve the business environment have been uneven. Corporations now have additional disclosure requirements for filing taxes, and it is harder to obtain a building permit. The government deficit is large and growing.

Foreign companies are now permitted to own land, but ambiguous foreign investment laws deter investors. Government corruption remains a serious problem; the Auditor General discovered during a special audit in February 2016 that $79 million had been embezzled from the Maldives Marketing and Public Relations Corporation.

ECONOMIC FREEDOM SCORE

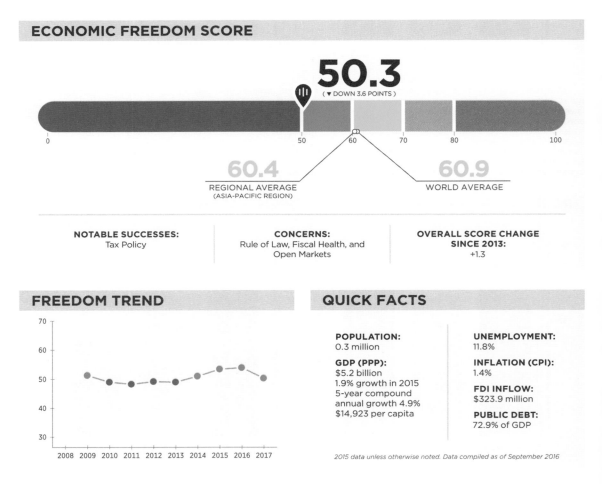

50.3
(▼ DOWN 3.6 POINTS)

0   50   60   70   80   100

60.4
REGIONAL AVERAGE
(ASIA-PACIFIC REGION)

60.9
WORLD AVERAGE

NOTABLE SUCCESSES:
Tax Policy

CONCERNS:
Rule of Law, Fiscal Health, and Open Markets

OVERALL SCORE CHANGE SINCE 2013:
+1.3

FREEDOM TREND

70
60
50
40
30

2008 2009 2010 2011 2012 2013 2014 2015 2016 2017

QUICK FACTS

POPULATION:
0.3 million

GDP (PPP):
$5.2 billion
1.9% growth in 2015
5-year compound
annual growth 4.9%
$14,923 per capita

UNEMPLOYMENT:
11.8%

INFLATION (CPI):
1.4%

FDI INFLOW:
$323.9 million

PUBLIC DEBT:
72.9% of GDP

2015 data unless otherwise noted. Data compiled as of September 2016

BACKGROUND: The military forced democratically elected President Mohamed Nasheed to step down in February 2012 after several weeks of anti-government street protests instigated by former dictator Maumoon Abdul Gayoom. In November 2013, Gayoom's half-brother Abdulla Yameen was elected president. Sixteen months later, Yameen's government sentenced former President Nasheed to 13 years in prison based on dubious allegations of terrorism, prompting large-scale protests among his supporters and cancellation of a planned state visit by India's prime minister. Nasheed was granted political asylum in London in May amid signs of increasing political repression by President Yameen. As calls for sanctions by Western countries have intensified, Yameen has turned increasingly toward Chinese and Saudi investment.

12 ECONOMIC FREEDOMS | MALDIVES

RULE OF LAW

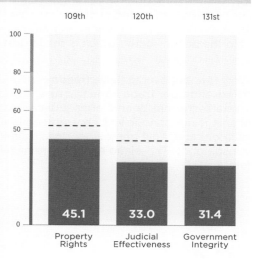

109th	120th	131st
Property Rights	Judicial Effectiveness	Government Integrity
45.1	33.0	31.4

Property rights are generally weak; most land is owned by the government and then leased to private owners or developers. Although legally independent, the judiciary is subject to influence amid numerous allegations of judicial impropriety and abuse of power. In 2016, former President Nasheed received a long prison sentence on a politically motivated terrorism charge, partly because he ordered the arrest of a corrupt judge in 2012.

GOVERNMENT SIZE

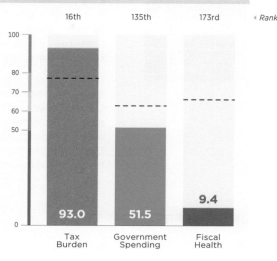

16th	135th	173rd	◄ Rank
Tax Burden	Government Spending	Fiscal Health	
93.0	51.5	9.4	

The government of the Maldives levies no personal income or corporate tax. Bank profits are subject to a profits tax. The overall tax burden equals 26.4 percent of total domestic income. Government spending has amounted to 40.2 percent of total output (GDP) over the past three years, and budget deficits have averaged 8.6 percent of GDP. Public debt is equivalent to 72.9 percent of GDP.

REGULATORY EFFICIENCY

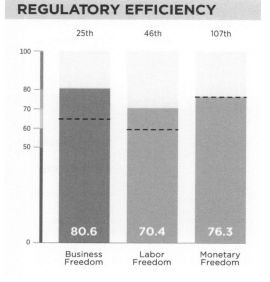

25th	46th	107th
Business Freedom	Labor Freedom	Monetary Freedom
80.6	70.4	76.3

Impediments to sustained private-sector growth and diversification remain considerable, in large part due to the lack of supportive policies and infrastructure. The large public sector employs much of the labor force. With the government facing an overall budget deficit of over 8 percent of GDP in 2016, the IMF recommended that it both find better ways to target welfare and food subsidies and eliminate electricity subsidies.

OPEN MARKETS

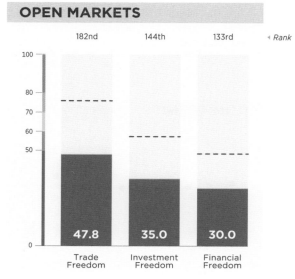

182nd	144th	133rd	◄ Rank
Trade Freedom	Investment Freedom	Financial Freedom	
47.8	35.0	30.0	

Trade is extremely important to the Maldives' economy; the value of exports and imports taken together equals 201 percent of GDP. The average applied tariff rate is 21.1 percent. The government screens foreign investment, and state-owned enterprises distort the economy. The shallow financial sector is dominated by banking. Costly credit and limited access to financial services impede development of a vibrant private sector.

MALDIVES

MICRONESIA

WORLD RANK: 132 | **REGIONAL RANK:** 30

ECONOMIC FREEDOM STATUS:
MOSTLY UNFREE

Micronesia faces considerable geographic and other challenges that arguably reduce its economic potential, but poor policy choices in critical areas of economic freedom have further retarded growth. A significant portion of economic activity is concentrated in the public sector, which is the largest source of employment.

Tariff barriers are relatively low, but overall trade freedom is limited by nontariff barriers and poor trade infrastructure. Development of the private sector has been marginal because of a business environment that is not conducive to entrepreneurial activity. The overall regulatory and legal framework remains inefficient and lacking in transparency. The island economy remains highly dependent on foreign aid.

ECONOMIC FREEDOM SCORE

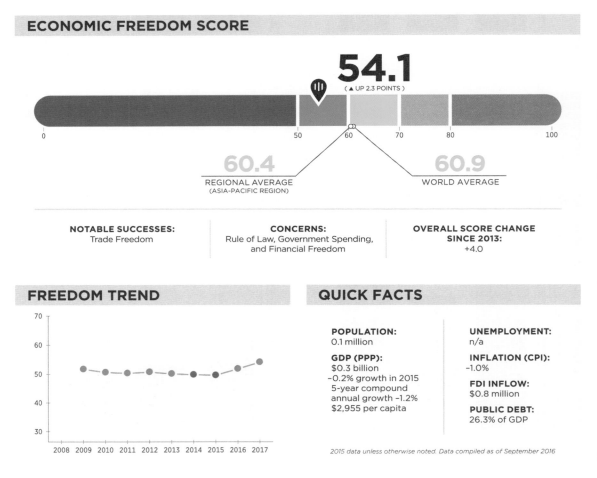

54.1
(▲ UP 2.3 POINTS)

0   50   60   70   80   100

60.4
REGIONAL AVERAGE
(ASIA–PACIFIC REGION)

60.9
WORLD AVERAGE

NOTABLE SUCCESSES:	CONCERNS:	OVERALL SCORE CHANGE SINCE 2013:
Trade Freedom	Rule of Law, Government Spending, and Financial Freedom	+4.0

FREEDOM TREND

(chart: y-axis 30–70; x-axis 2008–2017)

QUICK FACTS

POPULATION:
0.1 million

GDP (PPP):
$0.3 billion
–0.2% growth in 2015
5-year compound
annual growth –1.2%
$2,955 per capita

UNEMPLOYMENT:
n/a

INFLATION (CPI):
–1.0%

FDI INFLOW:
$0.8 million

PUBLIC DEBT:
26.3% of GDP

2015 data unless otherwise noted. Data compiled as of September 2016

BACKGROUND: Politically organized as a confederation of four states (the island groups of Pohnpei, Chuuk, Yap, and Kosrae), the 607-island South Pacific archipelago of Micronesia has a central government with limited powers. The most recent parliamentary election for Micronesia's small unicameral legislature took place in March 2015; in May 2015, the legislature's at-large members elected President Peter Christian to a four-year term. Under an amended compact, it receives about $130 million annually in direct assistance from the U.S.

12 ECONOMIC FREEDOMS | MICRONESIA

RULE OF LAW

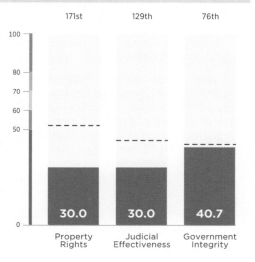

171st	129th	76th
Property Rights **30.0**	Judicial Effectiveness **30.0**	Government Integrity **40.7**

Property rights are only well protected for citizens and, to a lesser degree, for foreign nationals who have more than five year's residence in the country. The government generally respects the constitutionally independent judiciary, but the judicial system is chronically underfunded and subject to political influence. Civilian authorities maintain effective control of the police and investigate abuse and corruption.

GOVERNMENT SIZE

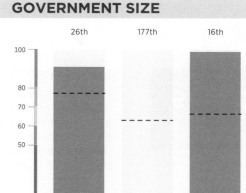

‹ Rank

26th	177th	16th
Tax Burden **90.7**	Government Spending **0.0**	Fiscal Health **98.6**

Micronesia's tax laws are administered and enforced erratically. The personal income tax rate is 10 percent, and the corporate tax rate is 21 percent. The overall tax burden equals 19.7 percent of total domestic income. Government spending has amounted to 60.2 percent of total output (GDP) over the past three years, and budget surpluses have averaged 5.7 percent of GDP. Public debt is equivalent to 26.3 percent of GDP.

REGULATORY EFFICIENCY

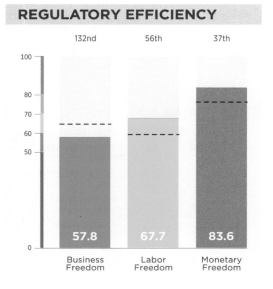

132nd	56th	37th
Business Freedom **57.8**	Labor Freedom **67.7**	Monetary Freedom **83.6**

Given the poor development of the physical and regulatory infrastructure, the formation or operation of private businesses is not easy. A large share of the workforce is employed in the informal sector. The government depends heavily on U.S. subsidies, which account for roughly 40 percent of annual revenue, and is looking to China for future support when the American payments end in 2023.

OPEN MARKETS

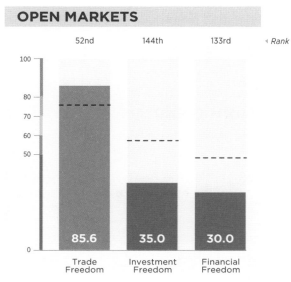

‹ Rank

52nd	144th	133rd
Trade Freedom **85.6**	Investment Freedom **35.0**	Financial Freedom **30.0**

Trade is important to Micronesia's economy; the value of exports and imports taken together equals 78 percent of GDP. The average applied tariff rate is 2.2 percent. Foreign investors may not own land, and investment in other economic sectors may be screened. Outmoded regulation, high credit costs, and scarce access to financing continue to constrain the small private sector. Much of the population remains outside of the formal banking sector.

MICRONESIA

MONGOLIA

In an effort to accelerate its transition to a competitive economy, Mongolia has adopted policies to liberalize markets and develop the financial sector. However, long-term economic development will still require further critical reforms. The evolving regulatory framework governing investment remains opaque, injecting uncertainty into investment decisions.

The weak rule of law and lingering corruption are additional drags on the economy. Institutional reforms and continued efforts to streamline public administration are critical to sustaining economic growth. Management of public finances has deteriorated notably, and growing budget deficits have pushed the level of public debt to more than 75 percent of GDP.

ECONOMIC FREEDOM SCORE

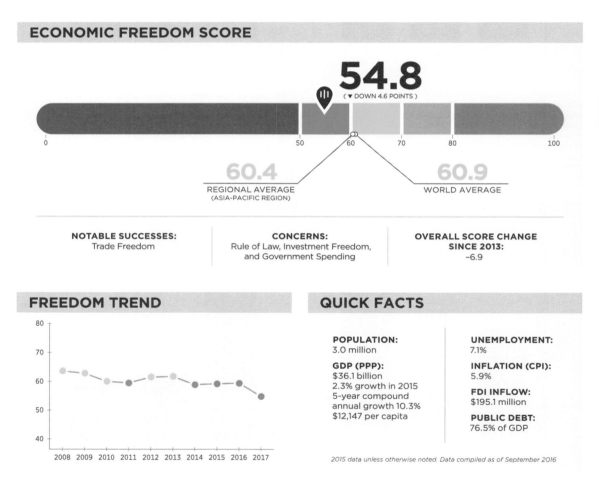

54.8
(▼ DOWN 4.6 POINTS)

0   50   60   70   80   100

60.4
REGIONAL AVERAGE
(ASIA–PACIFIC REGION)

60.9
WORLD AVERAGE

NOTABLE SUCCESSES:
Trade Freedom

CONCERNS:
Rule of Law, Investment Freedom, and Government Spending

OVERALL SCORE CHANGE SINCE 2013:
–6.9

FREEDOM TREND

80
70
60
50
40

2008 2009 2010 2011 2012 2013 2014 2015 2016 2017

QUICK FACTS

POPULATION:
3.0 million

GDP (PPP):
$36.1 billion
2.3% growth in 2015
5-year compound
annual growth 10.3%
$12,147 per capita

UNEMPLOYMENT:
7.1%

INFLATION (CPI):
5.9%

FDI INFLOW:
$195.1 million

PUBLIC DEBT:
76.5% of GDP

2015 data unless otherwise noted. Data compiled as of September 2016

BACKGROUND: Since the adoption of a new constitution in 1992, Mongolia has transformed from a closed society ruled by a single-party Communist system into an open society and a dynamic multi-party democracy. This transition has been accompanied by the gradual introduction of free-market reforms and relatively well-maintained political stability. While improving overall relations with the U.S., Japan, and South Korea, Mongolia has also maintained strong ties with Russia and China. President Tsakhiagiin Elbegdorj, whose Democratic Party coalition controls parliament, is serving his second term. Agriculture and mining remain the most important sectors of the economy. Uncertainty over investment rules has caused investment in the mineral sector to ebb and flow.

12 ECONOMIC FREEDOMS | MONGOLIA

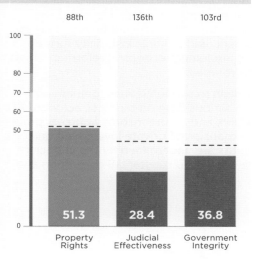

RULE OF LAW

88th	136th	103rd
Property Rights **51.3**	Judicial Effectiveness **28.4**	Government Integrity **36.8**

Property and contractual rights are recognized, but enforcement is weak. The government lacks the capacity to enforce intellectual property rights laws. The judiciary is independent but inefficient and vulnerable to political interference. Pervasive corruption stems from a political culture that places a high value on relationships. Graft is endemic, and weak institutions do not enforce anticorruption measures effectively.

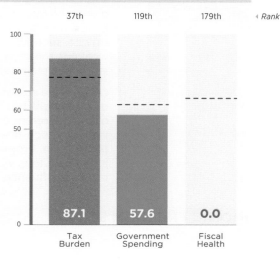

GOVERNMENT SIZE

◂ *Rank*

37th	119th	179th
Tax Burden **87.1**	Government Spending **57.6**	Fiscal Health **0.0**

The individual income tax rate is a flat 10 percent, and the top corporate tax rate is 25 percent. Other taxes include a value-added tax and an excise tax. The overall tax burden equals 23.7 percent of total domestic income. Government spending has amounted to 37.6 percent of total output (GDP) over the past three years, and budget deficits have averaged 9.4 percent of GDP. Public debt is equivalent to 76.5 percent of GDP.

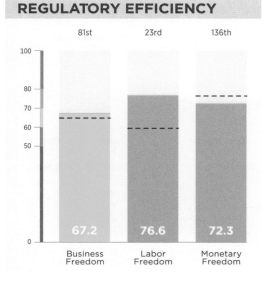

REGULATORY EFFICIENCY

81st	23rd	136th
Business Freedom **67.2**	Labor Freedom **76.6**	Monetary Freedom **72.3**

The regulatory framework continues to evolve, although the pace of reform has been sluggish. Labor regulations are relatively flexible, but the labor market lacks dynamism. The nonsalary cost of employing a worker is moderate, and dismissing an employee is not burdensome. Faced with a budget deficit, the government is contemplating the sale of some state-owned enterprises such as power plants, coal companies, and the stock exchange.

OPEN MARKETS

◂ *Rank*

109th	132nd	39th
Trade Freedom **74.9**	Investment Freedom **45.0**	Financial Freedom **60.0**

Trade is important to Mongolia's economy; the value of exports and imports taken together equals 87 percent of GDP. The average applied tariff rate is 5.0 percent. The judicial and regulatory systems impede foreign investment, and state-owned enterprises distort the economy. The limited availability of long-term loans and costly collateral requirements make access to credit a challenge for small and medium-size firms.

MONGOLIA

NEPAL

Nepal's economy lacks the entrepreneurial dynamism needed for stronger economic growth and long-term development. Overall, weak reform efforts have failed to stimulate broad-based poverty reduction. The state continues to hinder private-sector development, and political instability further weakens the capacity to implement economic reform or create a stable development environment.

Overall, the statist approach to economic management and development has been a serious drag on business activity. Lack of transparency, corruption, and a burdensome approval process impede much-needed expansion of private investment and production. Property rights are undermined by the inefficient judicial system, which is subject to substantial corruption and political influence.

ECONOMIC FREEDOM SCORE

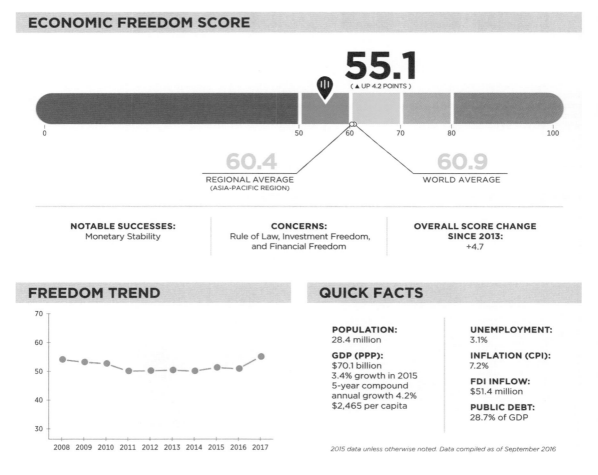

55.1
(▲ UP 4.2 POINTS)

0   50   60   70   80   100

60.4
REGIONAL AVERAGE
(ASIA–PACIFIC REGION)

60.9
WORLD AVERAGE

NOTABLE SUCCESSES:
Monetary Stability

CONCERNS:
Rule of Law, Investment Freedom, and Financial Freedom

OVERALL SCORE CHANGE SINCE 2013:
+4.7

FREEDOM TREND

70
60
50
40
30

2008 2009 2010 2011 2012 2013 2014 2015 2016 2017

QUICK FACTS

POPULATION:
28.4 million

GDP (PPP):
$70.1 billion
3.4% growth in 2015
5-year compound annual growth 4.2%
$2,465 per capita

UNEMPLOYMENT:
3.1%

INFLATION (CPI):
7.2%

FDI INFLOW:
$51.4 million

PUBLIC DEBT:
28.7% of GDP

2015 data unless otherwise noted. Data compiled as of September 2016

BACKGROUND: Political instability continues in Nepal, which has seen eight governments in the past decade. On September 20, 2015, Nepal finally approved a new constitution establishing itself as a federal republic and redrawing political boundaries. Ethnic Madhesis, who have close links to India, objected to the constitution and protested in street demonstrations. In July 2016, an impending vote of no confidence drove Prime Minister Khadga Prasad Oli to resign. The Nepali Congress party and the Communist Party of Nepal (Maoist-Center), which were allied against Oli, agreed to share rotating leadership of the government, and Communist Party chairman Pushpa Kamal Dahal became prime minister in August 2016. The dramatic drop in trade with India since adoption of the constitution has caused a fuel crisis in Nepal.

12 ECONOMIC FREEDOMS | NEPAL

RULE OF LAW

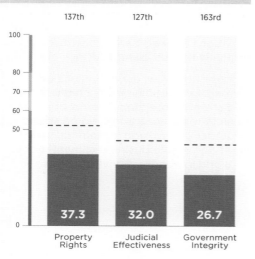

	137th	127th	163rd
	Property Rights	Judicial Effectiveness	Government Integrity
	37.3	32.0	26.7

Property rights are not protected effectively, and it can take years to resolve property disputes. The law provides for an independent judiciary, but courts remain vulnerable to political pressure, bribery, and intimidation. There are numerous reports of corrupt actions by government officials, political parties, and party-affiliated organizations. Corruption and impunity in general are problems within the Nepal Police and Armed Police Force.

GOVERNMENT SIZE

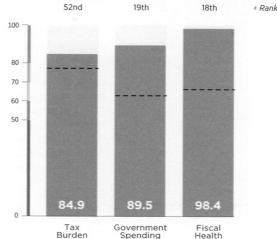

52nd	19th	18th	◄ Rank
Tax Burden	Government Spending	Fiscal Health	
84.9	89.5	98.4	

The top individual income and corporate tax rates are 25 percent. Other taxes include a value-added tax and a property tax. The overall tax burden equals 16.1 percent of total domestic income. Government spending has amounted to 18.7 percent of total output (GDP) over the past three years, and budget surpluses have averaged 1.5 percent of GDP. Public debt is equivalent to 28.7 percent of GDP.

REGULATORY EFFICIENCY

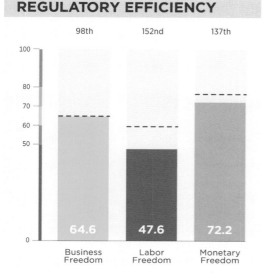

98th	152nd	137th
Business Freedom	Labor Freedom	Monetary Freedom
64.6	47.6	72.2

Despite some progress in streamlining the process for launching a business, other time-consuming requirements reduce the efficiency of the regulatory system. Nepal's labor regulations remain obsolete, and underemployment persists. In the wake of the devastating 2015 earthquake, Nepal has subsidized the rebuilding of homes, contingent on the use of earthquake-resistant methods and materials.

OPEN MARKETS

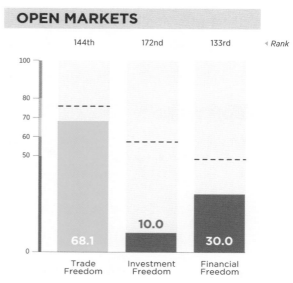

144th	172nd	133rd	◄ Rank
Trade Freedom	Investment Freedom	Financial Freedom	
68.1	10.0	30.0	

Trade is important to Nepal's economy; the value of exports and imports taken together equals 53 percent of GDP. The average applied tariff rate is 10.9 percent. The judicial and regulatory systems impede foreign investment, and state-owned enterprises distort the economy. Nepal's fragmented financial system remains vulnerable to government influence, and financial supervision is inadequate.

NEPAL

NEW ZEALAND

WORLD RANK: **3** | REGIONAL RANK: **3**

ECONOMIC FREEDOM STATUS:
FREE

New Zealand's strong commitment to economic freedom has resulted in a policy framework that encourages impressive economic resilience. Openness to global trade and investment are firmly institutionalized. The financial system has remained stable, and prudent regulations allowed banks to withstand the past global financial turmoil with little disruption.

Other institutional strengths of the Kiwi economy include relatively sound management of public finance, a high degree of monetary stability, and strong protection of property rights. The government continues to maintain a tight rein on spending, keeping public debt under control and sustaining overall fiscal health. A transparent and stable business climate makes New Zealand one of the world's friendliest environments for entrepreneurs.

ECONOMIC FREEDOM SCORE

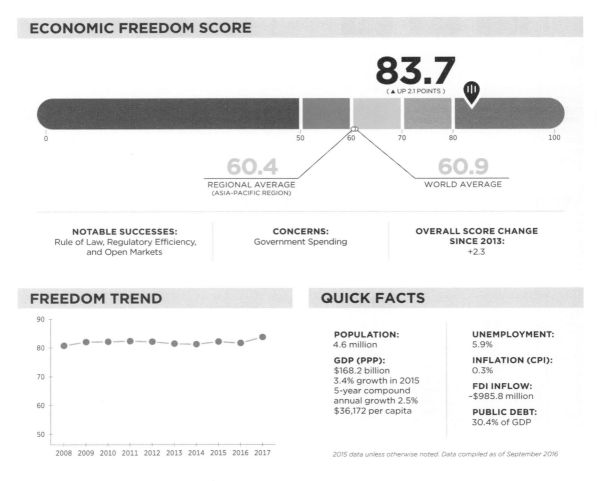

83.7
(▲ UP 2.1 POINTS)

0   50   60   70   80   100

60.4
REGIONAL AVERAGE
(ASIA–PACIFIC REGION)

60.9
WORLD AVERAGE

NOTABLE SUCCESSES:
Rule of Law, Regulatory Efficiency, and Open Markets

CONCERNS:
Government Spending

OVERALL SCORE CHANGE SINCE 2013:
+2.3

FREEDOM TREND

90
80
70
60
50

2008 2009 2010 2011 2012 2013 2014 2015 2016 2017

QUICK FACTS

POPULATION:
4.6 million

GDP (PPP):
$168.2 billion
3.4% growth in 2015
5-year compound annual growth 2.5%
$36,172 per capita

UNEMPLOYMENT:
5.9%

INFLATION (CPI):
0.3%

FDI INFLOW:
–$985.8 million

PUBLIC DEBT:
30.4% of GDP

2015 data unless otherwise noted. Data compiled as of September 2016

BACKGROUND: New Zealand is a parliamentary democracy and one of the Asia–Pacific region's most prosperous countries. After 10 years of Labor Party–dominated governments, the center-right National Party, led by Prime Minister John Key, returned to power in November 2008. Key was reelected in 2011 and 2014. In December 2016, Key resigned and endorsed his deputy, Bill English, who was elected to succeed him as prime minister. Far-reaching deregulation and privatization in the 1980s and 1990s largely liberated the economy. Agriculture is important, but so too are a flourishing manufacturing sector, thriving tourism, and a strong geothermal energy resource base. Following a sizable contraction during the global economic recession, the economy has been expanding since 2010.

12 ECONOMIC FREEDOMS | NEW ZEALAND

RULE OF LAW

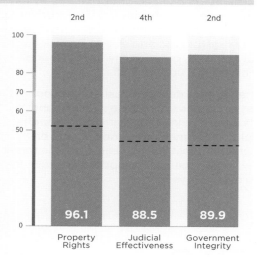

2nd	4th	2nd
96.1	88.5	89.9
Property Rights	Judicial Effectiveness	Government Integrity

Private property rights are strongly protected, and contracts are notably secure. The judicial system is independent and functions well. New Zealand ranked fourth out of 168 countries surveyed in Transparency International's 2015 *Corruption Perceptions Index*. The country is renowned for its efforts to penalize bribery and ensure a transparent, competitive, and corruption-free government procurement system.

GOVERNMENT SIZE

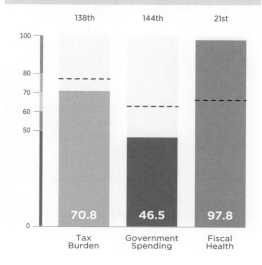

◄ Rank

138th	144th	21st
70.8	46.5	97.8
Tax Burden	Government Spending	Fiscal Health

The top income tax rate is 33 percent, and the top corporate tax rate is 28 percent. Other taxes include a goods and services tax and environmental taxes. The overall tax burden equals 32.4 percent of total domestic income. Government spending has amounted to 42.2 percent of total output (GDP) over the past three years, and budget deficits have averaged 0.5 percent of GDP. Public debt is equivalent to 30.4 percent of GDP.

REGULATORY EFFICIENCY

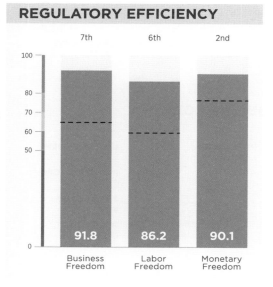

7th	6th	2nd
91.8	86.2	90.1
Business Freedom	Labor Freedom	Monetary Freedom

The entrepreneurial environment is one of the world's most efficient and competitive. Start-up companies enjoy great flexibility under licensing and other regulatory frameworks. The labor regulations facilitate a dynamic labor market. New Zealand, which has the lowest subsidies among OECD countries, removed all farm subsidies more than three decades ago and spurred the development of a vibrant and diversified agriculture sector.

OPEN MARKETS

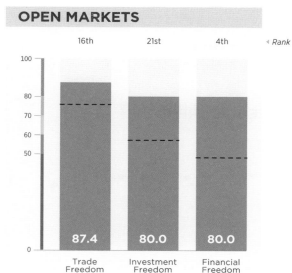

◄ Rank

16th	21st	4th
87.4	80.0	80.0
Trade Freedom	Investment Freedom	Financial Freedom

Trade is important to New Zealand's economy; the value of exports and imports taken together equals 55 percent of GDP. The average applied tariff rate is 1.3 percent. There are few barriers to foreign investment, although some investment may be subject to screening. The financial sector, dominated by banking, is well developed and competitive, offering a full range of financing instruments for entrepreneurial activity.

NEW ZEALAND

PAKISTAN

Pakistan has pursued reforms to improve its entrepreneurial environment and facilitate private-sector development. The financial sector has undergone modernization and restructuring. However, overall progress lags significantly behind other countries in the region. The tax system is complex and inefficient, although reforms to cut tax rates, broaden the tax base, and increase transparency have been undertaken.

The judicial system suffers from a serious backlog and poor security, and corruption continues to taint the judiciary and civil service. The state's excessive involvement in the economy and restrictions on foreign investment are serious drags on economic dynamism. Ongoing political instability and the threat of terrorist violence have made the business operating environment more challenging in recent years.

ECONOMIC FREEDOM SCORE

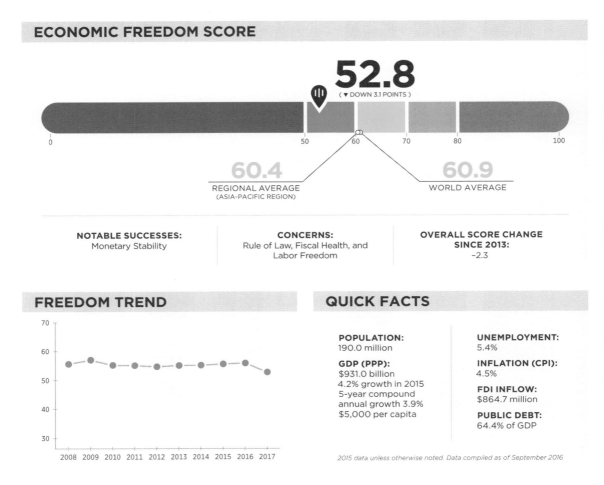

52.8
(▼ DOWN 3.1 POINTS)

0   50   60   70   80   100

60.4
REGIONAL AVERAGE
(ASIA-PACIFIC REGION)

60.9
WORLD AVERAGE

NOTABLE SUCCESSES:
Monetary Stability

CONCERNS:
Rule of Law, Fiscal Health, and Labor Freedom

OVERALL SCORE CHANGE SINCE 2013:
−2.3

FREEDOM TREND

70

60

50

40

30

2008 2009 2010 2011 2012 2013 2014 2015 2016 2017

QUICK FACTS

POPULATION:
190.0 million

GDP (PPP):
$931.0 billion
4.2% growth in 2015
5-year compound
annual growth 3.9%
$5,000 per capita

UNEMPLOYMENT:
5.4%

INFLATION (CPI):
4.5%

FDI INFLOW:
$864.7 million

PUBLIC DEBT:
64.4% of GDP

2015 data unless otherwise noted. Data compiled as of September 2016

BACKGROUND: Prime Minister Nawaz Sharif, elected in 2013, governs an unstable democracy that continues to face formidable threats from sectarian and terrorist violence. Tensions with India remain high, as evidenced by a January 2, 2016, attack by Pakistan-based militants on an Indian air base just six days after Indian Prime Minister Modi's goodwill visit to Lahore. U.S.–Pakistan relations have deteriorated as well. In April 2016, Congress blocked U.S. subsidies for Pakistan's purchase of additional F-16 fighter jets because of Islamabad's failure to include the Haqqani network in its crackdown on militants.

12 ECONOMIC FREEDOMS | PAKISTAN

RULE OF LAW

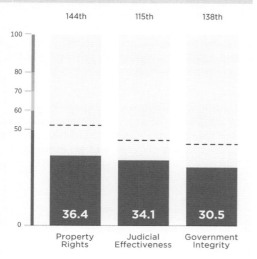

144th   115th   138th   ◀ Rank

Property Rights: **36.4**
Judicial Effectiveness: **34.1**
Government Integrity: **30.5**

Protection of property rights is weak. Although technically independent, the judiciary is subject to external influences, such as fear of reprisal from extremist elements in terrorism or blasphemy cases. Corruption is pervasive in politics, government, and law enforcement, and various politicians and public officeholders face allegations of corruption involving bribery, extortion, cronyism, nepotism, patronage, graft, and embezzlement.

GOVERNMENT SIZE

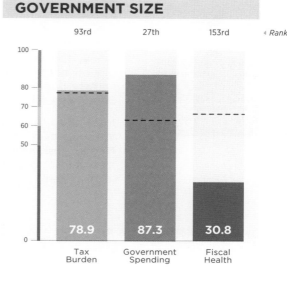

93rd   27th   153rd   ◀ Rank

Tax Burden: **78.9**
Government Spending: **87.3**
Fiscal Health: **30.8**

The top personal income tax rate is 30 percent, and the top corporate tax rate is 33 percent. The overall tax burden equals 11.0 percent of total domestic income. Government spending has amounted to 20.6 percent of total output (GDP) over the past three years, and budget deficits have averaged 6.2 percent of GDP. Public debt is equivalent to 64.4 percent of GDP.

REGULATORY EFFICIENCY

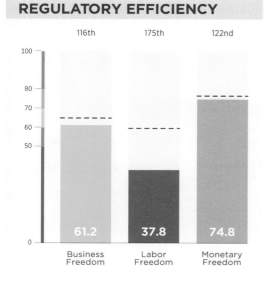

116th   175th   122nd

Business Freedom: **61.2**
Labor Freedom: **37.8**
Monetary Freedom: **74.8**

Progress in improving the entrepreneurial environment has been modest. The cost of completing licensing requirements is still burdensome. A large portion of the workforce is underemployed in the informal sector. The IMF has commended Pakistan for making substantial progress in reducing untargeted energy subsidies from 2.3 percent of GDP in FY 2011–2012 to a budgeted 0.4 percent for FY 2015–2016 but also says that additional cuts are needed.

OPEN MARKETS

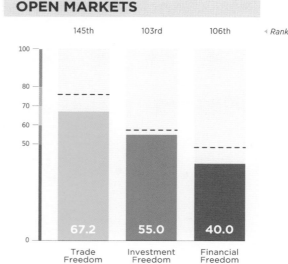

145th   103rd   106th   ◀ Rank

Trade Freedom: **67.2**
Investment Freedom: **55.0**
Financial Freedom: **40.0**

Trade is moderately important to Pakistan's economy; the value of exports and imports taken together equals 28 percent of GDP. The average applied tariff rate is 8.9 percent. The judicial and regulatory systems can deter foreign investment, and state-owned enterprises distort the economy. A majority of the commercial banks are now in private hands, but the sector remains vulnerable to government influence in terms of budgetary support.

PAKISTAN

PAPUA NEW GUINEA

WORLD RANK: 152

REGIONAL RANK: 37

ECONOMIC FREEDOM STATUS:
MOSTLY UNFREE

Papua New Guinea's economy has long been divided between a formal sector based on exports of natural resources and a large informal sector that relies on subsistence farming and other small-scale economic activity. The government intrudes in many aspects of the economy through state ownership and regulation, not only raising the costs of conducting entrepreneurial activity, but also discouraging broader-based development of the private sector.

In an effort to enhance regulatory efficiency, the government introduced an online business registration system early in 2016. Nonetheless, private-sector development is still held back by the lack of institutionalized open-market policies and an inefficient legal system.

ECONOMIC FREEDOM SCORE

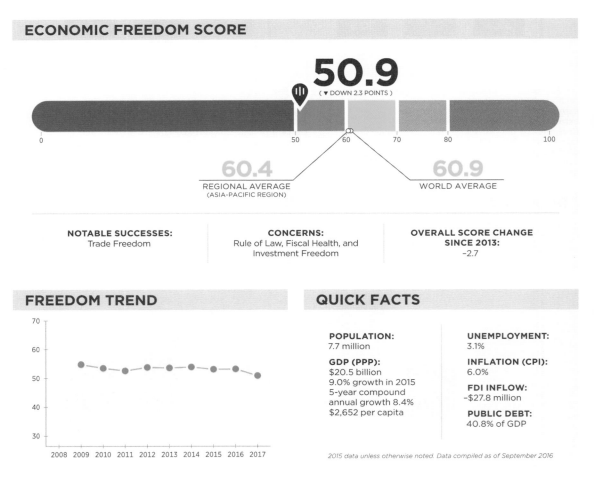

50.9
(▼ DOWN 2.3 POINTS)

0   50   60   70   80   100

60.4
REGIONAL AVERAGE
(ASIA-PACIFIC REGION)

60.9
WORLD AVERAGE

NOTABLE SUCCESSES:	CONCERNS:	OVERALL SCORE CHANGE
Trade Freedom	Rule of Law, Fiscal Health, and Investment Freedom	SINCE 2013: −2.7

FREEDOM TREND

70

60

50

40

30

2008 2009 2010 2011 2012 2013 2014 2015 2016 2017

QUICK FACTS

POPULATION:
7.7 million

GDP (PPP):
$20.5 billion
9.0% growth in 2015
5-year compound
annual growth 8.4%
$2,652 per capita

UNEMPLOYMENT:
3.1%

INFLATION (CPI):
6.0%

FDI INFLOW:
−$27.8 million

PUBLIC DEBT:
40.8% of GDP

2015 data unless otherwise noted. Data compiled as of September 2016

BACKGROUND: Papua New Guinea is a parliamentary democracy whose nearly 7.5 million people speak over 840 different languages. A year-long constitutional crisis subsided in August 2012 with the reelection of Prime Minister Peter O'Neill, whose People's National Congress Party won the most seats in parliament. Sir Michael Somare, O'Neill's chief rival, agreed to form a joint government. In 2014, O'Neill was embroiled in a legal battle over alleged misuse of government funds. Protests against O'Neill, including student protests in 2016 during which police opened fire on protesters, continue today. Elections will be held in 2017. Gold and copper mining, oil, and natural gas dominate the formal economy.

12 ECONOMIC FREEDOMS | PAPUA NEW GUINEA

RULE OF LAW

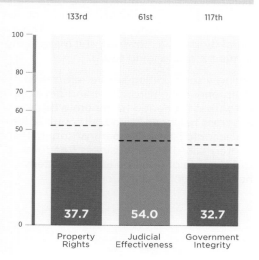

133rd	61st	117th
Property Rights	Judicial Effectiveness	Government Integrity
37.7	54.0	32.7

The law does not permit direct foreign ownership of land, and there are substantial delays both in the government's issuance of long-term leases and in other legal processes to facilitate acquisition and disposition of property rights. The judicial framework is inadequately resourced and underdeveloped. Pervasive corruption and nepotism fueled by large foreign investment windfalls in mining and petroleum are the biggest hindrances to development.

GOVERNMENT SIZE

◄ Rank

149th	105th	161st
Tax Burden	Government Spending	Fiscal Health
67.8	64.5	16.7

The top individual income tax rate is 42 percent, and the top corporate tax rate is 30 percent. Other taxes include a value-added tax and an excise tax. The overall tax burden equals 23.5 percent of total domestic income. Government spending has amounted to 34.4 percent of total output (GDP) over the past three years, and budget deficits have averaged 7.6 percent of GDP. Public debt is equivalent to 40.8 percent of GDP.

REGULATORY EFFICIENCY

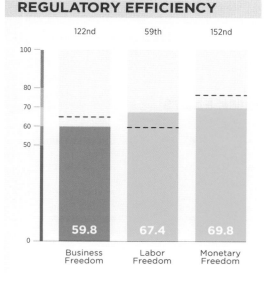

122nd	59th	152nd
Business Freedom	Labor Freedom	Monetary Freedom
59.8	67.4	69.8

The overall regulatory framework remains poor. Labor regulations are relatively flexible, but the formal labor market is not fully developed. Lower prices for liquefied natural gas have caused fiscal deficits to balloon, forcing drastic cuts in transportation, health care, and education subsidies. Heavily subsidized state-owned enterprises provide substandard services for power, water, banking, telecommunications, air travel, and seaports.

OPEN MARKETS

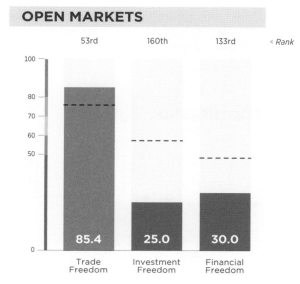

◄ Rank

53rd	160th	133rd
Trade Freedom	Investment Freedom	Financial Freedom
85.4	25.0	30.0

Trade is important to Papua New Guinea's economy; the value of exports and imports taken together equals 57 percent of GDP. The average applied tariff rate is 2.3 percent. Foreign investors may not own land, and investment in several other sectors is restricted. State-owned enterprises distort the economy. Financial intermediation varies across the country, and a large portion of the population remains unconnected to the banking system.

THE PHILIPPINES

Despite the challenging global economic environment, the Philippines has achieved notable economic expansion, driven by the economy's strong export performance and inflows of remittances that have bolstered private consumption. The absence of entrepreneurial dynamism, however, still makes long-term economic development a challenging task.

The government is pursuing a series of legislative reforms to enhance the overall entrepreneurial environment and develop the stronger private sector that is needed to generate broader-based job growth. Progress has been mixed, although some fiscal reforms have been accomplished. Deeper institutional reforms are required in interrelated areas: business freedom, investment freedom, and the rule of law. The judicial system remains weak and vulnerable to political influence.

WORLD RANK: **58** | REGIONAL RANK: **14**

ECONOMIC FREEDOM STATUS:
MODERATELY FREE

ECONOMIC FREEDOM SCORE

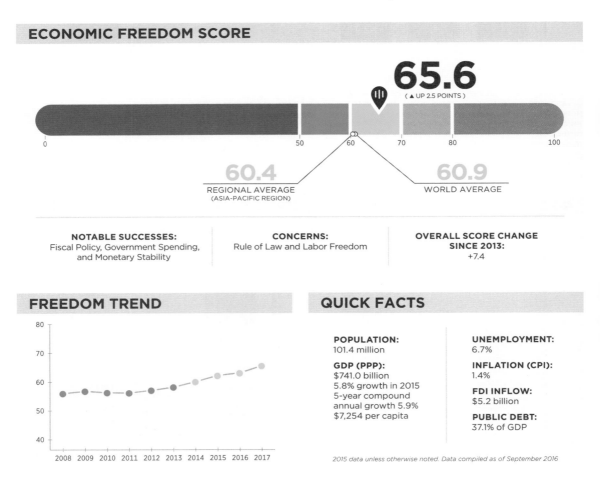

65.6
(▲ UP 2.5 POINTS)

0   50   60   70   80   100

60.4
REGIONAL AVERAGE
(ASIA-PACIFIC REGION)

60.9
WORLD AVERAGE

NOTABLE SUCCESSES:	CONCERNS:	OVERALL SCORE CHANGE
Fiscal Policy, Government Spending, and Monetary Stability	Rule of Law and Labor Freedom	SINCE 2013: +7.4

FREEDOM TREND

80

70

60

50

40

2008 2009 2010 2011 2012 2013 2014 2015 2016 2017

QUICK FACTS

POPULATION:
101.4 million

GDP (PPP):
$741.0 billion
5.8% growth in 2015
5-year compound
annual growth 5.9%
$7,254 per capita

UNEMPLOYMENT:
6.7%

INFLATION (CPI):
1.4%

FDI INFLOW:
$5.2 billion

PUBLIC DEBT:
37.1% of GDP

2015 data unless otherwise noted. Data compiled as of September 2016

BACKGROUND: The Philippines' diverse population, speaking more than 80 languages and dialects, is spread over 7,000 islands in the Western Pacific. During the six-year term of President Benigno Aquino III (2010–2016), the Philippines became one of the region's best-performing economies. Now the question is whether his successor, longtime mayor of Davao City Rodrigo Duterte, will maintain and expand his predecessor's successful policies. While agriculture is still a significant part of the economy, industrial production in areas like electronics, apparel, and shipbuilding has been growing rapidly. Remittances from overseas workers are equivalent to nearly 10 percent of GDP.

12 ECONOMIC FREEDOMS | THE PHILIPPINES

RULE OF LAW

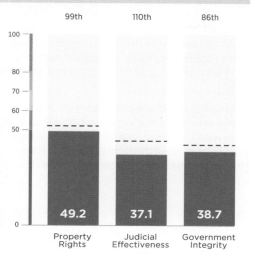

	99th	110th	86th
	49.2	37.1	38.7
	Property Rights	Judicial Effectiveness	Government Integrity

Implementation of laws protecting property rights is weak. Judicial independence is strong, but the rule of law is generally ineffectual. Courts are hampered by inefficiency, low pay, intimidation, and complex procedures. Corruption and cronyism are pervasive. A few dozen leading families hold a disproportionate share of land, corporate wealth, and political power. A culture of impunity is reinforced by the strong-arm tactics of the new president.

GOVERNMENT SIZE

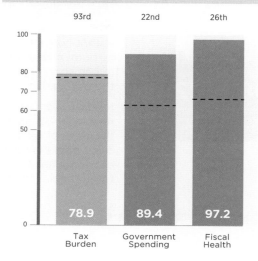

	93rd	22nd	26th	◀ Rank
	78.9	89.4	97.2	
	Tax Burden	Government Spending	Fiscal Health	

The top individual income tax rate is 32 percent, and the top corporate tax rate is 30 percent. Other taxes include a value-added tax and an environmental tax. The overall tax burden equals 13.6 percent of total domestic income. Government spending has amounted to 18.8 percent of total output (GDP) over the past three years, and budget surpluses have averaged 0.4 percent of GDP. Public debt is equivalent to 37.1 percent of GDP.

REGULATORY EFFICIENCY

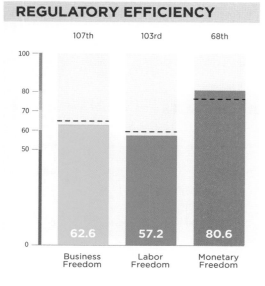

	107th	103rd	68th
	62.6	57.2	80.6
	Business Freedom	Labor Freedom	Monetary Freedom

Gradual improvement of the business regulatory environment includes reduction of the time and cost involved in fulfilling licensing requirements. The labor market remains structurally rigid, but existing regulations are not particularly burdensome. In 2016, the government used its authority to grant special agriculture subsidies in response to El Niño drought conditions. There are price controls on pharmaceuticals and some food and household fuel items.

OPEN MARKETS

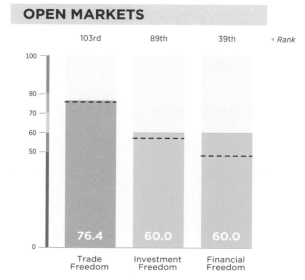

	103rd	89th	39th	◀ Rank
	76.4	60.0	60.0	
	Trade Freedom	Investment Freedom	Financial Freedom	

Trade is important to the Philippines' economy; the value of exports and imports taken together equals 61 percent of GDP. The average applied tariff rate is 4.3 percent. Many agricultural imports face additional barriers. Investment in several economic sectors is restricted. The financial sector remains relatively stable and sound. In 2016, the central bank announced that it would end a 17-year moratorium on the granting of new banking licenses.

SAMOA

The government of Samoa has lagged in reforming vital economic institutions. More vibrant economic growth is constrained by lingering structural weaknesses that continue to undermine economic freedom. Particularly because of persistent corruption, the rule of law is not firmly institutionalized through a well-functioning judicial system. Inefficient and high public spending has resulted in a considerable fiscal burden for the population.

Modest regulatory reforms, including simplification of the business start-up process, have led to increased efficiency. However, the pace of reform has slowed in recent years, and policies to open markets further have not been advanced. The Samoan economy has become more dependent on remittances and foreign aid.

ECONOMIC FREEDOM SCORE

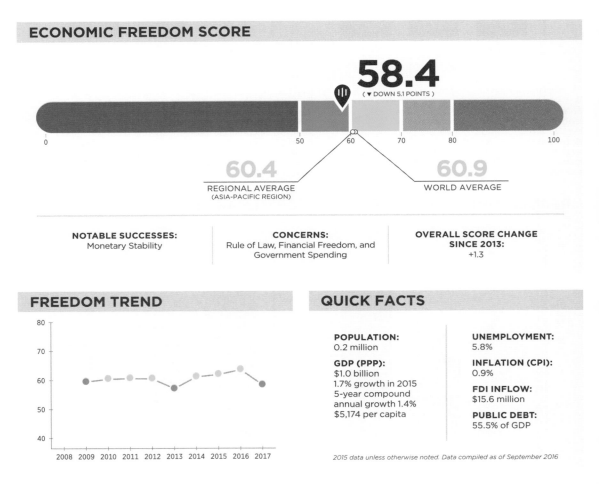

58.4
(▼ DOWN 5.1 POINTS)

0   50   60   70   80   100

60.4
REGIONAL AVERAGE
(ASIA-PACIFIC REGION)

60.9
WORLD AVERAGE

NOTABLE SUCCESSES:
Monetary Stability

CONCERNS:
Rule of Law, Financial Freedom, and Government Spending

OVERALL SCORE CHANGE SINCE 2013:
+1.3

FREEDOM TREND

80

70

60

50

40

2008 2009 2010 2011 2012 2013 2014 2015 2016 2017

QUICK FACTS

POPULATION:
0.2 million

GDP (PPP):
$1.0 billion
1.7% growth in 2015
5-year compound annual growth 1.4%
$5,174 per capita

UNEMPLOYMENT:
5.8%

INFLATION (CPI):
0.9%

FDI INFLOW:
$15.6 million

PUBLIC DEBT:
55.5% of GDP

2015 data unless otherwise noted. Data compiled as of September 2016

BACKGROUND: Samoa is a small South Pacific archipelago with a population of less than 200,000. Independent since 1962, it is now a multi-party, unicameral parliamentary democracy dominated politically by the Human Rights Protection Party (HRPP). A few politicians were found guilty of bribery during the 2011 parliamentary elections, but the HRPP remains in power. Current Prime Minister Tuilaepa Aiono Sailele Malielegaoi, in office since 1998, was reelected in March 2016. Two-thirds of the workforce is employed in the fishing and agricultural sector, which produces 90 percent of exports. Samoa's economy is based on fishing, agriculture, and tourism.

12 ECONOMIC FREEDOMS | SAMOA

RULE OF LAW

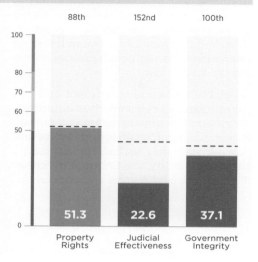

	88th	152nd	100th
	Property Rights	Judicial Effectiveness	Government Integrity
	51.3	22.6	37.1

The judiciary is independent, but a modern and well-functioning legal framework for land ownership and enforcement of property rights is not firmly in place. Official corruption is a major cause of public discontent. An associate minister was found guilty of forgery in January 2016 and later resigned from Parliament, but the recently reelected government has refused to set up an anticorruption tribunal.

GOVERNMENT SIZE

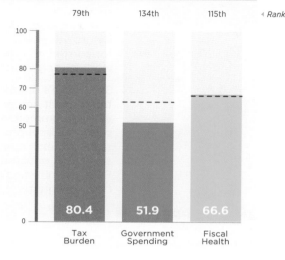

	79th	134th	115th	◄ Rank
	Tax Burden	Government Spending	Fiscal Health	
	80.4	51.9	66.6	

The top individual income and corporate tax rates are 27 percent. Other taxes include a value-added tax and excise taxes. The overall tax burden equals 22.4 percent of total domestic income. Government spending has amounted to 40 percent of total output (GDP) over the past three years, and budget deficits have averaged 4.1 percent of GDP. Public debt is equivalent to 55.5 percent of GDP.

REGULATORY EFFICIENCY

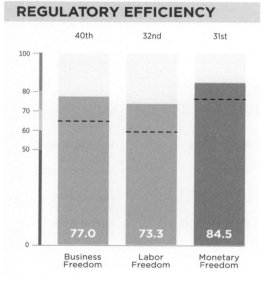

	40th	32nd	31st
	Business Freedom	Labor Freedom	Monetary Freedom
	77.0	73.3	84.5

The application of commercial codes is not always straightforward, and bureaucratic uncertainty continues to hamper the emergence of a vibrant private sector. The nonsalary cost of employing a worker is not costly, but the formal labor market is not fully developed. The government's response to IMF advice that it should privatize the highly subsidized electricity-generation company and other state-owned enterprises has been lackluster.

OPEN MARKETS

	126th	103rd	133rd	◄ Rank
	Trade Freedom	Investment Freedom	Financial Freedom	
	70.7	55.0	30.0	

Trade is important to Samoa's economy; the value of exports and imports taken together equals 78 percent of GDP. The average applied tariff rate is 9.7 percent. Foreign investors may not own land, and investment in some sectors of the economy is restricted. Samoa's small and underdeveloped financial sector is dominated by banking. A significant portion of the population remains unconnected to the formal banking system.

SAMOA

SINGAPORE

Prudent macroeconomic policy and a stable political and legal environment have been the keys to Singapore's continuing success in maintaining a strong and dynamic economy. Well-secured property rights promote entrepreneurship and productivity growth effectively. A strong tradition of minimum tolerance for corruption is institutionalized in an effective judicial framework, strongly sustaining the rule of law.

Singapore's openness to global trade and investment and its transparent and efficient regulatory environment encourage vibrant commercial activity, and the private sector is a prime source of economic resilience and competitiveness. However, state ownership and involvement in key sectors remain substantial. A government statutory entity, the Central Provident Fund, administers public housing, health care, and various other programs.

ECONOMIC FREEDOM SCORE

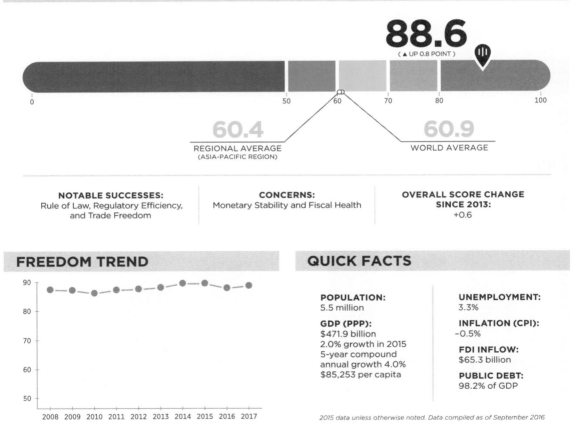

88.6
(▲ UP 0.8 POINT)

0   50   60   70   80   100

60.4
REGIONAL AVERAGE
(ASIA-PACIFIC REGION)

60.9
WORLD AVERAGE

NOTABLE SUCCESSES:
Rule of Law, Regulatory Efficiency, and Trade Freedom

CONCERNS:
Monetary Stability and Fiscal Health

OVERALL SCORE CHANGE SINCE 2013:
+0.6

FREEDOM TREND

90
80
70
60
50
2008 2009 2010 2011 2012 2013 2014 2015 2016 2017

QUICK FACTS

POPULATION:
5.5 million

GDP (PPP):
$471.9 billion
2.0% growth in 2015
5-year compound annual growth 4.0%
$85,253 per capita

UNEMPLOYMENT:
3.3%

INFLATION (CPI):
-0.5%

FDI INFLOW:
$65.3 billion

PUBLIC DEBT:
98.2% of GDP

2015 data unless otherwise noted. Data compiled as of September 2016

BACKGROUND: Singapore is a democratic state that has been ruled by only one party, the People's Action Party (PAP), since independence in 1965. In the September 2015 election, the PAP won 83 of the 89 parliamentary seats and 69.9 percent of the vote. Prime Minister Lee Hsien Loong has led the government since 2004. Certain civil liberties, such as freedom of assembly and freedom of speech, remain restricted, but the PAP has embraced economic liberalization and international trade. Singapore is one of the world's most prosperous nations. Its economy is dominated by services, but the country is also a major manufacturer of electronics and chemicals.

12 ECONOMIC FREEDOMS | SINGAPORE

RULE OF LAW

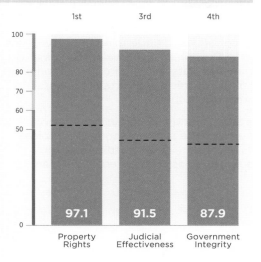

1st   3rd   4th

Property Rights	Judicial Effectiveness	Government Integrity
97.1	91.5	87.9

Property rights are enforced. In 2015, the World Bank ranked Singapore first in enforcement of contracts and 24th in registration of property. Commercial courts function well, but the government's overwhelmingly successful track record in court cases raises questions about judicial independence. Singapore is one of the world's least corrupt countries, although the power of deeply entrenched political elites continues to raise concerns.

GOVERNMENT SIZE

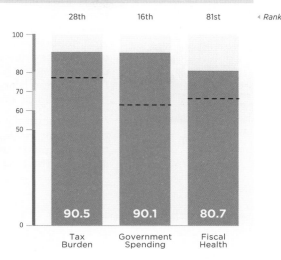

28th   16th   81st   ◄ Rank

Tax Burden	Government Spending	Fiscal Health
90.5	90.1	80.7

The top individual income tax rate has been raised to 22 percent. The top corporate tax rate is 17 percent. The overall tax burden equals 13.4 percent of total domestic income. Government spending has amounted to 18.2 percent of total output (GDP) over the past three years, and budget surpluses have averaged 3.3 percent of GDP. Public debt is equivalent to almost a full year's GDP.

REGULATORY EFFICIENCY

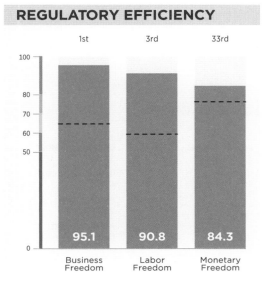

1st   3rd   33rd

Business Freedom	Labor Freedom	Monetary Freedom
95.1	90.8	84.3

The overall entrepreneurial environment remains one of the world's most transparent and efficient. The business start-up process is straightforward, with no minimum capital required. The labor market is vibrant and functions well, supported by flexible labor regulations. The government funds generous housing, transport, and health care subsidy programs and influences other prices through regulation and state-linked enterprises.

OPEN MARKETS

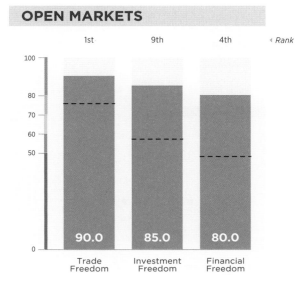

1st   9th   4th   ◄ Rank

Trade Freedom	Investment Freedom	Financial Freedom
90.0	85.0	80.0

Trade is extremely important to Singapore's economy; the value of exports and imports taken together equals 326 percent of GDP. The average applied tariff rate is 0.0 percent, and most sectors of the economy are open to foreign investment. The efficient and well-developed financial sector is highly competitive. The government continues its ownership in the sector but has steadily been opening the domestic market to foreign banks.

SINGAPORE

SOLOMON ISLANDS

WORLD RANK:
126

REGIONAL RANK:
27

ECONOMIC FREEDOM STATUS:
MOSTLY UNFREE

Economic dynamism and development in the Solomon Islands remain stifled by a number of serious deficiencies that include poor governance and an inefficient public sector. Underdeveloped legal and physical infrastructure, combined with political instability, continues to undermine the emergence of a vibrant private sector. Private-sector development is also undercut by the government's outsized role in the economy. The Solomon Islands' limited protection of property rights is a further drag on entrepreneurial activity.

These structural weaknesses limit dynamic business activity, and the agriculture sector remains the primary source of employment. Despite attempts at reform, widespread corruption increases the cost of doing business and deters investment.

ECONOMIC FREEDOM SCORE

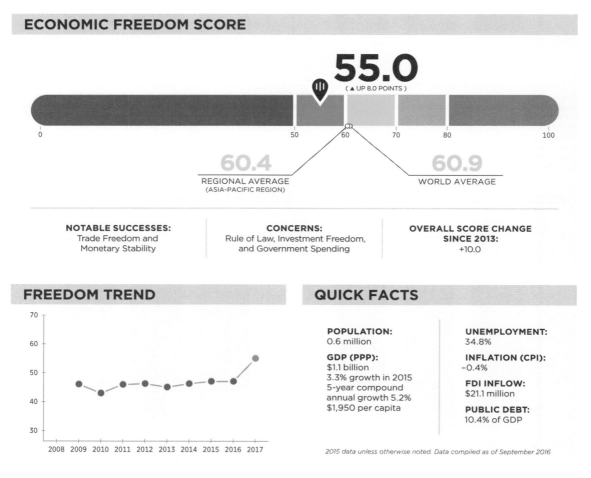

55.0
(▲ UP 8.0 POINTS)

0   50   60   70   80   100

60.4
REGIONAL AVERAGE
(ASIA-PACIFIC REGION)

60.9
WORLD AVERAGE

NOTABLE SUCCESSES:	CONCERNS:	OVERALL SCORE CHANGE
Trade Freedom and Monetary Stability	Rule of Law, Investment Freedom, and Government Spending	SINCE 2013: +10.0

FREEDOM TREND

70
60
50
40
30

2008 2009 2010 2011 2012 2013 2014 2015 2016 2017

QUICK FACTS

POPULATION:
0.6 million

GDP (PPP):
$1.1 billion
3.3% growth in 2015
5-year compound
annual growth 5.2%
$1,950 per capita

UNEMPLOYMENT:
34.8%

INFLATION (CPI):
–0.4%

FDI INFLOW:
$21.1 million

PUBLIC DEBT:
10.4% of GDP

2015 data unless otherwise noted. Data compiled as of September 2016

BACKGROUND: The Solomon Islands is a parliamentary democracy and one of Asia's poorest nations. Danny Philip's election as prime minister in 2010 seemingly stabilized a chaotic political environment, but allegations of corruption forced Philip to resign in 2011. Prime Minister Manasseh Sogavare has been in office since 2014. In recent years, Australia has had to intervene several times to defuse ethnic conflict. Australia, the European Union, Japan, New Zealand, and Taiwan provide significant financial aid. Most of the population lives in rural communities, and three-fourths of the workforce is engaged in subsistence farming and fishing. Economic growth depends largely on logging and exports of timber.

12 ECONOMIC FREEDOMS | SOLOMON ISLANDS

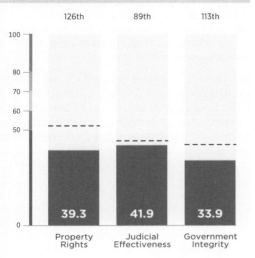

RULE OF LAW

	Property Rights	Judicial Effectiveness	Government Integrity
Rank	126th	89th	113th
Score	39.3	41.9	33.9

Land ownership is reserved for Solomon Islanders, and conflicts over land tenure have been a major source of civil unrest. The judiciary's lack of resources hinders the conduct of timely trials. Residents of rural areas have limited access to the formal justice system. Threats against judges and prosecutors have weakened the judicial system's independence and rigor. Government corruption is a pervasive problem, especially in the forestry and fishing sectors.

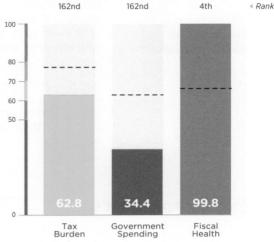

GOVERNMENT SIZE

	Tax Burden	Government Spending	Fiscal Health	◄ Rank
Rank	162nd	162nd	4th	
Score	62.8	34.4	99.8	

The top personal income tax rate is 40 percent, and the top corporate tax rate is 30 percent. Other taxes include a property tax and a sales tax. The overall tax burden equals 35.0 percent of total domestic income. Government spending has amounted to 46.8 percent of total output (GDP) over the past three years, and budget surpluses have averaged 1.9 percent of GDP. Public debt is equivalent to 10.4 percent of GDP.

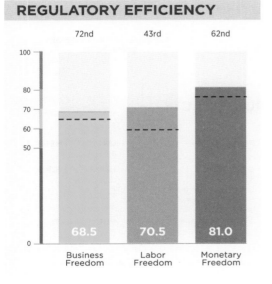

REGULATORY EFFICIENCY

	Business Freedom	Labor Freedom	Monetary Freedom
Rank	72nd	43rd	62nd
Score	68.5	70.5	81.0

The regulatory infrastructure continues to be undermined by bureaucratic bottlenecks. Despite the recognized need for business law reforms, policy action toward greater business freedom has been marginal. The formal labor market is not fully developed, and enforcement of the labor code is not effective. About one-third of total public spending subsidizes infrastructure development projects, many of which are funded by international donors.

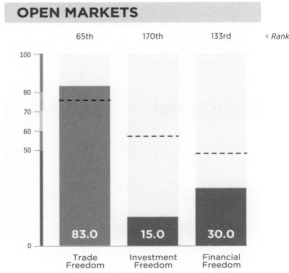

OPEN MARKETS

	Trade Freedom	Investment Freedom	Financial Freedom	◄ Rank
Rank	65th	170th	133rd	
Score	83.0	15.0	30.0	

Trade is important to the Solomon Islands' economy; the value of exports and imports taken together equals 98 percent of GDP. The average applied tariff rate is 8.5 percent. Foreign investment is screened by the government. Four state-owned enterprises have been privatized since 2008. The financial sector is underdeveloped and dominated by banking, and limited access to credit constrains business development.

SRI LANKA

Sri Lanka's economy has expanded at an average rate of about 6 percent over the past five years. The country has made a notable economic transition from fragility to relative stability. Political reconciliation and economic transformation have been strengthened by measures that support long-term development and competitiveness.

Economic reforms undertaken to improve Sri Lanka's macroeconomic stability and potential for growth include strengthening the management of public finance and structural reforms to foster a more dynamic private sector. However, a weak judiciary continues to undermine property rights, and the perceived level of corruption is debilitating.

WORLD RANK: **112** REGIONAL RANK: **25**

ECONOMIC FREEDOM STATUS:
MOSTLY UNFREE

ECONOMIC FREEDOM SCORE

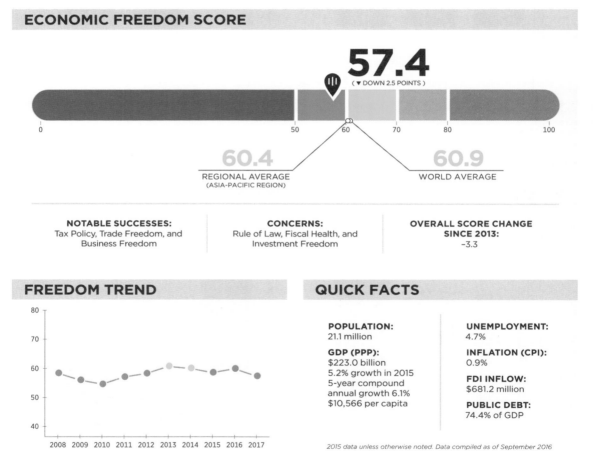

57.4
(▼ DOWN 2.5 POINTS)

0   50   60   70   80   100

60.4
REGIONAL AVERAGE
(ASIA-PACIFIC REGION)

60.9
WORLD AVERAGE

NOTABLE SUCCESSES:
Tax Policy, Trade Freedom, and Business Freedom

CONCERNS:
Rule of Law, Fiscal Health, and Investment Freedom

OVERALL SCORE CHANGE SINCE 2013:
−3.3

FREEDOM TREND

80
70
60
50
40

2008 2009 2010 2011 2012 2013 2014 2015 2016 2017

QUICK FACTS

POPULATION:
21.1 million

GDP (PPP):
$223.0 billion
5.2% growth in 2015
5-year compound annual growth 6.1%
$10,566 per capita

UNEMPLOYMENT:
4.7%

INFLATION (CPI):
0.9%

FDI INFLOW:
$681.2 million

PUBLIC DEBT:
74.4% of GDP

2015 data unless otherwise noted. Data compiled as of September 2016

BACKGROUND: President Mahinda Rajapaksa was voted out of office in January 2015. Prime Minister Maithripala Sirisena, who ran against him on pledges to restore parliamentary democracy and rein in corruption, formed a coalition government with the opposition United National Party (UNP) and reinstated presidential term limits. Parliamentary elections in August 2015 brought UNP leader Ranil Wickremesinghe to power as the new prime minister. Sirisena and Wickremesinghe have pledged to work together for ethnic reconciliation and in September 2015 co-sponsored a U.N. Human Rights Council resolution acknowledging that war crimes were committed by both the government and the Liberation Tigers of Tamil Eelam during the civil war that ended in 2009.

12 ECONOMIC FREEDOMS | SRI LANKA

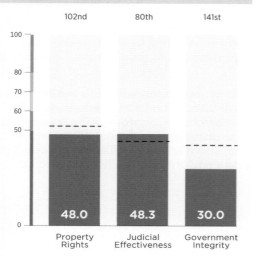

RULE OF LAW

102nd	80th	141st
Property Rights 48.0	Judicial Effectiveness 48.3	Government Integrity 30.0

Secured interests in property are generally recognized, and there is a fairly reliable registration system for recording private property, but many investors claim that protection can be flimsy. Judicial independence has improved under the new administration. Although corruption remains a concern, steps were taken in 2015 to strengthen enforcement of existing safeguards and uphold the current legal and administrative framework.

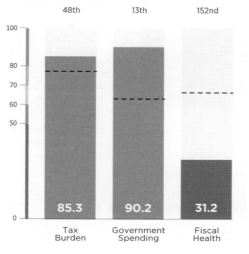

GOVERNMENT SIZE

48th	13th	152nd	◄ Rank
Tax Burden 85.3	Government Spending 90.2	Fiscal Health 31.2	

The top personal income tax rate is 24 percent, and the top corporate tax rate is 28 percent. Other taxes include a value-added tax. The overall tax burden equals 10.7 percent of total domestic income. Government spending has amounted to 18.1 percent of total output (GDP) over the past three years, and budget deficits have averaged 6.0 percent of GDP. Public debt is equivalent to 74.4 percent of GDP.

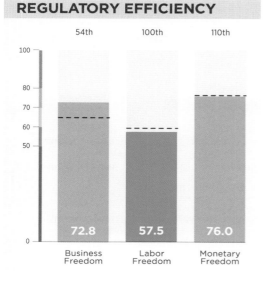

REGULATORY EFFICIENCY

54th	100th	110th
Business Freedom 72.8	Labor Freedom 57.5	Monetary Freedom 76.0

The business start-up process has been streamlined, and the number of licensing requirements has been reduced. Because the labor market lacks efficiency, there is an imbalance between labor supply and demand. In 2016, the IMF recommended that the government phase out some of its extensive system of price controls and subsidies that distort most sectors of the economy. The government's plan to privatize some industries faces public opposition.

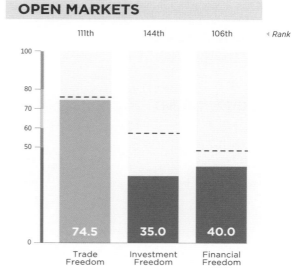

OPEN MARKETS

111th	144th	106th	◄ Rank
Trade Freedom 74.5	Investment Freedom 35.0	Financial Freedom 40.0	

Trade is moderately important to Sri Lanka's economy; the value of exports and imports taken together equals 48 percent of GDP. The average applied tariff rate is 5.3 percent. Investment in some sectors of the economy is restricted, and state-owned enterprises distort the economy. The financial sector remains underdeveloped. Nonperforming loans remain a problem in the banking system, and the allocation of credit is subject to state influence.

SRI LANKA

TAIWAN

WORLD RANK:
11

REGIONAL RANK:
5

ECONOMIC FREEDOM STATUS:
MOSTLY FREE

Taiwan's private sector has benefited from a relatively well-developed commercial code and open-market policies that facilitate the free flow of goods and capital. Small and medium-size enterprises have been the backbone of Taiwan's dynamic economic expansion. A sound legal framework is in place to provide strong protection of property rights and uphold the rule of law.

Although institutional and economic fundamentals are in place, further reforms to increase competition and openness will be critical to sustaining the momentum for growth. The level of state involvement in the export-oriented economy remains considerable. Privatization and market liberalization are ongoing, but progress has been slow and uneven. The financial sector remains fragmented.

ECONOMIC FREEDOM SCORE

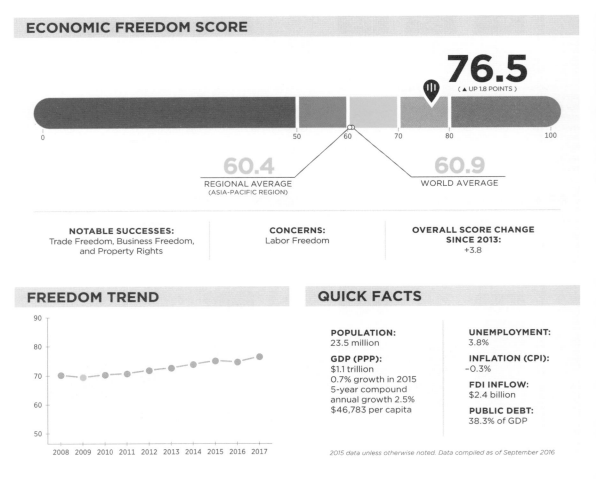

76.5
(▲ UP 1.8 POINTS)

0   50   60   70   80   100

60.4
REGIONAL AVERAGE
(ASIA-PACIFIC REGION)

60.9
WORLD AVERAGE

NOTABLE SUCCESSES:
Trade Freedom, Business Freedom, and Property Rights

CONCERNS:
Labor Freedom

OVERALL SCORE CHANGE SINCE 2013:
+3.8

FREEDOM TREND

90

80

70

60

50

2008 2009 2010 2011 2012 2013 2014 2015 2016 2017

QUICK FACTS

POPULATION:
23.5 million

GDP (PPP):
$1.1 trillion
0.7% growth in 2015
5-year compound annual growth 2.5%
$46,783 per capita

UNEMPLOYMENT:
3.8%

INFLATION (CPI):
−0.3%

FDI INFLOW:
$2.4 billion

PUBLIC DEBT:
38.3% of GDP

2015 data unless otherwise noted. Data compiled as of September 2016

BACKGROUND: Taiwan is a dynamic multi-party democracy, and its economy is one of the richest in Asia. The Democratic Progressive Party returned to power when Tsai Ing-wen was elected president in 2016. As a result of the election and the economic slowdown in China, tourism, an important source of economic growth, has declined. Taiwan is excluded from membership in the United Nations, other international organizations, and a variety of free trade arrangements as part of Beijing's efforts to pressure it into unification. Although internal opposition to engaging with China is considerable because of fears that sovereignty will be lost, recent economic arrangements bind the island closer to the mainland.

12 ECONOMIC FREEDOMS | TAIWAN

RULE OF LAW

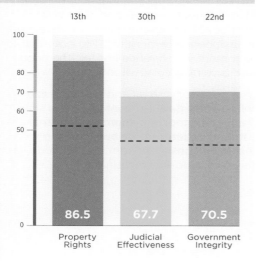

13th 30th 22nd

Property Rights	Judicial Effectiveness	Government Integrity
86.5	67.7	70.5

Property rights are generally protected, and contracts are enforced effectively. The judiciary is independent, and the court system is largely free of political interference. Although corruption is much less prevalent today, it remains a problem. Politics and big business are closely intertwined, and this leads to malfeasance in government procurement. In November 2015, a former New Taipei City deputy mayor was charged with taking $230,000 in bribes.

GOVERNMENT SIZE

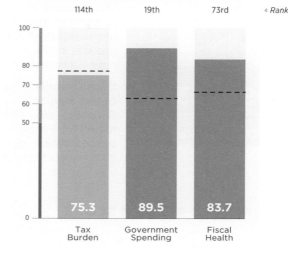

114th 19th 73rd ◄ Rank

Tax Burden	Government Spending	Fiscal Health
75.3	89.5	83.7

The top personal income tax rate has been raised to 45 percent. The top corporate tax rate is 17 percent. Other taxes include a value-added tax and an interest tax. The overall tax burden equals 12.3 percent of total domestic income. Government spending has amounted to 18.7 percent of total output (GDP) over the past three years, and budget deficits have averaged 2.9 percent of GDP. Public debt is equivalent to 38.3 percent of GDP.

REGULATORY EFFICIENCY

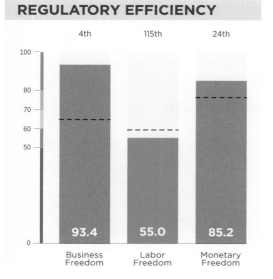

4th 115th 24th

Business Freedom	Labor Freedom	Monetary Freedom
93.4	55.0	85.2

The overall freedom to conduct business is relatively well protected under the transparent regulatory environment. The nonsalary cost of employing a worker is low, but regulations on work hours are not flexible. Taiwan law mandates price controls on electricity and salt, and the government regulates prices for fuels and pharmaceutical products. Other prices are determined largely by the market.

OPEN MARKETS

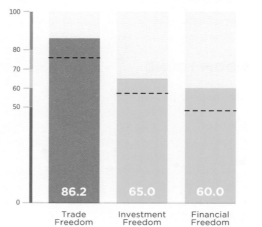

48th 73rd 39th ◄ Rank

Trade Freedom	Investment Freedom	Financial Freedom
86.2	65.0	60.0

Trade is extremely important to Taiwan's economy; the value of exports and imports taken together equals 111 percent of GDP. The average applied tariff rate is 1.9 percent, and some agricultural imports face additional barriers. Foreign investment is screened, and investment in some sectors is restricted. The financial sector continues to evolve, and the stock market is generally open to foreign participation. Foreign banks play a relatively small role.

TAIWAN

TAJIKISTAN

Tajikistan's many ongoing challenges include rebuilding infrastructure, improving the entrepreneurial environment, and attracting dynamic investment. Progress on reforms to foster sounder macroeconomic management and improvement of the business climate has been only marginal. The potential for growth is high, but government interference has left the economy vulnerable in a repressive political environment.

Despite some progress in privatizing small and medium-size public enterprises, private-sector development has been slow. Remittances continue to be an important source of external financing. Foreign investment is deterred by burdensome bureaucratic regulations and inconsistent administration. Tajikistan remains one of the world's most corrupt nations.

WORLD RANK:
109

REGIONAL RANK:
23

ECONOMIC FREEDOM STATUS:
MOSTLY UNFREE

ECONOMIC FREEDOM SCORE

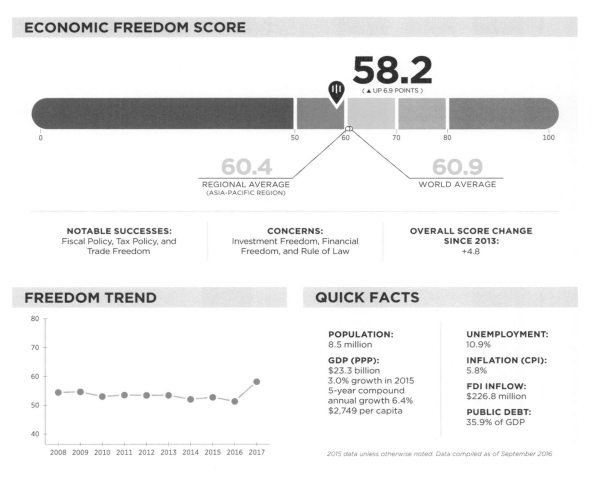

58.2
(▲ UP 6.9 POINTS)

0   50   60   70   80   100

60.4
REGIONAL AVERAGE
(ASIA-PACIFIC REGION)

60.9
WORLD AVERAGE

NOTABLE SUCCESSES:
Fiscal Policy, Tax Policy, and Trade Freedom

CONCERNS:
Investment Freedom, Financial Freedom, and Rule of Law

OVERALL SCORE CHANGE SINCE 2013:
+4.8

FREEDOM TREND

80

70

60

50

40

2008 2009 2010 2011 2012 2013 2014 2015 2016 2017

QUICK FACTS

POPULATION:
8.5 million

GDP (PPP):
$23.3 billion
3.0% growth in 2015
5-year compound annual growth 6.4%
$2,749 per capita

UNEMPLOYMENT:
10.9%

INFLATION (CPI):
5.8%

FDI INFLOW:
$226.8 million

PUBLIC DEBT:
35.9% of GDP

2015 data unless otherwise noted. Data compiled as of September 2016

BACKGROUND: President Emomali Rahmon has been in power since 1994. His ruling party won parliamentary elections in March 2015 that were criticized by international monitors. For the first time since 1991, the Communists and the Islamic Renaissance Party failed to clear the 5 percent threshold needed to win seats. Relations with neighboring Uzbekistan are strained, and the Russian military patrols the border with Afghanistan. Abuse of human rights is widespread. Tajikistan relies heavily on revenues from aluminum and cotton exports. It is estimated that the illegal drug trade and remittances from migrant workers, primarily in Russia, account for over 45 percent of GDP. Tajikistan has been negatively affected by the economic slowdown in Russia.

12 ECONOMIC FREEDOMS | TAJIKISTAN

RULE OF LAW

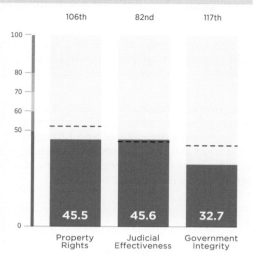

	106th	82nd	117th
	Property Rights	Judicial Effectiveness	Government Integrity
	45.5	45.6	32.7

Under Tajik law, all land belongs to the state. The judiciary lacks independence. Many judges are poorly trained and inexperienced, and bribery is reportedly widespread. Corruption is pervasive. Patronage networks and regional affiliations are central to political life. At least two of President Rahmon's children hold senior government posts, and various family members reportedly maintain extensive business interests in the country.

GOVERNMENT SIZE

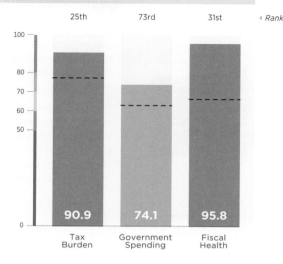

◄ Rank

	25th	73rd	31st
	Tax Burden	Government Spending	Fiscal Health
	90.9	74.1	95.8

The top individual income tax rate is 13 percent, and the statutory corporate tax rate is 15 percent. Other taxes include a value-added tax. The overall tax burden equals 22.8 percent of total domestic income. Government spending has amounted to 29.4 percent of total output (GDP) over the past three years, and budget deficits have averaged 1.0 percent of GDP. Public debt is equivalent to 35.9 percent of GDP.

REGULATORY EFFICIENCY

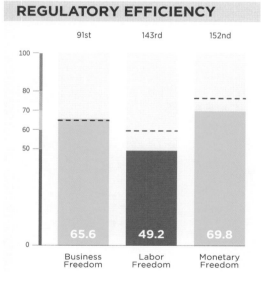

	91st	143rd	152nd
	Business Freedom	Labor Freedom	Monetary Freedom
	65.6	49.2	69.8

Entrepreneurial activity is hampered by state interference that increases regulatory costs and uncertainty through various bureaucratic impediments. Labor regulations are not flexible enough to facilitate dynamic employment growth. The government influences prices through regulation and large subsidies to numerous state-owned and state-trading enterprises. The economy is highly dollarized, and central bank institutional capacity is weak.

OPEN MARKETS

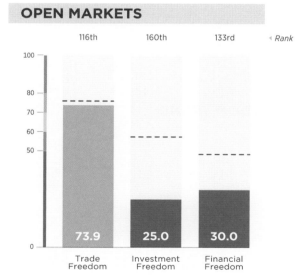

◄ Rank

	116th	160th	133rd
	Trade Freedom	Investment Freedom	Financial Freedom
	73.9	25.0	30.0

Trade is important to Tajikistan's economy; the value of exports and imports taken together equals 55 percent of GDP. The average applied tariff rate is 5.6 percent. All land is owned by the government. The government screens foreign investment, and state-owned enterprises distort the economy. The government's continuing interference and the financial sector's limited overall capacity are serious impediments to development of the private sector.

THAILAND

Thailand's government has taken measures to enhance regulatory efficiency and better integrate the economy into the global marketplace. The overall regulatory framework has gradually become more efficient and transparent, with procedures for business formation streamlined and the financial sector opened to competition. The level of trade freedom is relatively high, although nontariff barriers continue to undercut gains from trade.

Despite relatively solid economic fundamentals, serious challenges require deeper institutional reforms. Political instability continues to undermine the investment climate and hold economic activity far below potential levels. The judicial system remains vulnerable to political interference, and government integrity has been undermined by pervasive corruption.

WORLD RANK: **55**
REGIONAL RANK: **13**

ECONOMIC FREEDOM STATUS:
MODERATELY FREE

ECONOMIC FREEDOM SCORE

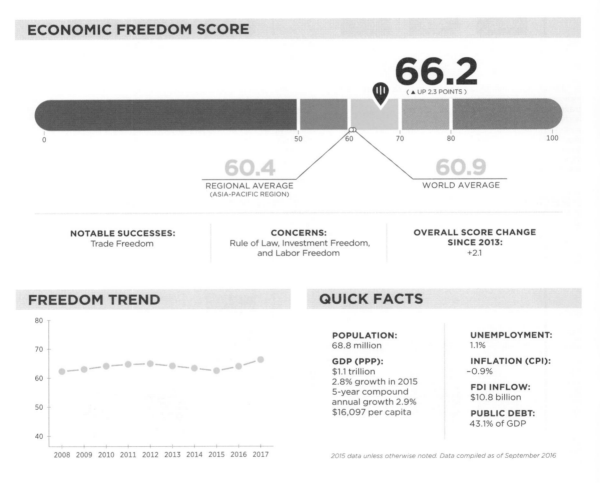

66.2
(▲ UP 2.3 POINTS)

0   50   60   70   80   100

60.4
REGIONAL AVERAGE
(ASIA-PACIFIC REGION)

60.9
WORLD AVERAGE

NOTABLE SUCCESSES:
Trade Freedom

CONCERNS:
Rule of Law, Investment Freedom, and Labor Freedom

OVERALL SCORE CHANGE SINCE 2013:
+2.1

FREEDOM TREND

(Chart values for years 2008–2017, vertical axis 40–80)

QUICK FACTS

POPULATION:
68.8 million

GDP (PPP):
$1.1 trillion
2.8% growth in 2015
5-year compound annual growth 2.9%
$16,097 per capita

UNEMPLOYMENT:
1.1%

INFLATION (CPI):
−0.9%

FDI INFLOW:
$10.8 billion

PUBLIC DEBT:
43.1% of GDP

2015 data unless otherwise noted. Data compiled as of September 2016

BACKGROUND: Thailand has had 19 military coups since becoming a constitutional monarchy in 1932. The period since the ouster and exile of Thaksin Shinawatra in 2006 has been particularly turbulent. Civilian government returned in 2007, and Pheu Thai, the legacy party of the Thaksin government, won an outright majority in the 2011 parliamentary elections. Thaksin's sister, Yingluck Shinawatra, became prime minister but was subsequently ousted from power in spring 2014 in a military coup led by former army commander Prayut Chan-ocha, who is now prime minister. New elections, initially expected to be held in October 2015, have been postponed first until 2016 and again until 2017 following a referendum on a new constitution.

12 ECONOMIC FREEDOMS | THAILAND

RULE OF LAW

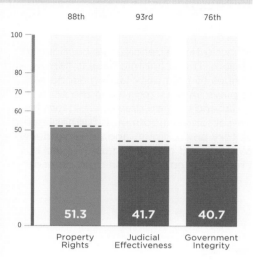

	88th	93rd	76th
Property Rights	51.3		
Judicial Effectiveness		41.7	
Government Integrity			40.7

The independent judiciary has generally been effective in enforcing property and contractual rights but has been criticized for political bias. Owners of intellectual property rights must still contend with widespread counterfeiting and piracy. Corruption is widespread at all levels of society, and bribery is viewed as a normal part of doing business. Low civil service salaries also reportedly encourage officials to accept illegal inducements.

GOVERNMENT SIZE

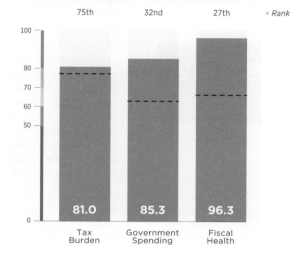

	75th	32nd	27th	◂ Rank
Tax Burden	81.0			
Government Spending		85.3		
Fiscal Health			96.3	

The top personal income tax rate is 35 percent, and the top corporate tax rate is 20 percent. Other taxes include a value-added tax and a property tax. The overall tax burden equals 16.5 percent of total domestic income. Government spending has amounted to 22.2 percent of total output (GDP) over the past three years, and budget deficits have averaged 0.1 percent of GDP. Public debt is equivalent to 43.1 percent of GDP.

REGULATORY EFFICIENCY

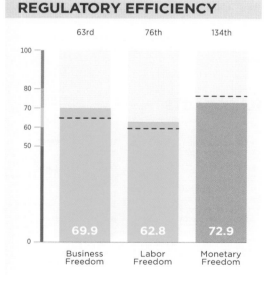

	63rd	76th	134th
Business Freedom	69.9		
Labor Freedom		62.8	
Monetary Freedom			72.9

Recent reforms have improved regulatory efficiency, although licensing requirements remain time-consuming. Labor regulations are relatively flexible, but informal labor activity remains substantial. The military government appears to have no intention of phasing out price controls on an extensive list of goods and services, including basic foods, cooking oils, and fertilizer, that have been in place for many years.

OPEN MARKETS

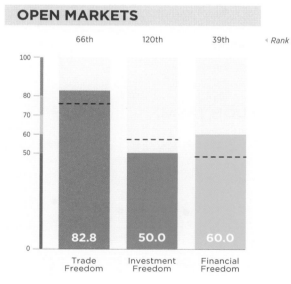

	66th	120th	39th	◂ Rank
Trade Freedom	82.8			
Investment Freedom		50.0		
Financial Freedom			60.0	

Trade is extremely important to Thailand's economy; the value of exports and imports taken together equals 132 percent of GDP. The average applied tariff rate is 3.6 percent. The government has undertaken measures to facilitate trade, but investment in several sectors of the economy is restricted. The financial system has undergone restructuring, and the regulatory framework has been strengthened. The stock exchange is active and open to foreign investors.

THAILAND

TIMOR-LESTE

WORLD RANK:
173

REGIONAL RANK:
42

ECONOMIC FREEDOM STATUS:
REPRESSED

Timor-Leste has made some progress toward macroeconomic stability since achieving independence in 2002. Gains in poverty reduction and income growth have been driven largely by development of the oil and gas sector.

However, structural and institutional deficiencies continue to constrain economic freedom. The economic base is narrow, and political instability continues to hold back lasting economic development. The state plays an outsized role in the economy with its increasing dependence on drawdowns from the Petroleum Fund. Private-sector development is further limited by a burdensome regulatory environment and an underdeveloped financial sector. Widespread corruption unchecked by a weak judicial system remains a considerable drag on economic activity.

ECONOMIC FREEDOM SCORE

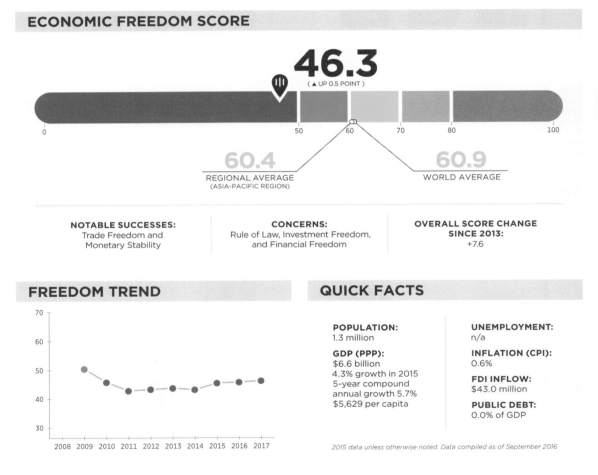

46.3
(▲ UP 0.5 POINT)

0   50   60   70   80   100

60.4
REGIONAL AVERAGE
(ASIA-PACIFIC REGION)

60.9
WORLD AVERAGE

NOTABLE SUCCESSES:
Trade Freedom and
Monetary Stability

CONCERNS:
Rule of Law, Investment Freedom,
and Financial Freedom

**OVERALL SCORE CHANGE
SINCE 2013:**
+7.6

FREEDOM TREND

70

60

50

40

30

2008 2009 2010 2011 2012 2013 2014 2015 2016 2017

QUICK FACTS

POPULATION:
1.3 million

GDP (PPP):
$6.6 billion
4.3% growth in 2015
5-year compound
annual growth 5.7%
$5,629 per capita

UNEMPLOYMENT:
n/a

INFLATION (CPI):
0.6%

FDI INFLOW:
$43.0 million

PUBLIC DEBT:
0.0% of GDP

2015 data unless otherwise noted. Data compiled as of September 2016

BACKGROUND: The Democratic Republic of Timor-Leste became independent in 2002, and successive governments have struggled to pacify the country. Revolutionary leader Xanana Gusmao, its first president, who had been prime minister since 2007, stepped down in February 2015 and appointed opposition leader Rui Araujo as his successor. Timor-Leste remains one of East Asia's poorest countries. Economic liberalization has mostly stalled, and the economy depends heavily on foreign aid. Oil and gas profits account for more than 95 percent of government revenue. The government deposits all oil income in the Petroleum Fund, which is not counted as part of GDP but is reflected in government revenue figures.

12 ECONOMIC FREEDOMS | TIMOR-LESTE

RULE OF LAW

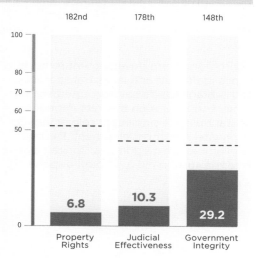

	182nd	178th	148th
	6.8	10.3	29.2
	Property Rights	Judicial Effectiveness	Government Integrity

Land reform remains an unresolved and contentious issue with rival property claims from the Portuguese, Indonesian, and post-independence eras. The overly complex legal regime reflects that same confusing pedigree. The weak judicial system suffers from a severe shortage of qualified personnel and has failed to demonstrate independence in some politically sensitive cases. Corruption and nepotism continue to be serious problems.

GOVERNMENT SIZE

	157th	103rd	159th	◄ Rank
	64.7	65.6	20.0	
	Tax Burden	Government Spending	Fiscal Health	

The top personal income and corporate tax rates are 10 percent. Most government revenue comes from offshore petroleum projects in the Timor Sea. Overall government revenue, including large petroleum receipts, equals 61.5 percent of total domestic income. Government spending has risen to more than 50 percent of total output (GDP) over the past three years, and budget deficits have averaged 46.6 percent of GDP. Timor-Leste has no public debt.

REGULATORY EFFICIENCY

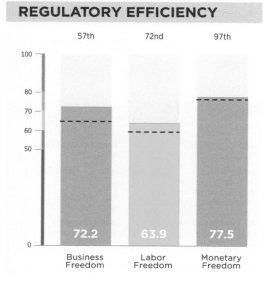

	57th	72nd	97th
	72.2	63.9	77.5
	Business Freedom	Labor Freedom	Monetary Freedom

The lack of consistency in enforcing regulations continues to discourage private-sector development. The minimum capital necessary to start a business is quite high. The public sector accounts for approximately half of nonagricultural employment, and the formal labor market remains underdeveloped. With state revenues reduced as a result of low world oil prices, the IMF has urged the government to curtail its large subsidy programs.

OPEN MARKETS

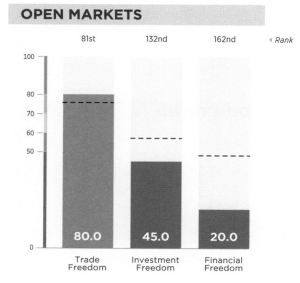

	81st	132nd	162nd	◄ Rank
	80.0	45.0	20.0	
	Trade Freedom	Investment Freedom	Financial Freedom	

Trade is extremely important to Timor-Leste's economy; the value of exports and imports taken together equals 111 percent of GDP. The average applied tariff rate is 2.5 percent. Foreign ownership of land is not allowed, and investment in other sectors of the economy is screened. Modest progress has been made in establishing an effective banking system, but the financial sector is still at a nascent stage of development.

TIMOR-LESTE

TONGA

Tonga's economy remains heavily dependent on foreign aid and overseas remittances. The dominance of the public sector has contributed to a low level of economic dynamism despite a workforce that is considered the best educated among the Pacific Island nations.

The institutional capacity for long-term development remains weak. The judicial system is inefficient and lacks transparency. Although trade-weighted average tariffs have dropped significantly, a lack of commitment to fully open markets impedes investment growth. The state plays a significant role in the economy, crowding out private-sector development. Despite improved oversight of government expenditures, Tonga's public debt poses a challenge to the sustainability of public spending.

ECONOMIC FREEDOM SCORE

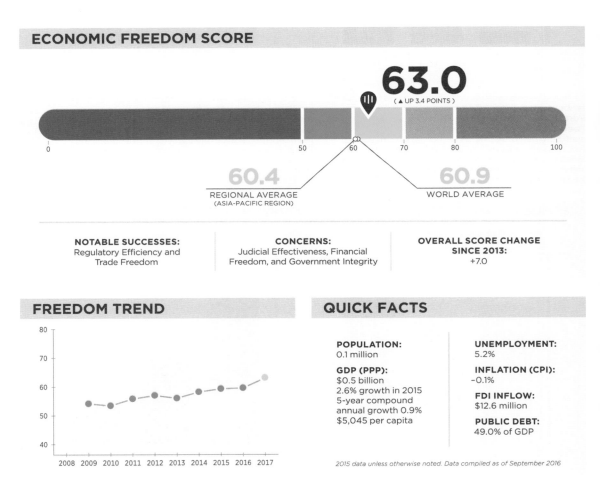

63.0
(▲ UP 3.4 POINTS)

0   50   60   70   80   100

60.4
REGIONAL AVERAGE
(ASIA-PACIFIC REGION)

60.9
WORLD AVERAGE

NOTABLE SUCCESSES:
Regulatory Efficiency and
Trade Freedom

CONCERNS:
Judicial Effectiveness, Financial
Freedom, and Government Integrity

**OVERALL SCORE CHANGE
SINCE 2013:**
+7.0

FREEDOM TREND

QUICK FACTS

POPULATION:
0.1 million

GDP (PPP):
$0.5 billion
2.6% growth in 2015
5-year compound
annual growth 0.9%
$5,045 per capita

UNEMPLOYMENT:
5.2%

INFLATION (CPI):
−0.1%

FDI INFLOW:
$12.6 million

PUBLIC DEBT:
49.0% of GDP

2015 data unless otherwise noted. Data compiled as of September 2016

BACKGROUND: The Kingdom of Tonga, the South Pacific's last Polynesian monarchy, has been independent since 1970. The royal family, hereditary nobles, and a few other landholders control politics. Tonga held its first elections in November 2010 under its newly formed constitutional monarchy. The Democratic Party of the Friendly Islands won a plurality in parliament, and Lord Siale'ataongo Tu'ivakano became Tonga's first elected prime minister. In 2014 elections, the Democratic Party of the Friendly Islands maintained power but elected a new prime minister, 'Akilisi Pohiva. Agriculture is the principal productive sector of the economy, and remittances from abroad are a significant source of income.

12 ECONOMIC FREEDOMS | TONGA

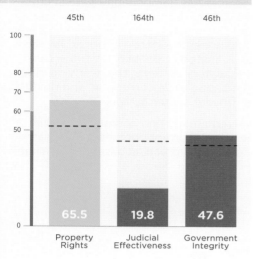

RULE OF LAW

	45th	164th	46th
	Property Rights	Judicial Effectiveness	Government Integrity
	65.5	19.8	47.6

Property rights are uncertain, and their enforcement is weak. The judicial system is generally independent but inadequately resourced. In 2014, public support for democratic reforms and dissatisfaction with widespread corruption among the Tongan nobility and their top associates led to the election of a reformist government that has struggled to implement policy while facing opposition from vested interests and a faction of nobles in the legislature.

GOVERNMENT SIZE

	40th	68th	86th	◄ Rank
	Tax Burden	Government Spending	Fiscal Health	
	86.9	74.4	79.6	

The top personal income tax rate is 20 percent, and the top corporate tax rate is 25 percent. Other taxes include a value-added tax and an interest tax. The overall tax burden equals 17.0 percent of total domestic income. Government spending has amounted to 29.2 percent of total output (GDP) over the past three years, and budget deficits have averaged 0.5 percent of GDP. Public debt is equivalent to 49.0 percent of GDP.

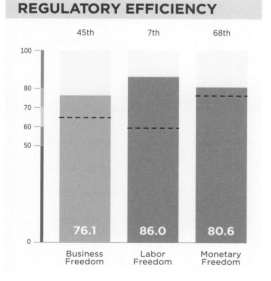

REGULATORY EFFICIENCY

	45th	7th	68th
	Business Freedom	Labor Freedom	Monetary Freedom
	76.1	86.0	80.6

A dynamic private sector has not emerged, partly because of inefficient implementation of a statutorily business-friendly regulatory environment. The formal labor sector is underdeveloped, and labor regulations are not enforced effectively. The foreign aid–dependent government is under pressure from international donors to scale back subsidies for electricity and loss-making state-owned enterprises that it uses to influence prices.

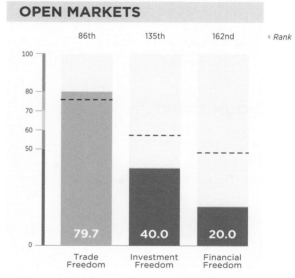

OPEN MARKETS

	86th	135th	162nd	◄ Rank
	Trade Freedom	Investment Freedom	Financial Freedom	
	79.7	40.0	20.0	

Trade is important to Tonga's economy; the value of exports and imports taken together equals 71 percent of GDP. The average applied tariff rate is 5.2 percent. Foreign investment in several sectors of the economy is restricted, and foreign investors may lease but not own land. The underdeveloped financial sector's limited ability to offer affordable credit undermines the development of a dynamic entrepreneurial sector.

TURKMENISTAN

The government of Turkmenistan's heavy involvement in leading economic sectors has dampened private-sector dynamism and led to economic stagnation in nonhydrocarbon sectors. The government restricts foreign investment to a few handpicked partners, and under the state-controlled financial system, access to credit is limited to political favorites. Burdensome and opaque regulatory systems, the nearly complete absence of property rights, pervasive corruption, and rigid labor regulations further limit private-sector activity.

While diversification will require the end of state control in several sectors, Turkmenistan's current competitive tax rates and open trade regime provide a practical base for sustainable long-term growth.

ECONOMIC FREEDOM SCORE

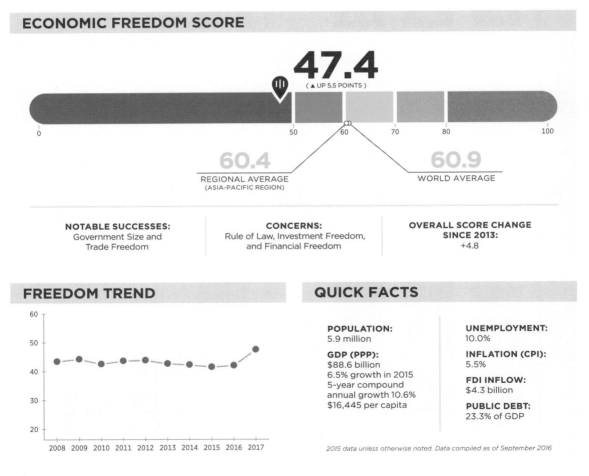

47.4
(▲ UP 5.5 POINTS)

0   50   60   70   80   100

60.4
REGIONAL AVERAGE
(ASIA–PACIFIC REGION)

60.9
WORLD AVERAGE

NOTABLE SUCCESSES:
Government Size and
Trade Freedom

CONCERNS:
Rule of Law, Investment Freedom,
and Financial Freedom

**OVERALL SCORE CHANGE
SINCE 2013:**
+4.8

FREEDOM TREND

60

50

40

30

20

2008 2009 2010 2011 2012 2013 2014 2015 2016 2017

QUICK FACTS

POPULATION:
5.9 million

GDP (PPP):
$88.6 billion
6.5% growth in 2015
5-year compound
annual growth 10.6%
$16,445 per capita

UNEMPLOYMENT:
10.0%

INFLATION (CPI):
5.5%

FDI INFLOW:
$4.3 billion

PUBLIC DEBT:
23.3% of GDP

2015 data unless otherwise noted. Data compiled as of September 2016

BACKGROUND: In 2012, President Gurbanguly Berdymukhammedov won a second five-year term with 97 percent of the vote in elections that international observers regarded as flawed. The presidency tightly controls the judiciary, the legislature, the economy, social services, and the mass media. Berdymukhammedov's policies are somewhat more open to the world than those of his predecessor, President-for-Life Saparmurad Niyazov, but the government still tends toward isolationism. Turkmenistan has intensive agriculture in irrigated oases, sizable oil resources, and the world's sixth-largest reserves of natural gas. Berdymukhammedov has encouraged some foreign investment in the energy sector, especially from Russia, China, and Iran. Turkmenistan's economy has been negatively affected by the economic slowdown in Russia.

12 ECONOMIC FREEDOMS | TURKMENISTAN

RULE OF LAW

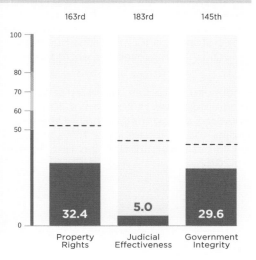

163rd	183rd	145th
Property Rights **32.4**	Judicial Effectiveness **5.0**	Government Integrity **29.6**

All land is owned by the government, and other ownership rights are limited. The judicial system is subservient to the president, who appoints and removes judges without legislative review. The legal system does not enforce contracts and property rights effectively. Laws are poorly developed, and judges are poorly trained and open to bribery. Corruption is widespread, and public officials are often forced to bribe their way into their positions.

GOVERNMENT SIZE

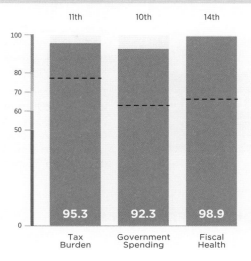

11th	10th	14th	◄ Rank
Tax Burden **95.3**	Government Spending **92.3**	Fiscal Health **98.9**	

The personal income tax rate is a flat 10 percent, and the corporate tax rate is 8 percent. Other taxes include a value-added tax and a property tax. The overall tax burden equals 17.4 percent of total domestic income. Government spending has amounted to 16 percent of total output (GDP) over the past three years, and budget surpluses have averaged 0.6 percent of GDP. Public debt is equivalent to 23.3 percent of GDP.

REGULATORY EFFICIENCY

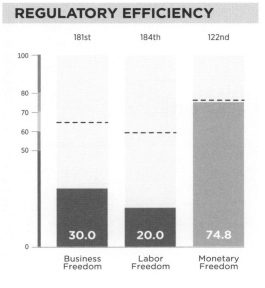

181st	184th	122nd
Business Freedom **30.0**	Labor Freedom **20.0**	Monetary Freedom **74.8**

Regulatory codes remain outmoded, and personal relations with government officials often play a role in overcoming bureaucratic red tape. The bloated public sector provides the majority of jobs, and labor regulations are outdated and not enforced effectively. Although citizens have received gas, electricity, and water free of charge since 1993, regional economic reverberations from deep recession in Russia have forced the state to cut those subsidies.

OPEN MARKETS

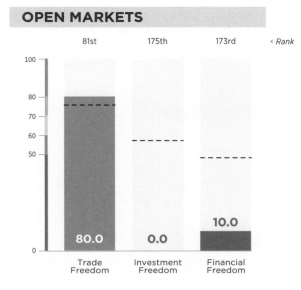

81st	175th	173rd	◄ Rank
Trade Freedom **80.0**	Investment Freedom **0.0**	Financial Freedom **10.0**	

Trade is important to Turkmenistan's economy; the value of exports and imports taken together equals 58 percent of GDP. The average applied tariff rate is 0.0 percent, but nontariff barriers impede trade. Private investors may not own land, and state-owned enterprises distort the economy. The government continues to control the financial system, and the flow of financial resources is severely restricted.

UZBEKISTAN

WORLD RANK:
148

REGIONAL RANK:
36

ECONOMIC FREEDOM STATUS:
MOSTLY UNFREE

Overall economic freedom in Uzbekistan has been held back by corruption and government intervention in various aspects of the economy. While structural reform has been uneven, recent efforts have improved the investment climate to some extent. An online one-stop shop to streamline business regulation, introduced in 2015, has improved the entrepreneurial environment.

The government has announced a program to privatize approximately 1,200 state-owned enterprises by the end of 2016. More than 300 were privatized during the first half of the year, but there is doubt regarding the transparency of this process. Uzbekistan also reduced its business corporate tax rate from 9 percent to 7.5 percent in 2016.

ECONOMIC FREEDOM SCORE

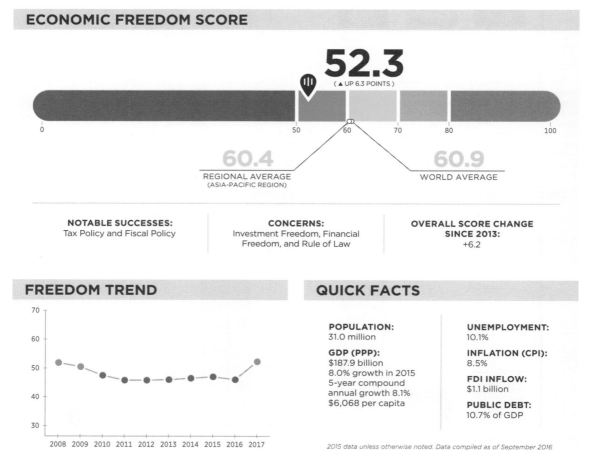

52.3
(▲ UP 6.3 POINTS)

0   50   60   70   80   100

60.4
REGIONAL AVERAGE
(ASIA-PACIFIC REGION)

60.9
WORLD AVERAGE

NOTABLE SUCCESSES:
Tax Policy and Fiscal Policy

CONCERNS:
Investment Freedom, Financial Freedom, and Rule of Law

OVERALL SCORE CHANGE SINCE 2013:
+6.2

FREEDOM TREND

70

60

50

40

30

2008 2009 2010 2011 2012 2013 2014 2015 2016 2017

QUICK FACTS

POPULATION:
31.0 million

GDP (PPP):
$187.9 billion
8.0% growth in 2015
5-year compound
annual growth 8.1%
$6,068 per capita

UNEMPLOYMENT:
10.1%

INFLATION (CPI):
8.5%

FDI INFLOW:
$1.1 billion

PUBLIC DEBT:
10.7% of GDP

2015 data unless otherwise noted. Data compiled as of September 2016

BACKGROUND: Islam Karimov ruled the country with an iron fist from the late 1980s until his death in 2016. He never reformed the highly subsidized, Soviet-era command economy. Karimov was succeeded by former prime minister and current President Shavkat Mirziyoyev, who committed to policy continuity but has shown some willingness to reform. Uzbekistan is dry and landlocked; 11 percent of the land is cultivated in irrigated river valleys. More than 60 percent of the population lives in densely populated rural communities. Uzbekistan is the world's fifth-largest cotton exporter and sixth-largest producer, but unsound cultivation practices have degraded the land and depleted water supplies. The economy also relies on natural gas and gold exports.

12 ECONOMIC FREEDOMS | UZBEKISTAN

RULE OF LAW

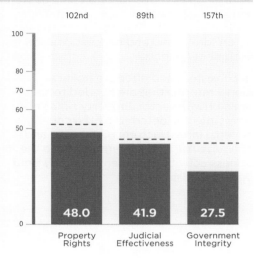

102nd   89th   157th

Property Rights **48.0** | Judicial Effectiveness **41.9** | Government Integrity **27.5**

Property ownership is generally respected, but it can be subverted by the government. There is no general system for registering liens on chattel property. Police, security services, and judges interpret the laws as they choose or according to political dictates, leaving little recourse to appeal. Corruption is pervasive. Uzbekistan was ranked 153rd out of 168 countries and territories surveyed in Transparency International's 2015 *Corruption Perceptions Index*.

GOVERNMENT SIZE

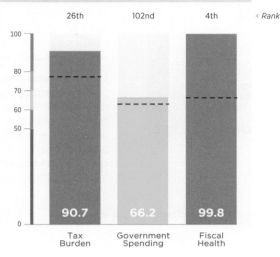

26th   102nd   4th   ◂ *Rank*

Tax Burden **90.7** | Government Spending **66.2** | Fiscal Health **99.8**

The top personal income tax rate is 22 percent. The top corporate tax rate has been cut to 7.5 percent. Other taxes include a value-added tax and a property tax. The overall tax burden equals 19.7 percent of total domestic income. Government spending has amounted to 33.6 percent of total output (GDP) over the past three years, and budget surpluses have averaged 1.8 percent of GDP. Public debt is equivalent to 10.7 percent of GDP.

REGULATORY EFFICIENCY

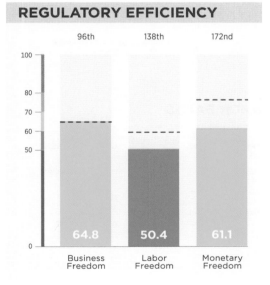

96th   138th   172nd

Business Freedom **64.8** | Labor Freedom **50.4** | Monetary Freedom **61.1**

The regulatory system suffers from a lack of transparency and clarity, and regulations are enforced inconsistently. The labor market lacks flexibility, and regulations undermine dynamic employment growth. The government effectively subsidizes many basic staples. It also controls interest rates and in 2016 imposed strict limits on the amount of hard currency that Uzbek citizens may withdraw while traveling abroad.

OPEN MARKETS

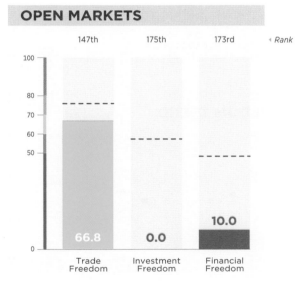

147th   175th   173rd   ◂ *Rank*

Trade Freedom **66.8** | Investment Freedom **0.0** | Financial Freedom **10.0**

Trade is moderately important to Uzbekistan's economy; the value of exports and imports taken together equals 43 percent of GDP. The average applied tariff rate is 6.6 percent. All land is owned by the government. Foreign investment is screened, and state-owned enterprises distort the economy. The financial sector is subject to heavy state intervention. The high cost of financing remains a key barrier to development of the private sector.

UZBEKISTAN

VANUATU

The government of Vanuatu's main policy focus over the past year has been on rebuilding key infrastructure (such as water and sanitation works, schools, and medical facilities) that was severely damaged by a cyclone in 2015. The island economy continues to rely heavily on foreign aid and concessional loans from international development agencies.

Overall, Vanuatu lacks a consistent and effective political commitment to institutional reforms that are needed to spark development of a dynamic private sector. Property rights are poorly protected, and investment is deterred by the country's inadequate physical and legal infrastructure. High tariffs and nontariff barriers to trade have held back integration into the global marketplace. Business activity is further limited by rigid labor regulations and widespread corruption.

WORLD RANK:
52

REGIONAL RANK:
12

ECONOMIC FREEDOM STATUS:
MODERATELY FREE

ECONOMIC FREEDOM SCORE

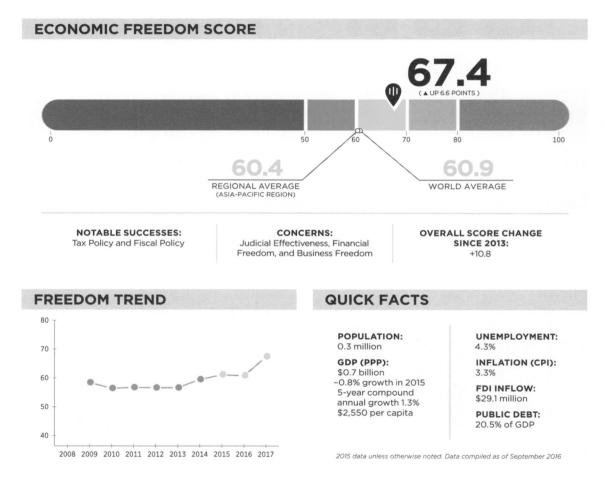

67.4
(▲ UP 6.6 POINTS)

0   50   60   70   80   100

60.4
REGIONAL AVERAGE
(ASIA-PACIFIC REGION)

60.9
WORLD AVERAGE

NOTABLE SUCCESSES:
Tax Policy and Fiscal Policy

CONCERNS:
Judicial Effectiveness, Financial Freedom, and Business Freedom

OVERALL SCORE CHANGE SINCE 2013:
+10.8

FREEDOM TREND

80

70

60

50

40

2008 2009 2010 2011 2012 2013 2014 2015 2016 2017

QUICK FACTS

POPULATION:
0.3 million

GDP (PPP):
$0.7 billion
−0.8% growth in 2015
5-year compound annual growth 1.3%
$2,550 per capita

UNEMPLOYMENT:
4.3%

INFLATION (CPI):
3.3%

FDI INFLOW:
$29.1 million

PUBLIC DEBT:
20.5% of GDP

2015 data unless otherwise noted. Data compiled as of September 2016

BACKGROUND: The South Pacific island Republic of Vanuatu achieved independence in 1980 and is today a parliamentary democracy divided between its English-speaking and French-speaking citizens. Charlot Salwai of the Reunification of Movements for Change party became prime minister in February 2016 following snap elections called after 14 members of parliament were convicted of bribery. Vanuatu is heavily dependent on tourism, which comprises 40 percent of the economy. In March 2015, Cyclone Pam destroyed thousands of homes and other buildings and killed more than a dozen people.

12 ECONOMIC FREEDOMS | VANUATU

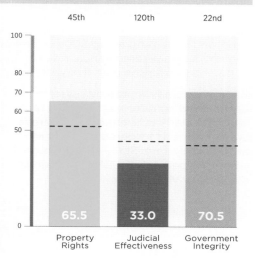

RULE OF LAW

45th — Property Rights — 65.5
120th — Judicial Effectiveness — 33.0
22nd — Government Integrity — 70.5

In 2016, Vanuatu appointed an ombudsman to deal with complaints about land registration procedures. The judiciary is largely independent but lacks the resources to retain qualified personnel. After 14 members of parliament charged with corruption were convicted in late 2015, a snap election in January 2016 resulted in an overhauled parliament and a new prime minister, but strong factionalism continues to undermine political stability.

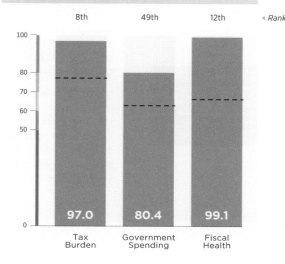

GOVERNMENT SIZE

8th — Tax Burden — 97.0
49th — Government Spending — 80.4
12th — Fiscal Health — 99.1
◄ Rank

Vanuatu imposes no individual or corporate income tax. Taxes include a value-added tax and import duties. The overall tax burden equals 17.2 percent of total domestic income. Government spending has amounted to 25.6 percent of total output (GDP) over the past three years, and budget deficits have averaged 0.2 percent of GDP. Public debt is equivalent to 20.5 percent of GDP.

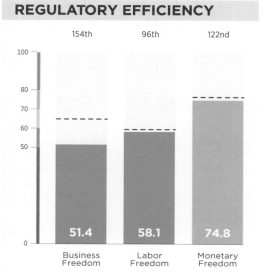

REGULATORY EFFICIENCY

154th — Business Freedom — 51.4
96th — Labor Freedom — 58.1
122nd — Monetary Freedom — 74.8

Bureaucratic procedures are complex and nontransparent, and completion of licensing requirements is costly. Labor codes are rigid and outmoded, and a formal labor market is not fully developed. The government still subsidizes 11 state-owned enterprises in such important economic areas as airports, banking, agriculture, and broadcasting. Most are poorly managed and lose money.

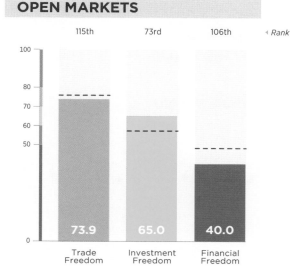

OPEN MARKETS

115th — Trade Freedom — 73.9
73rd — Investment Freedom — 65.0
106th — Financial Freedom — 40.0
◄ Rank

Trade is important to Vanuatu's economy; the value of exports and imports taken together equals 97 percent of GDP. The average applied tariff rate is 5.5 percent. Foreign investors may lease but not own land, and investment in other sectors of the economy may be screened by the government. Access to financing remains poor, and less than 15 percent of rural adults have access to formal banking services.

VANUATU

VIETNAM

Capitalizing on its gradual integration into the global trade and investment system, Vietnam has been transforming itself into a more market-oriented economy. Reforms have included partial privatization of state-owned enterprises, liberalization of the trade regime, and increasing recognition of private property rights. The economy has registered annual rates of growth averaging about 6 percent over the past five years.

Vietnam's overall economic freedom is limited by several key institutional factors. Despite ongoing reform efforts, the regulatory environment is not particularly efficient or transparent. Despite progress, investment remains hindered by opaque bureaucracy and a weak judicial system. State-owned enterprises still account for about 40 percent of GDP, hampering the emergence of a more dynamic private sector.

WORLD RANK: **147** **REGIONAL RANK:** **35**

ECONOMIC FREEDOM STATUS: **MOSTLY UNFREE**

ECONOMIC FREEDOM SCORE

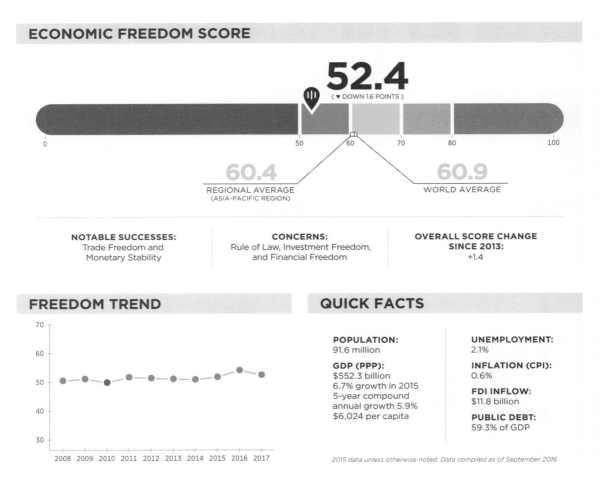

52.4
(▼ DOWN 1.6 POINTS)

0   50   60   70   80   100

60.4
REGIONAL AVERAGE
(ASIA-PACIFIC REGION)

60.9
WORLD AVERAGE

NOTABLE SUCCESSES:	CONCERNS:	OVERALL SCORE CHANGE SINCE 2013:
Trade Freedom and Monetary Stability	Rule of Law, Investment Freedom, and Financial Freedom	+1.4

FREEDOM TREND

70

60

50

40

30

2008 2009 2010 2011 2012 2013 2014 2015 2016 2017

QUICK FACTS

POPULATION:
91.6 million

GDP (PPP):
$552.3 billion
6.7% growth in 2015
5-year compound
annual growth 5.9%
$6,024 per capita

UNEMPLOYMENT:
2.1%

INFLATION (CPI):
0.6%

FDI INFLOW:
$11.8 billion

PUBLIC DEBT:
59.3% of GDP

2015 data unless otherwise noted. Data compiled as of September 2016

BACKGROUND: The Socialist Republic of Vietnam remains a Communist dictatorship characterized by political repression and the absence of civil liberties. Economic liberalization began in 1986 with the *doi moi* reforms, and Vietnam joined the World Trade Organization in 2007. Economic growth was among the fastest in the world during the decade-long tenure of prime minister Nguyễn Tấn Dũng but in 2016, after losing a contest for the highest position, that of General Secretary of the Communist Party of Vietnam, Dung was forced out. He was replaced as prime minister by Nguyễn Xuân Phúc. The economy is driven primarily by tourism and exports. In a major development, the U.S. lifted the long-standing arms embargo against Vietnam in 2016.

12 ECONOMIC FREEDOMS | VIETNAM

RULE OF LAW

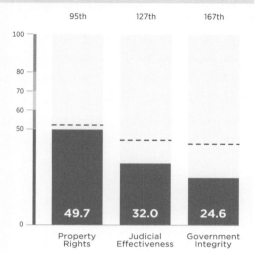

95th — 127th — 167th

Property Rights **49.7**, Judicial Effectiveness **32.0**, Government Integrity **24.6**

All land is collectively owned and managed by the state. Private property rights are not strongly respected, and resolution of disputes can take years. The underdeveloped judiciary is subordinate to the Communist Party of Vietnam, which controls the courts at all levels. Party membership is widely viewed as a way to enhance one's personal wealth and connections. Corruption and nepotism are rife within the party and in state-owned companies.

GOVERNMENT SIZE

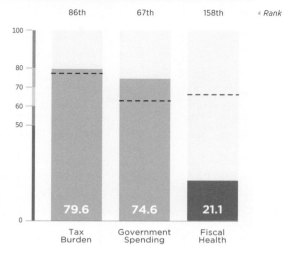

86th — 67th — 158th ◄ Rank

Tax Burden **79.6**, Government Spending **74.6**, Fiscal Health **21.1**

The top personal income tax rate is 35 percent, and the top corporate tax rate is 22 percent. Other taxes include a value-added tax and a property tax. The overall tax burden equals 18.2 percent of total domestic income. Government spending has amounted to 29.1 percent of total output (GDP) over the past three years, and budget deficits have averaged 6.7 percent of GDP. Public debt is equivalent to 59.3 percent of GDP.

REGULATORY EFFICIENCY

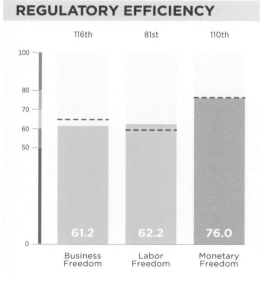

116th — 81st — 110th

Business Freedom **61.2**, Labor Freedom **62.2**, Monetary Freedom **76.0**

Administrative procedures have been streamlined, and the regulatory framework for smaller businesses has been improved. The labor market remains relatively rigid. Prices for air travel, water, electricity, telecommunications, postal service, and gasoline are set by the state, which also regulates prices for some natural resources, pharmaceuticals, and products produced by government-run enterprises such as health care, education, and some housing.

OPEN MARKETS

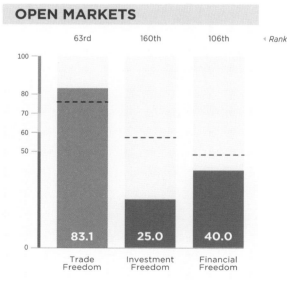

63rd — 160th — 106th ◄ Rank

Trade Freedom **83.1**, Investment Freedom **25.0**, Financial Freedom **40.0**

Trade is extremely important to Vietnam's economy; the value of exports and imports taken together equals 179 percent of GDP. The average applied tariff rate is 3.4 percent. Barriers to foreign investment remain significant, but they have been liberalized. Numerous state-owned enterprises distort the economy. The state remains heavily involved in the financial sector. The high level of nonperforming loans continues to limit the pace of credit growth.

VIETNAM

EUROPE

EUROPE

Europe has served as the testing ground for the two great economic philosophies of the past century and has witnessed the collapse of one of them: Communism, which proved unable to generate standards of living even remotely approximating those of capitalist Western Europe.

Now that the old Cold War rivalries have been eclipsed by a new technology-driven globalization, many of the large economies in Europe that were built on a quasi-market welfare state model are looking for ways to improve their competitiveness vis-a-vis fast-growing small economies like Ireland and Estonia that have surpassed them in economic efficiency.

The European region encompasses nations as diverse as Russia, Switzerland, Iceland, and Greece. The population-weighted average GDP per capita for the region stands at $31,661, with inflation generally under control. However, the European continent is plagued by higher unemployment rates than are historically typical and by a growing level of public debt.

Chart 1 shows the distribution of countries in Europe within the five categories of economic freedom. One of the world's five truly "free" economies (Switzerland) is in this region.

It is notable that 11 of the world's 20 freest countries are in Europe, which is the only region to have a distribution of economies that is skewed toward relatively high levels of economic freedom. Most countries in the region fall into the category of "mostly free" and "moderately free."

Seven countries (Croatia, Slovenia, Serbia, Belarus, Moldova, Russia, and Greece) have economies that are rated "mostly unfree." Ukraine, which continues to experience political and security turmoil, remains the region's least economically free economy.

Relatively extensive and long-established free-market institutions in a number of countries allow the region to score far above the world average in most categories of economic freedom. (See Table 1.) It is over 10 points ahead in both investment freedom and financial freedom. The region's average scores on property rights, judicial effectiveness, and government integrity lead the world averages by about 15 points or more.

However, taken as a whole, the Europe region still struggles with a variety of policy barriers to dynamic economic expansion, such as overly protective and costly labor regulations, higher tax burdens, various market-distorting subsidies, and continuing problems in public finance caused by years of public-sector expansion. The result has been stagnant economic growth, which has exacerbated the burden of fiscal deficits and mounting debt in a number of countries in the region.

Chart 2 shows the strongly positive correlation between high levels of economic freedom and high GDP per capita, but the freedom gap is less pronounced within Europe than it is in other regions. Europe has definitely benefited from economic competition over the centuries, which may help to

EUROPE: QUICK FACTS

TOTAL POPULATION: 823 million

POPULATION WEIGHTED AVERAGES

GDP PER CAPITA (PPP):	$31,661
GROWTH:	0.5%
5 YEAR GROWTH:	1.29%
INFLATION:	6.2%
UNEMPLOYMENT:	9.1%
PUBLIC DEBT:	66.3%

SOURCE: Terry Miller and Anthony B. Kim,
2017 Index of Economic Freedom
(Washington: The Heritage Foundation, 2017),
http://www.heritage.org/index.

☎ heritage.org

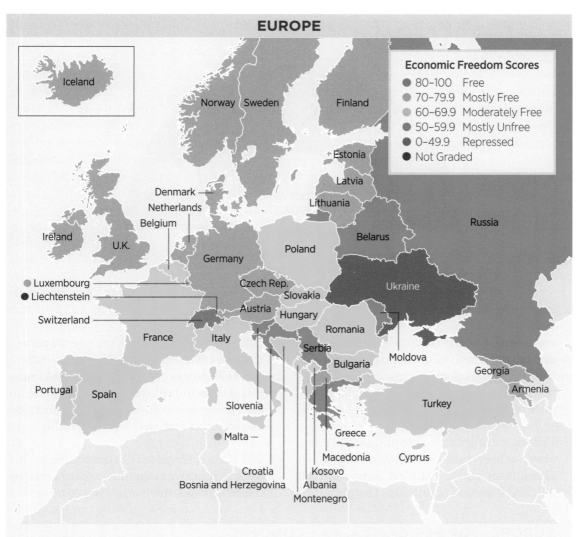

EUROPE

Economic Freedom Scores
- 80–100 Free
- 70–79.9 Mostly Free
- 60–69.9 Moderately Free
- 50–59.9 Mostly Unfree
- 0–49.9 Repressed
- Not Graded

SOURCE: Terry Miller and Anthony B. Kim, *2017 Index of Economic Freedom* (Washington: The Heritage Foundation, 2017), http://www.heritage.org/index.

☎ heritage.org

explain why economic repression is so rare in the West. However, that competition has still not generated enough reform in some of the Eastern European countries. Many post-Communist countries, such as Russia, Belarus, and Ukraine, are found in the "less free" end of the distribution.

As shown in Chart 3, around the region, countries with higher economic freedom tend to maintain cleaner environments and greater protection of ecosystem vitality.

In the 2017 *Index*, the scores of 30 countries in the European region have improved, and those of 14 have declined.

NOTABLE COUNTRIES

- Despite the challenging economic environment within the European Union, Germany continues to be one of the world's most powerful and dynamic economies. Business freedom and investment freedom

EUROPE: ECONOMIC FREEDOM SUMMARY

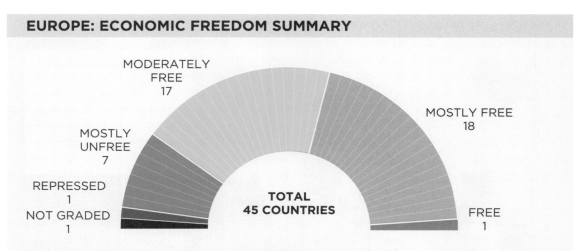

MODERATELY FREE 17

MOSTLY FREE 18

MOSTLY UNFREE 7

REPRESSED 1

NOT GRADED 1

TOTAL 45 COUNTRIES

FREE 1

SOURCE: Terry Miller and Anthony B. Kim, *2017 Index of Economic Freedom* (Washington: The Heritage Foundation, 2017), http://www.heritage.org/index.

Chart 1 ☎ heritage.org

are strong. Long-term competitiveness and entrepreneurial growth are supported by openness to global commerce, well-protected property rights, and a sound business regulatory environment.

- The increasing dynamism of Latvia's economy has been facilitated by openness to global trade and investment. Supported by efficient business regulations that promote

entrepreneurial activity, the overall commercial environment has become conducive to business creation and risk-taking. Fiscal consolidation in recent years has kept government spending under control and ensured macroeconomic stability.

- The United Kingdom has continued its efforts to improve economic performance by reducing taxes and containing government

EUROPE: GDP PER CAPITA, BY ECONOMIC FREEDOM CATEGORY

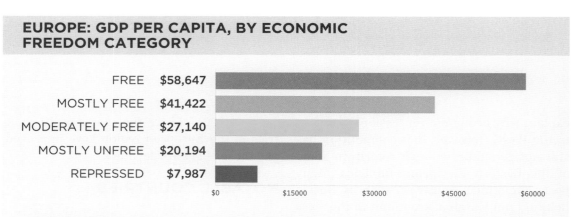

FREE	$58,647
MOSTLY FREE	$41,422
MODERATELY FREE	$27,140
MOSTLY UNFREE	$20,194
REPRESSED	$7,987

$0 $15000 $30000 $45000 $60000

SOURCES: Terry Miller and Anthony B. Kim, *2017 Index of Economic Freedom* (Washington: The Heritage Foundation, 2017), http://www.heritage.org/index, and International Monetary Fund, World Economic Outlook Database, April 2016, https://www.imf.org/external/pubs/ft/weo/2016/01/weodata/index.aspx (accessed December 13, 2016).

Chart 2 ☎ heritage.org

EUROPE: COMPONENTS OF ECONOMIC FREEDOM

LOWER THAN WORLD AVERAGE ●—⊣   ⊢—● HIGHER THAN WORLD AVERAGE

		AVERAGES		
		Region	World	
OVERALL		**68.0**	60.9	
RULE OF LAW	Property Rights	**70.2**	53.0	
	Judicial Effectiveness	**60.2**	45.0	
	Government Integrity	**57.8**	43.0	
GOVERNMENT SIZE	Tax Burden	**71.8**	77.1	
	Government Spending	**42.9**	63.4	
	Fiscal Health	**75.6**	68.0	
REGULATORY EFFICIENCY	Business Freedom	**74.9**	64.6	
	Labor Freedom	**60.0**	59.2	
	Monetary Freedom	**81.1**	76.4	
MARKET OPENNESS	Trade Freedom	**85.3**	75.9	
	Investment Freedom	**74.1**	57.2	
	Financial Freedom	**61.8**	48.2	

SOURCE: Terry Miller and Anthony B. Kim, *2017 Index of Economic Freedom* (Washington: The Heritage Foundation, 2017), http://www.heritage.org/index.

Table 1 ☎ heritage.org

EUROPE: ECONOMIC FREEDOM AND THE ENVIRONMENT

Category in the *2017 Index of Economic Freedom*

Environmental Performance Index Score

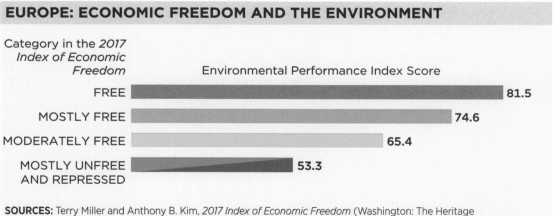

FREE	81.5
MOSTLY FREE	74.6
MODERATELY FREE	65.4
MOSTLY UNFREE AND REPRESSED	53.3

SOURCES: Terry Miller and Anthony B. Kim, *2017 Index of Economic Freedom* (Washington: The Heritage Foundation, 2017), http://www.heritage.org/index, and Yale University, "2016 Environmental Performance Index," http://epi.yale.edu/reports/2016-report (accessed December 13, 2016).

Chart 3 ☎ heritage.org

spending, and growth rates have picked up somewhat. The looming prospect of an exit from the European Union presents both major challenges and opportunities to improve regulatory and other policies that bear on economic freedom.

- Russia's economy is severely hampered by blatant disdain for the rule of law and rejection of any concept of limited government. The private sector remains marginalized by structural and institutional constraints caused by ever-growing government encroachment into the marketplace. Rising inflationary pressure jeopardizes macroeconomic stability.

- Spain's economy has experienced a notable rebound facilitated by structural reforms. Ongoing efforts have focused on reducing the inefficient and oversized government sector and reforming the labor market. Top income tax rates on individuals and corporations have been lowered as well. Spain's ongoing economic recovery, however, remains highly vulnerable to challenges related to ensuring fiscal stability and restoring the financial sector's competitiveness.

ECONOMIC FREEDOM IN EUROPE

World Rank	Regional Rank	Country	Overall Score	Change from 2016	Property Rights	Judicial Effectiveness	Government Integrity	Tax Burden	Government Spending	Fiscal Health	Business Freedom	Labor Freedom	Monetary Freedom	Trade Freedom	Investment Freedom	Financial Freedom
4	1	Switzerland	81.5	0.5	86.9	77.6	80.3	70.9	67.5	95.8	76.8	72.2	84.4	90.0	85	90
6	2	Estonia	79.1	1.9	82.6	82.8	69.9	81.2	55.8	99.8	77.0	56.9	85.7	87.0	90	80
9	3	Ireland	76.7	-0.6	85.8	78.3	78.3	72.7	57.1	60.3	80.3	73.6	87.6	87.0	90	70
12	4	United Kingdom	76.4	0.0	93.8	93.0	78.3	65.1	41.9	40.4	89.9	72.8	85.0	87.0	90	80
13	5	Georgia	76.0	3.4	55.1	66.5	65.0	87.3	74.4	93.5	87.2	75.9	78.2	88.6	80	60
14	6	Luxembourg	75.9	2.0	85.8	77.0	78.3	64.5	46.0	99.0	68.6	43.8	86.2	87.0	95	80
15	7	Netherlands	75.8	1.2	87.4	69.9	85.7	53.2	37.0	83.0	80.2	70.5	85.8	87.0	90	80
16	8	Lithuania	75.8	0.6	73.0	62.4	69.7	86.9	64.1	93.6	79.1	63.6	90.0	87.0	70	70
18	9	Denmark	75.1	-0.2	86.7	68.5	84.9	37.2	5.7	95.4	93.9	85.8	85.5	87.0	90	80
19	10	Sweden	74.9	2.9	88.6	82.2	87.4	44.4	21.7	93.4	90.8	53.2	85.3	87.0	85	80
20	11	Latvia	74.8	4.4	72.6	59.7	67.3	84.7	57.4	95.0	79.8	72.0	86.5	87.0	75	60
22	12	Iceland	74.4	1.1	85.0	71.5	71.5	70.9	41.1	90.6	90.2	62.6	81.2	88.0	80	60
24	13	Finland	74.0	1.4	90.6	82.7	90.0	66.6	0.0	77.3	90.2	53.4	85.1	87.0	85	80
25	14	Norway	74.0	3.2	86.7	83.3	88.3	55.6	38.5	98.4	89.5	48.8	75.8	87.7	75	60
26	15	Germany	73.8	-0.6	82.9	79.5	77.7	61.9	41.4	89.9	86.6	42.8	85.9	87.0	80	70
28	16	Czech Republic	73.3	0.1	70.3	55.9	55.9	82.9	45.3	92.0	67.2	77.7	85.8	87.0	80	80
30	17	Austria	72.3	0.6	86.0	81.8	75.2	50.3	19.3	79.7	76.9	67.6	83.4	87.0	90	70
31	18	Macedonia	70.7	3.2	67.0	61.4	52.0	91.9	68.9	72.6	81.5	66.7	80.8	86.1	60	60
33	19	Armenia	70.3	3.3	55.5	42.5	43.4	83.7	81.7	82.9	78.5	72.4	72.8	80.2	80	70
39	20	Romania	69.7	4.1	63.9	58.5	45.9	87.4	65.3	90.9	65.9	62.5	83.6	87.0	75	50
45	21	Poland	68.3	-1.0	60.8	58.0	55.5	76.0	46.9	76.1	67.8	61.5	84.7	87.0	75	70
46	22	Kosovo	67.9	6.5	70.3	58.0	45.9	93.5	77.8	88.9	68.8	65.3	80.0	70.8	65	30
47	23	Bulgaria	67.9	2.0	62.5	38.9	41.8	91.0	58.4	86.4	66.7	68.3	83.3	87.0	70	60
48	24	Cyprus	67.9	-0.8	75.4	60.7	53.6	73.0	48.8	72.9	75.8	58.6	83.3	87.0	75	50
49	25	Belgium	67.8	-0.6	83.3	69.3	71.5	44.1	9.6	66.3	82.0	61.1	84.9	87.0	85	70
50	26	Malta	67.7	1.0	67.7	62.9	53.6	62.8	44.9	85.1	62.5	57.2	83.5	87.0	85	60
56	27	Hungary	65.8	-0.2	60.1	51.8	41.5	79.3	25.3	79.3	64.0	64.4	91.7	87.0	75	70
57	28	Slovak Republic	65.7	-0.9	69.0	38.0	39.6	79.7	47.2	82.9	64.9	54.4	81.1	87.0	75	70
60	29	Turkey	65.2	3.1	61.3	52.5	40.7	75.5	57.7	95.7	64.3	48.5	72.2	79.4	75	60
65	30	Albania	64.4	-1.5	54.0	28.5	39.7	86.9	72.5	51.5	79.3	50.7	81.4	87.7	70	70
69	31	Spain	63.6	-4.9	71.2	53.9	57.2	62.5	41.4	26.9	66.9	55.3	85.5	87.0	85	70
72	32	France	63.3	1.0	85.0	72.7	69.7	47.6	2.0	57.0	78.0	44.1	81.6	82.0	70	70
77	33	Portugal	62.6	-2.5	73.3	68.9	59.0	59.8	25.1	32.1	86.4	43.4	85.9	87.0	70	60
79	34	Italy	62.5	1.3	74.6	55.4	44.7	54.9	22.3	66.9	69.8	52.9	86.9	87.0	85	50
83	35	Montenegro	62.0	-2.9	58.0	50.4	43.4	83.1	33.1	44.3	72.0	67.4	82.5	84.7	75	50
92	36	Bosnia and Herzegovina	60.2	1.6	41.2	40.0	32.7	83.5	33.7	89.3	47.4	59.3	84.0	86.6	65	60
95	37	Croatia	59.4	0.3	65.5	56.8	43.4	66.8	31.3	44.7	58.2	43.3	80.3	87.4	75	60

(CONTINUED ON NEXT PAGE)

ECONOMIC FREEDOM IN EUROPE

World Rank	Regional Rank	Country	Overall Score	Change from 2016	Property Rights	Judicial Effectiveness	Government Integrity	Tax Burden	Government Spending	Fiscal Health	Business Freedom	Labor Freedom	Monetary Freedom	Trade Freedom	Investment Freedom	Financial Freedom
97	38	Slovenia	59.2	-1.4	75.0	55.1	53.6	58.7	28.6	6.1	80.6	60.2	85.3	87.0	70	50
99	39	Serbia	58.9	-3.2	50.3	40.2	38.2	83.3	40.3	46.9	62.9	65.9	80.8	77.8	70	50
104	40	Belarus	58.6	9.8	50.9	56.3	37.6	89.8	48.7	92.8	71.3	74.6	60.4	80.6	30	10
110	41	Moldova	58.0	0.6	49.6	23.9	28.6	86.1	54.8	90.6	65.9	38.9	72.0	80.0	55	50
114	42	Russia	57.1	6.5	47.6	44.5	38.2	81.8	61.5	93.4	74.8	50.8	57.3	75.2	30	30
127	43	Greece	55.0	1.8	52.5	56.1	41.3	61.1	5.4	58.1	74.3	51.0	78.2	82.0	60	40
166	44	Ukraine	48.1	1.3	41.4	22.6	29.2	78.6	38.2	67.9	62.1	48.8	47.4	85.9	25	30
N/A	N/A	Liechtenstein	N/A	N/A	N/A	N/A	N/A	N/A	N/A	N/A	92.3	85.7	N/A	90.0	85	80

ALBANIA

Albania's transition to a more open and flexible economic system has been facilitated by substantial restructuring over the past decade. The country has made considerable progress in income growth and poverty reduction. A competitive trade regime supported by a relatively efficient regulatory framework has encouraged the development of a growing entrepreneurial sector.

Albania continues on a path of gradual economic recovery, confronting challenging external conditions, but more reform is needed to ensure the growth of economic freedom and encourage vibrant economic development. The judicial system remains inefficient and vulnerable to political interference, and corruption is still perceived as widespread. Expansionary government spending has led to budget deficits and growing public debt in recent years, but the deficits have been narrowing.

ECONOMIC FREEDOM SCORE

64.4
(▼ DOWN 1.5 POINTS)

0   50   60   70   80   100

60.9
WORLD AVERAGE

68.0
REGIONAL AVERAGE
(EUROPE REGION)

NOTABLE SUCCESSES:	CONCERNS:	OVERALL SCORE CHANGE SINCE 2013:
Trade Freedom, Tax Policy, and Monetary Stability	Judicial Effectiveness, Government Integrity, and Labor Freedom	–0.8

FREEDOM TREND

80

70

60

50

40

2008 2009 2010 2011 2012 2013 2014 2015 2016 2017

QUICK FACTS

POPULATION:
2.8 million

GDP (PPP):
$32.7 billion
2.6% growth in 2015
5-year compound
annual growth 1.9%
$11,300 per capita

UNEMPLOYMENT:
17.3%

INFLATION (CPI):
1.9%

FDI INFLOW:
$1.0 billion

PUBLIC DEBT:
71.9% of GDP

2015 data unless otherwise noted. Data compiled as of September 2016

BACKGROUND: Socialist Edi Rama was elected prime minister in June 2013, defeating eight-year conservative incumbent Sali Berisha. As promised, Rama secured European Union candidacy status in June 2014. Albania achieved full membership in NATO in April 2009 and continues to make a small contribution to the NATO-led mission in Afghanistan. A Strategic Partnership agreement with the U.S. is intended to increase cooperation, including improvements in the rule of law. The economy is dominated by agriculture, which employs about half of the workforce, and services, including tourism.

12 ECONOMIC FREEDOMS | ALBANIA

RULE OF LAW

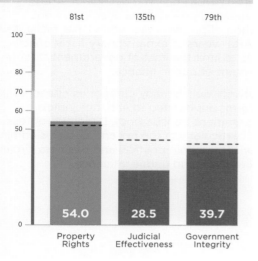

	81st	135th	79th
	Property Rights	Judicial Effectiveness	Government Integrity
	54.0	28.5	39.7

Development of property legislation has been piecemeal and uncoordinated. Real estate registration procedures are cumbersome. The judiciary, although constitutionally independent, is subject to political pressure and intimidation and has limited resources. A 2015 law bars convicted criminals from holding public office, but public administration continues to be plagued by inefficiency, incompetence, and widespread corruption.

GOVERNMENT SIZE

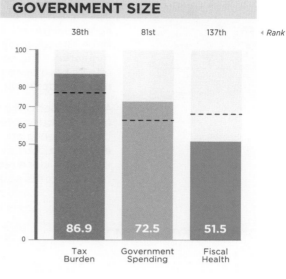

◄ Rank

	38th	81st	137th
	Tax Burden	Government Spending	Fiscal Health
	86.9	72.5	51.5

The top individual income tax rate is 23 percent, and the top corporate tax rate is 15 percent. Other taxes include a value-added tax and an inheritance tax. The overall tax burden equals 23.6 percent of total domestic income. Government spending has amounted to 30.3 percent of total output (GDP) over the past three years, and budget deficits have averaged 4.9 percent of GDP. Public debt is equivalent to 71.9 percent of GDP.

REGULATORY EFFICIENCY

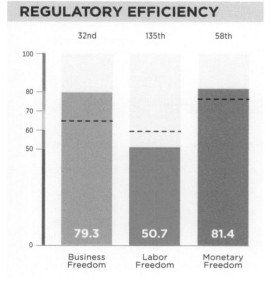

	32nd	135th	58th
	Business Freedom	Labor Freedom	Monetary Freedom
	79.3	50.7	81.4

Business start-up procedures have become less costly, and there is no longer a minimum capital requirement for setting up a company. Labor demand in the formal economy, which has a high level of self-employment, is significantly influenced by the public sector. The government is on course to phase out many subsidies and price controls for electricity, water, agricultural products, and railroad transportation.

OPEN MARKETS

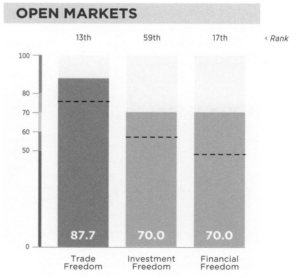

◄ Rank

	13th	59th	17th
	Trade Freedom	Investment Freedom	Financial Freedom
	87.7	70.0	70.0

Trade is important to Albania's economy; the value of exports and imports taken together equals 71 percent of GDP. The average applied tariff rate is 1.1 percent, and bureaucratic barriers deter international trade and investment. Most banks are foreign-owned. The banking system has benefited from increased competition and remains stable, but the number of nonperforming loans hinders credit growth.

ALBANIA

ARMENIA

WORLD RANK: **33** **REGIONAL RANK:** **19**

ECONOMIC FREEDOM STATUS:
MOSTLY FREE

Considerable diversification of Armenia's economic base has increased economic dynamism, and a decade of strong economic growth has reduced poverty and unemployment rates. Broad simplification of business procedures has facilitated regulatory efficiency. After years of expansionary fiscal policies, efforts have been made to limit the cost of government through more prudent management of public finance.

Armenia performs relatively well in many categories of economic freedom, but more reforms are needed to enhance judicial independence and government transparency. Despite progress in tackling corruption, particularly in the tax and customs administrations, close relationships within political and business circles raise concerns about cronyism and undue influence.

ECONOMIC FREEDOM SCORE

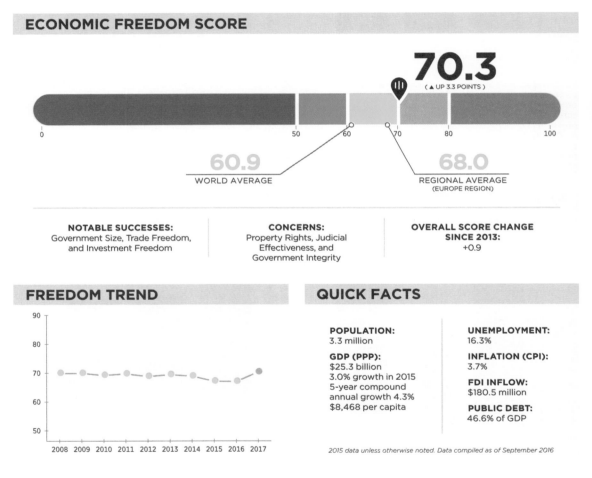

70.3
(▲ UP 3.3 POINTS)

0   50   60   70   80   100

60.9
WORLD AVERAGE

68.0
REGIONAL AVERAGE
(EUROPE REGION)

NOTABLE SUCCESSES:
Government Size, Trade Freedom, and Investment Freedom

CONCERNS:
Property Rights, Judicial Effectiveness, and Government Integrity

OVERALL SCORE CHANGE SINCE 2013:
+0.9

FREEDOM TREND

90
80
70
60
50

2008 2009 2010 2011 2012 2013 2014 2015 2016 2017

QUICK FACTS

POPULATION:
3.3 million

GDP (PPP):
$25.3 billion
3.0% growth in 2015
5-year compound
annual growth 4.3%
$8,468 per capita

UNEMPLOYMENT:
16.3%

INFLATION (CPI):
3.7%

FDI INFLOW:
$180.5 million

PUBLIC DEBT:
46.6% of GDP

2015 data unless otherwise noted. Data compiled as of September 2016

BACKGROUND: President Serzh Sargsyan of the center-right Republican Party won a second five-year term in 2013. A cease-fire in Armenia's 25-year occupation of Azerbaijan's Nagorno–Karabakh region has been in effect since 1994, but four days of intensive fighting in April 2016 left dozens dead on both sides. The economy relies on manufacturing, services, remittances, and agriculture. Armenia announced that it was suspending an association agreement with the European Union in September 2013 and joined the Russian-backed Eurasian Economic Union in 2015. A sluggish Russian economy, which accounts for 23 percent of Armenian exports, has inhibited growth. The government relies heavily on loans from the World Bank, the International Monetary Fund, the Asian Development Bank, and Russia.

12 ECONOMIC FREEDOMS | ARMENIA

RULE OF LAW

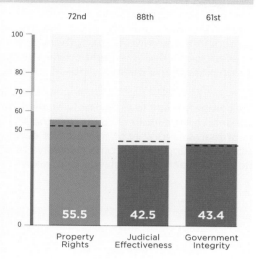

Armenian law protects secured interests in personal and real property. The judiciary lacks independence and transparency. All disputes involving contracts, ownership of property, or commercial matters are resolved in the courts of general jurisdiction, which handle both civil and criminal cases and have long backlogs. Pervasive corruption has been aggravated by Russia's consolidation of its influence over Armenia's economy and regional security.

GOVERNMENT SIZE

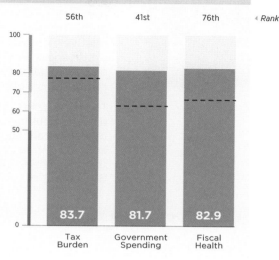

The top individual income tax rate is 26 percent, and the top corporate tax rate is 20 percent. Other taxes include a value-added tax and excise taxes. The overall tax burden equals 23.5 percent of total domestic income. Government spending has amounted to 24.7 percent of total output (GDP) over the past three years, and budget deficits have averaged 2.8 percent of GDP. Public debt is equivalent to 46.6 percent of GDP.

REGULATORY EFFICIENCY

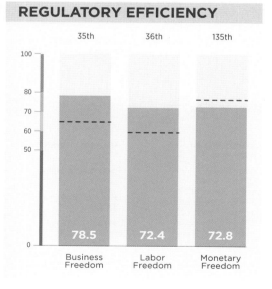

The regulatory framework is relatively efficient. The minimum capital requirement for business start-ups has been eliminated, and bankruptcy procedures have been modernized. The nonsalary cost of labor is moderate, but the informal labor market is sizable. The government and a Russian–Armenian billionaire jointly funded electricity subsidies for more than a year after massive public protests in June 2015 against a proposed rate increase.

OPEN MARKETS

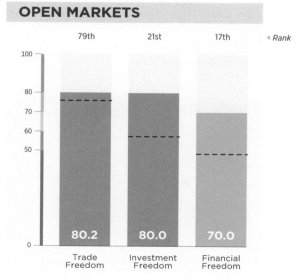

Trade is important to Armenia's economy; the value of exports and imports taken together equals 71 percent of GDP. The average applied tariff rate is 2.4 percent. Bureaucratic barriers interfere with international trade, and foreign citizens may not own land. The state no longer has a stake in any bank, but the banking sector, which accounts for over 90 percent of total financial-sector assets, still struggles to provide adequate long-term credit.

ARMENIA

AUSTRIA

WORLD RANK:
30

REGIONAL RANK:
17

ECONOMIC FREEDOM STATUS:
MOSTLY FREE

Austria's small but well-developed economy is highly global- ized and resilient, sustained by a skilled labor force, com- petitive manufacturing, and a large service sector. Openness to global trade and investment is firmly institutionalized, and the relatively efficient entrepreneurial framework strengthens com- petitiveness. Protection of property rights is traditionally strong, and the legal system is transparent and reliable. Anti-corruption measures are effective.

The corporate tax rate is comparatively low, but individuals face a 50 percent income tax and various indirect taxes. Austria's overall fiscal condition compares favorably to those of its euro- zone neighbors, but public spending has become excessive and unsustainable. Public debt has reached a post-war high above 85 percent of GDP.

ECONOMIC FREEDOM SCORE

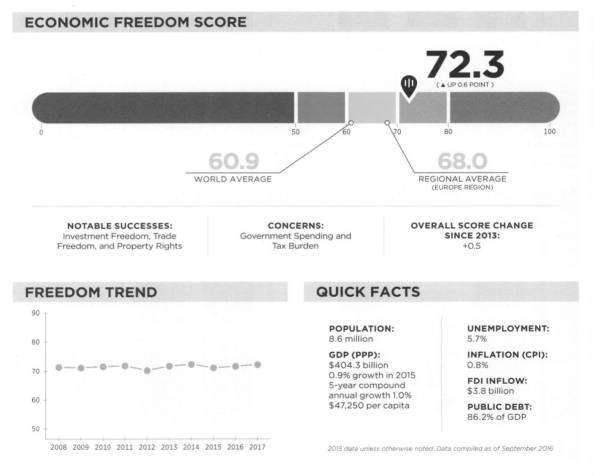

72.3
(▲ UP 0.6 POINT)

0   50   60   70   80   100

60.9
WORLD AVERAGE

68.0
REGIONAL AVERAGE
(EUROPE REGION)

NOTABLE SUCCESSES:
Investment Freedom, Trade Freedom, and Property Rights

CONCERNS:
Government Spending and Tax Burden

OVERALL SCORE CHANGE SINCE 2013:
+0.5

FREEDOM TREND

90

80

70

60

50

2008 2009 2010 2011 2012 2013 2014 2015 2016 2017

QUICK FACTS

POPULATION:
8.6 million

GDP (PPP):
$404.3 billion
0.9% growth in 2015
5-year compound annual growth 1.0%
$47,250 per capita

UNEMPLOYMENT:
5.7%

INFLATION (CPI):
0.8%

FDI INFLOW:
$3.8 billion

PUBLIC DEBT:
86.2% of GDP

2015 data unless otherwise noted. Data compiled as of September 2016

BACKGROUND: The center-left Social Democratic Party and center-right Austrian People's Party coalition, led by Social Democrat Federal Chancellor Christian Kern, lost seats in September 2013 but retained a governing majority. The results of the May 2016 runoff presidential election were annulled because of vot- ing irregularities. A new election was scheduled for October, but defective glue on mail-in ballots caused a further postponement. Austria has large service and industrial sectors and a small, highly developed agricultural sector. A large influx of young migrants may present an opportunity to alleviate the strain an aging population places on long-term labor markets and public finances, but assimilating migrants could also prove challenging.

12 ECONOMIC FREEDOMS | AUSTRIA

RULE OF LAW

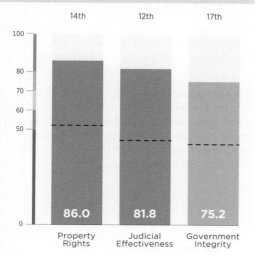

14th	12th	17th
86.0	81.8	75.2
Property Rights	Judicial Effectiveness	Government Integrity

Austria's land registry is a reliable and publicly accessible system for recording interests in property. The investment climate has been enhanced by the country's reputation for relatively high political stability and strong rule of law. The independent judiciary provides an effective means for protecting property rights (including intellectual property rights) and the contractual rights of nationals and foreigners. Corruption is relatively rare.

GOVERNMENT SIZE

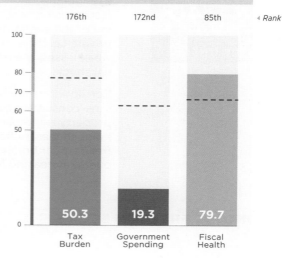

176th	172nd	85th	◄ Rank
50.3	19.3	79.7	
Tax Burden	Government Spending	Fiscal Health	

The top income tax rate is 50 percent, and the top corporate tax rate is 25 percent. High social security contributions are shared between employers and employees. The overall tax burden equals 43 percent of total domestic income. Government spending has amounted to 51.9 percent of total output (GDP) over the past three years, and budget deficits have averaged 1.9 percent of GDP. Public debt is equivalent to 86.2 percent of GDP.

REGULATORY EFFICIENCY

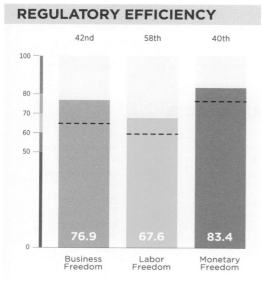

42nd	58th	40th
76.9	67.6	83.4
Business Freedom	Labor Freedom	Monetary Freedom

Austria's transparent and efficient regulatory framework facilitates business innovation and productivity growth. The cost of fringe benefits is among the highest in the world. VERBUND, 51 percent owned by the state and Austria's largest provider of power, lost a third of its market value in 2015 as a result of falling electricity prices and government subsidies for renewables in neighboring European countries.

OPEN MARKETS

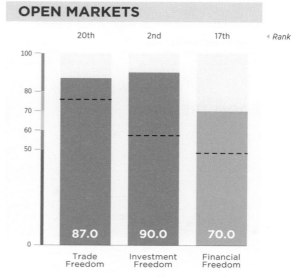

20th	2nd	17th	◄ Rank
87.0	90.0	70.0	
Trade Freedom	Investment Freedom	Financial Freedom	

Trade is extremely important to Austria's economy; the value of exports and imports taken together equals 102 percent of GDP. The average applied tariff rate is 1.5 percent. Austria is very open to trade and investment, but complex regulations may impede investment. The competitive and stable financial sector offers a wide range of services. There are no controls on currency transfers, access to foreign exchange, or repatriation of profits.

AUSTRIA

BELARUS

Belarus has achieved minor success in deregulation, but more liberal economic policies have not been a priority. Pervasive state involvement and control hamper the economy. Restructuring of the economic system has been very slow, and the small private sector is marginalized. Undercut by domestic structural weaknesses, the economy has little resilience against external shocks.

Corruption remains widespread, and the ineffective judiciary and time-consuming bureaucracy undermine the enforcement of property rights. Government interference with the private sector holds monetary freedom, investment freedom, and financial freedom far below average levels. Public debt has risen, partly due to increasing losses in the state-owned enterprises.

ECONOMIC FREEDOM SCORE

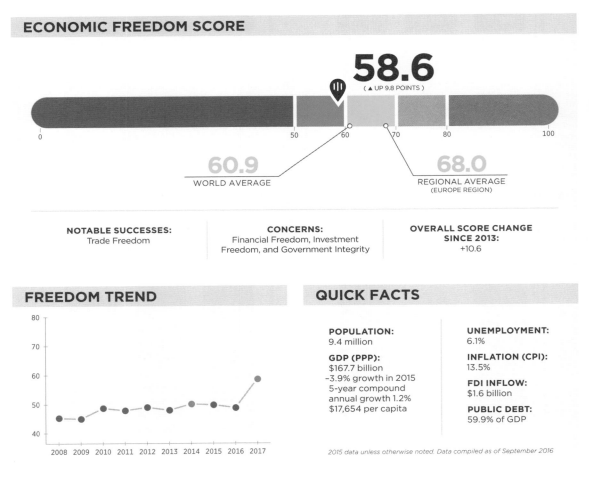

58.6
(▲ UP 9.8 POINTS)

0   50   60   70   80   100

60.9
WORLD AVERAGE

68.0
REGIONAL AVERAGE
(EUROPE REGION)

NOTABLE SUCCESSES:	CONCERNS:	OVERALL SCORE CHANGE SINCE 2013:
Trade Freedom	Financial Freedom, Investment Freedom, and Government Integrity	+10.6

FREEDOM TREND

80
70
60
50
40

2008 2009 2010 2011 2012 2013 2014 2015 2016 2017

QUICK FACTS

POPULATION:
9.4 million

GDP (PPP):
$167.7 billion
–3.9% growth in 2015
5-year compound
annual growth 1.2%
$17,654 per capita

UNEMPLOYMENT:
6.1%

INFLATION (CPI):
13.5%

FDI INFLOW:
$1.6 billion

PUBLIC DEBT:
59.9% of GDP

2015 data unless otherwise noted. Data compiled as of September 2016

BACKGROUND: President Alexander Lukashenko, in power since 1994, rules all branches of government. The U.N. Human Rights Council has appointed an investigator for Belarus. In a controversial move, the European Union has lifted sanctions against 170 people, including Lukashenko, that had been in place since the government crackdown on opposition figures in 2010. The two main opposition parties boycotted the rigged 2012 parliamentary elections. Lukashenko faced no serious competition in the October 2015 presidential election, which was neither free nor fair. Industries and state-controlled agriculture are not competitive. Moscow maintains huge influence in the government and the economy, which has been negatively affected by a faltering Russian economy. Belarus joined the Russia-backed Eurasian Economic Union in January 2015.

12 ECONOMIC FREEDOMS | BELARUS

RULE OF LAW

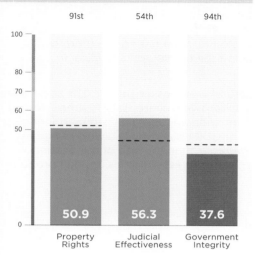

91st	54th	94th
Property Rights	Judicial Effectiveness	Government Integrity
50.9	56.3	37.6

Soviet-era property laws remain in effect. The constitution vests most power in the president, giving him control of the government, the courts, and even the legislative process by stating that presidential decrees have a higher legal force than ordinary legislation. The state controls 70 percent of the economy, feeding widespread corruption. Graft is also encouraged by an overall lack of government transparency and accountability.

GOVERNMENT SIZE

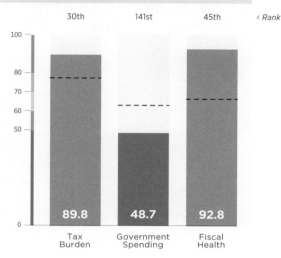

30th	141st	45th	◄ Rank
Tax Burden	Government Spending	Fiscal Health	
89.8	48.7	92.8	

The personal income tax rate is 13 percent. The top corporate tax rate remains 18 percent. Other taxes include excise taxes and a value-added tax. The overall tax burden equals 23.0 percent of total domestic income. Government spending has amounted to 41.3 percent of total output (GDP) over the past three years, and small budget surpluses have averaged 0.04 percent of GDP. Public debt is equivalent to 59.9 percent of GDP.

REGULATORY EFFICIENCY

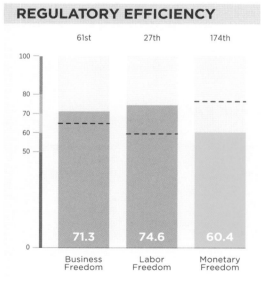

61st	27th	174th
Business Freedom	Labor Freedom	Monetary Freedom
71.3	74.6	60.4

Simplifying registration formalities and abolishing the minimum capital requirement have facilitated business formation. Procedural requirements for necessary permits have also been reduced. An efficient labor market is not fully developed. Heavily dependent on subsidized Russian energy, the government subsidizes its inefficient agricultural sector, but it cut some of those subsidies and liberalized food prices in 2016.

OPEN MARKETS

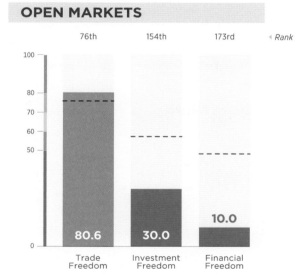

76th	154th	173rd	◄ Rank
Trade Freedom	Investment Freedom	Financial Freedom	
80.6	30.0	10.0	

Trade is extremely important to Belarus's economy; the value of exports and imports taken together equals 119 percent of GDP. The average applied tariff rate is 2.2 percent. State-owned enterprises distort the economy, and extensive government control severely limits investment and financial activity. Many industries are primarily or exclusively state-run to the detriment of private investment and enterprises.

BELARUS

BELGIUM

Generally friendly to free-market competition, Belgium's economy has long benefited from openness to global trade and investment. Among the notable reforms instituted during the past two years to address fiscal weaknesses and enhance competitiveness are pension reforms raising the retirement age and gradually reducing the employers' social security contribution.

However, lingering structural weaknesses persist. The tax system is burdensome, and the extensive welfare state is supported by a high level of government spending. Belgium's public spending rate (around 55 percent of GDP) is among the world's highest. Government debt is now larger than the size of the economy. Despite some progress, labor market rigidities impede productivity and job growth.

ECONOMIC FREEDOM SCORE

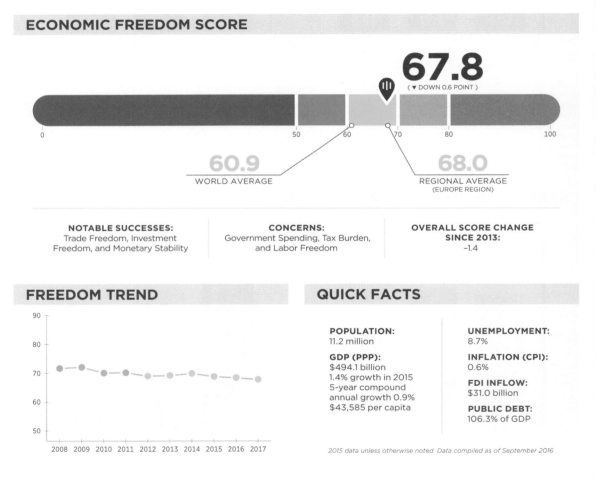

67.8
(▼ DOWN 0.6 POINT)

0   50   60   70   80   100

60.9
WORLD AVERAGE

68.0
REGIONAL AVERAGE
(EUROPE REGION)

NOTABLE SUCCESSES:
Trade Freedom, Investment Freedom, and Monetary Stability

CONCERNS:
Government Spending, Tax Burden, and Labor Freedom

OVERALL SCORE CHANGE SINCE 2013:
–1.4

FREEDOM TREND

90
80
70
60
50

2008 2009 2010 2011 2012 2013 2014 2015 2016 2017

QUICK FACTS

POPULATION:
11.2 million

GDP (PPP):
$494.1 billion
1.4% growth in 2015
5-year compound annual growth 0.9%
$43,585 per capita

UNEMPLOYMENT:
8.7%

INFLATION (CPI):
0.6%

FDI INFLOW:
$31.0 billion

PUBLIC DEBT:
106.3% of GDP

2015 data unless otherwise noted. Data compiled as of September 2016

BACKGROUND: Belgium is a federal state with three culturally different regions: Flanders, Wallonia, and the capital city of Brussels. Brussels also serves as the headquarters of NATO and the European Union. The center-right New Flemish Alliance won a plurality in the May 2014 federal elections, the first since electoral reform, and is part of a coalition government. Charles Michel of the liberal francophone Reformist Movement Party is Belgium's youngest prime minister since 1845. Neighboring countries have a strong political and economic impact on Belgium. Terrorist attacks in March 2016 have cost the nation billions in additional security measures and lost business and tax revenue. Tourism has been particularly affected.

12 ECONOMIC FREEDOMS | BELGIUM

RULE OF LAW

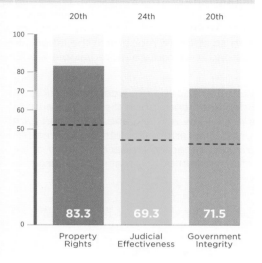

	20th	24th	20th

- Property Rights: 83.3
- Judicial Effectiveness: 69.3
- Government Integrity: 71.5

Property rights are well protected by law. Laws are well codified, and the independent judicial system functions slowly but professionally. Enforcement of intellectual property rights can be protracted. Corruption is relatively rare, and government efforts to address underlying fiscal and competitiveness weaknesses should further reduce opportunities for rent-seeking. The government prohibits and punishes bribery.

GOVERNMENT SIZE

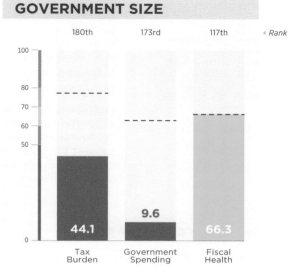

180th	173rd	117th	◀ Rank

- Tax Burden: 44.1
- Government Spending: 9.6
- Fiscal Health: 66.3

The top income tax rate is 50 percent, and the top corporate tax rate is 34 percent. Other taxes include a value-added tax and an estate tax. The overall tax burden equals 44.7 percent of total domestic income. Government spending has amounted to 54.9 percent of total output (GDP) over the past three years, and budget deficits have averaged 2.9 percent of GDP. Public debt is equivalent to 106.3 percent of GDP.

REGULATORY EFFICIENCY

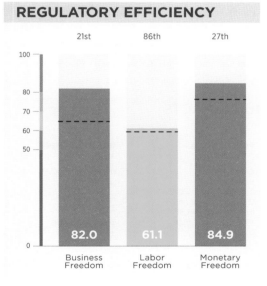

21st	86th	27th

- Business Freedom: 82.0
- Labor Freedom: 61.1
- Monetary Freedom: 84.9

The overall regulatory environment is efficient and transparent. With the cost of establishing a company reduced, starting a business takes less than five days and procedures. Employment regulations have gradually become less burdensome, but the nonsalary cost of hiring a worker remains high. The center-right federal government has focused on improving public finances (for example, by cutting subsidies on diesel fuel in 2016).

OPEN MARKETS

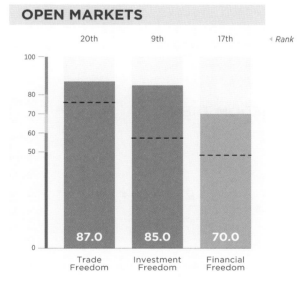

20th	9th	17th	◀ Rank

- Trade Freedom: 87.0
- Investment Freedom: 85.0
- Financial Freedom: 70.0

Trade is extremely important to Belgium's economy; the value of exports and imports taken together equals 167 percent of GDP. The average applied tariff rate is 1.5 percent, and there are relatively few barriers to trade and investment. Since the financial crisis that resulted in the restructuring of Dexia and Fortis banks, the banking sector has become smaller. However, it has recovered its resilience, and the number of nonperforming loans remains low.

BELGIUM

BOSNIA AND HERZEGOVINA

WORLD RANK:
92

REGIONAL RANK:
36

ECONOMIC FREEDOM STATUS:
MODERATELY FREE

Bosnia and Herzegovina's economic development has been driven by reconstruction efforts. Trade has been an engine of growth, but the overall entrepreneurial environment remains one of the region's most burdensome, hindering the emergence of a dynamic private sector. In an effort to modernize the labor market, a new labor law intended to introduce more flexible working practices was adopted in July 2015.

Inefficient and high government spending, weak protection of property rights, and widespread corruption discourage entrepreneurial activity. The rule of law is weak, and local courts are subject to substantial political interference. Intrusive bureaucracy and costly registration procedures reflect a history of central planning. The informal economy remains quite large.

ECONOMIC FREEDOM SCORE

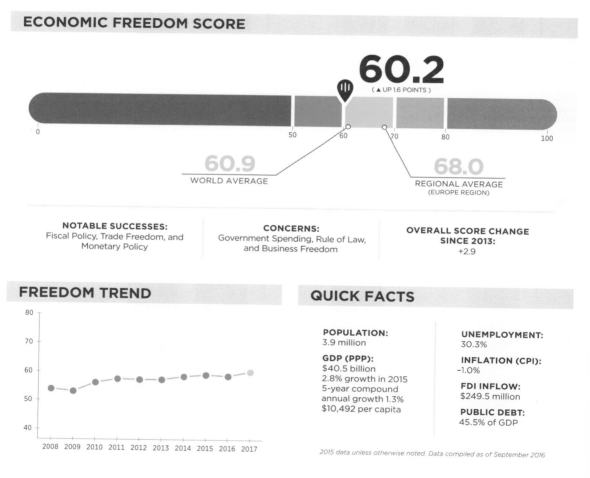

60.2
(▲ UP 1.6 POINTS)

0   50   60   70   80   100

60.9
WORLD AVERAGE

68.0
REGIONAL AVERAGE
(EUROPE REGION)

NOTABLE SUCCESSES:
Fiscal Policy, Trade Freedom, and Monetary Policy

CONCERNS:
Government Spending, Rule of Law, and Business Freedom

OVERALL SCORE CHANGE SINCE 2013:
+2.9

FREEDOM TREND

80
70
60
50
40

2008 2009 2010 2011 2012 2013 2014 2015 2016 2017

QUICK FACTS

POPULATION:
3.9 million

GDP (PPP):
$40.5 billion
2.8% growth in 2015
5-year compound annual growth 1.3%
$10,492 per capita

UNEMPLOYMENT:
30.3%

INFLATION (CPI):
–1.0%

FDI INFLOW:
$249.5 million

PUBLIC DEBT:
45.5% of GDP

2015 data unless otherwise noted. Data compiled as of September 2016

BACKGROUND: The 1995 Dayton Agreement ended three years of war in the former Yugoslavia and finalized Bosnia and Herzegovina's independence. Two separate entities exist under a loose central government: the Republika Srpska (Serbian) and Federation of Bosnia and Herzegovina (Muslim/Croat). The official results of a 2013 census, published in 2016, showed that the two entities remain ethnically split. A Stabilization and Association Agreement signed by Bosnia and Herzegovina and the European Union took effect in June 2015. In February 2016, Bosnia formally applied to join the EU. Bosnia also received a NATO Membership Action Plan in 2010 and is one of three official candidates for NATO membership.

12 ECONOMIC FREEDOMS | BOSNIA AND HERZEGOVINA

RULE OF LAW

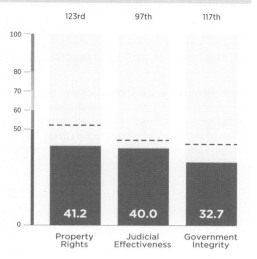

	123rd	97th	117th
	Property Rights	Judicial Effectiveness	Government Integrity
	41.2	40.0	32.7

Largely unreliable property registries leave transfers open to dispute and create a major barrier to the development of real property and mortgage markets. The complex system of government lends itself to deadlock and has bred a large informal economy. The judiciary remains susceptible to influence by nationalist political parties and pressure from the executive branch. Inefficiency and corruption are widespread at all levels of government.

GOVERNMENT SIZE

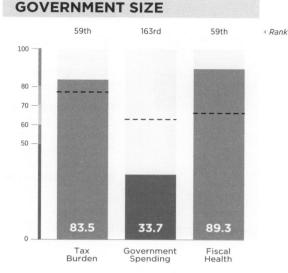

◄ Rank

	59th	163rd	59th
	Tax Burden	Government Spending	Fiscal Health
	83.5	33.7	89.3

The top income and corporate tax rates are 10 percent, but various governing entities have different tax policies. The overall tax burden equals 38.1 percent of total domestic income. Government spending has amounted to 47 percent of total output (GDP) over the past three years, and budget deficits have averaged 2 percent of GDP. Public debt is equivalent to 45.5 percent of GDP.

REGULATORY EFFICIENCY

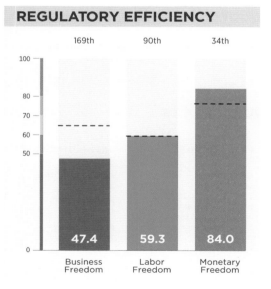

	169th	90th	34th
	Business Freedom	Labor Freedom	Monetary Freedom
	47.4	59.3	84.0

Regulatory inefficiency still impairs the business environment and limits the private investment needed for faster economic growth. Obtaining business licenses and launching a business remain vulnerable to bureaucratic delays. The recently adopted labor code is intended to enhance labor market flexibility. The government subsidizes energy and, according to the World Bank, targets its agricultural subsidies poorly.

OPEN MARKETS

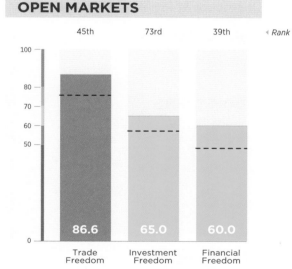

◄ Rank

	45th	73rd	39th
	Trade Freedom	Investment Freedom	Financial Freedom
	86.6	65.0	60.0

Trade is important to Bosnia and Herzegovina's economy; the value of exports and imports taken together equals 91 percent of GDP. The average applied tariff rate is 1.7 percent. The government's official policy is to treat foreign and domestic investors equally under the law. Foreign-owned banks account for over 80 percent of banking assets. Long-term lending is still hindered by insufficient enforcement of contracts.

BULGARIA

WORLD RANK: **47** REGIONAL RANK: **23**

ECONOMIC FREEDOM STATUS:
MODERATELY FREE

Bulgaria's transition to a more open and flexible economic system has been facilitated by substantial restructuring. Competitive flat tax rates and an open trade regime, supported by a relatively efficient regulatory framework, have encouraged development of a growing private sector. The financial sector demonstrated a relatively high level of resilience during the 2014 liquidity crisis.

The management of public finance has been relatively sound. The level of public debt continues to be among the lowest in the region, with budget deficits declining. However, deeper and more committed institutional reforms are needed in areas like judicial effectiveness and government integrity to help ensure long-term economic development.

ECONOMIC FREEDOM SCORE

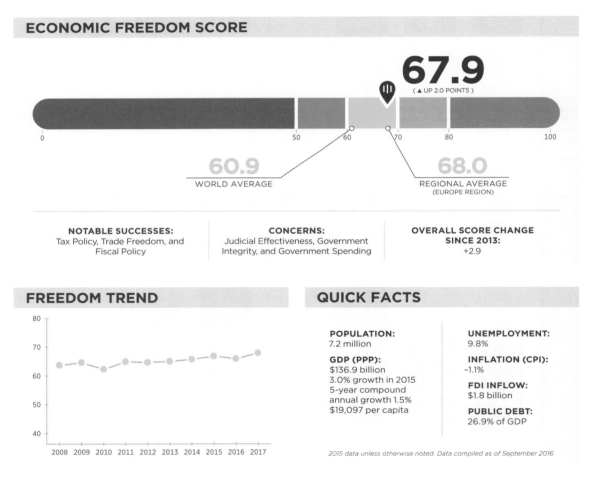

67.9
(▲ UP 2.0 POINTS)

0   50   60   70   80   100

60.9
WORLD AVERAGE

68.0
REGIONAL AVERAGE
(EUROPE REGION)

NOTABLE SUCCESSES:
Tax Policy, Trade Freedom, and Fiscal Policy

CONCERNS:
Judicial Effectiveness, Government Integrity, and Government Spending

OVERALL SCORE CHANGE SINCE 2013:
+2.9

FREEDOM TREND

80
70
60
50
40

2008 2009 2010 2011 2012 2013 2014 2015 2016 2017

QUICK FACTS

POPULATION:
7.2 million

GDP (PPP):
$136.9 billion
3.0% growth in 2015
5-year compound
annual growth 1.5%
$19,097 per capita

UNEMPLOYMENT:
9.8%

INFLATION (CPI):
–1.1%

FDI INFLOW:
$1.8 billion

PUBLIC DEBT:
26.9% of GDP

2015 data unless otherwise noted. Data compiled as of September 2016

BACKGROUND: From May 2013 to October 2014, Bulgaria held a European Parliament election and two national parliamentary elections. A year after the 2013 parliamentary election and amid protests against low living standards, high energy costs, and corruption, President Rosen Plevneliev dissolved the parliament because of banking instability. Boyko Borissov of the center-right GERB party formed a minority coalition government with the center-right Reformist bloc and became prime minister for the second time. Recovery from the eurozone crisis has been slow but steady. Tourism, information technology and telecommunications, agriculture, pharmaceuticals, and textiles are leading industries. Migrant flows are an issue, and Bulgaria has taken steps to secure its border with Turkey.

12 ECONOMIC FREEDOMS | BULGARIA

RULE OF LAW

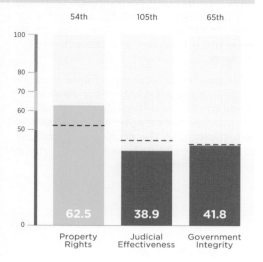

54th   105th   65th

Property Rights **62.5**
Judicial Effectiveness **38.9**
Government Integrity **41.8**

Property rights are not well protected. The judiciary has benefited from legal and institutional reforms associated with accession to the European Union, but practical gains in efficiency and accountability have been lacking. Public trust in the judicial system remains extremely low. The government has struggled to combat corruption within the business community, in the judiciary, and in its own ranks.

GOVERNMENT SIZE

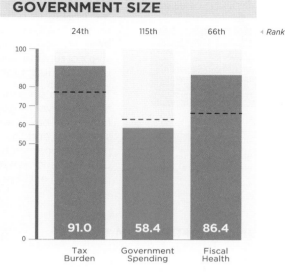

24th   115th   66th   ◄ Rank

Tax Burden **91.0**
Government Spending **58.4**
Fiscal Health **86.4**

The individual income and corporate tax rates are a flat 10 percent. Other taxes include a value-added tax and an estate tax. The overall tax burden equals 26.5 percent of total domestic income. Government spending has amounted to 37.2 percent of total output (GDP) over the past three years, and budget deficits have averaged 2.8 percent of GDP. Public debt is equivalent to 26.9 percent of GDP.

REGULATORY EFFICIENCY

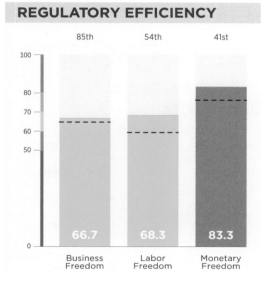

85th   54th   41st

Business Freedom **66.7**
Labor Freedom **68.3**
Monetary Freedom **83.3**

Launching a business has become less time-consuming, and licensing requirements have been eased, though the pace of change has lagged behind that of some other countries. Relatively flexible labor regulations enhance employment growth, but there is room for further reform. Government subsidies to the largely state-owned energy sector are being reduced gradually, and other state-owned enterprises (such as airports) are being privatized.

OPEN MARKETS

20th   59th   39th   ◄ Rank

Trade Freedom **87.0**
Investment Freedom **70.0**
Financial Freedom **60.0**

Trade is extremely important to Bulgaria's economy; the value of exports and imports taken together equals 131 percent of GDP. The average applied tariff rate is 1.5 percent. Officially, foreign and domestic investors are treated equally under the law. The banking sector has regained stability since the 2014 liquidity crisis, although the level of nonperforming loans remains high. Foreign banks account for more than 70 percent of total assets.

BULGARIA

CROATIA

WORLD RANK: **95** REGIONAL RANK: **37**

ECONOMIC FREEDOM STATUS:
MOSTLY UNFREE

Croatia lags behind many of its neighbors in structural economic reform, and institutional shortcomings continue to hold back entrepreneurial growth. Recent fiscal reforms have been limited in scope and depth. Political volatility and pervasive corruption undermine the rule of law, and protection of property rights remains weak.

The state's presence in private-sector activity remains intrusive, and the level of government spending is high. Few meaningful efforts have been made to reduce or control government spending, and the bloated public sector severely constrains private-sector dynamism, prolonging the economic downturn. Government ownership in such key sectors as transport, natural resources, and banking remains considerable.

ECONOMIC FREEDOM SCORE

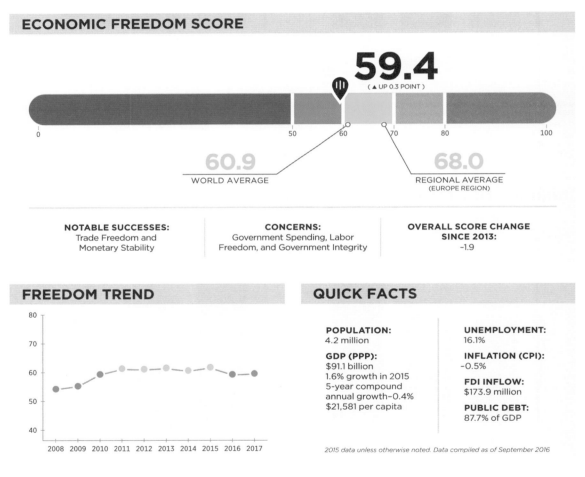

59.4
(▲ UP 0.3 POINT)

0   50   60   70   80   100

60.9
WORLD AVERAGE

68.0
REGIONAL AVERAGE
(EUROPE REGION)

NOTABLE SUCCESSES:
Trade Freedom and Monetary Stability

CONCERNS:
Government Spending, Labor Freedom, and Government Integrity

OVERALL SCORE CHANGE SINCE 2013:
-1.9

FREEDOM TREND

80

70

60

50

40

2008 2009 2010 2011 2012 2013 2014 2015 2016 2017

QUICK FACTS

POPULATION:
4.2 million

GDP (PPP):
$91.1 billion
1.6% growth in 2015
5-year compound annual growth–0.4%
$21,581 per capita

UNEMPLOYMENT:
16.1%

INFLATION (CPI):
-0.5%

FDI INFLOW:
$173.9 million

PUBLIC DEBT:
87.7% of GDP

2015 data unless otherwise noted. Data compiled as of September 2016

BACKGROUND: Croatia declared its independence in 1991, contributing to the breakup of Yugoslavia along ethnic and religious lines. Years of Croat–Serb conflict ended formally in 1995 with the Dayton Peace Accords. Croatia joined NATO in 2009 and the European Union in 2013. In October 2016, after months of political instability, President Kolinda Grabar-Kitarović appointed Andrej Plenković, leader of the center-right HDZ party, as prime minister after his party and a small populist group agreed to form a coalition government. Political uncertainty continues to endanger much-needed economic reform. Tourism and shipbuilding are major industries. While domestic demand has picked up in recent years, high indebtedness, a weak export base, and the slow pace of privatization continue to limit growth.

12 ECONOMIC FREEDOMS | CROATIA

RULE OF LAW

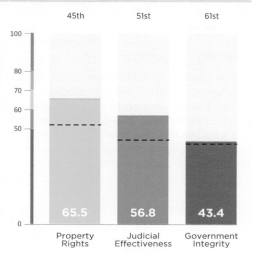

	45th	51st	61st

Property Rights: **65.5**
Judicial Effectiveness: **56.8**
Government Integrity: **43.4**

Private property rights are well established, but there can be ambiguous and conflicting claims in some title cases. Judicial independence is generally respected. A new appointments system has increased judicial professionalism, although the case backlog exceeds the EU average. Croatia received low scores in the Economist Intelligence Unit's 2015 *Democracy Index* in categories indicating popular dissatisfaction with failure to tackle corruption.

GOVERNMENT SIZE

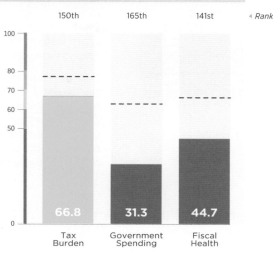

	150th	165th	141st	◄ Rank

Tax Burden: **66.8**
Government Spending: **31.3**
Fiscal Health: **44.7**

The top personal income tax rate is 40 percent, and the top corporate tax rate is 20 percent. Other taxes include a value-added tax and excise taxes. The overall tax burden equals 36.4 percent of total domestic income. Government spending has amounted to 47.9 percent of total output (GDP) over the past three years, and budget deficits have averaged 5.0 percent of GDP. Public debt is equivalent to 87.7 percent of GDP.

REGULATORY EFFICIENCY

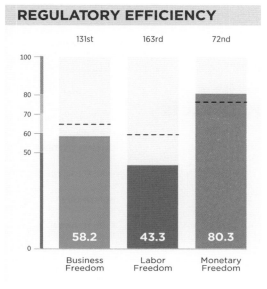

	131st	163rd	72nd

Business Freedom: **58.2**
Labor Freedom: **43.3**
Monetary Freedom: **80.3**

Despite reforms to streamline the procedures for establishing a business, the overall regulatory environment remains burdensome and inefficient. A new labor law passed in 2014 was an attempt to make the labor market flexible and dynamic. Political instability in 2016 further delayed progress on reforms to reduce spending and subsidies as required by the European Commission's Excessive Deficit Procedure.

OPEN MARKETS

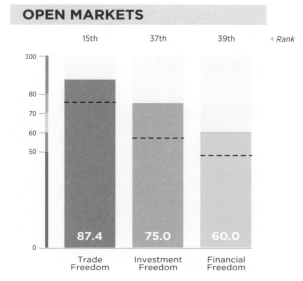

	15th	37th	39th	◄ Rank

Trade Freedom: **87.4**
Investment Freedom: **75.0**
Financial Freedom: **60.0**

Trade is important to Croatia's economy; the value of exports and imports taken together equals 96 percent of GDP. The average applied tariff rate is 1.3 percent. In general, the government does not screen or discriminate against foreign investment. State-owned enterprises distort the economy. The banking sector has remained stable and relatively well capitalized, but nonperforming loans remain a problem.

CROATIA

CYPRUS

WORLD RANK: **48** | REGIONAL RANK: **24**

ECONOMIC FREEDOM STATUS:
MODERATELY FREE

Cyprus has been emerging from a severe economic recession compounded by the collapse of its financial system in 2013. Economic policy has focused mainly on improving fiscal discipline and other structural reforms. Ending its IMF bailout program before term, Cyprus has made a considerable economic adjustment and turned around its economy.

Scoring high in many of the 12 economic freedoms, Cyprus does particularly well in trade freedom and monetary freedom. The regulatory framework is relatively transparent and efficient, the financial sector has become more stable and efficient, and the government has pursued policies that are more favorable to private-sector development. Following the banking sector's recovery, the government lifted all capital controls.

ECONOMIC FREEDOM SCORE

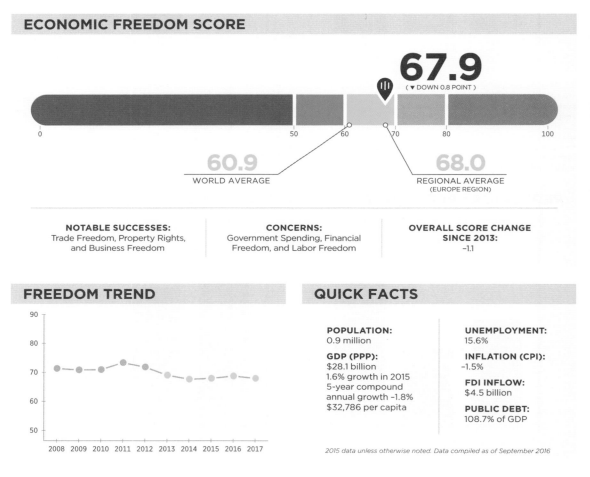

67.9
(▼ DOWN 0.8 POINT)

0   50   60   70   80   100

60.9
WORLD AVERAGE

68.0
REGIONAL AVERAGE
(EUROPE REGION)

NOTABLE SUCCESSES:
Trade Freedom, Property Rights, and Business Freedom

CONCERNS:
Government Spending, Financial Freedom, and Labor Freedom

OVERALL SCORE CHANGE SINCE 2013:
–1.1

FREEDOM TREND

90
80
70
60
50

2008 2009 2010 2011 2012 2013 2014 2015 2016 2017

QUICK FACTS

POPULATION:
0.9 million

GDP (PPP):
$28.1 billion
1.6% growth in 2015
5-year compound annual growth –1.8%
$32,786 per capita

UNEMPLOYMENT:
15.6%

INFLATION (CPI):
–1.5%

FDI INFLOW:
$4.5 billion

PUBLIC DEBT:
108.7% of GDP

2015 data unless otherwise noted. Data compiled as of September 2016

BACKGROUND: A U.N. buffer zone has separated the Greek Cypriot Republic of Cyprus from the Turkish Republic of Northern Cyprus since 1974. The Republic of Cyprus joined the European Union in 2004 and acts as the island's internationally recognized administration. Despite deep mutual hostility, Greek and Turkish leaders continue to negotiate on possible reunification through U.N.-brokered talks. Center-right Cyprus President Nicos Anastasiades has been head of state and head of government since taking office in February 2013. In May 2016, eight political parties won seats in parliament in an election that was marked by low voter turnout.

12 ECONOMIC FREEDOMS | CYPRUS

RULE OF LAW

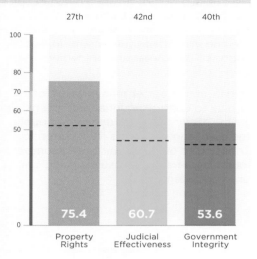

	27th	42nd	40th
	Property Rights 75.4	Judicial Effectiveness 60.7	Government Integrity 53.6

There are significant restrictions on ownership of real estate by non-EU residents, but a fast-track procedure for claims under €3,000 has simplified the enforcement of contracts. In the Republic of Cyprus, an independent and impartial judiciary operates according to the British tradition, upholding due process rights. Corruption, patronage, and a lack of transparency continue to flourish in the Turkish-controlled area.

GOVERNMENT SIZE

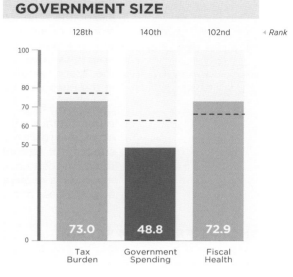

	128th	140th	102nd	◀ Rank
	Tax Burden 73.0	Government Spending 48.8	Fiscal Health 72.9	

The top personal income tax rate is 35 percent, and the top corporate tax rate is 12.5 percent. Other taxes include a value-added tax and a real estate tax. The overall tax burden equals 36.3 percent of total domestic income. Government spending has amounted to 41.3 percent of total output (GDP) over the past three years, and budget deficits have averaged 2.1 percent of GDP. Public debt is equivalent to 108.7 percent of GDP.

REGULATORY EFFICIENCY

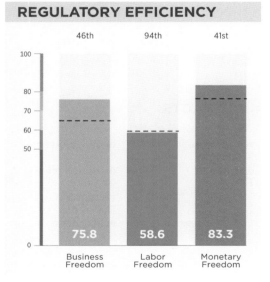

	46th	94th	41st
	Business Freedom 75.8	Labor Freedom 58.6	Monetary Freedom 83.3

The regulatory framework generally facilitates entrepreneurial activity. With no minimum capital requirement, it takes six procedures to launch a company. Relatively flexible labor regulations facilitate employment and productivity growth, although union power is quite strong. According to a 2016 IMF report, government subsidies in the first nine months of 2015 amounted to about 3 percent of GDP.

OPEN MARKETS

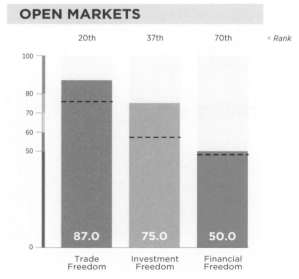

	20th	37th	70th	◀ Rank
	Trade Freedom 87.0	Investment Freedom 75.0	Financial Freedom 50.0	

Trade is extremely important to Cyprus's economy; the value of exports and imports taken together equals 108 percent of GDP. The average applied tariff rate is 1.5 percent. There is no general screening of foreign investment. State-owned enterprises distort the economy. The banking sector has restored stability and resilience in recent years, but nonperforming loans are equivalent to about 150 percent of GDP.

CYPRUS

CZECH REPUBLIC

WORLD RANK: **28** | REGIONAL RANK: **16**

ECONOMIC FREEDOM STATUS:
MOSTLY FREE

Implementation of critical reforms in many areas has gradually expanded the Czech Republic's vibrant private sector. Business start-up procedures have been streamlined, and a relatively efficient tax regime facilitates entrepreneurial growth. With openness to global trade and investment fully institutionalized, the Czech Republic has one of the lowest unemployment rates in the European Union.

Continuing fiscal consolidation and better management of public finance will be critical to controlling inflation and ensuring economic resilience. The eurozone crisis has dampened public support for adopting the euro, and prospects for its adoption remain uncertain. Contributing to overall stability and competitiveness, a relatively sound legal framework sustains judicial effectiveness and government integrity.

ECONOMIC FREEDOM SCORE

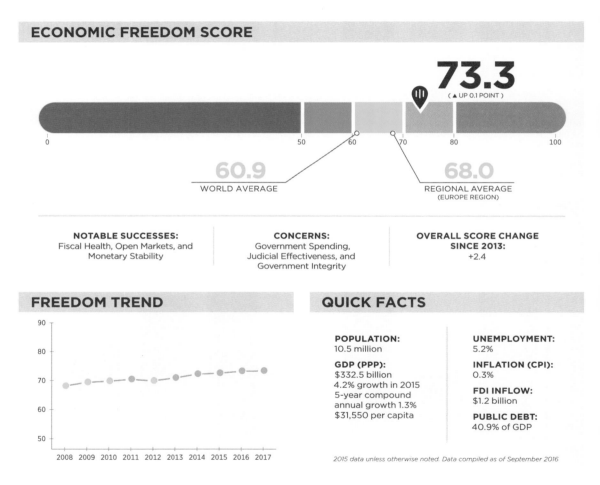

73.3
(▲ UP 0.1 POINT)

0   50   60   70   80   100

60.9
WORLD AVERAGE

68.0
REGIONAL AVERAGE
(EUROPE REGION)

NOTABLE SUCCESSES:
Fiscal Health, Open Markets, and Monetary Stability

CONCERNS:
Government Spending, Judicial Effectiveness, and Government Integrity

OVERALL SCORE CHANGE SINCE 2013:
+2.4

FREEDOM TREND

90
80
70
60
50

2008 2009 2010 2011 2012 2013 2014 2015 2016 2017

QUICK FACTS

POPULATION:
10.5 million

GDP (PPP):
$332.5 billion
4.2% growth in 2015
5-year compound
annual growth 1.3%
$31,550 per capita

UNEMPLOYMENT:
5.2%

INFLATION (CPI):
0.3%

FDI INFLOW:
$1.2 billion

PUBLIC DEBT:
40.9% of GDP

2015 data unless otherwise noted. Data compiled as of September 2016

BACKGROUND: The end of Czechoslovakia's Communist dictatorship in 1989 led to the election of dissident playwright Vaclav Havel as president. The Czech Republic separated from Slovakia in 1993 and joined NATO in 1999 and the European Union in 2004. The first directly elected president, Miloš Zeman of the center-left Czech Social Democrat Party, appointed a caretaker government in August 2013, and legislative elections followed in October. In January 2014, Zeman asked Social Democrat leader Bohuslav Sobotka to form a government. Polling shows low satisfaction with EU membership. In 2016, "Czechia" was officially registered at the United Nations as an alternate name for the country.

12 ECONOMIC FREEDOMS | CZECH REPUBLIC

RULE OF LAW

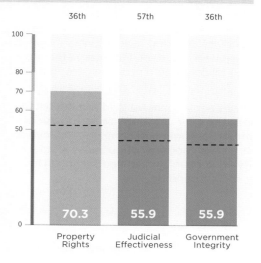

36th	57th	36th
70.3	55.9	55.9
Property Rights	Judicial Effectiveness	Government Integrity

Property rights are relatively well protected, and contracts are generally secure. The independence of the judiciary is largely respected, though its complexity and multilayered composition lead to the slow delivery of judgments. While corruption and political pressure are still present within law enforcement agencies, the Office of the Public Prosecutor has become more independent in recent years.

GOVERNMENT SIZE

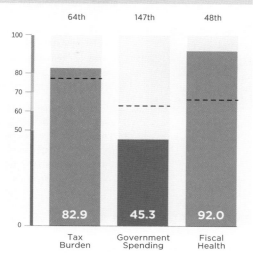

64th	147th	48th	◂ Rank
82.9	45.3	92.0	
Tax Burden	Government Spending	Fiscal Health	

The individual income tax rate is a flat 15 percent, and the standard corporate tax rate is 19 percent. Other taxes include a value-added tax and an inheritance tax. The overall tax burden equals 33.5 percent of total domestic income. Government spending has amounted to 42.7 percent of total output (GDP) over the past three years, and budget deficits have averaged 1.7 percent of GDP. Public debt is equivalent to 40.9 percent of GDP.

REGULATORY EFFICIENCY

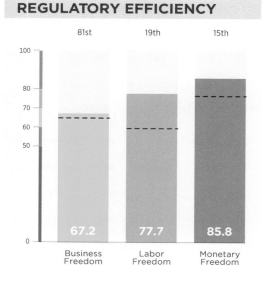

81st	19th	15th
67.2	77.7	85.8
Business Freedom	Labor Freedom	Monetary Freedom

Business formation and operation are possible without bureaucratic interference, and no minimum capital is required. Recent reforms have reduced the cost and number of procedures required to launch a company. The labor market is relatively flexible, and the unemployment rate continues to decline. The state energy program includes increased reliance on unsubsidized nuclear power, although subsidies for fossil fuels have increased.

OPEN MARKETS

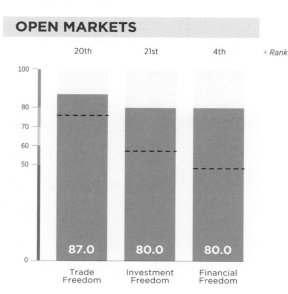

20th	21st	4th	◂ Rank
87.0	80.0	80.0	
Trade Freedom	Investment Freedom	Financial Freedom	

Trade is extremely important to the Czech Republic's economy; the value of exports and imports taken together equals 163 percent of GDP. The average applied tariff rate is 1.5 percent, and the government has reduced bureaucratic barriers to investment. The financial sector remains resilient. Banks are well capitalized and stable, and liquidity levels are gradually increasing.

CZECH REPUBLIC

DENMARK

WORLD RANK: **18** REGIONAL RANK: **9**

ECONOMIC FREEDOM STATUS:
MOSTLY FREE

Denmark's economy performs notably well in regulatory efficiency. Open-market policies sustain flexibility, competitiveness, and large flows of trade and investment, and the transparent and efficient regulatory and legal environment encourages robust entrepreneurial activity. Banking regulations are sensible, and lending practices have been prudent. Monetary stability is well maintained, and the judicial system provides strong protection for property rights.

Government spending has been expansive, and the overall tax regime needed to finance the ever-growing scope of government has become more burdensome and complex. However, such institutional assets as high degrees of business efficiency and regulatory flexibility have counterbalanced some of the shortcomings of heavy social spending.

ECONOMIC FREEDOM SCORE

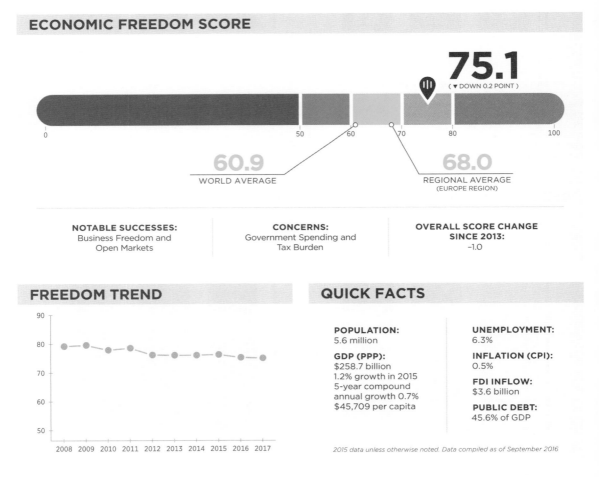

75.1
(▼ DOWN 0.2 POINT)

0   50   60   70   80   100

60.9
WORLD AVERAGE

68.0
REGIONAL AVERAGE
(EUROPE REGION)

NOTABLE SUCCESSES:
Business Freedom and
Open Markets

CONCERNS:
Government Spending and
Tax Burden

**OVERALL SCORE CHANGE
SINCE 2013:**
–1.0

FREEDOM TREND

90
80
70
60
50

2008 2009 2010 2011 2012 2013 2014 2015 2016 2017

QUICK FACTS

POPULATION:
5.6 million

GDP (PPP):
$258.7 billion
1.2% growth in 2015
5-year compound
annual growth 0.7%
$45,709 per capita

UNEMPLOYMENT:
6.3%

INFLATION (CPI):
0.5%

FDI INFLOW:
$3.6 billion

PUBLIC DEBT:
45.6% of GDP

2015 data unless otherwise noted. Data compiled as of September 2016

BACKGROUND: Lars Løkke Rasmussen's center-right Venstre party came in third in the June 2015 parliamentary elections, but Rasmussen became prime minister after forming a minority government. He also served as prime minister from 2009–2011. The center-left Social Democrats came in first in the election, and the Eurosceptic Danish People's Party came in second. Denmark has been a member of the European Union since 1973. Its economy depends heavily on foreign trade, and the private sector includes many small and medium-size companies. Measures put in place to decrease immigration, including delayed family reunification and temporary border controls, appear to be having an impact.

12 ECONOMIC FREEDOMS | DENMARK

RULE OF LAW

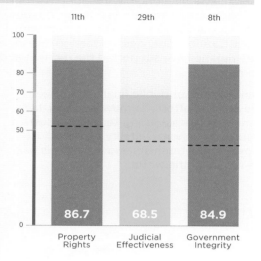

11th	29th	8th
Property Rights **86.7**	Judicial Effectiveness **68.5**	Government Integrity **84.9**

With a trustworthy, independent, and fair judicial system institutionalized throughout the economy, protection of property rights is strongly enforced. Intellectual property rights are respected, and enforcement is consistent with world standards. Levels of corruption are generally very low in Denmark, which was ranked first out of 168 countries surveyed in Transparency International's 2015 *Corruption Perceptions Index*.

GOVERNMENT SIZE

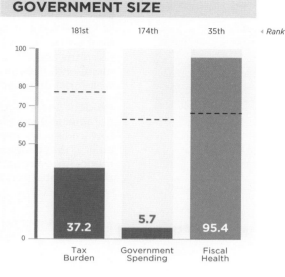

◄ Rank

181st	174th	35th
Tax Burden **37.2**	Government Spending **5.7**	Fiscal Health **95.4**

The top personal income tax rate is 56 percent, and the top corporate tax rate is 23.5 percent. Other taxes include a value-added tax and an inheritance tax. The overall tax burden equals 50.9 percent of total domestic income. Government spending has amounted to 56.1 percent of total output (GDP) over the past three years, and budget deficits have averaged 0.5 percent of GDP. Public debt is equivalent to 45.6 percent of GDP.

REGULATORY EFFICIENCY

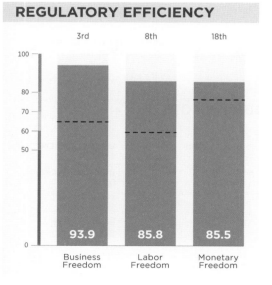

3rd	8th	18th
Business Freedom **93.9**	Labor Freedom **85.8**	Monetary Freedom **85.5**

The overall regulatory environment remains transparent and efficient. Launching a business takes fewer days and procedures than the world averages. Flexible and modern employment regulations sustain the labor market. Monetary stability is well established. Energy prices fell in 2016. Denmark has increased subsidies to maintain its renewable energy program but has declined to buy expensive new wind turbines.

OPEN MARKETS

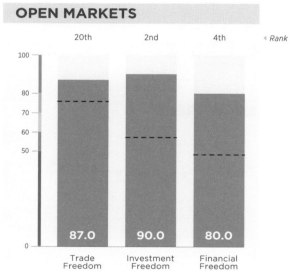

◄ Rank

20th	2nd	4th
Trade Freedom **87.0**	Investment Freedom **90.0**	Financial Freedom **80.0**

Trade is extremely important to Denmark's economy; the value of exports and imports taken together equals 100 percent of GDP. The average applied tariff rate is 1.5 percent, and there are few barriers to foreign trade and investment. The financial system is competitive and resilient. The banking sector, characterized by relatively prudent lending in a sound regulatory framework, has regained its stability after a period of uncertainty.

DENMARK

ESTONIA

WORLD RANK: **6** REGIONAL RANK: **2**

ECONOMIC FREEDOM STATUS:
MOSTLY FREE

Estonia's economy continues to benefit from government policies that sustain a high level of economic freedom. The rule of law remains strongly buttressed and enforced by an independent and efficient judicial system. A simplified tax system with flat rates and low indirect taxation, openness to foreign investment, and a liberal trade regime have supported the resilient and well-functioning economy.

Prudent and sound management of public finance has been notable. In particular, revitalized efforts to move even further toward limited government and ensure long-term fiscal sustainability have helped to sustain economic vitality. Fiscal adjustments have brought down budget deficits and kept levels of public debt among the lowest in the world.

ECONOMIC FREEDOM SCORE

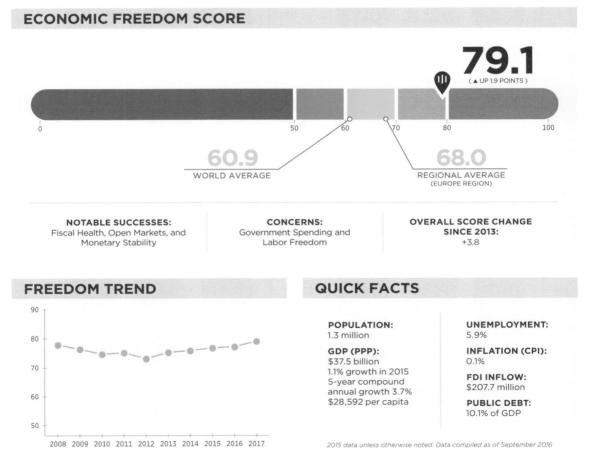

79.1
(▲ UP 1.9 POINTS)

0   50   60   70   80   100

60.9
WORLD AVERAGE

68.0
REGIONAL AVERAGE
(EUROPE REGION)

NOTABLE SUCCESSES:
Fiscal Health, Open Markets, and Monetary Stability

CONCERNS:
Government Spending and Labor Freedom

OVERALL SCORE CHANGE SINCE 2013:
+3.8

FREEDOM TREND

90
80
70
60
50

2008 2009 2010 2011 2012 2013 2014 2015 2016 2017

QUICK FACTS

POPULATION:
1.3 million

GDP (PPP):
$37.5 billion
1.1% growth in 2015
5-year compound annual growth 3.7%
$28,592 per capita

UNEMPLOYMENT:
5.9%

INFLATION (CPI):
0.1%

FDI INFLOW:
$207.7 million

PUBLIC DEBT:
10.1% of GDP

2015 data unless otherwise noted. Data compiled as of September 2016

BACKGROUND: Estonia regained its independence from the Soviet Union in 1991 and is a stable multiparty democracy. It joined NATO and the European Union in 2004 and the Organisation for Economic Co-operation and Development in 2010. In 2011, it became the first former Soviet state to adopt the euro. With a liberal investment climate, foreign investment has risen substantially since independence. In 2014, Estonia became the world's first country to issue "E-Residency" status to noncitizens, which makes it easier to do business in Estonia. Jüri Ratas, leader of the Centre Party, became prime minister in November 2016 after his party joined a coalition in a parliamentary power struggle to defeat the center-right, pro-market Reform Party of former Prime Minister Taavi Rõivas.

12 ECONOMIC FREEDOMS | ESTONIA

RULE OF LAW

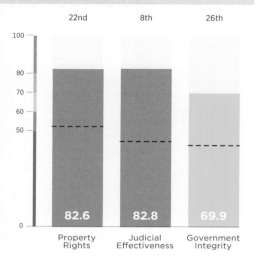

22nd	8th	26th	◄ Rank

Property Rights	Judicial Effectiveness	Government Integrity
82.6	**82.8**	**69.9**

Property rights and contracts are well enforced and secure. Commercial codes are applied consistently. The judiciary is independent and well insulated from government influence. The government has effective mechanisms to investigate and punish abuse and corruption. There have been no reports of impunity involving the security forces, but several high-ranking state officials have been convicted of corruption and criminal misconduct.

GOVERNMENT SIZE

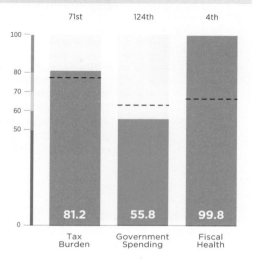

71st	124th	4th	◄ Rank

Tax Burden	Government Spending	Fiscal Health
81.2	**55.8**	**99.8**

The top personal income and corporate tax rates are 20 percent. Undistributed profits are not taxed. Other taxes include a value-added tax and excise taxes. The overall tax burden equals 32.9 percent of total domestic income. Government spending has amounted to 38.4 percent of total output (GDP) over the past three years, and budget surpluses have averaged 0.3 percent of GDP. Public debt is equivalent to 10.1 percent of GDP.

REGULATORY EFFICIENCY

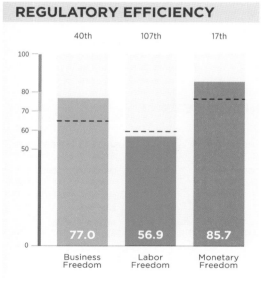

40th	107th	17th

Business Freedom	Labor Freedom	Monetary Freedom
77.0	**56.9**	**85.7**

The business start-up process is straightforward, and the cost of completing licensing requirements has been substantially reduced. Enhancing labor productivity and employment growth has been a key goal in ongoing efforts to reform the labor market. Estonian Air, a small airline, went out of business in late 2015 after the European Commission ruled that it benefited from unfair advantages because of heavy government subsidies.

OPEN MARKETS

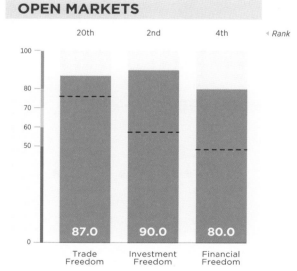

20th	2nd	4th	◄ Rank

Trade Freedom	Investment Freedom	Financial Freedom
87.0	**90.0**	**80.0**

Trade is extremely important to Estonia's economy; the value of exports and imports taken together equals 155 percent of GDP. The average applied tariff rate is 1.5 percent. Estonia is very open to foreign investment, but several state-owned enterprises distort the economy. The competitive banking sector provides a wide range of financial services with little state intervention.

ESTONIA

FINLAND

WORLD RANK: **24**   REGIONAL RANK: **13**

ECONOMIC FREEDOM STATUS:
MOSTLY FREE

Finland's economy is characterized by openness and transparency. The quality of the legal framework is among the world's highest, providing effective protection of property rights. The rule of law is well maintained, and a strong tradition of minimum tolerance for corruption continues.

Over the past five years, the economy has experienced economic slowdown and uncertainty. Efforts to restore economic growth, increase competitiveness, and reduce public debt continue to be at the top of the policy agenda. Government spending accounts for over half of GDP and has proven to be a drag on the economy instead of a stimulus, and public debt continues to rise.

ECONOMIC FREEDOM SCORE

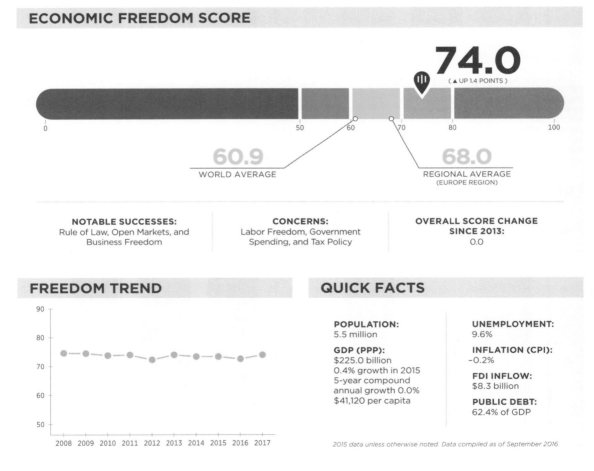

74.0
(▲ UP 1.4 POINTS)

0   50   60   70   80   100

60.9
WORLD AVERAGE

68.0
REGIONAL AVERAGE
(EUROPE REGION)

NOTABLE SUCCESSES:
Rule of Law, Open Markets, and Business Freedom

CONCERNS:
Labor Freedom, Government Spending, and Tax Policy

OVERALL SCORE CHANGE SINCE 2013:
0.0

FREEDOM TREND

90
80
70
60
50

2008 2009 2010 2011 2012 2013 2014 2015 2016 2017

QUICK FACTS

POPULATION:
5.5 million

GDP (PPP):
$225.0 billion
0.4% growth in 2015
5-year compound annual growth 0.0%
$41,120 per capita

UNEMPLOYMENT:
9.6%

INFLATION (CPI):
−0.2%

FDI INFLOW:
$8.3 billion

PUBLIC DEBT:
62.4% of GDP

2015 data unless otherwise noted. Data compiled as of September 2016

BACKGROUND: Prime Minister Juha Sipilä of the Centre Party formed a coalition with the Eurosceptic conservative Finns Party and center-right National Coalition Party following elections in April 2015. Finland joined the European Union in 1995 and adopted the euro in 1999. It became a member of NATO's Partnership for Peace in 1994 and sits on the Euro–Atlantic Council. In 2014, Finland became one of five nations to deepen their cooperation with NATO as enhanced opportunity partners. Recent Russian aggression against Ukraine has prompted renewed public debate about full NATO membership. Declining exports and flagging business for key Finnish companies have negatively affected the economy.

12 ECONOMIC FREEDOMS | FINLAND

RULE OF LAW

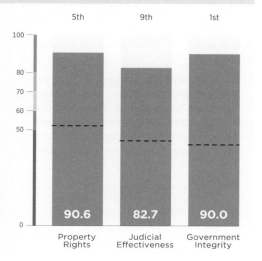

Finland has one of the world's strongest property rights protection regimes and adheres to many international agreements intended to protect intellectual property. Contractual agreements are strictly honored. The quality of the judiciary is generally high. Corruption is not a significant problem in Finland, which was ranked second out of 168 countries surveyed in Transparency International's 2015 *Corruption Perceptions Index*.

GOVERNMENT SIZE

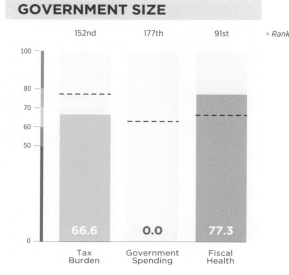

The top personal income tax rate is 31.8 percent, and the top corporate tax rate is 20 percent. Other taxes include a value-added tax and a tax on capital income. The overall tax burden equals 43.9 percent of total domestic income. Government spending has amounted to 58 percent of total output (GDP) over the past three years, and budget deficits have averaged 3.1 percent of GDP. Public debt is equivalent to 62.4 percent of GDP.

REGULATORY EFFICIENCY

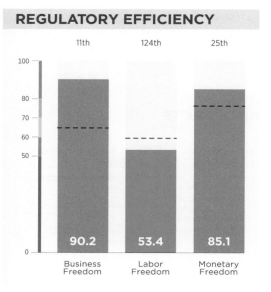

The efficient business framework is conducive to innovation and productivity growth. The labor market, however, is characterized by high costs and burdensome regulations. The nonsalary cost of employing a worker is high, and the severance payment scheme remains costly. The government has reduced spending on subsidies for wind power and has cut entitlements and welfare spending in response to increased deficits.

OPEN MARKETS

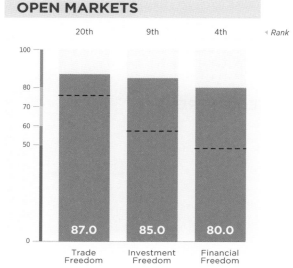

Trade is important to Finland's economy; the value of exports and imports taken together equals 74 percent of GDP. The average applied tariff rate is 1.5 percent. Finland generally welcomes foreign investment, but state-owned enterprises distort the economy. The financial sector, with sound regulations that encourage prudent lending practices, provides a wide range of services.

FINLAND

FRANCE

WORLD RANK:
72

REGIONAL RANK:
32

ECONOMIC FREEDOM STATUS:
MODERATELY FREE

France's economy has proven to be relatively resilient, with entrepreneurial activity facilitated by such institutional strengths as strong protection of property rights and a fairly efficient regulatory framework. Various reform measures have been adopted to increase the economy's competitiveness and flexibility, but overall progress has been marginal.

The state dominates major sectors of the economy and remains a large shareholder in many semipublic enterprises. Government spending accounts for more than half of total domestic output, and the budget has been chronically in deficit. Various stimulus measures have resulted in a deterioration of public finance, increasing the fiscal burdens imposed on French taxpayers.

ECONOMIC FREEDOM SCORE

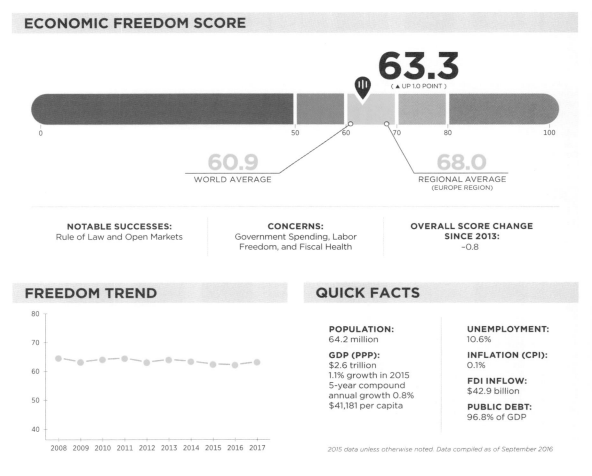

63.3
(▲ UP 1.0 POINT)

0   50   60   70   80   100

60.9
WORLD AVERAGE

68.0
REGIONAL AVERAGE
(EUROPE REGION)

NOTABLE SUCCESSES:
Rule of Law and Open Markets

CONCERNS:
Government Spending, Labor Freedom, and Fiscal Health

OVERALL SCORE CHANGE SINCE 2013:
−0.8

FREEDOM TREND

80
70
60
50
40

2008 2009 2010 2011 2012 2013 2014 2015 2016 2017

QUICK FACTS

POPULATION:
64.2 million

GDP (PPP):
$2.6 trillion
1.1% growth in 2015
5-year compound
annual growth 0.8%
$41,181 per capita

UNEMPLOYMENT:
10.6%

INFLATION (CPI):
0.1%

FDI INFLOW:
$42.9 billion

PUBLIC DEBT:
96.8% of GDP

2015 data unless otherwise noted. Data compiled as of September 2016

BACKGROUND: François Hollande was elected president in May 2012, and his Socialist Party has majority control of the National Assembly. Hollande's poor handling of the economy and public fears related to security have led to consistently low approval ratings. A recent spate of horrific terrorist attacks has shaken public confidence. France was a leading participant in NATO's March 2011 military engagement in Libya and has sent troops to Mali and the Central African Republic to counter advancing Islamic militants. France began airstrikes against ISIS in spring 2015 and remains a major contributor to the anti-ISIS coalition. The economy is diversified with tourism, manufacturing, and pharmaceuticals as major industries.

12 ECONOMIC FREEDOMS | FRANCE

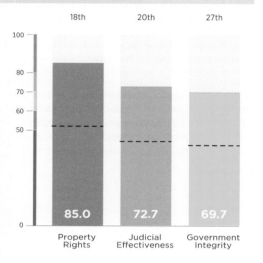

RULE OF LAW

18th   20th   27th

85.0 — Property Rights
72.7 — Judicial Effectiveness
69.7 — Government Integrity

Enforcement of property rights and contracts is secure, but regulation of real estate is complex and inefficient. France is a strong defender of intellectual property rights. An independent judiciary and the rule of law are firmly established. Although the government actively promotes transparency, accountability, and civic participation, corruption persists in such sectors as public works and the defense industry.

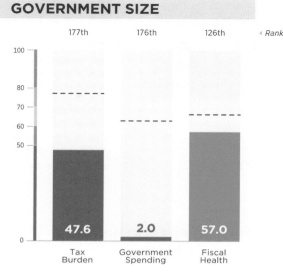

GOVERNMENT SIZE

177th   176th   126th   ◂ Rank

47.6 — Tax Burden
2.0 — Government Spending
57.0 — Fiscal Health

The top individual income tax rate is 45 percent, and the top corporate tax rate is 34.3 percent. Other taxes include a value-added tax. The overall tax burden equals 45.2 percent of total domestic income. Government spending has amounted to 57.1 percent of total output (GDP) over the past three years, and budget deficits have averaged 3.9 percent of GDP. Public debt is equivalent to 96.8 percent of GDP.

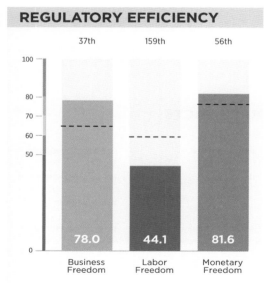

REGULATORY EFFICIENCY

37th   159th   56th

78.0 — Business Freedom
44.1 — Labor Freedom
81.6 — Monetary Freedom

The overall regulatory framework remains relatively efficient, but the labor market is burdened with rigid regulations and lacks the capacity to generate more vibrant employment growth. The government maintains an extensive system of subsidies and price controls that affect a number of products and services. France is the largest recipient of subsidies under the European Union's Common Agricultural Policy (CAP).

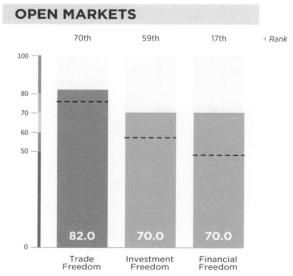

OPEN MARKETS

70th   59th   17th   ◂ Rank

82.0 — Trade Freedom
70.0 — Investment Freedom
70.0 — Financial Freedom

Trade is important to France's economy; the value of exports and imports taken together equals 61 percent of GDP. The average applied tariff rate is 1.5 percent. Investment in some sectors is restricted, and state-owned enterprises distort the economy. The financial sector accounts for about 4 percent of GDP. The banking sector is mostly in private hands, but the state still owns several important institutions.

FRANCE

GEORGIA

WORLD RANK: **13**   REGIONAL RANK: **5**

ECONOMIC FREEDOM STATUS:
MOSTLY FREE

Georgia's government has maintained strong momentum in liberalizing economic activity while taking steps to restore fiscal discipline. Public debt and budget deficits remain under control. Open-market policies, supported by competitively low tax rates and regulatory efficiency, have facilitated flows of trade and investment. Large-scale privatization has advanced, and anticorruption efforts have yielded some notable results.

With monetary stability and the overall soundness of fiscal health relatively well maintained, Georgia has enjoyed macroeconomic resilience. Nonetheless, deeper and more rapid institutional reforms to enhance judicial independence and effectiveness remain critical to ensuring further dynamic and lasting economic development.

ECONOMIC FREEDOM SCORE

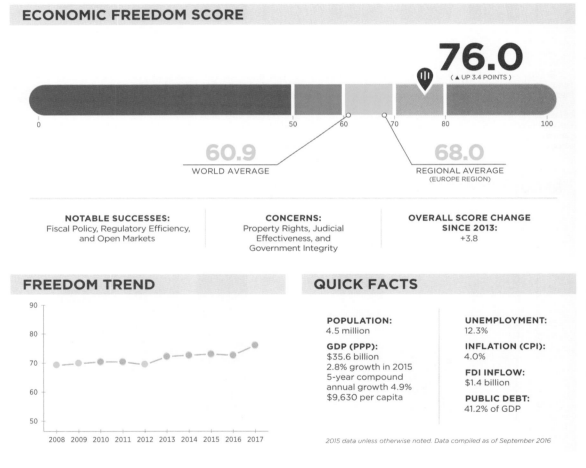

76.0
(▲ UP 3.4 POINTS)

0   50   60   70   80   100

60.9
WORLD AVERAGE

68.0
REGIONAL AVERAGE
(EUROPE REGION)

NOTABLE SUCCESSES:
Fiscal Policy, Regulatory Efficiency, and Open Markets

CONCERNS:
Property Rights, Judicial Effectiveness, and Government Integrity

OVERALL SCORE CHANGE SINCE 2013:
+3.8

FREEDOM TREND

90
80
70
60
50

2008 2009 2010 2011 2012 2013 2014 2015 2016 2017

QUICK FACTS

POPULATION:
4.5 million

GDP (PPP):
$35.6 billion
2.8% growth in 2015
5-year compound
annual growth 4.9%
$9,630 per capita

UNEMPLOYMENT:
12.3%

INFLATION (CPI):
4.0%

FDI INFLOW:
$1.4 billion

PUBLIC DEBT:
41.2% of GDP

2015 data unless otherwise noted. Data compiled as of September 2016

BACKGROUND: Russia invaded Georgia in 2008 and continues to occupy its South Ossetia and Abkhazia regions, which make up about 20 percent of Georgia's territory. In 2012, billionaire Bidzina Ivanishvili and his Georgian Dream coalition defeated President Mikheil Saakashvili's United National Movement. Victory by Prime Minister Giorgi Kvirikashvili and his Georgian Dream party in the 2016 parliamentary elections reinforced the party's political dominance. Georgia has been affected by the economic downturn in Russia and by low oil prices. Agriculture or related industries employ over half of the workforce. Georgia signed an Association Agreement with the European Union in June 2014 and is an official aspirant country for NATO membership.

12 ECONOMIC FREEDOMS | GEORGIA

RULE OF LAW

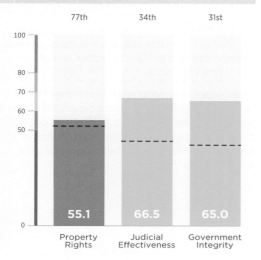

77th	34th	31st
Property Rights	Judicial Effectiveness	Government Integrity
55.1	66.5	65.0

Protection of property rights has improved, and the government has made enforcement of contracts easier. Although the constitution and law provide for an independent judiciary, there has been little progress in the past year on judicial reforms, and the government does not fully respect judicial independence. Georgia still struggles with the lingering effects of Soviet-era corruption as well as ongoing Russian influence.

GOVERNMENT SIZE

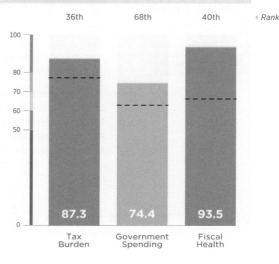

36th	68th	40th	◀ Rank
Tax Burden	Government Spending	Fiscal Health	
87.3	74.4	93.5	

The flat individual income tax rate is 20 percent, and the flat corporate tax rate is 15 percent. Other taxes include a value-added tax and a tax on dividends. The overall tax burden equals 25.3 percent of total domestic income. Government spending has amounted to 29.2 percent of total output (GDP) over the past three years, and budget deficits have averaged 1.4 percent of GDP. Public debt is equivalent to 41.2 percent of GDP.

REGULATORY EFFICIENCY

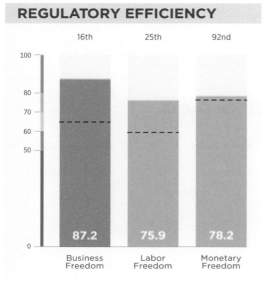

16th	25th	92nd
Business Freedom	Labor Freedom	Monetary Freedom
87.2	75.9	78.2

The regulatory environment is efficient. It takes only three procedures and three days to start a business, and no minimum capital is required. The nonsalary cost of hiring a worker is not burdensome, but the labor market lacks dynamism, and unemployment remains fairly high. Dollarization of the economy is high, and the local currency was devalued in 2015 but stabilized in 2016. Inflationary pressure has been kept under control.

OPEN MARKETS

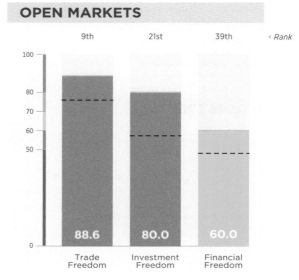

9th	21st	39th	◀ Rank
Trade Freedom	Investment Freedom	Financial Freedom	
88.6	80.0	60.0	

Trade is extremely important to Georgia's economy; the value of exports and imports taken together equals 110 percent of GDP. The average applied tariff rate is 0.7 percent. There are some restrictions on foreign ownership of agricultural land. With the banking sector growing and modernized, access to financing has improved. Capital markets continue to evolve, but the stock exchange remains small and underdeveloped.

GEORGIA

GERMANY

WORLD RANK: **26** REGIONAL RANK: **15**

ECONOMIC FREEDOM STATUS:
MOSTLY FREE

Despite the challenging economic environment within the European Union, Germany continues to be one of the world's most powerful and dynamic economies. Business freedom and investment freedom are strong. Long-term competitiveness and entrepreneurial growth are supported by openness to global commerce, well-protected property rights, and a sound business regulatory environment.

The German economy has gradually emerged from the effects of the global financial crisis, which had an acute negative impact both on Germany's public finances and on its economic growth. Actions required to hold the eurozone together have taken a toll, and the more recent migrant crisis has had huge political, economic, and societal impacts within the country.

ECONOMIC FREEDOM SCORE

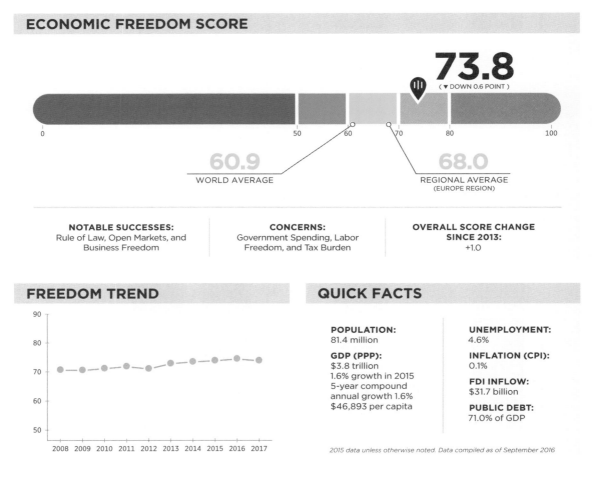

73.8
(▼ DOWN 0.6 POINT)

0   50   60   70   80   100

60.9
WORLD AVERAGE

68.0
REGIONAL AVERAGE
(EUROPE REGION)

NOTABLE SUCCESSES:
Rule of Law, Open Markets, and
Business Freedom

CONCERNS:
Government Spending, Labor
Freedom, and Tax Burden

**OVERALL SCORE CHANGE
SINCE 2013:**
+1.0

FREEDOM TREND

90

80

70

60

50

2008 2009 2010 2011 2012 2013 2014 2015 2016 2017

QUICK FACTS

POPULATION:
81.4 million

GDP (PPP):
$3.8 trillion
1.6% growth in 2015
5-year compound
annual growth 1.6%
$46,893 per capita

UNEMPLOYMENT:
4.6%

INFLATION (CPI):
0.1%

FDI INFLOW:
$31.7 billion

PUBLIC DEBT:
71.0% of GDP

2015 data unless otherwise noted. Data compiled as of September 2016

BACKGROUND: Chancellor Angela Merkel's Christian Democratic Union remains in power, governing in coalition with the Social Democratic Party since December 2013. With the government initially following an open-door policy, net immigration of foreign nations to Germany was 1.14 million in 2015. Merkel's CDU suffered losses in regional elections in March 2016, and parties with anti-immigration platforms gained strength. The ongoing migrant crisis has opened deep divisions in German society and exposed flaws in ideas like the Schengen Area that are at the heart of the European project. Germany remains, both politically and economically, the most influential nation in the EU.

12 ECONOMIC FREEDOMS | GERMANY

RULE OF LAW

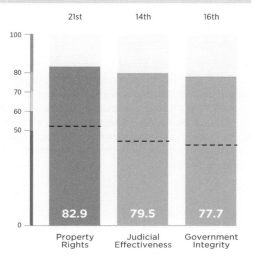

German law fully protects the property rights of German citizens and foreigners alike. Secured interests in property, both chattel and real, are recognized and enforced. Germany boasts a robust regime for the protection of intellectual property rights. The judiciary is independent, and the rule of law prevails. Corrupt acts by public officials are vigorously prosecuted and punished.

GOVERNMENT SIZE

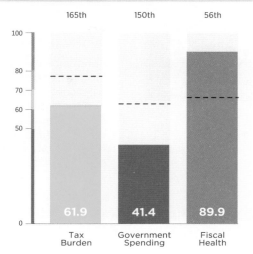

The top personal income tax rate is 45 percent. The federal corporate tax rate is 15.8 percent, but other taxes, including a solidarity tax, make the effective rate more than 30 percent. The overall tax burden equals 36.1 percent of total domestic income. Government spending has amounted to 44.2 percent of total output (GDP) over the past three years, and budget surpluses have averaged 0.4 percent of GDP. Public debt is equivalent to 71.0 percent of GDP.

REGULATORY EFFICIENCY

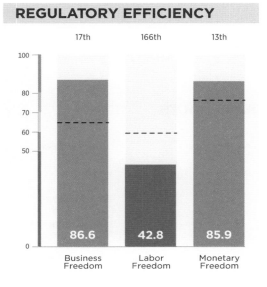

The efficient regulatory framework strongly facilitates entrepreneurial activity, allowing business operation to be as dynamic in Germany as anywhere else in the world. A nationwide statutory minimum wage was introduced in 2015. Monetary stability is well maintained, but electricity costs are among the highest in Europe because of the government's commitment to renewable energy.

OPEN MARKETS

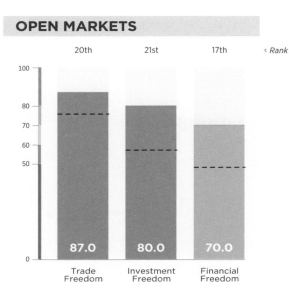

Trade is important to Germany's economy; the value of exports and imports taken together equals 86 percent of GDP. The average applied tariff rate is 1.5 percent. Barriers to foreign investment are low, but state-owned enterprises distort the economy. The well-functioning and modern financial sector offers a full range of services. The banking sector consists of the traditional three-tiered system of private, public, and cooperative banks.

GERMANY

GREECE

Greece has made progress in restoring macroeconomic stability and implementing much-needed initial fiscal adjustments. However, the public sector accounts for more than 50 percent of GDP, and the country continues to confront a daunting debt burden and severe erosion of competitiveness.

Serious challenges remain in such areas as government spending and labor freedom. The fiscal deficit remains approximately 4 percent of GDP, and public debt exceeds 170 percent of GDP. Fading business confidence and the lack of competitiveness are serious impediments to economic revival. The economy, stifled by powerful public unions, does not support entrepreneurship. The rigid labor market impedes productivity and job growth, and corruption continues to be a problem.

ECONOMIC FREEDOM SCORE

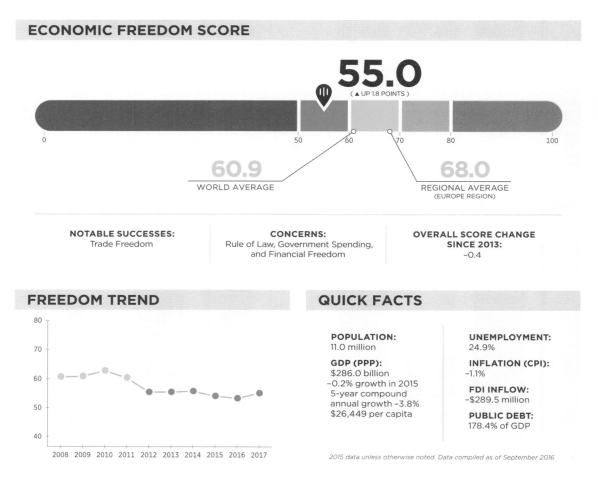

55.0
(▲ UP 1.8 POINTS)

0   50   60   70   80   100

60.9
WORLD AVERAGE

68.0
REGIONAL AVERAGE
(EUROPE REGION)

NOTABLE SUCCESSES:
Trade Freedom

CONCERNS:
Rule of Law, Government Spending,
and Financial Freedom

OVERALL SCORE CHANGE
SINCE 2013:
−0.4

FREEDOM TREND

80

70

60

50

40

2008 2009 2010 2011 2012 2013 2014 2015 2016 2017

QUICK FACTS

POPULATION:
11.0 million

GDP (PPP):
$286.0 billion
−0.2% growth in 2015
5-year compound
annual growth −3.8%
$26,449 per capita

UNEMPLOYMENT:
24.9%

INFLATION (CPI):
−1.1%

FDI INFLOW:
−$289.5 million

PUBLIC DEBT:
178.4% of GDP

2015 data unless otherwise noted. Data compiled as of September 2016

BACKGROUND: Greece joined NATO in 1952 and the European Union in 1981. It adopted the euro in 2002. Prime Minister Alexis Tsipras of the Coalition of the Radical Left (Syriza) was able to reestablish a coalition government following snap elections in September 2015. Greece remains mired in political and economic uncertainty. In May 2016, an IMF–EU deal on Greek debt relief led to the release of $11.5 billion in new bailout funds. Greece has been beset by a series of crippling strikes and protests in the face of new austerity measures and has had to deal with high numbers of migrants.

12 ECONOMIC FREEDOMS | GREECE

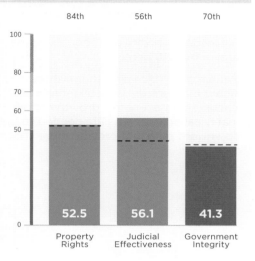

RULE OF LAW

84th   56th   70th

52.5   **56.1**   **41.3**

Property Rights | Judicial Effectiveness | Government Integrity

Greek laws extend protection of property rights to both foreign and Greek nationals, but protection of property rights is not strongly enforced. The judiciary is independent, but the court system is extremely slow. Corruption remains a problem in Greece. Although tax enforcement has become more robust in recent years, authorities have largely failed to prosecute tax evasion by economic elites.

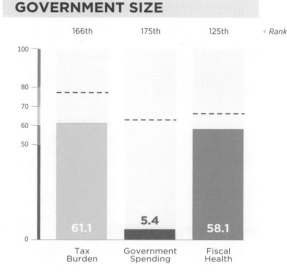

GOVERNMENT SIZE

166th   175th   125th   ◄ Rank

61.1   **5.4**   **58.1**

Tax Burden | Government Spending | Fiscal Health

The top personal income tax rate has been increased to 42 percent. The top corporate tax rate has been increased from 26 percent to 29 percent. The overall tax burden equals 35.9 percent of total domestic income. Government spending has amounted to 56.2 percent of total output (GDP) over the past three years, and budget deficits have averaged 3.7 percent of GDP. Public debt is equivalent to 178.4 percent of GDP.

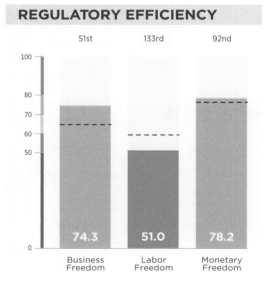

REGULATORY EFFICIENCY

51st   133rd   92nd

74.3   **51.0**   **78.2**

Business Freedom | Labor Freedom | Monetary Freedom

Sporadic efforts to enhance the business environment have been undermined by red tape and insufficient political commitment. Labor regulations are restrictive, and the economy continues to lack labor mobility. Resolution of the ongoing Greek debt crisis will require considerably more progress on planned privatizations of heavily subsidized and loss-making state-owned enterprises across a wide variety of economic sectors.

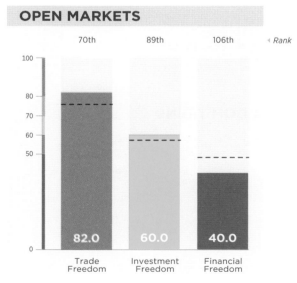

OPEN MARKETS

70th   89th   106th   ◄ Rank

82.0   **60.0**   **40.0**

Trade Freedom | Investment Freedom | Financial Freedom

Trade is important to Greece's economy; the value of exports and imports taken together equals 60 percent of GDP. The average applied tariff rate is 1.5 percent. Foreign and domestic investors are generally treated equally, but bureaucratic barriers may discourage investment. Nonperforming loans are about 50 percent of total banking-sector loans, the second highest level in the euro area.

GREECE

HUNGARY

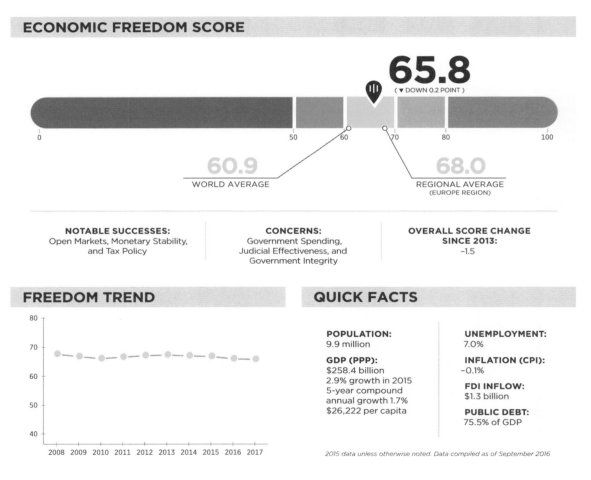

WORLD RANK: 56 | **REGIONAL RANK:** 27

ECONOMIC FREEDOM STATUS:
MODERATELY FREE

Hungary has implemented critical reforms in many areas. Licensing procedures have been streamlined, and the overall entrepreneurial environment is further aided by strong trade freedom, business freedom, and investment freedom. Since January 2016, the personal income tax rate has been lowered to a flat rate of 15 percent, down from 16 percent.

The economy has grown at a robust pace over the past few years and now has significant momentum. Consolidating public finances and further encouraging economic growth remain policy priorities. Additional fiscal adjustments are needed to put public debt on a firmly downward path and provide more space for vibrant private-sector activity.

ECONOMIC FREEDOM SCORE

65.8
(▼ DOWN 0.2 POINT)

0   50   60   70   80   100

60.9
WORLD AVERAGE

68.0
REGIONAL AVERAGE
(EUROPE REGION)

NOTABLE SUCCESSES:
Open Markets, Monetary Stability, and Tax Policy

CONCERNS:
Government Spending, Judicial Effectiveness, and Government Integrity

OVERALL SCORE CHANGE SINCE 2013:
–1.5

FREEDOM TREND

(chart: values near 65–68 from 2008 to 2017)

80
70
60
50
40

2008 2009 2010 2011 2012 2013 2014 2015 2016 2017

QUICK FACTS

POPULATION:
9.9 million

GDP (PPP):
$258.4 billion
2.9% growth in 2015
5-year compound annual growth 1.7%
$26,222 per capita

UNEMPLOYMENT:
7.0%

INFLATION (CPI):
–0.1%

FDI INFLOW:
$1.3 billion

PUBLIC DEBT:
75.5% of GDP

2015 data unless otherwise noted. Data compiled as of September 2016

BACKGROUND: Hungary has been a member of NATO since 1999 and a member of the European Union since 2004. In the April 2014 parliamentary election, held in accordance with a new constitution that took effect in January 2012, the center-right Fidesz–Hungarian Civic Alliance won the majority of seats, and Prime Minister Viktor Orbán, in office since May 2010, was able to form a new government. Robust exports and increased domestic demand have helped Hungary's economy to achieve strong growth. Public works programs, including building border fences, have succeeded in lowering unemployment but also have swallowed a growing percentage of GDP. Hard-currency indebtedness and a shortage of labor remain key vulnerabilities.

12 ECONOMIC FREEDOMS | HUNGARY

RULE OF LAW

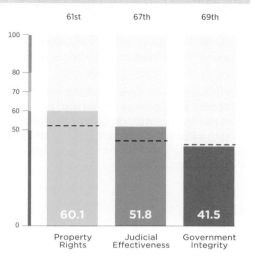

61st — Property Rights — 60.1
67th — Judicial Effectiveness — 51.8
69th — Government Integrity — 41.5

Citizens have the right to own property and establish private businesses, but cronyism remains a serious concern, and critics cite recent taxes targeted to drive out or take over foreign businesses. Judicial independence is increasingly threatened. Corruption remains a notable problem. Government allies lead state agencies that have anticorruption roles, and several companies with close ties to the government are supported primarily by public funds.

GOVERNMENT SIZE

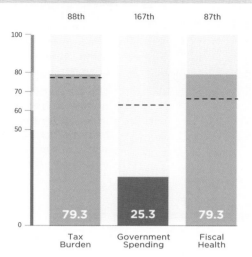

88th — Tax Burden — 79.3
167th — Government Spending — 25.3
87th — Fiscal Health — 79.3
◄ Rank

The personal income tax rate has been cut from 16 percent to a flat 15 percent. The top corporate tax rate is 19 percent. Other taxes include a value-added tax. The overall tax burden equals 38.5 percent of total domestic income. Government spending has amounted to 49.9 percent of total output (GDP) over the past three years, and budget deficits have averaged 2.4 percent of GDP. Public debt is equivalent to 75.5 percent of GDP.

REGULATORY EFFICIENCY

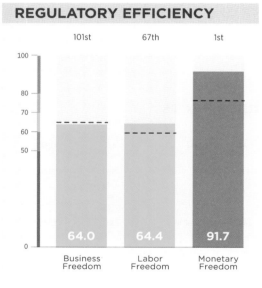

101st — Business Freedom — 64.0
67th — Labor Freedom — 64.4
1st — Monetary Freedom — 91.7

The regulatory framework allows business formation and operation to be efficient and dynamic. Bankruptcy proceedings are relatively straightforward. Labor regulations lack flexibility. Most prices are set by the market, but the government administers prices on tobacco and pharmaceuticals, surcharges in the state-run mobile payment system, and fees on connections to district heating systems, telecommunications, and electric companies.

OPEN MARKETS

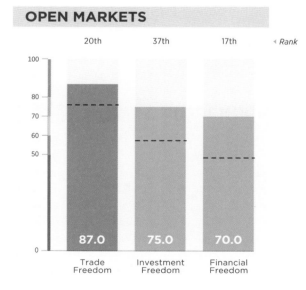

20th — Trade Freedom — 87.0
37th — Investment Freedom — 75.0
17th — Financial Freedom — 70.0
◄ Rank

Trade is extremely important to Hungary's economy; the value of exports and imports taken together equals 171 percent of GDP. The average applied tariff rate is 1.5 percent. There is no general screening of foreign investment. State-owned enterprises distort the economy. Credit to the private sector has continued to contract, and the number of nonperforming loans, while declining, remains significant.

HUNGARY

ICELAND

WORLD RANK:
22

REGIONAL RANK:
12

ECONOMIC FREEDOM STATUS:
MOSTLY FREE

Iceland's modern and competitive economy benefits from a strong commitment to open-market policies that facilitate dynamic flows of trade and investment. Transparent and efficient regulations are applied evenly in most cases and encourage vigorous private-sector entrepreneurial activity. Measures to lift capital controls imposed in the wake of the 2008 financial crisis are underway.

The strength of Iceland's economic and social institutions is reinforced by robust protection of property rights and an independent judiciary that enforces anticorruption measures. Management of public finance has been comparatively prudent, with continued attention to the size and scope of government. Monetary stability has been well maintained.

ECONOMIC FREEDOM SCORE

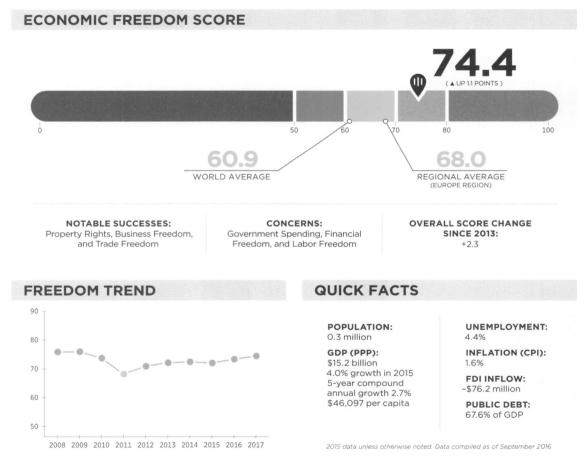

74.4
(▲ UP 1.1 POINTS)

0   50   60   70   80   100

60.9
WORLD AVERAGE

68.0
REGIONAL AVERAGE
(EUROPE REGION)

NOTABLE SUCCESSES:
Property Rights, Business Freedom, and Trade Freedom

CONCERNS:
Government Spending, Financial Freedom, and Labor Freedom

OVERALL SCORE CHANGE SINCE 2013:
+2.3

FREEDOM TREND

QUICK FACTS

POPULATION:
0.3 million

GDP (PPP):
$15.2 billion
4.0% growth in 2015
5-year compound annual growth 2.7%
$46,097 per capita

UNEMPLOYMENT:
4.4%

INFLATION (CPI):
1.6%

FDI INFLOW:
–$76.2 million

PUBLIC DEBT:
67.6% of GDP

2015 data unless otherwise noted. Data compiled as of September 2016

BACKGROUND: Sigurður Ingi Jóhannsson became prime minister in April 2016 following the resignation of Sigmundur Davíð Gunnlaugsson after revelations in the Panama Papers of ownership in an offshore company. The Progressive Party has ruled in a coalition with the Independence Party since parliamentary elections in April 2013. Public distrust of politicians helped propel Guðni Jóhannesson, an independent historian, to the largely ceremonial presidency following elections in June 2016. Iceland officially withdrew its application for membership in the European Union in March 2015. Its relationship with the EU includes free trade and movement of capital, labor, goods, and services within the region. Domestic consumption and tourism have fueled growth in recent years.

12 ECONOMIC FREEDOMS | ICELAND

RULE OF LAW

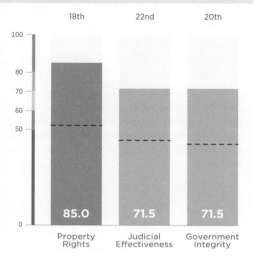

	18th	22nd	20th
	Property Rights	Judicial Effectiveness	Government Integrity
	85.0	71.5	71.5

Private property is well protected, but real property rights are mostly reserved to Icelandic citizens. Iceland has a solid legal institutional framework to enforce laws protecting intellectual property. The judiciary is independent, and accountability and transparency are institutionalized. Corruption is contained, although the prime minister stepped down in April 2016 following a tax scandal involving an offshore company that he set up with his wife.

GOVERNMENT SIZE

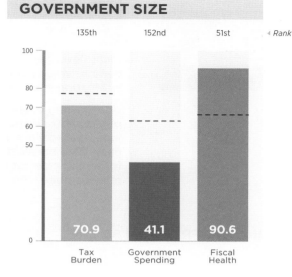

	135th	152nd	51st	◄ Rank
	Tax Burden	Government Spending	Fiscal Health	
	70.9	41.1	90.6	

The top personal income tax rate is 31.8 percent, and the flat corporate rate is 20 percent. Other taxes include a value-added tax and an estate tax. The overall tax burden equals 38.7 percent of total domestic income. Government spending has amounted to 44.3 percent of total output (GDP) over the past three years, and budget deficits have averaged 0.4 percent of GDP. Public debt is equivalent to 67.6 percent of GDP.

REGULATORY EFFICIENCY

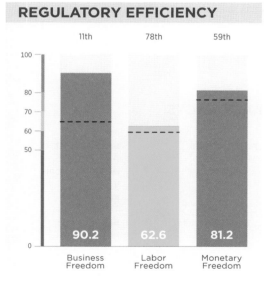

	11th	78th	59th
	Business Freedom	Labor Freedom	Monetary Freedom
	90.2	62.6	81.2

The transparent regulatory environment supports commercial activity, allowing business formation and operation to be efficient. The labor market, characterized by broad wage settlements and high unionization, lacks flexibility. A new law passed in June 2016 authorizes the central bank to impose reserve requirements on certain capital inflows as part of efforts to dismantle existing capital controls.

OPEN MARKETS

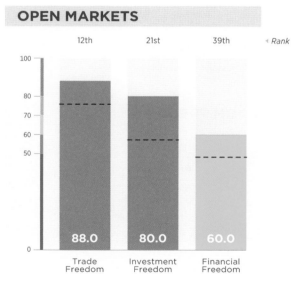

	12th	21st	39th	◄ Rank
	Trade Freedom	Investment Freedom	Financial Freedom	
	88.0	80.0	60.0	

Trade is extremely important to Iceland's economy; the value of exports and imports taken together equals 100 percent of GDP. The average applied tariff rate is 1.0 percent. Iceland has restructured and recapitalized its banking system since the 2008 banking crisis. Implementation of a plan to liberalize capital controls is in its final stages, with the majority of the controls to be eased or removed in 2017.

ICELAND

WORLD RANK:
9

REGIONAL RANK:
3

ECONOMIC FREEDOM STATUS:
MOSTLY FREE

IRELAND

Ireland's economic fundamentals remain strong, well supported by solid protection of property rights and an independent judiciary that enforces the rule of law effectively. Commitment to open-market policies that facilitate global trade and investment flows has been well institutionalized, and the economy has demonstrated admirable resilience in the face of recent years' international and domestic challenges.

Undertaking politically difficult reforms, including sharp cuts in public-sector wages and restructuring of the banking sector, Ireland has regained its macroeconomic stability and competitiveness. With the management of public finance back on a sounder footing, the deficit is declining, although the level of public debt remains quite high.

ECONOMIC FREEDOM SCORE

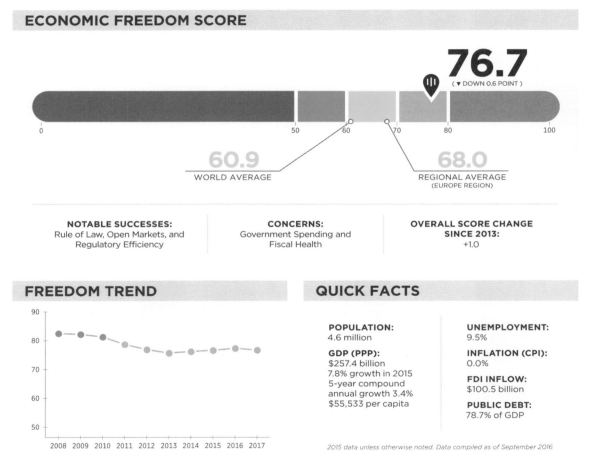

76.7
(▼ DOWN 0.6 POINT)

| 0 | 50 | 60 | 70 | 80 | 100 |

60.9
WORLD AVERAGE

68.0
REGIONAL AVERAGE
(EUROPE REGION)

NOTABLE SUCCESSES:
Rule of Law, Open Markets, and Regulatory Efficiency

CONCERNS:
Government Spending and Fiscal Health

OVERALL SCORE CHANGE SINCE 2013:
+1.0

FREEDOM TREND

| | 2008 | 2009 | 2010 | 2011 | 2012 | 2013 | 2014 | 2015 | 2016 | 2017 |

(chart, y-axis 50 to 90)

QUICK FACTS

POPULATION:
4.6 million

GDP (PPP):
$257.4 billion
7.8% growth in 2015
5-year compound
annual growth 3.4%
$55,533 per capita

UNEMPLOYMENT:
9.5%

INFLATION (CPI):
0.0%

FDI INFLOW:
$100.5 billion

PUBLIC DEBT:
78.7% of GDP

2015 data unless otherwise noted. Data compiled as of September 2016.

BACKGROUND: Prime Minister Enda Kenny of the center-right Fine Gael heads a minority government after losing a parliamentary majority in February 2016 elections. Ireland's highly industrialized economy performed extraordinarily well throughout the 1990s and most of the 2000s, encouraged by free-market policies that attracted investment capital, but the burst of a speculative housing bubble in 2008 generated a financial crisis. The 2010 National Recovery Plan was implemented after the government nationalized several banks, and Ireland accepted a $90 billion European Union–International Monetary Fund rescue package. Widening economic disparities between Dublin and the rest of the country have become a source of political debate.

12 ECONOMIC FREEDOMS | IRELAND

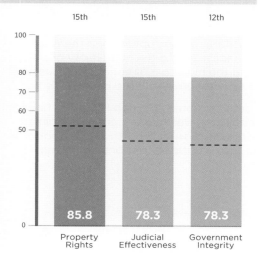

RULE OF LAW

15th	15th	12th
Property Rights **85.8**	Judicial Effectiveness **78.3**	Government Integrity **78.3**

Property rights are well protected, and secured interests in property are recognized and enforced. Contracts are secure, and expropriation is rare. Ireland's legal system is based on common law, and the judiciary is independent. Allegations of outright public corruption are investigated and prosecuted, but cronyism remains a recurring problem that affects all levels of Irish politics.

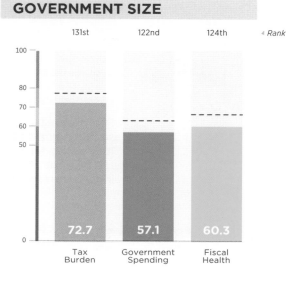

GOVERNMENT SIZE

131st	122nd	124th	◄ Rank
Tax Burden **72.7**	Government Spending **57.1**	Fiscal Health **60.3**	

The top personal income tax rate is 41 percent, and the top corporate tax rate is 12.5 percent. Other taxes include a value-added tax and a capital gains tax. The overall tax burden equals 29.9 percent of total domestic income. Government spending has amounted to 37.8 percent of total output (GDP) over the past three years, and budget deficits have averaged 3.7 percent of GDP. Public debt is equivalent to 78.7 percent of GDP.

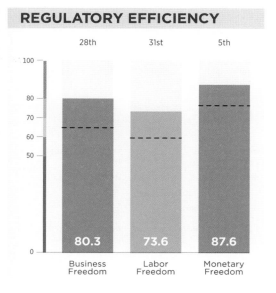

REGULATORY EFFICIENCY

28th	31st	5th
Business Freedom **80.3**	Labor Freedom **73.6**	Monetary Freedom **87.6**

The streamlined regulatory process is very conducive to dynamic investment and supports business decisions that enhance productivity. The nonsalary cost of employing a worker is low, and the severance payment system is not overly burdensome. In November 2015, the government rejected calls to impose rent controls but did act to restrict landlords to rent increases every two years instead of annually.

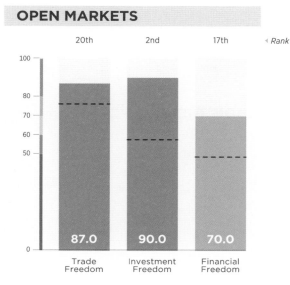

OPEN MARKETS

20th	2nd	17th	◄ Rank
Trade Freedom **87.0**	Investment Freedom **90.0**	Financial Freedom **70.0**	

Trade is extremely important to Ireland's economy; the value of exports and imports taken together equals 222 percent of GDP. The average applied tariff rate is 1.5 percent, and there are relatively few barriers to international trade and investment. Recapitalization and restructuring have taken place to restore banking-sector stability. The state still retains its ownership in banks, but there has been some divestment.

IRELAND

ITALY

Italy's economy has been mired in a protracted slowdown since 2011. Despite repeated attempts at reform, economic competitiveness has flagged. Much-needed structural reforms have not been implemented effectively, and the economy remains burdened by political interference, corruption, and the poor management of public finance. Due to the complexity of the regulatory framework and the high cost of conducting business, considerable economic activity remains in the informal sector.

Sharp increases in the debt burden and instability in the financial sector, aggravated by structural weaknesses, are undermining Italy's long-term development prospects. With public debt over 130 percent of GDP and growing, policy options are increasingly constrained.

WORLD RANK: **79** REGIONAL RANK: **34**

ECONOMIC FREEDOM STATUS:
MODERATELY FREE

ECONOMIC FREEDOM SCORE

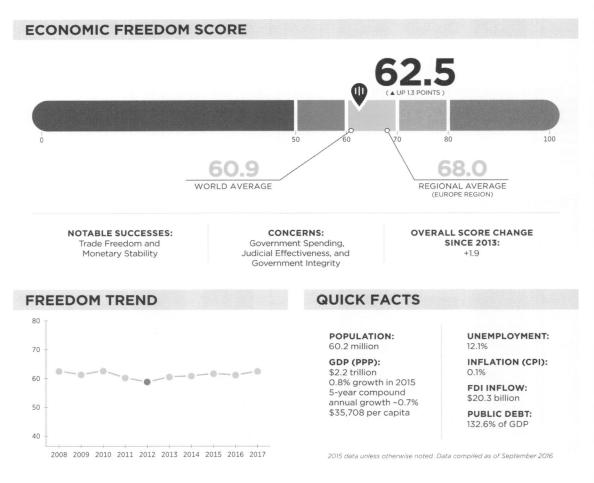

62.5
(▲ UP 1.3 POINTS)

0   50   60   70   80   100

60.9
WORLD AVERAGE

68.0
REGIONAL AVERAGE
(EUROPE REGION)

NOTABLE SUCCESSES:
Trade Freedom and
Monetary Stability

CONCERNS:
Government Spending,
Judicial Effectiveness, and
Government Integrity

**OVERALL SCORE CHANGE
SINCE 2013:**
+1.9

FREEDOM TREND

80
70
60
50
40

2008 2009 2010 2011 2012 2013 2014 2015 2016 2017

QUICK FACTS

POPULATION:
60.2 million

GDP (PPP):
$2.2 trillion
0.8% growth in 2015
5-year compound
annual growth −0.7%
$35,708 per capita

UNEMPLOYMENT:
12.1%

INFLATION (CPI):
0.1%

FDI INFLOW:
$20.3 billion

PUBLIC DEBT:
132.6% of GDP

2015 data unless otherwise noted. Data compiled as of September 2016

BACKGROUND: Matteo Renzi became Italy's youngest prime minister in February 2014, leading a coalition government of the center-left Democratic, New Centre-Right, Union of the Centre, and Civic Choice parties. Renzi tried to reform entitlements, taxes, and labor laws. He promised to resign if voters rejected a December 2016 referendum on constitutional reforms. They did, and he was replaced by Paolo Gentiloni. The populist 5 Star Movement won 19 of 20 cities and elected Rome's first woman mayor in June 2016 municipal elections. Italy has struggled with increased pressure from large numbers of Muslim migrants crossing the Mediterranean and Adriatic Seas.

12 ECONOMIC FREEDOMS | ITALY

RULE OF LAW

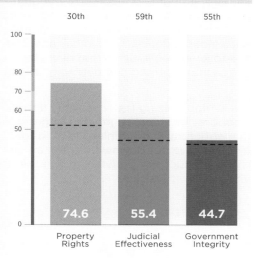

| 30th | 59th | 55th | ◄ Rank |

Property Rights	Judicial Effectiveness	Government Integrity
74.6	55.4	44.7

Property rights and contracts are secure, and the World Bank's *Doing Business* survey reports that a mandatory electronic filing system has improved the enforcement of contracts, but court procedures are slow. The legal system is vulnerable to political interference. Corruption and organized crime are significant impediments to investment and economic growth, costing an estimated €60 billion annually in wasted public resources.

GOVERNMENT SIZE

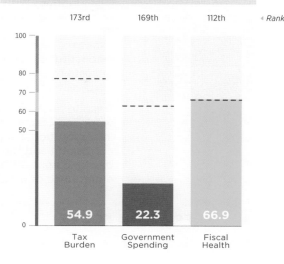

| 173rd | 169th | 112th | ◄ Rank |

Tax Burden	Government Spending	Fiscal Health
54.9	22.3	66.9

The top personal income tax rate is 43 percent, and the top corporate tax rate is 27.5 percent. Other taxes include a value-added tax and an inheritance tax. The overall tax burden equals 43.6 percent of total domestic income. Government spending has amounted to 50.9 percent of total output (GDP) over the past three years, and budget deficits have averaged 2.9 percent of GDP. Public debt is equivalent to 132.6 percent of GDP.

REGULATORY EFFICIENCY

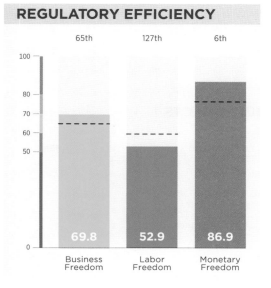

| 65th | 127th | 6th |

Business Freedom	Labor Freedom	Monetary Freedom
69.8	52.9	86.9

Organizing new investment and production remains a cumbersome and bureaucratic process. Inefficient public administration increases the cost of entrepreneurial activity. Systemic deficiencies in the labor market continue to hamper job growth. The government has the legal right to regulate prices but allows most to be set by the market except those for electricity, transportation, pharmaceuticals, telecommunications, water, and gas networks.

OPEN MARKETS

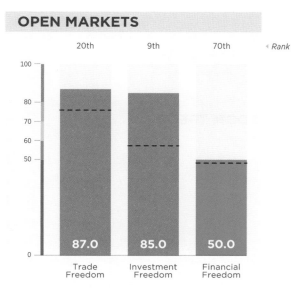

| 20th | 9th | 70th | ◄ Rank |

Trade Freedom	Investment Freedom	Financial Freedom
87.0	85.0	50.0

Trade is important to Italy's economy; the value of exports and imports taken together equals 57 percent of GDP. The average applied tariff rate is 1.5 percent. There is no general screening of foreign investment, and most sectors of the economy are open to investment. The financial sector has been under strain. Recapitalization and consolidation of banks have been underway, but progress remains constrained by the burden of nonperforming loans.

ITALY

KOSOVO

WORLD RANK: **46** | **REGIONAL RANK:** **22**

ECONOMIC FREEDOM STATUS:
MODERATELY FREE

Kosovo's transition to an open, market-based economy continues with an increasing degree of economic freedom. In a challenging regional economic environment, the landlocked economy has outperformed its neighbors, recording economic expansion every year since independence. Kosovo has adopted a constitutional fiscal rule to keep public debt from rising to unsustainable levels and has implemented competitively low corporate tax rates.

Despite notable progress in modernizing the regulatory framework and opening the economy to global commerce, lingering institutional and other structural shortcomings related to corruption and the rule of law have put downward pressure on overall competitiveness and productivity growth, limiting the emergence of a more vibrant private sector.

ECONOMIC FREEDOM SCORE

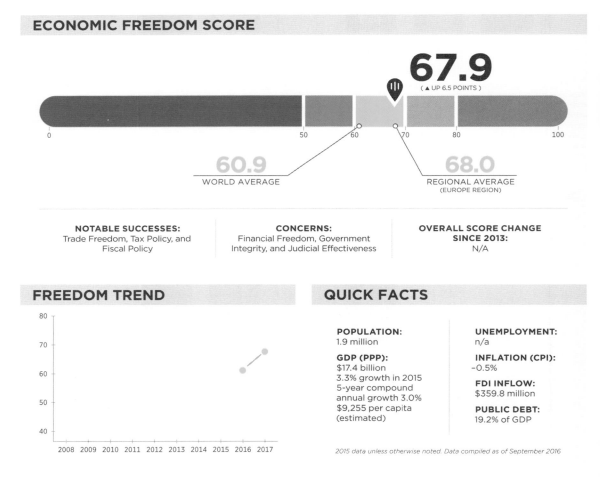

67.9
(▲ UP 6.5 POINTS)

0   50   60   70   80   100

60.9
WORLD AVERAGE

68.0
REGIONAL AVERAGE
(EUROPE REGION)

NOTABLE SUCCESSES:
Trade Freedom, Tax Policy, and Fiscal Policy

CONCERNS:
Financial Freedom, Government Integrity, and Judicial Effectiveness

OVERALL SCORE CHANGE SINCE 2013:
N/A

FREEDOM TREND

80
70
60
50
40

2008 2009 2010 2011 2012 2013 2014 2015 2016 2017

QUICK FACTS

POPULATION:
1.9 million

GDP (PPP):
$17.4 billion
3.3% growth in 2015
5-year compound
annual growth 3.0%
$9,255 per capita
(estimated)

UNEMPLOYMENT:
n/a

INFLATION (CPI):
−0.5%

FDI INFLOW:
$359.8 million

PUBLIC DEBT:
19.2% of GDP

2015 data unless otherwise noted. Data compiled as of September 2016

BACKGROUND: Kosovo is a parliamentary republic. Since gaining independence in February 2008, it has been recognized as a sovereign nation by 109 out of 193 members of the United Nations and 23 out of 28 members of the European Union. The 2013 Brussels Agreement helped to stabilize relations between Kosovo and Serbia, but NATO still maintains a peacekeeping force in the country. Parliamentary elections in June 2014 produced political deadlock. Isa Mustafa of the center-right Democratic League of Kosovo replaced Prime Minister Hashim Thaçi of the center-right Democratic Party in December 2014. Thaçi was elected to the largely ceremonial role of president in April 2016.

12 ECONOMIC FREEDOMS | KOSOVO

RULE OF LAW

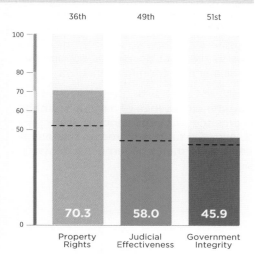

There are numerous property disputes between Kosovar Albanians and the Serb minority. The constitution provides for an independent judiciary, but courts do not always provide due process in practice. According to the European Commission, the administration of justice is slow, and there is insufficient accountability for judicial officials, who are prone to political interference. Corruption remains a problem.

GOVERNMENT SIZE

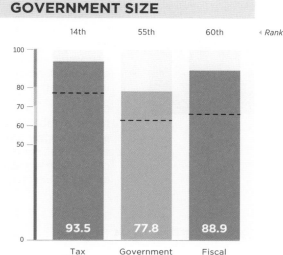

The top personal income tax and corporate tax rates are 10 percent. Other taxes include a value-added tax and a property tax. The overall tax burden equals 21.1 percent of total domestic income. Government spending has amounted to 27.2 percent of total output (GDP) over the past three years, and budget deficits have averaged 2.5 percent of GDP. Public debt is equivalent to 19.2 percent of GDP.

REGULATORY EFFICIENCY

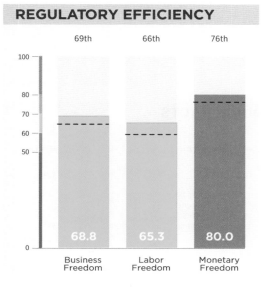

Regulatory efficiency has improved. Launching a business no longer requires minimum capital, and licensing requirements, although they still take over 100 days on average, have become less costly. The formal labor market is not fully developed, and informal labor activity remains substantial. Agricultural and energy-related subsidies from the government and international donors are massive, amounting to more than one-third of GDP.

OPEN MARKETS

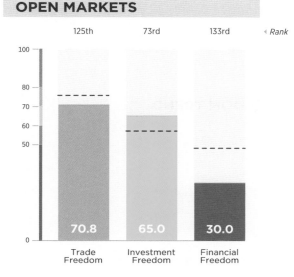

Trade is important to Kosovo's economy; the value of exports and imports taken together equals 69 percent of GDP. The average applied tariff rate is 7.1 percent. In general, foreign and domestic investors are treated equally under the law. State-owned enterprises distort the economy. The financial system continues to evolve. The banking sector, dominated by foreign banks, remains stable. Capital markets are underdeveloped.

KOSOVO

LATVIA

WORLD RANK: **20** | REGIONAL RANK: **11**

ECONOMIC FREEDOM STATUS:
MOSTLY FREE

The increasing dynamism of Latvia's economy has been facilitated by openness to global trade and investment. Supported by efficient business regulations that promote entrepreneurial activity, the overall commercial environment has become conducive to business creation and risk-taking. Fiscal consolidation in recent years has kept government spending under control and ensured macroeconomic stability.

Continued institutional reform to enhance transparency will be indispensable to ensuring the emergence of a more profitable private sector. Poor governance and inefficiency in state-owned enterprises remain problems. Corruption increases the overall cost of doing business and undermines government integrity and judicial effectiveness.

ECONOMIC FREEDOM SCORE

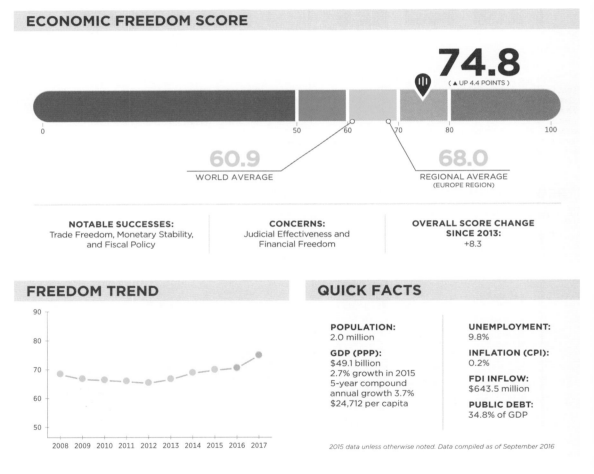

74.8
(▲ UP 4.4 POINTS)

0   50   60   70   80   100

60.9
WORLD AVERAGE

68.0
REGIONAL AVERAGE
(EUROPE REGION)

NOTABLE SUCCESSES:
Trade Freedom, Monetary Stability, and Fiscal Policy

CONCERNS:
Judicial Effectiveness and Financial Freedom

OVERALL SCORE CHANGE SINCE 2013:
+8.3

FREEDOM TREND

90
80
70
60
50

2008 2009 2010 2011 2012 2013 2014 2015 2016 2017

QUICK FACTS

POPULATION:
2.0 million

GDP (PPP):
$49.1 billion
2.7% growth in 2015
5-year compound annual growth 3.7%
$24,712 per capita

UNEMPLOYMENT:
9.8%

INFLATION (CPI):
0.2%

FDI INFLOW:
$643.5 million

PUBLIC DEBT:
34.8% of GDP

2015 data unless otherwise noted. Data compiled as of September 2016

BACKGROUND: Latvia regained its independence from the Soviet Union in 1991 and joined the European Union and NATO in 2004. Prime Minister Laimdota Straujuma of the Conservative Union resigned in December 2015 after proving unable to maintain the solidarity of the ruling coalition government. Māris Kučinskis of the centrist Liepāja Party (part of the Union of Greens and Farmers), who replaced her in February 2016, heads a three-party coalition that includes the Unity party, the National Alliance, and the Union of Greens and Farmers. The pro-Russian Harmony party is the biggest party despite not gaining power. Implementation of pro-market reforms has improved Latvia's economic standing and credit rating. Latvia joined the eurozone in 2014.

12 ECONOMIC FREEDOMS | LATVIA

RULE OF LAW

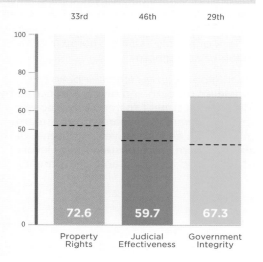

33rd — Property Rights — **72.6**
46th — Judicial Effectiveness — **59.7**
29th — Government Integrity — **67.3**

The World Bank's *Doing Business* survey reports that Latvia has made contract enforcement and property transfers easier by restructuring its courts and introducing other new procedures. Although judicial independence is generally respected and property rights are protected, the public distrusts the judicial system, which it views as inefficient, politicized, and corrupt. There are significant concerns regarding accountability for corruption.

GOVERNMENT SIZE

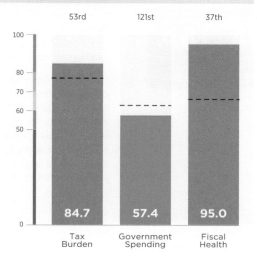

53rd — Tax Burden — **84.7**
121st — Government Spending — **57.4**
37th — Fiscal Health — **95.0**
◄ Rank

The individual income tax rate is a flat 23 percent, and the corporate tax rate is a flat 15 percent. Other taxes include a value-added tax and excise taxes. The overall tax burden equals 27.8 percent of total domestic income. Government spending has amounted to 37.7 percent of total output (GDP) over the past three years, and budget deficits have averaged 1.3 percent of GDP. Public debt is equivalent to 34.8 percent of GDP.

REGULATORY EFFICIENCY

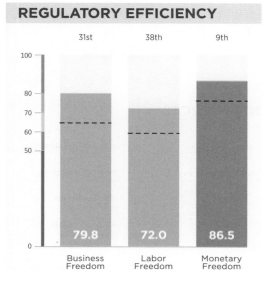

31st — Business Freedom — **79.8**
38th — Labor Freedom — **72.0**
9th — Monetary Freedom — **86.5**

The overall regulatory framework is relatively efficient. In general, rules regarding the formation and operation of private enterprises are easy and not burdensome. The nonsalary cost of employing a worker is relatively high, and dismissing an employee can be difficult. In 2016, the government told the IMF that it is making progress on governance reforms in state-owned enterprises and plans to liberalize the natural gas market in 2017.

OPEN MARKETS

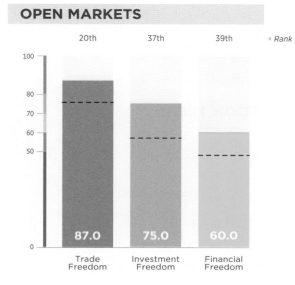

20th — Trade Freedom — **87.0**
37th — Investment Freedom — **75.0**
39th — Financial Freedom — **60.0**
◄ Rank

Trade is extremely important to Latvia's economy; the value of exports and imports taken together equals 119 percent of GDP. The average applied tariff rate is 1.5 percent. Foreign investment in some sectors is restricted, and state-owned enterprises distort the economy. The financial sector is dominated by banks and has undertaken significant regulatory adjustments since early 2009. Capital markets are not fully developed.

LATVIA

LIECHTENSTEIN

WORLD RANK: **N/A** | REGIONAL RANK: **N/A**

ECONOMIC FREEDOM STATUS:
NOT GRADED

Liechtenstein has a vibrant free-enterprise economy that is closely linked to Switzerland, whose currency it shares, and the European Union. Liechtenstein is a member of the European Free Trade Association, the Schengen Area, and the European Economic Area, but the lack of readily available comparable statistics precludes ranking of its economy.

Flexibility and openness to global commerce have been the cornerstones of Liechtenstein's modern and diversified economy. Minimal barriers to trade and investment foster vibrant economic activity, and a straightforward, transparent, and streamlined regulatory system supports an innovative entrepreneurial sector. Banking has benefited from Liechtenstein's high levels of political and social stability and its sound and transparent judicial system.

ECONOMIC FREEDOM SCORE

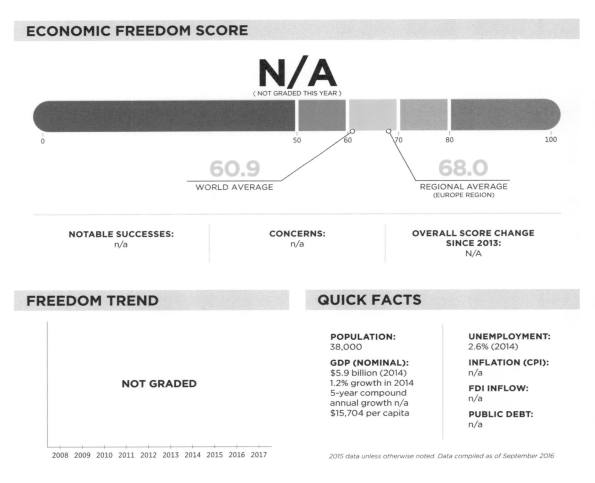

N/A
(NOT GRADED THIS YEAR)

0   50   60   70   80   100

60.9
WORLD AVERAGE

68.0
REGIONAL AVERAGE
(EUROPE REGION)

NOTABLE SUCCESSES:	CONCERNS:	OVERALL SCORE CHANGE SINCE 2013:
n/a	n/a	N/A

FREEDOM TREND

NOT GRADED

2008 2009 2010 2011 2012 2013 2014 2015 2016 2017

QUICK FACTS

POPULATION:
38,000

GDP (NOMINAL):
$5.9 billion (2014)
1.2% growth in 2014
5-year compound
annual growth n/a
$15,704 per capita

UNEMPLOYMENT:
2.6% (2014)

INFLATION (CPI):
n/a

FDI INFLOW:
n/a

PUBLIC DEBT:
n/a

2015 data unless otherwise noted. Data compiled as of September 2016

BACKGROUND: Prince of Liechtenstein Hans-Adam II is head of state, but his son Prince Alois wields considerable power as regent. The center-right Progressive Citizens' Party won the March 2013 parliamentary elections, and Prime Minister Adrian Hasler heads the government. Traditions of strict bank secrecy have helped financial institutions to attract funds, but the global financial crisis has led to a contraction in the banking sector. In 2009, the Organisation for Economic Co-operation and Development removed Liechtenstein from its list of uncooperative tax havens. In October 2015, Liechtenstein and the EU signed an agreement allowing for the automatic exchange of financial account information.

12 ECONOMIC FREEDOMS | LIECHTENSTEIN

RULE OF LAW

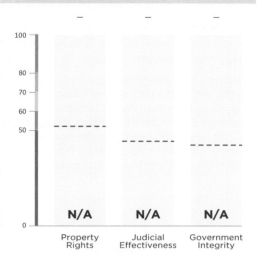

Property rights and contracts are secure. The judiciary is independent and impartial despite the appointment of judges by the hereditary monarch. Politics and society are largely free of corruption. Although Liechtenstein is a leading offshore tax haven and traditionally has maintained tight bank secrecy laws, the government has made efforts in recent years to increase transparency in banking.

GOVERNMENT SIZE

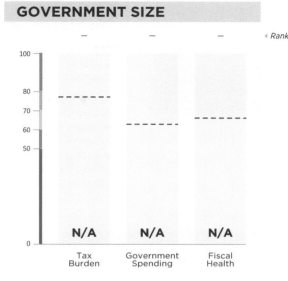

◄ Rank

Liechtenstein imposes relatively low taxes on both nationals and non-nationals. The tax reform law that became effective in January 2011 has made the tax system more modern and attractive. The corporate tax rate is now a flat 12.5 percent, and capital gains, inheritance, and gift taxes have been abolished. Although the fiscal system lacks transparency, government fiscal management has been relatively sound.

REGULATORY EFFICIENCY

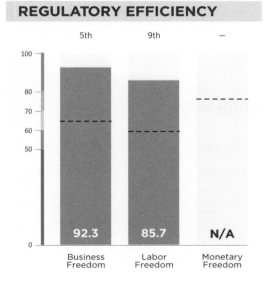

Establishing a business is fairly easy. Administrative procedures are straightforward, and regulations affecting business are transparent and applied consistently. Traditionally, unemployment has been very low. In recent years, labor market policies have focused on reducing youth unemployment. Liechtenstein has a de facto monetary union with Switzerland but no say with respect to the Swiss National Bank's monetary policies.

OPEN MARKETS

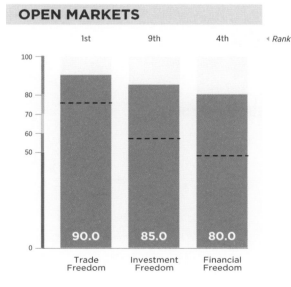

◄ Rank

Trade is extremely important to Liechtenstein's economy; the value of exports and imports taken together equals 122.5 percent of GDP. The average applied tariff rate is 0.0 percent. In general, foreign and domestic investors are treated equally, but foreign ownership of land is restricted. Liechtenstein is a major financial center, particularly in private banking.

LIECHTENSTEIN

LITHUANIA

WORLD RANK: **16** REGIONAL RANK: **8**

ECONOMIC FREEDOM STATUS:
MOSTLY FREE

Despite global and regional challenges, Lithuania's economy has demonstrated considerable resilience. Efforts to crack down on corruption and enhance fiscal soundness by revitalizing the commitment to limited government have borne fruit. Budgetary consolidation has kept government spending under control and has enhanced macroeconomic stability.

A new labor code scheduled to come into force in January 2017 should bring greater flexibility to Lithuania's labor market. Notable features of the law include new types of contracts, an increase in the legally permitted number of working hours, and reduced statutory notice periods and severance payments in cases of dismissal. Lithuania's relatively sound legal framework sustains judicial effectiveness and government integrity.

ECONOMIC FREEDOM SCORE

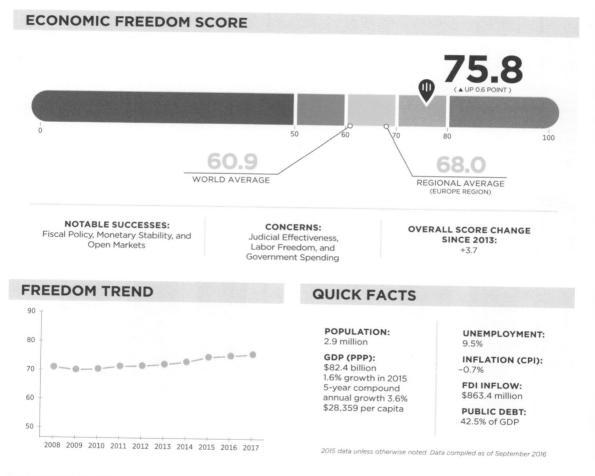

75.8
(▲ UP 0.6 POINT)

0   50   60   70   80   100

60.9
WORLD AVERAGE

68.0
REGIONAL AVERAGE
(EUROPE REGION)

NOTABLE SUCCESSES:
Fiscal Policy, Monetary Stability, and Open Markets

CONCERNS:
Judicial Effectiveness, Labor Freedom, and Government Spending

OVERALL SCORE CHANGE SINCE 2013:
+3.7

FREEDOM TREND

90
80
70
60
50

2008 2009 2010 2011 2012 2013 2014 2015 2016 2017

QUICK FACTS

POPULATION:
2.9 million

GDP (PPP):
$82.4 billion
1.6% growth in 2015
5-year compound annual growth 3.6%
$28,359 per capita

UNEMPLOYMENT:
9.5%

INFLATION (CPI):
-0.7%

FDI INFLOW:
$863.4 million

PUBLIC DEBT:
42.5% of GDP

2015 data unless otherwise noted. Data compiled as of September 2016

BACKGROUND: Lithuania, largest of the three Baltic States, regained its independence from the Soviet Union in 1991 and joined the European Union and NATO in 2004. Lithuania is a parliamentary republic with some attributes of a presidential system. Under President Dalia Grybauskaitė, reelected in May 2014, the country has worked to improve transparency in parliamentary elections, pass judicial reforms, and increase energy and financial security. Until recently, Lithuania depended heavily on Russia for natural gas. However, in 2016, Norway overtook Russia as Lithuania's top gas supplier thanks to the recent completion of the largest offshore liquefied natural gas terminal in the region.

12 ECONOMIC FREEDOMS | LITHUANIA

RULE OF LAW

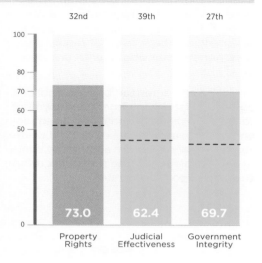

	32nd	39th	27th
	Property Rights	Judicial Effectiveness	Government Integrity
	73.0	**62.4**	**69.7**

Stronger legal structures and better enforcement have significantly improved the protection of intellectual property rights in Lithuania, and membership in the EU has strengthened judicial independence. However, many improvements are still needed. A series of civil service corruption scandals that emerged in early 2016 reinforced the public's poor perceptions of government efficiency and lack of confidence in political parties.

GOVERNMENT SIZE

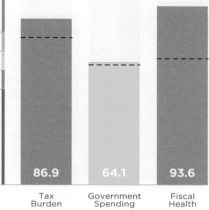

	38th	106th	39th	◂ Rank
	Tax Burden	Government Spending	Fiscal Health	
	86.9	**64.1**	**93.6**	

Lithuania's top individual income and corporate tax rates are 15 percent. Other taxes include an inheritance tax and a value-added tax. The overall tax burden equals 29.3 percent of total domestic income. Government spending has amounted to 34.6 percent of total output (GDP) over the past three years, and budget deficits have averaged 1.3 percent of GDP. Public debt is equivalent to 42.5 percent of GDP.

REGULATORY EFFICIENCY

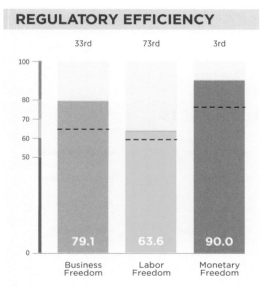

	33rd	73rd	3rd
	Business Freedom	Labor Freedom	Monetary Freedom
	79.1	**63.6**	**90.0**

The overall entrepreneurial framework has become fairly streamlined and efficient. Business formation and operation take place without bureaucratic interference. New labor regulations intended to enhance labor market flexibility have come into force. Lithuania scrapped its fuel subsidies in 2015 after connecting to Poland and Sweden's electric grid to import electricity at a lower cost, a move that saved consumers €90 million in 2016.

OPEN MARKETS

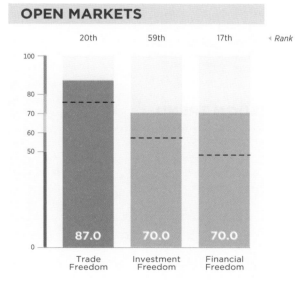

	20th	59th	17th	◂ Rank
	Trade Freedom	Investment Freedom	Financial Freedom	
	87.0	**70.0**	**70.0**	

Trade is extremely important to Lithuania's economy; the value of exports and imports taken together equals 155 percent of GDP. The average applied tariff rate is 1.5 percent. In general, the law treats foreign and domestic investors equally. State-owned enterprises distort the economy. The competitive financial sector offers a full range of services, and branch networks of commercial banks provide access to services throughout the country.

LITHUANIA

LUXEMBOURG

WORLD RANK: **14** | REGIONAL RANK: **6**

ECONOMIC FREEDOM STATUS:
MOSTLY FREE

Luxembourg's economic competitiveness is sustained by solid institutional foundations for an open-market system. The judiciary, independent and free of corruption, protects property rights and upholds the rule of law. The economy is open to global trade and investment, and high levels of regulatory transparency and efficiency encourage vibrant entrepreneurial activity.

The fiscal environment remains characterized by high public spending on social programs. Relatively stringent employment protection tends to undercut job mobility and dynamic employment growth. Fiscal consolidation and enhancement of Luxembourg's status as a global financial center are among the coalition government's main policy objectives. The recent tax reform package has lowered the top corporate tax rate.

ECONOMIC FREEDOM SCORE

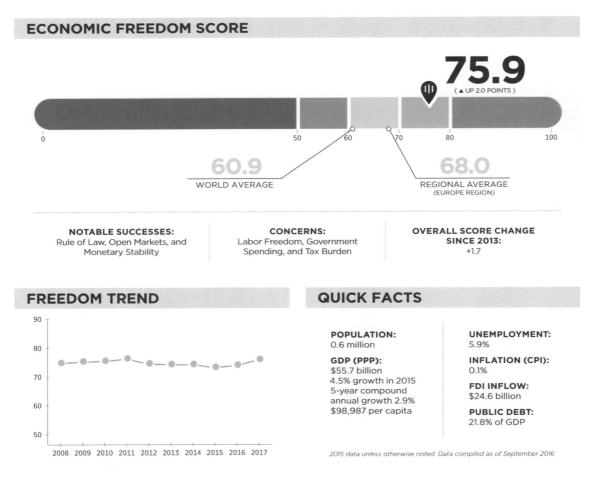

75.9
(▲ UP 2.0 POINTS)

0   50   60   70   80   100

60.9
WORLD AVERAGE

68.0
REGIONAL AVERAGE
(EUROPE REGION)

NOTABLE SUCCESSES:
Rule of Law, Open Markets, and Monetary Stability

CONCERNS:
Labor Freedom, Government Spending, and Tax Burden

OVERALL SCORE CHANGE SINCE 2013:
+1.7

FREEDOM TREND

90
80
70
60
50

2008 2009 2010 2011 2012 2013 2014 2015 2016 2017

QUICK FACTS

POPULATION:
0.6 million

GDP (PPP):
$55.7 billion
4.5% growth in 2015
5-year compound
annual growth 2.9%
$98,987 per capita

UNEMPLOYMENT:
5.9%

INFLATION (CPI):
0.1%

FDI INFLOW:
$24.6 billion

PUBLIC DEBT:
21.8% of GDP

2015 data unless otherwise noted. Data compiled as of September 2016

BACKGROUND: A founding member of the European Union in 1957 and the eurozone in 1999, the Grand Duchy of Luxembourg continues to promote European integration. Prime Minister Xavier Bettel of the Democratic Party was elected in December 2013, defeating the Christian Social People's Party that had been in power since 1979. Luxembourgers have one of the world's highest income levels, although the global economic crisis provoked the first recession in 60 years in 2009. Growth is strong, and unemployment remains well below the EU average. During the 20th century, Luxembourg evolved into a mixed manufacturing and services economy with a strong financial services sector.

12 ECONOMIC FREEDOMS | LUXEMBOURG

RULE OF LAW

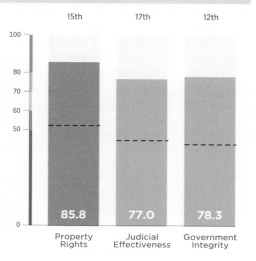

Private property rights are well protected, contracts are secure, and steps have been taken to implement and enforce the World Trade Organization's TRIPS (Trade-Related Aspects of Intellectual Property Rights) agreement. The judiciary is independent, and the legal framework strongly supports the rule of law. Luxembourg has laws, regulations, and penalties to combat corruption effectively, and they are enforced impartially.

GOVERNMENT SIZE

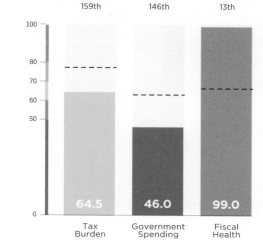

The top individual income tax rate is 42 percent, and the top corporate tax rate has been reduced from 21 percent to 19 percent. Other taxes include a value-added tax. The overall tax burden equals 37.8 percent of total domestic income. Government spending has amounted to 42.4 percent of total output (GDP) over the past three years, and budget surpluses have averaged 1.0 percent of GDP. Public debt is equivalent to 21.8 percent of GDP.

REGULATORY EFFICIENCY

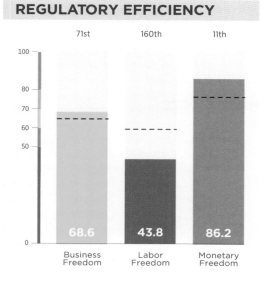

The overall freedom to start, operate, and close a business is relatively well protected under the transparent regulatory environment. However, labor regulations are costly, unemployment benefits are quite generous, and the minimum wage is high. Monetary stability has been well maintained. Luxembourg has a highly subsidized agricultural sector and the highest rate of fuel subsidies per citizen in Europe.

OPEN MARKETS

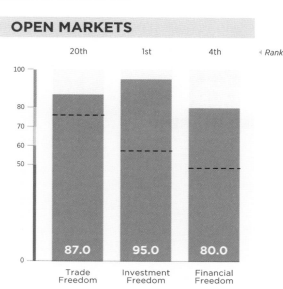

Trade is extremely important to Luxembourg's economy; the value of exports and imports taken together equals 391 percent of GDP. The average applied tariff rate is 1.5 percent. In general, foreign and domestic investors are treated equally under the law. The sophisticated banking sector is well capitalized, competitive, and supported by transparent and effective regulations. Many of the world's leading banks have subsidiaries in Luxembourg.

LUXEMBOURG

MACEDONIA

Improvements in Macedonia's regulatory framework have created a stable environment for foreign and domestic investment, but political instability has undercut vibrant growth. Although Macedonia depends primarily on economic activity in service sectors, new investment in automotive parts manufacturing is helping to diversify the economy. Businesses benefit from competitive flat tax rates and an open trade regime.

Greater structural reform is still needed, especially in the area of government corruption and bureaucracy. The legal framework is sound, but enforcement is slow and weak. Frequently changing business regulations and selective law enforcement hinder the confidence of foreign investors.

WORLD RANK: **31**

REGIONAL RANK: **18**

ECONOMIC FREEDOM STATUS:
MOSTLY FREE

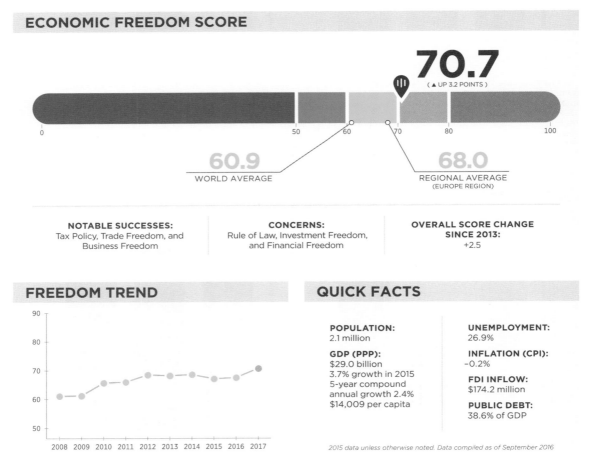

ECONOMIC FREEDOM SCORE

70.7
(▲ UP 3.2 POINTS)

0   50   60   70   80   100

60.9
WORLD AVERAGE

68.0
REGIONAL AVERAGE
(EUROPE REGION)

NOTABLE SUCCESSES:
Tax Policy, Trade Freedom, and Business Freedom

CONCERNS:
Rule of Law, Investment Freedom, and Financial Freedom

OVERALL SCORE CHANGE SINCE 2013:
+2.5

FREEDOM TREND

90

80

70

60

50

2008 2009 2010 2011 2012 2013 2014 2015 2016 2017

QUICK FACTS

POPULATION:
2.1 million

GDP (PPP):
$29.0 billion
3.7% growth in 2015
5-year compound annual growth 2.4%
$14,009 per capita

UNEMPLOYMENT:
26.9%

INFLATION (CPI):
−0.2%

FDI INFLOW:
$174.2 million

PUBLIC DEBT:
38.6% of GDP

2015 data unless otherwise noted. Data compiled as of September 2016

BACKGROUND: Macedonia gained its independence from the former Yugoslavia in 1991. Nikola Gruevski of the conservative Internal Macedonian Revolutionary Organization–Democratic Party for Macedonian National Unity resigned as prime minister in January 2016, embroiled in a wiretap scandal. Emil Dimitriev is serving as interim prime minister. The VMRO-DPMNE had prevailed in the April 2014 presidential and parliamentary elections in a coalition with the Albanian Democratic Union for Integration. The Social Democratic Union of Macedonia, the main opposition party, disputed the results and boycotted parliament. Macedonia completed NATO's Membership Action Plan in 2008, but Greece continues to block its accession because it objects to Macedonia's name. This dispute is also delaying Macedonia's accession to the European Union.

12 ECONOMIC FREEDOMS | MACEDONIA

RULE OF LAW

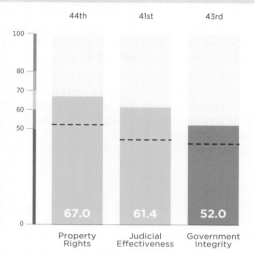

44th   41st   43rd

- Property Rights: **67.0**
- Judicial Effectiveness: **61.4**
- Government Integrity: **52.0**

Although the legal basis for protecting the ownership of movable, intellectual, and real property exists, implementation remains incomplete. The legal framework is sound, but law enforcement is weak, and the public doubts the government's willingness to prosecute corrupt officials. Political interference, inefficiency, cronyism, and corruption are pervasive.

GOVERNMENT SIZE

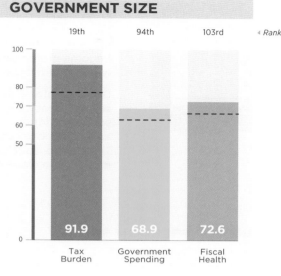

19th   94th   103rd   ◂ Rank

- Tax Burden: **91.9**
- Government Spending: **68.9**
- Fiscal Health: **72.6**

The individual income and corporate tax rates are a flat 10 percent. Other taxes include a value-added tax and a property transfer tax. The overall tax burden equals 24.6 percent of total domestic income. Government spending has amounted to 32.2 percent of total output (GDP) over the past three years, and budget deficits have averaged 3.9 percent of GDP. Public debt is equivalent to 38.6 percent of GDP.

REGULATORY EFFICIENCY

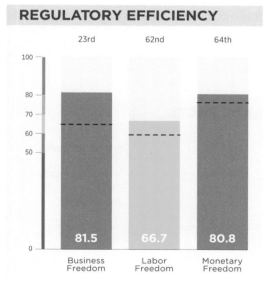

23rd   62nd   64th

- Business Freedom: **81.5**
- Labor Freedom: **66.7**
- Monetary Freedom: **80.8**

Streamlined processes for business formation and operation provide an environment that is fairly conducive to private investment and production. After years of high unemployment, recent reforms have focused on making the labor market more flexible. Almost half of government spending is allocated to social transfers designed in part to shore up support for the ruling parties. Subsidized hospitals are being built to attract "medical tourists."

OPEN MARKETS

50th   89th   39th   ◂ Rank

- Trade Freedom: **86.1**
- Investment Freedom: **60.0**
- Financial Freedom: **60.0**

Trade is extremely important to Macedonia's economy; the value of exports and imports taken together equals 113 percent of GDP. The average applied tariff rate is 2.0 percent. In general, foreign and domestic investments are treated equally. State-owned enterprises distort the economy. The financial sector has become more dynamic. Bank competition has increased, and the foreign presence accounts for more than 80 percent of total banking-sector assets.

MACEDONIA

MALTA

WORLD RANK:
50

REGIONAL RANK:
26

ECONOMIC FREEDOM STATUS:
MODERATELY FREE

Malta's overall entrepreneurial environment supports the development of a dynamic private sector. The judiciary, fairly independent and efficient, provides strong protection of property rights. The financial market is small but sound and has become more open to competition. The financial sector has weathered the global financial crisis relatively well.

Despite notable institutional competitiveness, Malta is weak in several areas of economic freedom. Tax rates and government spending, for example, are relatively high. Lingering corruption and rigid labor regulations add to the cost of doing business. The maintenance of fiscal health will require reasonable containment of the wage bill, social transfers, and pension funds.

ECONOMIC FREEDOM SCORE

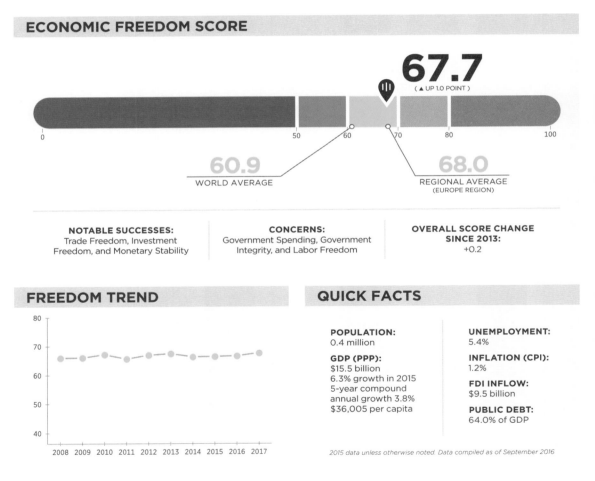

67.7
(▲ UP 1.0 POINT)

0   50   60   70   80   100

60.9
WORLD AVERAGE

68.0
REGIONAL AVERAGE
(EUROPE REGION)

NOTABLE SUCCESSES:
Trade Freedom, Investment Freedom, and Monetary Stability

CONCERNS:
Government Spending, Government Integrity, and Labor Freedom

OVERALL SCORE CHANGE SINCE 2013:
+0.2

FREEDOM TREND

80
70
60
50
40

2008 2009 2010 2011 2012 2013 2014 2015 2016 2017

QUICK FACTS

POPULATION:
0.4 million

GDP (PPP):
$15.5 billion
6.3% growth in 2015
5-year compound
annual growth 3.8%
$36,005 per capita

UNEMPLOYMENT:
5.4%

INFLATION (CPI):
1.2%

FDI INFLOW:
$9.5 billion

PUBLIC DEBT:
64.0% of GDP

2015 data unless otherwise noted. Data compiled as of September 2016

BACKGROUND: Malta joined the European Union in 2004 and the eurozone in 2008. Labour Party leader Joseph Muscat won the March 2013 elections and became prime minister. With few natural resources, Malta imports most of its food and fresh water and 100 percent of its energy. The economy depends on tourism, trade, and manufacturing. Well-trained workers, low labor costs, and membership in the EU attract foreign investment, but the government maintains a sprawling socialist bureaucracy, and the majority of spending is allocated to housing, education, and health care. The unemployment rate is one of the lowest in the EU. Substantial migration from North Africa and regional instability are growing concerns.

12 ECONOMIC FREEDOMS | MALTA

RULE OF LAW

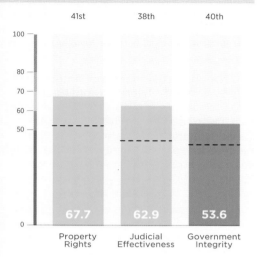

41st   38th   40th

67.7   62.9   53.6

Property Rights | Judicial Effectiveness | Government Integrity

Property rights are protected in Malta, and expropriation is unlikely, but foreigners do not have full rights to buy property. The judiciary is independent both constitutionally and in practice. The police and the Permanent Commission Against Corruption are responsible for combating official corruption and have prosecuted cases, but they do not publish information about such cases.

GOVERNMENT SIZE

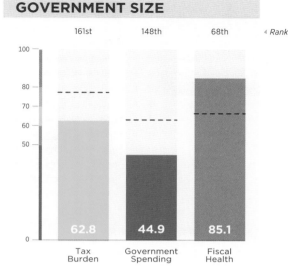

161st   148th   68th   ◄ Rank

62.8   44.9   85.1

Tax Burden | Government Spending | Fiscal Health

The top individual income and corporate tax rates are 35 percent. Other taxes include a value-added tax and a capital gains tax. The overall tax burden equals 35.6 percent of total domestic income. Government spending has amounted to 42.8 percent of total output (GDP) over the past three years, and budget deficits have averaged 2.0 percent of GDP. Public debt is equivalent to 64.0 percent of GDP.

MALTA

REGULATORY EFFICIENCY

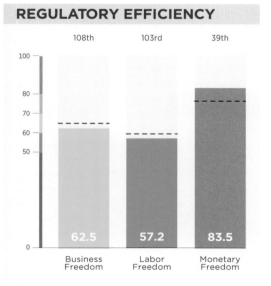

108th   103rd   39th

62.5   57.2   83.5

Business Freedom | Labor Freedom | Monetary Freedom

Existing regulations are relatively straightforward and applied uniformly most of the time. Transparent and effective policies and regulations have been adopted to foster competition. Labor regulations are relatively rigid, and there is a minimum wage. The government plans to reduce the fiscal deficit from around 2 percent of GDP in 2014 to almost zero by 2018, in part by reducing subsidies such as support for a state-owned airline.

OPEN MARKETS

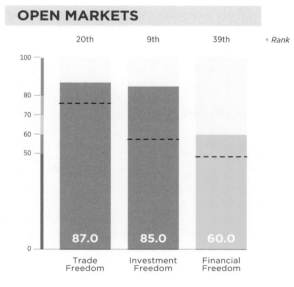

20th   9th   39th   ◄ Rank

87.0   85.0   60.0

Trade Freedom | Investment Freedom | Financial Freedom

Trade is extremely important to Malta's economy; the value of exports and imports taken together equals 101 percent of GDP. The average applied tariff rate is 1.5 percent. In general, foreign investment is not screened by the government. Many state-owned enterprises have been privatized. Supervision and regulation of the financial sector have gradually become more transparent and effective. The stock exchange is small but active.

MOLDOVA

WORLD RANK: 110
REGIONAL RANK: 41

ECONOMIC FREEDOM STATUS:
MOSTLY UNFREE

Moldova has gradually recovered from a sharp economic slowdown over the past three years, with growth driven largely by remittance-based consumption and modest credit expansion. Some new momentum has been generated for improving the business environment and further liberalizing the trade regime.

However, the transition to a more stable market-oriented economy remains fragile. The government's overall commitment to enhancing the entrepreneurial climate and advancing economic freedom has been uneven. Despite several privatizations, the public sector still plays a dominant role in the economy. The foundations of economic freedom are not firmly institutionalized, and the judiciary remains vulnerable to political interference and corruption.

ECONOMIC FREEDOM SCORE

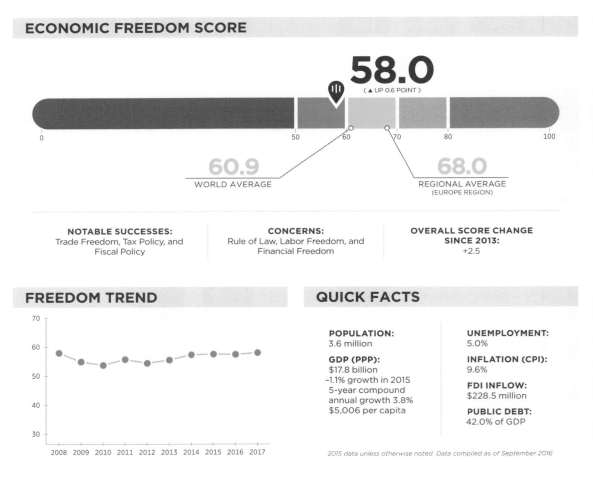

58.0
(▲ UP 0.6 POINT)

0   50   60   70   80   100

60.9
WORLD AVERAGE

68.0
REGIONAL AVERAGE
(EUROPE REGION)

NOTABLE SUCCESSES:
Trade Freedom, Tax Policy, and Fiscal Policy

CONCERNS:
Rule of Law, Labor Freedom, and Financial Freedom

OVERALL SCORE CHANGE SINCE 2013:
+2.5

FREEDOM TREND

70

60

50

40

30

2008 2009 2010 2011 2012 2013 2014 2015 2016 2017

QUICK FACTS

POPULATION:
3.6 million

GDP (PPP):
$17.8 billion
–1.1% growth in 2015
5-year compound
annual growth 3.8%
$5,006 per capita

UNEMPLOYMENT:
5.0%

INFLATION (CPI):
9.6%

FDI INFLOW:
$228.5 million

PUBLIC DEBT:
42.0% of GDP

2015 data unless otherwise noted. Data compiled as of September 2016

BACKGROUND: Moldova gained independence after the collapse of the Soviet Union in 1991 but faces a secessionist pro-Russian movement in its Transnistria region, currently home to more than 1,100 Russian troops. The country is poor, and excessive economic dependence on Russia threatens its sovereignty. The pro-Russia PSRM party won the most seats in the December 2014 parliamentary election. It was blocked from forming a government, however, by a pro–European integration coalition of the center-right Liberal Democratic Party, the Liberal Party, and the center-left Democratic Party of current Prime Minister Pavel Filip. Association agreements signed with the European Union in June 2014 include Deep and Comprehensive Free Trade Area (DCFTA) accords.

12 ECONOMIC FREEDOMS | MOLDOVA

RULE OF LAW

96th	150th	155th
Property Rights	Judicial Effectiveness	Government Integrity
49.6	23.9	28.6

Moldova has laws that formally protect all property rights. A system for recording property titles and mortgages is in place. The constitution provides for an independent judiciary, but the legal framework is ineffective, and reform efforts suffer from lack of funds. A major banking scandal that implicated high-ranking public figures and underlined the extent of corruption at all levels of government has led to mass protests.

GOVERNMENT SIZE

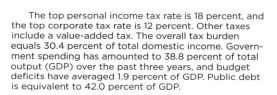

43rd	127th	51st	◄ Rank
Tax Burden	Government Spending	Fiscal Health	
86.1	54.8	90.6	

The top personal income tax rate is 18 percent, and the top corporate tax rate is 12 percent. Other taxes include a value-added tax. The overall tax burden equals 30.4 percent of total domestic income. Government spending has amounted to 38.8 percent of total output (GDP) over the past three years, and budget deficits have averaged 1.9 percent of GDP. Public debt is equivalent to 42.0 percent of GDP.

REGULATORY EFFICIENCY

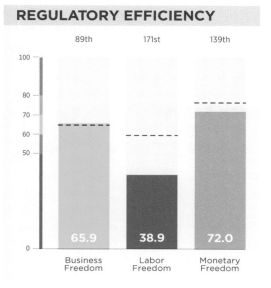

89th	171st	139th
Business Freedom	Labor Freedom	Monetary Freedom
65.9	38.9	72.0

Lingering bureaucracy and a lack of transparency often make the formation and operation of private enterprises costly and burdensome. Labor regulations are rigid. The nonsalary cost of employing a worker is high, and restrictions on work hours remain inflexible. The IMF reports that the cost of the bank bailout following a massive banking scam amounted to 12 percent of GDP, forcing the government to cut agricultural subsidies.

OPEN MARKETS

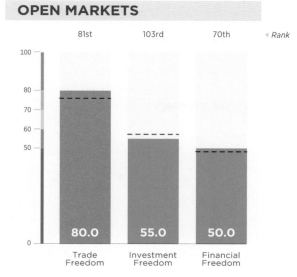

81st	103rd	70th	◄ Rank
Trade Freedom	Investment Freedom	Financial Freedom	
80.0	55.0	50.0	

Trade is extremely important to Moldova's economy; the value of exports and imports taken together equals 117 percent of GDP. The average applied tariff rate is 2.5 percent. In general, foreign and domestic investors are treated equally under the law. Long-term financing remains difficult. Overall, the financial sector is stable but shallow, and financial intermediation remains constrained by structural impediments.

MOLDOVA

MONTENEGRO

Montenegro's evolution into a modern, dynamic economy has made considerable gains. The trade regime is increasingly open, and the regulatory and legal frameworks governing investment and production have become more efficient, supporting the development of a growing private sector. Other previous reforms, which included further reduction of the already competitive flat tax rates and implementation of labor market reforms, have also contributed to an upsurge in entrepreneurship.

Despite the great strides made overall, Montenegro's economic freedom is still curtailed by the lack of institutional commitment to the strong protection of property rights or effective measures against corruption. The court system remains vulnerable to political interference and inefficiency.

ECONOMIC FREEDOM SCORE

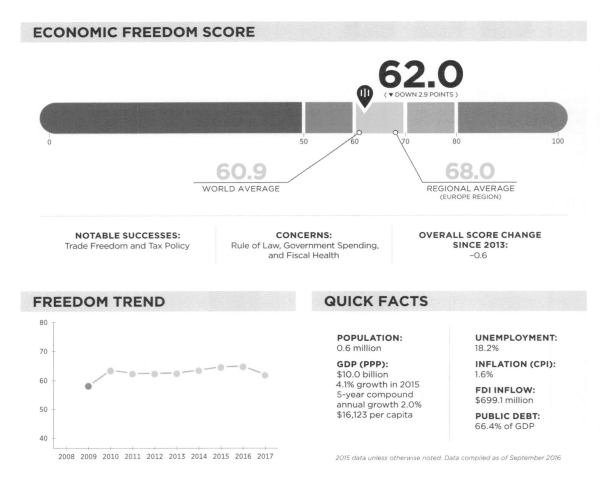

62.0
(▼ DOWN 2.9 POINTS)

0   50   60   70   80   100

60.9
WORLD AVERAGE

68.0
REGIONAL AVERAGE
(EUROPE REGION)

NOTABLE SUCCESSES:
Trade Freedom and Tax Policy

CONCERNS:
Rule of Law, Government Spending, and Fiscal Health

OVERALL SCORE CHANGE SINCE 2013:
–0.6

FREEDOM TREND

80
70
60
50
40

2008 2009 2010 2011 2012 2013 2014 2015 2016 2017

QUICK FACTS

POPULATION:
0.6 million

GDP (PPP):
$10.0 billion
4.1% growth in 2015
5-year compound
annual growth 2.0%
$16,123 per capita

UNEMPLOYMENT:
18.2%

INFLATION (CPI):
1.6%

FDI INFLOW:
$699.1 million

PUBLIC DEBT:
66.4% of GDP

2015 data unless otherwise noted. Data compiled as of September 2016

BACKGROUND: Montenegro declared its independence from Serbia in 2006, introduced significant privatization, and adopted the euro despite not being a member of the eurozone. Milo Đukanović has served as president or prime minister for nearly all of the past 25 years. Although his Democratic Party of Socialists won the most seats in the October 2016 parliamentary elections, it failed to secure a majority, and his longtime political ally Duško Marković became prime minister in a coalition government. Đukanović may seek the presidency again in 2018. He has steered Montenegro in a pro-Western direction and has accused Russia of financing opposition parties. Montenegro was formally invited to join NATO in May 2016 and would become the first nation to join since 2009.

12 ECONOMIC FREEDOMS | MONTENEGRO

RULE OF LAW

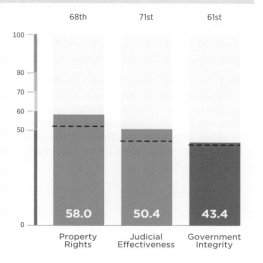

	68th	71st	61st
	Property Rights	Judicial Effectiveness	Government Integrity
	58.0	**50.4**	**43.4**

Foreigners may own real property. Trademark and copyright violations are a significant problem in the outerwear and apparel markets; unlicensed software can easily be found on the general market. Politicization of the judiciary is a long-standing problem. Corruption is pervasive in health care, education, and all levels of government including law enforcement. Impunity, political favoritism, nepotism, and selective prosecutions are common.

GOVERNMENT SIZE

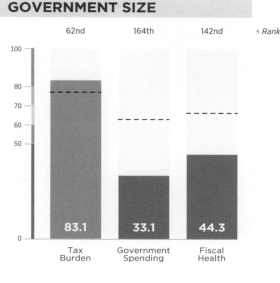

◄ Rank

	62nd	164th	142nd
	Tax Burden	Government Spending	Fiscal Health
	83.1	**33.1**	**44.3**

The personal income and corporate tax rates are a flat 9 percent. Other taxes include a value-added tax and an inheritance tax. The overall tax burden equals 39.1 percent of total domestic income. Government spending has amounted to 47.2 percent of total output (GDP) over the past three years, and budget deficits have averaged 5.4 percent of GDP. Public debt is equivalent to 66.4 percent of GDP.

REGULATORY EFFICIENCY

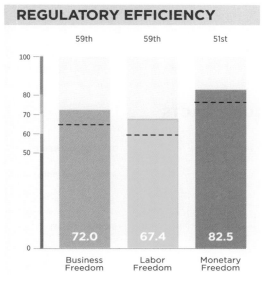

	59th	59th	51st
	Business Freedom	Labor Freedom	Monetary Freedom
	72.0	**67.4**	**82.5**

Procedures for setting up a business have been streamlined, and the number of licensing requirements has been reduced. Previous reforms reduced some of the labor market's rigidities, but there is room for further improvement. Now that the bankrupt, state-supported, Communist-era aluminum company KAP has been sold, the government hopes to sell other money-losing state-owned assets, but finding buyers for them will be difficult.

OPEN MARKETS

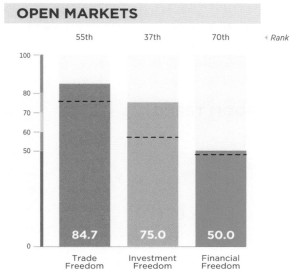

◄ Rank

	55th	37th	70th
	Trade Freedom	Investment Freedom	Financial Freedom
	84.7	**75.0**	**50.0**

Trade is extremely important to Montenegro's economy; the value of exports and imports taken together equals 104 percent of GDP. The average applied tariff rate is 2.6 percent. There are few formal barriers to foreign investment, and many state-owned enterprises have been privatized. The financial sector, though small and underdeveloped, is becoming more competitive, and the level of foreign banks' participation and investment is significant.

MONTENEGRO

NETHERLANDS

WORLD RANK:
15

REGIONAL RANK:
7

ECONOMIC FREEDOM STATUS:
MOSTLY FREE

The economy of the Netherlands benefits from a traditional emphasis on the rule of law and a robust legal framework. The judicial system, independent and free of corruption, provides strong protection of property rights. Openness to global trade and investment is well established, and the overall regulatory environment remains transparent and efficient.

Government spending has been expansive, but the coalition government has made some progress in narrowing the budget deficit. Cuts in health care and social security spending have helped to place public finances on a more secure footing. In an attempt to strengthen work incentives and reduce fiscal pressures, the government has introduced reforms in the labor market and pensions.

ECONOMIC FREEDOM SCORE

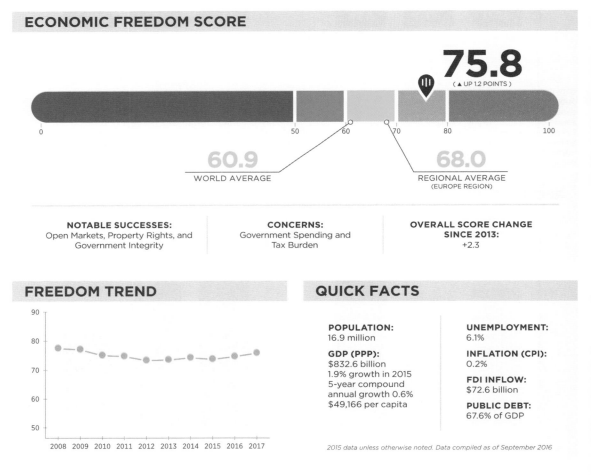

75.8
(▲ UP 1.2 POINTS)

0   50   60   70   80   100

60.9
WORLD AVERAGE

68.0
REGIONAL AVERAGE
(EUROPE REGION)

NOTABLE SUCCESSES:
Open Markets, Property Rights, and Government Integrity

CONCERNS:
Government Spending and Tax Burden

OVERALL SCORE CHANGE SINCE 2013:
+2.3

FREEDOM TREND

90
80
70
60
50

2008 2009 2010 2011 2012 2013 2014 2015 2016 2017

QUICK FACTS

POPULATION:
16.9 million

GDP (PPP):
$832.6 billion
1.9% growth in 2015
5-year compound
annual growth 0.6%
$49,166 per capita

UNEMPLOYMENT:
6.1%

INFLATION (CPI):
0.2%

FDI INFLOW:
$72.6 billion

PUBLIC DEBT:
67.6% of GDP

2015 data unless otherwise noted. Data compiled as of September 2016

BACKGROUND: The center-right coalition led by Prime Minister Mark Rutte collapsed in April 2012 when the Freedom Party's Geert Wilders refused to back Rutte's austerity package. Rutte's center-right People's Party for Freedom and Democracy and its principal coalition partner, the center-left Labor Party, won increased support during elections in September 2012. The Netherlands is a founding member of the European Union but under Rutte's leadership has been one of the most outspoken supporters of turning power back to EU member states. Euroscepticism is on the rise: In an April 2016 countrywide referendum, Dutch voters voted against approving an EU–Ukraine Association agreement.

12 ECONOMIC FREEDOMS | NETHERLANDS

RULE OF LAW

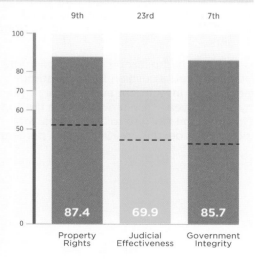

The legal framework ensures strong protection of private property rights and enforcement of contracts. Independent of political interference, the judiciary is respected and provides fair adjudication of disputes. There are few problems with political corruption. Effective anticorruption measures and minimal tolerance for corruption ensure government integrity. The Netherlands is a signatory to all major international anticorruption conventions.

GOVERNMENT SIZE

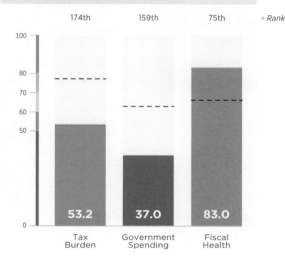

The top personal income tax rate is 52 percent, and the top corporate tax rate is 25 percent. Other taxes include a value-added tax and environmental taxes. The overall tax burden equals 36.7 percent of total domestic income. Government spending has amounted to 45.8 percent of total output (GDP) over the past three years, and budget deficits have averaged 2.2 percent of GDP. Public debt is equivalent to 67.6 percent of GDP.

REGULATORY EFFICIENCY

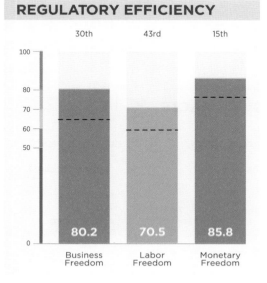

The overall regulatory framework is transparent and competitive. The efficient business framework is conducive to innovation and productivity growth. Monetary stability has been well maintained. Labor regulations are relatively rigid. The nonsalary cost of employing a worker is high, and dismissing an employee is relatively costly. Price controls are in place only for pharmaceuticals.

OPEN MARKETS

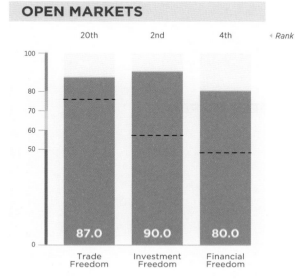

Trade is extremely important to the economy of the Netherlands; the value of exports and imports taken together equals 154 percent of GDP. The average applied tariff rate is 1.5 percent. There is no general screening of foreign investment, and investment in most sectors of the economy is not restricted. Sensible banking regulations facilitate dynamic entrepreneurial activity, and lending practices are prudent.

NETHERLANDS

NORWAY

WORLD RANK: **25** **REGIONAL RANK:** **14**

ECONOMIC FREEDOM STATUS:
MOSTLY FREE

Norway's competitive economy benefits from openness to global commerce and a regulatory environment that encourages entrepreneurial activity. Monetary stability is well maintained, and the independent judicial system provides strong protection of property rights.

The accumulation of assets from hydrocarbon production in the National Wealth Fund has provided a cushion for fiscal stimulus. In an effort to attract foreign investment and diversify the oil-dependent economy, a multi-year measure to reduce the top corporate tax rate has lowered the tax rate to 25 percent, with further planned reductions to 24 percent in 2017 and 23 percent in 2018.

ECONOMIC FREEDOM SCORE

74.0
(▲ UP 3.2 POINTS)

0   50   60   70   80   100

60.9
WORLD AVERAGE

68.0
REGIONAL AVERAGE
(EUROPE REGION)

NOTABLE SUCCESSES:
Rule of Law, Business Freedom, and Trade Freedom

CONCERNS:
Government Spending, Labor Freedom, and Tax Burden

OVERALL SCORE CHANGE SINCE 2013:
+3.5

FREEDOM TREND

90
80
70
60
50

2008 2009 2010 2011 2012 2013 2014 2015 2016 2017

QUICK FACTS

POPULATION:
5.2 million

GDP (PPP):
$356.2 billion
1.6% growth in 2015
5-year compound
annual growth 1.7%
$68,430 per capita

UNEMPLOYMENT:
4.2%

INFLATION (CPI):
2.2%

FDI INFLOW:
-$4.2 billion

PUBLIC DEBT:
27.9% of GDP

2015 data unless otherwise noted. Data compiled as of September 2016

BACKGROUND: Norway has been a member of NATO since 1949. Voters have twice rejected membership in the European Union, but Norway is a party to a European Free Trade Association agreement. Prime Minister Erna Solberg of the Conservative Party was elected in September 2013 and leads a center-right coalition minority government. Norway is one of the world's most prosperous countries. It saves a large portion of its petroleum-sector revenues, including dividends from the partially state-owned Statoil and taxes from oil and gas companies operating in Norway. Low oil prices have been a drag on the economy, and Norway made a withdrawal from its Government Pension Fund Global for the first time ever in March 2016.

12 ECONOMIC FREEDOMS | NORWAY

RULE OF LAW

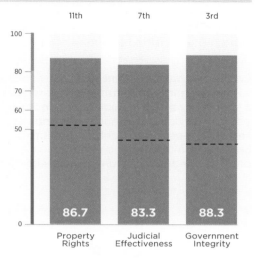

	11th	7th	3rd
	Property Rights	Judicial Effectiveness	Government Integrity
	86.7	83.3	88.3

Private property rights are securely protected, and commercial contracts are reliably enforced. The judiciary is independent, and the court system operates fairly at the local and national levels. Norway is one of the world's least corrupt countries and is ranked fifth out of 168 countries in Transparency International's 2015 *Corruption Perceptions Index*. Well-established anticorruption measures reinforce a cultural emphasis on government integrity.

GOVERNMENT SIZE

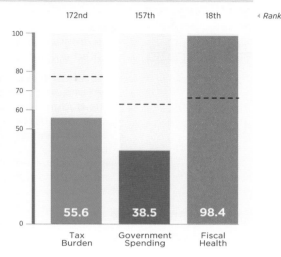

	172nd	157th	18th	◄ Rank
	Tax Burden	Government Spending	Fiscal Health	
	55.6	38.5	98.4	

The top personal income tax rate is 47.8 percent, and the corporate tax rate has been cut to 25 percent. Other taxes include a value-added tax and environmental taxes. The overall tax burden equals 39.1 percent of total domestic income. Government spending has amounted to 45.3 percent of total output (GDP) over the past three years, and budget surpluses have averaged 8.1 percent of GDP. Public debt is equivalent to 27.9 percent of GDP.

REGULATORY EFFICIENCY

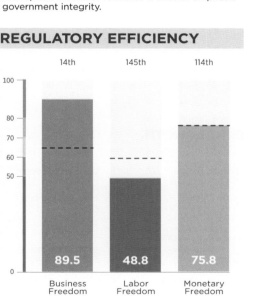

	14th	145th	114th
	Business Freedom	Labor Freedom	Monetary Freedom
	89.5	48.8	75.8

Norway's transparent and efficient regulatory framework facilitates entrepreneurial activity and innovation. The labor market lacks flexibility, but the nonsalary cost of employment is not high in comparison to other countries in the region. Monetary stability has been well maintained. The IMF has recommended that the government reduce its restrictive subsidies on agriculture and supply controls on the housing market.

OPEN MARKETS

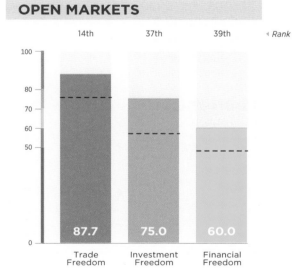

	14th	37th	39th	◄ Rank
	Trade Freedom	Investment Freedom	Financial Freedom	
	87.7	75.0	60.0	

Trade is important to Norway's economy; the value of exports and imports taken together equals 69 percent of GDP. The average applied tariff rate is 1.2 percent, and nontariff barriers restrict agricultural imports. State-owned enterprises distort the economy. Credit is allocated on market terms, and banks offer a wide array of services. The government retains ownership of Norway's largest financial institution.

NORWAY

POLAND

WORLD RANK: **45** | REGIONAL RANK: **21**

ECONOMIC FREEDOM STATUS:
MODERATELY FREE

Poland's economy has demonstrated a fairly high degree of macroeconomic resilience. Structural reforms that have included trade liberalization, implementation of a competitively low corporate tax rate, and modernization of the regulatory environment have facilitated the transition to a market-oriented economy.

Fiscal consolidation and prudent management of public finance are ongoing concerns. The government needs to further reduce the budget deficit and curb the growth of public debt. In 2016, an additional tax on financial-services companies was imposed to help finance increased social spending. Continued reform, particularly in strengthening the independence of the judiciary and eradicating corruption, is needed to ensure greater economic dynamism.

ECONOMIC FREEDOM SCORE

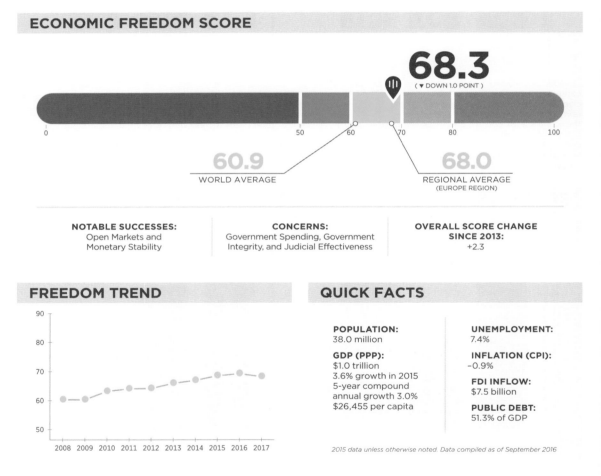

68.3
(▼ DOWN 1.0 POINT)

0   50   60   70   80   100

60.9
WORLD AVERAGE

68.0
REGIONAL AVERAGE
(EUROPE REGION)

NOTABLE SUCCESSES:
Open Markets and
Monetary Stability

CONCERNS:
Government Spending, Government
Integrity, and Judicial Effectiveness

**OVERALL SCORE CHANGE
SINCE 2013:**
+2.3

FREEDOM TREND

90
80
70
60
50

2008 2009 2010 2011 2012 2013 2014 2015 2016 2017

QUICK FACTS

POPULATION:
38.0 million

GDP (PPP):
$1.0 trillion
3.6% growth in 2015
5-year compound
annual growth 3.0%
$26,455 per capita

UNEMPLOYMENT:
7.4%

INFLATION (CPI):
-0.9%

FDI INFLOW:
$7.5 billion

PUBLIC DEBT:
51.3% of GDP

2015 data unless otherwise noted. Data compiled as of September 2016

BACKGROUND: Poland joined NATO in 1999 and the European Union in 2004. The center-right Civic Platform Party was ousted following parliamentary elections in October 2015. The conservative, Eurosceptic Law and Justice Party headed by Prime Minister Beata Szydlo won a parliamentary majority. Buoyed by its strong institutions, Poland was the only European country to experience economic growth during the 2009 credit crisis. Poland hosted the 2016 NATO Summit in Warsaw, and a rotational battalion of U.S. troops is to be deployed to Poland beginning in 2017. The private sector now accounts for two-thirds of GDP. A geographic split exists between a poor rural eastern region and the industrialized, more prosperous western region.

12 ECONOMIC FREEDOMS | POLAND

RULE OF LAW

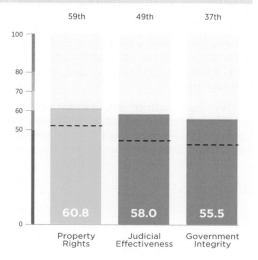

	59th	49th	37th

- Property Rights: 60.8
- Judicial Effectiveness: 58.0
- Government Integrity: 55.5

The legal system protects rights to acquire and dispose of property. The judiciary is independent but also slow to operate and sometimes subject to political pressure. Allegations of corruption occur most frequently in government contracting and the issuance of a regulation or permit that benefits a particular company. Incidents of such behavior have been decreasing and, if proven, are usually punished.

GOVERNMENT SIZE

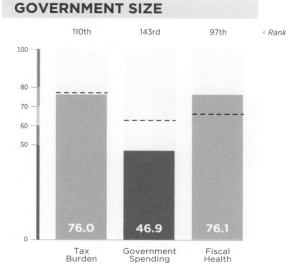

	110th	143rd	97th	◄ Rank

- Tax Burden: 76.0
- Government Spending: 46.9
- Fiscal Health: 76.1

The top income tax rate is 32 percent, and the corporate tax rate is a flat 19 percent. Other taxes include a value-added tax and a property tax. The overall tax burden equals 31.9 percent of total domestic income. Government spending has amounted to 42.1 percent of total output (GDP) over the past three years, and budget deficits have averaged 3.4 percent of GDP. Public debt is equivalent to 51.3 percent of GDP.

REGULATORY EFFICIENCY

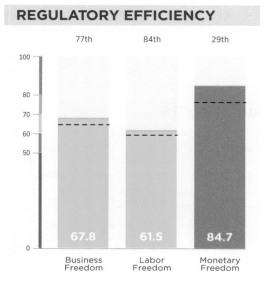

	77th	84th	29th

- Business Freedom: 67.8
- Labor Freedom: 61.5
- Monetary Freedom: 84.7

A new bankruptcy and insolvency code took effect in January 2016. The nonsalary cost of employing a worker is relatively high. Unions exercise considerable influence on contract termination and other labor issues. Poland, the largest recipient of EU subsidies, has few price controls but does administer prices on pharmaceuticals, taxi services, and goods and services in cases that are viewed as threatening the economy.

OPEN MARKETS

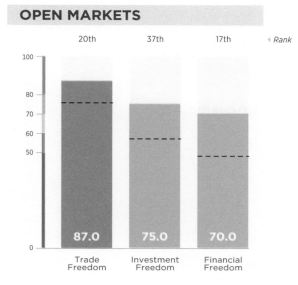

	20th	37th	17th	◄ Rank

- Trade Freedom: 87.0
- Investment Freedom: 75.0
- Financial Freedom: 70.0

Trade is important to Poland's economy; the value of exports and imports taken together equals 96 percent of GDP. The average applied tariff rate is 1.5 percent. Restrictions on ownership of agricultural land took effect in 2016, and state-owned enterprises distort the economy. The financial sector continues to expand. Credit is available on market terms, and foreign investors can access domestic financial markets.

POLAND

PORTUGAL

Portugal continues to face challenges that require urgent economic policy adjustment. Previous reforms, which had helped to modify and diversify the economy's productive base, have lost their momentum. Despite sound institutional settings such as an efficient business framework and an independent judicial system, the indebted and inefficient public sector has worn away the dynamism of the private sector and reduced the economy's overall competitiveness.

Reform priorities include reducing budget deficits that have elevated the level of public debt to more than 100 percent of GDP and enhancing the flexibility of the labor market. However, the pace of reform has slowed. The banking system remains weak.

WORLD RANK: **77** REGIONAL RANK: **33**

ECONOMIC FREEDOM STATUS:
MODERATELY FREE

ECONOMIC FREEDOM SCORE

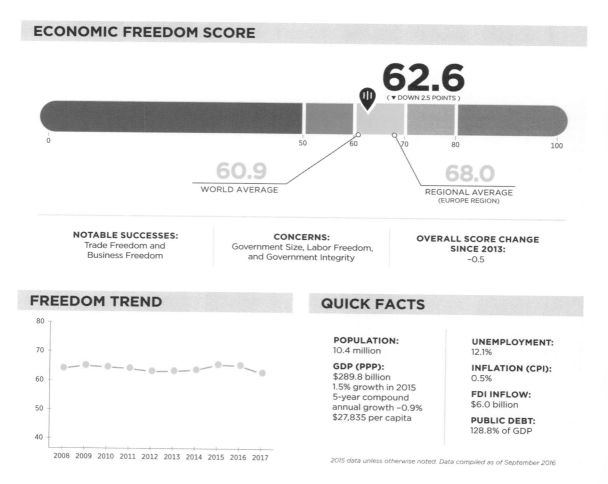

62.6
(▼ DOWN 2.5 POINTS)

0   50   60   70   80   100

60.9
WORLD AVERAGE

68.0
REGIONAL AVERAGE
(EUROPE REGION)

NOTABLE SUCCESSES:
Trade Freedom and
Business Freedom

CONCERNS:
Government Size, Labor Freedom,
and Government Integrity

**OVERALL SCORE CHANGE
SINCE 2013:**
–0.5

FREEDOM TREND

80
70
60
50
40

2008 2009 2010 2011 2012 2013 2014 2015 2016 2017

QUICK FACTS

POPULATION:
10.4 million

GDP (PPP):
$289.8 billion
1.5% growth in 2015
5-year compound
annual growth –0.9%
$27,835 per capita

UNEMPLOYMENT:
12.1%

INFLATION (CPI):
0.5%

FDI INFLOW:
$6.0 billion

PUBLIC DEBT:
128.8% of GDP

2015 data unless otherwise noted. Data compiled as of September 2016

BACKGROUND: The governing center-right coalition won the most seats in the October 2015 parliamentary elections but lost its majority. Shortly thereafter, Socialist former Lisbon Mayor António Costa joined leftist parties in the parliament to topple the government. In November 2015, Costa was appointed prime minister. The anti-austerity government has slowed economic reforms, causing friction with the European Union and International Monetary Fund. Adherence to strict budgetary discipline had allowed Portugal to move beyond the worst of its economic crisis, but growth has slowed, and Portugal failed to meet the EU-mandated deficit reduction target. Unemployment is high, especially among younger Portuguese, many of whom have moved abroad for work.

12 ECONOMIC FREEDOMS | PORTUGAL

RULE OF LAW

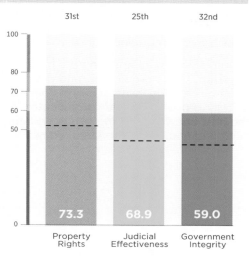

Property Rights	Judicial Effectiveness	Government Integrity
31st	25th	32nd
73.3	68.9	59.0

Registration of property is fairly easy and can be done quickly online. According to the World Bank's 2015 *Doing Business* report, registration is faster and simpler than in most other OECD countries. The constitution provides for an independent judiciary, but staff shortages and inefficiency have contributed to a considerable case backlog. Portugal continued to struggle with corruption scandals during the past year.

GOVERNMENT SIZE

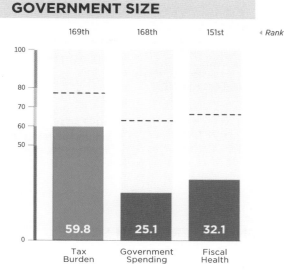

Tax Burden	Government Spending	Fiscal Health	◄ Rank
169th	168th	151st	
59.8	25.1	32.1	

The top personal income tax rate is 48 percent, and the top corporate tax rate is 21 percent. Other taxes include a value-added tax. The overall tax burden equals 34.4 percent of total domestic income. Government spending has amounted to 50 percent of total output (GDP) over the past three years, and budget deficits have averaged 5.5 percent of GDP. Public debt is equivalent to 128.8 percent of GDP.

REGULATORY EFFICIENCY

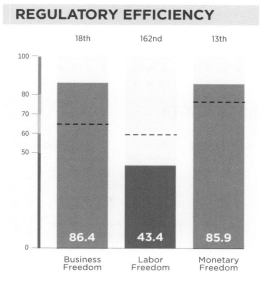

Business Freedom	Labor Freedom	Monetary Freedom
18th	162nd	13th
86.4	43.4	85.9

The overall regulatory framework is efficient. Rules regarding the formation and operation of private enterprises are relatively straightforward. Labor regulations on dismissals and the use of temporary contracts remain burdensome and costly. The continuing inefficient operation of remaining state-owned enterprises requires ongoing subsidization. A multi-year bailout of the banking system has cost the government billions.

OPEN MARKETS

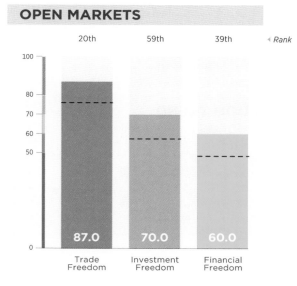

Trade Freedom	Investment Freedom	Financial Freedom	◄ Rank
20th	59th	39th	
87.0	70.0	60.0	

Trade is important to Portugal's economy; the value of exports and imports taken together equals 80 percent of GDP. The average applied tariff rate is 1.5 percent. In general, the government does not screen or discriminate against foreign investment. Despite some progress toward stability, the financial system continues to face substantial risks. The banking sector remains weak, and the share of nonperforming loans is rising.

PORTUGAL

ROMANIA

WORLD RANK:
39

REGIONAL RANK:
20

ECONOMIC FREEDOM STATUS:
MODERATELY FREE

Romania continues to recover from the recent global economic slowdown and has made fiscal sustainability a priority. Economic growth rates have improved, but the benefits have not been felt by all Romanians. The country continues to have the highest poverty rate in the European Union.

Progress on implementing reforms and improving the business environment has been uneven. The unpredictable and uneven regulatory system discourages foreign investors from doing business in Romania. Efforts to privatize state-owned enterprises have stalled in the past two years. Corruption is endemic at all levels of government and undermines the rule of law.

ECONOMIC FREEDOM SCORE

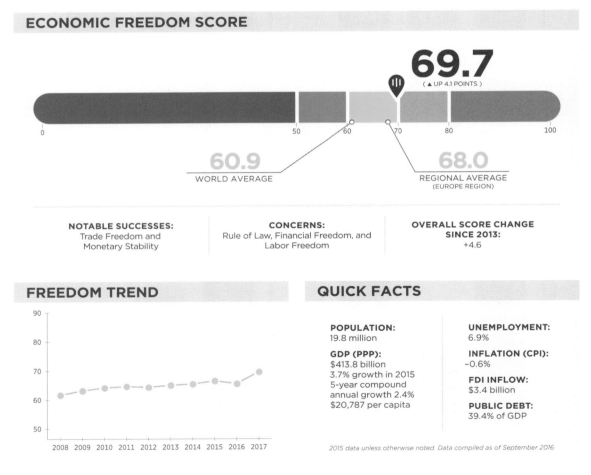

69.7
(▲ UP 4.1 POINTS)

0   50   60   70   80   100

60.9
WORLD AVERAGE

68.0
REGIONAL AVERAGE
(EUROPE REGION)

NOTABLE SUCCESSES:
Trade Freedom and
Monetary Stability

CONCERNS:
Rule of Law, Financial Freedom, and
Labor Freedom

**OVERALL SCORE CHANGE
SINCE 2013:**
+4.6

FREEDOM TREND

90
80
70
60
50

2008 2009 2010 2011 2012 2013 2014 2015 2016 2017

QUICK FACTS

POPULATION:
19.8 million

GDP (PPP):
$413.8 billion
3.7% growth in 2015
5-year compound
annual growth 2.4%
$20,787 per capita

UNEMPLOYMENT:
6.9%

INFLATION (CPI):
−0.6%

FDI INFLOW:
$3.4 billion

PUBLIC DEBT:
39.4% of GDP

2015 data unless otherwise noted. Data compiled as of September 2016

BACKGROUND: Former Prime Minister Victor Ponta of the center-left Social Democrat Party resigned in November 2015 following protests against government corruption that were sparked by a fatal nightclub fire. A caretaker government of technocrats managed the country for about a year until President Klaus Iohannis designated Prime Minister Sorin Grindeanu as the head of a new Social Democrat Party–led coalition government at the end of 2016. Romania's transition to a free-market economy began with the adoption of its new constitution in 1991. In the post–Cold War period, Romania developed closer ties with Western Europe and was accepted into NATO in 2004 and the EU in 2007. In addition to its strategic position on the Black Sea, Romania has extensive natural resources and a productive agriculture sector.

12 ECONOMIC FREEDOMS | ROMANIA

RULE OF LAW

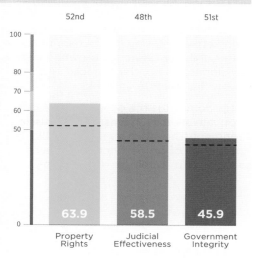

Romania's constitution guarantees the right to ownership of private property, and procedures for the enforcement of contracts have been streamlined. The inadequately resourced courts suffer from chronic corruption and political influence. Under pressure to meet the European Union's anticorruption requirements, authorities charged Prime Minister Victor Ponta with fraud, tax evasion, and money laundering. He resigned from office in November 2015.

GOVERNMENT SIZE

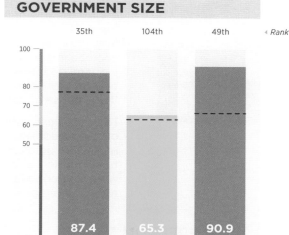

◄ Rank

Both the personal income and corporate tax rates are a flat 16 percent. Other taxes include a value-added tax and an environmental tax. The overall tax burden equals 27.4 percent of total domestic income. Government spending has amounted to 34 percent of total output (GDP) over the past three years, and budget deficits have averaged 1.9 percent of GDP. Public debt is equivalent to 39.4 percent of GDP.

REGULATORY EFFICIENCY

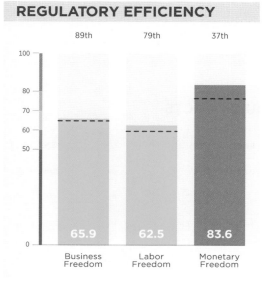

Enforcement of commercial regulations is not always consistent, and efficient procedures and rules for bankruptcy have not been fully implemented. Labor regulations remain rigid, although several amendments to improve the flexibility of the labor code have been adopted. The IMF has urged the government to reform inefficient and subsidized state-owned enterprises in the transportation and energy sectors.

OPEN MARKETS

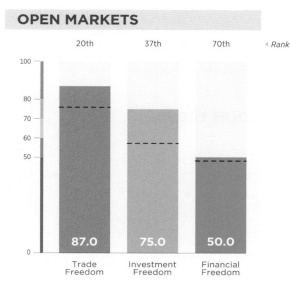

◄ Rank

Trade is important to Romania's economy; the value of exports and imports taken together equals 83 percent of GDP. The average applied tariff rate is 1.5 percent. The government does not screen or discriminate against foreign investment, but the regulatory and judicial systems may be deterrents. The banking sector is relatively sound and stable, with a high degree of capitalization. Foreign-owned banks account for over 70 percent of total assets.

ROMANIA

RUSSIA

Russia's economy is severely hampered by blatant disdain for the rule of law and for the concept of limited government. The private sector remains marginalized by structural and institutional constraints caused by ever-growing government encroachment into the marketplace. Rising inflationary pressure jeopardizes macroeconomic stability. Large state-owned institutions have increased their domination of the financial sector at the expense of private domestic and foreign banks.

The inefficient public sector dominates the economy. The risk of state meddling in the private sector remains high in Russia's repressive political environment. The judiciary is vulnerable to corruption, and the protection of property rights remains weak, undermining prospects for dynamic long-term economic development.

ECONOMIC FREEDOM SCORE

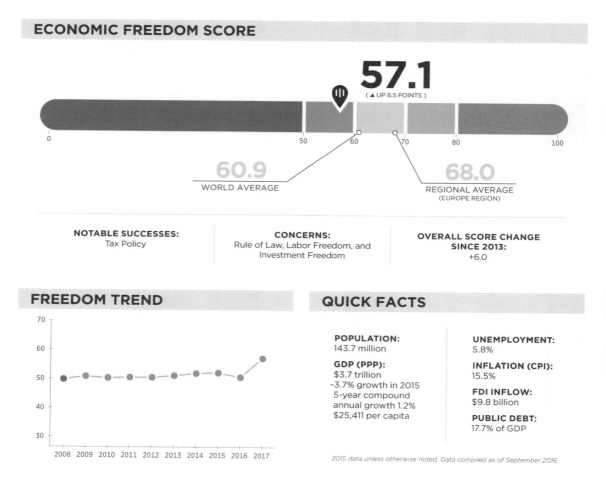

57.1
(▲ UP 6.5 POINTS)

0 — 50 — 60 — 70 — 80 — 100

60.9
WORLD AVERAGE

68.0
REGIONAL AVERAGE
(EUROPE REGION)

NOTABLE SUCCESSES:
Tax Policy

CONCERNS:
Rule of Law, Labor Freedom, and Investment Freedom

OVERALL SCORE CHANGE SINCE 2013:
+6.0

FREEDOM TREND

70

60

50

40

30

2008 2009 2010 2011 2012 2013 2014 2015 2016 2017

QUICK FACTS

POPULATION:
143.7 million

GDP (PPP):
$3.7 trillion
–3.7% growth in 2015
5-year compound
annual growth 1.2%
$25,411 per capita

UNEMPLOYMENT:
5.8%

INFLATION (CPI):
15.5%

FDI INFLOW:
$9.8 billion

PUBLIC DEBT:
17.7% of GDP

2015 data unless otherwise noted. Data compiled as of September 2016

BACKGROUND: Vladimir Putin was reelected president in March 2012 following hotly disputed December 2011 Duma elections. Russia illegally annexed Ukraine's Crimea Peninsula early in 2014 and continues to supply weapons and troops in Ukraine's Donbas region. Western economic sanctions have led to capital outflows. Russia's economy depends heavily on oil and gas exports. The low price of oil, the financial burden of annexing Crimea, and the desire to rearm the Russian military have strained public finances. The economy has been in recession since 2015. Russia's bid to join the Organisation for Economic Co-operation and Development has been postponed as a result of its recent actions in Ukraine.

12 ECONOMIC FREEDOMS | RUSSIA

RULE OF LAW

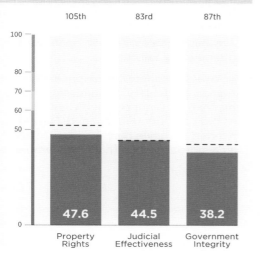

	105th	83rd	87th
	Property Rights	Judicial Effectiveness	Government Integrity
	47.6	44.5	38.2

Weak property rights are a significant impediment to economic progress and a deterrent to foreign investment. The rule of law is not maintained uniformly across the country, and the judiciary is vulnerable to political pressure and inconsistent in applying the law. Corruption in government and the business world is pervasive, and a growing lack of accountability enables bureaucrats to act with impunity.

GOVERNMENT SIZE

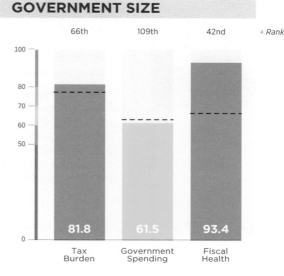

◄ Rank

	66th	109th	42nd
	Tax Burden	Government Spending	Fiscal Health
	81.8	61.5	93.4

The personal income tax rate is a flat 13 percent, and the top corporate tax rate is 20 percent. The overall tax burden equals 35.3 percent of total domestic income. Government spending has amounted to 35.8 percent of total output (GDP) over the past three years, and budget deficits have averaged 1.9 percent of GDP. Public debt is equivalent to 17.7 percent of GDP.

REGULATORY EFFICIENCY

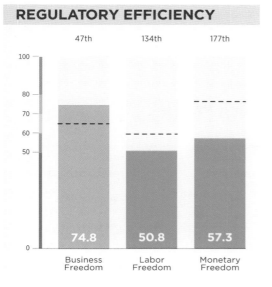

	47th	134th	177th
	Business Freedom	Labor Freedom	Monetary Freedom
	74.8	50.8	57.3

Burdensome regulations continue to hinder private-sector development. The regulatory system suffers from corruption and a lack of transparency. The rigid and outmoded labor code continues to limit employment and productivity growth. Pharmaceuticals are affected by price-setting. The nontransparent processes by which regulators set rates for utilities and transportation have turned rate-making reform into a major political issue.

OPEN MARKETS

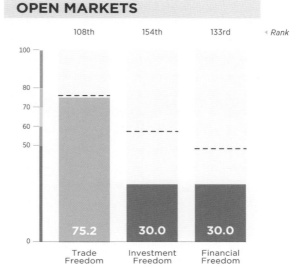

◄ Rank

	108th	154th	133rd
	Trade Freedom	Investment Freedom	Financial Freedom
	75.2	30.0	30.0

Trade is important to Russia's economy; the value of exports and imports taken together equals 51 percent of GDP. The average applied tariff rate is 4.9 percent, and export taxes interfere with trade. Foreign investment is screened, and investment in several sectors of the economy is capped. State-owned enterprises distort the economy. The financial sector is subject to government influence. State-owned banks dominate the banking sector.

RUSSIA

SERBIA

WORLD RANK: 99

REGIONAL RANK: 39

ECONOMIC FREEDOM STATUS: MOSTLY UNFREE

Serbia has implemented significant structural reforms in some parts of its economy. Facilitated by a process involving privatization and consolidation, the once-defunct banking sector has revived and continues to evolve. The economy's competitiveness is supported by low flat tax rates, relative openness to global trade, and ongoing regulatory reforms.

Despite progress, however, overall economic freedom in Serbia continues to be constrained by the lack of political will to undertake the bold reforms that are required. Inefficient government spending remains high and poorly managed. Deeper institutional reforms are needed to tackle bureaucracy, reduce corruption, and strengthen a judicial system that is vulnerable to political interference.

ECONOMIC FREEDOM SCORE

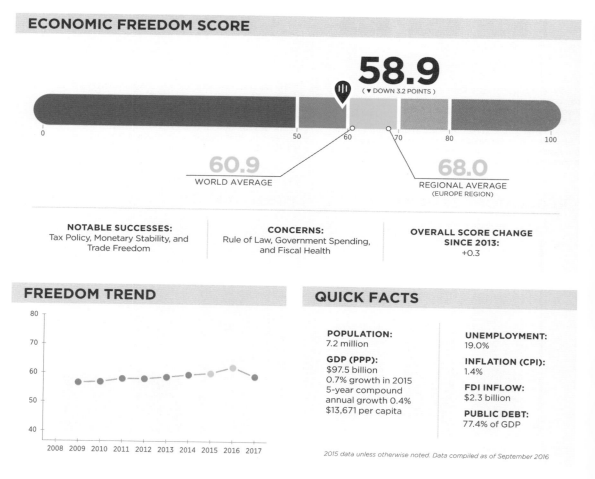

58.9 (▼ DOWN 3.2 POINTS)

0   50   60   70   80   100

60.9 WORLD AVERAGE

68.0 REGIONAL AVERAGE (EUROPE REGION)

NOTABLE SUCCESSES: Tax Policy, Monetary Stability, and Trade Freedom

CONCERNS: Rule of Law, Government Spending, and Fiscal Health

OVERALL SCORE CHANGE SINCE 2013: +0.3

FREEDOM TREND

80
70
60
50
40

2008 2009 2010 2011 2012 2013 2014 2015 2016 2017

QUICK FACTS

POPULATION: 7.2 million

GDP (PPP): $97.5 billion
0.7% growth in 2015
5-year compound annual growth 0.4%
$13,671 per capita

UNEMPLOYMENT: 19.0%

INFLATION (CPI): 1.4%

FDI INFLOW: $2.3 billion

PUBLIC DEBT: 77.4% of GDP

2015 data unless otherwise noted. Data compiled as of September 2016

BACKGROUND: Serbia signed a Stability and Association Agreement with the European Union in 2008 and applied for membership in 2009. An agreement between Serbia and Kosovo normalized relations in April 2013. Prime Minister Aleksandar Vucic's center-right Progressive Party won snap elections in April 2016. Parliamentary elections have been held frequently in Serbia; April's vote was the third election since 2012. Vucic has been in office since April 2014 and has been accused of silencing critical media outlets and opponents. The government supports seeking membership in the EU, but the country has had difficulty balancing its EU aspirations with its historical ties to Russia.

12 ECONOMIC FREEDOMS | SERBIA

RULE OF LAW

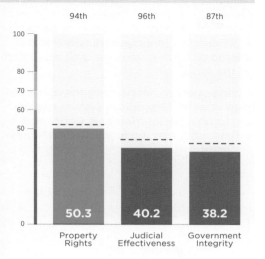

| 94th | 96th | 87th | ◄ Rank |

| Property Rights | Judicial Effectiveness | Government Integrity |
| 50.3 | 40.2 | 38.2 |

Serbian citizens and foreign investors enjoy full rights to ownership of private property, but enforcement of those rights can be extremely slow. The judiciary in Serbia operates independently, but endemic problems continue to plague the judicial system. Corruption remains a problem in many sectors, including the security, education, housing, and labor sectors, as well as in privatization processes and the judiciary.

GOVERNMENT SIZE

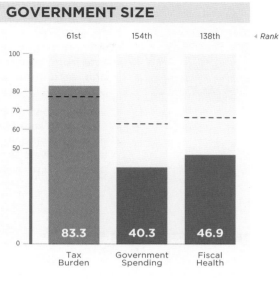

| 61st | 154th | 138th | ◄ Rank |

| Tax Burden | Government Spending | Fiscal Health |
| 83.3 | 40.3 | 46.9 |

The top personal income tax rate is 15 percent, and the corporate tax rate is a flat 15 percent. Other taxes include a value-added tax and a property tax. The overall tax burden equals 35.0 percent of total domestic income. Government spending has amounted to 44.6 percent of total output (GDP) over the past three years, and budget deficits have averaged 5.1 percent of GDP. Public debt is equivalent to 77.4 percent of GDP.

REGULATORY EFFICIENCY

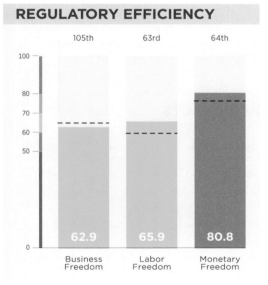

| 105th | 63rd | 64th |

| Business Freedom | Labor Freedom | Monetary Freedom |
| 62.9 | 65.9 | 80.8 |

Despite some progress in streamlining the process for launching a business, other time-consuming requirements reduce the regulatory system's efficiency. In an effort to make the labor market more flexible, the government recently introduced amendments to the rigid labor law that was implemented in 2005. The IMF program for Serbia emphasizes rationalization of state-owned enterprises to cut subsidies, but reforms are lagging.

OPEN MARKETS

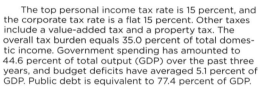
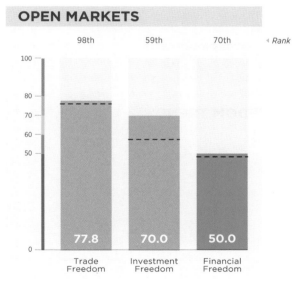

| 98th | 59th | 70th | ◄ Rank |

| Trade Freedom | Investment Freedom | Financial Freedom |
| 77.8 | 70.0 | 50.0 |

Trade is extremely important to Serbia's economy; the value of exports and imports taken together equals 105 percent of GDP. The average applied tariff rate is 6.1 percent. Legislation in 2015 liberalized Serbia's foreign investment climate, but state-owned enterprises distort the economy. Financial intermediation is relatively low, and the percentage of nonperforming loans in banks is one of the highest in the region.

SLOVAKIA

Openness to global trade and investment, facilitated by improvements in regulatory efficiency, has aided Slovakia's transition to a more market-based system. Recent changes in corporate taxation include reduction of the top corporate tax rate from 22 percent to 21 percent. Continued transformation and restructuring are needed to capitalize on the well-educated labor force and broaden the production base.

Progress on combating corruption and enhancing the quality of the public sector has been uneven. The judicial system remains inefficient and vulnerable to political interference. Corruption is still perceived as widespread, undermining judicial effectiveness and public trust in government.

ECONOMIC FREEDOM SCORE

65.7
(▼ DOWN 0.9 POINT)

0   50   60   70   80   100

60.9
WORLD AVERAGE

68.0
REGIONAL AVERAGE
(EUROPE REGION)

NOTABLE SUCCESSES:
Open Markets and Monetary Stability

CONCERNS:
Judicial Effectiveness, Government Integrity, and Government Spending

OVERALL SCORE CHANGE SINCE 2013:
–3.0

FREEDOM TREND

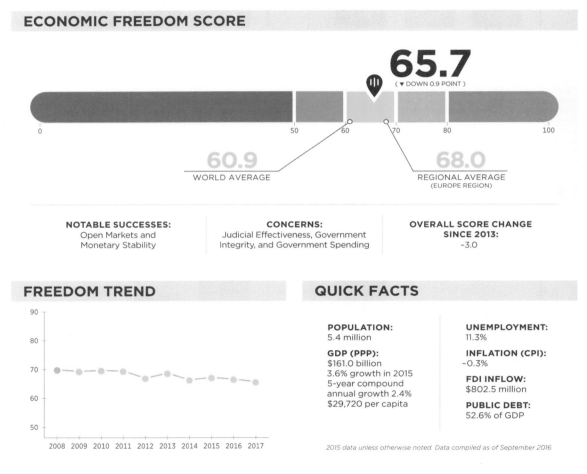

90
80
70
60
50

2008 2009 2010 2011 2012 2013 2014 2015 2016 2017

QUICK FACTS

POPULATION:
5.4 million

GDP (PPP):
$161.0 billion
3.6% growth in 2015
5-year compound annual growth 2.4%
$29,720 per capita

UNEMPLOYMENT:
11.3%

INFLATION (CPI):
–0.3%

FDI INFLOW:
$802.5 million

PUBLIC DEBT:
52.6% of GDP

2015 data unless otherwise noted. Data compiled as of September 2016

BACKGROUND: After Slovakia gained independence in 1993, market reforms made it one of Europe's rising economic stars. The country entered the European Union in 2004 and has been part of the eurozone since 2009. Unemployment remains high; 25 percent of young people are unemployed. Prime Minister Robert Fico has been in office since 2012. His center-left Direction-Social Democracy Party lost its parliamentary majority in March 2016 but returned to power as leader of a coalition government with three other parties. Andrej Kiska was elected president in 2014 as an Independent. Slovakia, which has rebuffed EU plans for mandatory migrant quotas, took over the rotating presidency of the Council of the European Union in July 2016.

12 ECONOMIC FREEDOMS | SLOVAKIA

RULE OF LAW

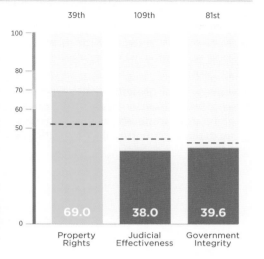

	39th	109th	81st
	Property Rights **69.0**	Judicial Effectiveness **38.0**	Government Integrity **39.6**

Secured interests in property and contractual rights are enforced. The constitution provides for an independent judiciary, but despite some reforms, the court system continues to suffer from corruption, intimidation of judges, and a significant backlog of cases. Concerns about corruption and a lack of government transparency contributed to the disappointing election results for the mainstream political parties in the March 2016 election.

GOVERNMENT SIZE

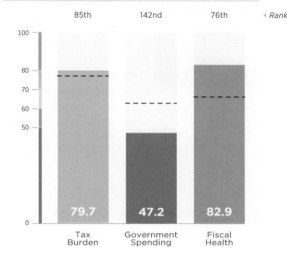

	85th	142nd	76th	◄ Rank
	Tax Burden **79.7**	Government Spending **47.2**	Fiscal Health **82.9**	

The top individual income tax rate is 25 percent, and the top corporate tax rate is 21 percent. Other taxes include a value-added tax and a property tax. The overall tax burden equals 31.0 percent of total domestic income. Government spending has amounted to 42 percent of total output (GDP) over the past three years, and budget deficits have averaged 2.7 percent of GDP. Public debt is equivalent to 52.6 percent of GDP.

REGULATORY EFFICIENCY

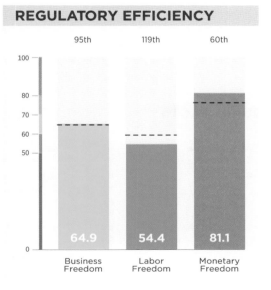

	95th	119th	60th
	Business Freedom **64.9**	Labor Freedom **54.4**	Monetary Freedom **81.1**

The process for launching a private enterprise is more streamlined, and licensing requirements have become less burdensome. The nonsalary cost of employing a worker is moderate. The severance payment system is not burdensome, but regulations on work hours remain relatively rigid. Although fuel prices at the pump are fully liberalized and determined by the market, the government adopted a €50 million "natural gas cash rebate" for households in 2016.

OPEN MARKETS

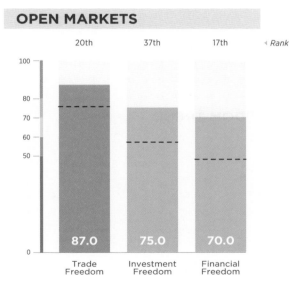

	20th	37th	17th	◄ Rank
	Trade Freedom **87.0**	Investment Freedom **75.0**	Financial Freedom **70.0**	

Trade is extremely important to the Slovak Republic's economy; the value of exports and imports taken together equals 185 percent of GDP. The average applied tariff rate is 1.5 percent. There is no general screening of or discrimination against foreign investment, but state-owned enterprises distort the economy. Most state-owned banks have been sold, and the presence of foreign banks is strong. Capital markets remain relatively small.

SLOVAKIA

SLOVENIA

WORLD RANK: **97** REGIONAL RANK: **38**

ECONOMIC FREEDOM STATUS:
MOSTLY UNFREE

Slovenia's record on structural reform has been uneven, and institutional weaknesses continue to undermine prospects for long-term economic development. In particular, the judicial system remains inefficient and vulnerable to political interference. Corruption continues to be perceived as widespread.

The overall regulatory framework has gradually been evolving to promote the emergence of a more vibrant private sector and encourage broad-based employment growth. Slovenia enjoys a comparatively high degree of trade freedom as tariff rates are quite low, but economic gains from trade are undercut by the lack of progress in the financial and investment areas, which are critical to sustaining open markets.

ECONOMIC FREEDOM SCORE

59.2
(▼ DOWN 1.4 POINTS)

0   50   60   70   80   100

60.9
WORLD AVERAGE

68.0
REGIONAL AVERAGE
(EUROPE REGION)

NOTABLE SUCCESSES:
Trade Freedom and
Monetary Stability

CONCERNS:
Government Size, Judicial
Effectiveness, and
Government Integrity

**OVERALL SCORE CHANGE
SINCE 2013:**
–2.5

FREEDOM TREND

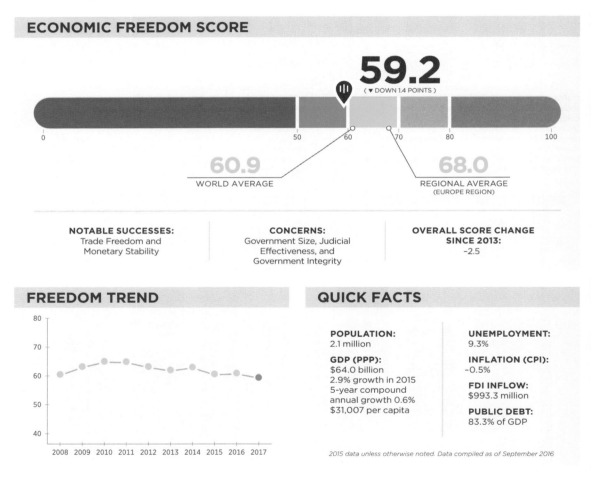

80
70
60
50
40

2008 2009 2010 2011 2012 2013 2014 2015 2016 2017

QUICK FACTS

POPULATION:
2.1 million

GDP (PPP):
$64.0 billion
2.9% growth in 2015
5-year compound
annual growth 0.6%
$31,007 per capita

UNEMPLOYMENT:
9.3%

INFLATION (CPI):
–0.5%

FDI INFLOW:
$993.3 million

PUBLIC DEBT:
83.3% of GDP

2015 data unless otherwise noted. Data compiled as of September 2016

BACKGROUND: Slovenia joined the European Union and NATO in 2004, adopted the euro in 2007, and joined the Organisation for Economic Co-operation and Development in 2010. Heavily affected by Europe's financial crisis, Slovenia staved off the need for international aid through a $3.5 billion package of bailouts for largely state-owned banks. Political instability has slowed the pace of privatization. Prime Minister Miro Cerar leads a center-left coalition government. His Modern Centre Party (SMC), a center-left party, won a plurality of seats in parliament in July 2014. Slovenia has been challenged by high numbers of migrants traversing the country and put tougher border restrictions in place in March 2016.

12 ECONOMIC FREEDOMS | SLOVENIA

RULE OF LAW

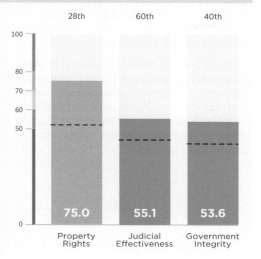

28th   60th   40th

| 75.0 | 55.1 | 53.6 |

Property Rights   Judicial Effectiveness   Government Integrity

Virtually all land has a clear title. Enforcement of private property rights is slow, but improved procedures and fee reductions have made transfers of property easier. The judicial system is sound and transparent but comparatively inefficient and inadequately resourced. Corruption, less prevalent in Slovenia than in many of its neighbors, often takes the form of conflicts of interest involving contracts between government officials and private businesses.

GOVERNMENT SIZE

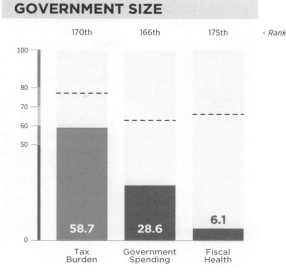

170th   166th   175th   ◄ Rank

| 58.7 | 28.6 | 6.1 |

Tax Burden   Government Spending   Fiscal Health

The top individual income tax rate is 50 percent, and the top corporate tax rate is 17 percent. Other taxes include a value-added tax and a property transfer tax. The overall tax burden equals 36.6 percent of total domestic income. Government spending has amounted to 48.8 percent of total output (GDP) over the past three years, and budget deficits have averaged 7.7 percent of GDP. Public debt is equivalent to 83.3 percent of GDP.

REGULATORY EFFICIENCY

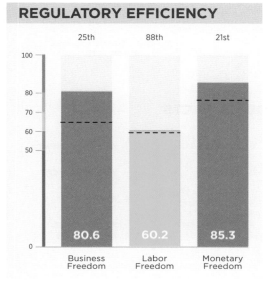

25th   88th   21st

| 80.6 | 60.2 | 85.3 |

Business Freedom   Labor Freedom   Monetary Freedom

Despite progress in streamlining the process for launching a business, other time-consuming requirements reduce the regulatory system's efficiency. The labor market remains saddled with rigid labor regulations that hamper dynamic employment growth. To rationalize public spending, the government is privatizing several state-run companies, but the reform process has been slow and complicated.

OPEN MARKETS

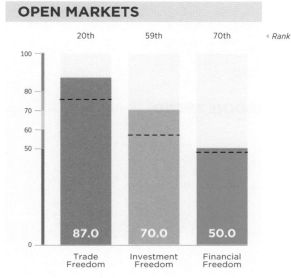

20th   59th   70th   ◄ Rank

| 87.0 | 70.0 | 50.0 |

Trade Freedom   Investment Freedom   Financial Freedom

Trade is extremely important to Slovenia's economy; the value of exports and imports taken together equals 146 percent of GDP. The average applied tariff rate is 1.5 percent. In general, foreign and domestic investors are treated equally under the law, but the regulatory and judicial systems may impede investment. Equity financing remains difficult for start-ups and smaller companies. Capital markets are relatively underdeveloped.

SLOVENIA

SPAIN

WORLD RANK: **69** | **REGIONAL RANK:** **31**

ECONOMIC FREEDOM STATUS:
MODERATELY FREE

Spain's economy has experienced a notable rebound facilitated by structural reforms. Ongoing efforts have focused on reducing the inefficient and oversized government sector and reforming the labor market. Top income tax rates on individuals and corporations have been lowered as well.

Spain's ongoing economic recovery, however, remains highly vulnerable to challenges related to ensuring fiscal stability and restoring the financial sector's competitiveness. Despite relatively sound economic institutions and transparent regulatory and judicial systems, the indebted public sector is still a drag on overall economic dynamism. A lack of progress in fiscal consolidation has resulted in a high level of public debt that is close to the size of the economy.

ECONOMIC FREEDOM SCORE

63.6
(▼ DOWN 4.9 POINTS)

0   50   60   70   80   100

60.9
WORLD AVERAGE

68.0
REGIONAL AVERAGE
(EUROPE REGION)

NOTABLE SUCCESSES:
Open Markets and Monetary Stability

CONCERNS:
Fiscal Health, Government Spending, and Judicial Effectiveness

OVERALL SCORE CHANGE SINCE 2013:
–4.4

FREEDOM TREND

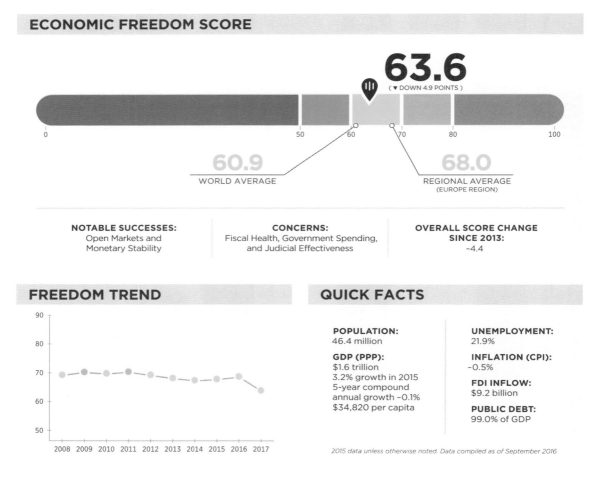

90
80
70
60
50

2008 2009 2010 2011 2012 2013 2014 2015 2016 2017

QUICK FACTS

POPULATION:
46.4 million

GDP (PPP):
$1.6 trillion
3.2% growth in 2015
5-year compound annual growth –0.1%
$34,820 per capita

UNEMPLOYMENT:
21.9%

INFLATION (CPI):
–0.5%

FDI INFLOW:
$9.2 billion

PUBLIC DEBT:
99.0% of GDP

2015 data unless otherwise noted. Data compiled as of September 2016

BACKGROUND: Although Prime Minister Mariano Rajoy's conservative Popular Party won a decisive plurality of parliamentary seats among the four major parties in the June 2016 elections, it did not secure an outright majority. Rajoy was not able to form a minority government to begin his second term in office until October. Despite the political turmoil, Spain's economic growth in 2016 was the fastest in the eurozone and new jobs were created. Nevertheless, unemployment remains a major problem, especially for young job-seekers, due to Spain's excessively rigid labor laws. Other problems include high debt levels, unsustainable pension obligations, and over-spending by regional governments.

12 ECONOMIC FREEDOMS | SPAIN

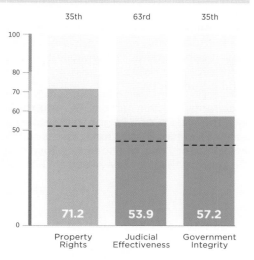

RULE OF LAW

	35th	63rd	35th
	71.2	53.9	57.2
	Property Rights	Judicial Effectiveness	Government Integrity

Spanish law protects property rights, although enforcement of contracts is slow. The courts have a solid record of investigating and prosecuting cases of corruption, but their high workload means that they are often overburdened. Spain enforces anticorruption laws on a generally uniform basis. In addition to public officials, several wealthy and well-connected business executives have been prosecuted successfully for corruption.

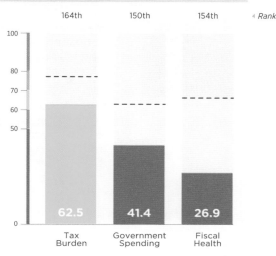

GOVERNMENT SIZE

	164th	150th	154th	◄ Rank
	62.5	41.4	26.9	
	Tax Burden	Government Spending	Fiscal Health	

The top individual income tax rate has been cut to 45 percent, and the top corporate tax rate has been cut to 25 percent. Other taxes include a value-added tax. The overall tax burden equals 33.2 percent of total domestic income. Government spending has amounted to 44.2 percent of total output (GDP) over the past three years, and budget deficits have averaged 5.8 percent of GDP. Public debt is equivalent to 99.0 percent of GDP.

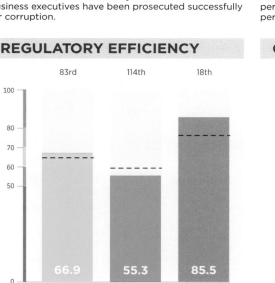

REGULATORY EFFICIENCY

	83rd	114th	18th
	66.9	55.3	85.5
	Business Freedom	Labor Freedom	Monetary Freedom

Procedures for setting up a business have been streamlined, and the number of licensing requirements has been reduced. Despite some progress, labor regulations remain restrictive. Price controls have all but disappeared except in sectors still controlled by the national government, such as farm insurance, stamps, public transport, and medicines. Regional governments also control a few prices in their jurisdictions.

OPEN MARKETS

	20th	9th	17th	◄ Rank
	87.0	85.0	70.0	
	Trade Freedom	Investment Freedom	Financial Freedom	

Trade is important to Spain's economy; the value of exports and imports taken together equals 64 percent of GDP. The average applied tariff rate is 1.5 percent. In general, foreign and domestic investors are treated equally under the law, and most sectors of the economy are open to foreign investment. The financial sector continues to improve its overall conditions, with the banking sector regaining stability. The share of nonperforming loans remains high.

SPAIN

SWEDEN

Sweden's economy performs notably well in regulatory efficiency, with open-market policies that sustain flexibility, competitiveness, and large flows of trade and investment. The transparent and efficient regulatory environment encourages robust entrepreneurial activity. Banking regulations are sensible, and lending practices have been prudent. The legal system provides strong protection for property rights, buttressing judicial effectiveness and government integrity.

Government spending accounts for over half of GDP, and the tax regime needed to finance the wide scope of government has become more burdensome. However, institutional assets such as high degrees of business efficiency and transparency have counterbalanced some of the shortcomings of heavy social spending.

WORLD RANK: **19** | REGIONAL RANK: **10**

ECONOMIC FREEDOM STATUS:
MOSTLY FREE

ECONOMIC FREEDOM SCORE

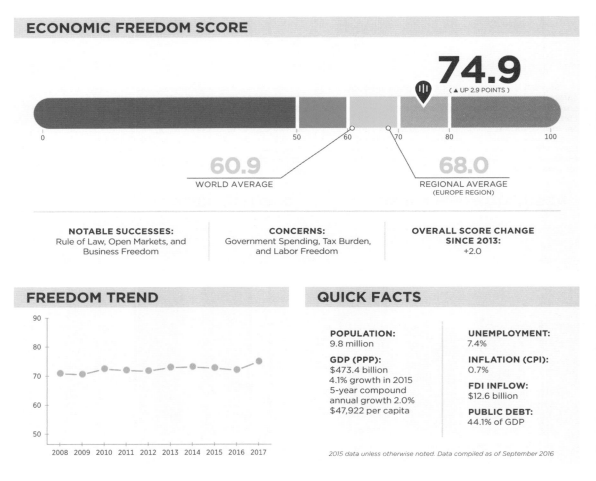

74.9
(▲ UP 2.9 POINTS)

0   50   60   70   80   100

60.9
WORLD AVERAGE

68.0
REGIONAL AVERAGE
(EUROPE REGION)

NOTABLE SUCCESSES:	CONCERNS:	OVERALL SCORE CHANGE
Rule of Law, Open Markets, and Business Freedom	Government Spending, Tax Burden, and Labor Freedom	SINCE 2013: +2.0

FREEDOM TREND

QUICK FACTS

POPULATION:
9.8 million

GDP (PPP):
$473.4 billion
4.1% growth in 2015
5-year compound
annual growth 2.0%
$47,922 per capita

UNEMPLOYMENT:
7.4%

INFLATION (CPI):
0.7%

FDI INFLOW:
$12.6 billion

PUBLIC DEBT:
44.1% of GDP

2015 data unless otherwise noted. Data compiled as of September 2016

BACKGROUND: Sweden joined the European Union in 1995 but rejected adoption of the euro in 2003. The public opposes membership in the eurozone. A general election was held in September 2014. After difficult negotiations, a new center-left Social Democratic Party–Green Party coalition government took office, led by Prime Minister Stefan Löfven. The government has cut spending and increased borrowing to cover the surging costs of unprecedented numbers of migrant arrivals in Sweden. Due to a number of security incidents in the region that have been linked to Russia, the debate about possible NATO membership has resurfaced, but it remains unlikely that Sweden will join the alliance in the near future.

12 ECONOMIC FREEDOMS | SWEDEN

RULE OF LAW

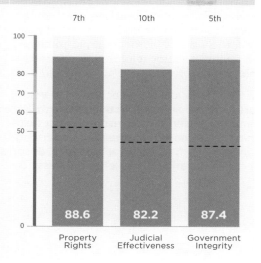

7th   10th   5th

Property Rights: 88.6
Judicial Effectiveness: 82.2
Government Integrity: 87.4

Property rights and enforcement of contracts are very secure. The rule of law is well maintained. The judicial system operates independently, impartially, and consistently. Rates of corruption are low, and Sweden was ranked third out of 168 countries and territories surveyed in Transparency International's 2015 *Corruption Perceptions Index*. Effective anticorruption measures discourage bribery of public officials and uphold government integrity.

GOVERNMENT SIZE

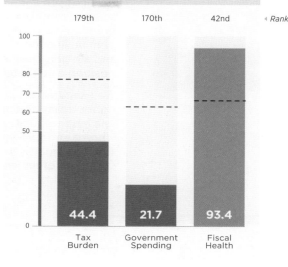

179th   170th   42nd   ◄ Rank

Tax Burden: 44.4
Government Spending: 21.7
Fiscal Health: 93.4

The top personal income tax rate is 57 percent, and the top corporate tax rate is 22 percent. Other taxes include a value-added tax and a capital gains tax. The overall tax burden equals 42.7 percent of total domestic income. Government spending has amounted to 51.1 percent of total output (GDP) over the past three years, and budget deficits have averaged 1.3 percent of GDP. Public debt is equivalent to 44.1 percent of GDP.

REGULATORY EFFICIENCY

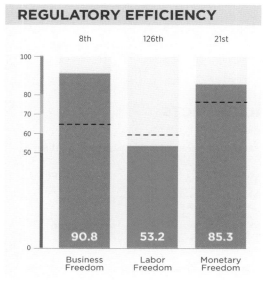

8th   126th   21st

Business Freedom: 90.8
Labor Freedom: 53.2
Monetary Freedom: 85.3

The efficient regulatory framework strongly facilitates entrepreneurial activity, allowing business formation and operation to be dynamic and innovative. The nonsalary cost of employing a worker is high, and dismissing an employee is costly and burdensome. There are few price controls, but state-owned liquor stores set prices for alcohol. The northern part of the country receives agriculture subsidies from the EU.

OPEN MARKETS

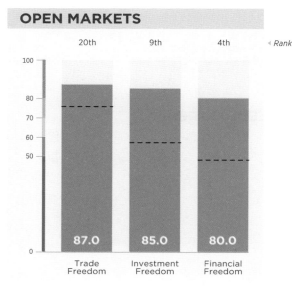

20th   9th   4th   ◄ Rank

Trade Freedom: 87.0
Investment Freedom: 85.0
Financial Freedom: 80.0

Trade is important to Sweden's economy; the value of exports and imports taken together equals 86 percent of GDP. The average applied tariff rate is 1.5 percent. Sweden is relatively open to foreign investment, but numerous state-owned enterprises distort the economy. Regulation of the financial system is transparent and largely consistent with international norms. Banks offer a full range of financial services.

SWEDEN

SWITZERLAND

WORLD RANK: 4 | **REGIONAL RANK:** 1

ECONOMIC FREEDOM STATUS:
FREE

Switzerland's openness to foreign trade and investment continues to stimulate a dynamic and resilient economy. With a sound regulatory environment and minimal barriers to entrepreneurial growth, the Swiss economy is one of the most competitive and innovative in the world. Macroeconomic stability and a highly developed financial sector reinforce the country's position as a global financial hub.

Well-secured property rights, including intellectual property rights, promote entrepreneurship and productivity growth. Flexible labor regulations and the absence of corruption also sustain vibrant entrepreneurship. Inflationary pressures are under control. The legal system, independent of political influence, ensures strong enforcement of contracts and judicial effectiveness.

ECONOMIC FREEDOM SCORE

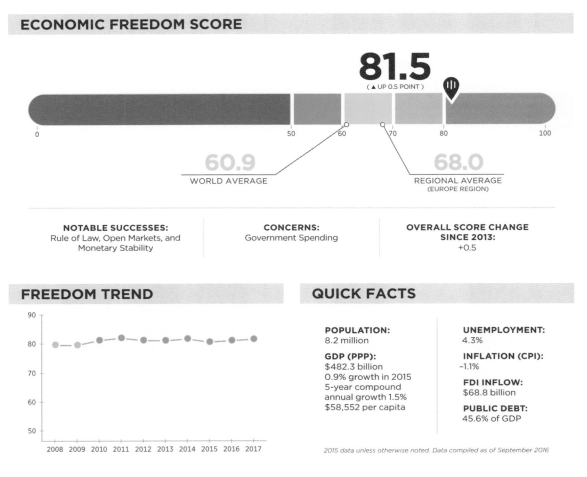

81.5
(▲ UP 0.5 POINT)

0   50   60   70   80   100

60.9
WORLD AVERAGE

68.0
REGIONAL AVERAGE
(EUROPE REGION)

NOTABLE SUCCESSES:
Rule of Law, Open Markets, and Monetary Stability

CONCERNS:
Government Spending

OVERALL SCORE CHANGE SINCE 2013:
+0.5

FREEDOM TREND

90
80
70
60
50

2008 2009 2010 2011 2012 2013 2014 2015 2016 2017

QUICK FACTS

POPULATION:
8.2 million

GDP (PPP):
$482.3 billion
0.9% growth in 2015
5-year compound
annual growth 1.5%
$58,552 per capita

UNEMPLOYMENT:
4.3%

INFLATION (CPI):
–1.1%

FDI INFLOW:
$68.8 billion

PUBLIC DEBT:
45.6% of GDP

2015 data unless otherwise noted. Data compiled as of September 2016

BACKGROUND: Switzerland's federal system of government disperses power widely, and executive authority is exercised by the seven-member Federal Council. Switzerland has a long tradition of openness to the world but jealously guards its independence and neutrality. It did not join the United Nations until 2002, and two referenda on membership in the European Union have failed by wide margins. Membership in the European Economic Area was rejected by referendum in 1992. The Eurosceptic Swiss People's Party, which favors tight controls on immigration, gained the largest number of seats in October 2015 parliamentary elections. In addition to banking, the economy relies heavily on precision manufacturing, metals, pharmaceuticals, chemicals, and electronics.

12 ECONOMIC FREEDOMS | SWITZERLAND

RULE OF LAW

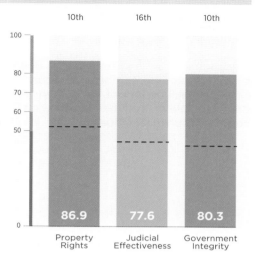

10th	16th	10th
86.9	77.6	80.3
Property Rights	Judicial Effectiveness	Government Integrity

Protection of property rights is strongly enforced, and an independent and fair judicial system is institutionalized throughout the economy. Intellectual property rights are respected and enforced. Commercial and bankruptcy laws are applied consistently and efficiently. The government is free from pervasive corruption. Switzerland was ranked first in the World Economic Forum's 2016 *Global Competitiveness Index*, in part because of its strong institutions.

GOVERNMENT SIZE

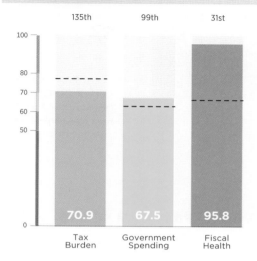

135th	99th	31st	◂ *Rank*
70.9	67.5	95.8	
Tax Burden	Government Spending	Fiscal Health	

Taxation is more burdensome at the cantonal levels than at the federal level. The top federal income tax rate is 11.5 percent, and the federal corporate tax rate is 8.5 percent. The overall tax burden equals 27.1 percent of total domestic income. Government spending has amounted to 32.9 percent of total output (GDP) over the past three years, and budget deficits have averaged 0.2 percent of GDP. Public debt is equivalent to 45.6 percent of GDP.

REGULATORY EFFICIENCY

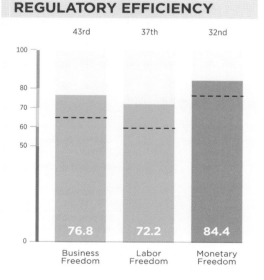

43rd	37th	32nd
76.8	72.2	84.4
Business Freedom	Labor Freedom	Monetary Freedom

The competitive and transparent regulatory framework strongly supports commercial activity, allowing the processes of business formation and operation to be efficient and dynamic. The nonsalary cost of employing a worker is moderate, but dismissing an employee can be costly. The government has the ability to intervene if it believes there is monopolistic pricing. Price and margin controls exist for all agricultural goods.

OPEN MARKETS

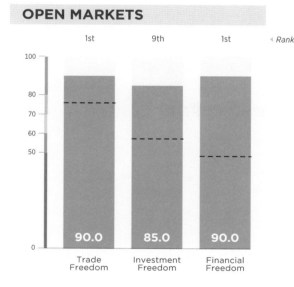

1st	9th	1st	◂ *Rank*
90.0	85.0	90.0	
Trade Freedom	Investment Freedom	Financial Freedom	

Trade is extremely important to Switzerland's economy; the value of exports and imports taken together equals 115 percent of GDP. The average applied tariff rate is 0.0 percent, but agricultural imports face barriers. In general, Switzerland's economy is open to foreign investment. The modern and highly developed financial sector provides a wide range of financing instruments. Banking remains well capitalized and sound.

SWITZERLAND

 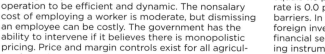

TURKEY

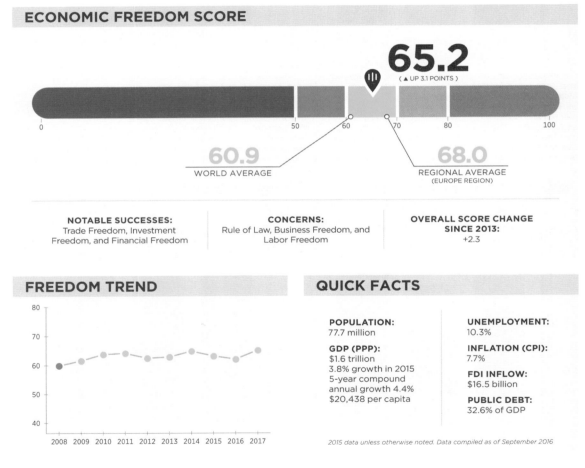

Turkey's economy has maintained overall macroeconomic stability despite ongoing political turmoil. Fiscal policy has been fairly prudent and has kept budget deficits and public debt under control, but inflationary pressures have increased. The financial sector remains stable and competitive.

However, prospects for economic growth in Turkey have been notably affected by political developments since the second half of 2016. Critical challenges include lack of transparency in government and erosion of the rule of law. The judicial system has become more susceptible to political influence.

WORLD RANK: **60** **REGIONAL RANK:** **29**

ECONOMIC FREEDOM STATUS:
MODERATELY FREE

ECONOMIC FREEDOM SCORE

65.2
(▲ UP 3.1 POINTS)

0 — 50 — 60 — 70 — 80 — 100

60.9
WORLD AVERAGE

68.0
REGIONAL AVERAGE
(EUROPE REGION)

NOTABLE SUCCESSES:
Trade Freedom, Investment Freedom, and Financial Freedom

CONCERNS:
Rule of Law, Business Freedom, and Labor Freedom

OVERALL SCORE CHANGE SINCE 2013:
+2.3

FREEDOM TREND

80
70
60
50
40

2008 2009 2010 2011 2012 2013 2014 2015 2016 2017

QUICK FACTS

POPULATION:
77.7 million

GDP (PPP):
$1.6 trillion
3.8% growth in 2015
5-year compound
annual growth 4.4%
$20,438 per capita

UNEMPLOYMENT:
10.3%

INFLATION (CPI):
7.7%

FDI INFLOW:
$16.5 billion

PUBLIC DEBT:
32.6% of GDP

2015 data unless otherwise noted. Data compiled as of September 2016

BACKGROUND: Turkey is a constitutionally secular republic, but President Recep Tayyip Erdogan's Justice and Development Party is pushing an Islamist agenda and eroding Turkey's Euro–Atlantic relations by cracking down on freedom of speech and the media. Elections held in June 2015 resulted in a hung parliament, but snap elections in November 2015 gave Erdogan's party a slim majority. An attempted military coup in July 2016 proved to be unsuccessful. During the subsequent state of emergency, Erdogan consolidated power by dismissing or arresting tens of thousands of public officials. Turkey has been a member of NATO since 1952. The European Union granted the country candidate status in 1999, but there is strong opposition from France, Germany, and Austria.

12 ECONOMIC FREEDOMS | TURKEY

RULE OF LAW

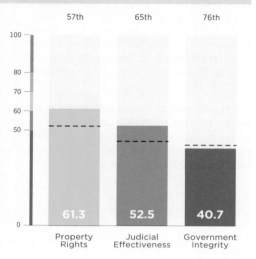

	57th	65th	76th
	Property Rights	Judicial Effectiveness	Government Integrity
	61.3	52.5	40.7

Property rights are generally enforced, although the courts are slow. The judiciary is independent but has shown that it can be swayed by the executive through appointments, promotions, and financing. That influence intensified after President Erdogan's purges of the military, judiciary, and police in the wake of the failed July 2016 military coup. Corruption, cronyism, and nepotism in government and in daily life are growing concerns.

GOVERNMENT SIZE

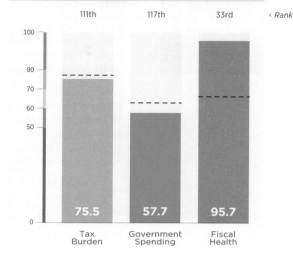

111th 117th 33rd ◀ Rank

	Tax Burden	Government Spending	Fiscal Health
	75.5	57.7	95.7

The top personal income tax rate is 35 percent, and the top corporate tax rate is 20 percent. Other taxes include a value-added tax and an environment tax. The overall tax burden equals 28.7 percent of total domestic income. Government spending has amounted to 37.6 percent of total output (GDP) over the past three years, and budget deficits have averaged 1.2 percent of GDP. Public debt is equivalent to 32.6 percent of GDP.

REGULATORY EFFICIENCY

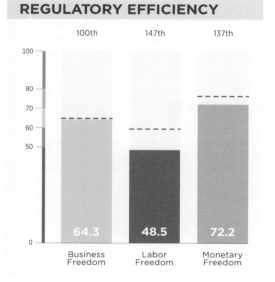

	100th	147th	137th
	Business Freedom	Labor Freedom	Monetary Freedom
	64.3	48.5	72.2

Bureaucratic red tape and ineffective enforcement of regulations continue to be substantial drags on entrepreneurship. The rigidity of the labor market limits the emergence of a more dynamic economy. The statutory minimum wage was raised by approximately 30 percent in January 2016. The government sets prices for products provided by state-owned enterprises and controls prices for some agricultural products and electricity.

OPEN MARKETS

88th 37th 39th ◀ Rank

	Trade Freedom	Investment Freedom	Financial Freedom
	79.4	75.0	60.0

Trade is important to Turkey's economy; the value of exports and imports taken together equals 59 percent of GDP. The average applied tariff rate is 2.8 percent. There is no general screening of or discrimination against foreign investment, and many state-owned enterprises have been privatized. The banking sector, which dominates the financial system, remains well capitalized and resilient. The presence of foreign banks is relatively small.

TURKEY

UKRAINE

Ukraine's economy has contracted deeply and remains very fragile. Ongoing disruptions of the country's productive and export capacities and significant capital outflows have put increasing pressure on the currency and reserves, severely undermining monetary stability. The overall soundness of fiscal policy has deteriorated substantially, and public deficits and debt have increased sharply. The rule of law remains fragile and is further undercut by judicial ineffectiveness.

A strong commitment to structural reforms to reduce corruption and open the economy further to Western investment and financial institutions will be crucial in helping to stabilize the economy. The government has launched a comprehensive set of reforms to restore growth, but progress is not yet evident.

ECONOMIC FREEDOM SCORE

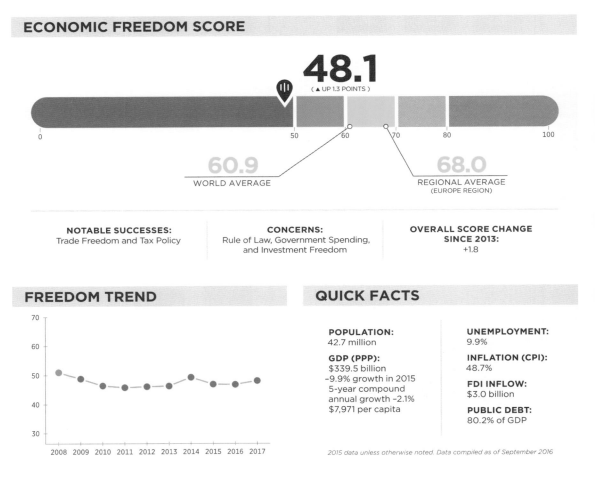

48.1
(▲ UP 1.3 POINTS)

0   50   60   70   80   100

60.9
WORLD AVERAGE

68.0
REGIONAL AVERAGE
(EUROPE REGION)

NOTABLE SUCCESSES:
Trade Freedom and Tax Policy

CONCERNS:
Rule of Law, Government Spending, and Investment Freedom

OVERALL SCORE CHANGE SINCE 2013:
+1.8

FREEDOM TREND

70
60
50
40
30

2008 2009 2010 2011 2012 2013 2014 2015 2016 2017

QUICK FACTS

POPULATION:
42.7 million

GDP (PPP):
$339.5 billion
–9.9% growth in 2015
5-year compound annual growth –2.1%
$7,971 per capita

UNEMPLOYMENT:
9.9%

INFLATION (CPI):
48.7%

FDI INFLOW:
$3.0 billion

PUBLIC DEBT:
80.2% of GDP

2015 data unless otherwise noted. Data compiled as of September 2016

BACKGROUND: Ukraine gained independence after the Soviet Union collapsed in 1991. Pro-Euro–Atlantic members of parliament ousted President Victor Yanukovych in February 2014, and Petro Poroshenko was elected to replace him in May. Parliamentary elections in October 2014 led to a pro-European government under Prime Minister Arseniy Yatesenyuk of the center-right People's Front. In April 2016, Yatesenyuk resigned and was replaced by Volodymyr Groysman. Russia has illegally annexed the Crimea, and Russian-backed separatists continue to destabilize the eastern part of the country. The shaky Minsk II ceasefire agreement remains in effect but is violated daily by the Russian-backed separatists.

12 ECONOMIC FREEDOMS | UKRAINE

RULE OF LAW

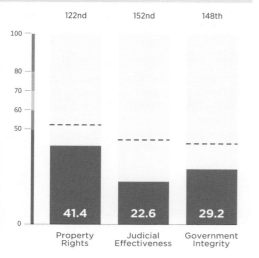

Property Rights	Judicial Effectiveness	Government Integrity
122nd	152nd	148th
41.4	22.6	29.2

Under Ukrainian law, property rights are protected, and mortgages and liens are recorded. The government that took office in April 2016 succeeded in passing constitutional reforms of the judiciary, one of Ukraine's weakest and least trusted public institutions. The IMF has urged the government to tackle high-level corruption, but a new anticorruption bureau has met strong resistance from vested interests across the institutions of state and society.

GOVERNMENT SIZE

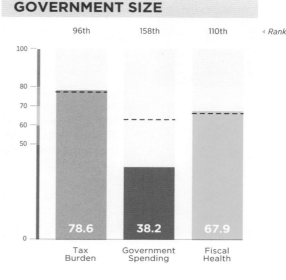

◄ Rank

Tax Burden	Government Spending	Fiscal Health
96th	158th	110th
78.6	38.2	67.9

The top individual income tax rate is 20 percent, and the top corporate tax rate is 18 percent. Other taxes include a value-added tax and a property tax. The overall tax burden equals 37.6 percent of total domestic income. Government spending has amounted to 45.4 percent of total output (GDP) over the past three years, and budget deficits have averaged 3.5 percent of GDP. Public debt is equivalent to 80.2 percent of GDP.

REGULATORY EFFICIENCY

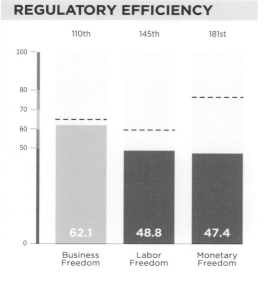

Business Freedom	Labor Freedom	Monetary Freedom
110th	145th	181st
62.1	48.8	47.4

The business start-up process has been streamlined, but completion of licensing requirements is still time-consuming. Overall, political instability continues to compound regulatory uncertainty in commercial transactions. The labor code is outmoded and lacks flexibility. The government has initiated a comprehensive reform agenda for the energy sector that is aimed at establishing market pricing for gas and heating.

OPEN MARKETS

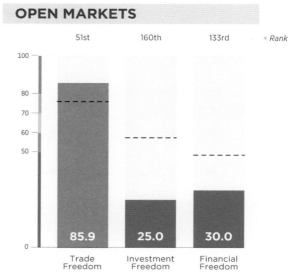

◄ Rank

Trade Freedom	Investment Freedom	Financial Freedom
51st	160th	133rd
85.9	25.0	30.0

Trade is extremely important to Ukraine's economy; the value of exports and imports taken together equals 108 percent of GDP. The average applied tariff rate is 2.1 percent. Conflict with Russia interferes with trade and investment flows, and state-owned enterprises distort the economy. The primarily cash-based economy suffers from a lack of sufficient capitalization. The large number of nonperforming loans is a drag on the banking system.

UKRAINE

UNITED KINGDOM

The United Kingdom has demonstrated good economic resilience with effective rule of law, an open trading environment, and a well-developed financial sector. A labor market that is relatively liberal by European standards has complemented one of the world's most efficient business and investment environments.

Fiscal consolidation has progressed through spending cuts that have reduced the fiscal deficit to a more manageable though still high level. The U.K. continues to benefit from strong institutional assets such as an independent judiciary and stable currency, and the services sector accounts for 75 percent of the nation's GDP.

ECONOMIC FREEDOM SCORE

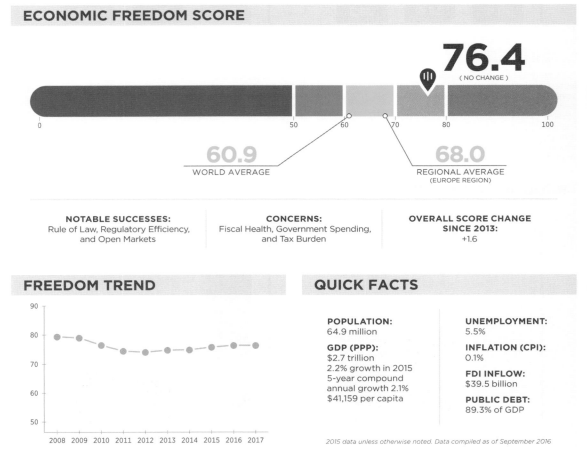

76.4
(NO CHANGE)

0   50   60   70   80   100

60.9
WORLD AVERAGE

68.0
REGIONAL AVERAGE
(EUROPE REGION)

NOTABLE SUCCESSES:	CONCERNS:	OVERALL SCORE CHANGE SINCE 2013:
Rule of Law, Regulatory Efficiency, and Open Markets	Fiscal Health, Government Spending, and Tax Burden	+1.6

FREEDOM TREND

QUICK FACTS

POPULATION:
64.9 million

GDP (PPP):
$2.7 trillion
2.2% growth in 2015
5-year compound
annual growth 2.1%
$41,159 per capita

UNEMPLOYMENT:
5.5%

INFLATION (CPI):
0.1%

FDI INFLOW:
$39.5 billion

PUBLIC DEBT:
89.3% of GDP

2015 data unless otherwise noted. Data compiled as of September 2016

BACKGROUND: Following the market reforms instituted by Prime Minister Margaret Thatcher in the 1980s, Britain experienced steady economic growth throughout the 1990s and is now the world's fifth-largest economy. Government spending grew significantly under successive Labour governments in the early 2000s but has moderated under Conservative governments since 2010. In June 2016, the U.K. voted in a popular referendum to leave the European Union. The exit vote resulted in the resignation of Prime Minister David Cameron, who was replaced by Theresa May. The overall policy direction of the May government, which has argued for an industrial policy, remains to be seen, but negotiating "Brexit" will undoubtedly be a top priority.

12 ECONOMIC FREEDOMS | UNITED KINGDOM

RULE OF LAW

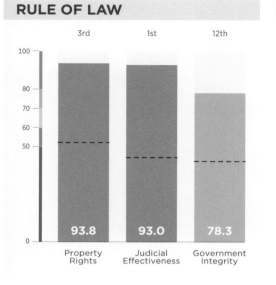

	3rd	1st	12th
	Property Rights	Judicial Effectiveness	Government Integrity
	93.8	93.0	78.3

GOVERNMENT SIZE

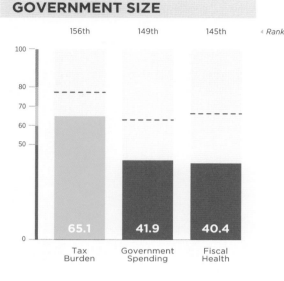

	156th	149th	145th	‹ Rank
	Tax Burden	Government Spending	Fiscal Health	
	65.1	41.9	40.4	

Private property rights and contracts are very secure, and the court system is efficient and independent. Protection of intellectual property rights is effective. The rule of law is well established, and the World Economic Forum's 2015–2016 *Global Competitiveness Report* ranked the U.K. sixth in the world for efficiency of dispute resolution through its legal framework. Isolated instances of bribery and corruption occur but are prosecuted vigorously.

The top personal income tax rate is 45 percent. The top corporate tax rate has been reduced to 20 percent. Other taxes include a value-added tax and an environment tax. The overall tax burden equals 32.6 percent of total domestic income. Government spending has amounted to 44 percent of total output (GDP) over the past three years, and budget deficits have averaged 5.2 percent of GDP. Public debt is equivalent to 89.3 percent of GDP.

REGULATORY EFFICIENCY

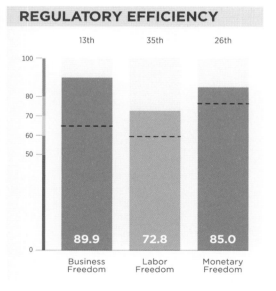

	13th	35th	26th
	Business Freedom	Labor Freedom	Monetary Freedom
	89.9	72.8	85.0

OPEN MARKETS

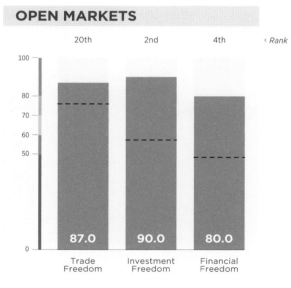

	20th	2nd	4th	‹ Rank
	Trade Freedom	Investment Freedom	Financial Freedom	
	87.0	90.0	80.0	

The regulatory environment is efficient and transparent. Starting a business takes less than a week. Bankruptcy proceedings are straightforward, and the labor market is relatively efficient. The U.K. has few price controls, but it does regulate rates for most utilities and partly controls the price of prescription drugs. In late 2015, the government cut subsidies for renewable wind energy.

Trade is important to the United Kingdom's economy; the value of exports and imports taken together equals 57 percent of GDP. The average applied tariff rate is 1.5 percent, and the economy is very open to foreign investment. The financial sector continues be one of most competitive in the world, but the state still holds ownership in some banks.

UNITED KINGDOM

MIDDLE EAST
—
NORTH AFRICA

MIDDLE EAST AND NORTH AFRICA

Stretching from Morocco's Atlantic shores to Iran and Yemen's beaches on the Arabian Sea, the Middle East and North Africa (MENA) region remains central to world affairs. The region encompasses some of the world's most ancient civilizations. Today, however, most of its economies are not free. Both blessed and in some ways cursed by enormous natural oil resources, most of the local populations are characterized by extreme concentrations of wealth and poverty. Most notably, the region continues to be a critical global hot spot for economic, political, and security vulnerabilities.

The population-weighted average GDP per capita for the region is approximately $18,803, with monetary stability relatively well maintained. However, in recent years, the MENA region has been suffering from low economic growth and plagued by a high level of unemployment.

Since early 2011, many countries in the region have experienced socioeconomic upheaval or outright conflict, and outcomes have been far from certain. The lives of many ordinary people have yet to change for the better. Of the Arab Spring economies, Tunisia and Egypt have shown the most encouraging results over the past year. However, Bahrain continues to be on a downward path in terms of economic freedom, and grading of economic freedom for Iraq, Libya, Syria, and Yemen remains suspended because of ongoing violence and unrest.

Chart 1 shows the distribution of countries in the MENA region within the five categories of economic freedom. The region does not have any economically "free" countries. The United Arab Emirates and Qatar are the region's two "mostly free" economies. The majority of the Middle East/North Africa region's 14 economies graded by the *Index* continue to be rated only "moderately free" or "mostly unfree," with the Algerian economy categorized as "repressed."

Structural and institutional problems abound throughout the region, and private-sector growth continues to lag far behind levels needed to provide adequate economic opportunities for growing populations. Despite the outflow of crude oil, actual trade flows remain very low, indicating a lack of economic dynamism. Taken as a whole, the MENA region's lack of job opportunities remains a serious problem, particularly for younger members of the labor force whose average unemployment rate is close to 25 percent.

The MENA region is the absolute world leader in one notable category: tax policy. (See Table 1.) The region's tax burden score is more than 10 points above the world average, a level reached because of the low income tax rates typical in the oil kingdoms. The region also scores slightly above the world average in such other areas as rule of law and regulatory efficiency, in part reflecting ongoing reform

MIDDLE EAST/NORTH AFRICA: QUICK FACTS

TOTAL POPULATION: 412.6 million

POPULATION WEIGHTED AVERAGES

GDP PER CAPITA (PPP):	$18,803
GROWTH:	0.2%
5 YEAR GROWTH:	2.0%
INFLATION:	9.1%
UNEMPLOYMENT:	10.7%
PUBLIC DEBT:	47.1%

SOURCE: Terry Miller and Anthony B. Kim, *2017 Index of Economic Freedom* (Washington: The Heritage Foundation, 2017), http://www.heritage.org/index.

☎ heritage.org

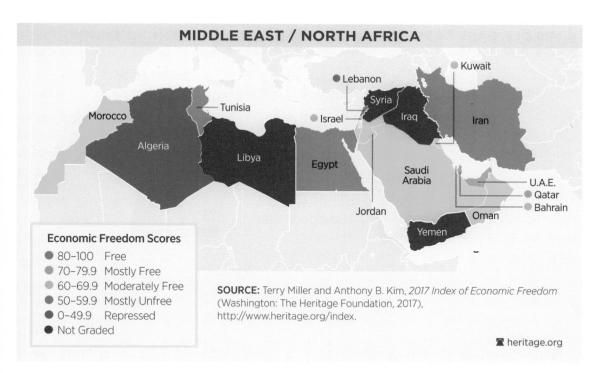

MIDDLE EAST / NORTH AFRICA

Economic Freedom Scores
- 80–100 Free
- 70–79.9 Mostly Free
- 60–69.9 Moderately Free
- 50–59.9 Mostly Unfree
- 0–49.9 Repressed
- Not Graded

SOURCE: Terry Miller and Anthony B. Kim, *2017 Index of Economic Freedom* (Washington: The Heritage Foundation, 2017), http://www.heritage.org/index.

☎ heritage.org

efforts that regional leaders are making to cut back on bribery and government malfeasance.

Given the extreme oil wealth within the region, which has little to do with economic freedom, it is somewhat surprising that the MENA countries also demonstrate in dramatic fashion the correlation between economic freedom and prosperity. Chart 2 illustrates the positive relationship between high levels of economic freedom and high GDP per capita. The ongoing transformation of innovative states such as the United Arab Emirates, Qatar, and Israel may yet light the way to broader-based economic growth and political stability regionally.

As shown in Chart 3, across the region, higher economic freedom is also strongly correlated with overall human development as measured by the United Nations Human Development Index, which measures life expectancy, literacy, education, and the standard of living.

In light of the disappointing impact of the Arab Spring, it is clear that mounting economic problems will not be solved simply by holding elections or allowing greater expressions of dissent. Existing policies and practices continue to restrict economic freedom. Costly energy and food subsidies, which place a considerable burden on budgets and stand in the way of sound sustainable economic development, are still on the rise as many governments in the region continue to rely on lavish spending to quell social and political unrest.

NOTABLE COUNTRIES

- Israel's economy has been on a path of economic expansion. With the productive base increasingly diversified and structural reforms ongoing, steady growth has averaged over 3 percent annually over the past five years. Economic competitiveness has been anchored in strong protection of property rights and facilitated by openness to global trade and investment. Israel has the world's highest concentration of high-technology start-ups per capita.

MIDDLE EAST/NORTH AFRICA: ECONOMIC FREEDOM SUMMARY

MOSTLY UNFREE
4

REPRESSED
1

NOT GRADED
4

MODERATELY
FREE
7

MOSTLY FREE
2

**TOTAL
18 COUNTRIES**

SOURCE: Terry Miller and Anthony B. Kim, *2017 Index of Economic Freedom* (Washington: The Heritage Foundation, 2017), http://www.heritage.org/index.

Chart 1 ☏ heritage.org

- Morocco continues to make gradual but notable progress in economic liberalization. The country's commitment to economic reform has encouraged the development of a dynamically evolving private sector. Policies that facilitate competitiveness and diversification of the productive base have contributed to economic expansion averaging around 4 percent annually over the past five years.

- Civil war has left Syria's economy in ruins and precludes assigning the country a rank in the 2017 *Index*. The devastation and chaos have inflicted a horrific human cost and caused enormous physical damage. Economic policy has focused on protecting the regime and maintaining the military's fighting capacity. With the escalating cost of the war compounded by a collapse in oil prices, the fiscal situation is dire.

MIDDLE EAST/NORTH AFRICA: GDP PER CAPITA, BY ECONOMIC FREEDOM CATEGORY

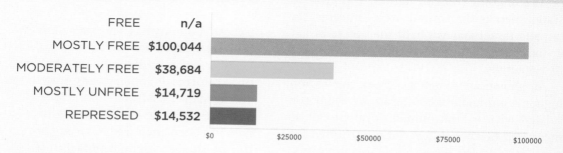

FREE	n/a
MOSTLY FREE	$100,044
MODERATELY FREE	$38,684
MOSTLY UNFREE	$14,719
REPRESSED	$14,532

SOURCES: Terry Miller and Anthony B. Kim, *2017 Index of Economic Freedom* (Washington: The Heritage Foundation, 2017), http://www.heritage.org/index, and International Monetary Fund, World Economic Outlook Database, April 2016, https://www.imf.org/external/pubs/ft/weo/2016/01/weodata/index.aspx (accessed December 13, 2016).

Chart 2 ☏ heritage.org

MIDDLE EAST/NORTH AFRICA: COMPONENTS OF ECONOMIC FREEDOM

LOWER THAN WORLD AVERAGE ●—| |—● HIGHER THAN WORLD AVERAGE

		AVERAGES		
		Region	World	
OVERALL		**61.9**	60.9	
RULE OF LAW	Property Rights	**55.7**	53.0	
	Judicial Effectiveness	**52.6**	45.0	
	Government Integrity	**43.8**	43.0	
GOVERNMENT SIZE	Tax Burden	**87.8**	77.1	
	Government Spending	**62.4**	63.4	
	Fiscal Health	**54.7**	68.0	
REGULATORY EFFICIENCY	Business Freedom	**67.8**	64.6	
	Labor Freedom	**60.2**	59.2	
	Monetary Freedom	**76.0**	76.4	
MARKET OPENNESS	Trade Freedom	**77.3**	75.9	
	Investment Freedom	**52.5**	57.2	
	Financial Freedom	**52.1**	48.2	

SOURCE: Terry Miller and Anthony B. Kim, *2017 Index of Economic Freedom* (Washington: The Heritage Foundation, 2017), http://www.heritage.org/index.

Table 1 ☎ heritage.org

- Economic dynamism is constrained in Tunisia by institutional weaknesses that remain unaddressed, primarily because political instability has hindered decisive government action. The regulatory regime, despite some improvements, remains burdensome and deters entrepreneurial activity. Deeper reforms to enhance governance and strengthen the critical pillars of economic freedom are needed to push the economy along a positive path of transition.

- Recent years' broad-based and dynamic growth in the United Arab Emirates has been underpinned by continuous efforts to strengthen the business climate, boost investment, and foster the emergence of a more vibrant and diverse private sector. The generally liberal trade regime has helped to sustain the momentum for growth. The UAE aims to be a regional financial hub, and its banking sector is resilient.

MIDDLE EAST/NORTH AFRICA: ECONOMIC FREEDOM AND HUMAN DEVELOPMENT

Each circle represents a nation in the *Index of Economic Freedom*

Human Development Index Score

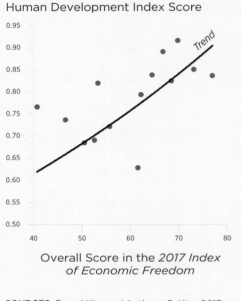

Overall Score in the *2017 Index of Economic Freedom*

SOURCES: Terry Miller and Anthony B. Kim, *2017 Index of Economic Freedom* (Washington: The Heritage Foundation, 2017), http://www.heritage.org/index, and U.N. Human Development Programme, International Human Development Indicators, http://hdr.undp.org/en/data (accessed December 13, 2016).

Chart 3 ☎ heritage.org

ECONOMIC FREEDOM IN MIDDLE EAST/NORTH AFRICA

World Rank	Regional Rank	Country	Overall Score	Change from 2016	Property Rights	Judicial Effectiveness	Government Integrity	Tax Burden	Government Spending	Fiscal Health	Business Freedom	Labor Freedom	Monetary Freedom	Trade Freedom	Investment Freedom	Financial Freedom
8	1	United Arab Emirates	76.9	4.3	76.7	85.0	74.2	96.4	67.4	99.2	81.1	80.9	78.4	83.5	40	60
29	2	Qatar	73.1	2.4	74.8	63.0	59.0	99.6	71.2	97.4	68.1	65.4	80.6	83.1	55	60
36	3	Israel	69.7	-1.0	71.9	82.0	47.6	61.0	50.5	71.8	69.9	64.3	84.9	88.0	75	70
44	4	Bahrain	68.5	-5.8	64.2	53.7	55.5	99.9	69.8	12.0	69.4	78.7	80.7	82.8	75	80
53	5	Jordan	66.7	-1.6	60.1	49.5	49.8	91.3	73.3	55.5	63.9	58.1	86.7	82.0	70	60
61	6	Kuwait	65.1	2.4	55.5	56.4	41.3	97.7	40.8	99.8	61.2	61.5	73.6	78.7	55	60
64	7	Saudi Arabia	64.4	2.3	62.0	65.0	45.9	99.7	54.5	65.7	73.8	68.5	70.1	78.2	40	50
82	8	Oman	62.1	-5.0	60.8	52.3	47.6	98.5	20.5	36.3	68.4	70.3	80.6	85.2	65	60
86	9	Morocco	61.5	0.2	55.0	41.9	37.1	71.7	69.4	55.0	67.7	33.8	82.7	84.0	70	70
123	10	Tunisia	55.7	-1.9	49.6	39.9	37.3	73.7	73.4	53.4	80.6	56.1	75.9	63.8	35	30
137	11	Lebanon	53.3	-6.2	43.8	25.3	23.3	91.8	76.1	0.0	51.5	49.5	78.4	84.4	65	50
144	12	Egypt	52.6	-3.4	35.4	56.3	32.7	86.1	63.0	4.6	66.8	51.3	69.6	70.2	55	40
155	13	Iran	50.5	7.0	32.4	36.0	29.6	81.1	92.7	94.9	64.8	54.5	55.5	54.5	0	10
172	14	Algeria	46.5	-3.6	38.2	29.6	31.7	81.1	51.0	19.8	62.1	49.5	67.0	63.3	35	30
N/A	N/A	Iraq	N/A	N/A	37.3	15.9	19.1	N/A	36.1	11.3	61.2	68.0	76.9	N/A	N/A	N/A
N/A	N/A	Libya	N/A	N/A	6.8	22.6	26.7	95	0	11.4	65.0	52.5	69.2	80.0	N/A	N/A
N/A	N/A	Syria	N/A	N/A	37.3	22.6	30.0	N/A	N/A	0.0	66.4	55.7	N/A	56.6	N/A	N/A
N/A	N/A	Yemen	N/A	N/A	37.3	22.6	17.4	N/A	77.2	10.6	51.4	54.2	59.7	N/A	N/A	N/A

ALGERIA

WORLD RANK:
172

REGIONAL RANK:
14

ECONOMIC FREEDOM STATUS:
REPRESSED

Institutional weaknesses continue to undermine prospects for sustained long-term economic development in Algeria. Lingering political uncertainty and a negative attitude toward foreign investment hamper fuller integration into the world economy, and policies to promote or sustain reform have been neglected or even reversed.

The government has made little progress in improving fiscal governance. Structural reforms to diversify the economic base have achieved only marginal progress, and policies to enhance regulatory efficiency and maintain open markets for the development of a more dynamic private sector have not advanced.

ECONOMIC FREEDOM SCORE

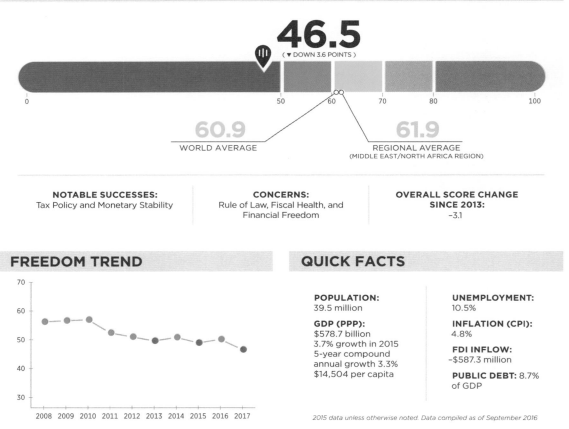

46.5
(▼ DOWN 3.6 POINTS)

0   50   60   70   80   100

60.9
WORLD AVERAGE

61.9
REGIONAL AVERAGE
(MIDDLE EAST/NORTH AFRICA REGION)

NOTABLE SUCCESSES:	CONCERNS:	OVERALL SCORE CHANGE
Tax Policy and Monetary Stability	Rule of Law, Fiscal Health, and Financial Freedom	SINCE 2013: −3.1

FREEDOM TREND

70

60

50

40

30

2008 2009 2010 2011 2012 2013 2014 2015 2016 2017

QUICK FACTS

POPULATION:
39.5 million

GDP (PPP):
$578.7 billion
3.7% growth in 2015
5-year compound
annual growth 3.3%
$14,504 per capita

UNEMPLOYMENT:
10.5%

INFLATION (CPI):
4.8%

FDI INFLOW:
−$587.3 million

PUBLIC DEBT: 8.7%
of GDP

2015 data unless otherwise noted. Data compiled as of September 2016

BACKGROUND: President Abdelaziz Bouteflika won a fourth term in April 2014 despite rarely appearing in public after a 2013 stroke. Reforms introduced after Arab Spring protests swept Tunisia and Libya included an end to almost two decades of state-of-emergency restrictions on civil liberties. In early 2016, the government passed a series of major constitutional amendments to strengthen Algeria's governing structure and deepen separation of powers. The socialist model adopted after independence from France in 1962 has hindered development, and the state still dominates the economy. Formal-sector unemployment and housing shortages are persistently high. Algeria is the world's eighth-largest gas exporter. Oil and natural gas account for over 90 percent of exports and around 40 percent of GDP.

12 ECONOMIC FREEDOMS | ALGERIA

RULE OF LAW

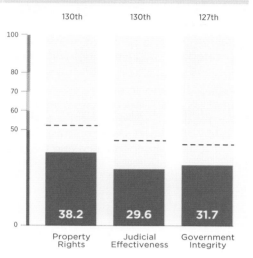

130th — Property Rights — **38.2**
130th — Judicial Effectiveness — **29.6**
127th — Government Integrity — **31.7**

Secured interests in property are generally enforceable, but most real property is in government hands, and conflicting title claims can make real estate transactions difficult. The judicial system is generally weak, slow, and opaque. High levels of corruption plague Algeria's business and public sectors, especially the energy sector. An estimated one-half of all economic transactions in Algeria occur in the informal sector.

GOVERNMENT SIZE

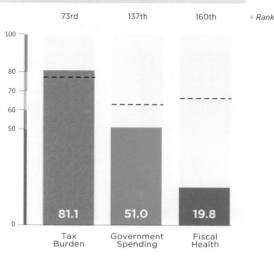

73rd — Tax Burden — **81.1**
137th — Government Spending — **51.0**
160th — Fiscal Health — **19.8** ◂ Rank

The top income tax rate is 35 percent, and the top corporate tax rate is 23 percent. Other major taxes include a value-added tax. The overall tax burden equals 11.7 percent of total domestic income. Government spending has amounted to 40.4 percent of total output (GDP) over the past three years, and budget deficits have averaged 7.7 percent of GDP. Public debt is equivalent to 8.7 percent of GDP.

REGULATORY EFFICIENCY

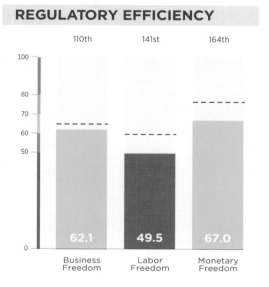

110th — Business Freedom — **62.1**
141st — Labor Freedom — **49.5**
164th — Monetary Freedom — **67.0**

Despite some enhancement of the business environment, significant bureaucratic impediments to entrepreneurial activity and economic development persist. The labor market remains rigid, contributing to high youth unemployment. In spite of continuing low global oil prices, the government has struggled to maintain costly but politically popular subsidies for basic foods, fuels, electricity, health care, and housing.

OPEN MARKETS

160th — Trade Freedom — **63.3**
144th — Investment Freedom — **35.0**
133rd — Financial Freedom — **30.0** ◂ Rank

Trade is important to Algeria's economy; the value of exports and imports taken together equals 63 percent of GDP. The average tariff rate is 8.4 percent. The government screens foreign investment, and its customs process is cumbersome. Capital markets are underdeveloped; private banks have grown, but the financial sector remains dominated by public banks.

ALGERIA

BAHRAIN

WORLD RANK: **44** REGIONAL RANK: **4**

ECONOMIC FREEDOM STATUS:
MODERATELY FREE

Despite challenging regional and domestic environments, Bahrain continues to be a financial and business hub in the Middle East and North Africa. High levels of global trade and investment activity are sustained by a competitive and efficient regulatory environment. Reforms in the existing Commercial Companies Law have facilitated foreign investment and ownership of companies.

Expansionary spending policy since 2009 has resulted in widening budget deficits and rising debt, undermining overall fiscal health. In addition to reining in public spending and implementing additional structural reforms, action to firmly institutionalize the rule of law and enhance judicial independence and transparency is urgently needed.

ECONOMIC FREEDOM SCORE

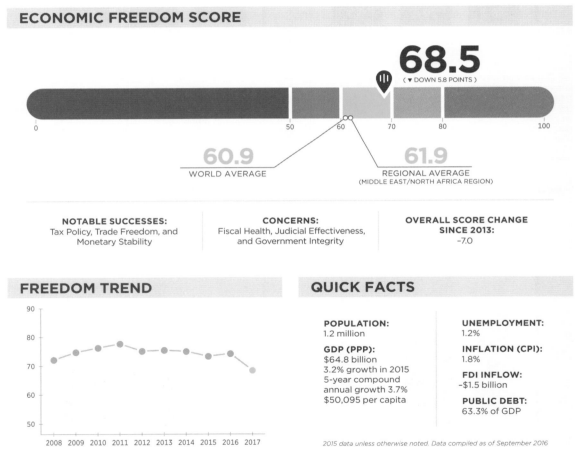

68.5
(▼ DOWN 5.8 POINTS)

0   50   60   70   80   100

60.9
WORLD AVERAGE

61.9
REGIONAL AVERAGE
(MIDDLE EAST/NORTH AFRICA REGION)

NOTABLE SUCCESSES:
Tax Policy, Trade Freedom, and Monetary Stability

CONCERNS:
Fiscal Health, Judicial Effectiveness, and Government Integrity

OVERALL SCORE CHANGE SINCE 2013:
–7.0

FREEDOM TREND

90
80
70
60
50

2008 2009 2010 2011 2012 2013 2014 2015 2016 2017

QUICK FACTS

POPULATION:
1.2 million

GDP (PPP):
$64.8 billion
3.2% growth in 2015
5-year compound annual growth 3.7%
$50,095 per capita

UNEMPLOYMENT:
1.2%

INFLATION (CPI):
1.8%

FDI INFLOW:
–$1.5 billion

PUBLIC DEBT:
63.3% of GDP

2015 data unless otherwise noted. Data compiled as of September 2016

BACKGROUND: Bahrain has been a constitutional monarchy since 2002. In 2011, Shia activists demanded a new constitution and greater political power. When modest concessions and efforts at dialogue failed to stem the demonstrations, King Hamad bin Isa Al Khalifa authorized a crackdown that was subsequently supported by Gulf Cooperation Council security forces. The government has sought to ease tensions through a national dialogue led by the crown prince and by introducing law enforcement, intelligence, and judicial reforms, but protests and sporadic violence continue. The oil industry continues to provide over 70 percent of budget revenues. Home to many multinational firms that do business in the region, Bahrain has a free trade agreement with the United States.

12 ECONOMIC FREEDOMS | BAHRAIN

RULE OF LAW

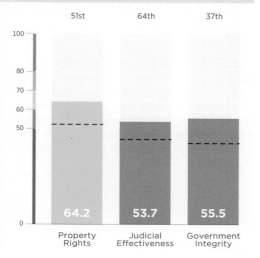

	51st	64th	37th
	Property Rights	Judicial Effectiveness	Government Integrity
	64.2	53.7	55.5

Bahrain's legal system adequately protects and facilitates the right to acquire and dispose of property. Expropriation is infrequent. The Al Khalifa royal family appoints all judges, and the judicial system is regarded as corrupt. Government tendering procedures are not always entirely transparent, and contracts are not always awarded based solely on price and technical merit. Petty corruption, however, is relatively rare.

GOVERNMENT SIZE

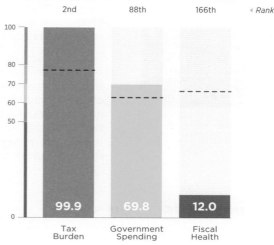

	2nd	88th	166th	◄ Rank
	Tax Burden	Government Spending	Fiscal Health	
	99.9	69.8	12.0	

Bahrain imposes no taxes on personal income. Most companies are not subject to a corporate tax, but a 46 percent tax is levied on oil companies. The overall tax burden equals 3.8 percent of total domestic income. Government spending has amounted to 31.7 percent of total output (GDP) over the past three years, and budget deficits have averaged 8.7 percent of GDP. Public debt is equivalent to 63.3 percent of GDP.

REGULATORY EFFICIENCY

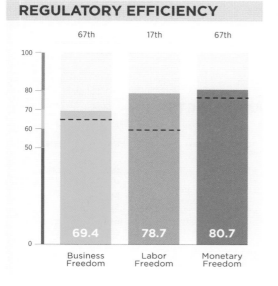

	67th	17th	67th
	Business Freedom	Labor Freedom	Monetary Freedom
	69.4	78.7	80.7

The regulatory framework is relatively streamlined, but minimum capital requirements for starting a firm are higher than the level of average annual income. Although there is no nationally mandated minimum wage, wage increases have exceeded overall productivity growth. In 2016, slumping global oil prices forced the government to reduce subsidies on gasoline, diesel and kerosene, natural gas for industrial users, food items, water, and electricity.

OPEN MARKETS

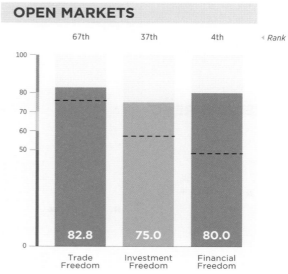

	67th	37th	4th	◄ Rank
	Trade Freedom	Investment Freedom	Financial Freedom	
	82.8	75.0	80.0	

Trade is extremely important to Bahrain's economy; the value of exports and imports taken together equals 115 percent of GDP. The average applied tariff rate is 3.6 percent, and domestic firms receive some preferences with respect to government procurement. The banking sector remains well-capitalized and liquid enough to navigate low oil prices. Foreign and domestic investors have access to a wide range of financial services.

BAHRAIN

EGYPT

WORLD RANK:
144

REGIONAL RANK:
12

ECONOMIC FREEDOM STATUS:
MOSTLY UNFREE

Egypt's economy has been experiencing an extended period of instability and uncertainty that reflects in no small measure the political turmoil of recent years. Weak institutional capacity and stiff opposition from interest groups has stymied some necessary economic reforms.

Nonetheless, the government has been keen to enhance the business environment and consolidate public finances through fiscal reforms, and confidence has improved. Recent policy choices include measures to induce more dynamic investment and spur much-needed private-sector job creation. Reform of fuel subsidies has been a notable achievement. The intensity of the government's commitment to institutional and structural reforms will be critical to future progress.

ECONOMIC FREEDOM SCORE

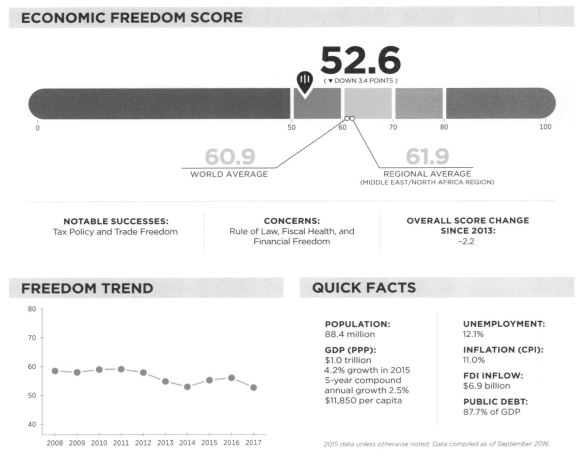

52.6
(▼ DOWN 3.4 POINTS)

0   50   60   70   80   100

60.9
WORLD AVERAGE

61.9
REGIONAL AVERAGE
(MIDDLE EAST/NORTH AFRICA REGION)

NOTABLE SUCCESSES:
Tax Policy and Trade Freedom

CONCERNS:
Rule of Law, Fiscal Health, and Financial Freedom

OVERALL SCORE CHANGE SINCE 2013:
−2.2

FREEDOM TREND

80
70
60
50
40

2008 2009 2010 2011 2012 2013 2014 2015 2016 2017

QUICK FACTS

POPULATION:
88.4 million

GDP (PPP):
$1.0 trillion
4.2% growth in 2015
5-year compound annual growth 2.5%
$11,850 per capita

UNEMPLOYMENT:
12.1%

INFLATION (CPI):
11.0%

FDI INFLOW:
$6.9 billion

PUBLIC DEBT:
87.7% of GDP

2015 data unless otherwise noted. Data compiled as of September 2016

BACKGROUND: The army ousted President Hosni Mubarak in 2011. The ensuing period of political instability included dissolution of the parliament in 2012, recurring street demonstrations, and an army coup that ousted the increasingly unpopular government of Mohamed Morsi of the Muslim Brotherhood's Freedom and Justice Party in 2013. A new constitution was approved by referendum in January 2014. Current President Abdel Fattah el-Sisi was elected in May 2014. Despite continued terrorist attacks, the vital tourism industry has begun to revive, and there are signs of increased investment and economic growth. Egypt has only a small amount of arable land, but farming is an important part of its relatively well-diversified economy.

12 ECONOMIC FREEDOMS | EGYPT

RULE OF LAW

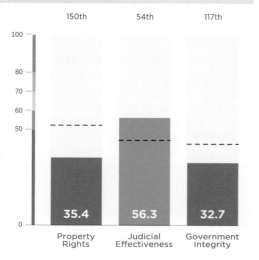

150th	54th	117th
Property Rights	Judicial Effectiveness	Government Integrity
35.4	56.3	32.7

Although protection of property rights is slightly improved overall, it weakened in the Sinai in 2015 due to government counterinsurgency efforts there. The rule of law remains highly unstable, and the judicial system has become more politicized, although the judiciary has become more efficient in resolving commercial disputes. Corruption pervades all levels of government, and official mechanisms for investigating and punishing it are very weak.

GOVERNMENT SIZE

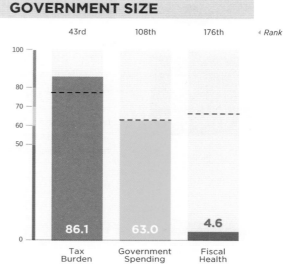

◄ Rank

43rd	108th	176th
Tax Burden	Government Spending	Fiscal Health
86.1	63.0	4.6

The top individual and corporate income tax rates are 25 percent. Other taxes include a property tax and a general sales tax. The overall tax burden equals 11.9 percent of total domestic income. Government spending has amounted to 35.1 percent of total output (GDP) over the past three years, and budget deficits have averaged 12.7 percent of GDP. Public debt is equivalent to 87.7 percent of GDP.

REGULATORY EFFICIENCY

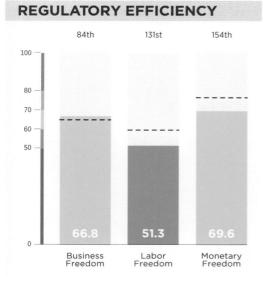

84th	131st	154th
Business Freedom	Labor Freedom	Monetary Freedom
66.8	51.3	69.6

Ongoing regulatory reforms have made starting a business less time-consuming, but without needed reforms in other critical areas, they have not had much real impact. In the absence of a well-functioning labor market, informal labor activity persists in many sectors. In 2016, the government increased prices for petroleum products and electricity as part of an effort to reduce the burden of energy subsidies on the state budget.

OPEN MARKETS

◄ Rank

131st	103rd	106th
Trade Freedom	Investment Freedom	Financial Freedom
70.2	55.0	40.0

Trade is moderately important to Egypt's economy; the value of exports and imports taken together equals 35 percent of GDP. The average applied tariff rate is 7.4 percent. Foreign investment in several sectors of the economy is restricted, and numerous state-owned enterprises distort the economy. The state's presence in the financial sector has been phased out, but modernization of the sector has progressed slowly.

EGYPT

IRAN

WORLD RANK: 155   **REGIONAL RANK:** 13

ECONOMIC FREEDOM STATUS:
MOSTLY UNFREE

Iran's intrusive state and institutional shortcomings continue to hold back more broadly based economic development. Deriving most of its revenue from the oil sector, the state owns and directly operates numerous enterprises and indirectly controls many companies affiliated with the security forces. The rule of law remains vulnerable to political interference and oppression.

The private sector is largely marginalized by the restrictive regulatory environment and government inefficiency and mismanagement. Modest efforts to enhance the business climate have occasionally been undone to maintain the status quo. The repressive climate stifles innovation.

ECONOMIC FREEDOM SCORE

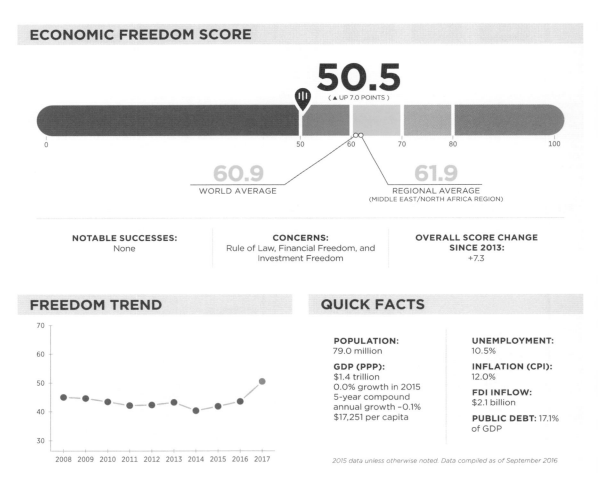

50.5
(▲ UP 7.0 POINTS)

0   50   60   70   80   100

60.9
WORLD AVERAGE

61.9
REGIONAL AVERAGE
(MIDDLE EAST/NORTH AFRICA REGION)

NOTABLE SUCCESSES:	CONCERNS:	OVERALL SCORE CHANGE
None	Rule of Law, Financial Freedom, and Investment Freedom	**SINCE 2013:** +7.3

FREEDOM TREND

70
60
50
40
30

2008 2009 2010 2011 2012 2013 2014 2015 2016 2017

QUICK FACTS

POPULATION:
79.0 million

GDP (PPP):
$1.4 trillion
0.0% growth in 2015
5-year compound
annual growth –0.1%
$17,251 per capita

UNEMPLOYMENT:
10.5%

INFLATION (CPI):
12.0%

FDI INFLOW:
$2.1 billion

PUBLIC DEBT: 17.1%
of GDP

2015 data unless otherwise noted. Data compiled as of September 2016

BACKGROUND: After the pro-Western shah was overthrown in 1979, radical Islamic forces established a theocratic government with religious authorities holding the most power. The president, who has limited powers, is elected every four years by popular vote in a process controlled by hard-line clerics who veto candidates that threaten the regime. Current President Hassan Rouhani, elected in 2013 as a pragmatist, has tried to steer a less confrontational path in dealing with foreign powers. Iran has the world's second-largest reserves of natural gas and fourth-largest reserves of crude oil. The relaxation of sanctions and reintegration into the international economy as a result of the July 2015 nuclear agreement are expected to bolster foreign investment and increase trade.

12 ECONOMIC FREEDOMS | IRAN

RULE OF LAW

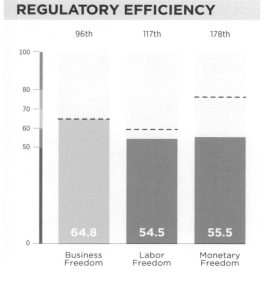

163rd	111th	145th	◂ Rank
Property Rights	Judicial Effectiveness	Government Integrity	
32.4	36.0	29.6	

The government has confiscated property belonging to religious minorities. The judicial system is not independent; the supreme leader directly appoints the head of the judiciary, who in turn appoints senior judges. Corruption is pervasive. The hard-line clerical establishment has gained great wealth through control of tax-exempt foundations that dominate many economic sectors.

GOVERNMENT SIZE

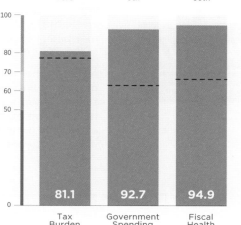

73rd	9th	38th	◂ Rank
Tax Burden	Government Spending	Fiscal Health	
81.1	92.7	94.9	

The top personal income tax rate is 35 percent. The top corporate tax rate is 25 percent. All property transfers are subject to a standard tax. The overall tax burden equals 6.4 percent of total domestic income. Government spending of tax and oil revenue has amounted to 15.5 percent of total output (GDP) over the past three years, and budget deficits have averaged 1.7 percent of GDP. Public debt is equivalent to 17.1 percent of GDP.

REGULATORY EFFICIENCY

96th	117th	178th	
Business Freedom	Labor Freedom	Monetary Freedom	
64.8	54.5	55.5	

The restrictive regulatory environment, exacerbated by the state's economic planning process and excessive bureaucracy, continues to hamper private investment and production. Labor regulations are restrictive, and the labor market remains stagnant. Price controls and subsidies that date from the early years of the Islamic Revolution have been reduced in scope in recent years.

OPEN MARKETS

175th	175th	173rd	◂ Rank
Trade Freedom	Investment Freedom	Financial Freedom	
54.5	0.0	10.0	

Trade is moderately important to Iran's economy; the value of exports and imports taken together equals 43 percent of GDP. The average applied tariff rate is 15.2 percent. International sanctions and domestic barriers limit foreign investment. Stringent government controls limit access to financing for businesses. State-owned commercial banks and specialized financial institutions account for a majority of banking-sector assets.

IRAN

IRAQ

WORLD RANK: **REGIONAL RANK:**
N/A | **N/A**

ECONOMIC FREEDOM STATUS:
NOT GRADED

The collapse of oil prices significantly damaged Iraq's long-term fiscal health, investment climate, and standard of living. Prime Minister Haider al-Abadi has enacted measures to reform state-owned enterprises, fight corruption, and reduce bureaucratic bottlenecks, but overall progress has been uneven and marginal. Due to the absence of reliable data, Iraq is not ranked in the 2017 *Index*.

Among other ongoing challenges, Iraq's economy lacks effective monetary and fiscal policies. The weak state of the financial system, coupled with its limited role within the economy, also makes development of a much-needed dynamic private sector extremely difficult and fragile. The main challenges are improving security and restoring the rule of law.

ECONOMIC FREEDOM SCORE

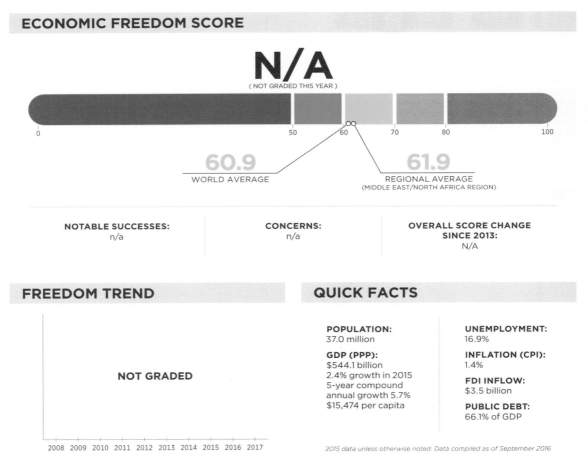

N/A
(NOT GRADED THIS YEAR)

0   50   60   70   80   100

60.9
WORLD AVERAGE

61.9
REGIONAL AVERAGE
(MIDDLE EAST/NORTH AFRICA REGION)

NOTABLE SUCCESSES:
n/a

CONCERNS:
n/a

OVERALL SCORE CHANGE SINCE 2013:
N/A

FREEDOM TREND

NOT GRADED

2008 2009 2010 2011 2012 2013 2014 2015 2016 2017

QUICK FACTS

POPULATION:
37.0 million

GDP (PPP):
$544.1 billion
2.4% growth in 2015
5-year compound
annual growth 5.7%
$15,474 per capita

UNEMPLOYMENT:
16.9%

INFLATION (CPI):
1.4%

FDI INFLOW:
$3.5 billion

PUBLIC DEBT:
66.1% of GDP

2015 data unless otherwise noted. Data compiled as of September 2016

BACKGROUND: Iraq has become increasingly unstable since 2013 due to the rise of the Islamic State (formerly known as the Islamic State in Iraq and Syria, or ISIS) and declining world oil prices. Prime Minister Nuri al-Maliki's party won the largest number of seats in the April 2014 parliamentary elections, but he alienated Sunni Arabs and Kurds with a heavy-handed sectarian agenda. He stepped down in August 2014 and was succeeded by Haider al-Abadi. The oil industry provides more than 90 percent of government revenue. The war against the Islamic State imposes a high cost on the economy, and the central government is corrupt and ineffective.

12 ECONOMIC FREEDOMS | IRAQ

RULE OF LAW

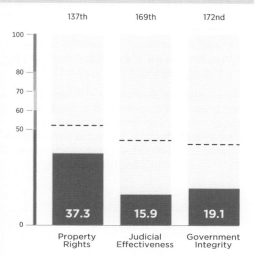

137th 169th 172nd

Property Rights: 37.3
Judicial Effectiveness: 15.9
Government Integrity: 19.1

Partly as a result of the state's limited administrative capacity, property rights are not well protected. The judiciary in Iraq is heavily influenced by political, tribal, and religious forces. Officials throughout the government often engage in corrupt practices with impunity, and investigation of corruption is politically influenced. Bribery, money laundering, nepotism, and misappropriation of public funds are commonplace.

GOVERNMENT SIZE

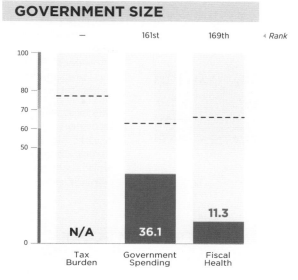

— 161st 169th ◄ Rank

Tax Burden: N/A
Government Spending: 36.1
Fiscal Health: 11.3

Individual and corporate income tax rates are capped at 15 percent. Tax revenue as a percentage of GDP is negligible due to high levels of evasion and lax enforcement. Public spending is estimated to equal more than half of total domestic output, and the budget records surpluses only because of oil revenue, which funds more than 90 percent of government expenses. Public debt is equivalent to 66.1 percent of GDP.

REGULATORY EFFICIENCY

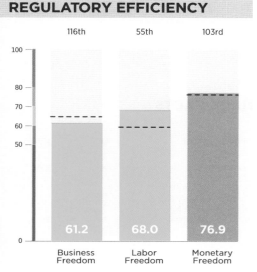

116th 55th 103rd

Business Freedom: 61.2
Labor Freedom: 68.0
Monetary Freedom: 76.9

The application of existing regulations has been inconsistent and nontransparent. In the absence of a well-functioning labor market, informal labor activity persists in many sectors. The government has struggled to comply with 2016 IMF requirements that it make politically difficult reductions in fuel and food subsidies even as it faces lower revenues from oil and instability caused by ISIS.

OPEN MARKETS

— — — ◄ Rank

Trade Freedom: N/A
Investment Freedom: N/A
Financial Freedom: N/A

Trade is important to Iraq's economy; the value of exports and imports taken together equals 50 percent of GDP. Judicial and regulatory system problems discourage foreign trade and investment, and numerous state-owned enterprises distort the economy. Iraq's cash-based economy lacks the infrastructure of a fully functioning financial system. The legal and institutional framework has not strengthened enough to deepen financial intermediation.

IRAQ

ISRAEL

Despite a very challenging external economic environment, Israel's economy has been on a path of economic expansion. With the productive base increasingly diversified and structural reforms ongoing, steady growth has averaged over 3 percent annually over the past five years. Economic competitiveness has been anchored in strong protection of property rights and facilitated by openness to global trade and investment.

Business start-ups have been well supported by efficient regulatory processes and effective policy coordination. Israel has the world's highest concentration of high-technology start-ups per capita. Contributing to overall stability, the sound judicial framework sustains the rule of law. Maintaining better management of public finance will be critical to ensuring economic resilience.

WORLD RANK: **36** | REGIONAL RANK: **3**

ECONOMIC FREEDOM STATUS:
MODERATELY FREE

ECONOMIC FREEDOM SCORE

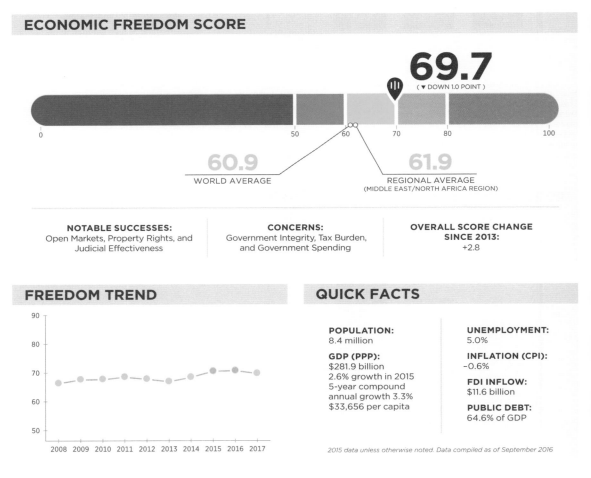

69.7
(▼ DOWN 1.0 POINT)

0   50   60   70   80   100

60.9
WORLD AVERAGE

61.9
REGIONAL AVERAGE
(MIDDLE EAST/NORTH AFRICA REGION)

NOTABLE SUCCESSES:
Open Markets, Property Rights, and Judicial Effectiveness

CONCERNS:
Government Integrity, Tax Burden, and Government Spending

OVERALL SCORE CHANGE SINCE 2013:
+2.8

FREEDOM TREND

QUICK FACTS

POPULATION:
8.4 million

GDP (PPP):
$281.9 billion
2.6% growth in 2015
5-year compound
annual growth 3.3%
$33,656 per capita

UNEMPLOYMENT:
5.0%

INFLATION (CPI):
–0.6%

FDI INFLOW:
$11.6 billion

PUBLIC DEBT:
64.6% of GDP

2015 data unless otherwise noted. Data compiled as of September 2016

BACKGROUND: Israel gained independence in 1948, and its vibrant democracy remains unique in the region. Prime Minister Benjamin Netanyahu, reelected in March 2015, leads a coalition government of right-leaning and religious parties. Israel has a modern market economy with a thriving high-technology sector that attracts considerable foreign investment. The recent discovery of large offshore natural gas deposits has improved both its energy security and its balance-of-payments prospects. Despite the 2006 war against Hezbollah in Lebanon and the 2008–2009, 2012, and 2014 wars against Hamas in Gaza, as well as the constant threat of terrorism, Israel's economy is fundamentally sound and dynamic.

12 ECONOMIC FREEDOMS | ISRAEL

RULE OF LAW

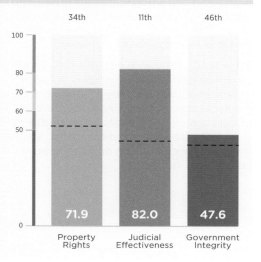

34th	11th	46th
Property Rights	Judicial Effectiveness	Government Integrity
71.9	82.0	47.6

GOVERNMENT SIZE

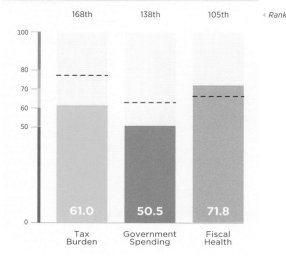

168th	138th	105th	◄ Rank
Tax Burden	Government Spending	Fiscal Health	
61.0	50.5	71.8	

Secured interests in property are recognized, and the system for recording titles is reliable. Israel's judicial system, based on British common law, enforces property and contractual rights effectively. Courts are independent. Bribery and other forms of corruption are illegal. A strong societal intolerance for graft underpins governance with relatively low levels of corruption and has strengthened the foundations of economic freedom.

The top personal income tax rate is 48 percent. The corporate tax rate has been cut to 25 percent. Other taxes include a value-added tax and a capital gains tax. The overall tax burden equals 31.1 percent of total domestic income. Government spending has amounted to 40.6 percent of total output (GDP) over the past three years, and budget deficits have averaged 3.5 percent of GDP. Public debt is equivalent to 64.6 percent of GDP.

REGULATORY EFFICIENCY

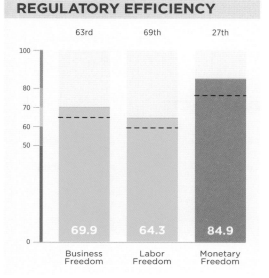

63rd	69th	27th
Business Freedom	Labor Freedom	Monetary Freedom
69.9	64.3	84.9

OPEN MARKETS

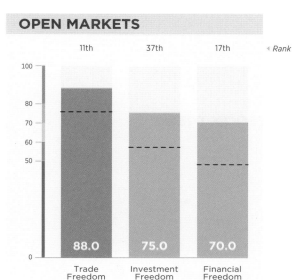

11th	37th	17th	◄ Rank
Trade Freedom	Investment Freedom	Financial Freedom	
88.0	75.0	70.0	

The overall regulatory framework promotes efficiency and entrepreneurial activity. The labor market needs more flexibility to accommodate the rapidly transforming economy, but the nonsalary cost of employing a worker is relatively low. Since widespread demonstrations in 2011, the government has maintained economically distorting price controls for many basic foods such as dairy products, eggs, bread, and salt and for basic banking services.

Trade is important to Israel's economy; the value of exports and imports taken together equals 59 percent of GDP. The average applied tariff rate is 1.0 percent. The government owns most of the land, and state-owned enterprises distort the economy. The financial sector facilitates a high level of capital liquidity. Banking remains concentrated, but commercial banks offer a range of financial services that support private-sector development.

ISRAEL

JORDAN

Economic freedom in Jordan has suffered in recent years with rising public debt and persistent budget deficits. The country has become home to a large number of refugees, putting further stress on the government's finances. Regional instability also disrupts trade routes and restricts tourism inflows.

The government has eliminated nearly all fuel subsidies, and many state-owned enterprises have been privatized. A three-year agreement with the International Monetary Fund concluded in August 2016 supports fiscal consolidation and structural reforms. Future adjustments are planned to focus on better-targeted capital spending and private-sector development. Overall economic freedom is curtailed by corruption and the judicial system's vulnerability to political influence.

WORLD RANK: **53**　REGIONAL RANK: **5**

ECONOMIC FREEDOM STATUS:
MODERATELY FREE

ECONOMIC FREEDOM SCORE

66.7
(▼ DOWN 1.6 POINTS)

0　　50　60　70　80　　100

60.9
WORLD AVERAGE

61.9
REGIONAL AVERAGE
(MIDDLE EAST/NORTH AFRICA REGION)

NOTABLE SUCCESSES:
Trade Freedom and
Monetary Stability

CONCERNS:
Judicial Effectiveness, Government
Integrity, and Fiscal Health

**OVERALL SCORE CHANGE
SINCE 2013:**
–3.7

FREEDOM TREND

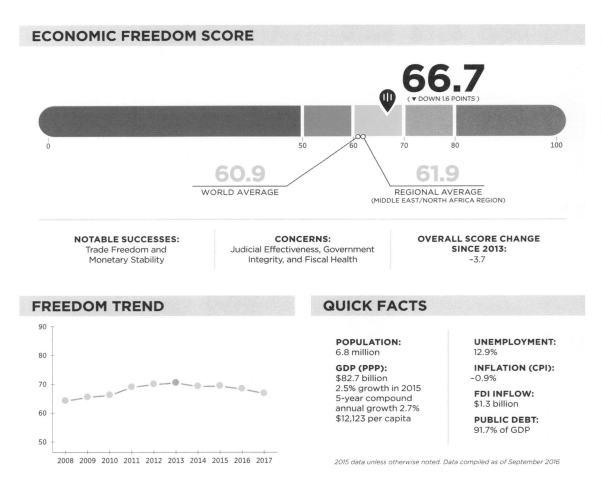

90

80

70

60

50

2008　2009　2010　2011　2012　2013　2014　2015　2016　2017

QUICK FACTS

POPULATION:
6.8 million

GDP (PPP):
$82.7 billion
2.5% growth in 2015
5-year compound
annual growth 2.7%
$12,123 per capita

UNEMPLOYMENT:
12.9%

INFLATION (CPI):
–0.9%

FDI INFLOW:
$1.3 billion

PUBLIC DEBT:
91.7% of GDP

2015 data unless otherwise noted. Data compiled as of September 2016

BACKGROUND: In 2011, constitutional monarch King Abdallah II responded to Arab Spring demonstrations by dismissing his cabinet and ceding greater authority to the judiciary and parliament. Since then, constitutional amendments aimed at restoring power to the crown have raised concerns that Arab Spring reforms were superficial. Foreign loans, international aid, and remittances from expatriate workers support the economy. In 2000, Jordan joined the World Trade Organization and signed a free trade agreement with the United States. The ongoing conflicts in Iraq and Syria have severely disrupted traditional economic activities and have exacerbated the challenges of governing an already diverse population.

12 ECONOMIC FREEDOMS | JORDAN

RULE OF LAW

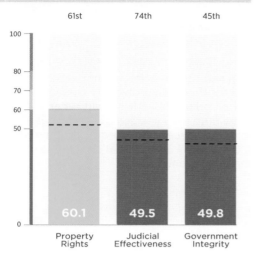

	61st	74th	45th
	Property Rights	Judicial Effectiveness	Government Integrity
	60.1	49.5	49.8

Property rights are respected for the most part. The judiciary is generally independent, but the king is the ultimate authority. The use of family, business, and other personal connections to advance business and interests, known in the Middle East as *wasta*, is endemic in Jordan. Weak investigative journalism, limited access to information, and a lack of institutional checks and balances undermine efforts to combat widespread corruption.

GOVERNMENT SIZE

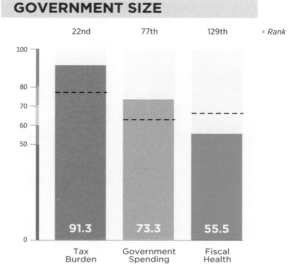

Rank

	22nd	77th	129th
	Tax Burden	Government Spending	Fiscal Health
	91.3	73.3	55.5

The top individual income tax rate is 14 percent. As of January 1, 2015, the standard corporate tax rate rose to 20 percent. The overall tax burden equals 16.7 percent of total domestic income. Government spending has amounted to 29.8 percent of total output (GDP) over the past three years, and budget deficits have averaged 4.2 percent of GDP. Public debt is equivalent to 91.7 percent of GDP.

REGULATORY EFFICIENCY

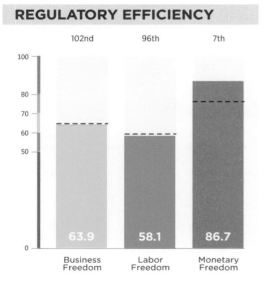

	102nd	96th	7th
	Business Freedom	Labor Freedom	Monetary Freedom
	63.9	58.1	86.7

Despite persistent bureaucratic obstacles and delays, reforms carried out in recent years have made business formation and operation more efficient and dynamic. Progress toward reforming bloated public-sector employment has been dismal. Under ongoing IMF agreements, the government has eliminated nearly all fuel subsidies and in 2016 pressed ahead with price increases to reduce losses at the state-owned electric and water companies.

OPEN MARKETS

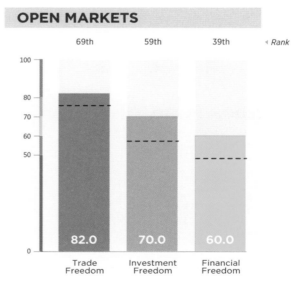

Rank

	69th	59th	39th
	Trade Freedom	Investment Freedom	Financial Freedom
	82.0	70.0	60.0

Trade is important to Jordan's economy; the value of exports and imports taken together equals 98 percent of GDP. The average applied tariff rate is 4.0 percent. The government screens foreign investment and restricts investment in some sectors of the economy. Along with financial-sector policies that are intended to enhance competition and efficiency, banking supervision and regulation generally conform to international standards.

JORDAN

KUWAIT

WORLD RANK: **61** | **REGIONAL RANK:** **6**

ECONOMIC FREEDOM STATUS:
MODERATELY FREE

Kuwait is trying to modernize the structure of its economy and scores relatively well in many of the 12 economic freedoms. The economy benefits from high levels of openness to global commerce and good monetary stability. Progress on enhancing the efficiency of business regulations, however, has been mixed.

The availability of high oil revenues has delayed privatization and other structural reforms that would diversify the economy; following the collapse of oil prices in 2015, Kuwait recorded a budget deficit for the first time in 15 years. Institutional deficiencies stemming from state bureaucracy and an entitlement culture stifle economic dynamism. The judicial system is subject to political influence and lacks transparency.

ECONOMIC FREEDOM SCORE

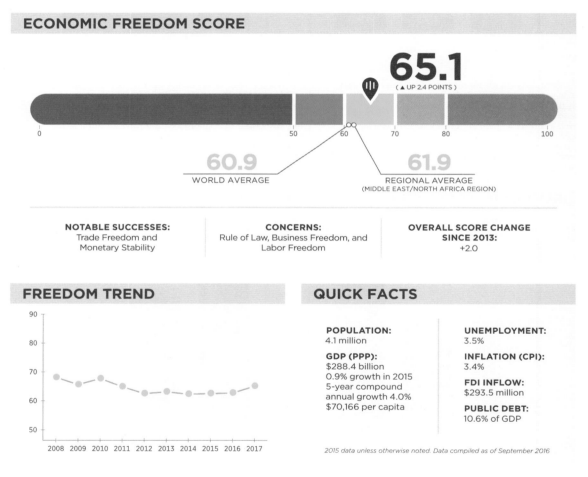

65.1
(▲ UP 2.4 POINTS)

0   50   60   70   80   100

60.9
WORLD AVERAGE

61.9
REGIONAL AVERAGE
(MIDDLE EAST/NORTH AFRICA REGION)

NOTABLE SUCCESSES:	CONCERNS:	OVERALL SCORE CHANGE
Trade Freedom and Monetary Stability	Rule of Law, Business Freedom, and Labor Freedom	SINCE 2013: +2.0

FREEDOM TREND

90

80

70

60

50

2008 2009 2010 2011 2012 2013 2014 2015 2016 2017

QUICK FACTS

POPULATION:
4.1 million

GDP (PPP):
$288.4 billion
0.9% growth in 2015
5-year compound
annual growth 4.0%
$70,166 per capita

UNEMPLOYMENT:
3.5%

INFLATION (CPI):
3.4%

FDI INFLOW:
$293.5 million

PUBLIC DEBT:
10.6% of GDP

2015 data unless otherwise noted. Data compiled as of September 2016

BACKGROUND: Kuwait, the first Gulf Arab country to establish an elected parliament, is a constitutional monarchy ruled by the al-Sabah dynasty. After Islamists scored major gains in parliamentary elections in February 2012, Emir Sabah al-Ahmad al-Jabr al-Sabah annulled the results and changed the election laws. This sparked protests and a boycott of the subsequent election, the results of which were annulled by the Constitutional Court. In July 2013 balloting, pro-government Sunni candidates won a significant majority. Kuwait controls roughly 6 percent of the world's oil reserves. Oil and gas account for nearly 60 percent of GDP and 94 percent of export revenues.

12 ECONOMIC FREEDOMS | KUWAIT

RULE OF LAW

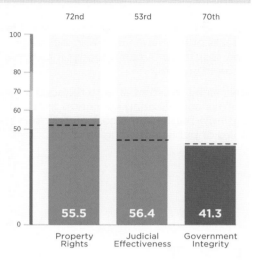

	72nd	53rd	70th

Property Rights **55.5**
Judicial Effectiveness **56.4**
Government Integrity **41.3**

Only citizens of Gulf Cooperation Council countries may own land. The legal system is not well developed, and foreigners face difficulties enforcing contract provisions in local courts. The emir appoints all judges. The ruling family has blocked attempts by the opposition in parliament to investigate corruption. Transparency in government spending and operations is inadequate, and the rule of law is weak.

GOVERNMENT SIZE

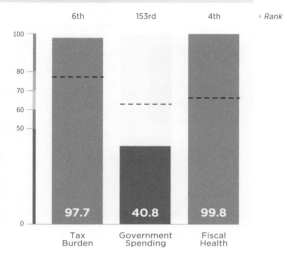

6th	153rd	4th	◂ Rank

Tax Burden **97.7**
Government Spending **40.8**
Fiscal Health **99.8**

Individual income is not taxed. Foreign-owned firms and joint ventures are the only businesses subject to the corporate income tax, which is a flat 15 percent. The overall tax burden equals 0.9 percent of total domestic income. Government spending has amounted to 44.4 percent of total output (GDP) over the past three years, and budget surpluses have averaged 20.6 percent of GDP. Public debt is equivalent to 10.6 percent of GDP.

REGULATORY EFFICIENCY

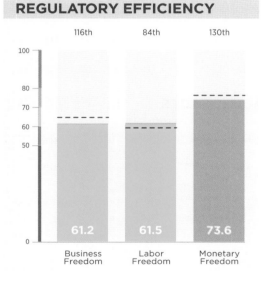

116th	84th	130th

Business Freedom **61.2**
Labor Freedom **61.5**
Monetary Freedom **73.6**

In an effort to enhance the economy's overall competitiveness, Kuwait has taken steps to improve its regulatory framework, but progress has been slow. The labor market is highly segmented. The public sector employs over 70 percent of the labor force. In 2016, public opposition slowed implementation of the government's five-year (2015–2019) development plan for the gradual phasing out of Kuwait's extensive system of subsidies.

OPEN MARKETS

89th	103rd	39th	◂ Rank

Trade Freedom **78.7**
Investment Freedom **55.0**
Financial Freedom **60.0**

Trade is important to Kuwait's economy; the value of exports and imports taken together equals 99 percent of GDP. The average applied tariff rate is 3.2 percent. Foreign investment may be screened by the government. The financial sector continues to evolve. The number of nonperforming loans is declining, and the banking sector remains well capitalized. Kuwait's stock exchange was privatized in 2016.

KUWAIT

LEBANON

WORLD RANK: **137** REGIONAL RANK: **11**

ECONOMIC FREEDOM STATUS:
MOSTLY UNFREE

Lebanon was once a leading regional center for finance and tourism, but its economy has fallen on hard times. The investment climate is undermined by political instability and continuing turmoil in Syria, rising sectarian tensions, and terrorism. The destabilizing spillover effects of the Syrian civil war, including the influx of over a million registered Syrian refugees, has had a negative impact on economic growth.

The fiscal deficit continues to be substantial, with reduced assistance from the Gulf countries complicating near-term financial management. The increasingly burdensome cost of debt service accounts for over one-third of public spending.

ECONOMIC FREEDOM SCORE

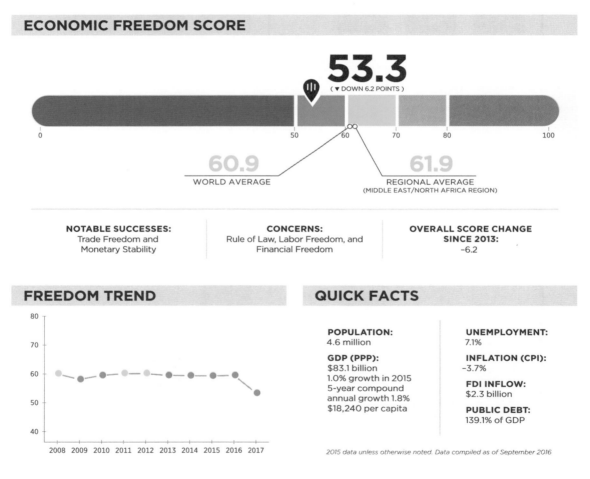

53.3
(▼ DOWN 6.2 POINTS)

0   50   60   70   80   100

60.9
WORLD AVERAGE

61.9
REGIONAL AVERAGE
(MIDDLE EAST/NORTH AFRICA REGION)

NOTABLE SUCCESSES:
Trade Freedom and Monetary Stability

CONCERNS:
Rule of Law, Labor Freedom, and Financial Freedom

OVERALL SCORE CHANGE SINCE 2013:
−6.2

FREEDOM TREND

80
70
60
50
40

2008 2009 2010 2011 2012 2013 2014 2015 2016 2017

QUICK FACTS

POPULATION:
4.6 million

GDP (PPP):
$83.1 billion
1.0% growth in 2015
5-year compound annual growth 1.8%
$18,240 per capita

UNEMPLOYMENT:
7.1%

INFLATION (CPI):
−3.7%

FDI INFLOW:
$2.3 billion

PUBLIC DEBT:
139.1% of GDP

2015 data unless otherwise noted. Data compiled as of September 2016

BACKGROUND: Lebanon has been destabilized since 1975 by civil war, Syrian occupation, and clashes between Israel and the powerful Shia Islamist group, Hezbollah, which is backed by Iran. Syria withdrew its army in 2005 after its government was implicated in the assassination of former Lebanese Prime Minister Rafiq Hariri. These sectarian tensions have led to complex power-sharing arrangements that hinder political cooperation on key government appointments and substantive policy issues. The Sunni-dominated Future Movement blocked the election by Lebanon's parliament of Michel Aoun, an 81-year-old former army general and Maronite Christian, as president for two years, until late October 2016. President Aoun was backed by Hezbollah.

12 ECONOMIC FREEDOMS | LEBANON

RULE OF LAW

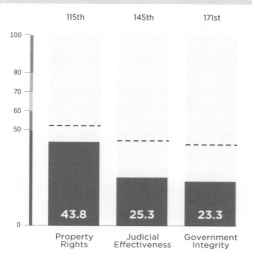

	115th	145th	171st
Property Rights	Judicial Effectiveness	Government Integrity
43.8	25.3	23.3

Lebanon has made transferring property more complex by increasing the time required for property registration. Political forces hold sway over an officially independent judiciary. The Supreme Judicial Council is composed of 10 judges, eight of whom are nominated by the president and the cabinet. Corruption is reportedly pervasive in government contracts (primarily in procurement and public works) and in taxation and real estate registration.

GOVERNMENT SIZE

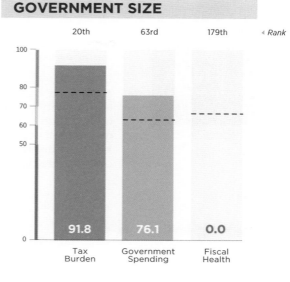

20th	63rd	179th	◀ Rank
Tax Burden	Government Spending	Fiscal Health
91.8	76.1	0.0

The top personal income tax rate is 20 percent, and the top corporate tax rate is 15 percent. Other taxes include a value-added tax and an inheritance tax. The overall tax burden equals 13.8 percent of total domestic income. Government spending has amounted to 28.2 percent of total output (GDP) over the past three years, and budget deficits have averaged 7.9 percent of GDP. Public debt is equivalent to 139.1 percent of GDP.

REGULATORY EFFICIENCY

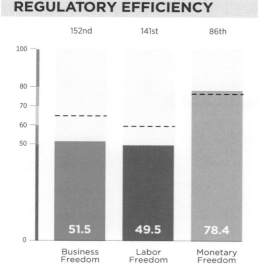

152nd	141st	86th
Business Freedom	Labor Freedom	Monetary Freedom
51.5	49.5	78.4

The overall freedom to establish and run a business remains limited by the poor regulatory environment. The cost of starting a business and completing licensing requirements is high. The labor market, undermined by political instability, continues to be stagnant. Although annual government transfers to the unprofitable state-owned power utility consume 15 percent of the budget, Lebanon continues to suffer from pervasive blackouts.

OPEN MARKETS

57th	73rd	70th	◀ Rank
Trade Freedom	Investment Freedom	Financial Freedom
84.4	65.0	50.0

Trade is extremely important to Lebanon's economy; the value of exports and imports taken together equals 122 percent of GDP. The average applied tariff rate is 2.8 percent. State-owned enterprises distort the economy, and the regulatory and judicial systems discourage foreign investment. Lebanon's financial sector used to be a regional hub, but ongoing political insecurity has subjected it to massive uncertainty and strain.

LEBANON

LIBYA

The level of economic freedom in Libya remains unrated because of a lack of reliable comparable data. Official government compilations of economic data are inadequate, and data reported by many of the international sources relied upon for *Index* grading remain incomplete.

Economic recovery since the overthrow of Muammar Qadhafi's regime has been fragile. Political instability, factional clashes, and security threats from domestic and foreign followers of the Islamic State are significant constraints on economic growth and meaningful development. The government faces major challenges in disarming and demobilizing militias, enforcing the rule of law, and reforming the state-dominated economy.

ECONOMIC FREEDOM SCORE

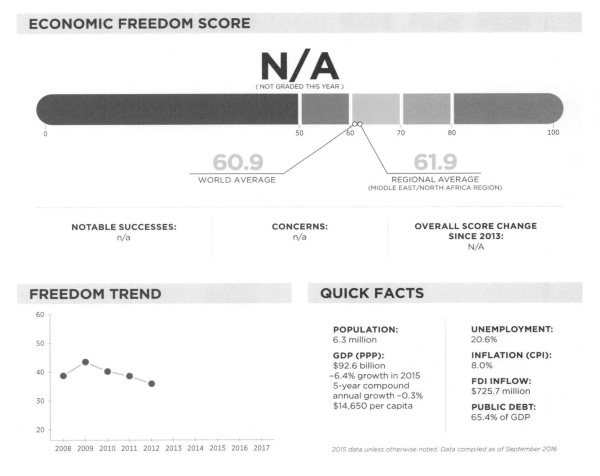

N/A
(NOT GRADED THIS YEAR)

0   50   60   70   80   100

60.9
WORLD AVERAGE

61.9
REGIONAL AVERAGE
(MIDDLE EAST/NORTH AFRICA REGION)

NOTABLE SUCCESSES:
n/a

CONCERNS:
n/a

**OVERALL SCORE CHANGE
SINCE 2013:**
N/A

FREEDOM TREND

60

50

40

30

20

2008 2009 2010 2011 2012 2013 2014 2015 2016 2017

QUICK FACTS

POPULATION:
6.3 million

GDP (PPP):
$92.6 billion
−6.4% growth in 2015
5-year compound
annual growth −0.3%
$14,650 per capita

UNEMPLOYMENT:
20.6%

INFLATION (CPI):
8.0%

FDI INFLOW:
$725.7 million

PUBLIC DEBT:
65.4% of GDP

2015 data unless otherwise noted. Data compiled as of September 2016

BACKGROUND: Dictator Muammar Qadhafi was overthrown in 2011, and political upheaval continues to this day. In June 2014, Libya held its second parliamentary election since the fall of Qadhafi; in November, the Supreme Constitutional Court ruled that the elected parliament was constitutionally illegitimate. Pro-Islamist militias allied with the Muslim Brotherhood have established parallel institutions. In March 2016, the U.N. brokered the establishment of a national unity government in Tripoli to replace the two rival administrations. Oil and natural gas provide about 80 percent of GDP, 95 percent of export revenues, and 99 percent of government revenues. Extremists have attacked oilfields and seized oil infrastructure, threatening government control of oil and gas revenues.

12 ECONOMIC FREEDOMS | LIBYA

RULE OF LAW

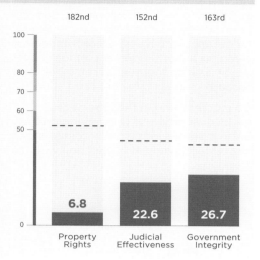

	182nd	152nd	163rd
	Property Rights	Judicial Effectiveness	Government Integrity
	6.8	22.6	26.7

Libyans have the right to own property and can start businesses, but regulations and protections are not upheld in practice. The World Bank's 2015 *Doing Business* report ranked Libya 188th out of 189 economies surveyed. Businesses and homes have been confiscated by militants, particularly in Libya's eastern regions and in Benghazi. Without a permanent constitution, the role of the judiciary remains unclear. Corruption is pervasive.

GOVERNMENT SIZE

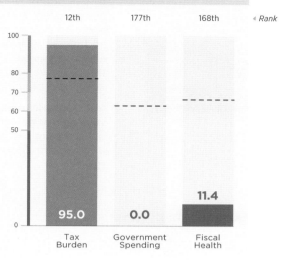

12th	177th	168th	◄ Rank
Tax Burden	Government Spending	Fiscal Health	
95.0	0.0	11.4	

The top income tax rate is 10 percent, but other taxes make the top rate much higher in practice. The top effective corporate tax rate is 20 percent. Taxation has not been enforced effectively since early 2011. Government spending has amounted to 74.7 percent of total output (GDP) over the past three years, and budget deficits have averaged 32.9 percent of GDP. Public debt is equivalent to 65.4 percent of GDP.

REGULATORY EFFICIENCY

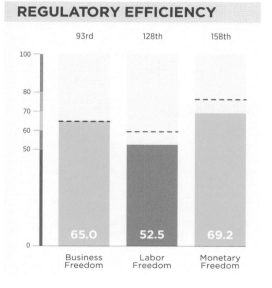

93rd	128th	158th
Business Freedom	Labor Freedom	Monetary Freedom
65.0	52.5	69.2

The existing regulatory framework is severely undermined by ongoing political instability and turmoil. The labor market remains destabilized, and the large informal sector is an important source of employment. Fearful of exacerbating social unrest, the central bank uses its large stock of foreign reserves to operate as a de facto ministry of finance, funding subsidies in the absence of a unified government.

OPEN MARKETS

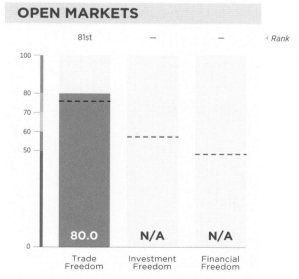

81st	—	—	◄ Rank
Trade Freedom	Investment Freedom	Financial Freedom	
80.0	N/A	N/A	

Trade is extremely important to Libya's economy; the value of exports and imports taken together equals 137 percent of GDP. Political instability is a major impediment to foreign trade and investment. The financial infrastructure has been significantly degraded by unstable political and economic conditions. Limited access to financing severely impedes any meaningful private business development.

LIBYA

MOROCCO

WORLD RANK: 86 | **REGIONAL RANK:** 9

ECONOMIC FREEDOM STATUS:
MODERATELY FREE

Morocco continues to make gradual but notable progress in economic liberalization. The country is benefiting from a commitment to economic reforms that encourage a dynamically evolving private sector. Policies that facilitate competitiveness and diversification of the productive base have contributed to economic expansion averaging around 4 percent annually over the past five years. However, a large segment of the labor force remains marginalized because of inflexible labor regulations.

Although Morocco is a strong reformer in the area of private-sector development, overall progress will depend on the government's willingness to confront long-standing challenges that require deeper reforms, particularly in connection with the rule of law.

ECONOMIC FREEDOM SCORE

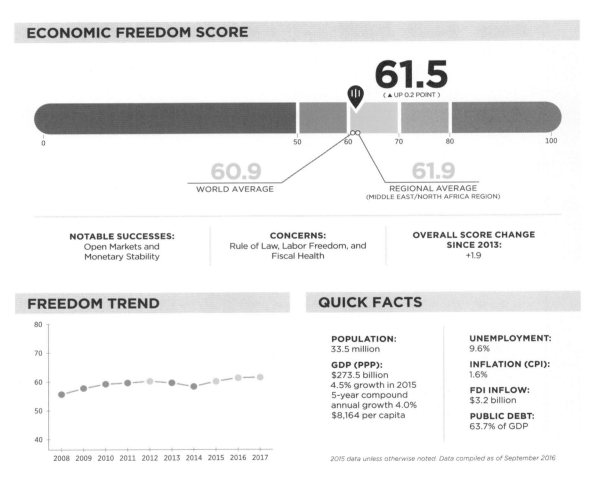

61.5
(▲ UP 0.2 POINT)

0   50   60   70   80   100

60.9
WORLD AVERAGE

61.9
REGIONAL AVERAGE
(MIDDLE EAST/NORTH AFRICA REGION)

NOTABLE SUCCESSES:
Open Markets and
Monetary Stability

CONCERNS:
Rule of Law, Labor Freedom, and
Fiscal Health

**OVERALL SCORE CHANGE
SINCE 2013:**
+1.9

FREEDOM TREND

80

70

60

50

40

2008 2009 2010 2011 2012 2013 2014 2015 2016 2017

QUICK FACTS

POPULATION:
33.5 million

GDP (PPP):
$273.5 billion
4.5% growth in 2015
5-year compound
annual growth 4.0%
$8,164 per capita

UNEMPLOYMENT:
9.6%

INFLATION (CPI):
1.6%

FDI INFLOW:
$3.2 billion

PUBLIC DEBT:
63.7% of GDP

2015 data unless otherwise noted. Data compiled as of September 2016

BACKGROUND: Morocco, a constitutional monarchy with an elected parliament, has been a key U.S. ally in the struggle against Islamist terrorism. Following popular protests in 2011, constitutional amendments proposed by a commission authorized by King Mohammed VI and approved by referendum were adopted to increase the power and independence of the prime minister and provide greater civil liberties. The king retains significant power as chief executive, however. In addition to a large tourism industry and a growing manufacturing sector, a nascent aeronautics industry has attracted foreign investment.

12 ECONOMIC FREEDOMS | MOROCCO

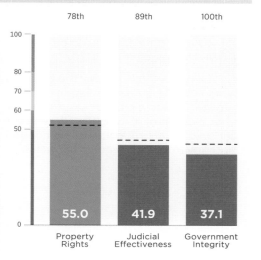

RULE OF LAW

	78th	89th	100th
	Property Rights	Judicial Effectiveness	Government Integrity
	55.0	41.9	37.1

The rates of land titling and land rights registration are low, although the 2016 World Bank *Doing Business* survey reported that new procedures have been put in place to speed property transfers. The judiciary is not independent of the palace, and the courts are regularly used to punish government opponents. Officials engage in corrupt practices with impunity. Corruption is a serious problem throughout government and law enforcement.

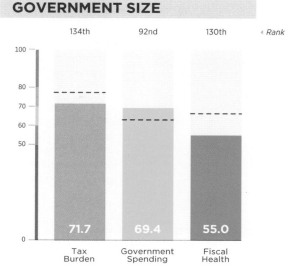

GOVERNMENT SIZE

	134th	92nd	130th	◄ Rank
	Tax Burden	Government Spending	Fiscal Health	
	71.7	69.4	55.0	

The top individual income tax rate is 38 percent, and the top corporate tax rate is 30 percent. Other taxes include a value-added tax and a gift tax. The overall tax burden equals 22.0 percent of total domestic income. Government spending has amounted to 31.9 percent of total output (GDP) over the past three years, and budget deficits have averaged 4.8 percent of GDP. Public debt is equivalent to 63.7 percent of GDP.

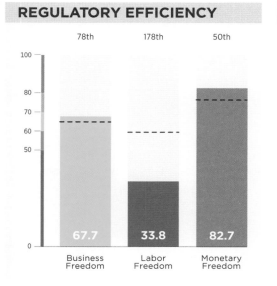

REGULATORY EFFICIENCY

	78th	178th	50th
	Business Freedom	Labor Freedom	Monetary Freedom
	67.7	33.8	82.7

Procedures for setting up and registering a private business have been streamlined in recent years. Despite some improvement, labor market rigidity continues to discourage dynamic employment growth. The elimination of fuel subsidies in 2015 provided critical fiscal space, but the government is likely to maintain subsidies on basic goods such as flour and sugar in the interest of preserving social stability.

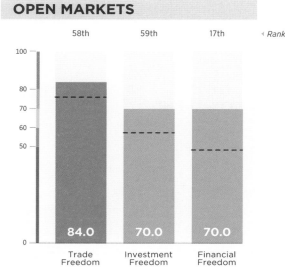

OPEN MARKETS

	58th	59th	17th	◄ Rank
	Trade Freedom	Investment Freedom	Financial Freedom	
	84.0	70.0	70.0	

Trade is important to Morocco's economy; the value of exports and imports taken together equals 81 percent of GDP. The average applied tariff rate is 3.0 percent. Foreign and domestic investors are generally treated equally under the law. The financial sector is competitive, and there is an ongoing campaign to increase modernization and transparency. The Casablanca Stock Exchange does not restrict foreign participation.

MOROCCO

OMAN

WORLD RANK: **82** REGIONAL RANK: **8**

ECONOMIC FREEDOM STATUS:
MODERATELY FREE

The government of Oman has tried to expand exports of liquefied natural gas and encourage foreign investment in petrochemicals, electric power, and telecommunications. It hopes to mitigate its dependence on declining oil resources through diversification that would reduce the oil sector's share from about 45 percent of GDP to 9 percent by 2020.

Greater structural reform is still needed to improve the business environment. Bureaucracy and cumbersome regulations hinder entrepreneurial activity, and state-owned enterprises distort the economy. The judiciary is not independent. Social welfare spending has strained the budget, and fiscal prudence will be needed as the population grows and government spending on welfare programs mounts.

ECONOMIC FREEDOM SCORE

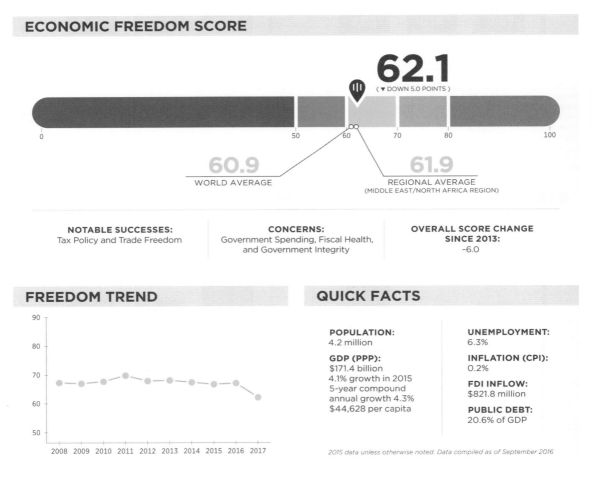

62.1
(▼ DOWN 5.0 POINTS)

0   50   60   70   80   100

60.9
WORLD AVERAGE

61.9
REGIONAL AVERAGE
(MIDDLE EAST/NORTH AFRICA REGION)

NOTABLE SUCCESSES:
Tax Policy and Trade Freedom

CONCERNS:
Government Spending, Fiscal Health, and Government Integrity

OVERALL SCORE CHANGE SINCE 2013:
–6.0

FREEDOM TREND

QUICK FACTS

POPULATION:
4.2 million

GDP (PPP):
$171.4 billion
4.1% growth in 2015
5-year compound
annual growth 4.3%
$44,628 per capita

UNEMPLOYMENT:
6.3%

INFLATION (CPI):
0.2%

FDI INFLOW:
$821.8 million

PUBLIC DEBT:
20.6% of GDP

2015 data unless otherwise noted. Data compiled as of September 2016

BACKGROUND: Oman, a relatively small oil-producing kingdom with one of the Arab world's smallest populations, has been ruled by Sultan Qaboos bin Said Al-Said since 1970. In early 2011, in response to widespread regional turmoil, the sultan changed cabinet ministers and promised political and economic reforms. A Consultative Council elected in October 2011 expanded regulatory and legislative powers. As part of the government's efforts to decentralize authority and allow greater citizen participation in local governance, Oman conducted its first municipal council elections in December 2012. Oman joined the World Trade Organization in 2000 and signed a free trade agreement with the United States in 2006.

12 ECONOMIC FREEDOMS | OMAN

RULE OF LAW

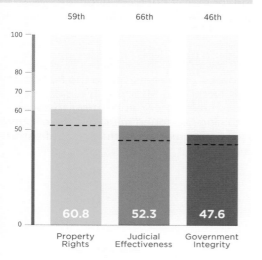

	59th	66th	46th
	60.8	52.3	47.6
	Property Rights	Judicial Effectiveness	Government Integrity

Property rights are well protected. The judiciary remains subordinate to the sultan and the Ministry of Justice, but authorities generally hold security personnel and other officials accountable for their actions. Several high-profile corruption cases involving government officials and executives of the state-owned oil company have been prosecuted in recent years, but many influential government officials are believed to have business-related conflicts of interest.

GOVERNMENT SIZE

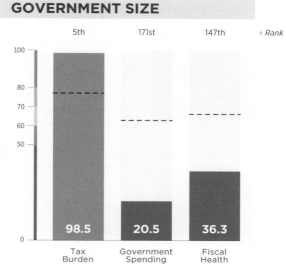

	5th	171st	147th	◄ Rank
	98.5	20.5	36.3	
	Tax Burden	Government Spending	Fiscal Health	

There is no individual income tax, and the top corporate tax rate is 12 percent. There is no consumption tax or value-added tax. The overall tax burden equals 2.6 percent of total domestic income. Government spending has amounted to 51.5 percent of total output (GDP) over the past three years, and budget deficits have averaged 6.3 percent of GDP. Public debt is equivalent to 20.6 percent of GDP.

REGULATORY EFFICIENCY

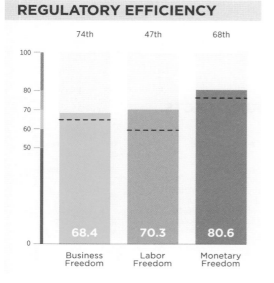

	74th	47th	68th
	68.4	70.3	80.6
	Business Freedom	Labor Freedom	Monetary Freedom

Although improving, the overall freedom to conduct a business remains limited by the inefficient regulatory environment. The nonsalary cost of employing a worker is low, but the labor laws enforce the "Omanization" policy that requires private-sector firms to meet quotas for hiring native Omani workers. Cuts in government subsidies for petroleum products have led to rises in fuel prices; other subsidies remain in place.

OPEN MARKETS

	54th	73rd	39th	◄ Rank
	85.2	65.0	60.0	
	Trade Freedom	Investment Freedom	Financial Freedom	

Trade is extremely important to Oman's economy; the value of exports and imports taken together equals 115 percent of GDP. The average applied tariff rate is 2.4 percent. There is no general screening of foreign investment. State-owned enterprises distort the economy. Most credit is offered at market rates, but the government uses subsidized loans to promote investment. The Muscat Securities Market is active and open to foreign investors.

OMAN

QATAR

WORLD RANK:
29

REGIONAL RANK:
2

ECONOMIC FREEDOM STATUS:
MOSTLY FREE

The oil and gas sectors remain the major drivers of Qatar's economy, accounting for over 50 percent of government revenue. This has left Qatar subject to external shocks, although growth in manufacturing and financial services has contributed to economic diversification.

Deeper structural reforms are critical to enhancing competitiveness, particularly as low oil prices have led to the first fiscal deficit in 15 years. In 2016, Qatar sold $9 billion in bonds, the largest Middle East bond issue in history, in an effort to cover the budget deficit. Maintaining the sound management of public finance is crucial as major government investments in infrastructure and other projects continue.

ECONOMIC FREEDOM SCORE

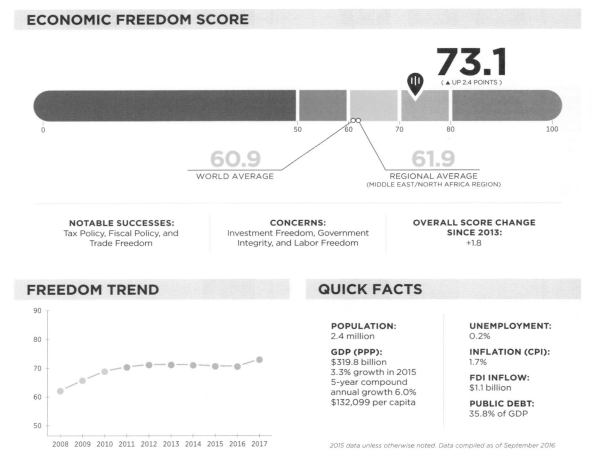

73.1
(▲ UP 2.4 POINTS)

0   50   60   70   80   100

60.9
WORLD AVERAGE

61.9
REGIONAL AVERAGE
(MIDDLE EAST/NORTH AFRICA REGION)

NOTABLE SUCCESSES:
Tax Policy, Fiscal Policy, and Trade Freedom

CONCERNS:
Investment Freedom, Government Integrity, and Labor Freedom

OVERALL SCORE CHANGE SINCE 2013:
+1.8

FREEDOM TREND

90
80
70
60
50

2008 2009 2010 2011 2012 2013 2014 2015 2016 2017

QUICK FACTS

POPULATION:
2.4 million

GDP (PPP):
$319.8 billion
3.3% growth in 2015
5-year compound
annual growth 6.0%
$132,099 per capita

UNEMPLOYMENT:
0.2%

INFLATION (CPI):
1.7%

FDI INFLOW:
$1.1 billion

PUBLIC DEBT:
35.8% of GDP

2015 data unless otherwise noted. Data compiled as of September 2016

BACKGROUND: The Al-Thani family has ruled Qatar since independence from Great Britain in 1971. Sheikh Tamim bin Hamad Al-Thani, in power since 2013, has emphasized such domestic issues as enhancing infrastructure, health care, and education. Qatar has largely avoided problems generated elsewhere by the Arab Spring uprisings, but it has been criticized for its support of radical Islamist groups. Qatar's proven oil reserves exceed 25 billion barrels, and its natural gas reserves are the world's third largest. After winning its bid to host the 2022 World Cup, the government expedited large infrastructure projects including roads, light rail transportation, a new port, stadiums, and other sporting facilities.

12 ECONOMIC FREEDOMS | QATAR

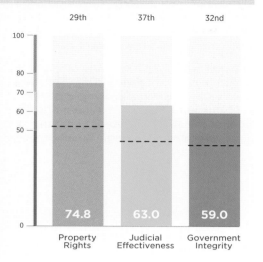

RULE OF LAW

29th	37th	32nd
Property Rights 74.8	Judicial Effectiveness 63.0	Government Integrity 59.0

Property rights for non-Qataris are limited. The judiciary is not independent in practice. The judicial system consists of Sharia courts (for family law) and civil law courts, which have jurisdiction over criminal, commercial, and civil cases. Critics cite a lack of transparency in government procurement, which favors personal connections. Qatar has faced ongoing allegations of corrupt practices in securing the winning bid to host the 2022 World Cup.

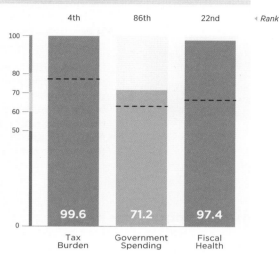

GOVERNMENT SIZE

4th	86th	22nd	◄ Rank
Tax Burden 99.6	Government Spending 71.2	Fiscal Health 97.4	

There is no income tax or domestic corporate tax. Foreign corporations operating in Qatar are subject to a flat 10 percent corporate rate. The overall tax burden equals 6.3 percent of total domestic income. Government spending has amounted to 31 percent of total output (GDP) over the past three years, and budget surpluses have averaged 15.0 percent of GDP. Public debt is equivalent to 35.8 percent of GDP.

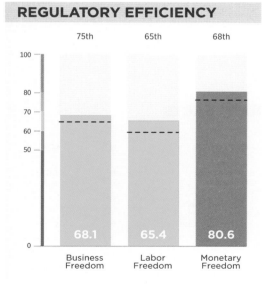

REGULATORY EFFICIENCY

75th	65th	68th
Business Freedom 68.1	Labor Freedom 65.4	Monetary Freedom 80.6

The process for launching a business and obtaining licenses has been made more streamlined. The labor force consists primarily of expatriate workers, and employment rules are relatively flexible. Fuel subsidies were scrapped in 2016 as liquefied natural gas revenues dropped and the emir criticized the dependency mindset created by years of heavy subsidization. The government has denied that it still subsidizes state-owned Qatar Airways.

OPEN MARKETS

63rd	103rd	39th	◄ Rank
Trade Freedom 83.1	Investment Freedom 55.0	Financial Freedom 60.0	

Trade is important to Qatar's economy; the value of exports and imports taken together equals 91 percent of GDP. The average applied tariff rate is 3.4 percent. Foreign investment in many sectors of the economy is capped, and state-owned enterprises distort the economy. The stable banking sector remains competitive, and investment laws have been amended to attract greater foreign investment in banking.

QATAR

SAUDI ARABIA

Saudi Arabia's regulatory efficiency and open-market policies have lagged behind those of other emerging economies. In a global economic environment of low oil prices over the past years, dynamic gains from free flows of trade and investment have likewise fallen short, leading to sizable budget deficits.

In April 2016, in a notable policy shift, the kingdom unveiled a significant economic reform plan, Saudi Vision 2030. The plan, which seeks to increase foreign investment and enhance the overall competitiveness of the Saudi Arabian economy, includes the sale of up to 5 percent of the state-owned oil company, ARAMCO, and economic diversification through development of the private sector.

WORLD RANK: **64**

REGIONAL RANK: **7**

ECONOMIC FREEDOM STATUS:
MODERATELY FREE

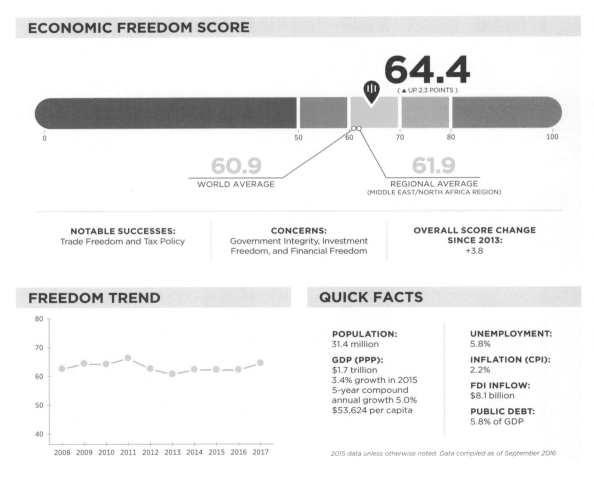

ECONOMIC FREEDOM SCORE

64.4
(▲ UP 2.3 POINTS)

0   50   60   70   80   100

60.9
WORLD AVERAGE

61.9
REGIONAL AVERAGE
(MIDDLE EAST/NORTH AFRICA REGION)

NOTABLE SUCCESSES:
Trade Freedom and Tax Policy

CONCERNS:
Government Integrity, Investment Freedom, and Financial Freedom

OVERALL SCORE CHANGE SINCE 2013:
+3.8

FREEDOM TREND

80
70
60
50
40

2008 2009 2010 2011 2012 2013 2014 2015 2016 2017

QUICK FACTS

POPULATION:
31.4 million

GDP (PPP):
$1.7 trillion
3.4% growth in 2015
5-year compound
annual growth 5.0%
$53,624 per capita

UNEMPLOYMENT:
5.8%

INFLATION (CPI):
2.2%

FDI INFLOW:
$8.1 billion

PUBLIC DEBT:
5.8% of GDP

2015 data unless otherwise noted. Data compiled as of September 2016

BACKGROUND: Saudi Arabia is an absolute monarchy ruled by King Salman bin Abdulaziz Al Saud, who became king following the death of his half-brother, King Abdullah, in January 2015. Oil revenues account for about 90 percent of export earnings and about 87 percent of government revenues. Saudi Arabia faces a rising threat from the Islamic State, which has recruited many young Saudis, as well as internal sectarian tensions between Sunni Muslims and the Shiite minority. Crown Prince Mohammad has taken the lead on security matters, including the Saudi-led coalition that intervened in Yemen in March 2015 to help the Yemeni government battle Iran-supported Houthi rebels.

12 ECONOMIC FREEDOMS | SAUDI ARABIA

RULE OF LAW

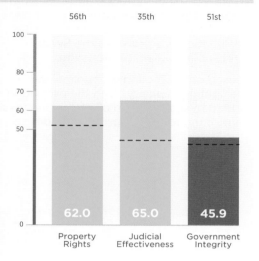

56th	35th	51st
Property Rights	Judicial Effectiveness	Government Integrity
62.0	65.0	45.9

Laws protecting private property are subject to Islamic practices. The slow and nontransparent judiciary is not independent and must coordinate its decisions with the executive branch. Despite some earlier moves to hold certain officials accountable, corruption remains a significant problem, and there is low transparency in the functioning of government as well as opacity about state budgets and financial practices.

GOVERNMENT SIZE

3rd	129th	118th	◄ Rank
Tax Burden	Government Spending	Fiscal Health	
99.7	54.5	65.7	

Saudi nationals or citizens of the Gulf Cooperation Council and corporations pay a 2.5 percent religious tax mandated by Islamic law. The overall tax burden equals 4.6 percent of total domestic income. Government spending has amounted to 39 percent of total output (GDP) over the past three years, and budget deficits have averaged 4.6 percent of GDP. Public debt is equivalent to 5.8 percent of GDP.

REGULATORY EFFICIENCY

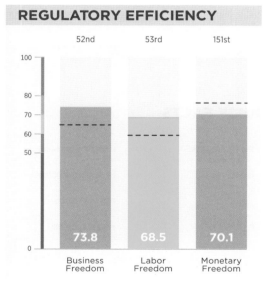

52nd	53rd	151st
Business Freedom	Labor Freedom	Monetary Freedom
73.8	68.5	70.1

With no minimum capital required, procedures for starting a business have been relatively streamlined. There is no mandated minimum wage, but wage increases have exceeded labor productivity. Oil prices must be at least $106 per barrel for Saudi Arabia to maintain its historically generous subsidies, for which Saudi nationals have paid zero taxes. In 2016, the government decreased some of those subsidies, but they still exceed regional averages.

OPEN MARKETS

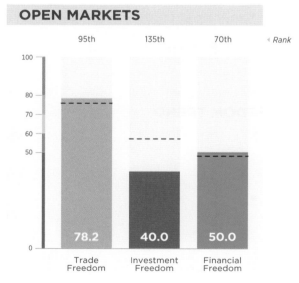

95th	135th	70th	◄ Rank
Trade Freedom	Investment Freedom	Financial Freedom	
78.2	40.0	50.0	

Trade is important to Saudi Arabia's economy; the value of exports and imports taken together equals 73 percent of GDP. The average applied tariff rate is 3.4 percent. Foreign investment is screened by the government, and state-owned enterprises distort the economy. Direct purchase of shares in Saudi companies listed on the stock exchange has been permitted since 2015, opening the market to foreign institutional investors.

SAUDI ARABIA

SYRIA

Civil war has left Syria's economy in ruins and precludes ranking it in the 2017 *Index*. The devastation and chaos have inflicted a horrific human cost and caused enormous damage to the economy. The rule of law is ravaged by extrajudicial killings, kidnappings, and torture. Inflation has grown as the Syrian pound has become an unreliable medium of exchange.

Economic policy has focused on protecting the regime and maintaining the military's fighting capacity. With the escalating cost of the war compounded by a collapse in oil prices, the fiscal situation is dire. The regime continues to prioritize spending on the military.

ECONOMIC FREEDOM SCORE

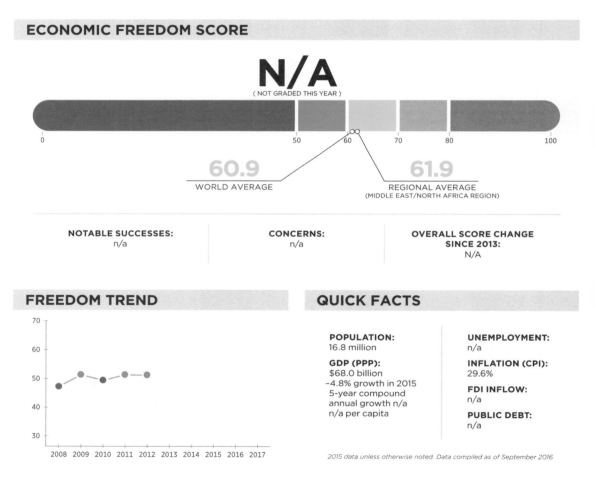

N/A
(NOT GRADED THIS YEAR)

0   50   60   70   80   100

60.9
WORLD AVERAGE

61.9
REGIONAL AVERAGE
(MIDDLE EAST/NORTH AFRICA REGION)

NOTABLE SUCCESSES:
n/a

CONCERNS:
n/a

OVERALL SCORE CHANGE SINCE 2013:
N/A

FREEDOM TREND

70

60

50

40

30

2008 2009 2010 2011 2012 2013 2014 2015 2016 2017

QUICK FACTS

POPULATION:
16.8 million

GDP (PPP):
$68.0 billion
–4.8% growth in 2015
5-year compound
annual growth n/a
n/a per capita

UNEMPLOYMENT:
n/a

INFLATION (CPI):
29.6%

FDI INFLOW:
n/a

PUBLIC DEBT:
n/a

2015 data unless otherwise noted. Data compiled as of September 2016

BACKGROUND: The Assad family has ruled Syria since Hafez al-Assad's military coup in 1970. Bashar al-Assad, who succeeded his father in 2000, failed to deliver on promises to open the socialist economy and ease political repression. A brutal crackdown after 2011's Arab Spring protests sparked an armed uprising against Assad that by 2012 had become a sectarian civil war with the predominantly Sunni rebels pitted against the Alawite-dominated regime. Assad's regime is heavily supported by Iran, Russia, and Hezbollah, while the U.S. and several of its allies back various Syrian rebel groups. The conflict has killed more than 400,000 Syrians and driven more than 4.5 million refugees out of the country.

12 ECONOMIC FREEDOMS | SYRIA

RULE OF LAW

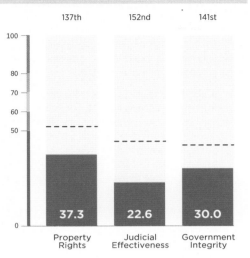

137th — Property Rights: **37.3**
152nd — Judicial Effectiveness: **22.6**
141st — Government Integrity: **30.0**

Rule of law is weak, and the government on occasion has seized political opponents' properties and businesses. All judges and prosecutors must belong to the Ba'ath Party and are beholden to the political leadership. Government institutions lacked public accountability and were plagued by corruption even before the civil war. Those who question state policies or use of public funds face harassment, imprisonment, or death.

GOVERNMENT SIZE

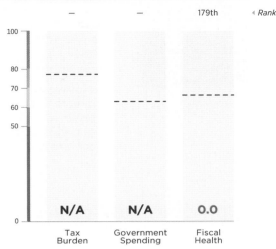

— Tax Burden: **N/A**
— Government Spending: **N/A**
179th — Fiscal Health: **0.0**

◀ Rank

The civil conflict has rendered fiscal policy and tax administration (if any) opaque. The overall budgetary situation remains dire in the near absence of a consistent flow of oil and tax revenues. In 2015, despite severe budget shortfalls, the Assad government issued a decree providing for an increase in the monthly salaries and pensions of all public-sector employees, exacerbating the already dismal fiscal situation.

REGULATORY EFFICIENCY

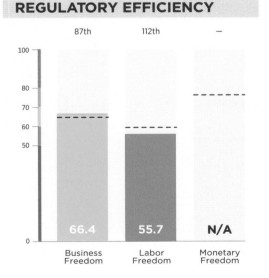

87th — Business Freedom: **66.4**
112th — Labor Freedom: **55.7**
— Monetary Freedom: **N/A**

Before the ongoing civil unrest, the business environment, lacking transparency and efficiency, had improved only marginally. Functioning labor markets are limited to certain parts of the country, subject to heavy state interference and control. To conserve resources for its fight against ISIS insurgents, the government has slashed electricity, water, diesel, and heating oil subsidies, angering Syrians who are already facing rampant inflation.

OPEN MARKETS

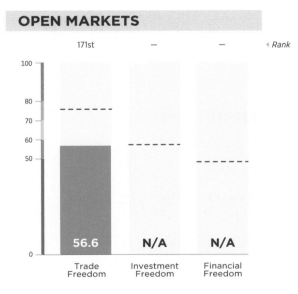

171st — Trade Freedom: **56.6**
— Investment Freedom: **N/A**
— Financial Freedom: **N/A**

◀ Rank

Syria's ongoing civil war deters international trade and investment. The average applied tariff rate is 14.2 percent. Political instability and repression have severely weakened the financial system, and foreign reserves have been almost exhausted. Despite the war, a number of foreign banks are in operation. In 2016, the Bahrain-based Islamic banking group Al Baraka became the largest privately owned bank in the country.

SYRIA

TUNISIA

Economic dynamism remains constrained in Tunisia by institutional weaknesses that remain unaddressed, primarily because political instability has hindered decisive government action. The regulatory regime, despite some improvements, remains burdensome and deters dynamic entrepreneurial activity. The closed trade regime and rigid labor markets largely prevent the emergence of a vibrant private sector.

Reforms adopted in past years have failed to deliver tangible benefits to the stagnant economic system or trigger more rapid growth. Deeper reforms to enhance governance and strengthen the critical pillars of economic freedom are needed to push the economy along a positive path of transition.

ECONOMIC FREEDOM SCORE

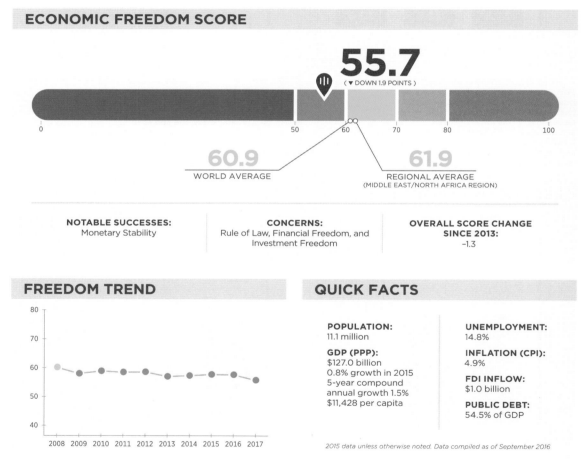

55.7
(▼ DOWN 1.9 POINTS)

0   50   60   70   80   100

60.9
WORLD AVERAGE

61.9
REGIONAL AVERAGE
(MIDDLE EAST/NORTH AFRICA REGION)

NOTABLE SUCCESSES:
Monetary Stability

CONCERNS:
Rule of Law, Financial Freedom, and Investment Freedom

OVERALL SCORE CHANGE SINCE 2013:
–1.3

FREEDOM TREND

80
70
60
50
40

2008 2009 2010 2011 2012 2013 2014 2015 2016 2017

QUICK FACTS

POPULATION:
11.1 million

GDP (PPP):
$127.0 billion
0.8% growth in 2015
5-year compound
annual growth 1.5%
$11,428 per capita

UNEMPLOYMENT:
14.8%

INFLATION (CPI):
4.9%

FDI INFLOW:
$1.0 billion

PUBLIC DEBT:
54.5% of GDP

2015 data unless otherwise noted. Data compiled as of September 2016

BACKGROUND: Tunisia, birthplace of the Arab Spring, ousted President Zine al-Abidine Ben Ali in January 2011. Shortly thereafter, the formerly banned Islamist Ennahda Party won the largest number of seats in the National Constituent Assembly. The Ennahda government stepped aside in 2014 following ratification of a new constitution in January and was succeeded by an interim technocratic government led by interim Prime Minister Mehdi Jomaa. During the second half of 2014, Tunisia held its first full parliamentary and presidential elections under the new constitution. Beji Caid Essebsi, former prime minister and leader of the Nidaa Tounes party that he founded in 2012, was elected president in December 2015. Despite notable progress in democratization, social unrest has continued.

12 ECONOMIC FREEDOMS | TUNISIA

RULE OF LAW

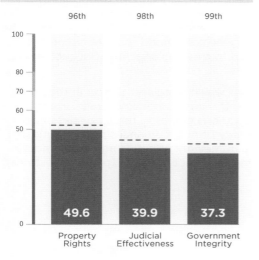

96th 98th 99th

Property Rights	Judicial Effectiveness	Government Integrity
49.6	39.9	37.3

Although the judiciary is generally independent, protection of property rights remains uneven, hindered by corruption and lengthy case backlogs. Governmental weakness encourages graft at lower levels of bureaucracy and law enforcement. Long-standing public resentment of efforts against smuggling along the Libyan border, which eliminated local jobs, intensified in 2016 after the construction of a border wall to block infiltration by terrorists.

GOVERNMENT SIZE

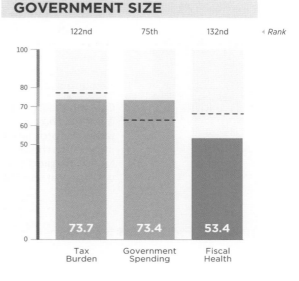

122nd 75th 132nd ◄ Rank

Tax Burden	Government Spending	Fiscal Health
73.7	73.4	53.4

The top personal income tax rate is 35 percent, and the top corporate tax rate is 30 percent. Other taxes include a value-added tax and a property transfer tax. The overall tax burden equals 22.5 percent of total domestic income. Government spending has amounted to 29.8 percent of total output (GDP) over the past three years, and budget deficits have averaged 5.0 percent of GDP. Public debt is equivalent to 54.5 percent of GDP.

REGULATORY EFFICIENCY

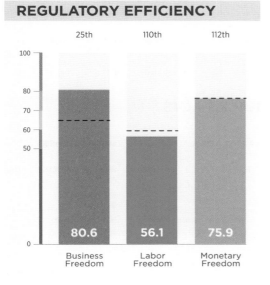

25th 110th 112th

Business Freedom	Labor Freedom	Monetary Freedom
80.6	56.1	75.9

Despite some progress, the regulatory framework still lacks transparency and efficiency. Completion of licensing requirements remains burdensome. The rigid labor market has been stagnant, failing to generate dynamic job growth. In 2016, social tensions triggered populist spending policies to placate a frustrated electorate, but low oil prices should permit the government to achieve its goal of phasing out fuel subsidies.

OPEN MARKETS

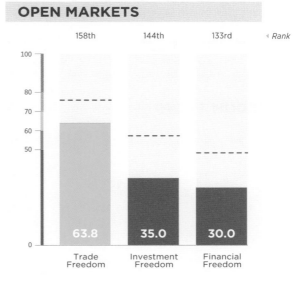

158th 144th 133rd ◄ Rank

Trade Freedom	Investment Freedom	Financial Freedom
63.8	35.0	30.0

Trade is extremely important to Tunisia's economy; the value of exports and imports taken together equals 102 percent of GDP. The average applied tariff rate is 13.1 percent. Foreign investors may not own agricultural land, and investment in other sectors may be subject to government screening. State-owned enterprises distort the economy. The weak financial sector is fragmented. Access to credit is limited, and capital markets are underdeveloped.

TUNISIA

UNITED ARAB EMIRATES

WORLD RANK:
8

REGIONAL RANK:
1

ECONOMIC FREEDOM STATUS:
MOSTLY FREE

Recent years' broad-based and dynamic growth in the United Arab Emirates has been underpinned by continuous efforts to strengthen the business climate, boost investment, and foster the emergence of a more vibrant and diverse private sector. The generally liberal trade regime has helped to sustain momentum for growth. The UAE aims to be a regional financial hub, and its banking sector is resilient.

Overall fiscal soundness is well maintained, although the non-oil deficit has widened as the government's overall surplus has fallen. Coordinating the various emirates' fiscal policies and improving the transparency of public finances remain critical tasks. Keeping the legal framework effective and independent will be vital to continuing to attract dynamic foreign investment.

ECONOMIC FREEDOM SCORE

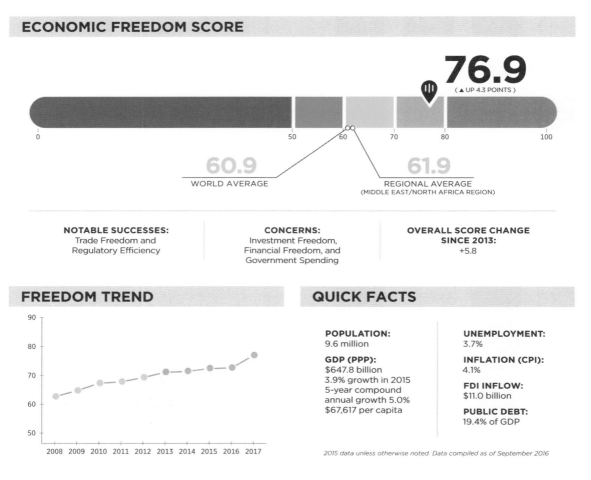

76.9
(▲ UP 4.3 POINTS)

0   50   60   70   80   100

60.9
WORLD AVERAGE

61.9
REGIONAL AVERAGE
(MIDDLE EAST/NORTH AFRICA REGION)

NOTABLE SUCCESSES:
Trade Freedom and
Regulatory Efficiency

CONCERNS:
Investment Freedom,
Financial Freedom, and
Government Spending

**OVERALL SCORE CHANGE
SINCE 2013:**
+5.8

FREEDOM TREND

90
80
70
60
50

2008 2009 2010 2011 2012 2013 2014 2015 2016 2017

QUICK FACTS

POPULATION:
9.6 million

GDP (PPP):
$647.8 billion
3.9% growth in 2015
5-year compound
annual growth 5.0%
$67,617 per capita

UNEMPLOYMENT:
3.7%

INFLATION (CPI):
4.1%

FDI INFLOW:
$11.0 billion

PUBLIC DEBT:
19.4% of GDP

2015 data unless otherwise noted. Data compiled as of September 2016

BACKGROUND: The United Arab Emirates is a federation of seven monarchies: Abu Dhabi, Ajman, Dubai, Fujairah, Ras Al-Khaimah, Sharjah, and Umm al-Qaiwain. The Federal Supreme Council (the seven rulers of the individual emirates) selects the president and vice president for five-year terms with no term limits. Abu Dhabi ruler Sheikh Khalifa bin Zayed al-Nahyan has been president since November 2004. In 2011, the government responded to protests calling for greater political participation by expanding the number of people allowed to vote in the September 2011 Federal National Council elections. Since 2012, the UAE has clamped down on social media activism.

12 ECONOMIC FREEDOMS | UNITED ARAB EMIRATES

RULE OF LAW

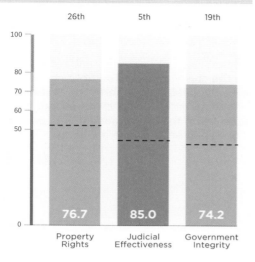

26th   5th   19th

Property Rights	Judicial Effectiveness	Government Integrity
76.7	85.0	74.2

Each emirate establishes its own land ownership procedures. Although the judiciary is not independent and court rulings are subject to review by the political leadership, the rule of law is generally well maintained, and the UAE is considered one of the region's less corrupt countries. A campaign to reform public services was launched in 2015, but the most significant government decisions are still taken only by the emirates' ruling families.

GOVERNMENT SIZE

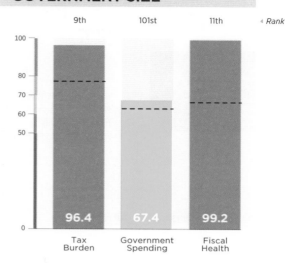

9th   101st   11th   ◂ Rank

Tax Burden	Government Spending	Fiscal Health
96.4	67.4	99.2

The UAE has no income tax and no federal-level corporate tax. There are different corporate tax rates for certain activities in some emirates. The overall tax burden equals 19.0 percent of total domestic income. Government spending has amounted to 33 percent of total output (GDP) over the past three years, and budget surpluses have averaged 3.5 percent of GDP. Public debt is equivalent to 19.4 percent of GDP.

REGULATORY EFFICIENCY

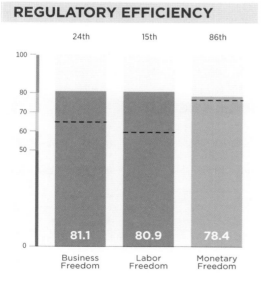

24th   15th   86th

Business Freedom	Labor Freedom	Monetary Freedom
81.1	80.9	78.4

There is no minimum capital requirement for establishing a business, and licensing requirements have been streamlined. Employment regulations are relatively flexible, and the nonsalary cost of employing a worker is not high. In 2016, the IMF commended the government for eliminating fuel subsidies, raising tariffs on water and electricity, and scaling back grants and transfers to government-run enterprises.

OPEN MARKETS

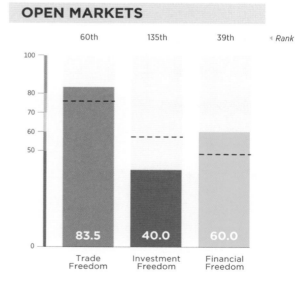

60th   135th   39th   ◂ Rank

Trade Freedom	Investment Freedom	Financial Freedom
83.5	40.0	60.0

Trade is extremely important to the UAE's economy; the value of exports and imports taken together equals 176 percent of GDP. The average applied tariff rate is 3.2 percent. In general, foreign investors may own majority stakes in companies outside of "free zones." State-owned enterprises distort the economy. The financial sector provides a full range of services, but the state presence is considerable. Capital markets are open and vibrant.

UNITED ARAB EMIRATES

YEMEN

Numerical grading of Yemen's overall economic freedom remains suspended in the 2017 *Index* because of a significant deterioration in the quality of publicly available economic statistics for the country. An intensifying civil conflict has devastated the economy, destroying critical infrastructure.

Yemen will require significant international assistance to stabilize its economy if and when the civil war ends. The fighting has created a mounting humanitarian crisis, food shortages, and tens of thousands of refugees. Yemen's limited oil and gas production has been severely disrupted, and the prolonged conflict continues to take a heavy toll on the already fragile economy.

ECONOMIC FREEDOM SCORE

N/A
(NOT GRADED THIS YEAR)

0   50   60   70   80   100

60.9
WORLD AVERAGE

61.9
REGIONAL AVERAGE
(MIDDLE EAST/NORTH AFRICA REGION)

NOTABLE SUCCESSES:	CONCERNS:	OVERALL SCORE CHANGE SINCE 2013:
n/a	n/a	N/A

FREEDOM TREND

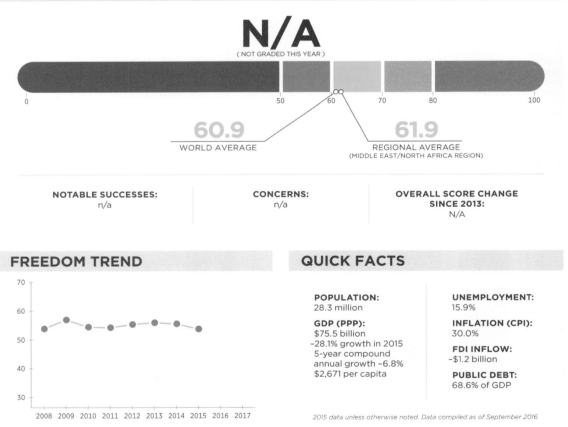

70

60

50

40

30

2008 2009 2010 2011 2012 2013 2014 2015 2016 2017

QUICK FACTS

POPULATION:
28.3 million

GDP (PPP):
$75.5 billion
−28.1% growth in 2015
5-year compound
annual growth −6.8%
$2,671 per capita

UNEMPLOYMENT:
15.9%

INFLATION (CPI):
30.0%

FDI INFLOW:
−$1.2 billion

PUBLIC DEBT:
68.6% of GDP

2015 data unless otherwise noted. Data compiled as of September 2016

BACKGROUND: The civil war in Yemen, one of the Arab world's least developed countries, has brought tentative efforts at modernization and integration into the global economy to a halt. The conflict's most immediate cause is a breakdown in relations between President Abd Rabbuh Mansour Hadi and the Houthis, a Zaydi Shia rebel movement. In March 2015, Saudi Arabia launched an intensive bombing campaign and ground intervention in an attempt to restore Hadi to power, but the Houthis have retained significant gains on the ground. Al-Qaeda in the Arabian Peninsula (AQAP) has exploited the conflict to seize parts of eastern Yemen and develop a working relationship with anti-Houthi tribal militias.

12 ECONOMIC FREEDOMS | YEMEN

RULE OF LAW

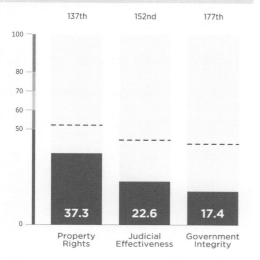

137th   152nd   177th

Property Rights	Judicial Effectiveness	Government Integrity
37.3	22.6	17.4

Property rights and business activity are impaired by insecurity and corruption. The nominally independent judiciary is weak and susceptible to interference from the executive branch. Authorities have a poor record of enforcing judicial rulings. Years of mismanagement and corruption, compounding the depletion of natural resources, had resulted in chronic poverty and underdevelopment even before the current conflict.

GOVERNMENT SIZE

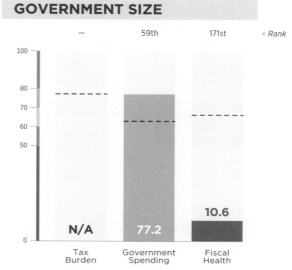

—   59th   171st   ◄ Rank

Tax Burden	Government Spending	Fiscal Health
N/A	77.2	10.6

Political turmoil and civil conflict have caused the economy to collapse. Oil and gas exports have been suspended, and the overall fiscal situation remains perilous with the impact of the escalating cost of the war compounded by a collapse in oil and tax revenue. Limited fiscal resources have been directed toward spending on the military and public-sector wages. Millions of Yemenis are at risk of famine.

REGULATORY EFFICIENCY

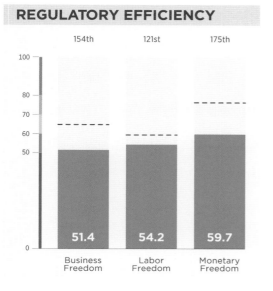

154th   121st   175th

Business Freedom	Labor Freedom	Monetary Freedom
51.4	54.2	59.7

The absence of a dynamic private sector results in chronic underemployment and a large informal sector. In 2014, in the midst of civil war, fiscal pressure caused by lower oil revenue forced the cash-strapped government in Sana'a to cut fuel subsidies. The ensuing popular backlash was exploited by the Houthis, a Zaydi Shia group from northern Yemen, but the Houthis could not afford to restore fuel subsidies after seizing the capital.

OPEN MARKETS

—   —   —   ◄ Rank

Trade Freedom	Investment Freedom	Financial Freedom
N/A	N/A	N/A

Trade is important to Yemen's economy; the value of exports and imports taken together equals 60 percent of GDP. The average applied tariff rate is 4.1 percent. Yemen's civil war impedes international trade and investment. The economy is largely cash based, and the small financial system remains dominated by the state. The ongoing conflict has increased the banking system's instability and fragility.

YEMEN

SUB-SAHARAN AFRICA

SUB-SAHARAN AFRICA

Sub-Saharan African countries are distributed primarily within the lower ranks of economic freedom. Nonetheless, a number of countries in the region have substantial growth momentum, and the positive economic results achieved through limited advances in economic freedom have created valuable impetus for the additional institutional reforms that are needed to ensure long-term economic development.

However, the region as a whole continues to underperform in following through on policy changes that would encourage the emergence of a more dynamic private sector. Structural transformation and modernization remain patchy in many African countries. Limited diversification has resulted in less broad-based growth, with exports often concentrated in sectors with little scope for sustained increases in productivity.

Regrettably, in some cases, the signs of repeated government failure continue to be overwhelming. The population-weighted average GDP per capita for the region is only $5,334, the lowest level of any region. Unemployment hovers at 7.7 percent.

SUB-SAHARAN AFRICA: QUICK FACTS

TOTAL POPULATION: 990.8 million

POPULATION WEIGHTED AVERAGES

GDP PER CAPITA (PPP):	$5,334
GROWTH:	4.5%
5 YEAR GROWTH:	5.3%
INFLATION:	6.5%
UNEMPLOYMENT:	7.7%
PUBLIC DEBT:	42.1%

SOURCE: Terry Miller and Anthony B. Kim, *2017 Index of Economic Freedom* (Washington: The Heritage Foundation, 2017), http://www.heritage.org/index.

☎ heritage.org

Chart 1 shows the distribution of countries in the Sub-Saharan African region among the five categories of economic freedom. Unlike regions that have a diverse range of free-market economies, in sub-Saharan Africa, there are only distinctions among less free economies. There is no "free" economy in the region, and Mauritius and Botswana are the only "moderately free" economies. A majority of the 47 graded nations are ranked either "mostly unfree" or "repressed." In fact, 11 of the world's 23 "repressed" economies are in Sub-Saharan Africa.

As shown in Table 1, the single factor for which the region scores higher than the world average is government size. Ironically, however, it is worse than average in terms of taxation, which might indicate that tax revenues are being stolen rather than spent on government services. Labor freedom is restricted, reflecting in part the region's lack of progress toward a modern and efficient labor market. Despite ongoing reform efforts in many countries, policies related to regulatory efficiency and open markets have not advanced strongly in comparison to other regions of the world.

More critically, uneven economic playing fields, exacerbated by the weak rule of law, continue to leave those who lack political connections with only limited prospects for a brighter future. The region's scores on property rights, judicial effectiveness, and government integrity are lower than world averages by 10 points or more.

Nevertheless, Chart 2 confirms that even in this region, the strong relationship between high levels of economic freedom and high GDP per capita holds true, although Equatorial Guinea, the oil-rich "repressed" economy, drives up the average GDP per capita for the region's least economically free countries.

Also noteworthy is the growing attention that has been given in recent years to the

SUB-SAHARAN AFRICA

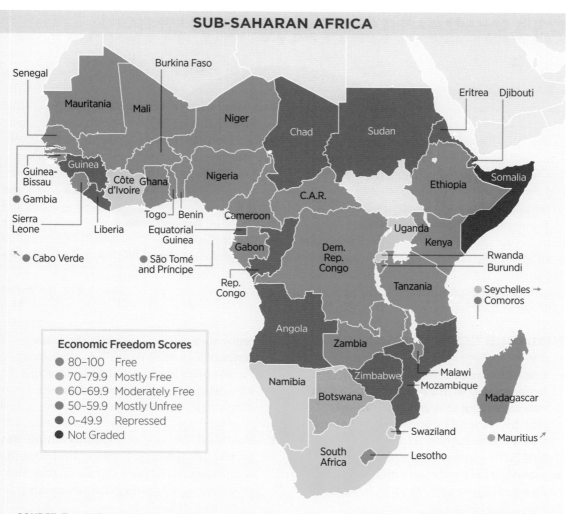

Economic Freedom Scores
- 80–100 Free
- 70–79.9 Mostly Free
- 60–69.9 Moderately Free
- 50–59.9 Mostly Unfree
- 0–49.9 Repressed
- Not Graded

SOURCE: Terry Miller and Anthony B. Kim, *2017 Index of Economic Freedom* (Washington: The Heritage Foundation, 2017), http://www.heritage.org/index.

☎ heritage.org

importance of ensuring food security, a critical dimension of fighting poverty, particularly in sub-Saharan Africa. More aid money cannot and will not safeguard food security. The task is multidimensional and closely linked to achieving agricultural development, economic growth, institutional stability, openness to trade, and overall social progress. It is ultimately about advancing and sustaining economic freedom so that a virtuous cycle of growth and development can occur meaningfully for a greater number of ordinary people. As shown in Chart 3, economic freedom is an indispensable ingredient in enhancing food security in the region.

It remains to be seen whether the region's leaders have the political will to undertake the fundamental economic reforms that are needed to translate narratives of "Africa Rising" into reality. There are some success stories, and they usually involve countries with greater freedom.

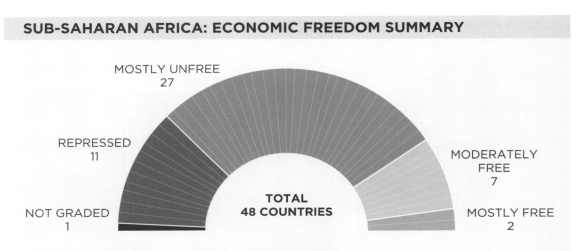

MOSTLY UNFREE
27

REPRESSED
11

NOT GRADED
1

**TOTAL
48 COUNTRIES**

MODERATELY
FREE
7

MOSTLY FREE
2

SOURCE: Terry Miller and Anthony B. Kim, *2017 Index of Economic Freedom* (Washington: The Heritage Foundation, 2017), http://www.heritage.org/index.

Chart 1 ☎ heritage.org

NOTABLE COUNTRIES

• Côte d'Ivoire's economic expansion has been notable with a robust GDP growth rate averaging around 6 percent over the past five years. The government has undertaken much-needed reforms to maintain and further enhance the potential for growth. These measures include strengthening management of public finances and

regulatory reforms to foster the emergence of a more dynamic private sector. Fiscal policy has focused on promoting investment as well as on funding other development needs.

• Nigeria, Africa's most populous nation, has sought to improve macroeconomic stability and develop its poor infrastructure, but severe economic policy distortions and

SUB-SAHARAN AFRICA: GDP PER CAPITA, BY ECONOMIC FREEDOM CATEGORY

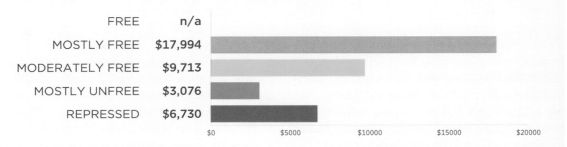

FREE	n/a
MOSTLY FREE	$17,994
MODERATELY FREE	$9,713
MOSTLY UNFREE	$3,076
REPRESSED	$6,730

SOURCES: Terry Miller and Anthony B. Kim, *2017 Index of Economic Freedom* (Washington: The Heritage Foundation, 2017), http://www.heritage.org/index, and International Monetary Fund, World Economic Outlook Database, April 2016, https://www.imf.org/external/pubs/ft/weo/2016/01/weodata/index.aspx (accessed December 13, 2016).

Chart 2 ☎ heritage.org

SUB-SAHARAN AFRICA: COMPONENTS OF ECONOMIC FREEDOM

LOWER THAN WORLD AVERAGE ●—| |—● HIGHER THAN WORLD AVERAGE

		AVERAGES		
		Region	World	
OVERALL		**55.0**	60.9	●—|
RULE OF LAW	Property Rights	**39.1**	53.0	●——|
	Judicial Effectiveness	**34.3**	45.0	●—|
	Government Integrity	**31.6**	43.0	●—|
GOVERNMENT SIZE	Tax Burden	**75.6**	77.1	●|
	Government Spending	**74.6**	63.4	|——●
	Fiscal Health	**62.1**	68.0	●—|
REGULATORY EFFICIENCY	Business Freedom	**52.6**	64.6	●——|
	Labor Freedom	**54.5**	59.2	●—|
	Monetary Freedom	**75.2**	76.4	●
MARKET OPENNESS	Trade Freedom	**68.3**	75.9	●—|
	Investment Freedom	**52.6**	57.2	●—|
	Financial Freedom	**39.8**	48.2	●——|

SOURCE: Terry Miller and Anthony B. Kim, *2017 Index of Economic Freedom* (Washington: The Heritage Foundation, 2017), http://www.heritage.org/index.

Table 1 ☎ heritage.org

a lack of transparency in the economic system continue to deter progress. The government has also struggled to end ongoing security threats in parts of the country that have exacerbated poverty and unemployment. The government's over-reliance on oil, which accounts for over 90 percent of export earnings, has exposed the economy to major risks amid declining oil prices.

- Performing far below its potential, South Africa's economy has been stifled by political instability and a weakening rule of law. The judicial system has become vulnerable to political interference, and numerous scandals and frequent political infighting have severely undermined government integrity. Private-sector growth remains constrained by structural and institutional impediments caused by growing government encroachment into the marketplace.

- Grading of Sudan's economic freedom has resumed in the 2017 *Index*, reflecting the improved availability and quality of key economic data. The petroleum sector provides some economic stability and foreign exchange earnings, but other parts of the economy are underdeveloped and face serious structural and institutional headwinds. Continued conflict with rebels and South Sudan promotes uncertainty and undermines investor confidence.

SUB-SAHARAN AFRICA: ECONOMIC FREEDOM AND FOOD SECURITY

Each circle represents a nation in the *Index of Economic Freedom*

Global Food Security Index Score

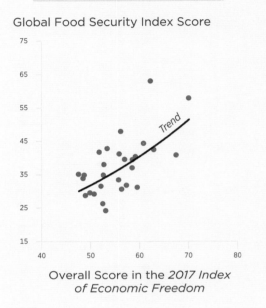

Overall Score in the *2017 Index of Economic Freedom*

SOURCES: Terry Miller and Anthony B. Kim, *2017 Index of Economic Freedom* (Washington: The Heritage Foundation, 2017), http://www.heritage.org/index, and The Economist Intelligence Unit, Global Food Security Index, June 2016, http://foodsecurityindex.eiu.com/ (accessed December 13, 2016).

Chart 3 ☎ heritage.org

- Togo has undertaken a series of economic reforms in recent years, restructuring its key banking, electricity, and transportation sectors. The corporate tax rate, formerly one of the region's highest, has been lowered. The government has also taken steps to divest public enterprises, and there are plans to privatize inefficient public banks. However, an inefficient business environment and weak public administration continue to undermine overall competitiveness.

ECONOMIC FREEDOM IN SUB-SAHARAN AFRICA

World Rank	Regional Rank	Country	Overall Score	Change from 2016	Property Rights	Judicial Effectiveness	Government Integrity	Tax Burden	Government Spending	Fiscal Health	Business Freedom	Labor Freedom	Monetary Freedom	Trade Freedom	Investment Freedom	Financial Freedom
21	1	Mauritius	74.7	0.0	64.4	72.6	44.3	92.0	81.5	74.9	78.2	68.8	81.1	88.7	80	70
34	2	Botswana	70.1	-1.0	58.1	54.0	57.6	77.1	61.2	99.4	68.8	68.6	77.9	83.8	65	70
51	3	Rwanda	67.6	4.5	64.4	68.8	45.9	79.8	77.3	83.3	59.0	81.8	80.0	70.3	60	40
75	4	Côte d'Ivoire	63.0	3.0	42.6	45.8	34.3	78.4	84.6	87.0	62.1	50.6	73.2	72.3	75	50
78	5	Namibia	62.5	0.6	53.8	50.6	41.3	65.2	55.6	66.4	67.6	84.4	77.2	83.5	65	40
81	6	South Africa	62.3	0.4	67.6	59.7	47.6	70.2	68.4	70.0	62.0	58.9	75.8	77.3	40	50
85	7	Seychelles	61.8	-0.4	55.2	42.6	44.3	78.8	63.9	90.7	63.4	55.9	78.3	83.4	55	30
88	8	Swaziland	61.1	1.4	53.5	33.3	30.9	74.8	71.6	93.2	57.5	64.4	75.6	88.9	50	40
91	9	Uganda	60.9	1.6	39.3	34.6	28.7	73.7	91.0	78.1	42.4	84.6	80.3	78.3	60	40
93	10	Burkina Faso	59.6	0.5	38.2	28.4	31.7	82.6	82.5	88.4	46.4	53.3	84.6	69.2	70	40
96	11	Benin	59.2	-0.1	36.0	29.4	31.3	68.6	85.9	71.3	51.9	52.4	85.4	68.7	80	50
102	12	Mali	58.6	2.1	36.7	33.8	34.3	69.4	88.0	87.8	44.2	51.1	83.0	70.1	65	40
103	13	Gabon	58.6	-0.4	35.9	26.7	37.6	77.0	81.0	96.1	50.6	58.4	83.0	61.8	55	40
105	14	Tanzania	58.6	0.1	33.8	28.8	29.2	80.3	89.5	76.6	50.1	64.3	69.6	76.0	55	50
113	15	Madagascar	57.4	-3.7	34.8	21.4	25.0	91.0	93.2	79.8	43.3	43.8	73.3	78.0	55	50
115	16	Nigeria	57.1	-0.4	35.3	33.2	12.2	85.2	95.2	87.2	48.9	73.9	71.3	62.3	40	40
116	17	Cabo Verde	56.9	-9.6	42.6	50.2	41.8	78.3	70.7	1.2	65.5	43.2	86.7	68.2	75	60
117	18	Congo, Dem. Rep. of	56.4	10.0	40.6	48.7	28.6	73.4	94.7	99.3	59.9	38.4	78.6	64.6	30	20
118	19	Ghana	56.2	-7.3	51.6	40.9	35.5	84.5	76.3	9.2	59.6	57.4	64.5	65.1	70	60
119	20	Guinea-Bissau	56.1	4.3	33.8	48.7	28.7	89.0	87.5	75.3	46.7	60.9	77.7	65.2	30	30
120	21	Senegal	55.9	-2.2	44.0	39.3	42.1	70.9	74.3	51.8	50.8	38.9	86.0	73.1	60	40
121	22	Comoros	55.8	3.4	37.3	22.6	30.0	64.6	81.2	98.6	58.5	50.6	81.5	70.2	45	30
122	23	Zambia	55.8	-3.0	49.6	39.8	35.0	73.1	81.6	21.6	66.6	48.2	70.7	78.3	55	50
124	24	São Tomé and Príncipe	55.4	-1.3	37.7	15.9	39.7	87.8	67.9	67.1	65.0	47.2	69.6	71.8	65	30
131	25	Mauritania	54.4	-0.4	22.5	13.8	29.2	81.2	73.2	77.1	64.4	57.4	81.9	62.3	50	40
134	26	Lesotho	53.9	3.3	51.6	50.9	39.6	55.7	0.0	92.2	52.2	57.7	76.4	80.2	50	40
135	27	Kenya	53.5	-4.0	45.1	42.7	24.7	78.5	77.9	14.4	50.0	62.4	73.8	67.2	55	50
136	28	Gambia	53.4	-3.7	39.1	38.8	38.2	74.9	74.3	3.2	52.8	65.6	63.8	65.0	75	50
138	29	Togo	53.2	-0.4	33.8	39.9	36.8	68.2	79.8	45.1	50.3	46.2	77.5	71.3	60	30
139	30	Burundi	53.2	-0.7	25.7	19.8	24.6	73.8	69.5	69.6	53.5	67.4	75.2	74.2	55	30
142	31	Ethiopia	52.7	1.2	32.6	29.6	37.6	77.1	90.3	86.5	50.0	57.2	65.7	65.1	20	20
145	32	Sierra Leone	52.6	0.3	37.4	27.0	18.9	81.3	90.2	76.2	49.6	29.7	71.1	69.4	60	20
149	33	Malawi	52.2	0.4	36.0	44.2	31.3	79.1	69.8	33.5	45.3	56.9	54.7	70.5	55	50
150	34	Cameroon	51.8	-2.4	43.5	29.6	17.4	75.4	84.4	60.9	44.3	47.8	80.1	53.4	35	50
151	35	Central African Republic	51.8	6.6	12.6	33.0	28.7	65.8	94.1	84.1	27.2	42.7	68.2	55.2	80	30
154	36	Niger	50.8	-3.5	33.8	22.6	35.0	76.3	73.4	38.5	39.1	46.1	83.3	66.4	55	40
158	37	Mozambique	49.9	-3.3	40.6	32.4	30.9	73.2	58.2	22.7	58.8	41.0	79.9	76.7	35	50

(CONTINUED ON NEXT PAGE)

ECONOMIC FREEDOM IN SUB-SAHARAN AFRICA

World Rank	Regional Rank	Country	Overall Score	Change from 2016	Property Rights	Judicial Effectiveness	Government Integrity	Tax Burden	Government Spending	Fiscal Health	Business Freedom	Labor Freedom	Monetary Freedom	Trade Freedom	Investment Freedom	Financial Freedom
161	38	Liberia	49.1	-3.1	33.6	41.0	31.4	83.6	60.1	36.2	53.1	48.5	71.8	60.1	50	20
162	39	Chad	49.0	2.7	30.6	24.1	24.6	46.0	87.2	74.6	27.5	44.9	74.3	54.7	60	40
164	40	Sudan	48.8	N/A	31.1	19.8	18.9	86.5	95.1	85.5	53.9	49.7	59.3	50.5	15	20
165	41	Angola	48.5	-0.4	36.4	19.8	12.8	87.7	58.6	70.7	58.5	40.4	70.6	56.7	30	40
169	42	Guinea	47.6	-5.7	15.6	13.1	27.5	69.1	78.4	34.2	55.8	54.8	71.1	61.2	50	40
171	43	Djibouti	46.7	-9.3	12.3	10.3	32.6	80.9	39.5	13.8	51.6	59.0	75.3	54.9	80	50
174	44	Equatorial Guinea	45.0	1.3	35.4	13.1	24.6	75.4	53.6	46.4	50.9	38.5	78.3	53.8	40	30
175	45	Zimbabwe	44.0	5.8	27.3	26.1	14.7	61.1	75.2	90.6	36.2	33.1	76.5	52.8	25	10
176	46	Eritrea	42.2	-0.5	36.4	10.3	27.5	81.3	74.7	0.0	56.7	69.7	61.0	69.2	0	20
177	47	Congo, Rep. of	40.0	-2.8	34.8	22.6	30.5	66.8	36.2	11.6	32.1	37.5	76.1	52.2	50	30
N/A	N/A	Somalia	N/A	N/A	6.8	N/A	11.6	100	N/A	0.0	92.3	91.8	N/A	N/A	N/A	N/A

ANGOLA

Angola's natural resource wealth has helped to attract foreign direct investment and facilitate a decade of notable economic growth. However, the economy recently suffered a major structural shock as a result of lower oil prices, and oil revenues are uncertain. Monopolies and quasi-monopolies still dominate the leading sectors. Modest reforms have somewhat modernized the regulatory environment.

Pervasive corruption and the lack of capable public institutions continue to undermine the implementation of other important reforms. Tariff and nontariff barriers and burdensome investment regulations hamper development of a more dynamic private sector and interfere with diversification of the economic base.

ECONOMIC FREEDOM SCORE

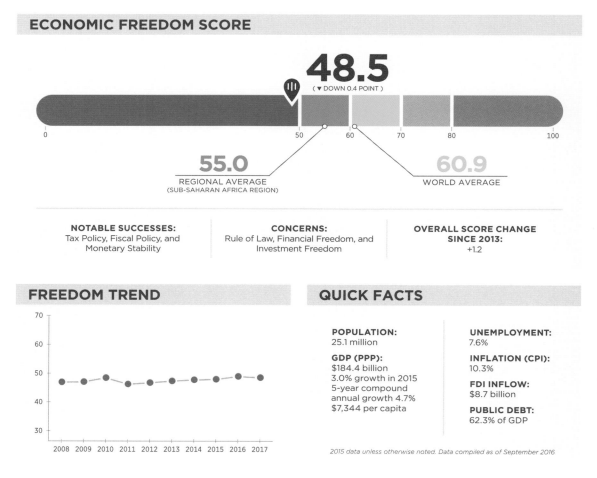

48.5
(▼ DOWN 0.4 POINT)

0   50   60   70   80   100

55.0
REGIONAL AVERAGE
(SUB-SAHARAN AFRICA REGION)

60.9
WORLD AVERAGE

NOTABLE SUCCESSES:
Tax Policy, Fiscal Policy, and
Monetary Stability

CONCERNS:
Rule of Law, Financial Freedom, and
Investment Freedom

**OVERALL SCORE CHANGE
SINCE 2013:**
+1.2

FREEDOM TREND

70

60

50

40

30

2008 2009 2010 2011 2012 2013 2014 2015 2016 2017

QUICK FACTS

POPULATION:
25.1 million

GDP (PPP):
$184.4 billion
3.0% growth in 2015
5-year compound
annual growth 4.7%
$7,344 per capita

UNEMPLOYMENT:
7.6%

INFLATION (CPI):
10.3%

FDI INFLOW:
$8.7 billion

PUBLIC DEBT:
62.3% of GDP

2015 data unless otherwise noted. Data compiled as of September 2016

BACKGROUND: José Eduardo dos Santos's Popular Movement for the Liberation of Angola won parliamentary elections in August 2012, the second such election since the end of the 27-year civil war in 2002. Angola is Africa's second-largest oil producer, with much of its proven reserves concentrated in Cabinda province, which is plagued by a separatist conflict. Despite the country's oil, diamonds, hydroelectric potential, and rich agricultural land, most Angolans remain poor and dependent on subsistence farming. The slump in global oil prices has battered the oil-dependent economy. As part of its response, the government borrowed more than $11 billion between November 2015 and June 2016. Angola served as a nonpermanent member of the United Nations Security Council for the 2015–2016 term.

12 ECONOMIC FREEDOMS | ANGOLA

RULE OF LAW

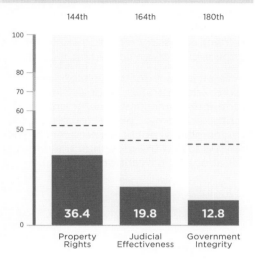

144th | 164th | 180th

Property Rights **36.4** | Judicial Effectiveness **19.8** | Government Integrity **12.8**

Protection of property rights is weak. Property registration is time-consuming and can be prohibitively expensive. The judiciary is subject to extensive political influence from the executive, and courts suffer from a lack of trained legal professionals, poor infrastructure, and a large case backlog. Government corruption is widespread. In June 2016, the president placed his eldest daughter in charge of Sonangol, the state-owned oil company.

GOVERNMENT SIZE

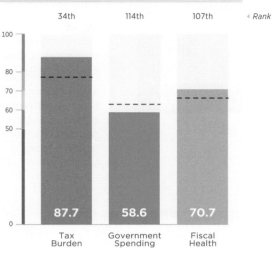

34th | 114th | 107th ◂ Rank

Tax Burden **87.7** | Government Spending **58.6** | Fiscal Health **70.7**

The top income tax rate is 17 percent. The top normal corporate tax rate is 30 percent, but rates for the mining and oil industries are as high as 50 percent. The overall tax burden equals 6.5 percent of total domestic income. Government spending has amounted to 37.1 percent of total output (GDP) over the past three years, and budget deficits have averaged 3.7 percent of GDP. Public debt is equivalent to 62.3 percent of GDP.

REGULATORY EFFICIENCY

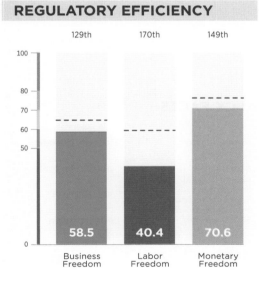

129th | 170th | 149th

Business Freedom **58.5** | Labor Freedom **40.4** | Monetary Freedom **70.6**

Despite the recent implementation of more streamlined business start-up procedures, burdensome regulations still hinder private-sector development. Overall, the regulatory system lacks clarity, and regulations are enforced inconsistently. The formal labor market is underdeveloped. In 2016, the government ended subsidies and raised prices significantly on gas, asphalt, and heavy and light oil; it continues to subsidize electricity.

OPEN MARKETS

170th | 154th | 106th ◂ Rank

Trade Freedom **56.7** | Investment Freedom **30.0** | Financial Freedom **40.0**

Trade is important to Angola's economy; the value of exports and imports taken together equals 75 percent of GDP. The average applied tariff rate is 11.7 percent. Quotas on some products deter imports, and all land is owned by the government. Banking continues to expand, but public use of banking services remains low; only about 10 percent of the population maintains a bank account. The capital market is underdeveloped.

ANGOLA

BENIN

WORLD RANK: **96** REGIONAL RANK: **11**

ECONOMIC FREEDOM STATUS:
MOSTLY UNFREE

Entrepreneurs in Benin benefit from a relatively stable political and macroeconomic environment. The government has introduced structural reforms to promote diversification and modernization. However, inefficient regulations and the lack of political momentum to fully implement necessary reforms remain serious obstacles to the advancement of economic freedom.

The most visible constraints on private-sector development are related to fiscal pressure, administrative complexities, and the lack of respect for contracts. Bureaucratic inefficiency and corruption affect much of the economy. Court enforcement of property rights remains vulnerable to political interference. The lack of economic freedom has fueled the growth of the informal sector, which accounts for about 60 percent of GDP.

ECONOMIC FREEDOM SCORE

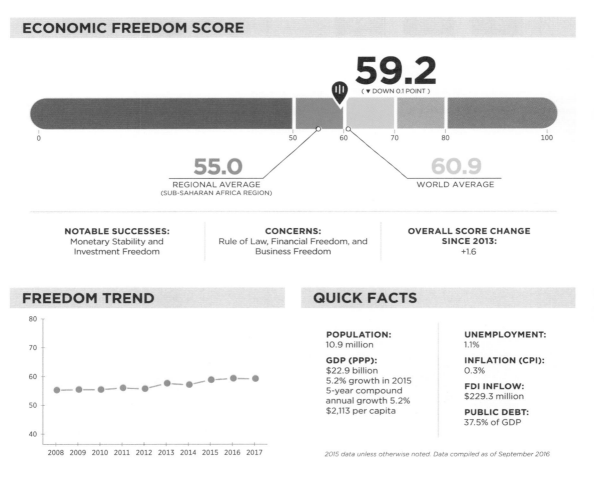

59.2
(▼ DOWN 0.1 POINT)

0   50   60   70   80   100

55.0
REGIONAL AVERAGE
(SUB-SAHARAN AFRICA REGION)

60.9
WORLD AVERAGE

NOTABLE SUCCESSES:
Monetary Stability and
Investment Freedom

CONCERNS:
Rule of Law, Financial Freedom, and
Business Freedom

**OVERALL SCORE CHANGE
SINCE 2013:**
+1.6

FREEDOM TREND

80
70
60
50
40

2008 2009 2010 2011 2012 2013 2014 2015 2016 2017

QUICK FACTS

POPULATION:
10.9 million

GDP (PPP):
$22.9 billion
5.2% growth in 2015
5-year compound
annual growth 5.2%
$2,113 per capita

UNEMPLOYMENT:
1.1%

INFLATION (CPI):
0.3%

FDI INFLOW:
$229.3 million

PUBLIC DEBT:
37.5% of GDP

2015 data unless otherwise noted. Data compiled as of September 2016

BACKGROUND: President Patrice Talon, a wealthy businessman, was elected in a runoff vote in March 2016 to succeed Thomas Boni Yayi, who stepped down pursuant to the constitution's two-term limit on the presidency. Talon ran as an independent and defeated Lionel Zinsou of the ruling Cowry Forces for an Emerging Benin party. One of Africa's largest cotton producers, Benin nevertheless remains underdeveloped and dependent on subsistence agriculture and regional trade, particularly with Nigeria. In September 2015, the government signed its second Millennium Challenge Corporation compact for $375 million to increase power generation in a country where two-thirds of the population lacks access to electricity.

12 ECONOMIC FREEDOMS | BENIN

RULE OF LAW

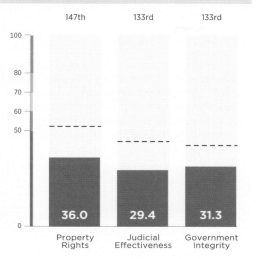

	147th	133rd	133rd
	Property Rights	Judicial Effectiveness	Government Integrity
	36.0	29.4	31.3

In 2016, the new government proposed reforms to increase state transparency and accountability and strengthen judicial independence. If they are adopted, a national Court of Accounts will be established to conduct thorough and independent reviews of public finances in the wake of a major embezzlement scandal in 2015. The courts are highly inefficient and susceptible to corruption, largely due to persistent lack of funding.

GOVERNMENT SIZE

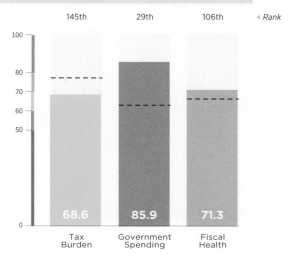

	145th	29th	106th	◄ Rank
	Tax Burden	Government Spending	Fiscal Health	
	68.6	85.9	71.3	

The top income tax rate is 45 percent. The top corporate tax rate is 30 percent, with oil companies subject to a 45 percent rate. Other taxes include a value-added tax. The overall tax burden equals 14.8 percent of total domestic income. Government spending has amounted to 21.7 percent of total output (GDP) over the past three years, and budget deficits have averaged 4.0 percent of GDP. Public debt is equivalent to 37.5 percent of GDP.

REGULATORY EFFICIENCY

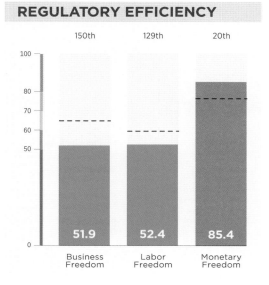

	150th	129th	20th
	Business Freedom	Labor Freedom	Monetary Freedom
	51.9	52.4	85.4

The overall entrepreneurial environment remains burdensome. Obtaining necessary business licenses is time-consuming and costly. Agriculture accounts for nearly 70 percent of the workforce, and outmoded employment regulations hinder overall job creation. The government subsidizes cotton production. Low-priced gasoline and diesel fuel are smuggled illegally from Nigeria and subsidized by the Nigerian government.

OPEN MARKETS

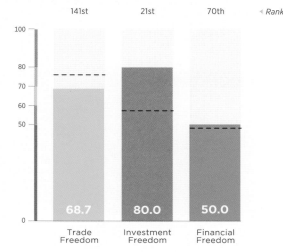

	141st	21st	70th	◄ Rank
	Trade Freedom	Investment Freedom	Financial Freedom	
	68.7	80.0	50.0	

Trade is important to Benin's economy; the value of exports and imports taken together equals 63 percent of GDP. The average applied tariff rate is 10.6 percent, and bureaucratic barriers to trade and investment have been reduced. Banking is highly concentrated and predominantly private, and foreign ownership is allowed. Despite the development of microfinance institutions, overall access to credit remains low.

BOTSWANA

Botswana's economy has rebounded from the 2008 global economic downturn. Good management of public finance has resulted in budget surpluses in recent years. The regulatory environment encourages growth, and openness to foreign investment and trade promotes competitiveness and resilience.

The financial sector is fairly well developed, with an independent central bank and little government intervention. The independent judiciary provides strong protection of property rights. In an effort to lessen dependence on diamond production, the government has instituted competitive corporate tax rates, streamlined the application process for business ventures, and committed to increased transparency.

ECONOMIC FREEDOM SCORE

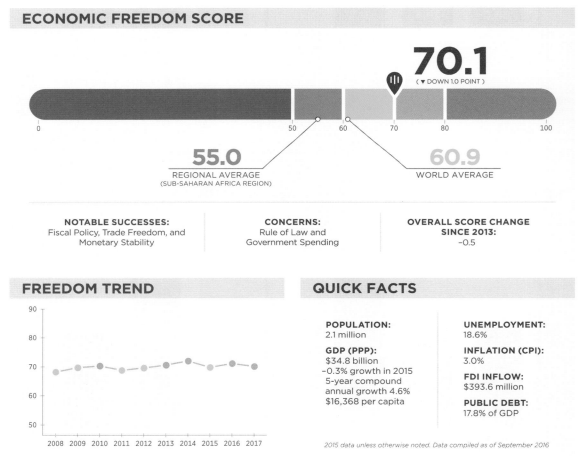

70.1
(▼ DOWN 1.0 POINT)

0   50   60   70   80   100

55.0
REGIONAL AVERAGE
(SUB-SAHARAN AFRICA REGION)

60.9
WORLD AVERAGE

NOTABLE SUCCESSES:
Fiscal Policy, Trade Freedom, and Monetary Stability

CONCERNS:
Rule of Law and Government Spending

OVERALL SCORE CHANGE SINCE 2013:
–0.5

FREEDOM TREND

90
80
70
60
50

2008 2009 2010 2011 2012 2013 2014 2015 2016 2017

QUICK FACTS

POPULATION:
2.1 million

GDP (PPP):
$34.8 billion
–0.3% growth in 2015
5-year compound annual growth 4.6%
$16,368 per capita

UNEMPLOYMENT:
18.6%

INFLATION (CPI):
3.0%

FDI INFLOW:
$393.6 million

PUBLIC DEBT:
17.8% of GDP

2015 data unless otherwise noted. Data compiled as of September 2016

BACKGROUND: The Botswana Democratic Party has governed this multi-party democracy since independence from Britain in 1966. The most recent elections, held in 2014, were the most competitive in the country's history. President Ian Khama won a second term in October 2014, though the BDP for the first time won less than 50 percent of the vote as opposition groups gained significant support from young and urban middle-class voters. Botswana and the U.S. cooperate closely on military issues and are in talks to have Botswana host a U.S. military airfield. Botswana has abundant natural resources, a market-oriented economy, and one of Africa's highest sovereign credit ratings. In an attempt to diversify the economy through tourism, Botswana focuses on conservation and developing its extensive nature preserves.

12 ECONOMIC FREEDOMS | BOTSWANA

RULE OF LAW

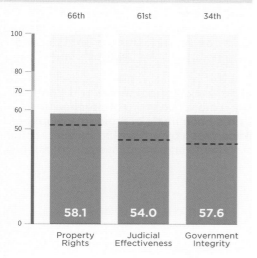

66th	61st	34th
Property Rights 58.1	Judicial Effectiveness 54.0	Government Integrity 57.6

Protection of property rights in Botswana is among the best in the region. The government generally respects judicial independence, but because of severe staffing shortages and a case backlog, courts do not provide timely trials. Botswana also is still rated the least corrupt country on the African continent, although there are almost no restrictions on the private business activities of public servants.

GOVERNMENT SIZE

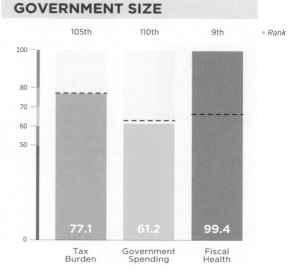

◁ Rank

105th	110th	9th
Tax Burden 77.1	Government Spending 61.2	Fiscal Health 99.4

The top personal income tax rate is 25 percent, and the top corporate tax rate is 22 percent. Other taxes include a property tax, an inheritance tax, and a value-added tax. The overall tax burden equals 34.4 percent of total domestic income. Government spending has amounted to 36 percent of total output (GDP) over the past three years, and budget surpluses have averaged 2.1 percent of GDP. Public debt is equivalent to 17.8 percent of GDP.

REGULATORY EFFICIENCY

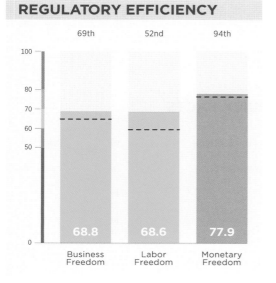

69th	52nd	94th
Business Freedom 68.8	Labor Freedom 68.6	Monetary Freedom 77.9

The regulatory environment protects the overall freedom to establish and run a business relatively well. A one-stop shop for entrepreneurs is in place, and the process for business closings has become easy and straightforward. Employment regulations are relatively flexible. One of the aims of the 2016–2017 draft budget is containment of subsidies and transfers to state-owned enterprises, but progress has been slow.

OPEN MARKETS

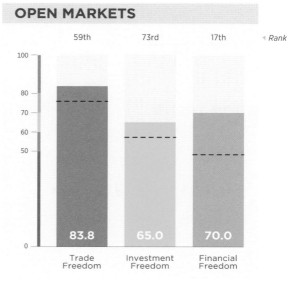

◁ Rank

59th	73rd	17th
Trade Freedom 83.8	Investment Freedom 65.0	Financial Freedom 70.0

Trade is important to Botswana's economy; the value of exports and imports taken together equals 99 percent of GDP. The average applied tariff rate is 0.6 percent. State-owned enterprises distort the economy, and foreign investment in some sectors is restricted. Generally adhering to global standards in the transparency of banking supervision, the financial sector provides considerable access to credit and has expanded.

BOTSWANA

BURKINA FASO

Relatively sound macroeconomic management facilitated by cotton and gold exports has enabled Burkina Faso to achieve annual growth rates of over 5 percent over the past five years. Earlier reforms have resulted in some positive trends, reducing poverty. Prospects for reinvigorating growth depend on how much the new democratically elected government can foster political stability.

Systemic weaknesses in protection of property rights continue to hinder development of a more dynamic entrepreneurial environment. Little progress has been made in fighting corruption. The weak rule of law, exacerbated by political turbulence, continues to undermine judicial effectiveness and investor confidence.

ECONOMIC FREEDOM SCORE

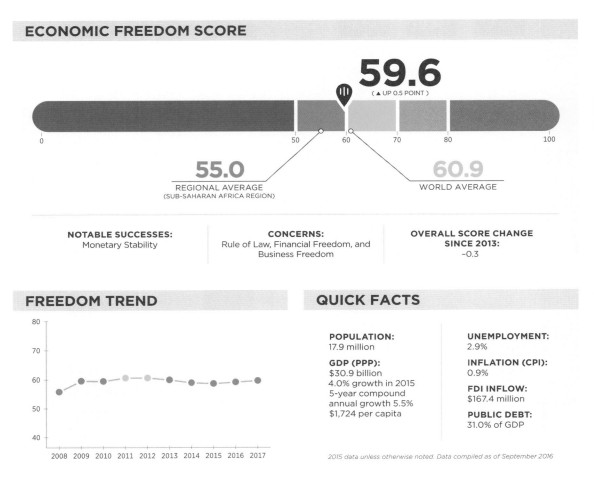

59.6
(▲ UP 0.5 POINT)

0   50   60   70   80   100

55.0
REGIONAL AVERAGE
(SUB-SAHARAN AFRICA REGION)

60.9
WORLD AVERAGE

NOTABLE SUCCESSES:
Monetary Stability

CONCERNS:
Rule of Law, Financial Freedom, and Business Freedom

OVERALL SCORE CHANGE SINCE 2013:
–0.3

FREEDOM TREND

80

70

60

50

40

2008 2009 2010 2011 2012 2013 2014 2015 2016 2017

QUICK FACTS

POPULATION:
17.9 million

GDP (PPP):
$30.9 billion
4.0% growth in 2015
5-year compound
annual growth 5.5%
$1,724 per capita

UNEMPLOYMENT:
2.9%

INFLATION (CPI):
0.9%

FDI INFLOW:
$167.4 million

PUBLIC DEBT:
31.0% of GDP

2015 data unless otherwise noted. Data compiled as of September 2016

BACKGROUND: Months of tumult that began after widespread protests forced longtime President Blaise Compaoré to resign ended with the first-round election of Roch Marc Christian Kaboré of the People's Movement for Progress in November 2015. Kaboré is the first president since 1966 to gain office without a coup. Landlocked Burkina Faso is one of the world's poorest countries. Youth literacy rates are well below the sub-Saharan Africa average, though enrolment in primary and secondary schools has risen over the past decade. In January 2016, terrorists from Al-Qaeda in the Islamic Maghreb and Al-Mourabitoun killed 30 people in the capital city of Ouagadougou in what the groups claimed was retaliation against French and other Western military activities in the region.

12 ECONOMIC FREEDOMS | BURKINA FASO

RULE OF LAW

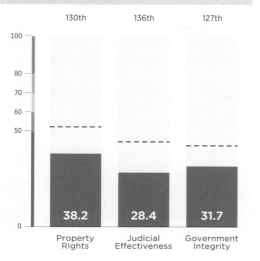

130th	136th	127th	◄
Property Rights 38.2	Judicial Effectiveness 28.4	Government Integrity 31.7	

Protection of private property is weak. Only about 5,000 land titles have been granted since 1960. Challenges faced by the new government include a weak judiciary, limited enforcement powers of anticorruption institutions, misappropriation of public funds, and the lack of an effective separation of powers. Courts lack resources and are often unwilling or unable to proceed effectively against many senior officials charged with corruption.

GOVERNMENT SIZE

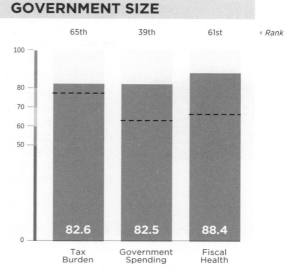

65th	39th	61st	◄ Rank
Tax Burden 82.6	Government Spending 82.5	Fiscal Health 88.4	

The top individual income and corporate tax rates are 27.5 percent. Other taxes include a value-added tax. The overall tax burden equals 15.2 percent of total domestic income. Government spending has amounted to 24.2 percent of total output (GDP) over the past three years, and budget deficits have averaged 2.5 percent of GDP. Public debt is equivalent to 31 percent of GDP.

REGULATORY EFFICIENCY

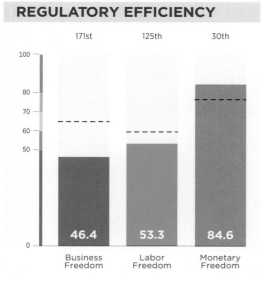

171st	125th	30th	
Business Freedom 46.4	Labor Freedom 53.3	Monetary Freedom 84.6	

Reforms to streamline regulation have been implemented and, although progress has been mixed, have helped to enhance the overall entrepreneurial environment. Measures to modernize the labor market and enhance its flexibility have progressed slowly. The state subsidizes fuels and electricity, maintains price supports for cotton, and influences other prices through the public sector.

OPEN MARKETS

139th	59th	106th	◄ Rank
Trade Freedom 69.2	Investment Freedom 70.0	Financial Freedom 40.0	

Trade is important to Burkina Faso's economy; the value of exports and imports taken together equals 69 percent of GDP. The average applied tariff rate is 7.9 percent. State-owned enterprises distort the economy. The government has pursued banking liberalization and restructuring, limiting its direct participation, but financial firms still lack the capacity to provide a full range of modern services.

BURUNDI

WORLD RANK:
139

REGIONAL RANK:
30

ECONOMIC FREEDOM STATUS:
MOSTLY UNFREE

Burundi's economy, hampered by extensive state controls and structural problems, lags in productivity growth and lacks dynamism. Despite a significant attempt to improve the regulatory environment for business, the overall absence of economic freedom continues to undermine entrepreneurial activity. Reform is fragile and has progressed unevenly.

Long-standing structural problems include inefficient management of public finance and a poor legal framework that undermines regulatory efficiency. The lack of enforcement of property rights and the weak rule of law have driven many people and enterprises into the informal sector. State interference in the economy and failure to sustain open markets have undercut trade and investment.

ECONOMIC FREEDOM SCORE

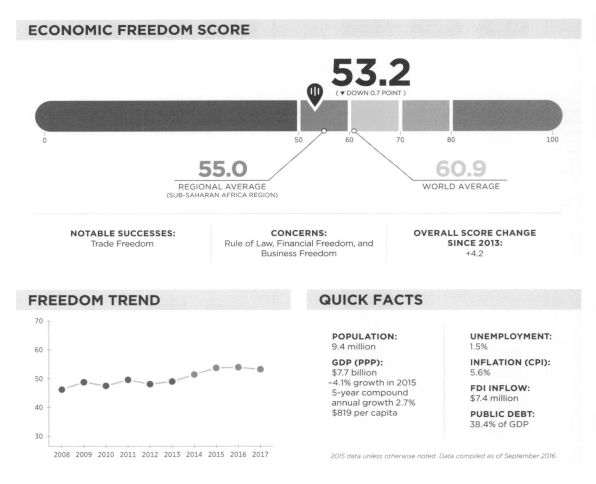

53.2
(▼ DOWN 0.7 POINT)

0   50   60   70   80   100

55.0
REGIONAL AVERAGE
(SUB-SAHARAN AFRICA REGION)

60.9
WORLD AVERAGE

NOTABLE SUCCESSES:
Trade Freedom

CONCERNS:
Rule of Law, Financial Freedom, and Business Freedom

OVERALL SCORE CHANGE SINCE 2013:
+4.2

FREEDOM TREND

70
60
50
40
30

2008 2009 2010 2011 2012 2013 2014 2015 2016 2017

QUICK FACTS

POPULATION:
9.4 million

GDP (PPP):
$7.7 billion
–4.1% growth in 2015
5-year compound
annual growth 2.7%
$819 per capita

UNEMPLOYMENT:
1.5%

INFLATION (CPI):
5.6%

FDI INFLOW:
$7.4 million

PUBLIC DEBT:
38.4% of GDP

2015 data unless otherwise noted. Data compiled as of September 2016

BACKGROUND: Pierre Nkurunziza was reelected president in July 2015, using a technicality to sidestep a two-term constitutional limit. His presidential run sparked violence that killed more than 450 people in tit-for-tat killings, including assassinations of prominent opposition members and high-ranking regime officials. Several Western countries have imposed sanctions on government officials and leaders of a rebel group formed to fight the regime. The economy is dominated by subsistence agriculture, and well over half of the population lives below the poverty line. As Western countries have grown reluctant to engage, in June 2016, Burundi's central bank signed an agreement with Russia's Gazprombank to explore possibilities for Russian investment in Burundi.

12 ECONOMIC FREEDOMS | BURUNDI

RULE OF LAW

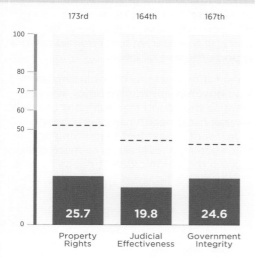

173rd   164th   167th

Property Rights: 25.7
Judicial Effectiveness: 19.8
Government Integrity: 24.6

Private property is vulnerable to government expropriation and armed banditry. The judiciary is nominally independent, but judges are subject to political pressure. One of the world's poorest nations, landlocked Burundi remains one of sub-Saharan Africa's most corrupt countries. Government procurement is conducted nontransparently amid frequent allegations of cronyism. Customs officials reportedly extort bribes.

GOVERNMENT SIZE

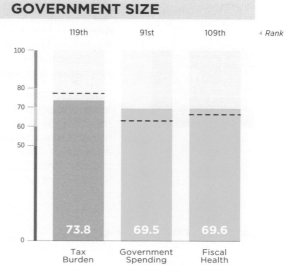

119th   91st   109th   ◄ Rank

Tax Burden: 73.8
Government Spending: 69.5
Fiscal Health: 69.6

The top individual income and corporate tax rates are 35 percent. A value-added tax recently replaced the general sales tax. The overall tax burden equals 12.9 percent of total domestic income. Government spending has amounted to 31.9 percent of total output (GDP) over the past three years, and budget deficits have averaged 4.1 percent of GDP. Public debt is equivalent to 38.4 percent of GDP.

REGULATORY EFFICIENCY

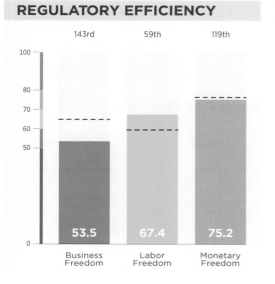

143rd   59th   119th

Business Freedom: 53.5
Labor Freedom: 67.4
Monetary Freedom: 75.2

The overall business environment remains severely constrained by burdensome regulations and inefficiency. Continuing instability and bureaucratic corruption impede entrepreneurial activity. In the absence of a modern labor market, the informal sector accounts for most employment. The state subsidizes fuel, rations subsidized electricity, and influences other prices through state-owned enterprises and agriculture-support programs.

OPEN MARKETS

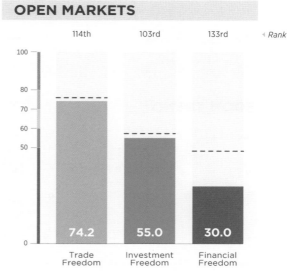

114th   103rd   133rd   ◄ Rank

Trade Freedom: 74.2
Investment Freedom: 55.0
Financial Freedom: 30.0

Trade is moderately important to Burundi's economy; the value of exports and imports taken together equals 40 percent of GDP. The average applied tariff rate is 5.4 percent. State-owned enterprises distort the economy. The underdeveloped financial sector provides a very limited range of services. The state dominates commercial banking, and many people still rely on microcredit or informal lending.

BURUNDI

CABO VERDE

WORLD RANK: **116**   **REGIONAL RANK:** **17**

ECONOMIC FREEDOM STATUS:
MOSTLY UNFREE

Cabo Verde has benefited from moderately well-maintained monetary stability and a relatively high level of market openness that facilitates engagement with the world through trade and investment. The small island economy benefits significantly from a sound and transparent legal framework that institutionalizes and supports the rule of law.

However, Cabo Verde's institutional strengths, including an independent judiciary and government transparency, are not matched by a commitment to the sound management of public finance. The country's overall fiscal health has been undermined by relatively high levels of government spending and deficits. With public debt reaching a level equal to more than 100 percent of GDP, reducing the chronic deficit needs to be a high priority.

ECONOMIC FREEDOM SCORE

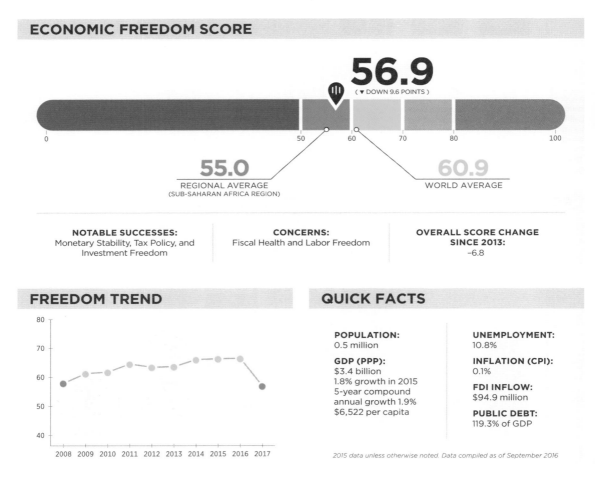

56.9
(▼ DOWN 9.6 POINTS)

0   50   60   70   80   100

55.0
REGIONAL AVERAGE
(SUB-SAHARAN AFRICA REGION)

60.9
WORLD AVERAGE

NOTABLE SUCCESSES:
Monetary Stability, Tax Policy, and Investment Freedom

CONCERNS:
Fiscal Health and Labor Freedom

OVERALL SCORE CHANGE SINCE 2013:
–6.8

FREEDOM TREND

80
70
60
50
40

2008 2009 2010 2011 2012 2013 2014 2015 2016 2017

QUICK FACTS

POPULATION:
0.5 million

GDP (PPP):
$3.4 billion
1.8% growth in 2015
5-year compound
annual growth 1.9%
$6,522 per capita

UNEMPLOYMENT:
10.8%

INFLATION (CPI):
0.1%

FDI INFLOW:
$94.9 million

PUBLIC DEBT:
119.3% of GDP

2015 data unless otherwise noted. Data compiled as of September 2016

BACKGROUND: Cabo Verde is a stable, multi-party parliamentary democracy. President Jorge Carlos Fonseca, the chief of state since 2011, appointed Ulisses Correia e Silva as prime minister after his Movement for Democracy party won the March 2016 parliamentary election. The Cabo Verde islands have few natural resources. Services dominate the economy, and most of the country's food is imported. Cabo Verde's expatriate population is larger than its domestic population. Ongoing economic reforms are intended to boost foreign investment and diversify the economy.

KEY: – – WORLD AVERAGE

12 ECONOMIC FREEDOMS | CABO VERDE

RULE OF LAW

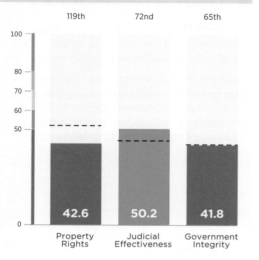

119th   72nd   65th

Property Rights	Judicial Effectiveness	Government Integrity
42.6	50.2	41.8

Private property is reasonably well protected. In 2016, the government made transfers of property less costly by lowering the property registration tax. The judiciary is constitutionally independent and generally respected, but the judicial system is inefficient, and a case backlog causes significant delays. Compared to other African nations, Cabo Verde has relatively high levels of transparency and relatively low levels of corruption.

GOVERNMENT SIZE

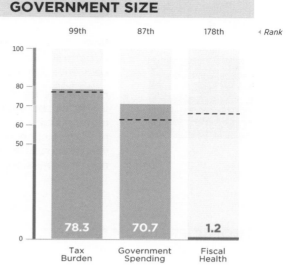

99th   87th   178th ◂ Rank

Tax Burden	Government Spending	Fiscal Health
78.3	70.7	1.2

The top personal income tax rate is 35 percent, and the top corporate tax rate is 25 percent. Other taxes include a value-added tax. The overall tax burden equals 18.0 percent of total domestic income. Government spending has amounted to 31.2 percent of total output (GDP) over the past three years, and budget deficits have averaged 7.0 percent of GDP. Public debt is equivalent to 119.3 percent of GDP.

REGULATORY EFFICIENCY

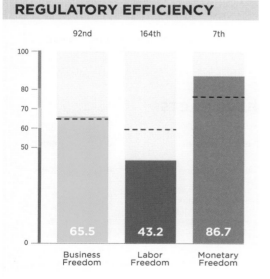

92nd   164th   7th

Business Freedom	Labor Freedom	Monetary Freedom
65.5	43.2	86.7

The overall business environment has become more efficient. The process for launching a business is more streamlined, and licensing requirements are less burdensome. Despite efforts to reform the labor market, the unemployment rate remains persistently high. The market determines most prices. The state subsidizes electricity and water, but subsidies to the state-owned, loss-making airline were reduced in 2016.

OPEN MARKETS

143rd   37th   39th ◂ Rank

Trade Freedom	Investment Freedom	Financial Freedom
68.2	75.0	60.0

Trade is moderately important to Cabo Verde's economy; the value of exports and imports taken together equals 38 percent of GDP. The average applied tariff rate is 10.9 percent. Nontariff barriers have been lowered, and foreign and domestic investors are generally treated equally under the law. The number of nonperforming loans in the banking system has decreased. Credit is generally allocated on market terms.

CABO VERDE

CAMEROON

WORLD RANK: 150   **REGIONAL RANK:** 34

ECONOMIC FREEDOM STATUS:
MOSTLY UNFREE

Cameroon's economy, although relatively diversified with services accounting for around 40 percent of GDP, is dominated by the public sector. Economic development continues to be hampered by the lack of private-sector dynamism. Modest structural reforms have done little to improve the overall business environment, which is not conducive to investment.

Entrepreneurs face lingering systemic challenges that include inefficient bureaucracy, an unreliable legal system, and poor infrastructure. Restrictions on trade through nontariff barriers raise costs, and the weak judicial system allows pervasive corruption that erodes incentives for long-term economic expansion.

ECONOMIC FREEDOM SCORE

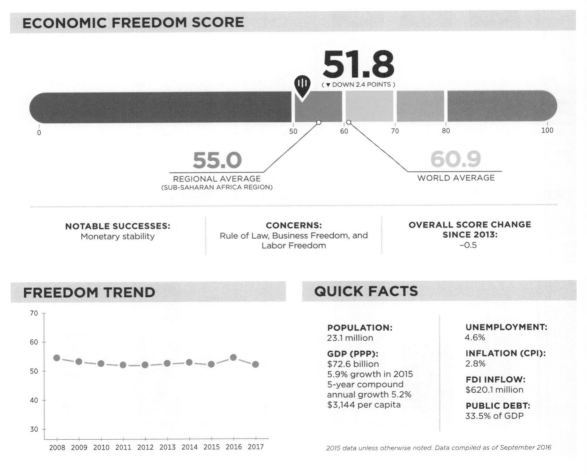

51.8
(▼ DOWN 2.4 POINTS)

0   50   60   70   80   100

55.0
REGIONAL AVERAGE
(SUB-SAHARAN AFRICA REGION)

60.9
WORLD AVERAGE

NOTABLE SUCCESSES:
Monetary stability

CONCERNS:
Rule of Law, Business Freedom, and Labor Freedom

OVERALL SCORE CHANGE SINCE 2013:
−0.5

FREEDOM TREND

70
60
50
40
30

2008 2009 2010 2011 2012 2013 2014 2015 2016 2017

QUICK FACTS

POPULATION:
23.1 million

GDP (PPP):
$72.6 billion
5.9% growth in 2015
5-year compound
annual growth 5.2%
$3,144 per capita

UNEMPLOYMENT:
4.6%

INFLATION (CPI):
2.8%

FDI INFLOW:
$620.1 million

PUBLIC DEBT:
33.5% of GDP

2015 data unless otherwise noted. Data compiled as of September 2016

BACKGROUND: President Paul Biya has ruled since 1982 and was reelected in October 2011 for another seven-year term in an election marred by irregularities. The country is battling the Nigerian Islamist terrorist group Boko Haram, which frequently attacks across the 1,230-mile Cameroon–Nigeria border. The economy is heavily regulated and dependent on exports of such commodities as oil, which accounts for about 40 percent of export earnings. The economy is further hobbled by inefficient parastatal companies in key industries. Cameroon is building a deep-sea port in Kribi and seeking to tap its great hydropower potential by building a dam and hydropower plant on the Lom River. Cameroon currently hosts more than 330,000 refugees, primarily from the Central African Republic and Nigeria.

12 ECONOMIC FREEDOMS | CAMEROON

RULE OF LAW

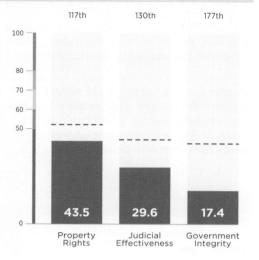

117th	130th	177th
43.5	29.6	17.4
Property Rights	Judicial Effectiveness	Government Integrity

Protection of real and intellectual property rights is weak, and the slow, inefficient judicial system is vulnerable to political interference. Corruption and cronyism are pervasive. Bribery is commonplace in all sectors, from gaining school admission to fixing traffic infractions. Revenues from oil, gas, and mining are not openly reported. A government anticorruption campaign has been used to remove potential political opponents.

GOVERNMENT SIZE

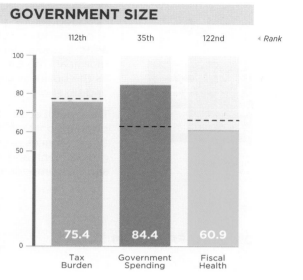

112th	35th	122nd	◄ Rank
75.4	84.4	60.9	
Tax Burden	Government Spending	Fiscal Health	

The top individual income tax rate is 35 percent, and the top corporate tax rate is 33 percent. Other taxes include a value-added tax and an inheritance tax. The overall tax burden equals 12.2 percent of total domestic income. Government spending has amounted to 22.8 percent of total output (GDP) over the past three years, and budget deficits have averaged 4.8 percent of GDP. Public debt is equivalent to 33.5 percent of GDP.

REGULATORY EFFICIENCY

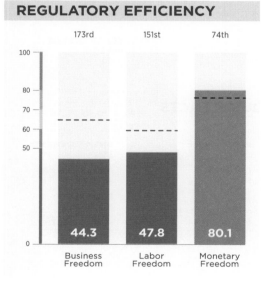

173rd	151st	74th
44.3	47.8	80.1
Business Freedom	Labor Freedom	Monetary Freedom

Private enterprises still face numerous impediments related to regulatory inefficiency and non-transparency. Despite some reforms, requirements for business entry and exit are time-consuming and costly. The labor market remains inefficient. Lower oil prices significantly reduced the cost of government subsidies for electricity, retail gasoline, diesel, and liquefied natural gas in 2016. Prices for food and other consumer goods are heavily regulated.

OPEN MARKETS

177th	144th	70th	◄ Rank
53.4	35.0	50.0	
Trade Freedom	Investment Freedom	Financial Freedom	

Trade is moderately important to Cameroon's economy; the value of exports and imports taken together equals 43 percent of GDP. The average applied tariff rate is 15.8 percent, and foreign and domestic investors are generally treated equally under the law. The cost of financing remains high, and access to credit is very limited in rural areas. There is a wide network of microfinance institutions.

CAMEROON

CENTRAL AFRICAN REPUBLIC

WORLD RANK: **151** REGIONAL RANK: **35**

ECONOMIC FREEDOM STATUS:
MOSTLY UNFREE

The Central African Republic is one of the world's least-developed countries. More than half of its people live in rural areas and depend on subsistence agriculture. Progress in developing a more stable climate for entrepreneurial activity has been only marginal. The CAR scores very poorly on such regulatory factors as the business and investment climate, labor market flexibility, and taxation.

The overall economic environment is further undermined by ongoing political and security challenges. The inability to deliver basic services reliably has severely eroded confidence in the government, and weak rule of law and pervasive corruption seriously impede prospects for economic development.

ECONOMIC FREEDOM SCORE

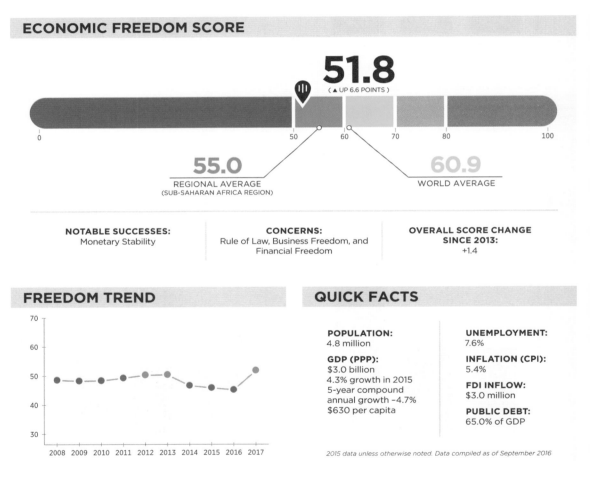

51.8
(▲ UP 6.6 POINTS)

0   50   60   70   80   100

55.0
REGIONAL AVERAGE
(SUB-SAHARAN AFRICA REGION)

60.9
WORLD AVERAGE

NOTABLE SUCCESSES:
Monetary Stability

CONCERNS:
Rule of Law, Business Freedom, and Financial Freedom

OVERALL SCORE CHANGE SINCE 2013:
+1.4

FREEDOM TREND

70
60
50
40
30

2008 2009 2010 2011 2012 2013 2014 2015 2016 2017

QUICK FACTS

POPULATION:
4.8 million

GDP (PPP):
$3.0 billion
4.3% growth in 2015
5-year compound
annual growth –4.7%
$630 per capita

UNEMPLOYMENT:
7.6%

INFLATION (CPI):
5.4%

FDI INFLOW:
$3.0 million

PUBLIC DEBT:
65.0% of GDP

2015 data unless otherwise noted. Data compiled as of September 2016

BACKGROUND: In early 2013, Muslim Seleka rebels led by Michel Djotodia ousted President François Bozizé. The sectarian violence that followed precipitated a French intervention in December 2013, and the U.N. deployed almost 12,000 peacekeepers starting in September 2014. Djotodia stepped down early in 2014 and was replaced by interim President Catherine Samba-Panza. Voters overwhelmingly approved a new constitution by referendum in December 2015, and former Prime Minister Faustin-Archange Touadéra was elected president in a runoff vote in February 2016. A cease-fire was signed in April 2015, but the violence, which has resulted in about 6,000 deaths and more than 800,000 refugees and internally displaced persons, continues. The CAR has abundant timber, diamonds, gold, and uranium.

12 ECONOMIC FREEDOMS | CENTRAL AFRICAN REPUBLIC

RULE OF LAW

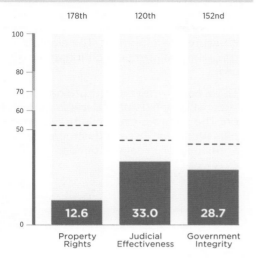

	178th	120th	152nd
	Property Rights **12.6**	Judicial Effectiveness **33.0**	Government Integrity **28.7**

Protection of property rights is weak. There have been numerous reports of armed militias entering homes without judicial authorization, seizing property without due process, and evicting residents both in the capital city of Bangui and throughout the countryside. The new government is struggling to provide basic protection and services. Ordinary citizens have very limited access to justice. Corruption remains pervasive.

GOVERNMENT SIZE

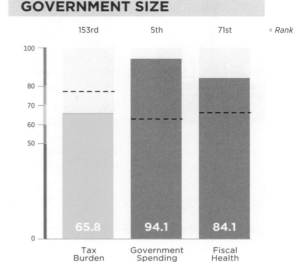

	153rd	5th	71st	◄ Rank
	Tax Burden **65.8**	Government Spending **94.1**	Fiscal Health **84.1**	

The top personal income tax rate is 50 percent, and the top corporate tax rate is 30 percent. Other taxes include a value-added tax. The overall tax burden equals 4.4 percent of total domestic income. Government spending has amounted to 14 percent of total output (GDP) over the past three years, and budget deficits have averaged 2.2 percent of GDP. Public debt is equivalent to 65.0 percent of GDP.

REGULATORY EFFICIENCY

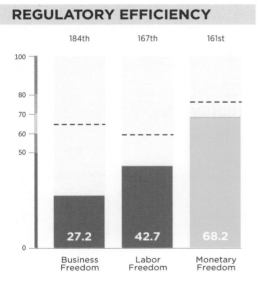

	184th	167th	161st
	Business Freedom **27.2**	Labor Freedom **42.7**	Monetary Freedom **68.2**

Establishing a business remains time-consuming, and other burdensome and opaque regulatory requirements increase the cost of conducting business. The labor market remains severely underdeveloped. Government distortions of the economy through subsidies and wage and price controls are exacerbated by persistent political volatility that undermines the functioning of state institutions.

OPEN MARKETS

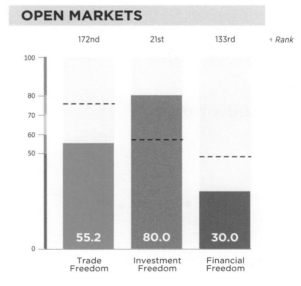

	172nd	21st	133rd	◄ Rank
	Trade Freedom **55.2**	Investment Freedom **80.0**	Financial Freedom **30.0**	

Trade is moderately important to the Central African Republic's economy; the value of exports and imports taken together equals 40 percent of GDP. The average applied tariff rate is 14.9 percent. The government taxes exports and restricts sugar imports. The financial system is underdeveloped, and access to financing for businesses remains very limited. Less than 1 percent of the population has access to banking services.

CHAD

Chad's economy has expanded at an average rate of almost 5 percent over the past five years, but the volatility of economic growth has undermined economic development and poverty reduction. The weakness of the overall regulatory and legal framework hinders private-sector development. The economy relies on oil and agriculture, with the former accounting for 60 percent of export revenues.

Entrepreneurs continue to be hamstrung by institutional shortcomings. The inefficient judicial system lacks independence and is vulnerable to corruption. The state's presence in the economy is still considerable. Despite significant fiscal adjustments in recent years, the budget remains chronically in deficit.

ECONOMIC FREEDOM SCORE

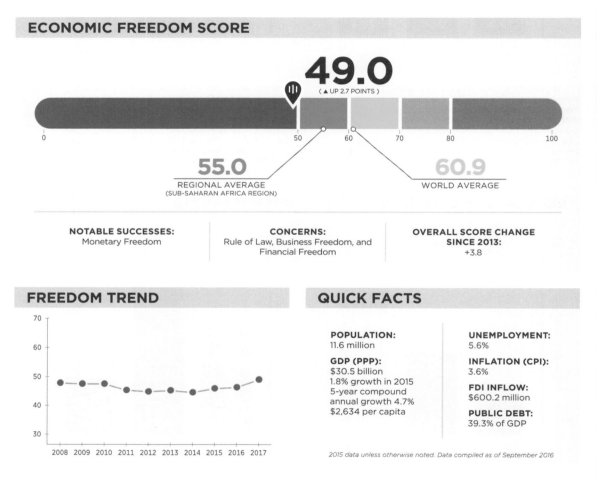

49.0
(▲ UP 2.7 POINTS)

| 0 | 50 | 60 | 70 | 80 | 100 |

55.0
REGIONAL AVERAGE
(SUB-SAHARAN AFRICA REGION)

60.9
WORLD AVERAGE

NOTABLE SUCCESSES:	CONCERNS:	OVERALL SCORE CHANGE
Monetary Freedom	Rule of Law, Business Freedom, and Financial Freedom	SINCE 2013: +3.8

FREEDOM TREND

(chart, values on y-axis: 70, 60, 50, 40, 30; x-axis years 2008 2009 2010 2011 2012 2013 2014 2015 2016 2017)

QUICK FACTS

POPULATION:
11.6 million

GDP (PPP):
$30.5 billion
1.8% growth in 2015
5-year compound
annual growth 4.7%
$2,634 per capita

UNEMPLOYMENT:
5.6%

INFLATION (CPI):
3.6%

FDI INFLOW:
$600.2 million

PUBLIC DEBT:
39.3% of GDP

2015 data unless otherwise noted. Data compiled as of September 2016

BACKGROUND: President Idriss Déby, who seized power as the leader of a rebel movement in 1990, won a fifth term in 2016. Voters approved a referendum scrapping presidential term limits in 2005, but Déby's 2016 reelection was preceded by large street protests against his rule. Déby has faced various armed revolts and survived Sudanese-supported rebel attacks on the capital of N'Djamena in 2006 and 2008. In 2010, Chad and Sudan normalized relations. Chad has sent security forces to assist peacekeeping missions in Sudan (Darfur), the Central African Republic, Mali, and the Democratic Republic of Congo and is the major component of the multinational force battling Boko Haram in Nigeria.

12 ECONOMIC FREEDOMS | CHAD

RULE OF LAW

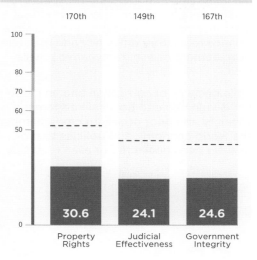

170th | 149th | 167th

Property Rights **30.6**
Judicial Effectiveness **24.1**
Government Integrity **24.6**

Protection of private property is inadequate, and fraud is common in property transactions. Costs for property registration range from 8 percent to 15 percent of property value. The rule of law is weak, and the judiciary lacks real independence. Corruption is endemic and prevails at all levels of government, from the siphoning off of oil wealth by the presidential cabinet to petty corruption in the police force and local bureaucracy.

GOVERNMENT SIZE

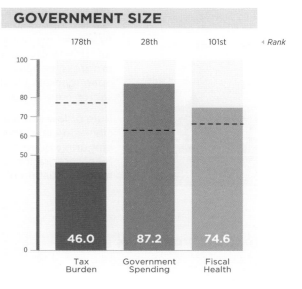

178th | 28th | 101st ◄ Rank

Tax Burden **46.0**
Government Spending **87.2**
Fiscal Health **74.6**

The top individual income tax rate is 60 percent, and the top corporate tax rate is 45 percent. Other taxes include a value-added tax and a property tax. The overall tax burden equals 6.8 percent of total domestic income. Government spending has amounted to 20.7 percent of total output (GDP) over the past three years, and budget deficits have averaged 3.7 percent of GDP. Public debt is equivalent to 39.3 percent of GDP.

REGULATORY EFFICIENCY

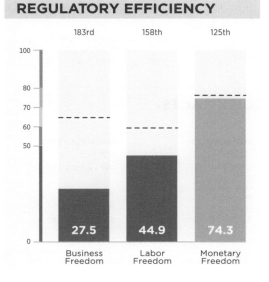

183rd | 158th | 125th

Business Freedom **27.5**
Labor Freedom **44.9**
Monetary Freedom **74.3**

The absence of modern commercial regulations imposes considerable costs on businesses, as do such other institutional deficiencies as a lack of access to financing. The labor market is mostly informal, and the workforce remains mostly unskilled. In 2016, spurred by permanently lower oil receipts, the government cut spending on some subsidies for state-owned enterprises.

OPEN MARKETS

174th | 89th | 106th ◄ Rank

Trade Freedom **54.7**
Investment Freedom **60.0**
Financial Freedom **40.0**

Trade is important to Chad's economy; the value of exports and imports taken together equals 67 percent of GDP. The average applied tariff rate is 15.1 percent. State-owned enterprises in several sectors distort the economy. Average citizens have little access to banking services, and high credit costs and scarce access to financing continue to constrain the small private sector.

CHAD

COMOROS

Chronic overdependence on foreign aid and a burdensome business environment continue to undermine prospects for sustained economic development in Comoros. With structural reforms to diversify the economic base achieving only marginal progress, policies to enhance regulatory efficiency and maintain open markets for the development of a more dynamic private sector have not advanced.

Rule of law remains fragile because of corruption and an inefficient judicial system that is vulnerable to political interference. Lingering political uncertainty and poor access to credit hamper fuller integration into the world economy, and policies to promote or sustain reforms have been neglected or even reversed.

WORLD RANK:
121

REGIONAL RANK:
22

ECONOMIC FREEDOM STATUS:
MOSTLY UNFREE

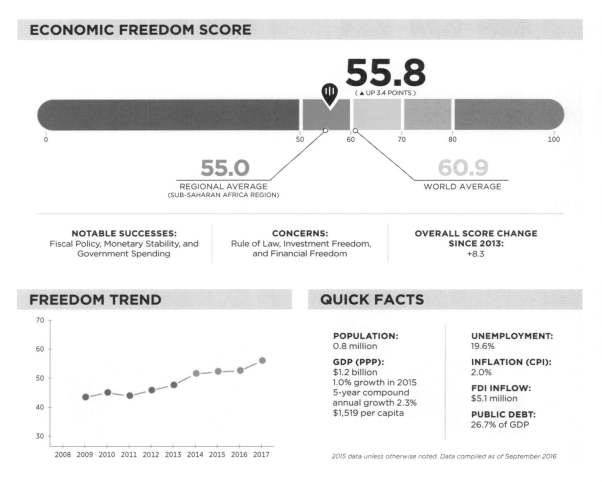

ECONOMIC FREEDOM SCORE

55.8
(▲ UP 3.4 POINTS)

0   50   60   70   80   100

55.0
REGIONAL AVERAGE
(SUB-SAHARAN AFRICA REGION)

60.9
WORLD AVERAGE

NOTABLE SUCCESSES:
Fiscal Policy, Monetary Stability, and Government Spending

CONCERNS:
Rule of Law, Investment Freedom, and Financial Freedom

OVERALL SCORE CHANGE SINCE 2013:
+8.3

FREEDOM TREND

70
60
50
40
30

2008 2009 2010 2011 2012 2013 2014 2015 2016 2017

QUICK FACTS

POPULATION:
0.8 million

GDP (PPP):
$1.2 billion
1.0% growth in 2015
5-year compound annual growth 2.3%
$1,519 per capita

UNEMPLOYMENT:
19.6%

INFLATION (CPI):
2.0%

FDI INFLOW:
$5.1 million

PUBLIC DEBT:
26.7% of GDP

2015 data unless otherwise noted. Data compiled as of September 2016

BACKGROUND: The three-island Union of the Comoros has experienced more than 20 coup attempts since independence in 1975, most recently in 2013. A 2001 constitution granted each island increased autonomy and stipulated that the presidency would rotate among the three islands. A 2009 referendum extended presidents' terms from four to five years and increased the central government's authority at the expense of local governments. President Ikililou Dhoinine stepped down peacefully in 2016, but the initial round of voting for his successor was marred by irregularities and isolated violence. Opposition politician and former President Azali Assoumani was eventually elected in a runoff vote. Comoros is a leading producer of ylang-ylang, cloves, and vanilla.

12 ECONOMIC FREEDOMS | COMOROS

RULE OF LAW

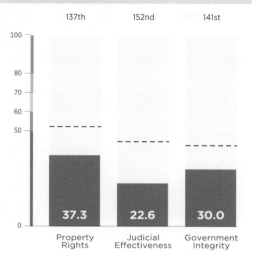

137th   152nd   141st

Property Rights	Judicial Effectiveness	Government Integrity
37.3	22.6	30.0

Property rights are not well protected, and contracts are weakly enforced. The judicial system, based on both Sharia (Islamic) law and the French legal code, is weak and subject to political influence. Corruption is reported at all levels of government and is exacerbated by internal political disputes and competition for resources among the administrations of the three islands.

GOVERNMENT SIZE

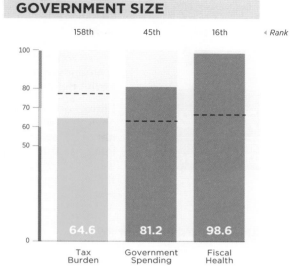

158th   45th   16th   ◄ Rank

Tax Burden	Government Spending	Fiscal Health
64.6	81.2	98.6

The top personal income tax rate is 30 percent, and the top corporate tax rate is 50 percent. Other taxes include a value-added tax and an insurance tax. The overall tax burden equals 11.8 percent of total domestic income. Government spending has amounted to 25 percent of total output (GDP) over the past three years, and budget surpluses have averaged 7.3 percent of GDP. Public debt is equivalent to 26.7 percent of GDP.

REGULATORY EFFICIENCY

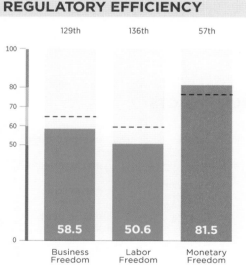

129th   136th   57th

Business Freedom	Labor Freedom	Monetary Freedom
58.5	50.6	81.5

The regulatory environment still imposes significant burdens on entrepreneurs. Minimum capital requirements to launch a company exceed the average level of annual income. With development of a modern labor market lagging, the informal sector accounts for most employment. The government subsidizes state-owned but poorly managed water, electricity, and oil utilities and controls other prices.

OPEN MARKETS

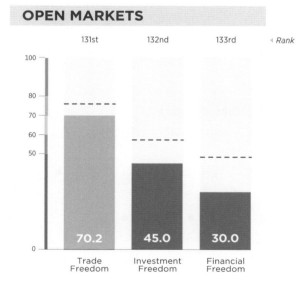

131st   132nd   133rd   ◄ Rank

Trade Freedom	Investment Freedom	Financial Freedom
70.2	45.0	30.0

Trade is important to the Comoros economy; the value of exports and imports taken together equals 80 percent of GDP. The average applied tariff rate is 7.4 percent. Foreign and domestic investors are generally treated equally under the law. The small financial sector still lacks adequate regulation or supervision. Banking is not well established, and many people are without bank accounts and rely on informal lending.

COMOROS

DEMOCRATIC REPUBLIC OF CONGO

Economic development in the Democratic Republic of Congo (DRC) has been severely undermined by decades of instability and violence. Poor economic management worsened by repeated political crises has constrained economic freedom and driven much of the population into persistent poverty. The government's inability to provide even basic public goods reliably further limits economic opportunity.

Entrepreneurial activity is curtailed by an uncertain regulatory environment and the absence of institutional support for or facilitation of private-sector development. Arbitrary taxation, poor infrastructure, marginal enforcement of property rights, and the weak rule of law have driven many people and enterprises into the informal sector, which accounts for more than 80 percent of economic activity.

WORLD RANK: 117

REGIONAL RANK: 18

ECONOMIC FREEDOM STATUS: MOSTLY UNFREE

ECONOMIC FREEDOM SCORE

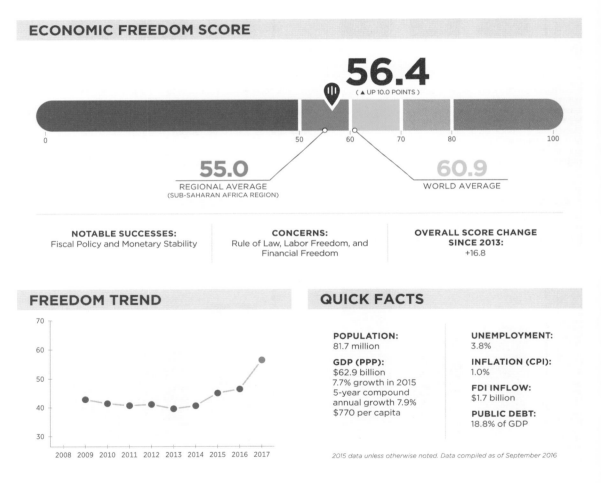

56.4
(▲ UP 10.0 POINTS)

0   50   60   70   80   100

55.0
REGIONAL AVERAGE
(SUB-SAHARAN AFRICA REGION)

60.9
WORLD AVERAGE

NOTABLE SUCCESSES:
Fiscal Policy and Monetary Stability

CONCERNS:
Rule of Law, Labor Freedom, and Financial Freedom

OVERALL SCORE CHANGE SINCE 2013:
+16.8

FREEDOM TREND

70
60
50
40
30

2008 2009 2010 2011 2012 2013 2014 2015 2016 2017

QUICK FACTS

POPULATION:
81.7 million

GDP (PPP):
$62.9 billion
7.7% growth in 2015
5-year compound annual growth 7.9%
$770 per capita

UNEMPLOYMENT:
3.8%

INFLATION (CPI):
1.0%

FDI INFLOW:
$1.7 billion

PUBLIC DEBT:
18.8% of GDP

2015 data unless otherwise noted. Data compiled as of September 2016

BACKGROUND: Rebel groups remain active, primarily in the eastern part of the country where the United Nations has a peacekeeping mission. Joseph Kabila, who in 2006 won the first multi-party election in 40 years, was reelected in December 2011 in a process rife with violence. His schemes to secure a constitutionally prohibited third term have sparked major protests that state security services have suppressed, often brutally. The DRC's immense natural resource wealth includes large deposits of rare earth minerals used in many technology products, but because of its political instability, the country remains among the least developed in the world.

12 ECONOMIC FREEDOMS | DEMOCRATIC REPUBLIC OF CONGO

RULE OF LAW

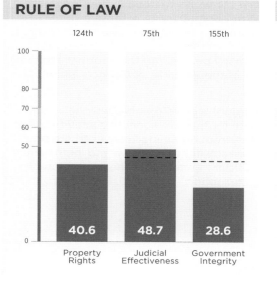

124th · 75th · 155th

- Property Rights: **40.6**
- Judicial Effectiveness: **48.7**
- Government Integrity: **28.6**

Protection of property rights is weak and dependent on a dysfunctional public administration and judicial system. Human rights abuses and banditry deter economic activity. Massive government corruption and weak rule of law remain prevalent. Clandestine trade in minerals and other natural resources in eastern Congo by armed rebel militias and elements of the army helps to finance violence and depletes government revenues.

GOVERNMENT SIZE

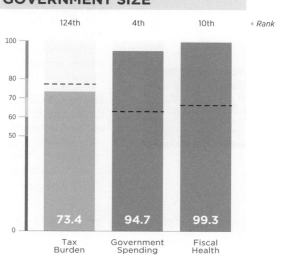

124th · 4th · 10th ◂ Rank

- Tax Burden: **73.4**
- Government Spending: **94.7**
- Fiscal Health: **99.3**

The top personal income tax rate is 30 percent, and the top corporate tax rate is 40 percent. Other taxes include a rental tax and a tax on vehicles. The overall tax burden equals 12.5 percent of total domestic income. Government spending has amounted to 13.2 percent of total output (GDP) over the past three years, and budget surpluses have averaged 2.1 percent of GDP. Public debt is equivalent to 18.8 percent of GDP.

REGULATORY EFFICIENCY

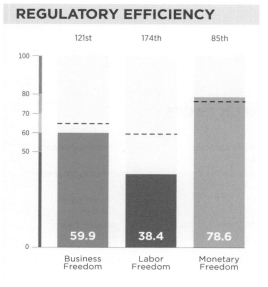

121st · 174th · 85th

- Business Freedom: **59.9**
- Labor Freedom: **38.4**
- Monetary Freedom: **78.6**

The regulatory system remains unfavorable for private entrepreneurship. Outmoded regulations increase the cost of running businesses and hamper private-sector development. Agriculture is the largest source of employment, and formal-sector employment is negligible. Prices are controlled and regulated by the government, which also heavily subsidizes electricity.

OPEN MARKETS

156th · 154th · 162nd ◂ Rank

- Trade Freedom: **64.6**
- Investment Freedom: **30.0**
- Financial Freedom: **20.0**

Trade is important to the Democratic Republic of Congo's economy; the value of exports and imports taken together equals 64 percent of GDP. The average applied tariff rate is 10.2 percent. Weak legal and regulatory systems impede foreign investment. The financial system provides a minimal range of banking services. Access to financing for entrepreneurial activity remains poor, and financial intermediation remains a luxury for most of the population.

REPUBLIC OF CONGO

Repressive governance continues to deprive the Congolese people of economic freedom. Despite extensive state controls from the period of state socialism, the government cannot provide basic public goods and infrastructure. Public-sector inefficiency has pushed many people into the informal economy, which accounts for most of the Republic of Congo's limited private-sector growth.

The lack of meaningful progress on reform has left the institutional capacity inadequate for modern economic activity. Many aspects of doing business, from obtaining licenses to attracting foreign investment, are subject to intrusive and inefficient regulations. The weak judiciary undermines the protection of property rights, fueling corruption.

WORLD RANK: **177** | REGIONAL RANK: **47**

ECONOMIC FREEDOM STATUS:
REPRESSED

ECONOMIC FREEDOM SCORE

40.0
(▼ DOWN 2.8 POINTS)

0   50   60   70   80   100

55.0
REGIONAL AVERAGE
(SUB-SAHARAN AFRICA REGION)

60.9
WORLD AVERAGE

NOTABLE SUCCESSES:
Monetary Stability

CONCERNS:
Rule of Law, Fiscal Health, and Business Freedom

OVERALL SCORE CHANGE SINCE 2013:
–3.5

FREEDOM TREND

(chart with values ranging from 40 to 45, years 2008 through 2017)

60

50

40

30

20

2008 2009 2010 2011 2012 2013 2014 2015 2016 2017

QUICK FACTS

POPULATION:
4.4 million

GDP (PPP):
$29.4 billion
2.5% growth in 2015
5-year compound
annual growth 4.0%
$6,722 per capita

UNEMPLOYMENT:
7.2%

INFLATION (CPI):
2.0%

FDI INFLOW:
$1.5 billion

PUBLIC DEBT:
64.9% of GDP

2015 data unless otherwise noted. Data compiled as of September 2016

BACKGROUND: The Republic of Congo became independent from France in 1960. Denis Sassou-Nguesso seized power in 1979 and governed the country as a Marxist–Leninist state before allowing a multi-party election in 1992. He lost that election to Pascal Lissouba, seized power again following a 1997 civil war, and then won flawed elections in 2002, 2009, and 2016. In 2015, the country held a referendum that modified the constitutional limits on a president's age and the number of terms he could serve, allowing Sassou-Nguesso to run again. Congo is one of sub-Saharan Africa's largest oil producers, but lack of infrastructure prevents exploitation of its natural gas reserves and hydropower potential.

12 ECONOMIC FREEDOMS | REPUBLIC OF CONGO

RULE OF LAW

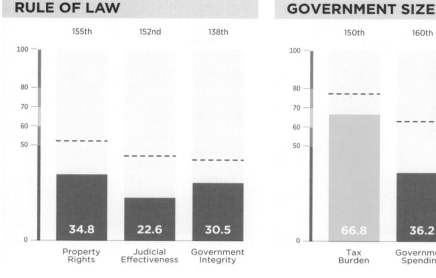

	155th	152nd	138th
	Property Rights	Judicial Effectiveness	Government Integrity
	34.8	22.6	30.5

Contract terms are not transparent, and "informal" tax collectors regularly solicit bribes. The judiciary is underfunded and crippled by institutional weakness and a lack of technical capability. Corruption remains pervasive in Congo. The state oil company is directly controlled by the president's family and advisers. In late 2015, because of suspected ill-gotten wealth, French judges ordered the seizure of properties tied to the president's family.

GOVERNMENT SIZE

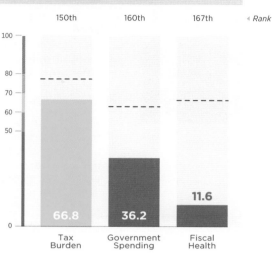

150th	160th	167th	◀ Rank
Tax Burden	Government Spending	Fiscal Health	
66.8	36.2	11.6	

The top individual income tax rate is 45 percent, and the top corporate tax rate is 34 percent. Other taxes include a value-added tax and a tax on rental values. The overall tax burden equals 11.7 percent of total domestic income. Government spending has amounted to 46.1 percent of total output (GDP) over the past three years, and budget deficits have averaged 7.1 percent of GDP. Public debt is equivalent to 64.9 percent of GDP.

REGULATORY EFFICIENCY

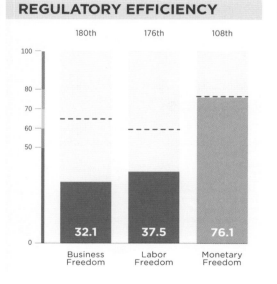

180th	176th	108th
Business Freedom	Labor Freedom	Monetary Freedom
32.1	37.5	76.1

The regulatory environment continues to be characterized by bureaucracy and a lack of transparency. Existing regulations are not enforced effectively. A modern labor market has not been developed, and the public sector remains the largest source of formal employment. In advance of the March 2016 presidential election, the government rejected IMF recommendations that it reduce spending on energy subsidies.

OPEN MARKETS

179th	120th	133rd	◀ Rank
Trade Freedom	Investment Freedom	Financial Freedom	
52.2	50.0	30.0	

Trade is extremely important to the Republic of Congo's economy; the value of exports and imports taken together equals 166 percent of GDP. The average applied tariff rate is 16.4 percent. In general, the government does not screen or discriminate against foreign investment. The underdeveloped financial sector remains hampered by state interference. Bank development has been stunted by poor management and nonperforming loans.

REPUBLIC OF CONGO

CÔTE D'IVOIRE

Côte d'Ivoire's economic expansion has been notable, with a robust GDP growth rate averaging around 6 percent over the past five years. The government has undertaken much-needed reforms to maintain and further enhance the potential for growth. These measures include strengthening management of public finances and regulatory reforms to foster the emergence of a more dynamic private sector. Fiscal policy has focused on promoting investment and funding other development needs.

Effective implementation of deeper institutional reforms related to the rule of law remains critical to reinforcing vibrant economic growth. Protection of property rights and anticorruption measures are not enforced effectively, and the judiciary remains vulnerable to political influence.

WORLD RANK: **75**   REGIONAL RANK: **4**

ECONOMIC FREEDOM STATUS:
MODERATELY FREE

ECONOMIC FREEDOM SCORE

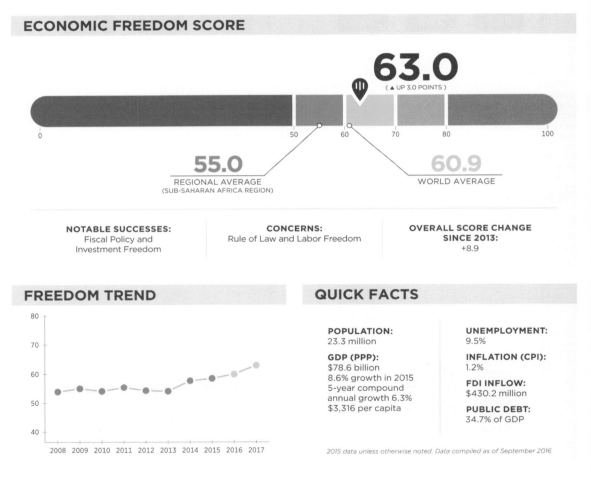

63.0
(▲ UP 3.0 POINTS)

0   50   60   70   80   100

55.0
REGIONAL AVERAGE
(SUB-SAHARAN AFRICA REGION)

60.9
WORLD AVERAGE

NOTABLE SUCCESSES:
Fiscal Policy and
Investment Freedom

CONCERNS:
Rule of Law and Labor Freedom

**OVERALL SCORE CHANGE
SINCE 2013:**
+8.9

FREEDOM TREND

80
70
60
50
40

2008 2009 2010 2011 2012 2013 2014 2015 2016 2017

QUICK FACTS

POPULATION:
23.3 million

GDP (PPP):
$78.6 billion
8.6% growth in 2015
5-year compound
annual growth 6.3%
$3,316 per capita

UNEMPLOYMENT:
9.5%

INFLATION (CPI):
1.2%

FDI INFLOW:
$430.2 million

PUBLIC DEBT:
34.7% of GDP

2015 data unless otherwise noted. Data compiled as of September 2016

BACKGROUND: In 2002, Côte d'Ivoire plunged into a civil war that lasted until peace largely returned in 2007, when rebel leader Guillaume Soro joined President Laurent Gbagbo's government as prime minister. After the 2010 presidential elections, Gbagbo refused to surrender power to internationally recognized winner Alassane Ouattara. U.N. and French forces removed Gbagbo, who is now facing trial at The Hague on charges of crimes against humanity. Ouattara won a second term in late 2015, and the U.N. plans to withdraw its troops by April 2017. Côte d'Ivoire is West Africa's second-largest economy and a leading producer of cocoa and cashews.

12 ECONOMIC FREEDOMS | CÔTE D'IVOIRE

RULE OF LAW

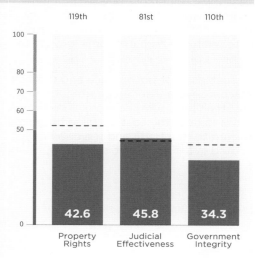

119th   81st   110th

42.6 Property Rights
45.8 Judicial Effectiveness
34.3 Government Integrity

Protection of property rights is fragile, and land titles are rare outside of urban areas, although the introduction of new alternative dispute resolution mechanisms has made it easier to enforce contracts. The judiciary is not independent, and judges are highly susceptible to external interference and bribes. Corruption persists in the judiciary, the police, the military, customs, contract awards, tax offices, and other government institutions.

GOVERNMENT SIZE

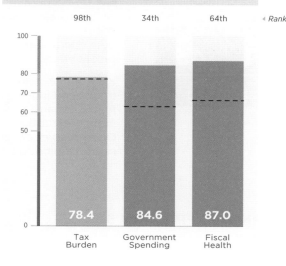

98th   34th   64th   ◂ Rank

78.4 Tax Burden
84.6 Government Spending
87.0 Fiscal Health

The top individual income tax rate is 36 percent, and the top corporate tax rate is 25 percent. Other taxes include a value-added tax and a tax on interest. The overall tax burden equals 15.5 percent of total domestic income. Government spending has amounted to 22.7 percent of total output (GDP) over the past three years, and budget deficits have averaged 2.6 percent of GDP. Public debt is equivalent to 34.7 percent of GDP.

REGULATORY EFFICIENCY

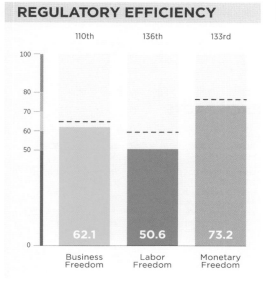

110th   136th   133rd

62.1 Business Freedom
50.6 Labor Freedom
73.2 Monetary Freedom

Considerable effort has been made to modernize the regulatory framework. The business start-up process has become more straightforward, and minimum capital requirements have been reduced. The nonsalary cost of employing a worker is relatively low. To lessen dependence on cocoa, the government encourages crop diversification by guaranteeing high prices for other crops while still guaranteeing a minimum price to cocoa farmers.

OPEN MARKETS

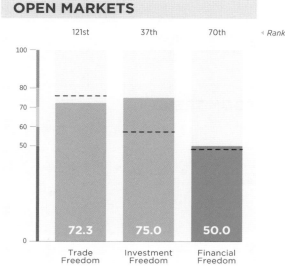

121st   37th   70th   ◂ Rank

72.3 Trade Freedom
75.0 Investment Freedom
50.0 Financial Freedom

Trade is important to Côte d'Ivoire's economy; the value of exports and imports taken together equals 88 percent of GDP. The average applied tariff rate is 6.3 percent. The government does not screen or discriminate against most foreign investment. The financial system is dominated by banking, which, despite some modernization and restructuring, still lacks the capacity to support rapid private-sector growth.

CÔTE D'IVOIRE

DJIBOUTI

WORLD RANK:
171

REGIONAL RANK:
43

ECONOMIC FREEDOM STATUS:
REPRESSED

Djibouti's economy is driven mainly by services, with industry accounting for less than 20 percent of GDP. Economic activity is centered on port facilities, the railway, and military bases. Increased investment, particularly in construction and port operations, has led to relatively high economic growth in recent years.

Institutional weaknesses such as poor governance and the lack of a sound judicial framework severely undercut vibrant economic expansion and constrain long-term economic development. Corruption continues to raise the cost of doing business. Open-market policies related to free trade and the free flow of capital are not deeply rooted in the economic system.

ECONOMIC FREEDOM SCORE

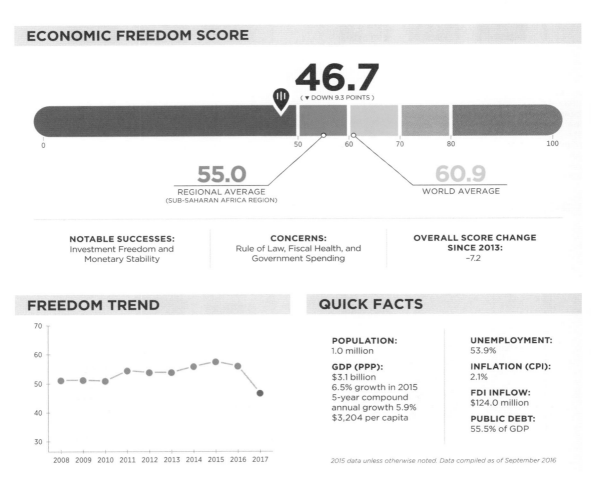

46.7
(▼ DOWN 9.3 POINTS)

0   50   60   70   80   100

55.0
REGIONAL AVERAGE
(SUB-SAHARAN AFRICA REGION)

60.9
WORLD AVERAGE

NOTABLE SUCCESSES:
Investment Freedom and Monetary Stability

CONCERNS:
Rule of Law, Fiscal Health, and Government Spending

OVERALL SCORE CHANGE SINCE 2013:
−7.2

FREEDOM TREND

70
60
50
40
30

2008 2009 2010 2011 2012 2013 2014 2015 2016 2017

QUICK FACTS

POPULATION:
1.0 million

GDP (PPP):
$3.1 billion
6.5% growth in 2015
5-year compound
annual growth 5.9%
$3,204 per capita

UNEMPLOYMENT:
53.9%

INFLATION (CPI):
2.1%

FDI INFLOW:
$124.0 million

PUBLIC DEBT:
55.5% of GDP

2015 data unless otherwise noted. Data compiled as of September 2016

BACKGROUND: President Ismael Omar Guelleh was reelected by a landslide to a fourth term in 2016 after getting parliament in 2010 to change a constitutional prohibition against more than two terms. Djibouti's strategic location at the mouth of the Red Sea makes its port facilities and railway key assets. The U.S. has its only permanent African base in Djibouti, and France and Japan have a military presence there as well. In early 2016, China began building "support facilities" for its army and navy in the port town of Obock. Djibouti has few natural resources and imports most of its food. The government relies on foreign assistance to finance development projects.

12 ECONOMIC FREEDOMS | DJIBOUTI

RULE OF LAW

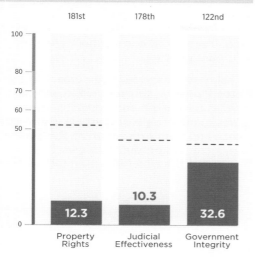

	181st	178th	122nd
Property Rights	Judicial Effectiveness	Government Integrity
12.3	10.3	32.6

Protection of private property is weak. Judicial proceedings and trials are time-consuming, prone to corruption, and politically manipulated. Sharia law prevails in family matters. Power remains heavily concentrated in the president's hands, and repression of political opposition has increased. Public officials do not have to disclose their assets. Government corruption is a serious problem, and efforts to curb it have had little success.

GOVERNMENT SIZE

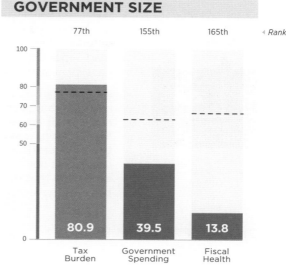

	77th	155th	165th	◄ Rank
Tax Burden	Government Spending	Fiscal Health
80.9	39.5	13.8

The top personal income tax rate is 30 percent, and the top corporate tax rate is 25 percent. Other taxes include a property tax and an excise tax. The overall tax burden equals 19.6 percent of total domestic income. Government spending has amounted to 44.9 percent of total output (GDP) over the past three years, and budget deficits have averaged 11.5 percent of GDP. Public debt is equivalent to 55.5 percent of GDP.

REGULATORY EFFICIENCY

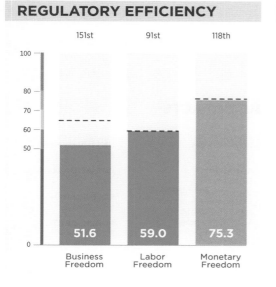

	151st	91st	118th
Business Freedom	Labor Freedom	Monetary Freedom
51.6	59.0	75.3

The regulatory system's lack of transparency and clarity injects considerable uncertainty into entrepreneurial decision-making. A modern labor market has not been fully developed. In 2016, the government and the Saudi Arabia–based Islamic Trade Finance Corporation, a subsidiary of the Islamic Development Bank, signed a $75 million agreement that the IMF warns will probably be used to finance Djibouti's fuel subsidies.

OPEN MARKETS

	173rd	21st	70th	◄ Rank
Trade Freedom	Investment Freedom	Financial Freedom
54.9	80.0	50.0

Trade is important to Djibouti's economy; the value of exports and imports taken together equals 58.7 percent of GDP. The average applied tariff rate is 17.6 percent. State-owned enterprises distort the economy. Credit is generally allocated on market terms, but access to credit for entrepreneurial activity is still limited by high costs and the lack of other available financing instruments.

DJIBOUTI

EQUATORIAL GUINEA

WORLD RANK:
174

REGIONAL RANK:
44

ECONOMIC FREEDOM STATUS:
REPRESSED

Oil has been the major source of high economic growth in Equatorial Guinea over the past five years. Overall economic development has been uneven, and poverty remains daunting. Privatization and liberalization half-measures have made little difference, and improving the investment and business climate remains an urgent priority.

Persistent institutional weaknesses impede development of a more vibrant private sector. Pervasive corruption and onerous regulations are major hurdles for foreign and domestic investment. The rule of law is weak, and private property is vulnerable to bureaucratic interference and even expropriation. Restrictive labor laws hamper employment and productivity growth. It is estimated that more than half of the workforce is employed in the informal economy.

ECONOMIC FREEDOM SCORE

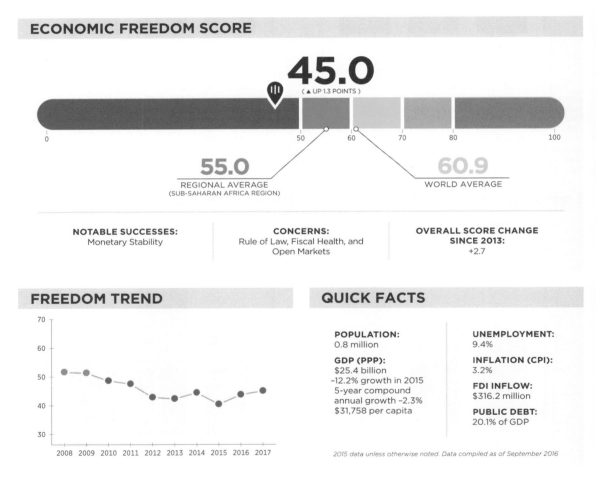

45.0
(▲ UP 1.3 POINTS)

0   50   60   70   80   100

55.0
REGIONAL AVERAGE
(SUB-SAHARAN AFRICA REGION)

60.9
WORLD AVERAGE

NOTABLE SUCCESSES:
Monetary Stability

CONCERNS:
Rule of Law, Fiscal Health, and Open Markets

OVERALL SCORE CHANGE SINCE 2013:
+2.7

FREEDOM TREND

Chart showing values from 2008 to 2017 ranging approximately between 40 and 52.

QUICK FACTS

POPULATION:
0.8 million

GDP (PPP):
$25.4 billion
–12.2% growth in 2015
5-year compound
annual growth –2.3%
$31,758 per capita

UNEMPLOYMENT:
9.4%

INFLATION (CPI):
3.2%

FDI INFLOW:
$316.2 million

PUBLIC DEBT:
20.1% of GDP

2015 data unless otherwise noted. Data compiled as of September 2016

BACKGROUND: President Teodoro Obiang Nguema Mbasogo seized power from his uncle in a coup in 1979. He most recently won reelection in April 2016 with 93 percent of the vote, a result that the opposition protested as fraudulent. In 2014, more than $30 million in assets allegedly purchased with embezzled funds was seized from Obiang's son by U.S. authorities. Human rights organizations criticize Obiang for similarly enriching himself through corrupt practices. Equatorial Guinea is one of Africa's fastest-growing economies and sub-Saharan Africa's third-largest oil producer. The government is trying to diversify its economy by developing its agricultural, fishing, financial services, and tourism sectors.

12 ECONOMIC FREEDOMS | EQUATORIAL GUINEA

RULE OF LAW

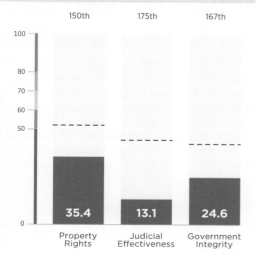

150th	175th	167th

- Property Rights: 35.4
- Judicial Effectiveness: 13.1
- Government Integrity: 24.6

Property rights are enforced selectively. Despite laws regarding the rights of property owners, the government can seize land with very little, if any, due process. Because the president is also the chief magistrate, the judicial system is not independent. Graft and nepotism are rampant. The government views domestic private firms without links to the regime as suspicious.

GOVERNMENT SIZE

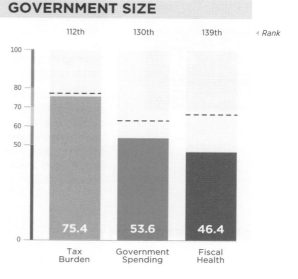

112th	130th	139th	◄ Rank

- Tax Burden: 75.4
- Government Spending: 53.6
- Fiscal Health: 46.4

The top personal income and corporate tax rates are 35 percent. Other taxes include a value-added tax and a tax on inheritance. The overall tax burden equals 2.8 percent of total domestic income. Government spending has amounted to 39.3 percent of total output (GDP) over the past three years, and budget deficits have averaged 5.7 percent of GDP. Public debt is equivalent to 20.1 percent of GDP.

REGULATORY EFFICIENCY

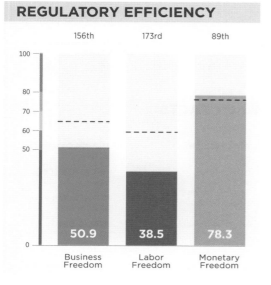

156th	173rd	89th

- Business Freedom: 50.9
- Labor Freedom: 38.5
- Monetary Freedom: 78.3

Cumbersome procedures and high compliance costs slow licensing and make starting a business more difficult. Existing labor regulations are outmoded and create challenging barriers to hiring. During the commodity boom, the government misused its substantial oil revenues to subsidize strategic sectors; now government revenues have plummeted as a result of plunging global oil prices and poor management of the oil sector.

OPEN MARKETS

176th	135th	133rd	◄ Rank

- Trade Freedom: 53.8
- Investment Freedom: 40.0
- Financial Freedom: 30.0

Trade is extremely important to Equatorial Guinea's economy; the value of exports and imports taken together equals 178 percent of GDP. The average applied tariff rate is 15.6 percent. Weak regulatory and judicial systems may discourage foreign investment. Credit costs are high, and access to financing is limited. The government controls long-term lending through the state-owned development bank.

EQUATORIAL GUINEA

ERITREA

Economic mismanagement and structural anomalies that severely undermine private-sector development have impeded productivity growth, dynamism, and overall economic growth in Eritrea. Long-standing structural problems include poor management of public finance and underdeveloped legal and regulatory frameworks.

Poor governance and the lack of commitment to reforms continue to hamper economic freedom in Eritrea. Monetary stability remains fragile, and inflation is very high, largely reflecting excessive money creation to fund fiscal deficits. Arbitrary taxation, poor infrastructure, marginal enforcement of property rights, and weak rule of law have driven many people and enterprises into the informal sector.

ECONOMIC FREEDOM SCORE

42.2
(▼ DOWN 0.5 POINT)

0   50   60   70   80   100

55.0
REGIONAL AVERAGE
(SUB-SAHARAN AFRICA REGION)

60.9
WORLD AVERAGE

NOTABLE SUCCESSES:	CONCERNS:	OVERALL SCORE CHANGE
Labor Freedom	Fiscal Health, Open Markets, and Rule of Law	**SINCE 2013:** +5.9

FREEDOM TREND

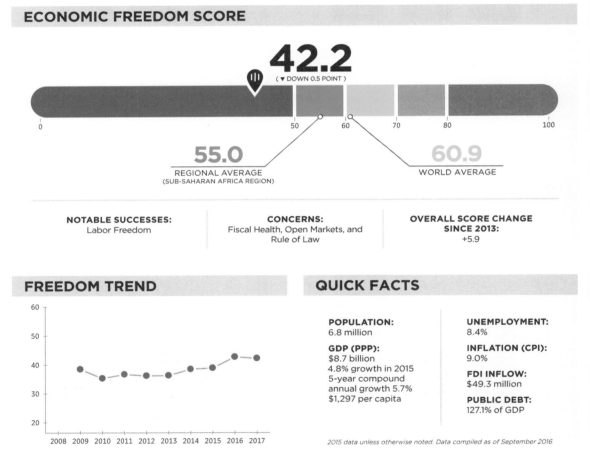

QUICK FACTS

POPULATION:
6.8 million

GDP (PPP):
$8.7 billion
4.8% growth in 2015
5-year compound
annual growth 5.7%
$1,297 per capita

UNEMPLOYMENT:
8.4%

INFLATION (CPI):
9.0%

FDI INFLOW:
$49.3 million

PUBLIC DEBT:
127.1% of GDP

2015 data unless otherwise noted. Data compiled as of September 2016

BACKGROUND: Isaias Afwerki has ruled this one-party state since 1993, when it voted for independence from Ethiopia after winning a 30-year war with its southern neighbor. A border dispute between Ethiopia and Eritrea occasionally flares into conflict, most recently in June 2016. According to the Committee to Protect Journalists, Eritrea is the world's most censored country, and the U.N. Human Rights Council determined in 2016 that the government was guilty of crimes against humanity, a finding that the Eritrean government rejects. Eritrea is also subject to U.N. military and economic sanctions for allegedly supporting armed groups in the Horn of Africa. Copper and gold are important exports, but military spending drains resources from the development of public infrastructure.

12 ECONOMIC FREEDOMS | ERITREA

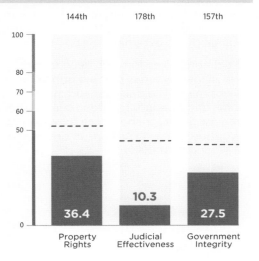

RULE OF LAW

144th	178th	157th
Property Rights	Judicial Effectiveness	Government Integrity
36.4	10.3	27.5

Protection of property rights is poor, and the state often expropriates private property without due process or compensation. The politicized judiciary, understaffed and unprofessional, has never ruled against the government. The one-party state, ruled by the autocratic regime of the president and his small circle of senior advisers and military commanders, is widely regarded as one of the world's most repressive. Corruption is a major problem.

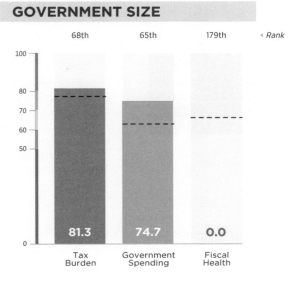

GOVERNMENT SIZE

68th	65th	179th	◄ *Rank*
Tax Burden	Government Spending	Fiscal Health	
81.3	74.7	0.0	

The top personal income and corporate tax rates are 30 percent. The overall tax burden is estimated to equal about 10 percent of total domestic income, but taxation remains erratic. Government spending has amounted to 29 percent of total output (GDP) over the past three years, and budget deficits have averaged 14.6 percent of GDP. Public debt is equivalent to 127.1 percent of GDP.

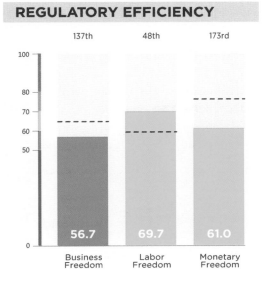

REGULATORY EFFICIENCY

137th	48th	173rd
Business Freedom	Labor Freedom	Monetary Freedom
56.7	69.7	61.0

The overall regulatory regime remains severely outdated and is not conducive to entrepreneurial activity. Procedures for establishing and running a business are opaque and costly. Monetary stability has been weak. Labor regulations are not enforced effectively in the absence of a well-functioning labor market. Subsidies and price controls have been a core feature of Eritrea's command economy.

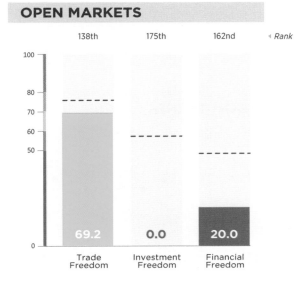

OPEN MARKETS

138th	175th	162nd	◄ *Rank*
Trade Freedom	Investment Freedom	Financial Freedom	
69.2	0.0	20.0	

Trade is important to Eritrea's economy; the value of exports and imports taken together equals 52.9 percent of GDP. The average applied tariff rate is 5.4 percent. Foreign investment in several sectors of the economy is restricted, and state-owned enterprises distort the economy. The financial system remains very underdeveloped. All banks are majority-owned by the state, and private-sector involvement remains limited.

ERITREA

ETHIOPIA

WORLD RANK: **142** REGIONAL RANK: **31**

ECONOMIC FREEDOM STATUS:
MOSTLY UNFREE

Despite the global economic downturn, Ethiopia's economy has recorded annual economic expansion of around 10 percent over the past five years, facilitated by improved infrastructure and more effective mining and farming techniques. However, growth remains highly vulnerable to external shocks.

Progress toward greater economic freedom has been uneven. Ethiopia underperforms in many key areas that are critical to long-term economic development. The business and investment regime is burdensome and opaque. The poor quality and efficiency of government services are made worse by weak rule of law and pervasive corruption. State distortions in prices and interest rates undermine monetary stability.

ECONOMIC FREEDOM SCORE

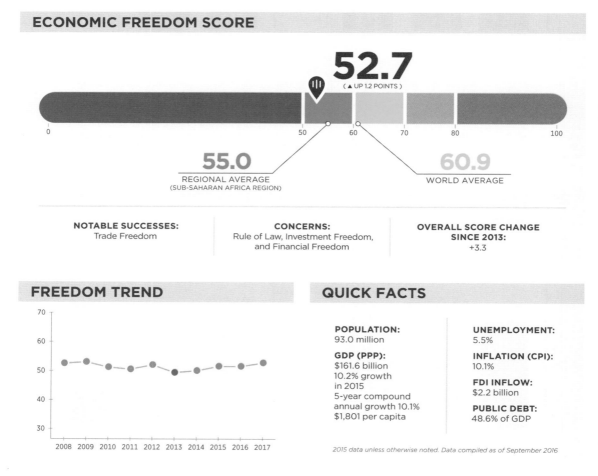

52.7
(▲ UP 1.2 POINTS)

0   50   60   70   80   100

55.0
REGIONAL AVERAGE
(SUB-SAHARAN AFRICA REGION)

60.9
WORLD AVERAGE

NOTABLE SUCCESSES:
Trade Freedom

CONCERNS:
Rule of Law, Investment Freedom, and Financial Freedom

OVERALL SCORE CHANGE SINCE 2013:
+3.3

FREEDOM TREND

70

60

50

40

30

2008 2009 2010 2011 2012 2013 2014 2015 2016 2017

QUICK FACTS

POPULATION:
93.0 million

GDP (PPP):
$161.6 billion
10.2% growth
in 2015
5-year compound
annual growth 10.1%
$1,801 per capita

UNEMPLOYMENT:
5.5%

INFLATION (CPI):
10.1%

FDI INFLOW:
$2.2 billion

PUBLIC DEBT:
48.6% of GDP

2015 data unless otherwise noted. Data compiled as of September 2016

BACKGROUND: Prime Minister Hailemariam Desalegn's political coalition claimed all 547 seats in May 2015 parliamentary elections held in an atmosphere of government intimidation. Little remains of democracy since the passage of laws that repress political opposition, tighten control of civil society, suppress independent media, and control online activity. Demonstrations by the marginalized Oromo tribe against government plans to expand the capital city of Addis Ababa into Oromo lands flared again in late 2015 and into 2016, with security personnel allegedly killing hundreds of protesters. Ethiopia's long-running border dispute with Eritrea led to a sharp military engagement between the two countries in June 2016. Strong economic growth has reduced the percentage of the population living in poverty.

12 ECONOMIC FREEDOMS | ETHIOPIA

RULE OF LAW

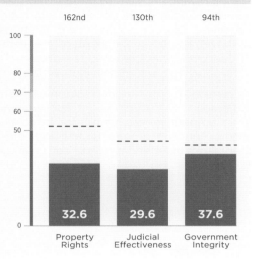

162nd   130th   94th

- Property Rights: 32.6
- Judicial Effectiveness: 29.6
- Government Integrity: 37.6

The state retains ownership of all land, with use rights for landholders. The judiciary is officially independent, but its judgments rarely deviate from government policy. Corruption remains a significant problem. Ruling Ethiopian People's Revolutionary Democratic Front officials who dominate state institutions reportedly enjoy preferential access to credit, land leases, and jobs. Lower-level officials solicit bribes in return for processing documents.

GOVERNMENT SIZE

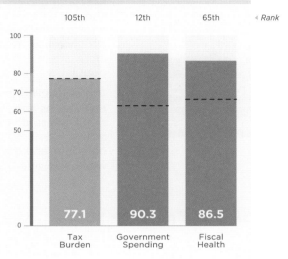

105th   12th   65th   ◂ Rank

- Tax Burden: 77.1
- Government Spending: 90.3
- Fiscal Health: 86.5

The top individual income tax rate is 35 percent, and the top corporate tax rate is 30 percent. Other taxes include a value-added tax and a capital gains tax. The overall tax burden equals 12.7 percent of total domestic income. Government spending has amounted to 18 percent of total output (GDP) over the past three years, and budget deficits have averaged 2.3 percent of GDP. Public debt is equivalent to 48.6 percent of GDP.

REGULATORY EFFICIENCY

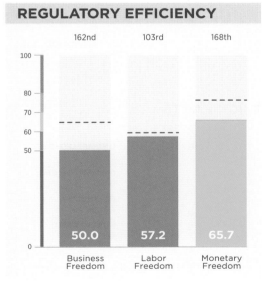

162nd   103rd   168th

- Business Freedom: 50.0
- Labor Freedom: 57.2
- Monetary Freedom: 65.7

Establishing a business has become less time-consuming, but other regulatory requirements remain opaque, increasing the cost of conducting business. The underdeveloped labor market hinders employment growth, trapping much of the labor force in the informal economy. The IMF has recommended that indirect subsidies be replaced with direct transfers to increase efficiency in addressing the needs of the most vulnerable households.

OPEN MARKETS

153rd   166th   162nd   ◂ Rank

- Trade Freedom: 65.1
- Investment Freedom: 20.0
- Financial Freedom: 20.0

Trade is moderately important to Ethiopia's economy; the value of exports and imports taken together equals 37 percent of GDP. The average applied tariff rate is 10.0 percent. Ethiopia is not a member of the World Trade Organization. All land belongs to the state. The government influences lending and funds state-led development projects. The state has allowed the private sector to participate in banking but restricts foreign ownership.

ETHIOPIA

GABON

WORLD RANK: **103** REGIONAL RANK: **13**

ECONOMIC FREEDOM STATUS:
MOSTLY UNFREE

Economic growth in Gabon has slowed. The government's continued reliance on oil revenue has led to budget shortfalls, and efforts to encourage diversification are underway. However, efforts to improve the business environment, reduce regulations, and increase investment have progressed inconsistently. Recent increases in economic freedom have not reached the greater population, and many of Gabon's people remain in poverty.

The regulatory structure remains highly bureaucratic. Investment restrictions and the rigid system for starting an enterprise make it difficult to do business. Competitiveness is hindered by costly tariffs and nontariff barriers. The legal process is slow and cumbersome, and the judiciary lacks independence and consistency when applying the law.

ECONOMIC FREEDOM SCORE

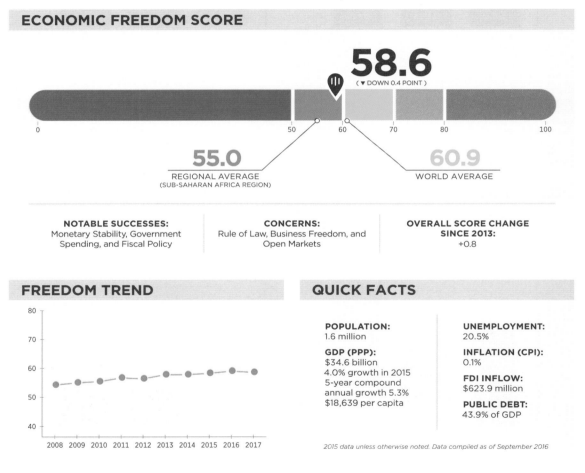

58.6
(▼ DOWN 0.4 POINT)

0   50   60   70   80   100

55.0
REGIONAL AVERAGE
(SUB-SAHARAN AFRICA REGION)

60.9
WORLD AVERAGE

NOTABLE SUCCESSES:
Monetary Stability, Government Spending, and Fiscal Policy

CONCERNS:
Rule of Law, Business Freedom, and Open Markets

OVERALL SCORE CHANGE SINCE 2013:
+0.8

FREEDOM TREND

80
70
60
50
40

2008 2009 2010 2011 2012 2013 2014 2015 2016 2017

QUICK FACTS

POPULATION:
1.6 million

GDP (PPP):
$34.6 billion
4.0% growth in 2015
5-year compound
annual growth 5.3%
$18,639 per capita

UNEMPLOYMENT:
20.5%

INFLATION (CPI):
0.1%

FDI INFLOW:
$623.9 million

PUBLIC DEBT:
43.9% of GDP

2015 data unless otherwise noted. Data compiled as of September 2016

BACKGROUND: In 2009, Ali Bongo Ondimba became president, succeeding his father, Omar Bongo, who had ruled Gabon for more than 40 years. Opposition leaders accused the Bongo family of electoral fraud to ensure dynastic succession. In 2011, Bongo's Gabonese Democratic Party (PDG) took 95 percent of the seats in parliamentary elections that were boycotted by the opposition. There are no presidential term limits in Gabon, and Bongo secured his second seven-year term in the heavily disputed August 2016 elections. Due to the oil wealth of a few, Gabon has one of Africa's highest average per capita incomes, but most Gabonese are poor.

12 ECONOMIC FREEDOMS | GABON

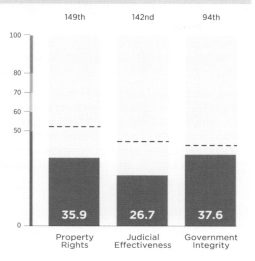

RULE OF LAW

149th | 142nd | 94th

- Property Rights: 35.9
- Judicial Effectiveness: 26.7
- Government Integrity: 37.6

Protection of property rights and contracts is not strongly enforced. The judiciary is inefficient and not independent. Public frustration with the dominant PDG party's cronyism grew during the boom years, when increased petroleum revenues failed to produce improved living standards for much of the population because of rampant corruption. Payoffs are common in the commercial and business arenas, particularly in the energy sector.

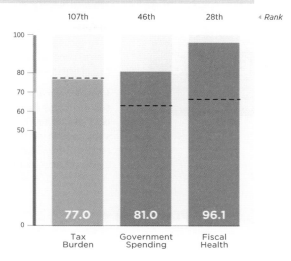

GOVERNMENT SIZE

107th | 46th | 28th ◀ Rank

- Tax Burden: 77.0
- Government Spending: 81.0
- Fiscal Health: 96.1

The top individual income tax rate is 35 percent, and the top corporate tax rate is 30 percent. Other taxes include a value-added tax. The overall tax burden equals 13.1 percent of total domestic income. Government spending has amounted to 25.2 percent of total output (GDP) over the past three years, and budget surpluses have averaged 0.7 percent of GDP. Public debt is equivalent to 43.9 percent of GDP.

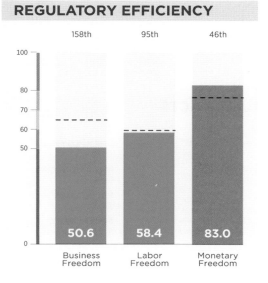

REGULATORY EFFICIENCY

158th | 95th | 46th

- Business Freedom: 50.6
- Labor Freedom: 58.4
- Monetary Freedom: 83.0

The regulatory framework still confronts potential entrepreneurs with significant bureaucratic and procedural hurdles. Labor regulations are outdated and applied inconsistently. In accordance with IMF recommendations, Gabon eliminated fuel subsidies in February 2016 after a dramatic drop in oil revenues, but the state continues to influence prices through subsidies to state-owned enterprises and direct control of the prices of other products.

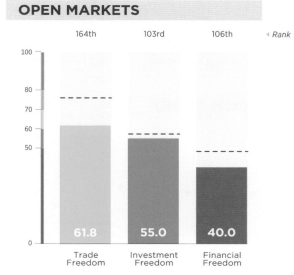

OPEN MARKETS

164th | 103rd | 106th ◀ Rank

- Trade Freedom: 61.8
- Investment Freedom: 55.0
- Financial Freedom: 40.0

Trade is important to Gabon's economy; the value of exports and imports taken together equals 74 percent of GDP. The average applied tariff rate is 14.1 percent. The government screens foreign investment, and investment is discouraged by the judicial and regulatory regimes. The underdeveloped financial sector remains state-controlled. Credit costs are high, and access to financing is scarce.

GABON

THE GAMBIA

The Gambia relies primarily on agriculture, tourism, and remittances to support its economy, leaving itself vulnerable to global market shocks. Gradual reforms in fiscal policies have helped to improve stability and growth in the economy. The Gambia has a fairly open foreign investment system, but serious government corruption and human rights issues hinder investment inflows.

Tariffs on imports, including additional duties on certain agricultural goods during harvesting season, undermine competition and decrease choices for individuals. Corruption remains pervasive, and protection of property rights is weak, undermining the rule of law. State-owned enterprises are present in many sectors, and supporting them is a major source of the government's debt.

WORLD RANK: **136**
REGIONAL RANK: **28**

ECONOMIC FREEDOM STATUS:
MOSTLY UNFREE

ECONOMIC FREEDOM SCORE

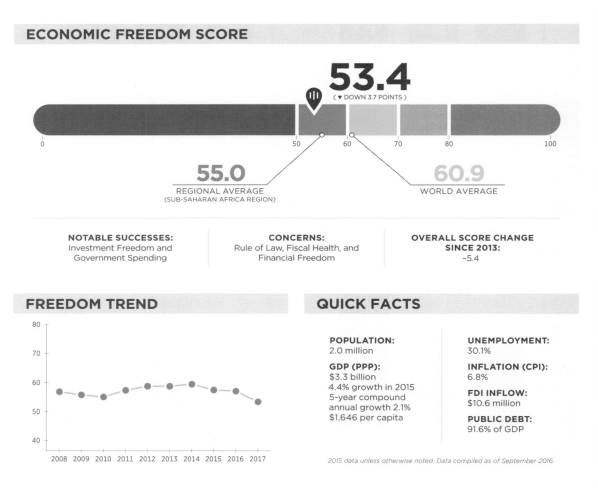

53.4
(▼ DOWN 3.7 POINTS)

0   50   60   70   80   100

55.0
REGIONAL AVERAGE
(SUB-SAHARAN AFRICA REGION)

60.9
WORLD AVERAGE

NOTABLE SUCCESSES:
Investment Freedom and Government Spending

CONCERNS:
Rule of Law, Fiscal Health, and Financial Freedom

OVERALL SCORE CHANGE SINCE 2013:
−5.4

FREEDOM TREND

80
70
60
50
40

2008 2009 2010 2011 2012 2013 2014 2015 2016 2017

QUICK FACTS

POPULATION:
2.0 million

GDP (PPP):
$3.3 billion
4.4% growth in 2015
5-year compound annual growth 2.1%
$1,646 per capita

UNEMPLOYMENT:
30.1%

INFLATION (CPI):
6.8%

FDI INFLOW:
$10.6 million

PUBLIC DEBT:
91.6% of GDP

2015 data unless otherwise noted. Data compiled as of September 2016

BACKGROUND: President Yahya Jammeh, who came to power in a bloodless coup in 1994, won his fourth term in 2011 in flawed elections. His Alliance for Patriotic Reorientation and Construction won a major victory in the 2012 legislative elections, which were boycotted by opposition parties. Despite constitutional guarantees of a number of basic rights, Jammeh's regime is one of the most authoritarian on the continent, a fact that led the U.S. to expel The Gambia from the African Growth and Opportunity Act and the Millennium Challenge Corporation. Government revenue depends heavily on peanut exports, leaving the state vulnerable to price fluctuations and market shocks.

12 ECONOMIC FREEDOMS | THE GAMBIA

RULE OF LAW

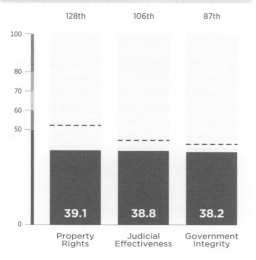

128th	106th	87th
Property Rights	Judicial Effectiveness	Government Integrity
39.1	38.8	38.2

Protection of property rights is weak. There are multiple overlapping land tenure systems, and many properties are subject to expropriation by the government. Although the constitution provides for an independent judiciary, the president selects and dismisses judges, and they usually defer to his wishes. The judicial system recognizes both customary law and Sharia (Islamic) law. Official corruption and impunity are serious problems.

GOVERNMENT SIZE

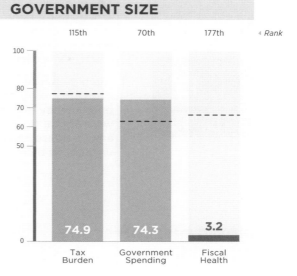

◄ Rank

115th	70th	177th
Tax Burden	Government Spending	Fiscal Health
74.9	74.3	3.2

The top personal income tax rate is 35 percent, and the top corporate tax rate is 32 percent. Other taxes include a capital gains tax and a sales tax. The overall tax burden equals 16.1 percent of total domestic income. Government spending has amounted to 29.2 percent of total output (GDP) over the past three years, and budget deficits have averaged 8.3 percent of GDP. Public debt is equivalent to 91.6 percent of GDP.

REGULATORY EFFICIENCY

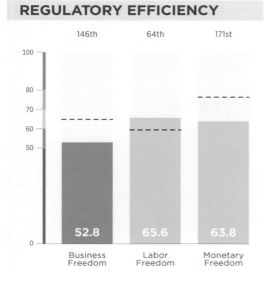

146th	64th	171st
Business Freedom	Labor Freedom	Monetary Freedom
52.8	65.6	63.8

Regulatory inefficiency continues to hamper the business environment. Chronically high unemployment and underemployment persist in the inefficient labor market. The large financial deficits of the National Water and Electricity Company and other public enterprises are a particularly acute problem; in 2015, one state-owned enterprise was instructed to sell imported fertilizer at below cost.

OPEN MARKETS

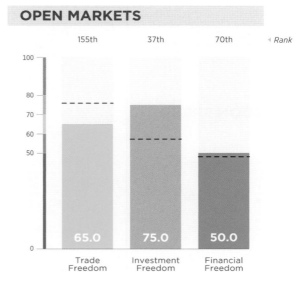

◄ Rank

155th	37th	70th
Trade Freedom	Investment Freedom	Financial Freedom
65.0	75.0	50.0

Trade is important to The Gambia's economy; the value of exports and imports taken together equals 58 percent of GDP. The average applied tariff rate is 12.5 percent. Foreign and domestic investors are generally treated equally under the law. Credit to the private sector has gradually increased, although supervision and regulation remain deficient. Capital markets consist only of government securities; there is no stock exchange.

THE GAMBIA

GHANA

A number of structural and institutional shortcomings still plague Ghana's economy and hold back prospects for more dynamic economic development. Continuing fiscal deficits have pushed public debt to over 70 percent of GDP, trapping the country in a cycle of debt service and borrowing.

The high burdens of government regulation and political favoritism are a drag on overall competitiveness. A cumbersome bureaucracy dissuades potential entrepreneurs and interferes with vibrant flows of goods and services. Undermining judicial effectiveness and government integrity, corruption remains unchecked by reform measures that are not enforced effectively.

ECONOMIC FREEDOM SCORE

56.2
(▼ DOWN 7.3 POINTS)

0   50   60   70   80   100

55.0
REGIONAL AVERAGE
(SUB-SAHARAN AFRICA REGION)

60.9
WORLD AVERAGE

NOTABLE SUCCESSES:
Trade Freedom

CONCERNS:
Rule of Law, Fiscal Health, and Labor Freedom

OVERALL SCORE CHANGE SINCE 2013:
–5.1

FREEDOM TREND

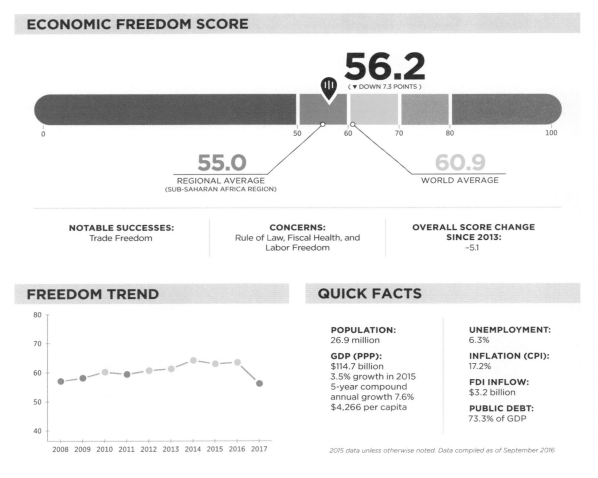

80

70

60

50

40

2008 2009 2010 2011 2012 2013 2014 2015 2016 2017

QUICK FACTS

POPULATION:
26.9 million

GDP (PPP):
$114.7 billion
3.5% growth in 2015
5-year compound
annual growth 7.6%
$4,266 per capita

UNEMPLOYMENT:
6.3%

INFLATION (CPI):
17.2%

FDI INFLOW:
$3.2 billion

PUBLIC DEBT:
73.3% of GDP

2015 data unless otherwise noted. Data compiled as of September 2016

BACKGROUND: Ghana has been a stable democracy since 1992. In December 2016, President John Dramani Mahama lost his bid for re-election to Nana Akufo-Addo. Ghana is Africa's second-biggest gold producer and second-largest cocoa producer. It is also rich in diamonds and oil. Most of its foreign debt was canceled in 2005 under the Heavily Indebted Poor Countries program, but government spending later ballooned. Coupled with plunging oil prices, this led to an economic crisis that forced the government to negotiate a $920 million extended credit facility from the IMF in April 2015. Ghana is locked in a dispute with Côte d'Ivoire over ownership of maritime oil fields, and a final ruling from an international court is expected in 2017.

12 ECONOMIC FREEDOMS | GHANA

RULE OF LAW

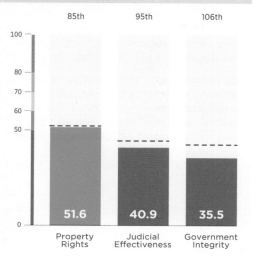

	85th	95th	106th
	Property Rights	Judicial Effectiveness	Government Integrity
	51.6	40.9	35.5

Property rights are recognized and enforced, but the process for obtaining clear title to land is often difficult, complicated, and lengthy. Scarce resources compromise and delay the judicial process, and poorly paid judges are tempted by bribes. Political corruption continues to be a problem despite robust legal and institutional frameworks to combat it, active media coverage, and the government's willingness to investigate major scandals.

GOVERNMENT SIZE

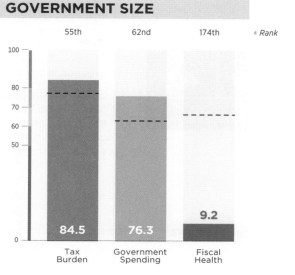

	55th	62nd	174th	◂ Rank
	Tax Burden	Government Spending	Fiscal Health	
	84.5	76.3	9.2	

The top personal income and corporate tax rates are 25 percent. Other taxes include a value-added tax, a national health insurance levy, and a capital gains tax. The overall tax burden equals 17.2 percent of total domestic income. Government spending has amounted to 28.1 percent of total output (GDP) over the past three years, and budget deficits have averaged 10.0 percent of GDP. Public debt is equivalent to 73.3 percent of GDP.

REGULATORY EFFICIENCY

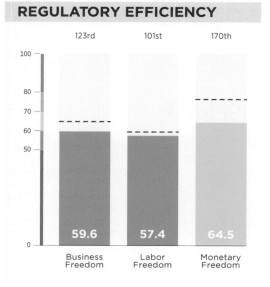

	123rd	101st	170th
	Business Freedom	Labor Freedom	Monetary Freedom
	59.6	57.4	64.5

Recent years' reforms have yielded reductions in the number of bureaucratic procedures, but the overall process for establishing and running a private enterprise is cumbersome. Labor regulations remain restrictive and outmoded. The government slashed electricity and water subsidies late in 2015 and reduced fuel subsidies early in 2016, but the approach of the November 2016 elections increased populist spending pressures.

OPEN MARKETS

	153rd	59th	39th	◂ Rank
	Trade Freedom	Investment Freedom	Financial Freedom	
	65.1	70.0	60.0	

Trade is important to Ghana's economy; the value of exports and imports taken together equals 99 percent of GDP. The average applied tariff rate is 10.0 percent, and foreign investment in several economic sectors is restricted. The financial system has undergone restructuring and transformation, and the supervisory framework is relatively strong. Bank credit to the private sector has increased, and capital markets are developing.

GHANA

GUINEA

WORLD RANK: **169** **REGIONAL RANK:** **42**

ECONOMIC FREEDOM STATUS:
REPRESSED

Advancement of economic freedom in Guinea has been uneven. Dynamic gains from relatively high openness to global trade are largely undercut by lack of progress in improving the investment regime and regulatory efficiency. The lack of a consistent commitment to structural reform continues to prevent more dynamic investment in the mining sector.

Guinea has lagged notably in promoting the effective rule of law. The judicial system remains vulnerable to political interference, and property rights are not strongly protected. Lingering corruption further undermines judicial effectiveness and government integrity, impeding more vibrant private-sector economic activity.

ECONOMIC FREEDOM SCORE

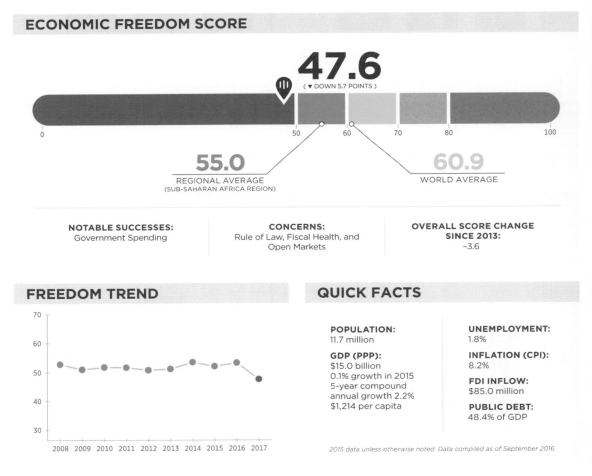

47.6
(▼ DOWN 5.7 POINTS)

0   50   60   70   80   100

55.0
REGIONAL AVERAGE
(SUB-SAHARAN AFRICA REGION)

60.9
WORLD AVERAGE

NOTABLE SUCCESSES:
Government Spending

CONCERNS:
Rule of Law, Fiscal Health, and Open Markets

OVERALL SCORE CHANGE SINCE 2013:
–3.6

FREEDOM TREND

70
60
50
40
30

2008 2009 2010 2011 2012 2013 2014 2015 2016 2017

QUICK FACTS

POPULATION:
11.7 million

GDP (PPP):
$15.0 billion
0.1% growth in 2015
5-year compound
annual growth 2.2%
$1,214 per capita

UNEMPLOYMENT:
1.8%

INFLATION (CPI):
8.2%

FDI INFLOW:
$85.0 million

PUBLIC DEBT:
48.4% of GDP

2015 data unless otherwise noted. Data compiled as of September 2016

BACKGROUND: In 2010, Alpha Condé won Guinea's first presidential election since independence from France in 1958, but the election was marred by irregularities and political violence. Condé's Rally of the Guinean People won a majority of seats in flawed parliamentary elections in 2013, and Condé easily won a second five-year term in October 2015 in elections boycotted by the opposition. The 2014 West Africa Ebola outbreak badly damaged Guinea's health care system and economy. An ambitious recovery plan unveiled by the government in 2015 includes measures designed to rebuild the health care system and the country's infrastructure, diversify the economy, and improve governance. Guinea has two-thirds of the world's bauxite reserves and large deposits of iron ore, gold, and diamonds.

12 ECONOMIC FREEDOMS | GUINEA

RULE OF LAW

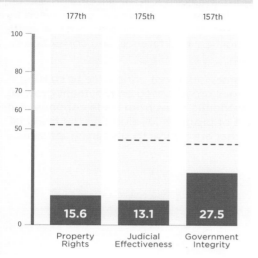

177th   175th   157th

- Property Rights: **15.6**
- Judicial Effectiveness: **13.1**
- Government Integrity: **27.5**

Both foreigners and citizens have the right to own property and businesses. However, enforcement of these rights depends on a corrupt and inefficient legal and administrative system. In addition, land sales and business contracts generally lack transparency. Public institutions are characterized by a pervasive culture of impunity and corruption.

GOVERNMENT SIZE

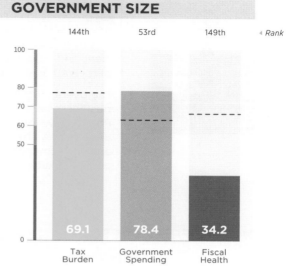

144th   53rd   149th   ◄ *Rank*

- Tax Burden: **69.1**
- Government Spending: **78.4**
- Fiscal Health: **34.2**

The top personal income tax rate is 40 percent, and the top corporate tax rate is 35 percent. Other taxes include a value-added tax and an inheritance tax. The overall tax burden equals 16.2 percent of total domestic income. Government spending has amounted to 26.8 percent of total output (GDP) over the past three years, and budget deficits have averaged 6.2 percent of GDP. Public debt is equivalent to 48.4 percent of GDP.

REGULATORY EFFICIENCY

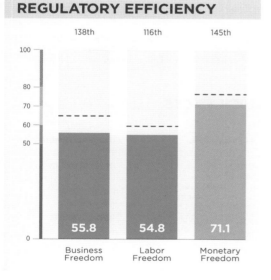

138th   116th   145th

- Business Freedom: **55.8**
- Labor Freedom: **54.8**
- Monetary Freedom: **71.1**

Private enterprises face numerous hurdles in incorporating and operating. The labor market remains underdeveloped, and the public sector still accounts for most formal employment. With inflation easing in 2016 due to lower world food and oil prices, the government resisted populist pressure to increase domestic fuel subsidies but delayed implementation of a planned automatic fuel pricing mechanism.

OPEN MARKETS

165th   120th   106th   ◄ *Rank*

- Trade Freedom: **61.2**
- Investment Freedom: **50.0**
- Financial Freedom: **40.0**

Trade is important to Guinea's economy; the value of exports and imports taken together equals 78 percent of GDP. The average applied tariff rate is 11.9 percent. The judicial and regulatory systems may impede foreign investment. The underdeveloped financial sector continues to provide a very limited range of services. Many people still rely on informal lending and have no bank accounts.

GUINEA

GUINEA-BISSAU

WORLD RANK:
119

REGIONAL RANK:
20

ECONOMIC FREEDOM STATUS:
MOSTLY UNFREE

Limited attempts at structural reform have generated uneven progress in Guinea–Bissau's economic development, and any emergence of private-sector dynamism remains constrained by institutionalized weaknesses. The judicial system remains inefficient and vulnerable to political interference, and corruption is perceived as widespread.

The overall regulatory framework is not conducive to starting businesses and discourages broad-based employment growth. Potentially significant economic gains from trade continue to be undercut by the absence of progress in reforming the financial and investment sectors that are critical to sustaining efficient open markets.

ECONOMIC FREEDOM SCORE

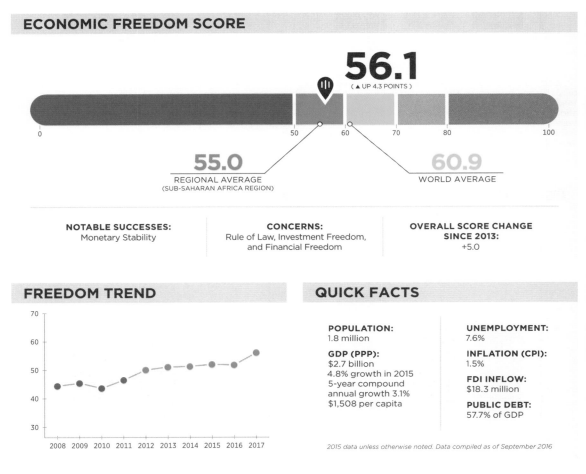

56.1
(▲ UP 4.3 POINTS)

0   50   60   70   80   100

55.0
REGIONAL AVERAGE
(SUB-SAHARAN AFRICA REGION)

60.9
WORLD AVERAGE

NOTABLE SUCCESSES:
Monetary Stability

CONCERNS:
Rule of Law, Investment Freedom, and Financial Freedom

OVERALL SCORE CHANGE SINCE 2013:
+5.0

FREEDOM TREND

70
60
50
40
30

2008 2009 2010 2011 2012 2013 2014 2015 2016 2017

QUICK FACTS

POPULATION:
1.8 million

GDP (PPP):
$2.7 billion
4.8% growth in 2015
5-year compound
annual growth 3.1%
$1,508 per capita

UNEMPLOYMENT:
7.6%

INFLATION (CPI):
1.5%

FDI INFLOW:
$18.3 million

PUBLIC DEBT:
57.7% of GDP

2015 data unless otherwise noted. Data compiled as of September 2016

BACKGROUND: Guinea–Bissau has been wracked by conflict since independence in 1974, including a civil war in the late 1990s and multiple military coups, most recently in April 2012. In May 2014, José Mário Vaz was elected president of the former Portuguese colony. In August 2015, Vaz dismissed Prime Minister Domingos Simões Pereira, head of the ruling African Party for the Independence of Guinea and Cape Verde (PAIGC), sparking a political crisis. Vaz quickly dismissed several successor governments and by November 2016, had named Umaro Sissoco Embaló to serve as the country's fifth prime minister within a two-year period. Guinea–Bissau is highly dependent on subsistence agriculture, the export of cashew nuts, and foreign assistance, which normally comprises about 80 percent of the country's budget.

12 ECONOMIC FREEDOMS | GUINEA-BISSAU

RULE OF LAW

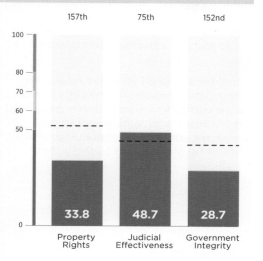

	157th	75th	152nd
	Property Rights	Judicial Effectiveness	Government Integrity
	33.8	**48.7**	**28.7**

Although the government has made transferring property easier by lowering the property registration tax, protection of property rights is generally weak. The judiciary has little independence and is barely operational. Judges are poorly trained, inadequately and irregularly paid, and subject to corruption. Guinea–Bissau's status as a transit hub for cocaine trafficking from South America to Europe exacerbates its endemic corruption.

GOVERNMENT SIZE

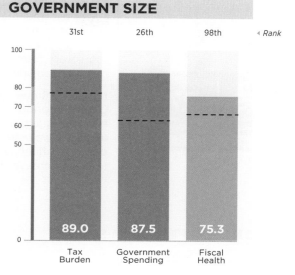

31st   26th   98th   ◄ Rank

	Tax Burden	Government Spending	Fiscal Health
	89.0	**87.5**	**75.3**

The top personal income tax rate is 20 percent, and the top corporate tax rate is 25 percent. The sales tax is down to 10 percent on certain commodities. The overall tax burden equals 8.7 percent of total domestic income. Government spending has amounted to 20.4 percent of total output (GDP) over the past three years, and budget deficits have averaged 3.4 percent of GDP. Public debt is equivalent to 57.7 percent of GDP.

REGULATORY EFFICIENCY

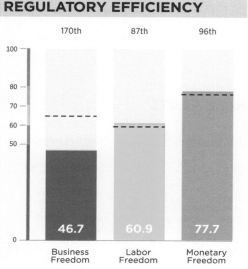

170th   87th   96th

	Business Freedom	Labor Freedom	Monetary Freedom
	46.7	**60.9**	**77.7**

The opaque regulatory environment discourages entrepreneurial activity, virtually precluding any significant private-sector development. Much of the labor force is employed in the public sector or the informal economy. Although the government has removed all fuel subsidies, in 2015, the IMF urged it to review its fuel pricing mechanism to ensure that international prices are fully passed through and criticized "indiscriminate" electricity subsidies.

OPEN MARKETS

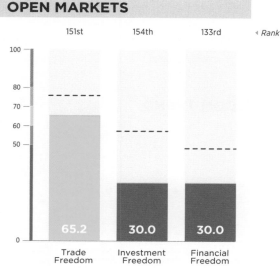

151st   154th   133rd   ◄ Rank

	Trade Freedom	Investment Freedom	Financial Freedom
	65.2	**30.0**	**30.0**

Trade is moderately important to Guinea–Bissau's economy; the value of exports and imports taken together equals 37 percent of GDP. The average applied tariff rate is 9.9 percent. The law treats foreign and domestic investment equally. High credit costs and scarce access to financing impede entrepreneurial activity, although bank credits to the private sector have increased. In late 2015, the government bailed out two commercial banks.

GUINEA–BISSAU

KENYA

Kenya's economy has shown moderate resilience in the face of external and internal challenges, and reform efforts are continuing in several areas. The government has enacted laws to improve the business environment, and the overall regulatory framework for launching a business has become more streamlined.

Kenya continues to lag in maintaining an effective rule of law. Overall economic freedom is limited by weak protection of property rights and by extensive corruption. Corruption is perceived as pervasive, and the judicial system remains vulnerable to political influence. Public-sector employees' continuing demands for pay increases have added fiscal pressures to the budget.

WORLD RANK: **135**
REGIONAL RANK: **27**
ECONOMIC FREEDOM STATUS:
MOSTLY UNFREE

ECONOMIC FREEDOM SCORE

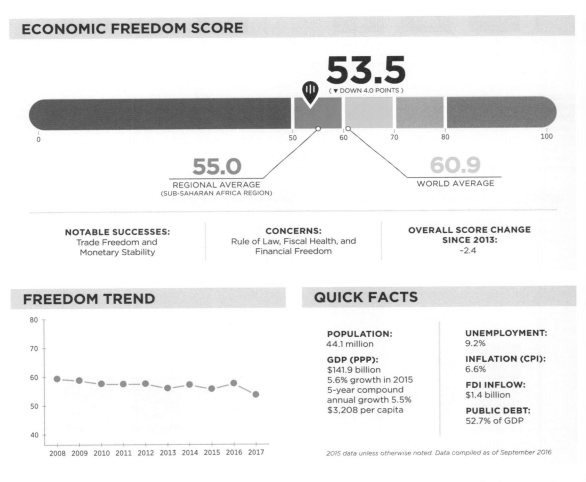

53.5
(▼ DOWN 4.0 POINTS)

0   50   60   70   80   100

55.0
REGIONAL AVERAGE
(SUB-SAHARAN AFRICA REGION)

60.9
WORLD AVERAGE

NOTABLE SUCCESSES:
Trade Freedom and
Monetary Stability

CONCERNS:
Rule of Law, Fiscal Health, and
Financial Freedom

**OVERALL SCORE CHANGE
SINCE 2013:**
–2.4

FREEDOM TREND

80
70
60
50
40

2008 2009 2010 2011 2012 2013 2014 2015 2016 2017

QUICK FACTS

POPULATION:
44.1 million

GDP (PPP):
$141.9 billion
5.6% growth in 2015
5-year compound
annual growth 5.5%
$3,208 per capita

UNEMPLOYMENT:
9.2%

INFLATION (CPI):
6.6%

FDI INFLOW:
$1.4 billion

PUBLIC DEBT:
52.7% of GDP

2015 data unless otherwise noted. Data compiled as of September 2016

BACKGROUND: In 2013, Uhuru Kenyatta won the first presidential election under a constitution promulgated in 2010. In 2014 and 2016, the International Criminal Court dropped charges against Kenyatta and Deputy President William Ruto involving crimes against humanity stemming from post-election violence in 2007. Kenya invaded Somalia in 2011 to counter the Islamist group al-Shabaab and in 2012 joined the African Union coalition battling the terrorist organization there. Since the invasion, Kenya has suffered a surge of terrorist attacks. The country recently discovered about a billion barrels of oil reserves that can be extracted profitably. Plans for a Uganda-to-Kenya oil pipeline fell through in April 2016, leading Kenya to sign a pipeline agreement with Ethiopia.

12 ECONOMIC FREEDOMS | KENYA

RULE OF LAW

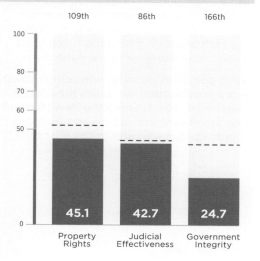

| 109th | 86th | 166th |

- Property Rights: 45.1
- Judicial Effectiveness: 42.7
- Government Integrity: 24.7

More than 10 percent of the land in Kenya lacks clear title, although electronic document management at the land registry has been improved. The judiciary demonstrates independence and impartiality, but courts are undermined by weak capacity and resource constraints. Corruption is pervasive and entrenched, and Kenya is ranked among the world's most corrupt countries by Transparency International.

GOVERNMENT SIZE

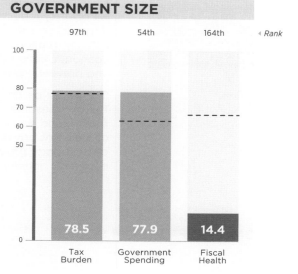

◄ Rank

| 97th | 54th | 164th |

- Tax Burden: 78.5
- Government Spending: 77.9
- Fiscal Health: 14.4

The top income and corporate tax rates are 30 percent. Other taxes include a value-added tax and a tax on interest. The overall tax burden equals 18.7 percent of total domestic income. Government spending has amounted to 27.1 percent of total output (GDP) over the past three years, and budget deficits have averaged 7.2 percent of GDP. Public debt is equivalent to 52.7 percent of GDP.

REGULATORY EFFICIENCY

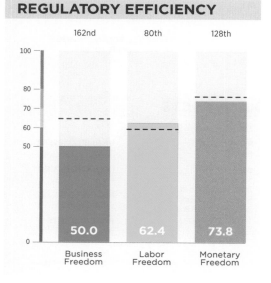

| 162nd | 80th | 128th |

- Business Freedom: 50.0
- Labor Freedom: 62.4
- Monetary Freedom: 73.8

The entrepreneurial environment has become more streamlined, and no minimum capital is required for launching a business. The nonsalary cost of employing a worker is relatively low, but dismissing an employee can be costly. The government continues to regulate prices through subsidies, agricultural marketing boards, and state-owned enterprises. Aid from international donors is funding development of geothermal power.

OPEN MARKETS

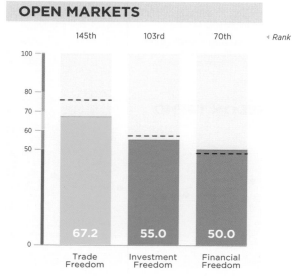

◄ Rank

| 145th | 103rd | 70th |

- Trade Freedom: 67.2
- Investment Freedom: 55.0
- Financial Freedom: 50.0

Trade is moderately important to Kenya's economy; the value of exports and imports taken together equals 45 percent of GDP. The average applied tariff rate is 8.9 percent. Foreign ownership in some sectors is restricted, and state-owned enterprises distort the economy. The growing financial sector has become more open to competition, and its overall stability is relatively well maintained. Over 40 commercial banks are in operation.

KENYA

LESOTHO

WORLD RANK: **134** REGIONAL RANK: **26**

ECONOMIC FREEDOM STATUS:
MOSTLY UNFREE

Lesotho has made considerable gains in income growth and poverty reduction, but a large portion of its population still depends on subsistence farming, and dynamic private-sector activity remains limited. The state is heavily involved in most economic activity, fueling high levels of government spending and preventing the emergence of entrepreneurial dynamism.

Significant barriers to trade constrain poverty-alleviating growth. The burdensome regulatory environment increases the cost of foreign and domestic investment, constraining the development of a vibrant private sector. Significant corruption and the poor protection of property rights continue to add to the cost of economic activity.

ECONOMIC FREEDOM SCORE

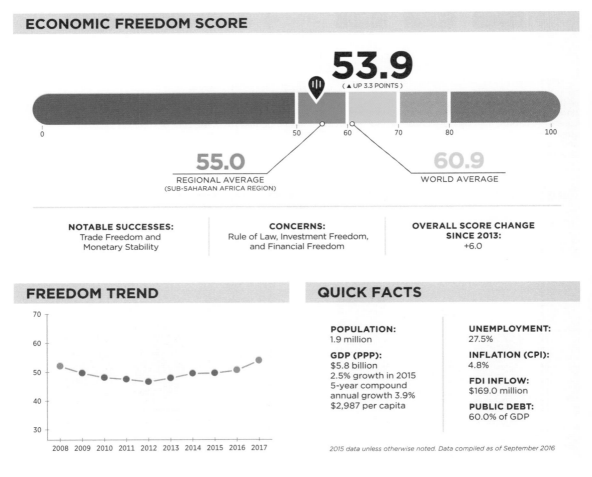

53.9
(▲ UP 3.3 POINTS)

0   50   60   70   80   100

55.0
REGIONAL AVERAGE
(SUB-SAHARAN AFRICA REGION)

60.9
WORLD AVERAGE

NOTABLE SUCCESSES:
Trade Freedom and
Monetary Stability

CONCERNS:
Rule of Law, Investment Freedom,
and Financial Freedom

**OVERALL SCORE CHANGE
SINCE 2013:**
+6.0

FREEDOM TREND

70

60

50

40

30

2008 2009 2010 2011 2012 2013 2014 2015 2016 2017

QUICK FACTS

POPULATION:
1.9 million

GDP (PPP):
$5.8 billion
2.5% growth in 2015
5-year compound
annual growth 3.9%
$2,987 per capita

UNEMPLOYMENT:
27.5%

INFLATION (CPI):
4.8%

FDI INFLOW:
$169.0 million

PUBLIC DEBT:
60.0% of GDP

2015 data unless otherwise noted. Data compiled as of September 2016

BACKGROUND: Lesotho is a parliamentary constitutional monarchy, and King Letsie III is ceremonial head of state. Thomas Thabane, elected prime minister in May 2012, fled in August 2014 after an attempted coup. He returned following a deal brokered by the South African government but fled again along with other opposition leaders in May 2015. General elections in February 2015 were largely viewed as free and fair, and Pakalitha Mosisili is now prime minister. Rights groups have accused the government of human rights abuses, and a prominent editor of a local paper narrowly survived an assassination attempt in July 2016. Principal exports include diamonds and water. Lesotho has one of the world's highest HIV rates.

12 ECONOMIC FREEDOMS | LESOTHO

RULE OF LAW

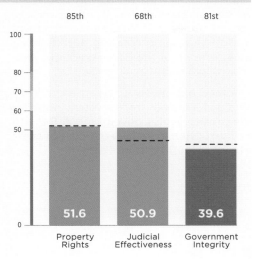

Protection of private property rights is ineffective, but expropriation is unlikely. Legal structures to protect intellectual property rights are comparatively strong. The judiciary is relatively independent but politicized and chronically underfunded. Corruption remains a problem in all areas of government and public services, and there is little that citizens can do to hold the government to account. Management of public finances lacks transparency.

GOVERNMENT SIZE

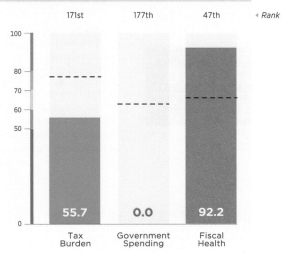

The top personal income tax rate is 35 percent, and the top corporate tax rate is 25 percent. Other taxes include a value-added tax and a tax on dividends. The overall tax burden equals 50.8 percent of total domestic income. Government spending has amounted to 60.7 percent of total output (GDP) over the past three years, and budget deficits have averaged 0.6 percent of GDP. Public debt is equivalent to 60.0 percent of GDP.

REGULATORY EFFICIENCY

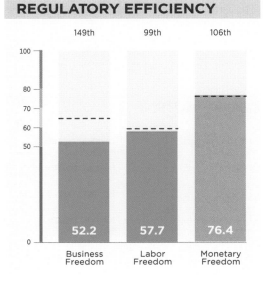

Red tape and outmoded commercial laws continue to limit the overall efficiency of the regulatory system. The labor market remains rigid and not fully developed, driving a large share of the labor force into the informal economy. The government increased food subsidies again in 2016 in response to drought, and it influences other prices through state-owned enterprises. Monetary stability is affected by the volatility of the South African rand.

OPEN MARKETS

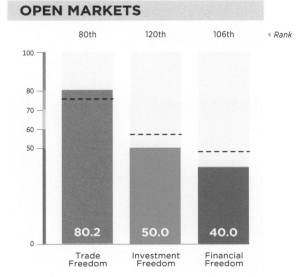

Trade is extremely important to Lesotho's economy; the value of exports and imports taken together equals 136 percent of GDP. The average applied tariff rate is 2.4 percent. Customs procedures have been improved. Investment in some sectors of the economy is restricted. Much of the population lacks adequate access to banking services. The high cost of credit hinders entrepreneurial activity and the development of a vibrant private sector.

LESOTHO

LIBERIA

WORLD RANK:
161

REGIONAL RANK:
38

ECONOMIC FREEDOM STATUS:
REPRESSED

A reform-minded government has placed Liberia on a path of growth despite numerous challenges. Reforms have dismantled some barriers to trade, simplified business licensing, and eased credit restrictions. In recent years, the government's core economic policy has focused on promoting broad-based economic growth in the aftermath of the Ebola epidemic and reviving health facilities within a tight fiscal space.

The rule of law is not enforced effectively across the country, and weak property rights and a lack of transparency in the legal system seriously impede private-sector development. Despite reform efforts, systemic corruption increases the cost of business and deters much-needed long-term investment.

ECONOMIC FREEDOM SCORE

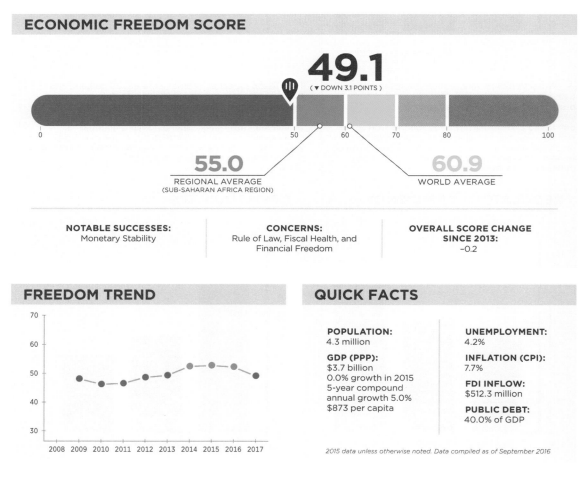

49.1
(▼ DOWN 3.1 POINTS)

0   50   60   70   80   100

55.0
REGIONAL AVERAGE
(SUB-SAHARAN AFRICA REGION)

60.9
WORLD AVERAGE

NOTABLE SUCCESSES:
Monetary Stability

CONCERNS:
Rule of Law, Fiscal Health, and Financial Freedom

OVERALL SCORE CHANGE SINCE 2013:
–0.2

FREEDOM TREND

70

60

50

40

30

2008 2009 2010 2011 2012 2013 2014 2015 2016 2017

QUICK FACTS

POPULATION:
4.3 million

GDP (PPP):
$3.7 billion
0.0% growth in 2015
5-year compound
annual growth 5.0%
$873 per capita

UNEMPLOYMENT:
4.2%

INFLATION (CPI):
7.7%

FDI INFLOW:
$512.3 million

PUBLIC DEBT:
40.0% of GDP

2015 data unless otherwise noted. Data compiled as of September 2016

BACKGROUND: In the early 1990s, civil war killed 250,000 Liberians. A peace agreement was reached in 1995, and rebel leader Charles Taylor was elected president in 1997. He was forced to step down in 2003 and was found guilty of war crimes in 2012. Ellen Johnson Sirleaf, president since 2006, was awarded the Nobel Peace Prize in 2011. The country is fragile, but the U.N. peacekeeping mission authorized in 2003 officially transferred peacekeeping responsibilities to Liberia in July 2016. Liberia is rich in natural resources, including rubber, mineral resources, and iron ore. It was one of the countries hit hardest by the 2014 Ebola outbreak in West Africa.

12 ECONOMIC FREEDOMS | LIBERIA

RULE OF LAW

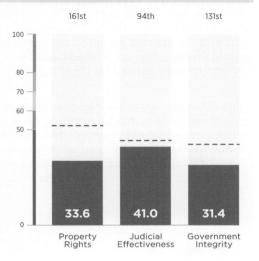

	161st	94th	131st

Property Rights: 33.6
Judicial Effectiveness: 41.0
Government Integrity: 31.4

Property rights are not strongly protected, and the rule of law remains uneven across the country, exacerbated by a precarious physical security environment. The judiciary is weak and inadequately resourced. Overall, the poor functioning of government reflects endemic corruption and a lack of administrative capacity. On the positive side, Liberia was the first African state to comply with the Extractive Industries Transparency Initiative.

GOVERNMENT SIZE

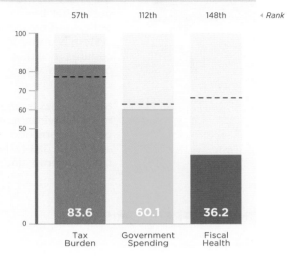

	57th	112th	148th	◄ Rank

Tax Burden: 83.6
Government Spending: 60.1
Fiscal Health: 36.2

Liberia's top individual income and corporate tax rates are 25 percent. Other taxes include a property tax and a goods and services tax. The overall tax burden equals 19.7 percent of total domestic income. Government spending has amounted to 36.5 percent of total output (GDP) over the past three years, and budget deficits have averaged 6.2 percent of GDP. Public debt is equivalent to 40.0 percent of GDP.

REGULATORY EFFICIENCY

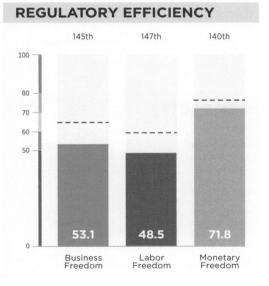

	145th	147th	140th

Business Freedom: 53.1
Labor Freedom: 48.5
Monetary Freedom: 71.8

Despite some legislative efforts to modernize the regulatory framework, private investment and production remain severely hampered by bureaucratic inefficiency. With the labor market not fully developed, a large portion of the workforce is engaged in the informal sector. Following the Ebola crisis, the government increased subsidies for education and health care and received higher levels of subsidized food aid from international donors.

OPEN MARKETS

	167th	120th	162nd	◄ Rank

Trade Freedom: 60.1
Investment Freedom: 50.0
Financial Freedom: 20.0

Trade is extremely important to Liberia's economy; the value of exports and imports taken together equals 112 percent of GDP. The average applied tariff rate is 6.1 percent. Foreign investment in several sectors of the economy is restricted, and foreign investors may not own land. A large part of the population remains outside of the formal banking sector, and the inefficient legal framework deters use of financial institutions.

LIBERIA

MADAGASCAR

WORLD RANK: **113** | REGIONAL RANK: **15**

ECONOMIC FREEDOM STATUS:
MOSTLY UNFREE

Despite some gains in much-needed economic development, much of the progress made in reducing poverty in Madagascar has been undermined by poor management of economic policy and the ongoing risk of political instability. The judicial system is underdeveloped, and convoluted administrative procedures facilitate corruption. Privatization has halted because of the unfavorable investment climate caused by chronic political turmoil.

Nonetheless, some notable reforms have enhanced the entrepreneurial environment. Procedures for launching a business have been streamlined, and minimum capital requirements have been abolished. Tax rates on individual and corporate income have been lowered, and the overall tax system has been simplified.

ECONOMIC FREEDOM SCORE

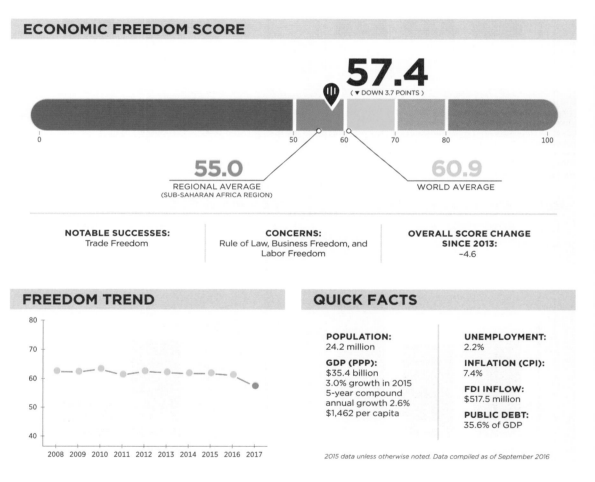

57.4
(▼ DOWN 3.7 POINTS)

0   50   60   70   80   100

55.0
REGIONAL AVERAGE
(SUB-SAHARAN AFRICA REGION)

60.9
WORLD AVERAGE

NOTABLE SUCCESSES:
Trade Freedom

CONCERNS:
Rule of Law, Business Freedom, and Labor Freedom

OVERALL SCORE CHANGE SINCE 2013:
–4.6

FREEDOM TREND

80

70

60

50

40

2008 2009 2010 2011 2012 2013 2014 2015 2016 2017

QUICK FACTS

POPULATION:
24.2 million

GDP (PPP):
$35.4 billion
3.0% growth in 2015
5-year compound
annual growth 2.6%
$1,462 per capita

UNEMPLOYMENT:
2.2%

INFLATION (CPI):
7.4%

FDI INFLOW:
$517.5 million

PUBLIC DEBT:
35.6% of GDP

2015 data unless otherwise noted. Data compiled as of September 2016

BACKGROUND: After decades of military coups, political violence, and corruption, the former French colony of Madagascar has become more stable, although there has been frequent turnover in the prime minister's office. Hery Rajaonarimampianina was elected president in January 2014 after years of political instability sparked by a 2009 coup. In January 2015, General Jean Ravelonarivo succeeded Roger Kolo as prime minister when Kolo and his government resigned after less than a year in office. Ravelonarivo subsequently resigned after serving approximately 15 months and was replaced by Olivier Mahafaly Solonandrasana. Given the country's relative stability, international organizations and foreign donors have restored ties that they had severed after the 2009 coup.

12 ECONOMIC FREEDOMS | MADAGASCAR

RULE OF LAW

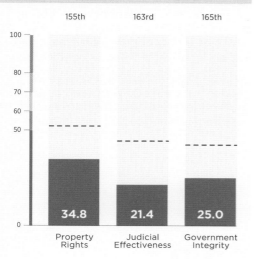

	155th	163rd	165th
	Property Rights	Judicial Effectiveness	Government Integrity
	34.8	21.4	25.0

Madagascar has continued French colonial land tenure policies, including presumed state ownership of all land and the central government as sole provider of legitimate land titles. The 2016 World Bank *Doing Business* survey reports that property transfer taxes have been reduced. High levels of corruption exist in nearly all sectors, especially the judiciary, police, taxation, customs, land, trade, mining, industry, environment, education, and health care.

GOVERNMENT SIZE

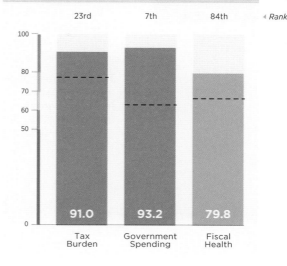

	23rd	7th	84th	◂ Rank
	Tax Burden	Government Spending	Fiscal Health	
	91.0	93.2	79.8	

The top individual income and corporate tax rates are 20 percent. Other taxes include a value-added tax and a capital gains tax. The overall tax burden equals 9.9 percent of total domestic income. Government spending has amounted to 15 percent of total output (GDP) over the past three years, and budget deficits have averaged 3.3 percent of GDP. Public debt is equivalent to 35.6 percent of GDP.

REGULATORY EFFICIENCY

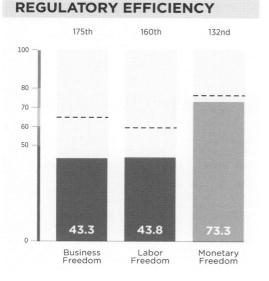

	175th	160th	132nd
	Business Freedom	Labor Freedom	Monetary Freedom
	43.3	43.8	73.3

The overall climate for entrepreneurial activity is held back by a lack of progress on reform. Procedures for setting up a business have been simplified, but other regulatory requirements are generally costly. The outmoded labor regulations are restrictive and not conducive to development of a dynamic labor market. Although the government has told the IMF repeatedly that it would reduce fuel price subsidies, it has not done so.

OPEN MARKETS

	96th	103rd	70th	◂ Rank
	Trade Freedom	Investment Freedom	Financial Freedom	
	78.0	55.0	50.0	

Trade is important to Madagascar's economy; the value of exports and imports taken together equals 70 percent of GDP. The average applied tariff rate is 6.0 percent. Judicial and regulatory barriers deter foreign investment, and state-owned enterprises distort the economy. The relatively high costs of financing and scarce access to credit are barriers to the development of a more dynamic private sector.

MADAGASCAR

MALAWI

In June 2016, the International Monetary Fund announced that it will extend its loan program for Malawi, including an extra $76.8 million to help the country battle hunger brought on by one of the worst droughts in southern Africa's history, for a further six months. Malawi's economy depends on its agriculture sector, which is often subject to adverse weather conditions.

The government has run large fiscal deficits in recent years, and the costs of debt service are rising. Corruption is endemic in several areas of the government and a deterrent to foreign investment. The judicial system is independent, but it is also slow and inefficient.

ECONOMIC FREEDOM SCORE

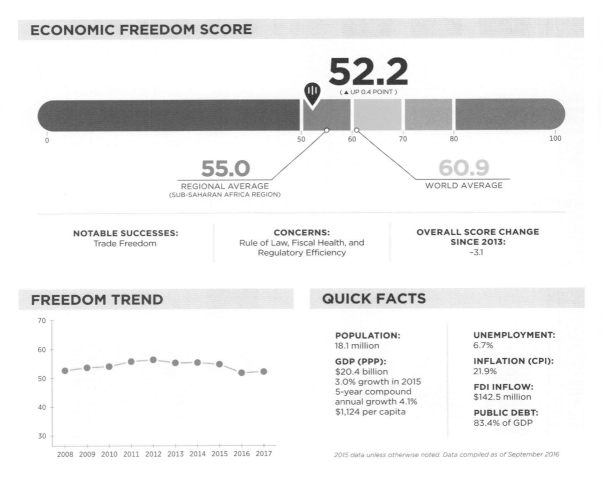

52.2
(▲ UP 0.4 POINT)

0   50   60   70   80   100

55.0
REGIONAL AVERAGE
(SUB-SAHARAN AFRICA REGION)

60.9
WORLD AVERAGE

NOTABLE SUCCESSES:
Trade Freedom

CONCERNS:
Rule of Law, Fiscal Health, and
Regulatory Efficiency

**OVERALL SCORE CHANGE
SINCE 2013:**
–3.1

FREEDOM TREND

70
60
50
40
30

2008 2009 2010 2011 2012 2013 2014 2015 2016 2017

QUICK FACTS

POPULATION:
18.1 million

GDP (PPP):
$20.4 billion
3.0% growth in 2015
5-year compound
annual growth 4.1%
$1,124 per capita

UNEMPLOYMENT:
6.7%

INFLATION (CPI):
21.9%

FDI INFLOW:
$142.5 million

PUBLIC DEBT:
83.4% of GDP

2015 data unless otherwise noted. Data compiled as of September 2016

BACKGROUND: Malawi achieved independence from the British in 1964 and was ruled as a one-party state by Dr. Hastings Kamuzu Banda for 30 years. President Bingu wa Mutharika, elected in 2004 and reelected in 2009, died in April 2012 and was replaced by Vice President Joyce Banda. In May 2014, Peter Mutharika, brother of the late president, won the presidency in elections of questionable legitimacy. Malawi is one of Africa's most densely populated countries. More than half of the population lives below the poverty line, and over 85 percent depend on subsistence agriculture. Tobacco, tea, and sugar are the most important exports.

12 ECONOMIC FREEDOMS | MALAWI

RULE OF LAW

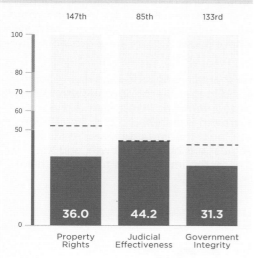

	147th	85th	133rd
	Property Rights **36.0**	Judicial Effectiveness **44.2**	Government Integrity **31.3**

Despite efforts to improve the land tenure system, customary rules still prevail, and occupants hold no legally binding titles. More than half of the arable land is untitled. The judicial system is independent but inefficient. Serious weaknesses include poor record keeping; a shortage of judges, attorneys, and other trained personnel; heavy caseloads; and a lack of resources. There have been recent allegations of rampant state corruption.

GOVERNMENT SIZE

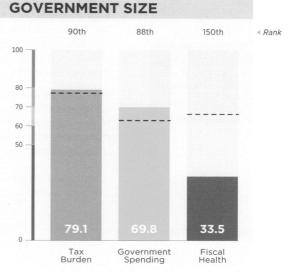

	90th	88th	150th ◄ Rank
	Tax Burden **79.1**	Government Spending **69.8**	Fiscal Health **33.5**

The top individual income and corporate tax rates are 30 percent. Other taxes include a value-added tax and an inheritance tax. The overall tax burden equals 16.9 percent of total domestic income. Government spending has amounted to 31.7 percent of total output (GDP) over the past three years, and budget deficits have averaged 5.7 percent of GDP. Public debt is equivalent to 83.4 percent of GDP.

REGULATORY EFFICIENCY

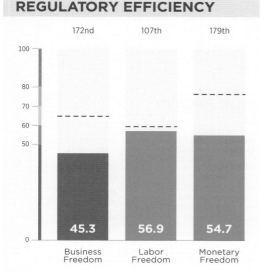

	172nd	107th	179th
	Business Freedom **45.3**	Labor Freedom **56.9**	Monetary Freedom **54.7**

Malawi has taken steps to improve its regulatory framework, but progress has been slow. Although the public sector is a large employer, most of the population remains employed outside of the formal sector, primarily in agriculture. The government outlined plans to reduce farm subsidies in fiscal year 2015–2016, but because of heavy political resistance to reform, those plans have failed to materialize.

OPEN MARKETS

	129th	103rd	70th ◄ Rank
	Trade Freedom **70.5**	Investment Freedom **55.0**	Financial Freedom **50.0**

Trade is important to Malawi's economy; the value of exports and imports taken together equals 62 percent of GDP. The average applied tariff rate is 4.8 percent. Foreign ownership of land is restricted, and state-owned enterprises distort the economy. Malawi's developing financial sector remains dominated by banking, but expensive credit and the lack of equitable access to finance continue to hinder private-sector development.

MALAWI

MALI

Mali has undertaken some significant reforms to diversify its economy and reduce rural poverty. Tax administration has been improved, and the cotton markets are moving toward privatization. Restraints on government spending and relatively stable monetary policy have allowed space for a growing entrepreneurial sector.

Substantial strides in other areas are needed to ensure significant poverty reduction and long-run economic growth. While Mali encourages foreign and domestic investment in theory, dynamic private-sector growth is impeded by the perception of widespread corruption, poor infrastructure, and regional instability. Rigid labor regulations hurt job growth, and the underdeveloped financial sector limits access to finance, hampering investment.

ECONOMIC FREEDOM SCORE

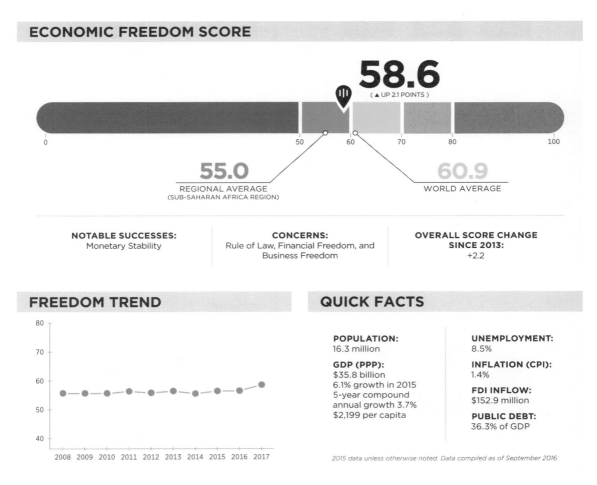

58.6
(▲ UP 2.1 POINTS)

0   50   60   70   80   100

55.0
REGIONAL AVERAGE
(SUB-SAHARAN AFRICA REGION)

60.9
WORLD AVERAGE

NOTABLE SUCCESSES:
Monetary Stability

CONCERNS:
Rule of Law, Financial Freedom, and Business Freedom

OVERALL SCORE CHANGE SINCE 2013:
+2.2

FREEDOM TREND

80

70

60

50

40

2008 2009 2010 2011 2012 2013 2014 2015 2016 2017

QUICK FACTS

POPULATION:
16.3 million

GDP (PPP):
$35.8 billion
6.1% growth in 2015
5-year compound annual growth 3.7%
$2,199 per capita

UNEMPLOYMENT:
8.5%

INFLATION (CPI):
1.4%

FDI INFLOW:
$152.9 million

PUBLIC DEBT:
36.3% of GDP

2015 data unless otherwise noted. Data compiled as of September 2016

BACKGROUND: After President Amadou Toumani Touré was ousted in a March 2012 military coup, Tuareg separatists and al-Qaeda–linked militants took control of northern Mali and declared independence. French armed forces restored government control in the major cities in January 2013, and former Prime Minister Ibrahim Boubacar Keita won the presidency in a second round of balloting in August. In June 2015, the government signed a peace accord with an alliance of Tuareg separatist groups, but clashes between the separatists and pro-government militias soon resumed. French troops remain in the country along with a U.N. peacekeeping operation that has suffered more peacekeepers killed than any other current U.N. peacekeeping mission.

12 ECONOMIC FREEDOMS | MALI

RULE OF LAW

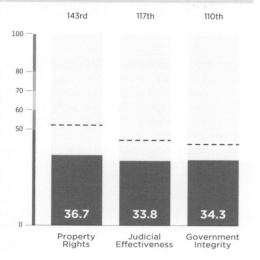

143rd   117th   110th

Property Rights	Judicial Effectiveness	Government Integrity
36.7	33.8	34.3

Property rights are not always adequately protected. The judicial system is inefficient and prone to corruption. Pervasive government corruption was a factor in the short-lived Islamist takeover in northern Mali. State authority in parts of the North is still tenuous, and corruption remains a problem throughout the government, public procurement, and both public and private contracting, where demands for bribes are frequently reported.

GOVERNMENT SIZE

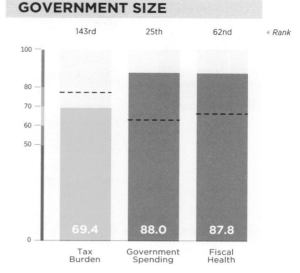

143rd   25th   62nd   ◀ Rank

Tax Burden	Government Spending	Fiscal Health
69.4	88.0	87.8

The top individual income tax rate is 40 percent, and the top corporate tax rate is 35 percent. Other taxes include a value-added tax. The overall tax burden equals 15.3 percent of total domestic income. Government spending has amounted to 20 percent of total output (GDP) over the past three years, and budget deficits have averaged 2.4 percent of GDP. Public debt is equivalent to 36.3 percent of GDP.

REGULATORY EFFICIENCY

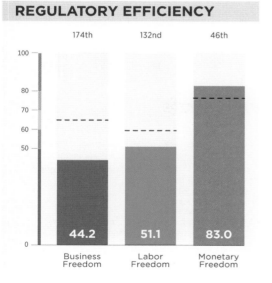

174th   132nd   46th

Business Freedom	Labor Freedom	Monetary Freedom
44.2	51.1	83.0

Despite some progress, the regulatory framework does not encourage much-needed economic diversification or private-sector development efficiently. Labor regulations, although not fully enforced, are relatively rigid. The government has eliminated fuel subsidies through market pricing. In the electricity sector, subsidies have been reduced by de facto rate increases, but significant untargeted subsidies remain in effect.

OPEN MARKETS

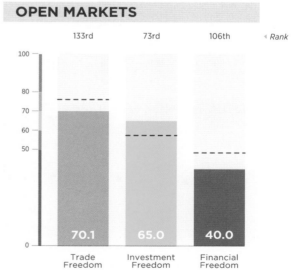

133rd   73rd   106th   ◀ Rank

Trade Freedom	Investment Freedom	Financial Freedom
70.1	65.0	40.0

Trade is important to Mali's economy; the value of exports and imports taken together equals 51 percent of GDP. The average applied tariff rate is 7.4 percent. In general, the law treats foreign and domestic investment equally, but state-owned enterprises distort the economy. Mali has an underdeveloped financial sector. Financial intermediation of transactions is relatively rare, and limited access to financing hampers entrepreneurial activity.

MALI

MAURITANIA

WORLD RANK:
131

REGIONAL RANK:
25

ECONOMIC FREEDOM STATUS:
MOSTLY UNFREE

Overall institutional weaknesses continue to limit economic dynamism and perpetuate poverty in Mauritania. Regulatory reforms implemented in recent years to enhance the entrepreneurial environment have been undercut by ongoing political instability.

Although Mauritania's economy has expanded from its limited productive base, it suffers from serious institutional weaknesses, and growth remains fragile. Pervasive corruption undermines the rule of law and is exacerbated by an inefficient and politically vulnerable judicial system. Open-market policies to promote dynamic investment have not been fully institutionalized, and tariffs and other restrictions inhibit potential entrepreneurs from participating efficiently in the global economy.

ECONOMIC FREEDOM SCORE

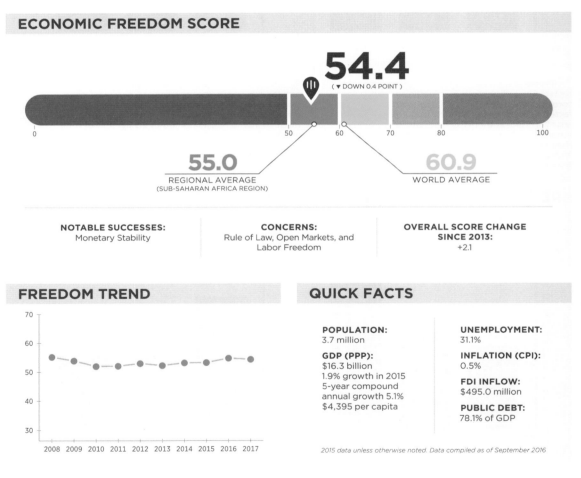

54.4
(▼ DOWN 0.4 POINT)

0   50   60   70   80   100

55.0
REGIONAL AVERAGE
(SUB-SAHARAN AFRICA REGION)

60.9
WORLD AVERAGE

NOTABLE SUCCESSES:
Monetary Stability

CONCERNS:
Rule of Law, Open Markets, and Labor Freedom

OVERALL SCORE CHANGE SINCE 2013:
+2.1

FREEDOM TREND

70

60

50

40

30

2008 2009 2010 2011 2012 2013 2014 2015 2016 2017

QUICK FACTS

POPULATION:
3.7 million

GDP (PPP):
$16.3 billion
1.9% growth in 2015
5-year compound annual growth 5.1%
$4,395 per capita

UNEMPLOYMENT:
31.1%

INFLATION (CPI):
0.5%

FDI INFLOW:
$495.0 million

PUBLIC DEBT:
78.1% of GDP

2015 data unless otherwise noted. Data compiled as of September 2016

BACKGROUND: Amidst political tensions from three major groups (Arabic-speaking descendants of slaves, Arabic-speaking "White Moors," and Sub-Saharan ethnic groups) a military junta ruled Mauritania until 1992, when the first multi-party elections were held. In 2008, General Mohamed Ould Abdel Aziz overthrew President Sidi Ould Abdallahi. Aziz was subsequently elected president in a 2009 election that was boycotted by the opposition. He was re-elected in 2014. In 1981, Mauritania became the last country in the world to outlaw slavery, but as much as 20 percent of the population remains enslaved. Mauritania is threatened by the terrorist group al-Qaeda in the Islamic Maghreb (AQIM). Large offshore gas fields discovered near the border with Senegal have raised hopes that Mauritania could become a significant source of gas.

12 ECONOMIC FREEDOMS | MAURITANIA

RULE OF LAW

176th	174th	148th	◄

Property Rights	Judicial Effectiveness	Government Integrity
22.5	13.8	29.2

There is a well-developed property registration system for land and real estate in most areas of the country, but there are many controversial land tenure issues in the South along the Senegal River. The chaotic and corrupt judicial system is heavily influenced by the government. Corruption is most pervasive in government procurement but is also common in the distribution of official documents, fishing licenses, bank loans, and tax payments.

GOVERNMENT SIZE

71st	78th	93rd	◄ Rank

Tax Burden	Government Spending	Fiscal Health
81.2	73.2	77.1

The top individual income tax rate is 30 percent, and the top corporate tax rate is 25 percent. Other taxes include a value-added tax. The overall tax burden equals 18.9 percent of total domestic income. Government spending has amounted to 29.9 percent of total output (GDP) over the past three years, and budget deficits have averaged 2.6 percent of GDP. Public debt is equivalent to 78.1 percent of GDP.

REGULATORY EFFICIENCY

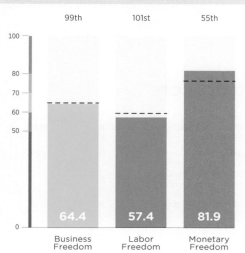

99th	101st	55th

Business Freedom	Labor Freedom	Monetary Freedom
64.4	57.4	81.9

Bureaucratic procedures are complex and non-transparent. Obtaining necessary business licenses is time-consuming and costly. The absence of a well-functioning labor market has led to chronically high unemployment and severe underemployment. In view of fiscally unsustainable subsidies, the IMF is pressuring the government to raise fuel prices and electricity tariffs and adopt automatic price mechanisms to depoliticize the price-setting process.

OPEN MARKETS

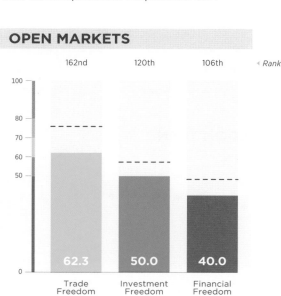

162nd	120th	106th	◄ Rank

Trade Freedom	Investment Freedom	Financial Freedom
62.3	50.0	40.0

Trade is extremely important to Mauritania's economy; the value of exports and imports taken together equals 104 percent of GDP. The average applied tariff rate is 11.4 percent. There are few formal barriers to foreign investment, but state-owned enterprises distort the economy. Limited access to credit and the high costs of financing continue to impede entrepreneurial activity. Progress in modernizing the financial sector has been sluggish.

MAURITANIA

MAURITIUS

An efficient and transparent regulatory environment supports relatively broad-based economic development in Mauritius, and competitive tax rates and a fairly flexible labor code facilitate private-sector growth. The open trade and investment regime is underpinned by relatively well-protected property rights and a nondiscriminatory legal system.

Privatization of state-owned monopolies has slowed, but the state does not play an overwhelming role in the economy, minimizing the drag on dynamic business activity. Corruption is relatively rare. Public financial management is generally sound, and a law requires that government debt must be reduced to below 50 percent of GDP by 2018.

ECONOMIC FREEDOM SCORE

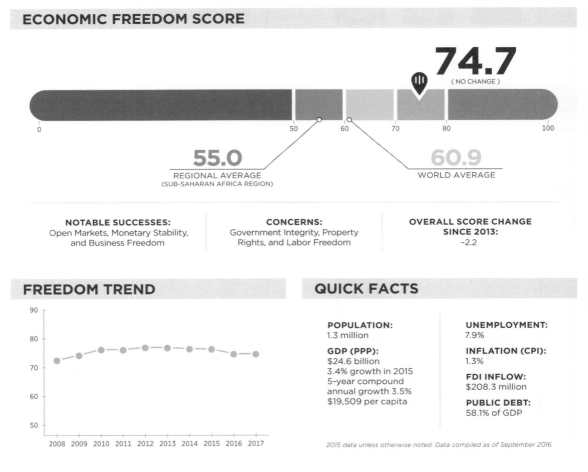

74.7
(NO CHANGE)

0   50   60   70   80   100

55.0
REGIONAL AVERAGE
(SUB-SAHARAN AFRICA REGION)

60.9
WORLD AVERAGE

NOTABLE SUCCESSES:	CONCERNS:	OVERALL SCORE CHANGE SINCE 2013:
Open Markets, Monetary Stability, and Business Freedom	Government Integrity, Property Rights, and Labor Freedom	−2.2

FREEDOM TREND

QUICK FACTS

POPULATION:
1.3 million

GDP (PPP):
$24.6 billion
3.4% growth in 2015
5-year compound
annual growth 3.5%
$19,509 per capita

UNEMPLOYMENT:
7.9%

INFLATION (CPI):
1.3%

FDI INFLOW:
$208.3 million

PUBLIC DEBT:
58.1% of GDP

2015 data unless otherwise noted. Data compiled as of September 2016

BACKGROUND: Independent since 1968, Mauritius is the only African country to be ranked a "full democracy" by the Economist Intelligence Unit. Sir Anerood Jugnauth became prime minister for the third time in December 2014, and Ameenah Gurib-Fakim was elected to the presidency in June 2015, the first woman to hold the largely ceremonial role. The government is trying to modernize the sugar and textile industries while promoting diversification into such areas as information technology and financial and business services. Services and tourism remain the main economic drivers. Maritime security is a priority, and the government signed a deal with Britain's Royal Navy in 2012 to transfer suspected pirates to Mauritius for prosecution.

12 ECONOMIC FREEDOMS | MAURITIUS

RULE OF LAW

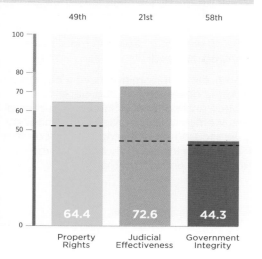

	49th	21st	58th
	64.4	72.6	44.3
	Property Rights	Judicial Effectiveness	Government Integrity

Property rights are respected, but enforcement of intellectual property laws is relatively weak. The judiciary continues to be independent, and the legal system is generally nondiscriminatory and transparent. In 2016, the World Economic Forum's *Global Competitiveness Index* reported a slight improvement in the country's institutions, which are among the strongest in Africa. The government prosecutes corruption, albeit inconsistently.

GOVERNMENT SIZE

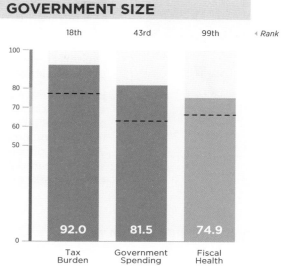

	18th	43rd	99th	‹ Rank
	92.0	81.5	74.9	
	Tax Burden	Government Spending	Fiscal Health	

The personal income and corporate tax rates are a flat 15 percent. Other taxes include a value-added tax. The overall tax burden equals 18.6 percent of total domestic income. Government spending has amounted to 24.9 percent of total output (GDP) over the past three years, and budget deficits have averaged 3.4 percent of GDP. Public debt is equivalent to 58.1 percent of GDP.

REGULATORY EFFICIENCY

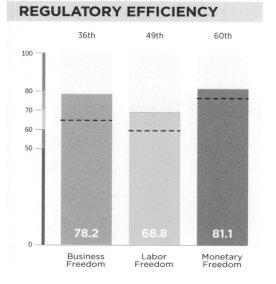

	36th	49th	60th
	78.2	68.8	81.1
	Business Freedom	Labor Freedom	Monetary Freedom

The overall regulatory framework has undergone a series of reforms aimed at facilitating entrepreneurial activity in recent years. Labor regulations are relatively flexible. The Economist Intelligence Unit reports that transfers to state-owned enterprises and poorly targeted welfare benefits will continue to consume considerable fiscal resources and that implementation of state-owned enterprise reforms will be slow.

OPEN MARKETS

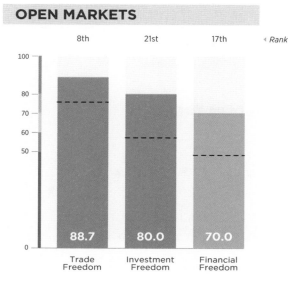

	8th	21st	17th	‹ Rank
	88.7	80.0	70.0	
	Trade Freedom	Investment Freedom	Financial Freedom	

Trade is extremely important to the economy of Mauritius; the value of exports and imports taken together equals 109 percent of GDP. The average applied tariff rate is 0.6 percent, and there are few nontariff barriers to trade. Foreign investment in some sectors is restricted. The financial sector remains competitive, and its contribution to GDP has risen steadily. Private banks dominate the sector and allocate credit on market terms.

MAURITIUS

MOZAMBIQUE

Mozambique has undertaken reforms to encourage economic development, although progress has been very gradual. Private-sector involvement in the economy is substantial, but privatization of state-owned enterprises has slowed. Foreign capital is treated the same as domestic capital in most cases, and trade liberalization has progressed.

Lingering institutional and fiscal shortcomings have a negative effect on long-term economic development. Judicial enforcement is subject to corruption and political influence. The regulatory environment remains inefficient and burdensome. In recent years, the government has focused on restoring macroeconomic stability, particularly in view of an increasingly burdensome external debt and liquidity risks confronting the country.

ECONOMIC FREEDOM SCORE

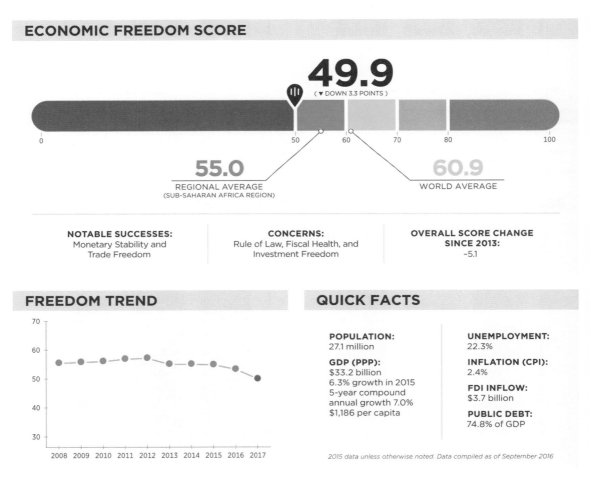

49.9
(▼ DOWN 3.3 POINTS)

0   50   60   70   80   100

55.0
REGIONAL AVERAGE
(SUB-SAHARAN AFRICA REGION)

60.9
WORLD AVERAGE

NOTABLE SUCCESSES:
Monetary Stability and
Trade Freedom

CONCERNS:
Rule of Law, Fiscal Health, and
Investment Freedom

**OVERALL SCORE CHANGE
SINCE 2013:**
–5.1

FREEDOM TREND

70

60

50

40

30

2008 2009 2010 2011 2012 2013 2014 2015 2016 2017

QUICK FACTS

POPULATION:
27.1 million

GDP (PPP):
$33.2 billion
6.3% growth in 2015
5-year compound
annual growth 7.0%
$1,186 per capita

UNEMPLOYMENT:
22.3%

INFLATION (CPI):
2.4%

FDI INFLOW:
$3.7 billion

PUBLIC DEBT:
74.8% of GDP

2015 data unless otherwise noted. Data compiled as of September 2016

BACKGROUND: The Mozambique Liberation Front (FRELIMO) party, headed since 2015 by President Filipe Nyusi, has been in power since independence from Portugal in 1975. Following independence, there was a 16-year civil war between FRELIMO and the rebel Mozambican National Resistance (RENAMO) movement that ended with the Rome Peace Accords in 1992. In October 2013, after several armed clashes with FRE-LIMO troops, RENAMO announced that it was pulling out of the peace accord. Despite a new peace deal in September 2014, violence has continued, and thousands have fled to Malawi. Previously undisclosed debts of about $1.4 billion amassed by the former government came to light in 2016, prompting donors to suspend budgetary support.

12 ECONOMIC FREEDOMS | MOZAMBIQUE

RULE OF LAW

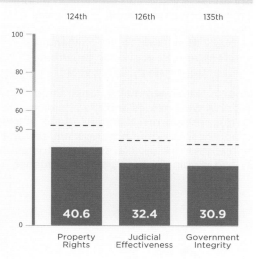

	124th	126th	135th
	Property Rights	Judicial Effectiveness	Government Integrity
	40.6	32.4	30.9

Although property rights are recognized by the government, they are not strongly respected, and enforcement of property law is inefficient and uneven. The judiciary is understaffed, inadequately trained, and subject to political influence. Corruption and extortion by police are widespread, and impunity remains a serious problem. Senior government officials often have conflicts of interest between their public roles and their private business interests.

GOVERNMENT SIZE

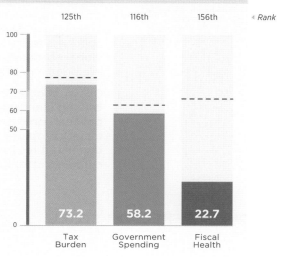

	125th	116th	156th	◄ Rank
	Tax Burden	Government Spending	Fiscal Health	
	73.2	58.2	22.7	

The top individual income and corporate tax rates are 32 percent. Other taxes include a value-added tax and an inheritance tax. The overall tax burden equals 25.1 percent of total domestic income. Government spending has amounted to 37.3 percent of total output (GDP) over the past three years, and budget deficits have averaged 6.4 percent of GDP. Public debt is equivalent to 74.8 percent of GDP.

REGULATORY EFFICIENCY

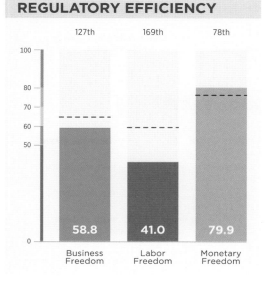

	127th	169th	78th
	Business Freedom	Labor Freedom	Monetary Freedom
	58.8	41.0	79.9

Despite some improvement, the overall business environment continues to restrain economic growth. A recently passed labor law was intended to make the labor market more flexible, but it also increased overtime restrictions. Although the government has divested ownership of small businesses, it maintains interests in large enterprises such as an aluminum smelter and the country's largest bank and has expanded the state-owned energy company.

OPEN MARKETS

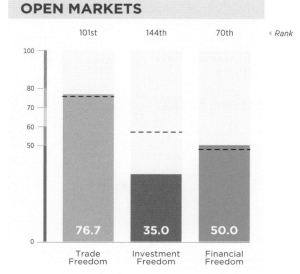

	101st	144th	70th	◄ Rank
	Trade Freedom	Investment Freedom	Financial Freedom	
	76.7	35.0	50.0	

Trade is important to Mozambique's economy; the value of exports and imports taken together equals 92 percent of GDP. The average applied tariff rate is 4.2 percent. All land is owned by the government, and state-owned enterprises distort the economy. Dominated by banking, the financial sector continues to evolve. The state retains shares in the banking sector, and a government-owned investment bank funnels funding to state projects.

MOZAMBIQUE

WORLD RANK: **78** | REGIONAL RANK: **5**

ECONOMIC FREEDOM STATUS:
MODERATELY FREE

NAMIBIA

Namibia's economy has benefited from a relatively high degree of regulatory efficiency and engagement in global commerce. The overall regulatory environment is fairly well organized and straightforward. With simplified and low tariffs, openness to trade is relatively high. Despite the challenging global economic environment, annual economic growth has averaged more than 5 percent over the past five years.

Overall economic freedom in Namibia remains constrained by long-standing institutional weaknesses and the absence of political commitment to deeper reforms. Namibia is weak in protecting property rights, and despite some progress, anticorruption measures lack effectiveness. The judicial system enforces contracts inconsistently and is vulnerable to political influence.

ECONOMIC FREEDOM SCORE

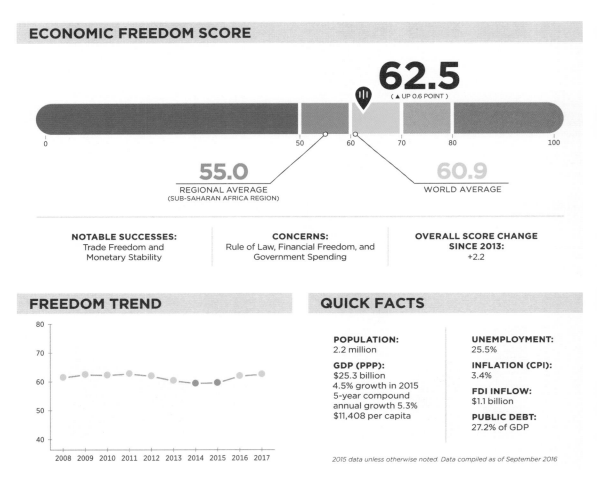

62.5
(▲ UP 0.6 POINT)

0   50   60   70   80   100

55.0
REGIONAL AVERAGE
(SUB-SAHARAN AFRICA REGION)

60.9
WORLD AVERAGE

NOTABLE SUCCESSES:
Trade Freedom and
Monetary Stability

CONCERNS:
Rule of Law, Financial Freedom, and
Government Spending

**OVERALL SCORE CHANGE
SINCE 2013:**
+2.2

FREEDOM TREND

80

70

60

50

40

2008 2009 2010 2011 2012 2013 2014 2015 2016 2017

QUICK FACTS

POPULATION:
2.2 million

GDP (PPP):
$25.3 billion
4.5% growth in 2015
5-year compound
annual growth 5.3%
$11,408 per capita

UNEMPLOYMENT:
25.5%

INFLATION (CPI):
3.4%

FDI INFLOW:
$1.1 billion

PUBLIC DEBT:
27.2% of GDP

2015 data unless otherwise noted. Data compiled as of September 2016

BACKGROUND: Namibia has been politically stable since independence from South Africa in 1990. President Hage Geingob won a five-year term in 2014. The ruling South West Africa People's Organization (SWAPO) has won every parliamentary election by large majorities since 1990. The mining sector brings in more than 50 percent of foreign exchange earnings, and the country is projected to become the world's second-largest uranium producer after a Chinese-owned mine is fully on line. Namibia has one of the highest credit ratings in Africa. Its economy is closely linked to South Africa's economy, and its dollar has been pegged to the South African rand since 1993.

12 ECONOMIC FREEDOMS | NAMIBIA

RULE OF LAW

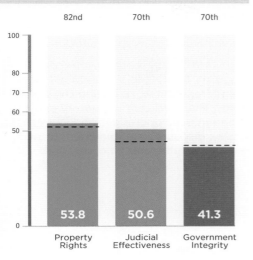

82nd   70th   70th

- Property Rights: **53.8**
- Judicial Effectiveness: **50.6**
- Government Integrity: **41.3**

Property rights are constitutionally guaranteed, but the parliament can legally expropriate property and regulate the property rights of foreign nationals. The rule of law remains weak, and the judicial system suffers from a lack of resources and chronic delays. The president's strong anticorruption drive, backed by exemplary action, has helped the fight against graft, but significant weaknesses in transparency and government accountability persist.

GOVERNMENT SIZE

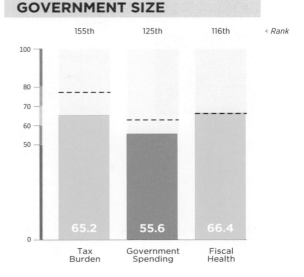

155th   125th   116th   ◂ Rank

- Tax Burden: **65.2**
- Government Spending: **55.6**
- Fiscal Health: **66.4**

The top individual income tax rate is 37 percent, and the top corporate tax rate is 34 percent. Other taxes include a value-added tax. The overall tax burden equals 30.9 percent of total domestic income. Government spending has amounted to 38.5 percent of total output (GDP) over the past three years, and budget deficits have averaged 4.5 percent of GDP. Public debt is equivalent to 27.2 percent of GDP.

REGULATORY EFFICIENCY

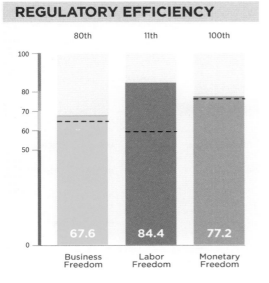

80th   11th   100th

- Business Freedom: **67.6**
- Labor Freedom: **84.4**
- Monetary Freedom: **77.2**

The overall regulatory framework has become more efficient and streamlined, but the pace of reform has slowed. Enforcement of commercial regulations is fairly effective and consistent. Labor regulations are relatively flexible, but the labor market lacks dynamism. Subsidies and transfers intended for educational assistance, medical care for public servants, and roads and infrastructure are expected to increase by nearly 1 percent of GDP.

OPEN MARKETS

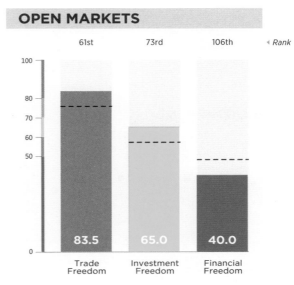

61st   73rd   106th   ◂ Rank

- Trade Freedom: **83.5**
- Investment Freedom: **65.0**
- Financial Freedom: **40.0**

Trade is extremely important to Namibia's economy; the value of exports and imports taken together equals 100 percent of GDP. The average applied tariff rate is 0.8 percent. Foreign investment is screened by the government, and state-owned enterprises distort the economy. Financial intermediation remains uneven across the country, and scarce access to credit and banking services discourages more robust entrepreneurial activity.

NIGER

Niger has recorded annual economic expansion of around 6 percent, driven mainly by minerals exports, over the past five years. Sustaining growth over the longer term will be difficult, however, because of a lack of economic dynamism. The economy remains highly vulnerable to external shocks.

Niger's overall progress toward greater economic freedom has been uneven and sluggish. The financial system remains underdeveloped, weak, and fragmented, reflecting the small size of the formal economy. The inefficient regulatory and legal environment constrains commercial operations and investment. Outmoded labor regulations discourage employment growth, and the judicial system remains vulnerable to corruption.

ECONOMIC FREEDOM SCORE

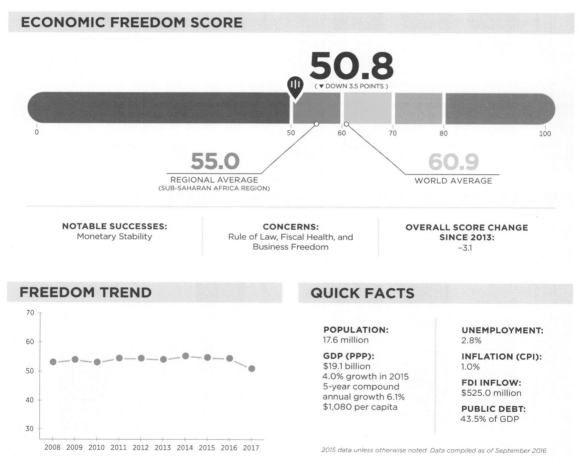

50.8
(▼ DOWN 3.5 POINTS)

0   50   60   70   80   100

55.0
REGIONAL AVERAGE
(SUB-SAHARAN AFRICA REGION)

60.9
WORLD AVERAGE

NOTABLE SUCCESSES:
Monetary Stability

CONCERNS:
Rule of Law, Fiscal Health, and Business Freedom

OVERALL SCORE CHANGE SINCE 2013:
−3.1

FREEDOM TREND

QUICK FACTS

POPULATION:
17.6 million

GDP (PPP):
$19.1 billion
4.0% growth in 2015
5-year compound
annual growth 6.1%
$1,080 per capita

UNEMPLOYMENT:
2.8%

INFLATION (CPI):
1.0%

FDI INFLOW:
$525.0 million

PUBLIC DEBT:
43.5% of GDP

2015 data unless otherwise noted. Data compiled as of September 2016

BACKGROUND: The military overthrew President Mamadou Tandja in a February 2010 coup after Tandja tried to extend his rule beyond the constitutionally mandated two terms. Mahamadou Issoufou of the opposition Nigerien Party for Democracy and Socialism won subsequent elections in 2011 and was reelected in a controversial March 2016 runoff vote after his chief rival, Hama Amadou, was imprisoned before the election on charges of child trafficking. In 2015, Niger joined a multinational coalition fighting the Nigerian terrorist group Boko Haram, and thousands of Nigeriens have been displaced by Boko Haram violence. Niger also faces a restive Tuareg population in the North and spillover violence from conflicts in Libya and Mali.

12 ECONOMIC FREEDOMS | NIGER

RULE OF LAW

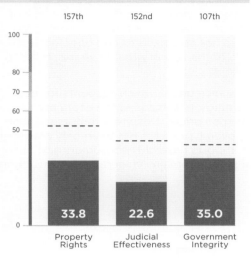

157th   152nd   107th

Property Rights	Judicial Effectiveness	Government Integrity
33.8	22.6	35.0

Interests in property are enforced when the land-holder is known, but property disputes are common, especially in rural areas subject to customary land titles. The rule of law remains hampered by an ineffective judicial framework and a weak court system that is vulnerable to political pressure. High rates of illiteracy among Nigeriens, many of whom are semi-nomadic, have contributed to a political culture that is overly tolerant of corruption.

GOVERNMENT SIZE

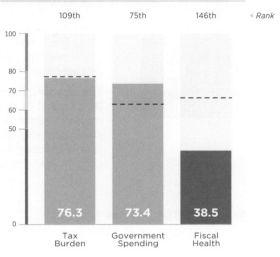

109th   75th   146th   ◂ Rank

Tax Burden	Government Spending	Fiscal Health
76.3	73.4	38.5

The top personal income tax rate is 35 percent, and the top corporate tax rate is 30 percent. Other taxes include a tax on interest and a capital gains tax. The overall tax burden equals 15.5 percent of total domestic income. Government spending has amounted to 29.8 percent of total output (GDP) over the past three years, and budget deficits have averaged 6.0 percent of GDP. Public debt is equivalent to 43.5 percent of GDP.

REGULATORY EFFICIENCY

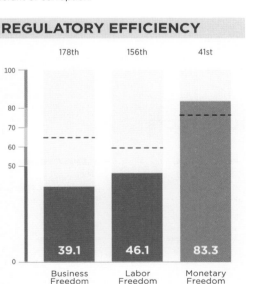

178th   156th   41st

Business Freedom	Labor Freedom	Monetary Freedom
39.1	46.1	83.3

Much-needed private-sector development has been hampered by the inadequate regulatory framework. Outmoded and inconsistent regulations impose substantial costs on business operations. The labor market is poorly developed, and much of the labor force works in the informal sector. Government-provided food subsidies cost an estimated 3.7 percent of GDP. The government also subsidizes natural gas in an effort to slow deforestation.

OPEN MARKETS

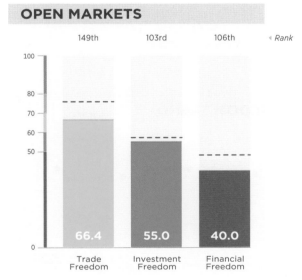

149th   103rd   106th   ◂ Rank

Trade Freedom	Investment Freedom	Financial Freedom
66.4	55.0	40.0

Trade is important to Niger's economy; the value of exports and imports taken together equals 57 percent of GDP. The average applied tariff rate is 9.3 percent. Investment in some sectors of the economy may be screened or capped, and state-owned enterprises distort the economy. Despite some progress, financing options for starting private businesses are limited. Overall bank credit to the private sector remains low.

NIGER

NIGERIA

WORLD RANK: **115**   REGIONAL RANK: **16**

ECONOMIC FREEDOM STATUS:
MOSTLY UNFREE

Nigeria, Africa's most populous nation, has sought to improve its macroeconomic stability and develop its poor infrastructure, but severe economic policy distortions and a lack of transparency in the economic system continue to impair progress. The government also has struggled to end ongoing security threats in some parts of the country that have exacerbated poverty and unemployment.

The government's overreliance on oil, which accounts for over 90 percent of export earnings, has exposed the economy to major risks amid declining oil prices. Despite attempts to diversify Nigeria's industries, overall progress has been only marginal. State-imposed bans on imports have hurt consumers and businesses, and the judicial system remains vulnerable to corruption.

ECONOMIC FREEDOM SCORE

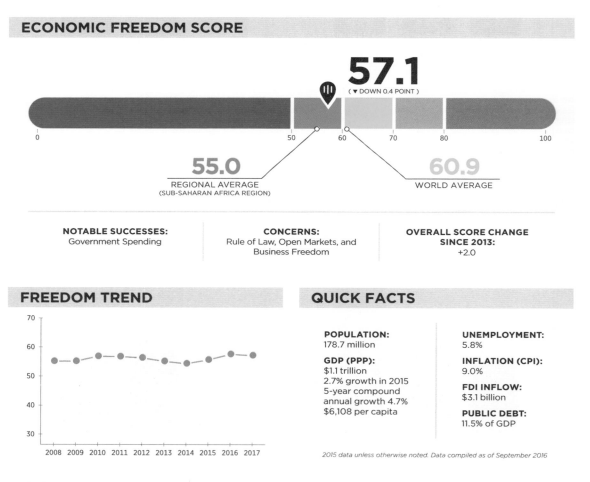

57.1
(▼ DOWN 0.4 POINT)

0   50   60   70   80   100

55.0
REGIONAL AVERAGE
(SUB-SAHARAN AFRICA REGION)

60.9
WORLD AVERAGE

NOTABLE SUCCESSES:
Government Spending

CONCERNS:
Rule of Law, Open Markets, and Business Freedom

OVERALL SCORE CHANGE SINCE 2013:
+2.0

FREEDOM TREND

70
60
50
40
30

2008 2009 2010 2011 2012 2013 2014 2015 2016 2017

QUICK FACTS

POPULATION:
178.7 million

GDP (PPP):
$1.1 trillion
2.7% growth in 2015
5-year compound
annual growth 4.7%
$6,108 per capita

UNEMPLOYMENT:
5.8%

INFLATION (CPI):
9.0%

FDI INFLOW:
$3.1 billion

PUBLIC DEBT:
11.5% of GDP

2015 data unless otherwise noted. Data compiled as of September 2016

BACKGROUND: In May 2015, in Nigeria's first peaceful transfer of power among parties since independence, former military ruler Muhammadu Buhari defeated incumbent President Goodluck Jonathan. Critical challenges include an Islamist insurgency and budgetary shortfalls caused by plunging oil prices. Before the May election, Nigeria, Chad, Niger, and Cameroon pushed the terrorist group Boko Haram out of its major strongholds. However, Boko Haram attacks have continued, primarily in northeast Nigeria, and militants in the oil-rich Niger Delta region have revived a campaign of attacks against the oil sector. In 2014, Nigeria surpassed South Africa as Africa's largest economy.

12 ECONOMIC FREEDOMS | NIGERIA

RULE OF LAW

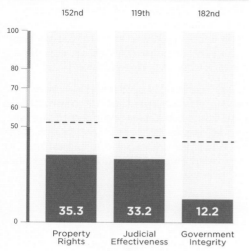

152nd   119th   182nd

Property Rights **35.3**, Judicial Effectiveness **33.2**, Government Integrity **12.2**

Protection of property rights is weak, although the World Bank's 2016 *Doing Business* survey reported that fees for property transfers had been reduced. The judiciary has some independence but is hobbled by political interference, corruption, and a lack of funding. Corruption is rarely investigated or prosecuted, and impunity remains widespread at all levels of government. Protectionism driven by currency devaluation has led to increased smuggling.

GOVERNMENT SIZE

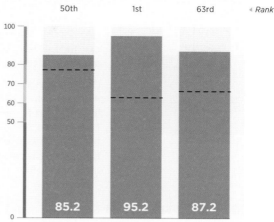

50th   1st   63rd ◂ Rank

Tax Burden **85.2**, Government Spending **95.2**, Fiscal Health **87.2**

The top individual income tax rate is 24 percent, and the top corporate tax rate is 30 percent. Other taxes include a value-added tax and a capital gains tax. The overall tax burden equals 2.8 percent of total domestic income. Government spending has amounted to 12.6 percent of total output (GDP) over the past three years, and budget deficits have averaged 2.8 percent of GDP. Public debt is equivalent to 11.5 percent of GDP.

REGULATORY EFFICIENCY

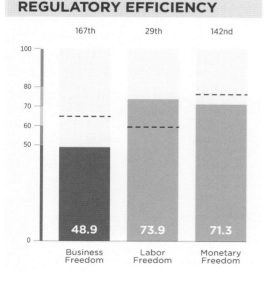

167th   29th   142nd

Business Freedom **48.9**, Labor Freedom **73.9**, Monetary Freedom **71.3**

Despite recent reforms, the structural changes that are needed to develop a more vibrant private sector have not emerged, and the oil sector still dominates overall economic activity. In the absence of dynamic nonenergy growth, a more vibrant labor market has not emerged. To tackle chronic shortages, the government cut gasoline subsidies in May 2016 by 67 percent. Nigeria regulates prices on electricity.

OPEN MARKETS

161st   135th   106th ◂ Rank

Trade Freedom **62.3**, Investment Freedom **40.0**, Financial Freedom **40.0**

Trade is moderately important to Nigeria's economy; the value of exports and imports taken together equals 31 percent of GDP. The average applied tariff rate is 11.3 percent. In general, foreign and domestic investors are treated equally, but the judicial and regulatory systems impede foreign investment. The banks are highly exposed to the energy sector, and nonperforming loans have been increasing rapidly.

NIGERIA

RWANDA

Rwanda's adoption of structural reforms has facilitated the emergence of entrepreneurial activity and transformed the once conflict-ridden country into a more open economy. Personal and corporate tax rates are moderate. With a sound regulatory framework that is conducive to private-sector development, Rwanda has achieved annual economic growth of approximately 7 percent over the past three years.

Overall economic freedom, however, is held back by lingering institutional weaknesses that are interrelated. Although foreign investment is welcome, political instability is a major deterrent. There have been ongoing efforts to strengthen the financial sector, create infrastructure, and improve expenditure management, but tangible progress has been elusive. The judicial system lacks independence and transparency.

WORLD RANK: **51** REGIONAL RANK: **3**

ECONOMIC FREEDOM STATUS:
MODERATELY FREE

ECONOMIC FREEDOM SCORE

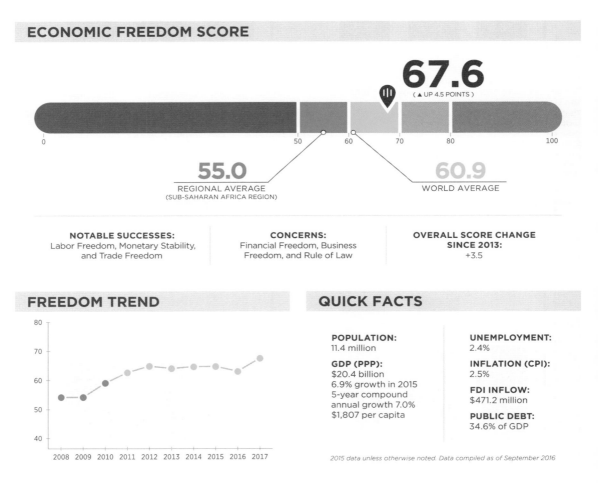

67.6
(▲ UP 4.5 POINTS)

| 0 | 50 | 60 | 70 | 80 | 100 |

55.0
REGIONAL AVERAGE
(SUB-SAHARAN AFRICA REGION)

60.9
WORLD AVERAGE

NOTABLE SUCCESSES:
Labor Freedom, Monetary Stability, and Trade Freedom

CONCERNS:
Financial Freedom, Business Freedom, and Rule of Law

OVERALL SCORE CHANGE SINCE 2013:
+3.5

FREEDOM TREND

| | 2008 | 2009 | 2010 | 2011 | 2012 | 2013 | 2014 | 2015 | 2016 | 2017 |

QUICK FACTS

POPULATION:
11.4 million

GDP (PPP):
$20.4 billion
6.9% growth in 2015
5-year compound
annual growth 7.0%
$1,807 per capita

UNEMPLOYMENT:
2.4%

INFLATION (CPI):
2.5%

FDI INFLOW:
$471.2 million

PUBLIC DEBT:
34.6% of GDP

2015 data unless otherwise noted. Data compiled as of September 2016

BACKGROUND: Paul Kagame's Tutsi-led Rwandan Patriotic Front (RPF) seized power in July 1994 in the wake of the state-sponsored genocide that killed an estimated 800,000 people, mostly Tutsis. Kagame has been president since 2000. He was reelected in August 2010 amid allegations of fraud, intimidation, and violence, and his RPF won a resounding victory in the September 2013 parliamentary elections. In 2015, in a move that drew criticism from countries concerned about Kagame's increasingly authoritarian rule, Rwandans voted overwhelmingly to amend the constitution to allow Kagame in theory to govern until 2034. Although it still remains widespread, poverty has been declining rapidly.

12 ECONOMIC FREEDOMS | RWANDA

RULE OF LAW

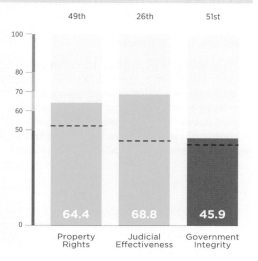

49th   26th   51st

- Property Rights: **64.4**
- Judicial Effectiveness: **68.8**
- Government Integrity: **45.9**

The law protects and facilitates the acquisition and disposition of private rights in property. There have been some recent improvements in the judicial system, including improved training and revisions of the legal code, but the judiciary has yet to secure full independence from the executive. Rwanda is among the least corrupt countries in Africa and is ranked 44th in the world in Transparency International's 2015 *Corruption Perceptions Index.*

GOVERNMENT SIZE

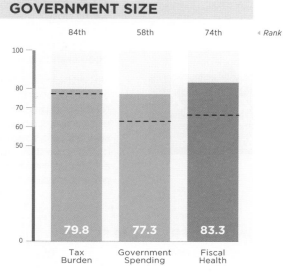

84th   58th   74th   ◂ *Rank*

- Tax Burden: **79.8**
- Government Spending: **77.3**
- Fiscal Health: **83.3**

The top personal income and corporate tax rates are 30 percent. Other taxes include a value-added tax and a property transfer tax. The overall tax burden equals 14.9 percent of total domestic income. Government spending has amounted to 27.5 percent of total output (GDP) over the past three years, and budget deficits have averaged 3.0 percent of GDP. Public debt is equivalent to 34.6 percent of GDP.

REGULATORY EFFICIENCY

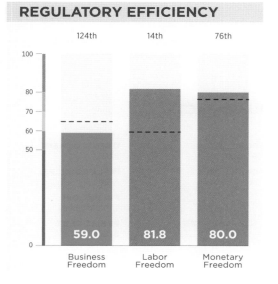

124th   14th   76th

- Business Freedom: **59.0**
- Labor Freedom: **81.8**
- Monetary Freedom: **80.0**

Regulatory reform measures have contributed to a more favorable business environment, although the pace of reform has slowed in recent years. Labor regulations are relatively flexible, but a more vibrant formal labor market has yet to develop. The government subsidizes agriculture, maintains price controls, and subsidizes power for the 20 percent of the population that has access to electricity.

OPEN MARKETS

130th   89th   106th   ◂ *Rank*

- Trade Freedom: **70.3**
- Investment Freedom: **60.0**
- Financial Freedom: **40.0**

Trade is moderately important to Rwanda's economy; the value of exports and imports taken together equals 45 percent of GDP. The average applied tariff rate is 7.4 percent. Foreign investors may lease but not own land. Many state-owned enterprises have been privatized. The financial sector continues to evolve, but the high costs of financing and limited access to credit still pose serious challenges for potential entrepreneurs.

RWANDA

SÃO TOMÉ AND PRÍNCIPE

São Tomé and Príncipe has undertaken structural reforms to boost government efficiency and enhance the business environment. A streamlined business formation process has enhanced regulatory efficiency, and the corporate tax rate has been significantly reduced to a flat 25 percent.

Nevertheless, institutional weaknesses continue to constrain overall economic freedom. The judicial system lacks the capacity to defend property rights effectively. Widespread corruption undermines prospects for long-term economic development. High public spending perpetuates fiscal burdens. A lack of commitment to open-market policies impedes growth in trade and investment and thwarts the emergence of a more dynamic private sector.

ECONOMIC FREEDOM SCORE

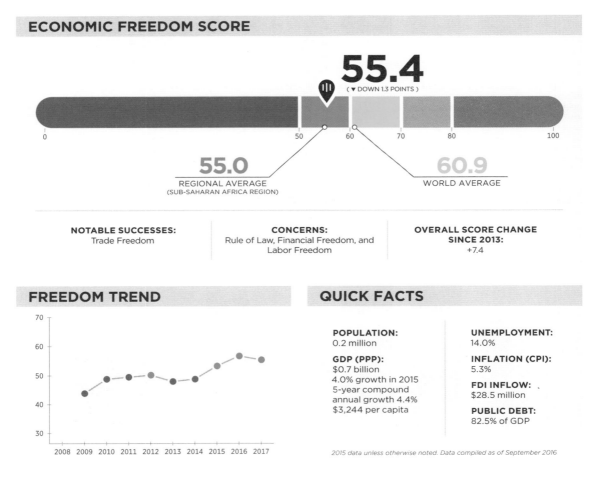

55.4
(▼ DOWN 1.3 POINTS)

0   50   60   70   80   100

55.0
REGIONAL AVERAGE
(SUB-SAHARAN AFRICA REGION)

60.9
WORLD AVERAGE

NOTABLE SUCCESSES:
Trade Freedom

CONCERNS:
Rule of Law, Financial Freedom, and Labor Freedom

OVERALL SCORE CHANGE SINCE 2013:
+7.4

FREEDOM TREND

70
60
50
40
30

2008 2009 2010 2011 2012 2013 2014 2015 2016 2017

QUICK FACTS

POPULATION:
0.2 million

GDP (PPP):
$0.7 billion
4.0% growth in 2015
5-year compound
annual growth 4.4%
$3,244 per capita

UNEMPLOYMENT:
14.0%

INFLATION (CPI):
5.3%

FDI INFLOW:
$28.5 million

PUBLIC DEBT:
82.5% of GDP

2015 data unless otherwise noted. Data compiled as of September 2016

BACKGROUND: Evaristo Carvalho won the presidency in a runoff election in August 2016 that was marred by accusations of irregularities and a boycott by incumbent President Manuel Pinto da Costa, who had served two separate terms following independence from Portugal in 1975. Previously, the supreme court had overturned results showing that Carvalho had won a narrow victory in the first round of voting. Patrice Trovoada, a Carvalho ally, is prime minister. Cocoa production, an economic mainstay, has declined in recent years, but there is tourism potential. São Tomé is dependent on foreign assistance. It is developing oil fields in the Gulf of Guinea jointly with Nigeria, but production will not begin for several years.

12 ECONOMIC FREEDOMS | SÃO TOMÉ AND PRÍNCIPE

RULE OF LAW

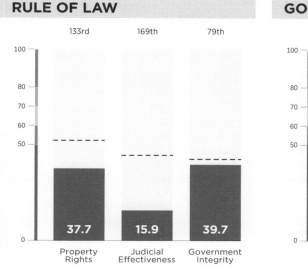

	133rd	169th	79th

Property Rights: 37.7
Judicial Effectiveness: 15.9
Government Integrity: 39.7

Property rights are not protected effectively. The judiciary is independent but weak and susceptible to political influence. Although there are criminal penalties for official corruption, the government reportedly does not enforce applicable laws effectively. The World Bank's 2015 Worldwide Governance Indicators confirmed that corruption is a problem. Many citizens view police as ineffective and corrupt.

GOVERNMENT SIZE

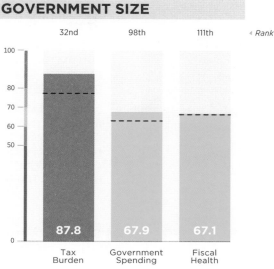

32nd	98th	111th	◄ Rank

Tax Burden: 87.8
Government Spending: 67.9
Fiscal Health: 67.1

The top personal income tax rate is 20 percent, and the corporate tax rate is a flat 25 percent. Other taxes include a sales tax and a dividend tax. The overall tax burden equals 14.1 percent of total domestic income. Government spending has amounted to 32.7 percent of total output (GDP) over the past three years, and budget deficits have averaged 3.5 percent of GDP. Public debt is equivalent to 82.5 percent of GDP.

REGULATORY EFFICIENCY

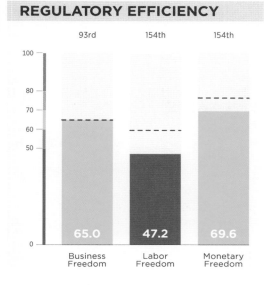

93rd	154th	154th

Business Freedom: 65.0
Labor Freedom: 47.2
Monetary Freedom: 69.6

Launching a business is time-consuming, and regulatory requirements increase the overall cost of entrepreneurial activity. Existing labor regulations are not enforced effectively. The government made an IMF commitment to introduce an automatic pricing mechanism for fuel beginning in June 2016 and to pursue power subsidy reform, but implementation has been hindered by powerful vested interests that profit from the status quo.

OPEN MARKETS

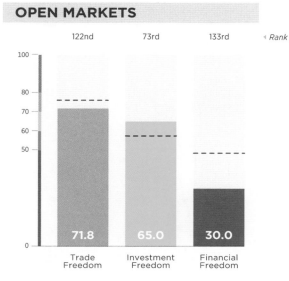

122nd	73rd	133rd	◄ Rank

Trade Freedom: 71.8
Investment Freedom: 65.0
Financial Freedom: 30.0

Trade is important to São Tomé and Príncipe's economy; the value of exports and imports taken together equals 55 percent of GDP. The average applied tariff rate is 9.1 percent. In general, foreign and domestic investors are treated equally under the law, and most sectors of the economy are open to foreign investment. Much of the population still lacks access to formal banking services, and financing for business expansion is very limited.

SÃO TOMÉ AND PRÍNCIPE

SENEGAL

Senegal has experienced uneven progress in economic freedom. The regulatory framework discourages dynamism and tends to curb development of the private sector. Despite some improvement in streamlining business formation, government bureaucracy and the lack of transparency create a poor entrepreneurial climate, and a lack of commitment to open markets hinders integration into the global marketplace.

Implementation of deeper institutional reforms to improve the foundations of economic freedom is critical to Senegal's prospects for long-term economic development and greater poverty reduction. Systemic weaknesses persist in the protection of property rights and the effective enforcement of anticorruption measures. The judiciary remains vulnerable to political influence.

ECONOMIC FREEDOM SCORE

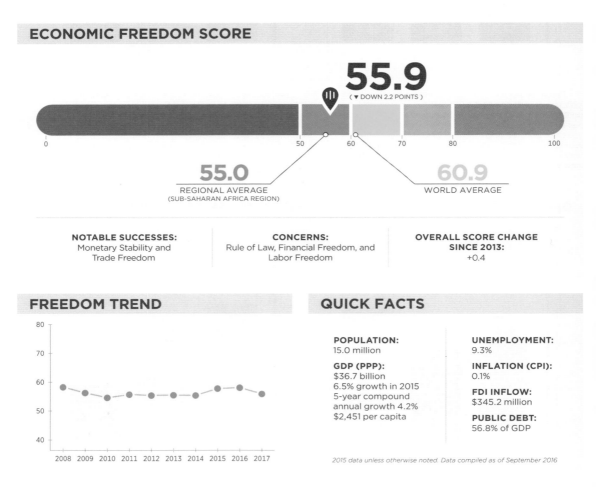

55.9
(▼ DOWN 2.2 POINTS)

| 0 | 50 | 60 | 70 | 80 | 100 |

55.0
REGIONAL AVERAGE
(SUB-SAHARAN AFRICA REGION)

60.9
WORLD AVERAGE

NOTABLE SUCCESSES:	CONCERNS:	OVERALL SCORE CHANGE
Monetary Stability and Trade Freedom	Rule of Law, Financial Freedom, and Labor Freedom	SINCE 2013: +0.4

FREEDOM TREND

| | 2008 | 2009 | 2010 | 2011 | 2012 | 2013 | 2014 | 2015 | 2016 | 2017 |

QUICK FACTS

POPULATION:
15.0 million

GDP (PPP):
$36.7 billion
6.5% growth in 2015
5-year compound
annual growth 4.2%
$2,451 per capita

UNEMPLOYMENT:
9.3%

INFLATION (CPI):
0.1%

FDI INFLOW:
$345.2 million

PUBLIC DEBT:
56.8% of GDP

2015 data unless otherwise noted. Data compiled as of September 2016

BACKGROUND: President Macky Sall of the Alliance for the Republic–Yakaar party won election in March 2012, defeating two-term incumbent Abdoulaye Wade, whose third-term bid sparked street protests. In March 2016, at Sall's urging, the country passed a constitutional referendum shortening presidential terms from seven to five years, prohibiting more than two terms, and reducing presidential power in favor of the National Assembly. In April 2014, after more than 30 years of conflict between the government and southern separatists, the leader of the rebel Movement of Democratic Forces of Casamance declared a unilateral cease-fire that remains in force. About 75 percent of the workforce is engaged in agriculture or fishing.

12 ECONOMIC FREEDOMS | SENEGAL

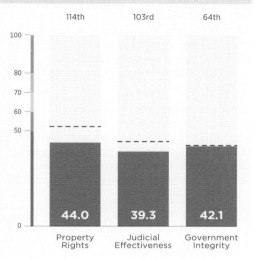

RULE OF LAW

114th	103rd	64th
Property Rights	Judicial Effectiveness	Government Integrity
44.0	**39.3**	**42.1**

Property titling procedures are uneven across the country. The judiciary is independent but inadequately resourced and subject to external influences. President Sall's reformist policy agenda includes restoring fiscal responsibility and pursuing former ministers accused of graft, but the public remains frustrated by perceived official corruption and by slow progress on efforts to address popular demand for political and social reform.

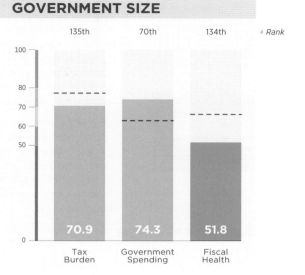

GOVERNMENT SIZE

135th	70th	134th	◂ Rank
Tax Burden	Government Spending	Fiscal Health	
70.9	**74.3**	**51.8**	

The top individual income tax rate is 40 percent, and the top corporate tax rate is 30 percent. Other taxes include a value-added tax and an insurance tax. The overall tax burden equals 20.2 percent of total domestic income. Government spending has amounted to 29.3 percent of total output (GDP) over the past three years, and budget deficits have averaged 5.1 percent of GDP. Public debt is equivalent to 56.8 percent of GDP.

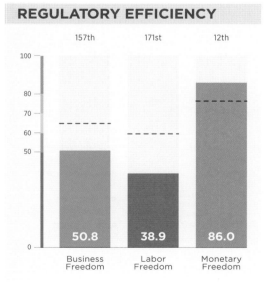

REGULATORY EFFICIENCY

157th	171st	12th
Business Freedom	Labor Freedom	Monetary Freedom
50.8	**38.9**	**86.0**

Although the process for establishing a business has become more streamlined, start-up costs remain substantial. The overall regulatory environment is vulnerable to arbitrary decision-making and corruption. A formal urban labor market has been slow to develop. The IMF has advised reductions in unproductive public spending and has appealed for progress in the implementation of energy reform, but the government continues to fund costly subsidies.

OPEN MARKETS

118th	89th	106th	◂ Rank
Trade Freedom	Investment Freedom	Financial Freedom	
73.1	**60.0**	**40.0**	

Trade is important to Senegal's economy; the value of exports and imports taken together equals 74 percent of GDP. Foreign investment may be screened. Most sectors of the economy are open to investment, but bureaucratic barriers may impede foreign investment. The underdeveloped financial system is dominated by banking, which is highly concentrated, and the government retains its shares in a number of banks.

SENEGAL

SEYCHELLES

Reforms of the Seychelles economy's evolving entrepreneurial framework have focused on improving overall regulatory efficiency. The government has previously implemented major tax reforms, cutting and simplifying personal and corporate taxes. Although privatization has been slow, efforts to enhance transparency and improve the governance of state-owned enterprises have continued. Additional regulatory reform will be critical to improving competitiveness.

Undermining the gains from an improved regulatory environment, however, is a lack of commitment to open-market policies that continues to hold back dynamic growth in trade and investment. Institutional weaknesses stemming from an inefficient legal framework and pervasive corruption severely hamper the emergence of a dynamic private sector beyond the tourism sector.

WORLD RANK: **85**
REGIONAL RANK: **7**

ECONOMIC FREEDOM STATUS:
MODERATELY FREE

ECONOMIC FREEDOM SCORE

61.8
(▼ DOWN 0.4 POINT)

0   50   60   70   80   100

55.0
REGIONAL AVERAGE
(SUB-SAHARAN AFRICA REGION)

60.9
WORLD AVERAGE

NOTABLE SUCCESSES:
Fiscal Policy, Trade Freedom, and Monetary Stability

CONCERNS:
Rule of Law, Financial Freedom, and Investment Freedom

OVERALL SCORE CHANGE SINCE 2013:
+6.9

FREEDOM TREND

QUICK FACTS

POPULATION:
0.1 million

GDP (PPP):
$2.4 billion
4.4% growth in 2015
5-year compound annual growth 4.9%
$26,277 per capita

UNEMPLOYMENT:
n/a

INFLATION (CPI):
4.0%

FDI INFLOW:
$194.5 million

PUBLIC DEBT:
68.1% of GDP

2015 data unless otherwise noted. Data compiled as of September 2016

BACKGROUND: The Seychelles People's Progressive Front, now known as the People's Party, has ruled the archipelago country of Seychelles since 1977 when France-Albert René seized power in a bloodless coup. In 2004, René ceded power to Vice President James Michel. Michel was elected to five-year terms in 2006, 2011, and 2015 after a runoff vote. In October 2016, President Michel resigned and transferred power to Vice President Danny Faure, who will serve the remaining four years of Michel's term. Seychelles enjoys a relatively stable economic environment with lucrative fishing and tourism industries. In July 2015, the World Bank classified Seychelles as a "high income" country.

12 ECONOMIC FREEDOMS | SEYCHELLES

RULE OF LAW

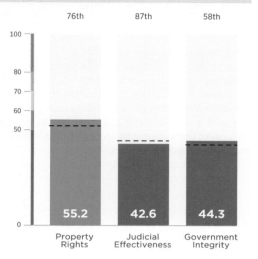

76th	87th	58th
55.2	**42.6**	**44.3**
Property Rights	Judicial Effectiveness	Government Integrity

The courts enforce interests in real property, including mortgages and liens. The World Bank's 2016 *Doing Business* survey ranked Seychelles 67th out of 189 countries in its Registering Property index. The judicial branch is independent, but well-connected individuals are perceived as receiving special treatment in the courts. A lack of transparency enables corruption in privatization and other government programs.

GOVERNMENT SIZE

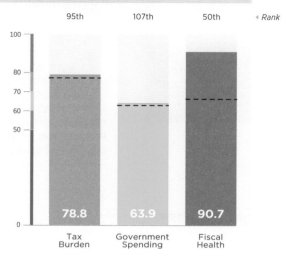

95th	107th	50th	◂ *Rank*
78.8	**63.9**	**90.7**	
Tax Burden	Government Spending	Fiscal Health	

The personal income tax rate is a flat 15 percent. The top corporate tax rate is 33 percent. Other taxes include an interest tax, a vehicle tax, and a value-added tax. The overall tax burden equals 28.4 percent of total domestic income. Government spending has amounted to 34.7 percent of total output (GDP) over the past three years, and budget surpluses have averaged 2.0 percent of GDP. Public debt is equivalent to 68.1 percent of GDP.

REGULATORY EFFICIENCY

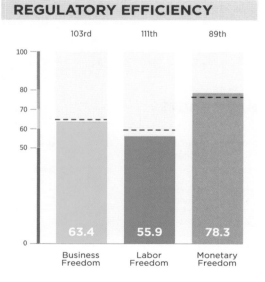

103rd	111th	89th
63.4	**55.9**	**78.3**
Business Freedom	Labor Freedom	Monetary Freedom

The regulatory framework still includes considerable bureaucratic and procedural hurdles for potential entrepreneurs. The formal labor market is not fully developed, and the inefficient public sector accounts for approximately 40 percent of total employment. The state-owned airline added new destinations in 2015 despite large operating losses, and Seychelles Public Transport Corporation recorded losses in 2015 despite a government subsidy.

OPEN MARKETS

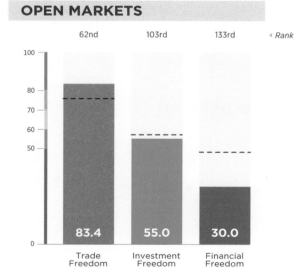

62nd	103rd	133rd	◂ *Rank*
83.4	**55.0**	**30.0**	
Trade Freedom	Investment Freedom	Financial Freedom	

Trade is extremely important to the Seychelles economy; the value of exports and imports taken together equals 181 percent of GDP. Seychelles joined the World Trade Organization in 2015. Foreign investment in some sectors of the economy is restricted. The banking sector consists of both state-owned and foreign financial institutions. Limited financing options for the private sector undermine business development.

SEYCHELLES

SIERRA LEONE

WORLD RANK: **145** | REGIONAL RANK: **32**

ECONOMIC FREEDOM STATUS:
MOSTLY UNFREE

In an effort to move away from dependence on diamond production, Sierra Leone has taken measures to improve its legal and physical infrastructure. It has also taken steps to improve tax administration and the management of public debt.

Significant structural weaknesses, however, continue to strain the fragile economy. Poverty reduction and economic growth are hampered by a restrictive regulatory environment, inadequate infrastructure, and weak enforcement of contracts. The financial system is still recovering from civil war and lacks the capacity to provide sufficient credit for vibrant business activity. Pervasive corruption and nearly nonexistent property rights are significant drags on private-sector dynamism.

ECONOMIC FREEDOM SCORE

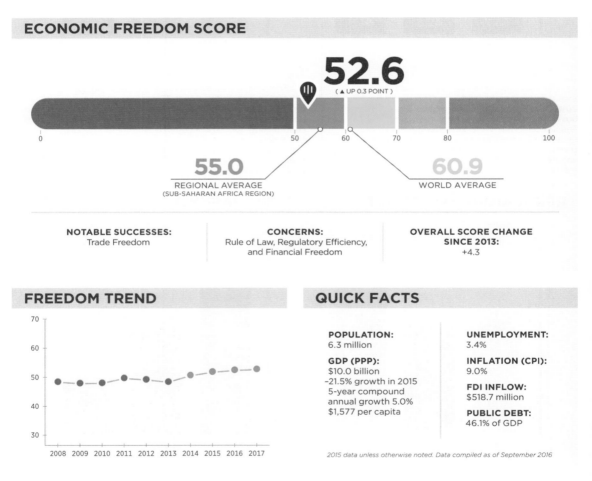

52.6
(▲ UP 0.3 POINT)

| 0 | 50 | 60 | 70 | 80 | 100 |

55.0
REGIONAL AVERAGE
(SUB-SAHARAN AFRICA REGION)

60.9
WORLD AVERAGE

NOTABLE SUCCESSES:
Trade Freedom

CONCERNS:
Rule of Law, Regulatory Efficiency, and Financial Freedom

OVERALL SCORE CHANGE SINCE 2013:
+4.3

FREEDOM TREND

QUICK FACTS

POPULATION:
6.3 million

GDP (PPP):
$10.0 billion
–21.5% growth in 2015
5-year compound
annual growth 5.0%
$1,577 per capita

UNEMPLOYMENT:
3.4%

INFLATION (CPI):
9.0%

FDI INFLOW:
$518.7 million

PUBLIC DEBT:
46.1% of GDP

2015 data unless otherwise noted. Data compiled as of September 2016

BACKGROUND: Opposition candidate Ernest Bai Koroma of the All People's Congress, elected president in 2007 in Sierra Leone's first peaceful transition of power since independence from Britain in 1961, was reelected in 2012. Despite some institutional progress since the end of a decade-long civil war in 2002, living standards remain very low, and basic infrastructure is lacking throughout the country. Because mining is the primary industry and mineral exports generate most foreign exchange, Sierra Leone is vulnerable to fluctuations in commodity prices. Gem-quality diamonds account for nearly half of exports and for high rates of economic growth. The 2014 Ebola epidemic in West Africa killed nearly 4,000 Sierra Leoneans.

12 ECONOMIC FREEDOMS | SIERRA LEONE

RULE OF LAW

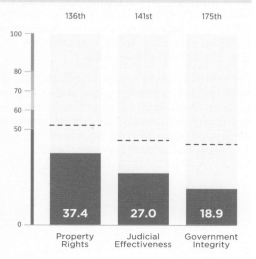

136th	141st	175th
Property Rights	Judicial Effectiveness	Government Integrity
37.4	27.0	18.9

There is no land titling system. The judiciary has demonstrated a degree of independence, but low salaries, lack of police professionalism, and inadequate resources still impede judicial effectiveness. Corruption remains endemic at every level of government: Even funds to fight Ebola have vanished. Perceptions of corruption, as reported in November 2015 by Transparency International's Global Corruption Barometer, are among the highest in Africa.

GOVERNMENT SIZE

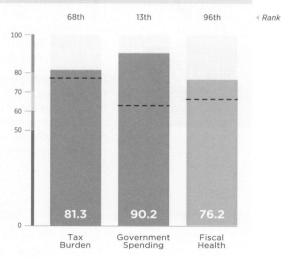

◄ Rank

68th	13th	96th
Tax Burden	Government Spending	Fiscal Health
81.3	90.2	76.2

The top individual income and corporate tax rates are 30 percent. Other taxes include a goods and services tax and an interest tax. The overall tax burden equals 8.3 percent of total domestic income. Government spending has amounted to 18.1 percent of total output (GDP) over the past three years, and budget deficits have averaged 3.5 percent of GDP. Public debt is equivalent to 46.1 percent of GDP.

REGULATORY EFFICIENCY

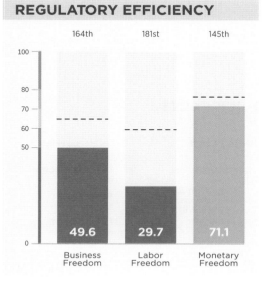

164th	181st	145th
Business Freedom	Labor Freedom	Monetary Freedom
49.6	29.7	71.1

Despite recent years' reform measures, the overall regulatory environment lacks efficiency and transparency. With much of the labor force employed in the informal sector, outmoded and inflexible labor regulations are rather futile in application. In 2015, the IMF advised the government to take advantage of lower oil prices and cut subsidies; in 2016, it reported that the authorities had failed to adhere to their commitments in this area.

OPEN MARKETS

◄ Rank

137th	89th	162nd
Trade Freedom	Investment Freedom	Financial Freedom
69.4	60.0	20.0

Trade is important to Sierra Leone's economy; the value of exports and imports taken together equals 59 percent of GDP. The average applied tariff rate is 10.3 percent. In general, foreign and domestic investors are treated equally under the law. State-owned enterprises distort the economy. The financial system was undermined by prolonged economic and political instability, and the recovery process has been sluggish.

SIERRA LEONE

SOMALIA

Violence and political unrest have prevented Somalia from developing a coherent and coordinated domestic marketplace. The central government controls only part of the country, and formal economic activity is largely relegated to urban areas like Mogadishu. The lack of accurate economic statistics precludes ranking Somalia in this edition of the *Index*.

Lack of central authority makes the rule of law inconsistent and fragmented, with different militias, authorities, and tribes applying varying legal frameworks. Traditional customs like Sharia law have become more entrenched. The level of corruption remains high, and the lack of transparency and formal bookkeeping means that government revenues are easily embezzled.

WORLD RANK: **N/A** REGIONAL RANK: **N/A**

ECONOMIC FREEDOM STATUS:
NOT GRADED

ECONOMIC FREEDOM SCORE

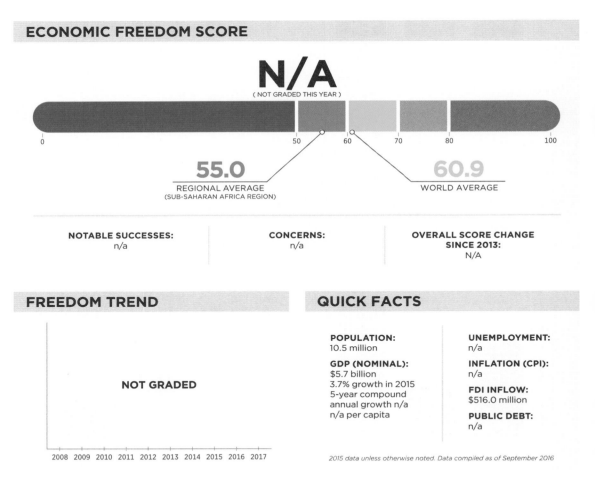

N/A
(NOT GRADED THIS YEAR)

0   50   60   70   80   100

55.0
REGIONAL AVERAGE
(SUB-SAHARAN AFRICA REGION)

60.9
WORLD AVERAGE

NOTABLE SUCCESSES:
n/a

CONCERNS:
n/a

OVERALL SCORE CHANGE SINCE 2013:
N/A

FREEDOM TREND

NOT GRADED

2008 2009 2010 2011 2012 2013 2014 2015 2016 2017

QUICK FACTS

POPULATION:
10.5 million

GDP (NOMINAL):
$5.7 billion
3.7% growth in 2015
5-year compound
annual growth n/a
n/a per capita

UNEMPLOYMENT:
n/a

INFLATION (CPI):
n/a

FDI INFLOW:
$516.0 million

PUBLIC DEBT:
n/a

2015 data unless otherwise noted. Data compiled as of September 2016

BACKGROUND: Since the collapse of longtime dictator Siad Barre's regime in 1991, various peacekeeping forces have protected a succession of weak and short-lived governments. The current AMISOM multinational force was inaugurated in 2007. A provisional constitution was passed in August 2012, and Hassan Sheikh Mohamud was elected president in September. The Islamist terrorist group al-Shabaab has been pushed from its most important strongholds, but it remains a potent threat. Somalia's GDP and living standards are among the lowest in the world, and the population depends on foreign aid and remittances. Economic growth is slowly expanding beyond Mogadishu. Livestock, agriculture, and fishing are economic mainstays.

12 ECONOMIC FREEDOMS | SOMALIA

RULE OF LAW

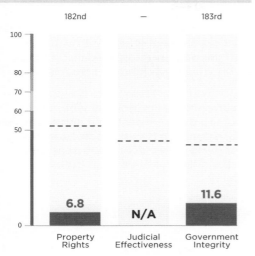

182nd — 183rd

- Property Rights: **6.8**
- Judicial Effectiveness: **N/A**
- Government Integrity: **11.6**

Disputes over real property are at the core of ongoing civil unrest, marked by many conflicts over land, land grabs by warlords, and huge displacements of local populations, especially in South Central Somalia. The civilian judicial system is largely nonfunctional across the country. Corruption is rampant. Somalia was tied with North Korea for last place among the 168 countries surveyed in Transparency International's 2015 *Corruption Perceptions Index.*

GOVERNMENT SIZE

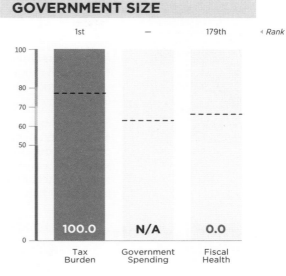

1st — 179th ◀ *Rank*

- Tax Burden: **100.0**
- Government Spending: **N/A**
- Fiscal Health: **0.0**

There is no effective national government that can provide basic services. Other than the collection of very limited duties and taxes, little formal fiscal policy is in place. A new income tax law has been submitted to parliament for approval, but the lack of productive economic activity severely constrains the government's ability to generate revenues.

REGULATORY EFFICIENCY

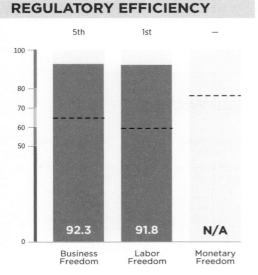

5th 1st —

- Business Freedom: **92.3**
- Labor Freedom: **91.8**
- Monetary Freedom: **N/A**

An outmoded regulatory environment and inadequate infrastructure deter the formation and operation of businesses. The labor market is dominated by informal hiring practices. Somalia has a nascent financial sector and no control over monetary policy, but its informal agricultural, construction, and telecommunications sectors have seen modest growth without subsidies.

OPEN MARKETS

— — — ◀ *Rank*

- Trade Freedom: **N/A**
- Investment Freedom: **N/A**
- Financial Freedom: **N/A**

Trade is important to Somalia's economy; the value of exports and imports taken together equals 76 percent of GDP. Much of the population remains outside of the formal trade and banking sectors, and private investment remains extremely limited. Somali diaspora remittances continue to be an important source of foreign exchange and economic support for the majority of Somalis.

SOMALIA

SOUTH AFRICA

WORLD RANK: **81** | REGIONAL RANK: **6**

ECONOMIC FREEDOM STATUS:
MODERATELY FREE

Performing far below its potential, South Africa's economy has been stifled by political instability and a weakening rule of law. The judicial system has become vulnerable to political interference, and numerous scandals and frequent political infighting have severely undermined government integrity. Private-sector growth remains constrained by structural and institutional impediments caused by growing government encroachment into the marketplace.

Persistent uncertainties surrounding key government policies are additional impediments to private investment and expansion of the production base. Undermining overall macroeconomic stability, a combination of rising public debt, inefficient state-owned enterprises, and spending pressures contributes to increasing fiscal vulnerability.

ECONOMIC FREEDOM SCORE

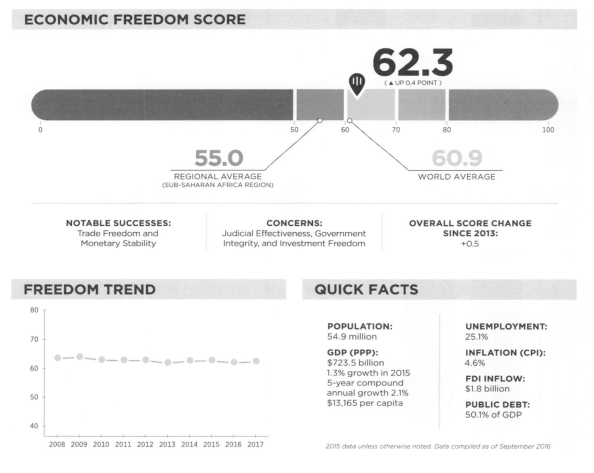

62.3
(▲ UP 0.4 POINT)

0   50   60   70   80   100

55.0
REGIONAL AVERAGE
(SUB-SAHARAN AFRICA REGION)

60.9
WORLD AVERAGE

NOTABLE SUCCESSES:
Trade Freedom and
Monetary Stability

CONCERNS:
Judicial Effectiveness, Government
Integrity, and Investment Freedom

**OVERALL SCORE CHANGE
SINCE 2013:**
+0.5

FREEDOM TREND

QUICK FACTS

POPULATION:
54.9 million

GDP (PPP):
$723.5 billion
1.3% growth in 2015
5-year compound
annual growth 2.1%
$13,165 per capita

UNEMPLOYMENT:
25.1%

INFLATION (CPI):
4.6%

FDI INFLOW:
$1.8 billion

PUBLIC DEBT:
50.1% of GDP

2015 data unless otherwise noted. Data compiled as of September 2016

BACKGROUND: Jacob Zuma of the African National Congress was elected president by the ANC-controlled National Assembly in 2009 and then reelected for another five years in May 2014. The ANC has dominated politics since the end of apartheid in 1994. South Africa is Africa's second-largest economy and one of the world's largest producers and exporters of gold and platinum. Yet many South Africans are poor, and the mining industry has been hurt by falling commodity prices and bitter labor strikes that have driven up production costs. Rates of formal-sector unemployment and crime are high, and the quality of public education is poor. Access to infrastructure and basic services is lacking.

12 ECONOMIC FREEDOMS | SOUTH AFRICA

RULE OF LAW

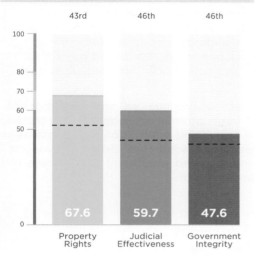

Property rights are relatively well protected, and contracts are generally secure. The World Economic Forum's 2015–2016 *Global Competitiveness Index* reports that South Africa benefits from strong institutions and a robust and independent legal framework. Corruption hampers the functioning of government, however, and enforcement of anticorruption statutes is inadequate. The process of tendering public contracts can be politically driven and opaque.

GOVERNMENT SIZE

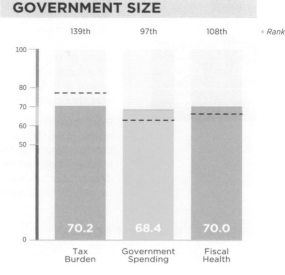

The top personal income tax rate has been raised to 41 percent. The top corporate tax rate is 28 percent. Other taxes include a value-added tax and a capital gains tax. The overall tax burden equals 22.6 percent of total domestic income. Government spending has amounted to 32.4 percent of total output (GDP) over the past three years, and budget deficits have averaged 4.0 percent of GDP. Public debt is equivalent to 50.1 percent of GDP.

REGULATORY EFFICIENCY

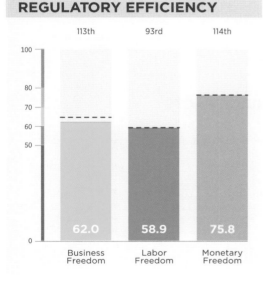

Progress in diversifying South Africa's economic base has been limited and uneven, indicating a need for regulatory changes that would encourage more dynamic private-sector development. Labor market rigidity has contributed to persistently high unemployment rates. The government has abolished price controls on all but a handful of items such as coal, petroleum and petroleum products, and utilities.

OPEN MARKETS

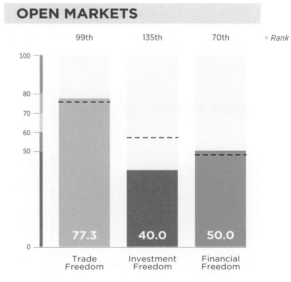

Trade is important to South Africa's economy; the value of exports and imports taken together equals 63 percent of GDP. The average applied tariff rate is 3.9 percent. Numerous state-owned enterprises distort the economy, and recent efforts to ban foreign ownership of land and facilitate expropriation discourage foreign investment. The financial sector is one of the largest among emerging markets and includes sophisticated banking and bond markets.

SOUTH AFRICA

SUDAN

Grading of Sudan's economic freedom has resumed in the 2017 *Index*, reflecting the improved availability and quality of key economic data. The petroleum sector provides some economic stability and foreign exchange earnings, but other parts of the economy are underdeveloped and face serious structural and institutional headwinds. Continued conflict with rebels and South Sudan promotes uncertainty and undermines investor confidence.

Poor governance and inefficient regulations impede further economic diversification. A large informal economy remains trapped by business regulations that inhibit registration and a rigid labor market that discourages formal hiring. High tariffs limit imports and protect domestic industry, and investment remains reserved largely for the hydrocarbon sector.

ECONOMIC FREEDOM SCORE

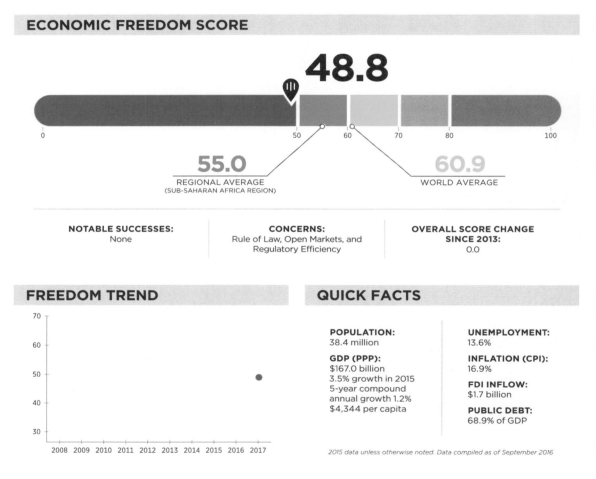

48.8

0   50   60   70   80   100

55.0
REGIONAL AVERAGE
(SUB-SAHARAN AFRICA REGION)

60.9
WORLD AVERAGE

NOTABLE SUCCESSES:	CONCERNS:	OVERALL SCORE CHANGE
None	Rule of Law, Open Markets, and Regulatory Efficiency	SINCE 2013: 0.0

FREEDOM TREND

70
60
50
40
30

2008 2009 2010 2011 2012 2013 2014 2015 2016 2017

QUICK FACTS

POPULATION:
38.4 million

GDP (PPP):
$167.0 billion
3.5% growth in 2015
5-year compound
annual growth 1.2%
$4,344 per capita

UNEMPLOYMENT:
13.6%

INFLATION (CPI):
16.9%

FDI INFLOW:
$1.7 billion

PUBLIC DEBT:
68.9% of GDP

2015 data unless otherwise noted. Data compiled as of September 2016

BACKGROUND: Omar Hassan al-Bashir has been president since 1989 after coming to power in a military coup. He faces two international arrest warrants based on charges of war crimes, crimes against humanity, and genocide in the Darfur conflict that has killed over 200,000 people and displaced over 2 million since 2003. Cross-border violence, political instability, poor infrastructure, weak property rights, and corruption hinder development. Following the secession of South Sudan in 2011, Sudan lost two-thirds of its oil revenue to the South. A June 2015 U.N. report of an upsurge of violence in Darfur has raised concerns that the conflict may be heating up again.

12 ECONOMIC FREEDOMS | SUDAN

RULE OF LAW

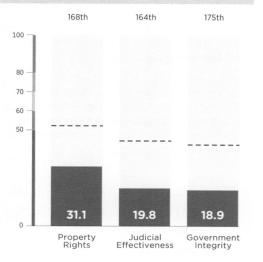

	168th	164th	175th
Property Rights	Judicial Effectiveness	Government Integrity
31.1	19.8	18.9

There is little respect for private property. The judiciary is not independent, and the legal framework has been severely hampered by years of political conflict. Sudan, one of the world's most corrupt nations, was ranked 165th among the 168 countries surveyed in Transparency International's 2015 *Corruption Perceptions Index*. Power and resources are concentrated in and around Khartoum, while outlying states are neglected and impoverished.

GOVERNMENT SIZE

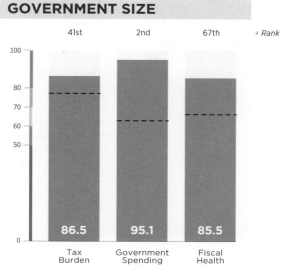

41st 2nd 67th ◄ Rank

Tax Burden	Government Spending	Fiscal Health
86.5	95.1	85.5

The top personal income tax rate is 10 percent, and the top corporate tax rate is 35 percent. The overall tax burden equals 5.2 percent of total domestic income. Government spending has amounted to 12.8 percent of total output (GDP) over the past three years, and budget deficits have averaged 1.8 percent of GDP. Public debt is equivalent to 68.9 percent of GDP.

REGULATORY EFFICIENCY

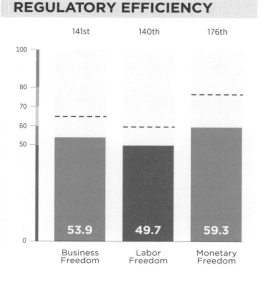

141st 140th 176th

Business Freedom	Labor Freedom	Monetary Freedom
53.9	49.7	59.3

The entrepreneurial environment is not conducive to private-sector development. The labor market remains underdeveloped, and much of the labor force is employed in the informal sector. Early in 2016, the government cut cooking gas, jet fuel, and fuel oil subsidies by ending a government monopoly over these products as global oil prices slid, opening the market to the private sector.

OPEN MARKETS

181st 170th 162nd ◄ Rank

Trade Freedom	Investment Freedom	Financial Freedom
50.5	15.0	20.0

Trade is moderately important to Sudan's economy; the value of exports and imports taken together equals 19 percent of GDP. The average applied tariff rate is 14.7 percent. International economic sanctions restrict investment, and state-owned enterprises distort the economy. A large portion of the population remains outside of the formal banking sector, and access to credit remains limited.

SUDAN

SWAZILAND

I nefficient regulatory and legal frameworks have deterred development of more dynamic private investment and production in Swaziland. Privatization has progressed only marginally. Averaging annual growth of around 2 percent over the past five years, Swaziland's economic performance has lagged behind that of other economies in the region.

Bureaucratic inefficiency and corruption affect many aspects of the economy, discouraging more vibrant activity. The most visible constraints on the emergence of economic dynamism are related to poor management of public finance, administrative complexities, and a lack of respect for contracts. Court enforcement of property rights is vulnerable to political interference.

ECONOMIC FREEDOM SCORE

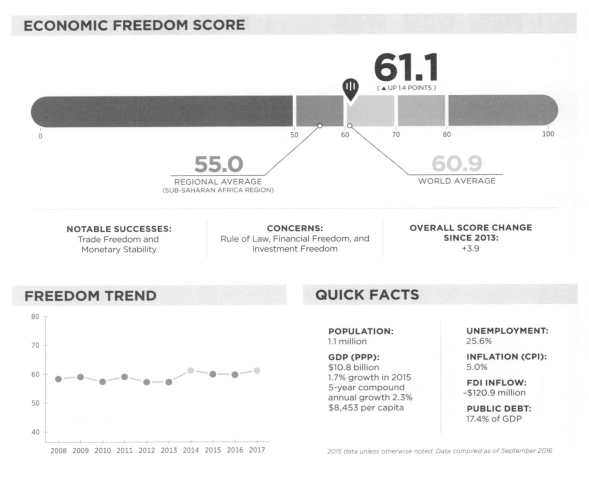

61.1
(▲ UP 1.4 POINTS)

0 — 50 — 60 — 70 — 80 — 100

55.0
REGIONAL AVERAGE
(SUB-SAHARAN AFRICA REGION)

60.9
WORLD AVERAGE

NOTABLE SUCCESSES:
Trade Freedom and
Monetary Stability

CONCERNS:
Rule of Law, Financial Freedom, and
Investment Freedom

**OVERALL SCORE CHANGE
SINCE 2013:**
+3.9

FREEDOM TREND

80
70
60
50
40

2008 2009 2010 2011 2012 2013 2014 2015 2016 2017

QUICK FACTS

POPULATION:
1.1 million

GDP (PPP):
$10.8 billion
1.7% growth in 2015
5-year compound
annual growth 2.3%
$8,453 per capita

UNEMPLOYMENT:
25.6%

INFLATION (CPI):
5.0%

FDI INFLOW:
–$120.9 million

PUBLIC DEBT:
17.4% of GDP

2015 data unless otherwise noted. Data compiled as of September 2016

BACKGROUND: King Mswati III rules Africa's last absolute monarchy. Political parties are banned, and rights groups accuse the government of imprisoning journalists and pro-democracy activists. Parliamentary candidates are handpicked by chiefs who are loyal to the king, and international observers declared the most recent elections, held in September 2013, not credible. In June 2014, responding to crackdowns on peaceful demonstrations and a lack of protection of workers' rights, the U.S. disqualified Swaziland from receiving the market-access benefits available under the African Growth and Opportunity Act. Because about one-third of Swaziland's garment and textile exports at the time went to the U.S., the AGOA disqualification forced Swaziland to reorient some of its exports regionally.

12 ECONOMIC FREEDOMS | SWAZILAND

RULE OF LAW

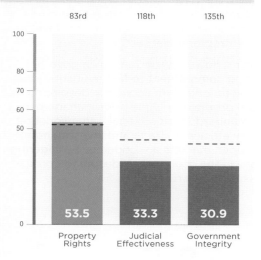

83rd   118th   135th

Property Rights	Judicial Effectiveness	Government Integrity
53.5	33.3	30.9

The right to own property is protected by law, but most Swazis reside on Swazi Nation Land that is not covered by this constitutional protection, and 60 percent of land does not have clear title. The constitution provides for an independent judiciary, but the king's power to appoint judges limits judicial independence. Corruption is a major problem. Areas most affected include public contracting, government appointments, and school admissions.

GOVERNMENT SIZE

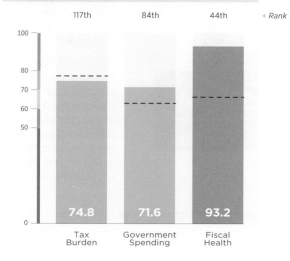

117th   84th   44th   ◄ Rank

Tax Burden	Government Spending	Fiscal Health
74.8	71.6	93.2

The top individual income tax rate is 33 percent, and the top corporate tax rate is 27.5 percent. Other taxes include a fuel tax and a sales tax. The overall tax burden equals 26.0 percent of total domestic income. Government spending has amounted to 30.8 percent of total output (GDP) over the past three years, and budget deficits have averaged 2.0 percent of GDP. Public debt is equivalent to 17.4 percent of GDP.

REGULATORY EFFICIENCY

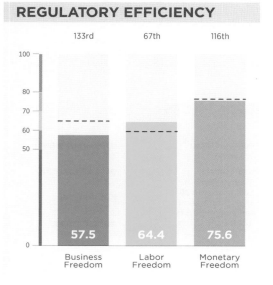

133rd   67th   116th

Business Freedom	Labor Freedom	Monetary Freedom
57.5	64.4	75.6

Saddled with an inefficient regulatory environment, Swaziland's private sector faces considerable challenges. Various regulatory requirements increase the overall cost of carrying out sustainable entrepreneurial activity. A formal labor market has not been fully developed. In 2015, the IMF called for reductions in subsidies and transfers, but policymaking is ultimately in the hands of the king, and significant economic reform appears unlikely.

OPEN MARKETS

7th   120th   106th   ◄ Rank

Trade Freedom	Investment Freedom	Financial Freedom
88.9	50.0	40.0

Trade is important to Swaziland's economy; the value of exports and imports taken together equals 77 percent of GDP. The average applied tariff rate is 0.6 percent. Foreign investment is screened by the government, and foreign investment in land is restricted. In addition, state-owned enterprises distort the economy. Overall supervision of the banking sector is weak, and the sector remains subject to government influence.

TANZANIA

Tanzania has made progress in achieving income growth and poverty reduction over the past decade. While small in size, the financial sector has undergone modernization, and credit is increasingly allocated at market rates, supporting the development of a more vibrant entrepreneurial sector.

Despite these recent gains, however, the Tanzanian government seems to lack strong commitment to further institutional reforms that are essential to long-term economic development. Long-standing structural problems include poor management of public finance and an underdeveloped legal framework that interferes with regulatory efficiency. Trade and investment policies needed to sustain open markets are undercut by lingering government interference in the economy. Widespread corruption further undermines the weak rule of law.

WORLD RANK: **105** REGIONAL RANK: **14**

ECONOMIC FREEDOM STATUS:
MOSTLY UNFREE

ECONOMIC FREEDOM SCORE

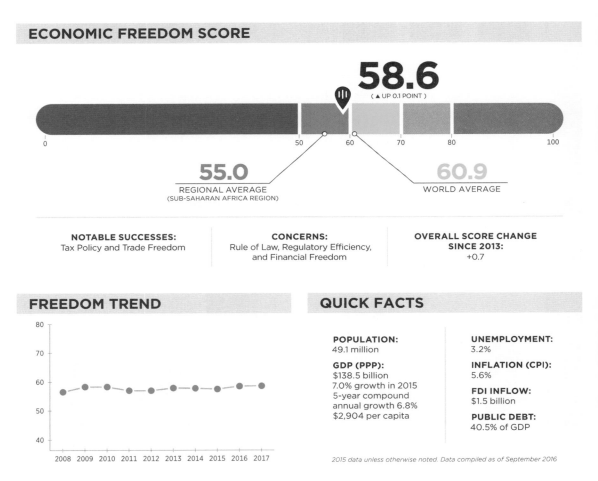

58.6
(▲ UP 0.1 POINT)

0   50   60   70   80   100

55.0
REGIONAL AVERAGE
(SUB-SAHARAN AFRICA REGION)

60.9
WORLD AVERAGE

NOTABLE SUCCESSES:
Tax Policy and Trade Freedom

CONCERNS:
Rule of Law, Regulatory Efficiency, and Financial Freedom

OVERALL SCORE CHANGE SINCE 2013:
+0.7

FREEDOM TREND

80

70

60

50

40

2008 2009 2010 2011 2012 2013 2014 2015 2016 2017

QUICK FACTS

POPULATION:
49.1 million

GDP (PPP):
$138.5 billion
7.0% growth in 2015
5-year compound
annual growth 6.8%
$2,904 per capita

UNEMPLOYMENT:
3.2%

INFLATION (CPI):
5.6%

FDI INFLOW:
$1.5 billion

PUBLIC DEBT:
40.5% of GDP

2015 data unless otherwise noted. Data compiled as of September 2016

BACKGROUND: John Magufuli of the Chama Cha Mapinduzi (CCM) party was elected president in October 2015, succeeding Jakaya Kikwete, also of the CCM. Their party and its earlier iterations have been in power since independence in 1961. In 2016, the United States froze some aid to Tanzania after declaring that elections won by the ruling party in the semiautonomous island of Zanzibar were fraudulent. The country has a high HIV/AIDS rate. In 2016, a large field of helium gas was discovered in Tanzania, and efforts to exploit the find are ongoing.

12 ECONOMIC FREEDOMS | TANZANIA

RULE OF LAW

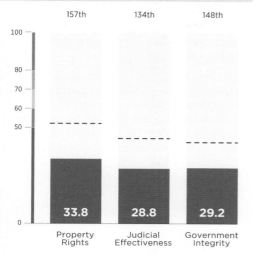

157th 134th 148th

Property Rights	Judicial Effectiveness	Government Integrity
33.8	28.8	29.2

Complex land laws have been accompanied by a high incidence of land disputes. The inadequately resourced and corrupt judiciary remains subject to political influence. Although corruption continues to be pervasive in all aspects of political and commercial life, the new president, who campaigned on an anti-graft platform and promised to establish an anticorruption court, has undertaken reforms to enhance institutional effectiveness.

GOVERNMENT SIZE

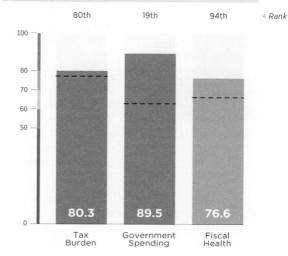

80th 19th 94th ◂ Rank

Tax Burden	Government Spending	Fiscal Health
80.3	89.5	76.6

The top personal income and corporate tax rates are 30 percent. Other taxes include a value-added tax and a tax on interest. The overall tax burden equals 13.2 percent of total domestic income. Government spending has amounted to 18.7 percent of total output (GDP) over the past three years, and budget deficits have averaged 3.5 percent of GDP. Public debt is equivalent to 40.5 percent of GDP.

REGULATORY EFFICIENCY

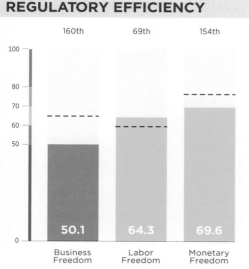

160th 69th 154th

Business Freedom	Labor Freedom	Monetary Freedom
50.1	64.3	69.6

The business environment remains hampered by inefficient regulations. Although requirements for launching a business are not time-consuming, the licensing process costs over five times the average level of annual income. Labor regulations are not flexible enough to support a vibrant labor market. The International Monetary Fund reported in 2016 that the public electricity utility TANESCO remains financially unsustainable.

OPEN MARKETS

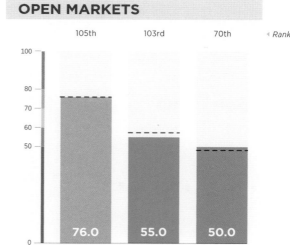

105th 103rd 70th ◂ Rank

Trade Freedom	Investment Freedom	Financial Freedom
76.0	55.0	50.0

Trade is important to Tanzania's economy; the value of exports and imports taken together equals 50 percent of GDP. The average applied tariff rate is 7.0 percent. Foreign investment in land is restricted, and investment in other sectors may be screened. State-owned enterprises distort the economy. The financial sector continues to evolve. Credit is allocated largely at market rates, and a range of commercial credit instruments is available to the private sector.

TANZANIA

TOGO

WORLD RANK:
138

REGIONAL RANK:
29

ECONOMIC FREEDOM STATUS:
MOSTLY UNFREE

Togo has undertaken a series of economic reforms in recent years, restructuring its key banking, electricity, and transportation sectors. The corporate tax rate, formerly one of the region's highest, has been lowered. The government has also taken steps to divest public enterprises. There are plans to privatize inefficient public banks.

However, an inefficient business environment and weak public administration continue to undermine overall competitiveness. A significant proportion of economic activity occurs in the informal sector. Togo still depends heavily on foreign aid. Foreign direct investment is allowed only in certain sectors, and regulatory and judicial systems are vulnerable to corruption and political interference.

ECONOMIC FREEDOM SCORE

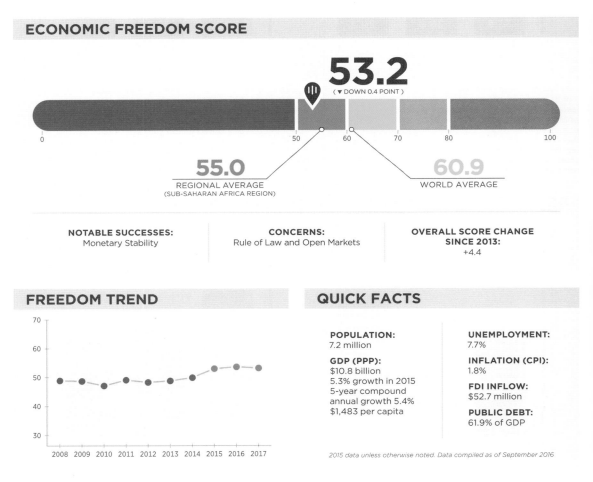

53.2
(▼ DOWN 0.4 POINT)

0   50   60   70   80   100

55.0
REGIONAL AVERAGE
(SUB-SAHARAN AFRICA REGION)

60.9
WORLD AVERAGE

NOTABLE SUCCESSES:
Monetary Stability

CONCERNS:
Rule of Law and Open Markets

**OVERALL SCORE CHANGE
SINCE 2013:**
+4.4

FREEDOM TREND

70

60

50

40

30

2008 2009 2010 2011 2012 2013 2014 2015 2016 2017

QUICK FACTS

POPULATION:
7.2 million

GDP (PPP):
$10.8 billion
5.3% growth in 2015
5-year compound
annual growth 5.4%
$1,483 per capita

UNEMPLOYMENT:
7.7%

INFLATION (CPI):
1.8%

FDI INFLOW:
$52.7 million

PUBLIC DEBT:
61.9% of GDP

2015 data unless otherwise noted. Data compiled as of September 2016

BACKGROUND: Togo's military appointed Faure Gnassingbé to the presidency in 2005 following the death of his father, who had ruled for nearly 40 years. Under pressure from the Economic Community of West African States and the African Union, he stepped down two months later, but he won the subsequent presidential election in April 2005. In 2012, Gnassingbé dissolved the ruling Rally of the Togolese People party and formed the Union for the Republic, which still dominates the political landscape. In April 2015, he secured a third five-year term. With one of West Africa's few natural deep-water ports, Togo's secure territorial waters have become a relatively safe zone for international shippers.

12 ECONOMIC FREEDOMS | TOGO

RULE OF LAW

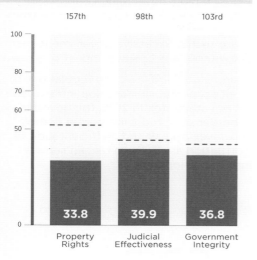

157th   98th   103rd

- Property Rights: **33.8**
- Judicial Effectiveness: **39.9**
- Government Integrity: **36.8**

Protection of real property is frequently contentious; the relevant statutes are comprised of poorly defined mixtures of civil code and traditional laws and can lead to legal fights over inheritances. Despite some recent reforms, property registration is still very cumbersome. Contracts are difficult to enforce. The opaque judicial system lacks resources and is heavily influenced by the presidency. Graft and corruption remain serious problems.

GOVERNMENT SIZE

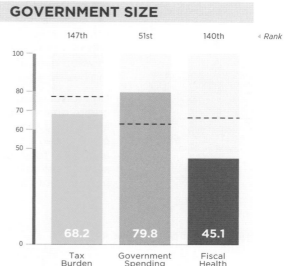

147th   51st   140th   ◂ *Rank*

- Tax Burden: **68.2**
- Government Spending: **79.8**
- Fiscal Health: **45.1**

The top individual income tax rate is 45 percent, and the top corporate tax rate is 27 percent. Other taxes include a value-added tax and a property tax. The overall tax burden equals 20.7 percent of total domestic income. Government spending has amounted to 26 percent of total output (GDP) over the past three years, and budget deficits have averaged 5.4 percent of GDP. Public debt is equivalent to 61.9 percent of GDP.

REGULATORY EFFICIENCY

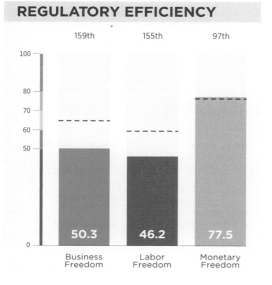

159th   155th   97th

- Business Freedom: **50.3**
- Labor Freedom: **46.2**
- Monetary Freedom: **77.5**

Recent reforms to enhance the entrepreneurial environment have reduced the time and cost involved in launching a business. The labor market lacks dynamism, and informal labor activity remains substantial. In 2016, lower oil prices allowed the government to reduce fuel subsidies, but these subsidies remain a burden on the budget and are expected to rise in the medium term as international oil prices increase.

OPEN MARKETS

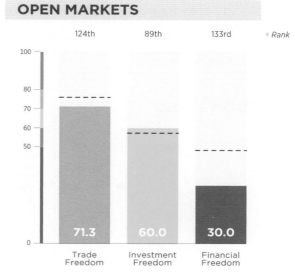

124th   89th   133rd   ◂ *Rank*

- Trade Freedom: **71.3**
- Investment Freedom: **60.0**
- Financial Freedom: **30.0**

Trade is extremely important to Togo's economy; the value of exports and imports taken together equals 107 percent of GDP. The average applied tariff rate is 9.4 percent. Foreign ownership of land is restricted; otherwise, foreign and domestic investors are generally treated equally under the law. Capital transactions are subject to some controls or government approval. Despite progress, the underdeveloped banking system lacks liquidity.

TOGO

UGANDA

The strong commitment to economic liberalization that made Uganda one of the most rapidly developing countries in Africa during the 1980s has noticeably diminished. Bureaucracy and expensive business licensing requirements discourage development of the private sector. Excessive government spending has led to rising debt without any positive impact on growth.

Uganda is currently revising a range of laws and regulations to create greater government accountability, develop infrastructure, and build a more vibrant private sector. In 2016, the government constructed a one-stop border post, reducing border compliance time for exports. However, a weak and inefficient judicial system and pervasive corruption are likely to remain serious impediments to sustainable development.

WORLD RANK:
91

REGIONAL RANK:
9

ECONOMIC FREEDOM STATUS:
MODERATELY FREE

ECONOMIC FREEDOM SCORE

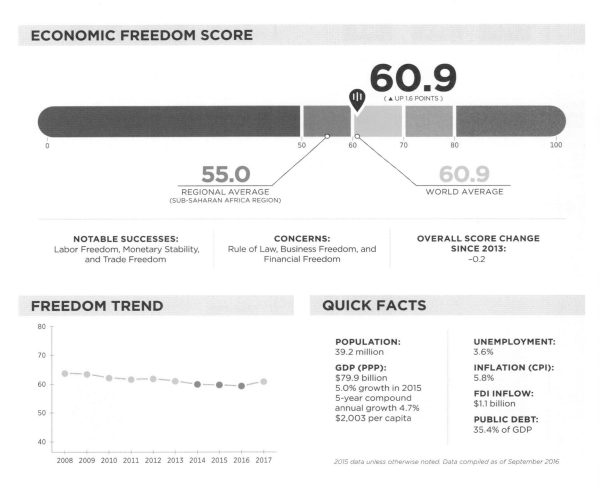

60.9
(▲ UP 1.6 POINTS)

0   50   60   70   80   100

55.0
REGIONAL AVERAGE
(SUB-SAHARAN AFRICA REGION)

60.9
WORLD AVERAGE

NOTABLE SUCCESSES:
Labor Freedom, Monetary Stability, and Trade Freedom

CONCERNS:
Rule of Law, Business Freedom, and Financial Freedom

OVERALL SCORE CHANGE SINCE 2013:
−0.2

FREEDOM TREND

80
70
60
50
40

2008 2009 2010 2011 2012 2013 2014 2015 2016 2017

QUICK FACTS

POPULATION:
39.2 million

GDP (PPP):
$79.9 billion
5.0% growth in 2015
5-year compound annual growth 4.7%
$2,003 per capita

UNEMPLOYMENT:
3.6%

INFLATION (CPI):
5.8%

FDI INFLOW:
$1.1 billion

PUBLIC DEBT:
35.4% of GDP

2015 data unless otherwise noted. Data compiled as of September 2016

BACKGROUND: President Yoweri Museveni and his National Resistance Movement have ruled Uganda since 1986 when Museveni, at the head of a rebel force, toppled President Tito Okello, who had seized power in a 1985 military coup. In February 2016, Museveni won a fifth term in elections that the international community viewed as tainted by government intimidation. The main opposition leader, Kizza Besigye, was arrested a number of times during the election cycle and later was charged with treason. Uganda has significant natural wealth, including gold, recently discovered oil, and rich agricultural lands from which more than two-thirds of the workforce derives employment.

12 ECONOMIC FREEDOMS | UGANDA

RULE OF LAW

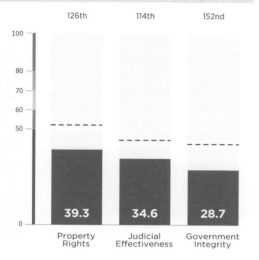

126th   114th   152nd

Property Rights	Judicial Effectiveness	Government Integrity
39.3	34.6	28.7

Property rights are guaranteed by law, but implementation of existing regulations lacks effectiveness and consistency. Businesses and individuals have great difficulty acquiring clear titles to land. Executive and military influence undermines judicial independence. Power is concentrated in the hands of the ruling party, the security forces, and especially the president, who retains office through deeply flawed elections. Corruption is rarely prosecuted.

GOVERNMENT SIZE

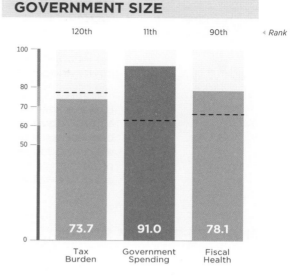

120th   11th   90th   ◂ *Rank*

Tax Burden	Government Spending	Fiscal Health
73.7	91.0	78.1

The top individual income tax rate is 40 percent, and the top corporate tax rate is 30 percent. Other taxes include a value-added tax and a property tax. The overall tax burden equals 11.4 percent of total domestic income. Government spending has amounted to 17.3 percent of total output (GDP) over the past three years, and budget deficits have averaged 3.5 percent of GDP. Public debt is equivalent to 35.4 percent of GDP.

REGULATORY EFFICIENCY

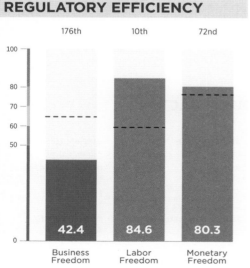

176th   10th   72nd

Business Freedom	Labor Freedom	Monetary Freedom
42.4	84.6	80.3

The overall regulatory framework remains poor. Although there is no minimum capital requirement, establishing a business is costly and time-consuming. Labor regulations are relatively flexible. The government does not subsidize fuel, and lower world oil prices have been passed on to consumers in the form of more economical gasoline and electricity prices.

OPEN MARKETS

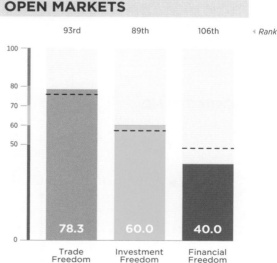

93rd   89th   106th   ◂ *Rank*

Trade Freedom	Investment Freedom	Financial Freedom
78.3	60.0	40.0

Trade is moderately important to Uganda's economy; the value of exports and imports taken together equals 47 percent of GDP. The average applied tariff rate is 5.9 percent. Foreign investors may lease but not own land; otherwise, foreign and domestic investors are generally treated equally under the law. The financial system is dominated by banking, which is increasingly open to competition, and access to financial services has been expanding.

UGANDA

ZAMBIA

Previous reform measures, coupled with relative political stability, have enabled Zambia's economy to maintain steady expansion averaging more than 5 percent over the past five years. The government's policy agenda has focused on reducing inflation, bringing down the fiscal deficit, and developing power and transport infrastructure to facilitate diversification of the economy.

However, overall progress in reforming governance, developing a more robust private sector, and diversifying the economy has been sluggish and mixed. Lingering institutional shortcomings, which include inefficient legal and regulatory frameworks, weak protection of property rights, and corruption, continue to undercut prospects for long-term development.

ECONOMIC FREEDOM SCORE

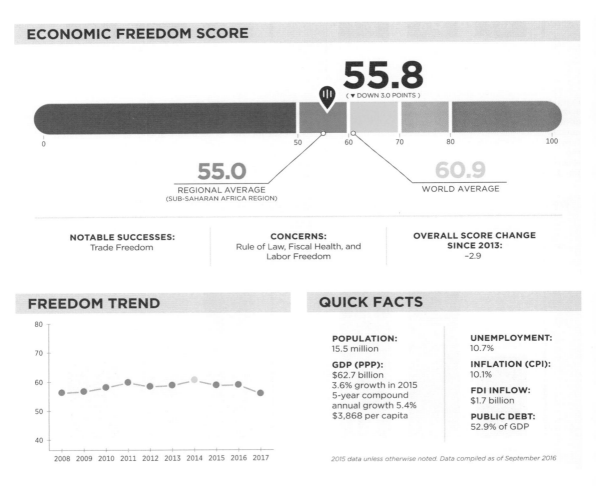

55.8
(▼ DOWN 3.0 POINTS)

0   50   60   70   80   100

55.0
REGIONAL AVERAGE
(SUB-SAHARAN AFRICA REGION)

60.9
WORLD AVERAGE

NOTABLE SUCCESSES:	CONCERNS:	OVERALL SCORE CHANGE SINCE 2013:
Trade Freedom	Rule of Law, Fiscal Health, and Labor Freedom	−2.9

FREEDOM TREND

80
70
60
50
40

2008 2009 2010 2011 2012 2013 2014 2015 2016 2017

QUICK FACTS

POPULATION:
15.5 million

GDP (PPP):
$62.7 billion
3.6% growth in 2015
5-year compound
annual growth 5.4%
$3,868 per capita

UNEMPLOYMENT:
10.7%

INFLATION (CPI):
10.1%

FDI INFLOW:
$1.7 billion

PUBLIC DEBT:
52.9% of GDP

2015 data unless otherwise noted. Data compiled as of September 2016

BACKGROUND: Zambia, traditionally one of the most politically stable countries in southern Africa, has successfully undergone five peaceful transfers of presidential power since the end of one-party rule in 1991. Edgar Lungu of the Patriotic Front narrowly won a January 2015 presidential special election held to replace Michael Sata, who died in office in October 2014. Zambia is revising its constitution to reduce presidential powers and institute a 50-plus-one vote for presidential elections, among other measures. Plummeting copper prices, reduced Chinese demand for commodities, and intense drought that reduced the country's hydroelectric power generation made the Zambian kwacha one of the world's most poorly performing currencies in 2015.

12 ECONOMIC FREEDOMS | ZAMBIA

RULE OF LAW

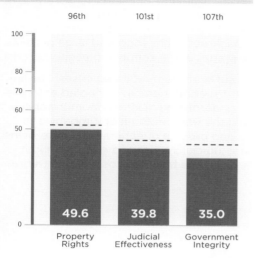

96th — Property Rights — 49.6
101st — Judicial Effectiveness — 39.8
107th — Government Integrity — 35.0

Protection of property rights and enforcement of contracts are weak. The rule of law remains uneven across the country. The inefficient judicial system is poorly resourced and politically influenced. Checks and balances on the president are inadequate. Although some steps were taken in 2015 to improve openness and transparency, widespread corruption, graft, and mismanagement continue to hinder the functioning of the government.

GOVERNMENT SIZE

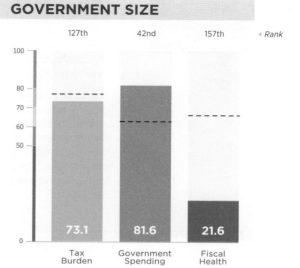

127th — Tax Burden — 73.1
42nd — Government Spending — 81.6
157th — Fiscal Health — 21.6

◄ Rank

The top personal income and corporate tax rates are 35 percent. Other taxes include a value-added tax and a property transfer tax. The overall tax burden equals 15.5 percent of total domestic income. Government spending has amounted to 24.8 percent of total output (GDP) over the past three years, and budget deficits have averaged 6.7 percent of GDP. Public debt is equivalent to 52.9 percent of GDP.

REGULATORY EFFICIENCY

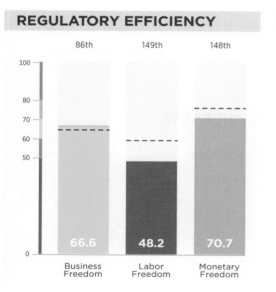

86th — Business Freedom — 66.6
149th — Labor Freedom — 48.2
148th — Monetary Freedom — 70.7

The regulatory environment does not promote entrepreneurial activity. Requirements for commercial licenses are time-consuming and costly, and enforcement of regulations is inconsistent. With unskilled labor abundant, an efficient labor market has not developed. Inflation has been rising as revenue shortfalls have forced subsidy cuts and price increases for electricity, fuel, and other goods.

OPEN MARKETS

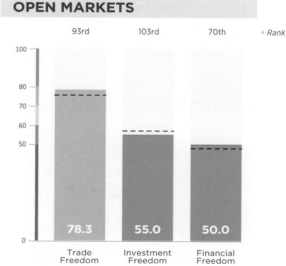

93rd — Trade Freedom — 78.3
103rd — Investment Freedom — 55.0
70th — Financial Freedom — 50.0

◄ Rank

Trade is important to Zambia's economy; the value of exports and imports taken together equals 73 percent of GDP. The average applied tariff rate is 3.4 percent, and additional barriers restrict agricultural trade. Foreign investment is screened by the government. In general, foreign investors may lease but not own land. Financial intermediation is rare, and credit to the private sector remains scarce.

ZAMBIA

WORLD RANK:
175

REGIONAL RANK:
45

ECONOMIC FREEDOM STATUS:
REPRESSED

ZIMBABWE

Zimbabwe's economy is characterized by instability and volatility, both of which are hallmarks of excessive government interference and mismanagement. Massive corruption and disastrous economic policies have plunged Zimbabwe into poverty. The government's near bankruptcy has triggered large protests over unpaid civil service wages and a continuing economic crisis.

The financial system has suffered from repeated crises. The lingering effects of years of hyperinflation have crippled entrepreneurial activity, severely undermining macroeconomic stability. The government has used the Reserve Bank of Zimbabwe to finance deficit spending and provide direct loans to state-owned enterprises. An inefficient judicial system and general lack of transparency severely exacerbate business costs and entrepreneurial risk.

ECONOMIC FREEDOM SCORE

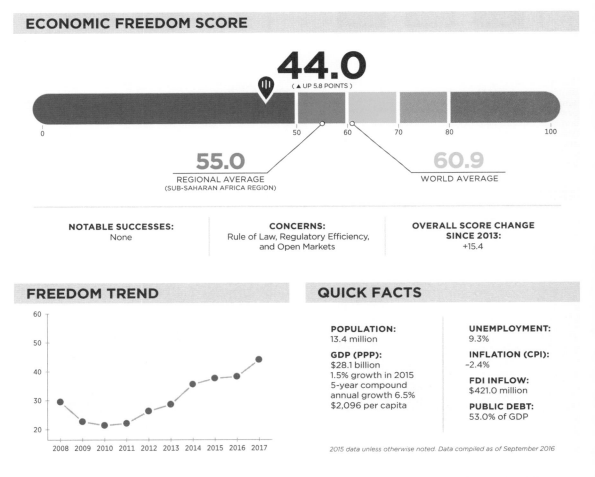

44.0
(▲ UP 5.8 POINTS)

0   50   60   70   80   100

55.0
REGIONAL AVERAGE
(SUB-SAHARAN AFRICA REGION)

60.9
WORLD AVERAGE

NOTABLE SUCCESSES:	CONCERNS:	OVERALL SCORE CHANGE SINCE 2013:
None	Rule of Law, Regulatory Efficiency, and Open Markets	+15.4

FREEDOM TREND

QUICK FACTS

POPULATION:
13.4 million

GDP (PPP):
$28.1 billion
1.5% growth in 2015
5-year compound
annual growth 6.5%
$2,096 per capita

UNEMPLOYMENT:
9.3%

INFLATION (CPI):
–2.4%

FDI INFLOW:
$421.0 million

PUBLIC DEBT:
53.0% of GDP

2015 data unless otherwise noted. Data compiled as of September 2016

BACKGROUND: In March 2013, Zimbabweans approved a new constitution to roll back presidential power. In July 2013, however, President Robert Mugabe of the Zimbabwe African National Union–Patriotic Front (ZANU–PF) won a seventh term in power since his first election as prime minister in 1980. In 1987, Mugabe consolidated power as president. Zimbabwe's next presidential and legislative elections are due to be held in 2018, but Mugabe's increasing frailty has touched off a bitter succession struggle within ZANU–PF. Inflation reached 500 billion percent in 2008, forcing the country to scrap the Zimbabwean dollar and allow use of other currencies, including the U.S. dollar.

12 ECONOMIC FREEDOMS | ZIMBABWE

RULE OF LAW

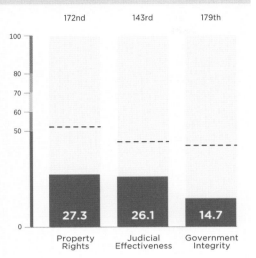

172nd	143rd	179th
Property Rights	Judicial Effectiveness	Government Integrity
27.3	26.1	14.7

The government enforces property rights with respect to residential and commercial properties in cities, but not with respect to agricultural land. While Zimbabwe continues to struggle with the internal factionalism of both ruling and opposition parties, the judiciary has shown increasing independence by deciding against powerful political interests, including ruling party elites. Nevertheless, corruption remains a severe problem at every level of government.

GOVERNMENT SIZE

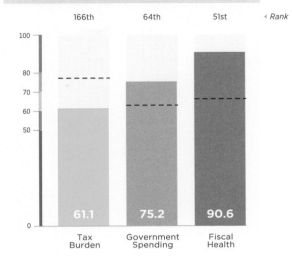

166th	64th	51st	◂ Rank
Tax Burden	Government Spending	Fiscal Health	
61.1	75.2	90.6	

The top personal income tax rate is 51.5 percent, and the top corporate tax rate is 25 percent. Other taxes include a value-added tax and a capital gains tax. The overall tax burden equals 24.8 percent of total domestic income. Government spending has amounted to 28.7 percent of total output (GDP) over the past three years, and budget deficits have averaged 1.5 percent of GDP. Public debt is equivalent to 53.0 percent of GDP.

REGULATORY EFFICIENCY

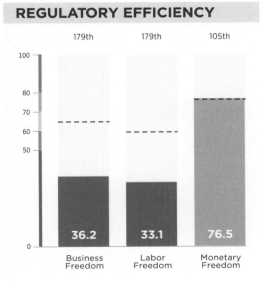

179th	179th	105th
Business Freedom	Labor Freedom	Monetary Freedom
36.2	33.1	76.5

The overall regulatory environment is opaque and vulnerable to government intervention. Because of the government's failed economic policies and continuing control, the formal labor market is not functioning. The IMF left in December 2015 with little sign of a genuine change in the government's prioritization of its political agenda over economic management. In 2016, the government reimposed import and currency controls.

OPEN MARKETS

178th	160th	173rd	◂ Rank
Trade Freedom	Investment Freedom	Financial Freedom	
52.8	25.0	10.0	

Trade is important to Zimbabwe's economy; the value of exports and imports taken together equals 75 percent of GDP. The average applied tariff rate is 13.6 percent. The government screens and limits foreign investment. Expropriation of land has been called a disaster, and state-owned enterprises distort the economy. Government intervention, inadequate supervision, and political instability have severely undermined the financial system.

ZIMBABWE

APPENDIX

INDEX OF ECONOMIC FREEDOM SCORES, 1995–2017

Country	1995	1996	1997	1998	1999	2000	2001	2002	2003	2004	2005	2006	2007	2008	2009	2010	2011	2012	2013	2014	2015	2016	2017
Afghanistan	N/A	N/A	N/A	N/A	N/A	N/A	N/A	N/A	N/A	N/A	N/A	N/A	N/A	N/A	N/A	N/A	N/A	N/A	N/A	N/A	N/A	N/A	48.9
Albania	49.7	53.8	54.8	53.9	53.4	53.6	56.6	56.8	56.8	58.5	57.8	60.3	61.4	62.4	63.7	66.0	64.0	65.1	65.2	66.9	65.7	65.9	64.4
Algeria	55.7	54.5	54.9	55.8	57.2	56.8	57.3	61.0	57.7	58.1	53.2	55.7	55.4	56.2	56.6	56.9	52.4	51.0	49.6	50.8	48.9	50.1	46.5
Angola	27.4	24.4	24.2	24.9	23.7	24.3	N/A	N/A	N/A	N/A	N/A	43.5	44.7	46.9	47.0	48.4	46.2	46.7	47.3	47.7	47.9	48.9	48.5
Argentina	68.0	74.7	73.3	70.9	70.6	70.0	68.6	65.7	56.3	53.9	51.7	53.4	54.0	54.2	52.3	51.2	51.7	48.0	46.7	44.6	44.1	43.8	50.4
Armenia	N/A	42.2	46.7	49.6	56.4	65.0	66.4	68.0	67.3	70.3	69.8	70.6	68.6	69.9	69.9	69.2	69.7	68.8	69.4	68.9	67.1	67.0	70.3
Australia	74.1	74.0	75.5	75.6	76.4	77.1	77.4	77.3	77.4	77.9	79.0	79.9	81.1	82.2	82.6	82.6	82.5	83.1	82.6	82.0	81.4	80.3	81.0
Austria	70.0	68.9	65.2	65.4	64.0	68.4	68.1	67.4	67.6	67.6	68.8	71.1	71.6	71.4	71.2	71.6	71.9	70.3	71.8	72.4	71.2	71.7	72.3
Azerbaijan	N/A	30.0	34.0	43.1	47.4	49.8	50.3	53.3	54.1	53.4	54.4	53.2	54.6	55.3	58.0	58.8	59.7	58.9	59.7	61.3	61.0	60.2	63.6
Bahamas	71.8	74.0	74.5	74.5	74.7	73.9	74.8	74.4	73.5	72.1	72.6	72.3	72.0	71.1	70.3	67.3	68.0	68.0	70.1	69.8	68.7	70.9	61.1
Bahrain	76.2	76.4	76.1	75.6	75.2	75.7	75.9	75.6	76.3	75.1	71.2	71.6	71.2	72.2	74.8	76.3	77.7	75.2	75.5	75.1	73.4	74.3	68.5
Bangladesh	40.9	51.1	49.9	52.0	50.0	48.9	51.2	51.9	49.3	50.0	47.5	52.9	46.7	44.2	47.5	51.1	53.0	53.2	52.6	54.1	53.9	53.3	55.0
Barbados	N/A	62.3	64.5	67.9	66.7	69.5	71.5	73.6	71.3	69.4	70.1	71.9	70.0	71.3	71.5	68.3	68.5	69.0	69.3	68.3	67.9	68.3	54.5
Belarus	40.4	38.7	39.8	38.0	35.4	41.3	38.0	39.0	39.7	43.1	46.7	47.5	47.0	45.3	45.0	48.7	47.9	49.0	48.0	50.1	49.8	48.8	58.6
Belgium	N/A	66.0	64.6	64.7	62.9	63.5	63.8	67.6	68.1	68.7	69.0	71.8	72.5	71.7	72.1	70.1	70.2	69.0	69.2	69.9	68.8	68.4	67.8
Belize	62.9	61.6	64.3	59.1	60.7	63.3	65.9	65.6	63.5	62.8	64.5	64.7	63.3	63.0	63.0	61.5	63.8	61.9	57.3	56.7	56.8	57.4	58.6
Benin	N/A	54.5	61.3	61.7	60.6	61.5	60.1	57.3	54.9	54.6	52.3	54.0	55.1	55.2	55.4	55.4	56.0	55.7	57.6	57.1	58.8	59.3	59.2
Bhutan	N/A	N/A	N/A	N/A	N/A	N/A	N/A	N/A	N/A	N/A	N/A	N/A	N/A	N/A	57.7	57.0	57.6	56.6	55.0	56.7	57.4	59.5	58.4
Bolivia	56.8	65.2	65.1	68.8	65.6	65.0	68.0	65.1	64.3	64.5	58.4	57.8	54.2	53.1	53.6	49.4	50.0	50.2	47.9	48.4	46.8	47.4	47.7
Bosnia and Herzegovina	N/A	N/A	N/A	29.4	29.4	45.1	36.6	37.4	40.6	44.7	48.8	55.6	54.4	53.9	53.1	56.2	57.5	57.3	57.3	58.4	59.0	58.6	60.2
Botswana	56.8	61.6	59.1	62.8	62.9	65.8	66.8	66.2	68.6	69.9	69.3	68.8	68.1	68.2	69.7	70.3	68.8	69.6	70.6	72.0	69.8	71.1	70.1
Brazil	51.4	48.1	52.6	52.3	61.3	61.1	61.9	61.5	63.4	62.0	61.7	60.9	56.2	56.2	56.7	55.6	56.3	57.9	57.7	56.9	56.6	56.5	52.9
Brunei	N/A	N/A	N/A	N/A	N/A	N/A	N/A	N/A	N/A	N/A	N/A	N/A	N/A	N/A	N/A	N/A	N/A	N/A	N/A	69.0	68.9	67.3	69.8
Bulgaria	50.0	48.6	47.6	45.7	46.2	47.3	51.9	57.1	57.0	59.2	62.3	64.1	62.7	63.7	64.6	62.3	64.9	64.7	65.0	65.7	66.8	65.9	67.9
Burkina Faso	N/A	49.4	54.0	54.5	55.0	55.7	56.7	58.8	58.9	58.0	56.6	55.8	55.1	55.7	59.5	59.4	60.6	60.6	59.9	58.9	58.6	59.1	59.6
Burma	N/A	45.1	45.4	45.7	46.4	47.9	46.1	45.5	44.9	43.6	40.5	40.0	41.0	39.5	37.7	36.7	37.8	38.7	39.2	46.5	46.9	48.7	52.5
Burundi	N/A	N/A	45.4	44.7	41.1	42.6	N/A	N/A	N/A	N/A	N/A	48.7	46.9	46.2	48.8	47.5	49.6	48.1	49.0	51.4	53.7	53.9	53.2
Cabo Verde	N/A	49.7	47.7	48.0	50.7	51.9	56.3	57.6	56.1	58.1	57.8	58.6	56.5	57.9	61.3	61.8	64.6	63.5	63.7	66.1	66.4	66.5	56.9
Cambodia	N/A	N/A	52.8	59.8	59.9	59.3	59.6	60.7	63.7	61.1	60.0	56.7	55.9	55.9	56.6	56.6	57.9	57.6	58.5	57.4	57.5	57.9	59.5
Cameroon	51.3	45.7	44.6	48.0	50.3	49.9	53.3	52.8	52.7	52.3	53.0	54.6	55.6	54.3	53.0	52.3	51.8	51.8	52.3	52.6	51.9	54.2	51.8

INDEX OF ECONOMIC FREEDOM SCORES, 1995–2017

Country	1995	1996	1997	1998	1999	2000	2001	2002	2003	2004	2005	2006	2007	2008	2009	2010	2011	2012	2013	2014	2015	2016	2017
Canada	69.4	70.3	67.9	68.5	69.3	70.5	71.2	74.6	74.8	75.3	75.8	77.4	78.0	80.2	80.5	80.4	80.8	79.9	79.4	80.2	79.1	78.0	78.5
Central African Republic	N/A	N/A	N/A	N/A	N/A	N/A	N/A	N/A	N/A	57.5	56.5	54.2	50.6	48.6	48.3	48.4	49.3	50.3	50.4	46.7	45.9	45.2	51.8
Chad	N/A	N/A	45.1	46.6	47.2	46.8	46.4	49.2	52.6	53.1	52.1	50.0	50.1	47.8	47.5	47.5	45.3	44.8	45.2	44.5	45.9	46.3	49.0
Chile	71.2	72.6	75.9	74.9	74.1	74.7	75.1	77.8	76.0	76.9	77.8	78.0	77.7	78.6	78.3	77.2	77.4	78.3	79.0	78.7	78.5	77.7	76.5
China	52.0	51.3	51.7	53.1	54.8	56.4	52.6	52.8	52.6	52.5	53.7	53.6	52.0	53.1	53.2	51.0	52.0	51.2	51.9	52.5	52.7	52.0	57.4
Colombia	64.5	64.3	66.4	65.5	65.3	63.3	65.6	64.2	64.2	61.2	59.6	60.4	59.9	62.2	62.3	65.5	68.0	68.0	69.6	70.7	71.7	70.8	69.7
Comoros	N/A	N/A	N/A	N/A	N/A	N/A	N/A	N/A	N/A	N/A	N/A	N/A	N/A	N/A	43.3	44.9	43.8	45.7	47.5	51.4	52.1	52.4	55.8
Congo, Dem. Rep. of	41.4	39.5	39.5	40.6	34.0	34.8	N/A	N/A	N/A	N/A	N/A	N/A	N/A	N/A	42.8	41.4	40.7	41.1	39.6	40.6	45.0	46.4	56.4
Congo, Rep. of	N/A	40.3	42.2	33.8	41.6	40.6	44.3	45.3	47.7	45.9	46.2	43.8	44.4	45.3	45.4	43.2	43.6	43.8	43.5	43.7	42.7	42.8	40.0
Costa Rica	68.0	66.4	65.6	65.6	67.4	68.4	67.6	67.5	67.0	66.4	66.1	65.9	64.0	64.2	66.4	65.9	67.3	68.0	67.0	66.9	67.2	67.4	65.0
Côte d'Ivoire	53.4	49.9	50.5	51.3	51.7	50.2	54.8	57.3	56.7	57.8	56.6	56.2	54.9	53.9	55.0	54.1	55.4	54.3	54.1	57.7	58.5	60.0	63.0
Croatia	N/A	48.0	46.7	51.7	53.1	53.6	50.7	51.1	53.3	53.1	51.9	53.6	53.4	54.1	55.1	59.2	61.1	60.9	61.3	60.4	61.5	59.1	59.4
Cuba	27.8	27.8	27.8	28.2	29.7	31.3	31.6	32.4	35.1	34.4	35.5	29.3	28.6	27.5	27.9	26.7	27.7	28.3	28.5	28.7	29.6	29.8	33.9
Cyprus	N/A	67.7	67.9	68.2	67.8	67.2	71.0	73.0	73.3	74.1	71.9	71.8	71.7	71.3	70.8	70.9	73.3	71.8	69.0	67.6	67.9	68.7	67.9
Czech Republic	67.8	68.1	68.8	68.4	69.7	68.6	70.2	66.5	67.5	67.0	64.6	66.4	67.4	68.1	69.4	69.8	70.4	69.9	70.9	72.2	72.5	73.2	73.3
Denmark	N/A	67.3	67.5	67.5	68.1	68.3	68.3	71.1	73.2	72.4	75.3	75.4	77.0	79.2	79.6	77.9	78.6	76.2	76.1	76.1	76.3	75.3	75.1
Djibouti	N/A	N/A	54.5	55.9	57.1	55.1	58.3	57.8	55.7	55.6	55.2	53.2	52.4	51.2	51.3	51.0	54.5	53.9	53.9	55.9	57.5	56.0	46.7
Dominica	N/A	N/A	N/A	N/A	N/A	N/A	N/A	N/A	N/A	N/A	N/A	N/A	N/A	N/A	62.6	63.2	63.3	61.6	63.9	65.2	66.1	67.0	63.7
Dominican Republic	55.8	58.1	53.5	58.1	58.1	59.0	59.1	58.6	57.8	54.6	55.1	56.3	56.8	57.7	59.2	60.3	60.0	60.2	59.7	61.3	61.0	61.0	62.9
Ecuador	57.7	60.1	61.0	62.8	62.9	59.8	55.1	53.1	54.1	54.4	52.9	54.6	55.3	55.2	52.5	49.3	47.1	48.3	46.9	48.0	49.2	48.6	49.3
Egypt	45.7	52.0	54.5	55.8	58.0	51.7	51.5	54.1	55.3	55.5	55.8	53.2	54.4	58.5	58.0	59.0	59.1	57.9	54.8	52.9	55.2	56.0	52.6
El Salvador	69.1	70.1	70.5	70.2	75.1	76.3	73.0	73.0	71.5	71.2	71.5	69.6	68.9	68.5	69.8	69.9	68.8	68.7	66.7	66.2	65.7	65.1	64.1
Equatorial Guinea	N/A	N/A	N/A	N/A	45.1	45.6	47.9	46.4	53.1	53.3	53.3	51.5	53.2	51.6	51.3	48.6	47.5	42.8	42.3	44.4	40.4	43.7	45.0
Eritrea	N/A	N/A	N/A	N/A	N/A	N/A	N/A	N/A	N/A	N/A	N/A	N/A	N/A	N/A	38.5	35.3	36.7	36.2	36.3	38.5	38.9	42.7	42.2
Estonia	65.2	65.4	69.1	72.5	73.8	69.9	76.1	77.6	77.7	77.4	75.2	74.9	78.0	77.9	76.4	74.7	75.2	73.2	75.3	75.9	76.8	77.2	79.1
Ethiopia	42.6	45.9	48.1	49.2	46.7	50.2	48.9	49.8	48.8	54.5	51.1	50.9	53.6	52.5	53.0	51.2	50.5	52.0	49.4	50.0	51.5	51.5	52.7
Fiji	54.7	57.4	58.0	58.2	58.4	57.8	53.7	53.9	54.7	58.0	58.2	58.4	60.8	61.8	61.0	60.3	60.4	57.3	57.2	58.7	59.0	58.8	63.4
Finland	N/A	63.7	65.2	63.5	63.9	64.3	69.7	73.6	73.7	73.4	71.0	72.9	74.0	74.6	74.5	73.8	74.0	72.3	74.0	73.4	73.4	72.6	74.0

INDEX OF ECONOMIC FREEDOM SCORES, 1995–2017

Country	1995	1996	1997	1998	1999	2000	2001	2002	2003	2004	2005	2006	2007	2008	2009	2010	2011	2012	2013	2014	2015	2016	2017
France	64.4	63.7	59.1	58.9	59.1	57.4	58.0	58.0	59.2	60.9	60.5	61.1	62.1	64.7	63.3	64.2	64.6	63.2	64.1	63.5	62.5	62.3	63.3
Gabon	57.5	55.7	58.8	59.2	60.5	58.2	55.0	58.0	58.7	57.1	54.8	56.1	54.8	54.2	55.0	55.4	56.7	56.4	57.8	57.8	58.3	59.0	58.6
Gambia	N/A	N/A	52.9	53.4	52.1	52.7	56.6	57.7	56.3	55.3	56.5	57.3	57.7	56.9	55.8	55.1	57.4	58.8	58.8	59.5	57.5	57.1	53.4
Georgia	N/A	44.1	46.5	47.9	52.5	54.3	58.3	56.7	58.6	58.9	57.1	64.5	69.3	69.2	69.8	70.4	70.4	69.4	72.2	72.6	73.0	72.6	76.0
Germany	69.8	69.1	67.5	64.3	65.6	65.7	69.5	70.4	69.7	69.5	68.1	70.8	70.8	70.6	70.5	71.1	71.8	71.0	72.8	73.4	73.8	74.4	73.8
Ghana	55.6	57.7	56.7	57.0	57.9	58.1	58.0	57.2	58.2	59.1	56.5	55.6	57.6	57.0	58.1	60.2	59.4	60.7	61.3	64.2	63.0	63.5	56.2
Greece	61.2	60.5	59.6	60.6	61.0	61.0	63.4	59.1	58.8	59.1	59.0	60.1	58.7	60.6	60.8	62.7	60.3	55.4	55.4	55.7	54.0	53.2	55.0
Guatemala	62.0	63.7	65.7	65.8	66.2	64.3	65.1	62.3	62.3	59.6	59.5	59.1	60.5	59.8	59.4	61.0	61.9	60.9	60.0	61.2	60.4	61.8	63.0
Guinea	59.4	58.5	52.9	61.0	59.4	58.2	58.4	52.9	54.6	56.1	57.4	52.8	54.5	52.8	51.0	51.8	51.7	50.8	51.2	53.5	52.1	53.3	47.6
Guinea-Bissau	N/A	N/A	N/A	N/A	33.5	34.7	42.5	42.3	43.1	42.6	46.0	46.5	46.1	44.4	45.4	43.6	46.5	50.1	51.1	51.3	52.0	51.8	56.1
Guyana	45.7	50.1	53.2	52.7	53.3	52.4	53.3	54.3	50.3	53.0	56.5	56.6	53.7	48.8	48.4	48.4	49.4	51.3	53.8	55.7	55.5	55.4	58.5
Haiti	43.0	41.0	45.8	45.7	45.9	45.7	47.1	47.9	50.6	51.2	48.4	49.2	51.4	49.0	50.5	50.8	52.1	50.7	48.1	48.9	51.3	51.3	49.6
Honduras	57.0	56.6	56.0	56.2	56.7	57.6	57.0	58.7	60.4	55.3	55.3	57.4	59.1	58.9	58.7	58.3	58.6	58.8	58.4	57.1	57.4	57.7	58.8
Hong Kong	88.6	90.5	88.6	88.0	88.5	89.5	89.9	89.4	89.8	90.0	89.5	88.6	89.9	89.7	90.0	89.7	89.7	89.9	89.3	90.1	89.6	88.6	89.8
Hungary	55.2	56.8	55.3	56.9	59.6	64.4	65.6	64.5	63.0	62.7	63.5	65.0	64.8	67.6	66.8	66.1	66.6	67.1	67.3	67.0	66.8	66.0	65.8
Iceland	N/A	N/A	70.5	71.2	71.4	74.0	73.4	73.1	73.5	72.1	76.6	75.8	76.0	75.8	75.9	73.7	68.2	70.9	72.1	72.4	72.0	73.3	74.4
India	45.1	47.4	49.7	49.7	50.2	47.4	49.0	51.2	51.2	51.5	54.2	52.2	53.9	54.1	54.4	53.8	54.6	54.6	55.2	55.7	54.6	56.2	52.6
Indonesia	54.9	61.0	62.0	61.5	61.5	55.2	52.5	54.8	55.8	52.1	52.9	51.9	53.2	53.2	53.4	55.5	56.0	56.4	56.9	58.5	58.1	59.4	61.9
Iran	N/A	36.1	34.5	36.0	36.8	36.1	35.9	36.4	43.2	42.8	50.5	45.0	45.0	45.0	44.6	43.4	42.1	42.3	43.2	40.3	41.8	43.5	50.5
Iraq	N/A	17.2	17.2	17.2	17.2	17.2	17.2	15.6	N/A	N/A	N/A	N/A	N/A	N/A	N/A	N/A	N/A	N/A	N/A	N/A	N/A	N/A	N/A
Ireland	68.5	68.5	72.6	73.7	74.6	76.1	81.2	80.5	80.9	80.3	80.8	82.2	82.6	82.5	82.2	81.3	78.7	76.9	75.7	76.2	76.6	77.3	76.7
Israel	61.5	62.0	62.7	68.0	68.3	65.5	66.1	66.9	62.7	61.4	62.6	64.4	64.8	66.3	67.6	67.7	68.5	67.8	66.9	68.4	70.5	70.7	69.7
Italy	61.2	60.8	58.1	59.1	61.6	61.9	63.0	63.6	64.3	64.2	64.9	62.0	62.8	62.6	61.4	62.7	60.3	58.8	60.6	60.9	61.7	61.2	62.5
Jamaica	64.4	66.7	67.7	67.1	64.7	65.5	63.7	61.7	67.0	66.7	67.0	66.4	65.5	65.7	65.2	65.5	65.7	65.1	66.8	66.7	67.7	67.5	69.5
Japan	75.0	72.6	70.3	70.2	69.1	70.7	70.9	66.7	67.6	64.3	67.3	73.3	72.7	73.0	72.8	72.9	72.8	71.6	71.8	72.4	73.3	73.1	69.6
Jordan	62.7	60.8	63.6	66.8	67.4	67.5	68.3	66.2	65.3	66.1	66.7	63.7	64.5	64.1	65.4	66.1	68.9	69.9	70.4	69.2	69.3	68.3	66.7
Kazakhstan	N/A	N/A	N/A	41.7	47.3	50.4	51.8	52.4	52.3	49.7	53.9	60.2	59.6	61.1	60.1	61.0	62.1	63.6	63.0	63.7	63.3	63.6	69.0
Kenya	54.5	56.4	60.1	58.4	58.2	59.7	57.6	58.2	58.6	57.7	57.9	59.7	59.6	59.3	58.7	57.5	57.4	57.5	55.9	57.1	55.6	57.5	53.5
Kiribati	N/A	N/A	N/A	N/A	N/A	N/A	N/A	N/A	N/A	N/A	N/A	N/A	N/A	N/A	45.7	43.7	44.8	46.9	45.9	46.3	46.4	46.2	50.9
North Korea	8.9	8.9	8.9	8.9	8.9	8.9	8.9	8.9	8.9	8.9	8.0	4.0	3.0	3.0	2.0	1.0	1.0	1.0	1.5	1.0	1.3	2.3	4.9

Country	1995	1996	1997	1998	1999	2000	2001	2002	2003	2004	2005	2006	2007	2008	2009	2010	2011	2012	2013	2014	2015	2016	2017
South Korea	72.0	73.0	69.8	73.3	69.7	69.7	69.1	69.5	68.3	67.8	66.4	67.5	67.8	68.6	68.1	69.9	69.8	69.9	70.3	71.2	71.5	71.7	74.3
Kosovo	N/A	N/A	N/A	N/A	N/A	N/A	N/A	N/A	N/A	N/A	N/A	N/A	N/A	N/A	N/A	N/A	N/A	N/A	N/A	N/A	N/A	61.4	67.9
Kuwait	N/A	66.1	64.8	66.3	69.5	69.7	68.2	65.4	66.7	63.6	64.6	66.5	66.4	68.1	65.6	67.7	64.9	62.5	63.1	62.3	62.5	62.7	65.1
Kyrgyz Republic	N/A	N/A	N/A	51.8	54.8	55.7	53.7	51.7	56.8	58.0	56.6	61.0	60.2	61.1	61.8	61.3	61.1	60.2	59.6	61.1	61.3	59.6	61.1
Laos	N/A	38.5	35.1	35.2	35.2	36.8	33.5	36.8	41.0	42.0	44.4	47.5	50.3	50.3	50.4	51.1	51.3	50.0	50.1	51.2	51.4	49.8	54.0
Latvia	N/A	55.0	62.4	63.4	64.2	63.4	66.4	65.0	66.0	67.4	66.3	66.9	67.9	68.3	66.6	66.2	65.8	65.2	66.5	68.7	69.7	70.4	74.8
Lebanon	N/A	63.2	63.9	59.0	59.1	56.1	61.0	57.1	56.7	56.9	57.2	57.5	60.4	60.0	58.1	59.5	60.1	60.1	59.5	59.4	59.3	59.5	53.3
Lesotho	N/A	47.0	47.2	48.4	48.2	48.4	50.6	48.9	52.0	50.3	53.9	54.7	53.2	52.1	49.7	48.1	47.5	46.6	47.9	49.5	49.6	50.6	53.9
Liberia	N/A	N/A	N/A	N/A	N/A	N/A	N/A	N/A	N/A	N/A	N/A	N/A	N/A	N/A	N/A	46.2	46.5	48.6	49.3	52.4	52.7	52.2	49.1
Libya	N/A	31.7	28.9	32.0	32.3	34.7	34.0	35.4	34.6	31.5	32.8	33.2	37.0	38.7	43.5	40.2	38.6	35.9	N/A	N/A	N/A	N/A	N/A
Liechtenstein	N/A	N/A	N/A	N/A	N/A	N/A	N/A	N/A	N/A	N/A	N/A	N/A	N/A	N/A	N/A	N/A	N/A	N/A	N/A	N/A	N/A	N/A	N/A
Lithuania	N/A	49.7	57.3	59.4	61.5	61.9	65.5	66.1	69.7	72.4	70.5	71.8	71.5	70.9	70.0	70.3	71.3	71.5	72.1	73.0	74.7	75.2	75.8
Luxembourg	N/A	72.5	72.8	72.7	72.4	76.4	80.1	79.4	79.9	78.9	76.3	75.3	74.6	74.7	75.2	75.4	76.2	74.5	74.2	74.2	73.2	73.9	75.9
Macau	N/A	N/A	N/A	N/A	N/A	N/A	N/A	N/A	N/A	N/A	N/A	N/A	N/A	N/A	72.0	72.5	73.1	71.8	71.7	71.3	70.3	70.1	70.7
Macedonia	N/A	N/A	N/A	N/A	N/A	N/A	N/A	58.0	60.1	56.8	56.1	59.2	60.6	61.1	61.2	65.7	66.0	68.5	68.2	68.6	67.1	67.5	70.7
Madagascar	51.6	52.2	53.8	51.8	52.8	54.4	53.9	56.8	62.8	60.9	63.1	61.0	61.1	62.4	62.2	63.2	61.2	62.4	62.0	61.7	61.7	61.1	57.4
Malawi	54.7	56.2	53.4	54.1	54.0	57.4	56.2	56.9	53.2	53.6	53.6	55.4	52.9	52.7	53.7	54.1	55.8	56.4	55.3	55.4	54.8	51.8	52.2
Malaysia	71.9	69.9	66.8	68.2	68.9	66.0	60.2	60.1	61.1	59.9	61.9	61.6	63.8	63.9	64.6	64.8	66.3	66.4	66.1	69.6	70.8	71.5	73.8
Maldives	N/A	N/A	N/A	N/A	N/A	N/A	N/A	N/A	N/A	N/A	N/A	N/A	N/A	N/A	51.3	49.0	48.3	49.2	49.0	51.0	53.4	53.9	50.3
Mali	52.4	57.0	56.4	57.3	58.4	60.3	60.1	61.1	58.6	56.6	57.3	54.1	54.7	55.6	55.6	55.6	56.3	55.8	56.4	55.5	56.4	56.5	58.6
Malta	56.3	55.8	57.9	61.2	59.3	58.3	62.9	62.2	61.1	63.3	68.9	67.3	66.1	66.0	66.1	67.2	65.7	67.0	67.5	66.4	66.5	66.7	67.7
Mauritania	N/A	45.5	47.0	43.7	42.8	46.0	48.5	52.5	59.0	61.8	59.4	55.7	53.6	55.2	53.9	52.0	52.1	53.0	52.3	53.2	53.3	54.8	54.4
Mauritius	N/A	N/A	N/A	N/A	68.5	67.2	66.4	67.7	64.4	64.3	67.2	67.4	69.4	72.6	74.3	76.3	76.2	77.0	76.9	76.5	76.4	74.7	74.7
Mexico	63.1	61.2	57.1	57.9	58.5	59.3	60.6	63.0	65.3	66.0	65.2	64.7	66.0	66.2	65.8	68.3	67.8	65.3	67.0	66.8	66.8	65.2	63.6
Micronesia	N/A	N/A	N/A	N/A	N/A	N/A	N/A	N/A	N/A	N/A	N/A	N/A	N/A	N/A	51.7	50.6	50.3	50.7	50.1	49.8	49.6	51.8	54.1
Moldova	33.0	52.5	48.9	53.5	56.1	59.6	54.9	57.4	60.0	57.1	57.4	58.0	58.7	57.9	54.9	53.7	55.7	54.4	55.5	57.3	57.5	57.4	58.0
Mongolia	47.8	47.4	52.9	57.3	58.6	58.5	56.0	56.7	57.7	56.5	59.7	62.4	60.3	63.6	62.8	60.0	59.5	61.5	61.7	58.9	59.2	59.4	54.8
Montenegro	N/A	N/A	N/A	N/A	N/A	N/A	N/A	N/A	N/A	N/A	N/A	N/A	N/A	N/A	58.2	63.6	62.5	62.5	62.6	63.6	64.7	64.9	62.0
Morocco	62.8	64.3	64.7	61.1	63.8	63.2	63.9	59.0	57.8	56.7	52.2	51.5	56.4	55.6	57.7	59.2	59.6	60.2	59.6	58.3	60.1	61.3	61.5
Mozambique	45.5	48.4	44.0	43.0	48.9	52.2	59.2	57.7	58.6	57.2	54.6	51.9	54.7	55.4	55.7	56.0	56.8	57.1	55.0	55.0	54.8	53.2	49.9

Country	1995	1996	1997	1998	1999	2000	2001	2002	2003	2004	2005	2006	2007	2008	2009	2010	2011	2012	2013	2014	2015	2016	2017
Namibia	N/A	N/A	61.6	66.1	66.1	66.7	64.8	65.1	67.3	62.4	61.4	60.7	63.5	61.4	62.4	62.2	62.7	61.9	60.3	59.4	59.6	61.9	62.5
Nepal	N/A	50.3	53.6	53.5	53.1	51.3	51.6	52.3	51.5	51.2	51.4	53.7	54.4	54.1	53.2	52.7	50.1	50.2	50.4	50.1	51.3	50.9	55.1
Netherlands	N/A	69.7	70.4	69.2	70.2	70.4	73.0	75.1	74.6	74.5	72.9	75.4	75.5	77.4	77.0	75.0	74.7	73.3	73.5	74.2	73.7	74.6	75.8
New Zealand	N/A	78.1	79.0	79.2	81.7	80.9	81.1	80.7	81.1	81.5	82.3	82.0	81.4	80.7	82.0	82.1	82.3	82.1	81.4	81.2	82.1	81.6	83.7
Nicaragua	42.5	54.1	53.3	53.8	54.0	56.9	58.0	61.1	62.6	61.4	62.5	63.8	62.7	60.8	59.8	58.3	58.8	57.9	56.6	58.4	57.6	58.6	59.2
Niger	N/A	45.8	46.6	47.5	48.6	45.9	48.9	48.2	54.2	54.6	54.1	52.5	53.2	52.9	53.8	52.9	54.3	54.3	53.9	55.1	54.6	54.3	50.8
Nigeria	47.3	47.4	52.8	52.3	55.7	53.1	49.6	50.9	49.5	49.2	48.4	48.7	55.6	55.1	55.1	56.8	56.7	56.3	55.1	54.3	55.6	57.5	57.1
Norway	N/A	65.4	65.1	68.0	68.6	70.1	67.1	67.4	67.2	66.2	64.5	67.9	67.9	68.6	70.2	69.4	70.3	68.8	70.5	70.9	71.8	70.8	74.0
Oman	70.2	65.4	64.5	64.9	64.9	64.1	67.7	64.0	64.6	66.9	66.5	63.7	65.8	67.3	67.0	67.7	69.8	67.9	68.1	67.4	66.7	67.1	62.1
Pakistan	57.6	58.4	56.0	53.2	53.0	56.4	56.0	55.8	55.0	54.9	53.3	57.9	57.2	55.6	57.0	55.2	55.1	54.7	55.1	55.2	55.6	55.9	52.8
Panama	71.6	71.8	72.4	72.6	72.6	71.6	70.6	68.5	68.4	65.3	64.3	65.6	64.6	64.7	64.7	64.8	64.9	65.2	62.5	63.4	64.1	64.8	66.3
Papua New Guinea	N/A	58.6	56.7	55.2	56.3	55.8	57.2	N/A	N/A	N/A	N/A	N/A	N/A	N/A	54.8	53.5	52.6	53.8	53.6	53.9	53.1	53.2	50.9
Paraguay	65.9	67.1	67.3	65.2	63.7	64.0	60.3	59.6	58.2	56.7	53.4	55.6	58.3	60.0	61.0	61.3	62.3	61.8	61.1	62.0	61.1	61.5	62.4
Peru	56.9	62.5	63.8	65.0	69.2	68.7	69.6	64.8	64.6	64.7	61.3	60.5	62.7	63.8	64.6	67.6	68.6	68.7	68.2	67.4	67.7	67.4	68.9
Philippines	55.0	60.2	62.2	62.8	61.9	62.5	60.9	60.7	61.3	59.1	54.7	56.3	56.0	56.0	56.8	56.3	56.2	57.1	58.2	60.1	62.2	63.1	65.6
Poland	50.7	57.8	56.8	59.2	59.6	60.0	61.8	65.0	61.8	58.7	59.6	59.3	58.1	60.3	60.3	63.2	64.1	64.2	66.0	67.0	68.6	69.3	68.3
Portugal	62.4	64.5	63.6	65.0	65.6	65.5	66.0	65.4	64.9	64.9	62.4	62.9	64.0	63.9	64.9	64.4	64.0	63.0	63.1	63.5	65.3	65.1	62.6
Qatar	N/A	N/A	N/A	N/A	62.0	62.0	60.0	61.9	65.9	66.5	63.5	62.4	62.9	62.2	65.8	69.0	70.5	71.3	71.3	71.2	70.8	70.7	73.1
Romania	42.9	46.2	50.8	54.4	50.1	52.1	50.0	48.7	50.6	50.0	52.1	58.2	61.2	61.7	63.2	64.2	64.7	64.4	65.1	65.5	66.6	65.6	69.7
Russia	51.1	51.6	48.6	52.8	54.5	51.8	49.8	48.7	50.8	52.8	51.3	52.4	52.2	49.8	50.8	50.3	50.5	50.5	51.1	51.9	52.1	50.6	57.1
Rwanda	N/A	N/A	38.3	39.1	39.8	42.3	45.4	50.4	47.8	53.3	51.7	52.8	52.4	54.2	54.2	59.1	62.7	64.9	64.1	64.7	64.8	63.1	67.6
Saint Lucia	N/A	N/A	N/A	N/A	N/A	N/A	N/A	N/A	N/A	N/A	N/A	N/A	N/A	N/A	68.8	70.5	70.8	71.3	70.4	70.7	70.2	70.0	65.0
Saint Vincent and the Grenadines	N/A	N/A	N/A	N/A	N/A	N/A	N/A	N/A	N/A	N/A	N/A	N/A	N/A	N/A	64.3	66.9	66.9	66.5	66.7	67.0	68.0	68.8	65.2
Samoa	N/A	47.6	51.5	49.9	58.7	60.8	63.1	N/A	N/A	N/A	N/A	N/A	N/A	N/A	59.5	60.4	60.6	60.5	57.1	61.1	61.9	63.5	58.4
São Tomé and Príncipe	N/A	N/A	N/A	N/A	N/A	N/A	N/A	N/A	N/A	N/A	N/A	N/A	N/A	N/A	43.8	48.8	49.5	50.2	48.0	48.8	53.3	56.7	55.4
Saudi Arabia	N/A	68.3	68.7	69.3	65.5	66.5	62.2	65.3	63.2	60.4	63.0	63.0	60.9	62.5	64.3	64.1	66.2	62.5	60.6	62.2	62.1	62.1	64.4
Senegal	N/A	58.2	58.1	59.7	60.6	58.9	58.7	58.6	58.1	58.9	57.9	56.2	58.1	58.3	56.3	54.6	55.7	55.4	55.5	55.4	57.8	58.1	55.9
Serbia	N/A	N/A	N/A	N/A	N/A	N/A	N/A	46.6	43.5	N/A	N/A	N/A	N/A	N/A	56.6	56.9	58.0	58.0	58.6	59.4	60.0	62.1	58.9

INDEX OF ECONOMIC FREEDOM SCORES, 1995–2017

Country	1995	1996	1997	1998	1999	2000	2001	2002	2003	2004	2005	2006	2007	2008	2009	2010	2011	2012	2013	2014	2015	2016	2017
Seychelles	N/A	N/A	N/A	N/A	N/A	N/A	N/A	N/A	N/A	N/A	N/A	N/A	N/A	N/A	47.8	47.9	51.2	53.0	54.9	56.2	57.5	62.2	61.8
Sierra Leone	49.8	52.3	45.0	47.7	47.2	44.2	N/A	N/A	42.2	43.6	44.8	45.2	47.0	48.3	47.8	47.9	49.6	49.1	48.3	50.5	51.7	52.3	52.6
Singapore	86.3	86.5	87.3	87.0	86.9	87.7	87.8	87.4	88.2	88.9	88.6	88.0	87.1	87.3	87.1	86.1	87.2	87.5	88.0	89.4	89.4	87.8	88.6
Slovak Republic	60.4	57.6	55.5	57.5	54.2	53.8	58.5	59.8	59.0	64.6	66.8	69.8	69.6	70.0	69.4	69.7	69.5	67.0	68.7	66.4	67.2	66.6	65.7
Slovenia	N/A	50.4	55.6	60.7	61.3	58.3	61.8	57.8	57.7	59.2	59.6	61.9	59.6	60.2	62.9	64.7	64.6	62.9	61.7	62.7	60.3	60.6	59.2
Solomon Islands	N/A	N/A	N/A	N/A	N/A	N/A	N/A	N/A	N/A	N/A	N/A	N/A	N/A	N/A	46.0	42.9	45.9	46.2	45.0	46.2	47.0	47.0	55.0
Somalia	N/A	25.6	25.6	27.8	27.8	27.8	N/A	N/A	N/A	N/A	N/A	N/A	N/A	N/A	N/A	N/A	N/A	N/A	N/A	N/A	N/A	N/A	N/A
South Africa	60.7	62.5	63.2	64.3	63.3	63.7	63.8	64.0	67.1	66.3	62.9	63.7	63.5	63.4	63.8	62.8	62.7	62.7	61.8	62.5	62.6	61.9	62.3
Spain	62.8	59.6	59.6	62.6	65.1	65.9	68.1	68.8	68.8	68.9	67.0	68.2	69.2	69.1	70.1	69.6	70.2	69.1	68.0	67.2	67.6	68.5	63.6
Sri Lanka	60.6	62.5	65.5	64.6	64.0	63.2	66.0	64.0	62.5	61.6	61.0	58.7	59.4	58.4	56.0	54.6	57.1	58.3	60.7	60.0	58.6	59.9	57.4
Sudan	39.4	39.2	39.9	38.3	39.6	47.2	N/A	N/A	N/A	N/A	N/A	N/A	N/A	N/A	N/A	N/A	N/A	N/A	N/A	N/A	N/A	N/A	48.8
Suriname	N/A	36.7	35.9	39.9	40.1	45.8	44.3	48.0	46.9	47.9	51.9	55.1	54.8	54.3	54.1	52.5	53.1	52.6	52.0	54.2	54.2	53.8	48.0
Swaziland	63.3	58.6	59.4	62.0	62.1	62.6	63.6	60.9	59.6	58.6	59.4	61.4	60.1	58.4	59.1	57.4	59.1	57.2	57.2	61.2	59.9	59.7	61.1
Sweden	61.4	61.8	63.3	64.0	64.2	65.1	66.6	70.8	70.0	70.1	69.8	70.9	69.3	70.8	70.5	72.4	71.9	71.7	72.9	73.1	72.7	72.0	74.9
Switzerland	N/A	76.8	78.6	79.0	79.1	76.8	76.0	79.3	79.0	79.5	79.3	78.9	78.0	79.5	79.4	81.1	81.9	81.1	81.0	81.6	80.5	81.0	81.5
Syria	N/A	42.3	43.0	42.2	39.0	37.2	36.6	36.3	41.3	40.6	46.3	51.2	48.3	47.2	51.3	49.4	51.3	51.2	N/A	N/A	N/A	N/A	N/A
Taiwan	74.2	74.1	70.0	70.4	71.5	72.5	72.8	71.3	71.7	69.6	71.3	69.7	69.4	70.3	69.5	70.4	70.8	71.9	72.7	73.9	75.1	74.7	76.5
Tajikistan	N/A	N/A	N/A	41.1	41.2	44.8	46.8	47.3	46.5	48.7	50.4	52.6	53.6	54.4	54.6	53.0	53.5	53.4	53.4	52.0	52.7	51.3	58.2
Tanzania	57.3	57.5	59.3	59.6	60.0	56.0	54.9	58.3	56.9	60.1	56.3	58.5	56.8	56.5	58.3	58.3	57.0	57.0	57.9	57.8	57.5	58.5	58.6
Thailand	71.3	71.0	66.1	67.3	66.9	66.6	68.9	69.1	65.8	63.7	62.5	63.3	63.5	62.3	63.0	64.1	64.7	64.9	64.1	63.3	62.4	63.9	66.2
Timor-Leste	N/A	N/A	N/A	N/A	N/A	N/A	N/A	N/A	N/A	N/A	N/A	N/A	N/A	N/A	50.5	45.8	42.8	43.3	43.7	43.2	45.5	45.8	46.3
Togo	N/A	N/A	N/A	N/A	48.2	46.4	45.3	45.2	46.8	47.0	48.2	47.3	49.7	48.9	48.7	47.1	49.1	48.3	48.8	49.9	53.0	53.6	53.2
Tonga	N/A	N/A	N/A	N/A	N/A	N/A	N/A	N/A	N/A	N/A	N/A	N/A	N/A	N/A	54.1	53.4	55.8	57.0	56.0	58.2	59.3	59.6	63.0
Trinidad and Tobago	N/A	69.2	71.3	72.0	72.4	74.5	71.8	70.1	68.8	71.3	71.5	70.4	70.6	69.5	68.0	65.7	66.5	64.4	62.3	62.7	64.1	62.9	61.2
Tunisia	63.4	63.9	63.8	63.9	61.1	61.3	60.8	60.2	58.1	58.4	55.4	57.5	60.3	60.1	58.0	58.9	58.5	58.6	57.0	57.3	57.7	57.6	55.7
Turkey	58.4	56.7	60.8	60.9	59.2	63.4	60.6	54.2	51.9	52.8	50.6	57.0	57.4	59.9	61.6	63.8	64.2	62.5	62.9	64.9	63.2	62.1	65.2
Turkmenistan	N/A	N/A	N/A	35.0	36.1	37.6	41.8	43.2	51.3	50.7	47.6	43.8	43.0	43.4	44.2	42.5	43.6	43.8	42.6	42.2	41.4	41.9	47.4
Uganda	62.9	66.2	66.6	64.7	64.8	58.2	60.4	61.0	60.1	64.1	62.9	63.9	63.1	63.8	63.5	62.2	61.7	61.9	61.1	59.9	59.7	59.3	60.9
Ukraine	39.9	40.6	43.5	40.4	43.7	47.8	48.5	48.2	51.1	53.7	55.8	54.4	51.5	51.0	48.8	46.4	45.8	46.1	46.3	49.3	46.9	46.8	48.1

Country	1995	1996	1997	1998	1999	2000	2001	2002	2003	2004	2005	2006	2007	2008	2009	2010	2011	2012	2013	2014	2015	2016	2017
United Arab Emirates	N/A	71.6	71.9	72.2	71.5	74.2	74.9	73.6	73.4	67.2	65.2	62.2	62.6	62.6	64.7	67.3	67.8	69.3	71.1	71.4	72.4	72.6	76.9
United Kingdom	77.9	76.4	76.4	76.5	76.2	77.3	77.6	78.5	77.5	77.7	79.2	80.4	79.9	79.4	79.0	76.5	74.5	74.1	74.8	74.9	75.8	76.4	76.4
United States	76.7	76.7	75.6	75.4	75.5	76.4	79.1	78.4	78.2	78.7	79.9	81.2	81.2	81.0	80.7	78.0	77.8	76.3	76.0	75.5	76.2	75.4	75.1
Uruguay	62.5	63.7	67.5	68.6	68.5	69.3	70.7	68.7	69.8	66.7	66.9	65.3	68.4	67.9	69.1	69.8	70.0	69.9	69.7	69.3	68.6	68.8	69.7
Uzbekistan	N/A	N/A	N/A	31.5	33.8	38.1	38.2	38.5	38.3	39.1	45.8	48.7	51.5	51.9	50.5	47.5	45.8	45.8	46.0	46.5	47.0	46.0	52.3
Vanuatu	N/A	N/A	N/A	N/A	N/A	N/A	N/A	N/A	N/A	N/A	N/A	N/A	N/A	N/A	58.4	56.4	56.7	56.6	56.6	59.5	61.1	60.8	67.4
Venezuela	59.8	54.5	52.8	54.0	56.1	57.4	54.6	54.7	54.8	46.7	45.2	44.6	47.9	44.7	39.9	37.1	37.6	38.1	36.1	36.3	34.3	33.7	27.0
Vietnam	41.7	40.2	38.6	40.4	42.7	43.7	44.3	45.6	46.2	46.1	48.1	50.5	49.8	50.4	51.0	49.8	51.6	51.3	51.0	50.8	51.7	54.0	52.4
Yemen	49.8	49.6	48.4	46.1	43.3	44.5	44.3	48.6	50.3	50.5	53.8	52.6	54.1	53.8	56.9	54.4	54.2	55.3	55.9	55.5	53.7	N/A	N/A
Zambia	55.1	59.6	62.1	62.7	64.2	62.8	59.5	59.6	55.3	54.9	55.0	56.8	56.2	56.2	56.6	58.0	59.7	58.3	58.7	60.4	58.7	58.8	55.8
Zimbabwe	48.5	46.7	48.0	44.6	47.2	48.7	38.8	36.7	36.7	34.4	35.2	33.5	32.0	29.5	22.7	21.4	22.1	26.3	28.6	35.5	37.6	38.2	44.0

METHODOLOGY

The *Index of Economic Freedom* focuses on four key aspects of the economic environment over which governments typically exercise policy control:

- **Rule of law,**
- **Government size,**
- **Regulatory efficiency**, and
- **Market openness.**

In assessing conditions in these four categories, the *Index* measures 12 specific components of economic freedom, each of which is graded on a scale from 0 to 100. Scores on these 12 components of economic freedom, which are calculated from a number of sub-variables, are equally weighted and averaged to produce an overall economic freedom score for each economy.

The following sections provide detailed descriptions of the formulas and methodology used to compute the scores for each of the 12 components of economic freedom.

RULE OF LAW

Property Rights

The property rights component assesses the extent to which a country's legal framework allows individuals to freely accumulate private property, secured by clear laws that are enforced effectively by the government. Relying on a mix of survey data and independent assessments, it provides a quantifiable measure of the degree to which a country's laws protect private property rights and the extent to which those laws are respected. It also assesses the likelihood that private property will be expropriated by the state.

The more effective the legal protection of property, the higher a country's score will be. Similarly, the greater the chances of government expropriation of property, the lower a country's score will be.

The score for this component is derived by averaging scores for the following five sub-factors, all of which are weighted equally:

- Physical property rights,
- Intellectual property rights,
- Strength of investor protection,
- Risk of expropriation, and
- Quality of land administration.

Each of these sub-factors is derived from numerical data sets that are normalized for comparative purposes using the following equation:

$$\text{Sub-factor Score } i = 100(\text{Sub-factorMax} - \text{Sub-factor}i)/(\text{Sub-factorMax} - \text{Sub-factorMin})$$

where Sub-factor*i* represents the original data for country *i*; Sub-factorMax and Sub-factorMin represent the upper and lower bounds for the corresponding data set; and Sub-factor Score *i* represents the computed sub-factor score for country *i*.

For a few countries, comparable data were not available for every sub-factor. In those cases, a score was computed for the missing sub-factor based on the relative percentile ranking of that country on the other sub-factors.

Sources. The *Index* relies on the following sources for assessing property rights: World Economic Forum, *World Competitiveness Report*; World Bank, *Doing Business*; and Credendo Group, *Country Risk Assessment*.

Judicial Effectiveness

Well-functioning legal frameworks are essential for protecting the rights of all citizens against unlawful acts by others, including by governments and powerful private parties. Judicial effectiveness requires efficient and fair judicial systems to ensure that laws are fully respected, with appropriate legal actions taken against violations. The score for the judicial effectiveness component is derived by averaging scores for the following three sub-factors, all of which are weighted equally:

- Judicial independence,
- Quality of the judicial process, and
- Likelihood of obtaining favorable judicial decisions.

Each of these sub-factors is derived from numerical data sets that are normalized for comparative purposes using the following equation:

$$\text{Sub-factor Score } i = 100(\text{Sub-factorMax} - \text{Sub-factor}i)/(\text{Sub-factorMax} - \text{Sub-factorMin})$$

where Sub-factor*i* represents the original data for country *i*; Sub-factorMax and Sub-factorMin represent the upper and lower bounds for the corresponding data set; and Sub-factor Score *i* represents the computed sub-factor score for country *i*.

For a few countries, comparable data were not available for every sub-factor. In each of these cases, a score was computed for the missing sub-factor based on the country's relative percentile ranking on the other sub-factors.

Sources. The *Index* relies on the following sources for assessing judicial effectiveness: World Economic Forum, *World Competitiveness Report*; World Bank, *Doing Business*.

Government Integrity

Corruption erodes economic freedom by introducing insecurity and uncertainty into economic relations. Of greatest concern is the systemic corruption of government institutions and decision-making by such practices as bribery, extortion, nepotism, cronyism, patronage, embezzlement, and graft. The lack of government integrity caused by such practices reduces economic vitality by increasing costs and shifting resources into unproductive lobbying activities.

The score for this component is derived by averaging scores for the following six sub-factors, all of which are weighted equally:

- Public trust in politicians,
- Irregular payments and bribes,
- Transparency of government policymaking,
- Absence of corruption,
- Perceptions of corruption, and
- Governmental and civil service transparency.

Each of these sub-factors is derived from numerical data sets that are normalized for comparative purposes using the following equation:

$$\text{Sub-factor Score } i = 100(\text{Sub-factorMax} - \text{Sub-factor}i)/(\text{Sub-factorMax} - \text{Sub-factorMin})$$

where Sub-factor$i$ represents the original data for country i; Sub-factorMax and Sub-factorMin represent the upper and lower bounds for the corresponding data set; and Sub-factor Score i represents the computed sub-factor score for country i.

For a few countries, comparable data were not available for every sub-factor. In each of these cases, a score was computed for the missing sub-factor based on the country's relative percentile ranking on the other sub-factors.

Sources. The *Index* relies on the following sources for assessing government integrity: World Economic Forum, *World Competitiveness Report*; World Justice Project, *Rule of Law Index*; Transparency International, *Corruption Perceptions Index*; TRACE International, *The Trace Matrix*.

GOVERNMENT SIZE

Tax Burden

Tax burden is a composite measure that reflects marginal tax rates on both personal and corporate income and the overall level of taxation (including direct and indirect taxes imposed by all levels of government) as a percentage of gross domestic product (GDP). The component score is derived from three quantitative sub-factors:

- The top marginal tax rate on individual income,
- The top marginal tax rate on corporate income, and
- The total tax burden as a percentage of GDP.

Each of these numerical variables is weighted equally as one-third of the component score. This equal weighting allows a country to achieve a score as high as 67 based on two of the factors even if it receives a score of 0 on the third.

Tax burden scores are calculated with a quadratic cost function to reflect the diminishing revenue returns from very high rates of taxation. The data for each sub-factor are converted to a 100-point scale using the following equation:

$$\text{Tax Burden}_{ij} = 100 - \alpha \, (\text{Factor}_{ij})^2$$

where Tax Burden$_{ij}$ represents the tax burden in country i for factor j; Factor$_{ij}$ represents the value (a percentage expressed on a scale of 0 to 100) in country i for factor j; and α is a coefficient set equal to 0.03. The minimum score for each sub-factor is zero, which is not represented in the printed equation but was utilized because it means that no single high tax burden will make the other two sub-factors irrelevant.

As an example, in the 2017 *Index*, Mauritius has a flat rate of 15 percent for both individual and corporate tax rates, which yields a score of 93.3 for each of the two factors. Mauritius's overall tax burden as a portion of GDP is 18.6 percent, yielding a tax burden factor score of 89.6. When the three factors are averaged together, Mauritius's overall tax burden score becomes 92.

Sources. The *Index* relies on the following sources for information on tax rate data, in order of priority: Deloitte, *International Tax and Business Guide Highlights*; International Monetary Fund, *Staff Country Report*, "Selected Issues and Statistical Appendix," and *Staff Country Report*, "Article IV Consultation"; PricewaterhouseCoopers, *Worldwide Tax Summaries*; countries' investment agencies; other government authorities (embassy confirmations and/or the country's treasury or tax authority); and Economist Intelligence Unit, *Country Commerce* and *Country Finance*.

For information on tax burden as a percentage of GDP, the primary sources are Organisation for Economic Co-operation and Development data; Eurostat, Government Finance Statistics data; African Development Bank and Organisation for Economic Co-operation and Development, *African Economic Outlook*; International Monetary Fund, *Staff Country Report*, "Selected Issues," and *Staff Country Report*, "Article IV Consultation"; Asian Development Bank, *Key Indicators for Asia and the Pacific*; United Nations Economic Commission for Latin America, *Economic Survey of Latin America and the Caribbean*; and individual contacts from government agencies and multinational organizations such as the IMF and the World Bank.

Government Spending

The government spending component captures the burden imposed by government expenditures, which includes consumption by the state and all transfer payments related to various entitlement programs.

No attempt has been made to identify an optimal level of government spending. The ideal level will vary from country to country, depending on factors that range from culture to geography to level of economic development. At some point, however, government spending becomes an unavoidable burden as growth in the size and scope of the public sector leads inevitably to misallocation of resources and loss of economic efficiency. Volumes of research have shown that excessive government spending that causes chronic budget deficits and the accumulation of public debt is one of the most serious drags on economic dynamism.

The *Index* methodology treats zero government spending as the benchmark. As a result, underdeveloped countries, particularly those with little government capacity, may receive artificially high scores. However, such governments, which can provide few if any public goods, are likely to receive low scores on some of the other components of economic freedom (such as property rights, financial freedom, and investment freedom) that measure aspects of government effectiveness.

Government spending has a major impact on economic freedom, but it is just one of many important components. The scale for scoring government spending is nonlinear, which means that government spending that is close to zero is lightly penalized, while levels of government spending that exceed 30 percent of GDP lead to much worse scores in a quadratic fashion (for example, doubling spending yields four times less freedom). Only extraordinarily large levels of government spending (for example, over 58 percent of GDP) receive a score of zero.

The equation used for computing a country's government spending score is:

$$GE_i = 100 - \alpha \, (Expenditures_i)^2$$

where GE_i represents the government expenditure score in country i; $Expenditures_i$ represents the average total government spending at all levels as a percentage of GDP for the most recent three years ; and α is a coefficient to control for variation among scores (set at 0.03). The minimum component score is zero.

In most cases, the *Index* uses general government expenditure data that include all levels of government such as federal, state, and local. In cases where data on general government spending are not available, data on central government expenditures are used instead.

Sources. The *Index* relies on the following sources for information on government intervention in the economy, in order of priority: Organisation for Economic Co-operation and Development data; Eurostat data; African Development Bank and Organisation for Economic Co-operation and Development, *African Economic Outlook*; International Monetary Fund, *Staff Country Report*, "Selected Issues and Statistical Appendix," *Staff Country Report*, "Article IV Consultation," and *World Economic Outlook Database*; Asian Development Bank, *Key Indicators for Asia and the Pacific*; African Development Bank, *The ADB Statistics Pocketbook*; official government publications of each country; and United Nations Economic Commission for Latin America, *Economic Survey of Latin America and the Caribbean.*

Fiscal Health

Widening deficits and a growing debt burden, both of which are caused by poor government budget management, lead to the erosion of a country's overall fiscal health. Deteriorating fiscal health, in turn, is associated with macroeconomic instability and economic uncertainty.

Debt is an accumulation of budget deficits over time. In theory, debt financing of public spending could make a positive contribution to productive investment and ultimately to economic growth. However, mounting public debt driven by persistent budget deficits, particularly spending that merely boosts government consumption or transfer payments, often undermines overall productivity growth and leads ultimately to economic stagnation rather than growth.

The score for the fiscal health component is based on two sub-factors, which are weighted as follows in calculating the overall component score:

- Average deficits as a percentage of GDP for the most recent three years (80 percent of score) and
- Debt as a percentage of GDP (20 percent of score).

The equation used for computing a country's fiscal health sub-factor scores is:

$$Sub\text{-}factor\ Score_i = 100 - \alpha \, (Sub\text{-}factor_i)^2$$

where Sub-factor Score$_i$ represents the deficit or debt score in country i; Sub-factor$_i$ represents the factor value as a portion of GDP; and α is a coefficient to control for variation among scores (set at 2 for deficit and 0.01 for debt). The minimum component score is zero.

In most cases, the *Index* uses general government deficit and debt data that include all levels of government such as federal, state, and local. In cases where such general government data are not available, data on central government expenditures are used instead.

Sources. The *Index* relies on the following sources for information on government intervention in the economy: International Monetary Fund, *World Economic Outlook Database, Staff Country Report,* "Selected Issues and Statistical Appendix," and *Staff Country Report,* "Article IV Consultation"; Asian Development Bank, *Key Indicators for Asia and the Pacific*; African Development Bank, *The ADB Statistics Pocketbook*; Economist Intelligence Unit, Data Tool; and official government publications of each country.

REGULATORY EFFICIENCY

Business Freedom

The business freedom component measures the extent to which the regulatory and infrastructure environments constrain the efficient operation of businesses. The quantitative score is derived from an array of factors that affect the ease of starting, operating, and closing a business.

The business freedom score for each country is a number between 0 and 100, with 100 indicating the freest business environment. The score is based on 13 sub-factors, all of which are weighted equally, using data from the World Bank's *Doing Business* report:

- Starting a business—procedures (number);
- Starting a business—time (days);
- Starting a business—cost (% of income per capita);
- Starting a business—minimum capital (% of income per capita);
- Obtaining a license—procedures (number);[1]
- Obtaining a license—time (days);
- Obtaining a license—cost (% of income per capita);
- Closing a business—time (years);
- Closing a business—cost (% of estate);
- Closing a business—recovery rate (cents on the dollar);
- Getting electricity—procedures (number);
- Getting electricity—time (days); and
- Getting electricity—cost (% of income per capita).[2]

Each of these sub-factors is converted to a scale of 0 to 100, after which the average of the converted values is computed. The result represents the country's business freedom score in comparison to the business freedom scores of other countries.

Each sub-factor is converted to a scale of 0 to 100 using the following equation:

$$\text{Sub-factor Score}_i = 50 \text{ Sub-factor}_{average}/\text{Sub-factor}_i$$

which is based on the ratio of the country data for each sub-factor relative to the world average, multiplied by 50. For example, on average worldwide, it takes 14 procedures to get necessary licenses. Canada's 12 licensing procedures are a sub-factor value that is better than the average, resulting in a ratio of 1.17. That ratio multiplied by 50 equals the final sub-factor score of 58.3.

For the six countries that are not covered by the World Bank's *Doing Business* report, business freedom is scored by analyzing business regulations based on qualitative information from reliable and internationally recognized sources.[3]

Sources. The *Index* relies on the following sources in determining business freedom scores, in order of priority: World Bank, *Doing Business*; Economist Intelligence Unit, *Country*

Commerce; U.S. Department of Commerce, *Country Commercial Guide*; and official government publications of each country.

Labor Freedom

The labor freedom component is a quantitative measure that considers various aspects of the legal and regulatory framework of a country's labor market, including regulations concerning minimum wages, laws inhibiting layoffs, severance requirements, and measurable regulatory restraints on hiring and hours worked, plus the labor force participation rate as an indicative measure of employment opportunities in the labor market.[4]

Seven quantitative sub-factors are equally weighted, with each counted as one-seventh of the labor freedom component:[5]

- Ratio of minimum wage to the average value added per worker,
- Hindrance to hiring additional workers,
- Rigidity of hours,
- Difficulty of firing redundant employees,
- Legally mandated notice period,
- Mandatory severance pay, and
- Labor force participation rate.

In constructing the labor freedom score, each of the seven sub-factors is converted to a scale of 0 to 100 based on the following equation:

$$\text{Sub-factor Score}_i = 50 \, \text{Sub-factor}_{average}/\text{Sub-factor}_i$$

where country *i* data are calculated relative to the world average and then multiplied by 50. The seven sub-factor scores are then averaged for each country, yielding an overall labor freedom score.

For the six countries that are not covered by the World Bank's *Doing Business* report, the labor freedom component is scored by looking at labor market flexibility based on qualitative information from other reliable and internationally recognized sources.[6]

Sources. The *Index* relies on the following sources for data on labor freedom, in order of priority: World Bank, *Doing Business*; International Labour Organization, *Statistics and Databases*; World Bank, *World Development Indicators*; Economist Intelligence Unit, *Country Commerce*; U.S. Department of Commerce, *Country Commercial Guide*; and official government publications of each country.

Monetary Freedom

Monetary freedom combines a measure of price stability with an assessment of price controls. Both inflation and price controls distort market activity. Price stability without sector-specific government intervention is the ideal state for the free market.

The score for the monetary freedom component is based on two sub-factors:

- The weighted average inflation rate for the most recent three years and
- Price controls.

The weighted average inflation rate for the most recent three years serves as the primary input into an equation that generates the base score for monetary freedom. The extent of price controls is then assessed as a penalty deduction of up to 20 points from the base score. The two equations used to convert inflation rates into the final monetary freedom score are:

$$\text{Weighted Avg. Inflation}_i = \theta_1 \text{Inflation}_{it} + \theta_2 \text{Inflation}_{it-1} + \theta_3 \text{Inflation}_{it-2}$$

$$\text{Monetary Freedom}_i = 100 - \alpha \sqrt{\text{Weighted Avg. Inflation}_i} - \text{PC penalty}_i$$

where θ_1 through θ_3 (thetas 1–3) represent three numbers that sum to 1 and are exponentially smaller in sequence (in this case, values of 0.665, 0.245, and 0.090, respectively); Inflation_{it} is the absolute value of the annual inflation rate in country i during year t as measured by the Consumer Price Index; α represents a coefficient that stabilizes the variance of scores; and the price control (PC) penalty is an assigned value of 0–20 penalty points based on the extent of price controls.

The convex (square root) functional form was chosen to create separation among countries with low inflation rates. A concave functional form would essentially treat all hyperinflations as equally bad, whether they were 100 percent price increases annually or 100,000 percent, whereas the square root provides much more gradation. The α coefficient is set to equal 6.333, which converts a 10 percent inflation rate into a freedom score of 80.0 and a 2 percent inflation rate into a score of 91.0.

Sources. The *Index* relies on the following sources for data on monetary policy, in order of priority: International Monetary Fund, *International Financial Statistics Online*; International Monetary Fund, *World Economic Outlook* and *Staff Country Report*, "Article IV Consultation"; Economist Intelligence Unit, *ViewsWire* and Data Tool; various World Bank country reports and blogs; various news and magazine articles; and official government publications of each country.

OPEN MARKETS

Trade Freedom

Trade freedom is a composite measure of the extent of tariff and nontariff barriers that affect imports and exports of goods and services. The trade freedom score is based on two inputs:

- The trade-weighted average tariff rate and
- Nontariff barriers (NTBs).

Different imports entering a country can (and often do) face different tariffs. The weighted average tariff uses weights for each tariff based on the share of imports for each good. Weighted average tariffs are a purely quantitative measure and account for the calculation of the base trade freedom score using the following equation:

$$\text{Trade Freedom}_i = 100(\text{Tariff}_{max} - \text{Tariff}_i)/(\text{Tariff}_{max} - \text{Tariff}_{min}) - \text{NTB}_i$$

where Trade Freedom_i represents the trade freedom in country i; Tariff_{max} and Tariff_{min} represent the upper and lower bounds for tariff rates (%); and Tariff_i represents the weighted average tariff rate (%) in country i. The minimum tariff is naturally zero percent, and the upper bound was set as 50 percent. An NTB penalty is then subtracted from the base score. The penalty of 5, 10, 15, or 20 points is assigned according to the following scale:

- **20**—NTBs are used extensively across many goods and services and/or act to impede a significant amount of international trade.
- **15**—NTBs are widespread across many goods and services and/or act to impede a majority of potential international trade.
- **10**—NTBs are used to protect certain goods and services and impede some international trade.
- **5**—NTBs are uncommon, protecting few goods and services, and/or have a very limited impact on international trade.
- **0**—NTBs are not used to limit international trade.

We determine the extent of NTBs in a country's trade policy regime using both qualitative and quantitative information. Restrictive rules that hinder trade vary widely, and their overlapping and shifting nature makes their complexity difficult to gauge. The categories of NTBs considered in our penalty include:

- **Quantity restrictions**—import quotas; export limitations; voluntary export restraints; import–export embargoes and bans; countertrade; etc.
- **Price restrictions**—antidumping duties; countervailing duties; border tax adjustments; variable levies/tariff rate quotas.
- **Regulatory restrictions**—licensing; domestic content and mixing requirements; sanitary and phytosanitary standards (SPSs); safety and industrial standards regulations; packaging, labeling, and trademark regulations; advertising and media regulations.
- **Customs restrictions**—advance deposit requirements; customs valuation procedures; customs classification procedures; customs clearance procedures.
- **Direct government intervention**—subsidies and other aid; government industrial policies; government-financed research and other technology policies; competition policies; government procurement policies; state trading, government monopolies, and exclusive franchises.

As an example, Bahrain received a trade freedom score of 82.8. By itself, Bahrain's trade-weighted average tariff of 3.6 percent would have yielded a score of 92.8, but the existence of NTBs in Bahrain reduced its score by 10 points.

Gathering tariff statistics to make a consistent cross-country comparison is a challenging task. Unlike data on inflation, for instance, some countries do not report their weighted average tariff rate or simple average tariff rate every year.

To preserve consistency in grading the trade freedom component, the *Index* uses the most recently reported weighted average tariff rate for a country from our primary source. If another reliable source reports more updated information on the country's tariff rate, this fact is noted, and the grading of this component may be reviewed if there is strong evidence that the most recently reported weighted average tariff rate is outdated.

The most comprehensive and consistent information on weighted average applied tariff rates is published by the World Bank. When the weighted average applied tariff rate is not available, the *Index* uses the country's average applied tariff rate; and when the country's average applied tariff rate is not available, the weighted average or the simple average of most favored nation (MFN) tariff rates is used.[7] In the very few cases where data on duties and customs revenues are not available, data on international trade taxes or an estimated effective tariff rate are used instead. In all cases, an effort is made to clarify the type of data used in the corresponding write-up for the trade freedom component.

Sources. The *Index* relies on the following sources to determine scores for trade policy, in order of priority: World Bank, *World Development Indicators*; World Trade Organization, *Trade Policy Review*; Office of the U.S. Trade Representative, *National Trade Estimate Report on Foreign Trade Barriers*; World Bank, *Doing Business*; U.S. Department of Commerce, *Country Commercial Guide*; Economist Intelligence Unit, *Country Commerce*; World Economic Forum, *The Global Enabling Trade Report*; and official government publications of each country.

Investment Freedom

In an economically free country, there would be no constraints on the flow of investment capital. Individuals and firms would be allowed to move their resources into and out of specific activities, both internally and across the country's borders, without restriction. Such an ideal country would receive a score of 100 on the investment freedom component of the *Index*.

In practice, however, most countries have a variety of restrictions on investment. Some have different rules for foreign and domestic investment. Some restrict access to foreign exchange. Some impose restrictions on payments, transfers, and capital transactions. In some, certain industries are closed to foreign investment.

The *Index* evaluates a variety of regulatory restrictions that typically are imposed on investment. Points, as indicated below, are deducted from the ideal score of 100 for each of the restrictions found in a country's investment regime. It is not necessary for a government to impose all of the listed restrictions at the maximum level to eliminate investment freedom. The few governments that impose so many restrictions that they total more than 100 points in deductions have had their scores set at zero.

Investment Restrictions

National treatment of foreign investment
- No national treatment, prescreening   25 points deducted
- Some national treatment, some prescreening   15 points deducted
- Some national treatment or prescreening   5 points deducted

Foreign investment code
- No transparency and burdensome bureaucracy   20 points deducted
- Inefficient policy implementation and bureaucracy   10 points deducted
- Some investment laws and practices nontransparent
  or inefficiently implemented   5 points deducted

Restrictions on land ownership
- All real estate purchases restricted   15 points deducted
- No foreign purchases of real estate   10 points deducted
- Some restrictions on purchases of real estate   5 points deducted

Sectoral investment restrictions
- Multiple sectors restricted   20 points deducted
- Few sectors restricted   10 points deducted
- One or two sectors restricted   5 points deducted

Expropriation of investments without fair compensation
- Common with no legal recourse   25 points deducted
- Common with some legal recourse   15 points deducted
- Uncommon but occurs   5 points deducted

Foreign exchange controls
- No access by foreigners or residents   25 points deducted
- Access available but heavily restricted   15 points deducted
- Access available with few restrictions   5 points deducted

Capital controls
- No repatriation of profits; all transactions require government approval   25 points deducted
- Inward and outward capital movements require approval and face some restrictions   15 points deducted
- Most transfers approved with some restrictions   5 points deducted

Up to an additional 20 points may be deducted for security problems, a lack of basic investment infrastructure, or other government policies that indirectly burden the investment process and limit investment freedom.

Sources. The *Index* relies on the following sources for data on capital flows and foreign investment, in order of priority: official government publications of each country; U.S. Department of State, *Investment Climate Statements*; Economist Intelligence Unit, *Country Commerce*; Office of the U.S. Trade Representative, *National Trade Estimate Report on Foreign Trade Barriers*; World Bank, *Investing Across Borders*; Organisation for Economic Co-operation and Development, *Services Trade Restrictiveness Index*; and U.S. Department of Commerce, *Country Commercial Guide*.

Financial Freedom

Financial freedom is an indicator of banking efficiency as well as a measure of independence from government control and interference in the financial sector. State ownership of banks and other financial institutions such as insurers and capital markets reduces competition and generally lowers the level of access to credit.

In an ideal banking and financing environment characterized by a minimum level of government interference, independent central bank supervision and regulation of financial institutions are limited to enforcing contractual obligations and preventing fraud. Credit is allocated on market terms, and the government does not own financial institutions. Financial institutions provide various types of financial services to individuals and companies. Banks are free to extend credit, accept deposits, and conduct operations in foreign currencies. Foreign financial institutions operate freely and are treated the same as domestic institutions.

The *Index* scores an economy's financial freedom by looking at five broad areas:

- The extent of government regulation of financial services,
- The degree of state intervention in banks and other financial firms through direct and indirect ownership,
- Government influence on the allocation of credit,
- The extent of financial and capital market development, and
- Openness to foreign competition.

These five areas are considered to assess an economy's overall level of financial freedom that ensures easy and effective access to financing opportunities for people and businesses in the economy. An overall score on a scale of 0 to 100 is given to an economy's financial freedom through deductions from the ideal score of 100.

- **90—Minimal government interference.** Regulation of financial institutions is minimal but may extend beyond enforcing contractual obligations and preventing fraud.
- **80—Nominal government interference.** Government ownership of financial institutions is a small share of overall sector assets. Financial institutions face almost no restrictions on their ability to offer financial services.
- **70—Limited government interference.** Credit allocation is influenced by the government, and private allocation of credit faces almost no restrictions. Government ownership of financial institutions is sizeable. Foreign financial institutions are subject to few restrictions.
- **60—Moderate government interference.** Banking and financial regulations are somewhat burdensome. The government exercises ownership and control of financial institutions with a significant share of overall sector assets. The ability of financial institutions to offer financial services is subject to some restrictions.
- **50—Considerable government interference.** Credit allocation is significantly influenced by the government, and private allocation of credit faces significant barriers. The ability of financial institutions to offer financial services is subject to significant restrictions. Foreign financial institutions are subject to some restrictions.
- **40—Strong government interference.** The central bank is subject to government influence, its supervision of financial institutions is heavy-handed, and its ability to enforce contracts and prevent fraud is weak. The government exercises active ownership and control of financial institutions with a large minority share of overall sector assets.
- **30—Extensive government interference.** Credit allocation is influenced extensively by the government. The government owns or controls a majority of financial institutions or is in a dominant position. Financial institutions are heavily restricted, and bank formation faces significant barriers. Foreign financial institutions are subject to significant restrictions.
- **20—Heavy government interference.** The central bank is not independent, and its supervision of financial institutions is repressive. Foreign financial institutions are discouraged or highly constrained.
- **10—Near-repressive.** Credit allocation is controlled by the government. Bank formation is restricted. Foreign financial institutions are prohibited.
- **0—Repressive.** Supervision and regulation are designed to prevent private financial institutions from functioning. Private financial institutions are nonexistent.

Sources. The *Index* relies on the following sources for data on banking and finance, in order of priority: Economist Intelligence Unit, *Country Commerce* and *Country Finance*; International Monetary Fund, *Staff Country Report*, "Selected Issues," and *Staff Country Report*, "Article IV Consultation"; Organisation for Economic Co-operation and Development, *Economic Survey*; official government publications of each country; U.S. Department of Commerce, *Country Commercial Guide*; Office of the U.S. Trade Representative, *National Trade Estimate Report on Foreign Trade Barriers*; U.S. Department of State, *Investment Climate Statements*; World Bank, *World Development Indicators*; and various news and magazine articles on banking and finance.

GENERAL METHODOLOGICAL PARAMETERS

Period of Study. For the current *Index of Economic Freedom*, scores are generally based on data for the period covering the second half of 2015 through the first half of 2016. To the extent possible, the information considered for each variable was current as of June 30, 2016. It is important to understand, however, that some component scores are based on historical information. For example, the monetary freedom component uses a three-year weighted average rate of inflation from January 1, 2013, to December 31, 2015.

Equal Weight. In the *Index of Economic Freedom*, the 12 components of economic freedom are weighted equally so that the overall score will not be biased toward any one component or policy direction. It is clear that the 12 economic freedoms interact, but the exact mechanisms of this interaction are not clearly definable: Is a minimum threshold for each one essential? Is it possible for one to maximize if others are minimized? Are they dependent or exclusive, complements or supplements?

These are valid questions, but they are beyond the scope of our fundamental mission. The purpose of the *Index* is to reflect the economic and entrepreneurial environment in every country studied in as balanced a way as possible. The *Index* has never been designed specifically to explain economic growth or any other dependent variable; that is ably done by researchers elsewhere. The raw data for each component are provided so that others can study, weight, and integrate as they see fit.

Using the Most Currently Available Information. Analyzing economic freedom annually enables the *Index* to include the most recent information as it becomes available country by country. A data cutoff date is used so that all countries are treated fairly. As described above, the period of study for the current year's *Index* considers all information as of the last day of June of the previous year (in this case, June 30, 2016). Any new legislative changes or policy actions effective after that date have no positive or negative impact on scores or rankings.[8]

DEFINING THE COUNTRY PAGES' "QUICK FACTS"

Each country page includes "Quick Facts," a statistical profile including the country's main economic and demographic indicators. In order to facilitate comparisons among countries, the GDP and GDP per capita figures in the "Quick Facts" section have been adjusted to reflect purchasing power parity (PPP). Caution should be used interpreting changes in these figures over time, as PPP conversion rates are subject to regular revision by the IMF and World Bank. In order to provide accurate estimates of annual and five-year GDP growth rates, these figures have been calculated using constant U.S. dollars for the most recent available years. Exact definitions and sources for each category of data reported are as follows:

Population: 2015 data from World Bank, *World Development Indicators Online*. For some countries, other sources include the country's statistical agency and/or central bank.

GDP: Gross domestic product (total production of goods and services) adjusted to reflect purchasing power parity. The primary source is International Monetary Fund, *World Economic Outlook Database, 2016*. The secondary source for GDP data is World Bank, *World Development Indicators Online*. Other sources include a country's statistical agency and/or central bank.

GDP growth rate: The annual percentage growth rate of real GDP derived from constant currency units. Annual percent changes are year-on-year. The primary source is International Monetary Fund, *World Economic Outlook Database, 2016*. Secondary sources include World Bank, *World Development Indicators Online*; Economist Intelligence Unit, Data Tool; and a country's statistical agency and/or central bank.

GDP five-year average annual growth: The average growth rate measured over a specified period of time. The five-year annual growth rate is measured using data from 2011 to 2015, based on real GDP growth rates. The primary source is International Monetary Fund, *World Economic Outlook Database, 2016*. Secondary sources are World Bank, *World Development Indicators Online*, and Economist Intelligence Unit, Data Tool.

GDP per capita: Gross domestic product (adjusted for PPP) divided by total population. The sources for these data are International Monetary Fund, *World Economic Outlook Database*, 2016; World Bank, *World Development Indicators Online*; U.S. Central Intelligence Agency, *The World Factbook 2016*; and a country's statistical agency and/or central bank.

Unemployment rate: A measure of the portion of the workforce that is not employed but is actively seeking work. Data are from International Labour Organization, *Global Employment Trends 2016*.

Inflation: The annual percent change in consumer prices as measured for 2015 (or the most recent available year). The primary source for 2015 data is International Monetary Fund, *World Economic Outlook Database, 2016*. Secondary sources are Economist Intelligence Unit, Data Tool; Asian Development Bank, *Asian Development Outlook 2016*; and a country's statistical agency and/or central bank.

Foreign direct investment (FDI) inward flow: The total annual inward flow of FDI in current 2015 U.S. dollars, reported in millions. FDI flows are defined as investments that acquire a lasting management interest (10 percent or more of voting stock) in a local enterprise by an investor operating in another country. Such investment is the sum of equity capital, reinvestment of earnings, other long-term capital, and short-term capital as shown in the balance of payments and both short-term and long-term international loans. Data are from United Nations Conference on Trade and Development, *World Investment Report 2016*.

Public debt: Gross government debt as a percentage of GDP, which indicates the cumulative total of all government borrowings less repayments that are denominated in a country's currency. Public debt is different from external debt, which reflects the foreign currency liabilities of both the private and public sectors and must be financed out of foreign exchange earnings. The primary sources for 2015 data are International Monetary Fund, *World Economic Outlook Database, 2016*; International Monetary Fund, *Article IV Staff Reports*, 2013–2016; and a country's statistical agency.

COMMONLY USED ACRONYMS

CARICOM: Caribbean Community and Common Market, composed of Antigua and Barbuda, the Bahamas, Barbados, Belize, Dominica, Grenada, Guyana, Haiti, Jamaica, Montserrat, Saint Lucia, Saint Kitts and Nevis, Saint Vincent and the Grenadines, Suriname, and Trinidad and Tobago.

CEMAC: Central African Economic and Monetary Community, which includes Cameroon, the Central African Republic, Chad, the Republic of Congo, Equatorial Guinea, and Gabon.

EU: European Union, consisting of Austria, Belgium, Bulgaria, Cyprus, Croatia, the Czech Republic, Denmark, Estonia, Finland, France, Germany, Greece, Hungary, Ireland, Italy, Latvia, Lithuania, Luxembourg, Malta, the Netherlands, Poland, Portugal, Romania, Slovakia, Slovenia, Spain, and Sweden.

IMF: International Monetary Fund, established in 1945 to help stabilize countries during crises; now includes 188 member countries.

OECD: Organisation for Economic Co-operation and Development, an international organization of developed countries, founded in 1948; now includes 34 member countries.

SACU: Southern African Customs Union, consisting of Botswana, Lesotho, Namibia, South Africa, and Swaziland.

WTO: World Trade Organization, founded in 1995 as the central organization dealing with the rules of trade between nations and based on signed agreements among member countries. As of November 2016, there were 164 member economies.

ENDNOTES:

1. Obtaining a license indicates necessary procedures, time, and cost in getting construction permits.

2. Infrastructure services such as roads, water, and power supplies are critical to the overall business climate of an economy. Among the key infrastructures, according to a recent World Bank study, securing electricity connection is often considered the most important aspect of facilitating private business. In an effort to measure business freedom more comprehensively, the 2016 *Index* adopted three sub-factors related to "getting electricity." Although the overall impact of this methodological refinement is minimal, the reader is urged to exercise caution in comparing business freedom scores over time.

3. The six countries that are not covered by the World Bank's *Doing Business* study are Burma, Cuba, North Korea, Libya, Macau, and Turkmenistan.

4. The assessment of labor freedom dates from the 2005 *Index* because of the limited availability of quantitative data before that time. In the 2016 *Index*, the labor freedom measurement added labor force participation rates to its sub-factors. According to the International Labour Organization, the labor force participation rate is defined as "a measure of the proportion of a country's working-age population that engages actively in the labour market, either by working or looking for work; it provides an indication of the size of the supply of labour available to engage in the production of goods and services, relative to the population at working age." "KILM 1. Labour Force Participation Rate," in International Labour Organization, *Key Indicators of the Labour Market, Eighth Edition* (Geneva: International Labour Office, 2014), p. 29, http://kilm.ilo.org/2011/download/kilmcompleteEN.pdf. In light of the labor freedom assessment's being refined with the addition of labor force participation rates, the reader is urged to use caution in comparing labor freedom scores over time.

5. The first six sub-factors specifically examine labor regulations that affect "the hiring and redundancy of workers and the rigidity of working hours." For more detailed information on the data, see "Employing Workers," in World Bank, *Doing Business*, http://www.doingbusiness.org/MethodologySurveys/EmployingWorkers.aspx. Reporting only raw data, the *Doing Business 2011* study discontinued all of the sub-indices of "Employing Workers": the difficulty of hiring index, the rigidity of hours index, and the difficulty of redundancy index. For the labor freedom component of the 2014 *Index*, the three indices were reconstructed by *Index* authors according to the methodology used previously by the *Doing Business* study.

6. See note 4, *supra*.

7. MFN is now referred to as permanent normal trade relations (PNTR).

8. Given the fact that the *Index* is published several months after the cutoff date for evaluation, more recent economic events cannot be factored into the scores. In the past editions, however, such occurrences have been uncommon. The impact of policy changes and more recently available macroeconomic statistics since the second half of 2016 have not affected the rankings for the 2017 *Index* but almost certainly will show up in scores for the next edition.

MAJOR WORKS CITED

The 2017 *Index of Economic Freedom* relies on data from multiple internationally recognized sources to present a representation of economic freedom in each country that is as comprehensive, impartial, and accurate as possible. The following sources provided the primary information for analyzing and scoring the 12 components of economic freedom.

In addition, the authors and analysts used supporting documentation and information from various government agencies and sites on the Internet, news reports and journal articles, and official responses to inquiries. All statistical and other information received from government sources was verified with independent, credible third-party sources.

African Development Bank, *Statistics Pocketbook 2016*; available at http://www.afdb.org/en/knowledge/publications/the-afdb-statistics-pocketbook/.

African Development Bank and Organisation for Economic Co-operation and Development, *African Economic Outlook 2016*; available at http://www.africaneconomicoutlook.org/en/.

African Financial Markets Initiative, *Country Profiles*; available at http://www.africanbondmarkets.org/en/country-profiles/.

Asian Development Bank, *Asian Development Outlook 2016: Asia's Potential Growth*; available at https://www.adb.org/publications/asian-development-outlook-2016-asia-potential-growth.

————, *Key Indicators for Asia and the Pacific 2016*; available at https://www.adb.org/publications/key-indicators-asia-and-pacific-2016.

Country statistical agencies, central banks, and ministries of finance, economy, and trade; available at http://unstats.un.org/unsd/methods/inter-natlinks/sd_natstat.asp; http://www.census.gov/aboutus/stat_int.html; and http://www.bis.org/cbanks.htm.

Deloitte, International Tax and Business Guide, *Country Highlights*; available at https://www.dits.deloitte.com/.

Economist Intelligence Unit, Ltd., *Country Commerce*, London, U.K., 2011–2016.

————, *Country Finance*, London, U.K., 2011–2016.

————, *Country Report*, London, U.K., 2011–2016.

European Bank for Reconstruction and Development, *Country Strategies*, 2011–2016; available at http://www.ebrd.com/pages/country.shtml.

European Commission, Eurostat, *European Statistics*; available at http://epp.eurostat.ec.europa.eu/portal/page/portal/statistics/themes.

International Monetary Fund, *Article IV Consultation Staff Reports*, various countries, Washington, DC, 2011–2016; available at http://www.imf.org/external/ns/cs.aspx?id=51.

————, *Country Information*; available at http://www.imf.org/external/country/index.htm.

————, *Selected Issues and Statistical Appendix*, various countries, Washington, DC, 2011–2016.

————, World Economic Outlook Database, April 2016; available at https://www.imf.org/external/pubs/ft/weo/2016/01/weodata/index.aspx.

Low Tax Network, various countries; available at http://www.lowtax.net.

Organisation for Economic Co-operation and Development, *OECD Economic Outlook*, Vol. 2016, Issue 1 (June1, 2016); available at http://www.oecd.org/eco/outlook/economic-outlook-june-2016.htm.

————, *OECD Statistics Portal*; available at http://stats.oecd.org/source/.

————, OECD Web site; available at www.oecd.org/home.

PricewaterhouseCoopers, *Worldwide Tax Summaries*; available with registration at http://www.pwc.com/gx/en/tax/corporate-tax/worldwide-tax-summaries/taxsummaries.jhtml.

Transparency International, *The Corruption Perceptions Index*, Berlin, Germany, 2000–2015; available at http://www.transparency.org/cpi2015.

United Nations Conference on Trade and Development, *World Investment Report 2016: Investor Nationality: Policy Challenges*; available at http://unctad.org/en/pages/PublicationWebflyer.aspx?publicationid=1555.

United States Central Intelligence Agency, *The World Factbook 2016*; available at https://www.cia.gov/library/publications/the-world-factbook/index.html.

United States Department of Commerce, *Country Commercial Guides*, Washington, DC, 2011–2016; available at http://www.buyusainfo.net/adsearch.cfm?search_type=int&loadnav=no.

United States Department of State, *Country Reports on Human Rights Practices for 2015*, released by the Bureau of Democracy, Human Rights, and Labor, April 2016; available at http://www.state.gov/j/drl/rls/hrrpt/humanrightsreport/index.htm#wrapper.

————, *Investment Climate Statements: 2011–2016*, released by the Bureau of Economic and Business Affairs; available at http://www.state.gov/e/eb/rls/othr/ics/.

United States Trade Representative, Office of the, *2016 National Trade Estimate Report on Foreign Trade Barriers*, Washington, DC, 2016; available at https://ustr.gov/about-us/policy-offices/press-office/reports-and-publications/2016/2016-national-trade-estimate.

World Bank, *World Bank World Development Indicators Online*, Washington, DC; available at http://data.worldbank.org/data-catalog/world-development-indicators.

————, *Country Briefs and Trade-at-a-Glance (TAAG) Tables*, Washington, DC; available at http://web.worldbank.org/WBSITE/EXTERNAL/TOPICS/ TRADE/0,,contentMDK:22421950~pagePK:148956~piPK:216618~theSitePK:239071,00.html.

————, *Doing Business*; available at www.doingbusiness.org.

World Trade Organization, *Trade Policy Reviews*, 1996–2016; available at https://www.wto.org/english/tratop_e/tpr_e/tpr_e.htm.

OUR INTERNATIONAL PARTNERS

Institute of Economic Affairs

2 Lord North Street,
Westminster
London, SWIP 3LB
United Kingdom
Phone: +44-20-7700-8900
Fax: +44-20-7799-2137
E-mail: iea@iea.org.uk
Web: www.iea.org.uk

Instituto Bruno Leoni

Piazza Cavour 3
3-10123 Torino
Italy
Phone: +39 (011) 1978 1215
Fax: +39 (011) 1978 1216
E-mail: info@brunoleoni.it
Web: www.brunoleoni.it

IME
Institute for Market Economics

**Institute for
Market Economics**

1000 Sofia
10 Patriarh Evtimii Blvd. fl. 2,
Bulgaria
Phone: +359-2-952-62-66
E-mail: mail@ime.bg
Web: www.ime.bg/en

ADRIATIC INSTITUTE
FOR PUBLIC POLICY

**Adriatic Institute
for Public Policy**

Markovici 15, Srdoci
51000 Rijeka, Croatia
Phone: +385-51-626-582
Fax: +385-1-655-7177
E-mail: AdriaticIPP@aol.com
Web: www.adriatricinstitute.org

F. A. Hayek
Foundation

Nadácia F. A. Hayeka

Jašíkova 6
821 03 Bratislava
(BC Kerametal)
Slovakia
Phone: +421-2-48-291-585
Fax: +421-248-291-243
E-mail: hayek@hayek.sk
Web: www.hayek.sk

Lithuanian
Free
Market
Institute

**Lithuanian Free
Market Institute**

Šeimyniškių St. 3A
LT-09312 Vilnius
Lithuania
Phone: +370-5-250-0280
E-mail: LFMI@freema.org
Web: www.en.llri.lt

Fundación Libertad

Fundación Libertad

Mitre 170
2000 Rosario Santa Fe
Argentina
Phone: +54 341 4105000
E-mail: prensa@libertad.org.ar
Web: www.libertad.org.ar

LIBERTAD
DESARROLLO

**Fundación Libertad
y Desarrollo**

Alcántara 498, Las Condes
Santiago, Chile
Phone: + (56-2) 377-4800
E-mail: lyd@lyd.com
Web: www.lyd.com

Instituto de Ciencia Política (ICP)

Calle 70 No. 7A-29
Bogotá, Colombia
Phone: + (571) 317 7979
E-mail: info@icpcolombia.org
Web: www.icpcolombia.org

Instituto de Desarrollo del Pensamiento Patria Soñada

Guarania 2152 entre Próceres
de Mayo y Año 1811
Teléfono: (+595 21) 210 159
info@instituto.org.py
Web: www.instituto.org.py/idpps

Centro de Investigaciones Sobre la Libre Empresa, A.C.

Camelia 329 Col. Florida C.P.
01030 México D.F.
Phone: +56.62.42.50
E-mail: instituto@cisle.org.mx
Web: www.cisle.org.mx

Centro de Investigación y Estudios Legales (CITEL)

Avenida Coronel Pedro
Portillo 521
San Isidro 15076
Perú
Phone: +511-222-3286
E-mail: info@citel.org
Web: www.citel.org

Fundación para el Análisis y los Estudios Sociales (FAES)

C/ María de Molina 40
6ª planta
28006 – Madrid
Phone: +34 91 567 6857
Fax: + (34) 91 575 46 95
E-mail:
fundacionfaes@fundacionfaes.org
Web: www.fundacionfaes.org

Centro de Divulgación del Conocimiento Económico (CEDICE)

Avenida Andrés Eloy Blanco
(Este 2)
Edificio Cámara de Comercio de
Caracas, Nivel Auditorio
Los Caobos, Caracas
Venezuela
Phone: +58 21 671 3357
Web: www.cedice.org.ve